# THE EMERGENCE OF A
## SCIENTIFIC CULTURE

# The Emergence of a Scientific Culture

*Science and the Shaping
of Modernity, 1210–1685*

STEPHEN GAUKROGER

CLARENDON PRESS · OXFORD

# OXFORD
UNIVERSITY PRESS

Great Clarendon Street, Oxford OX2 6DP

Oxford University Press is a department of the University of Oxford.
It furthers the University's objective of excellence in research, scholarship,
and education by publishing worldwide in

Oxford New York

Auckland Cape Town Dar es Salaam Hong Kong Karachi
Kuala Lumpur Madrid Melbourne Mexico City Nairobi
New Delhi Shanghai Taipei Toronto

With offices in

Argentina Austria Brazil Chile Czech Republic France Greece
Guatemala Hungary Italy Japan Poland Portugal Singapore
South Korea Switzerland Thailand Turkey Ukraine Vietnam

Oxford is a registered trademark of Oxford University Press
in the UK and in certain other countries

Published in the United States
by Oxford University Press Inc., New York

© Stephen Gaukroger 2006

The moral rights of the authors have been asserted
Database right Oxford University Press (maker)

First published 2006

British Library Cataloguing in Publication Data
Data available

Library of Congress Cataloging in Publication Data
Data available

Typeset by Laserwords Private Limited, Chennai, India
Printed in Great Britain
on acid-free paper by
Biddles Ltd., King's Lynn, Norfolk

ISBN 0–19–929644–8   978–0–19–929644–6

1 3 5 7 9 10 8 6 4 2

# *Preface*

Since the publication of Darwin's *The Origin of Species* in 1859, there has been much discussion of the value and standing of science, but comparatively little attention has been paid to how scientific values emerged in the West, with the result that they have often taken on the quality of timeless *sui generis* standards. Yet one striking thing about the way in which science in the West has developed from the seventeenth century onwards is just how distinctive its growth is, compared to that of any earlier or contemporary scientific cultures. In particular, issues of legitimation arise that are absent from other scientific cultures, and these shape the enterprise in distinct and novel ways. Above all, they make possible the ideal of modelling all cognitive values on scientific ones, which is one of the most distinctive features of modern Western culture. The early stages of this development are the topic of this book.

I have been thinking about these issues since first encountering the work of Hans Blumenberg in the early 1980s, although it was not until 1995 that I began serious work on the present project, of which this volume is the first of a projected five. In the earliest incarnation of the undertaking, one of my main aims was to compare the development of a scientific culture in the West with successful scientific programmes that had quite different cultural effects, namely those of China and medieval Islam, as well as with science in the Iberian peninsula, where the same scientific programme that was taking root in Northern Europe was developed with quite different cultural consequences. The direction that the project has taken subsequently has meant that these comparative questions have slipped into the background, but asking them has certainly helped guide my thinking. Comparison with China made me realize that the success of science in the West in the early-modern era might be due to its close association with religion, rather than any attempt to dissociate itself from religion; comparison with Iberian science helped me realize just how contingent and precarious any association between scientific values and modern culture was in the early-modern era; and comparison with medieval Arabic science made me realize just how peculiar and anomalous the development of science in the West was, and in particular how distinctive its legitimatory programme was.

The title page announces 1210 and 1685 as the *termini* of this book, and the choice perhaps needs explanation. The former is the date of the first Paris condemnation of Aristotle, the reintroduction of whose works into the West precipitated a transformation of Western intellectual culture, making natural philosophy the key to an understanding of the world and our place in it. I have occasionally gone further back, sometimes in detail, to classical, Hellenistic, and Patristic cultures, but only where this is needed in order to understand later developments. The date 1685, by contrast, is not marked by an event and is a little rubbery, in that there are some formative developments whose origins predate 1685 that I have deferred to the next volume. Nevertheless, between 1686 and 1691 seminal works by Newton, Varignon, Locke,

Leibniz, Ray, Fontenelle and others appear that ushered in a new era of thinking about natural-philosophical questions and their significance, and 1685 roughly marks a natural divide.

In the course of writing, I have inevitably built up many intellectual debts. For ideas, advice, thoughts, and constructive criticisms, I would particularly like to thank: Peter Anstey, Constance Blackwell, Des Clarke, Floris Cohen, Conal Condren, John Cottingham, Beatriz Domingues, Ofer Gal, Dan Garber, Peter Harrison, Ian Hunter, Rob Iliffe, Helen Irving, Susan James, Jamie Kassler, Ian Maclean, Noel Malcolm, Victor Navarro Brotóns, Simon Schaffer, Wilhelm Schmidt-Biggemann, Ulrich Schneider, Richard Serjeantson, Steven Shapin, Nathan Sivin, John Ward, Catherine Wilson, Rachel Yuen-Collingridge, and above all John Schuster, with whom I have discussed questions of natural philosophy to my great benefit over a period of thirty years.

It goes without saying that a project of this scale requires considerable momentum and I would have been greatly hindered in undertaking it without very generous support from the Australian Research Council over many years, which has provided me with near-ideal conditions. Work on the book has been pursued primarily at the University of Sydney, but generous hospitality has been provided by the School of Advanced Study at the University of the London during the first half of 2005, where I was able to take advantage of the wonderful library of the Warburg Institute.

Material from the book has been presented, over a ten-year period, at invited talks, conference presentations, and public lectures at the University of California at Davis, Cambridge University, University of Chicago, Columbia University, University of Copenhagen, University College Cork, University of Edinburgh, University of Helsinki, University of Hong Kong, Bogaziçi University Istanbul, University of Leeds, Imperial College London, the School of Advanced Study at the University of London, All Souls' College Oxford, Princeton University, University of Queensland, Federal University of Rio de Janeiro, the Russian Academy of Sciences (Moscow), University of Sydney, University of Uppsala, University of Utrecht, and the Warburg Institute.

I have drawn on earlier writings in some sections of the book. In particular, an abridged version of Ch. 1 was published in *Critical Quarterly* (2005); early versions of parts of Ch. 6 have appeared as 'The Autonomy of Natural Philosophy: From Truth to Impartiality', in Peter Anstey and John Schuster (eds.), *The Science of Nature in the Seventeenth Century* (Dordrecht: Kluwer, 2005); and early versions of parts of Ch. 6 and 7 as 'The *Persona* of the Natural Philosopher', in Conal Condren, Stephen Gaukroger, and Ian Hunter (eds.), *The Philosopher in Early Modern Europe* (Cambridge: Cambridge University Press, 2006).

# Contents

# Introduction

In his *Essai sur l'étude de la littérature* (1761), Gibbon set out to trace the origins of a fundamental shift in intellectual values in the West. During the previous hundred years, he noted, physics and mathematics had gradually come to replace the study of *belles lettres*[1] as the pre-eminent form of learning. Indeed, this was just the kind of thing that Meric Casaubon had feared and warned against a hundred years earlier. 'I hope it will not be required', Casaubon writes, that learning generally and divinity in particular 'shall be tried by the *Mathematicks*, and made subservient to them; which yet the temper of some men of this age doth seem to threaten, which scarce will allow anything else worth a man's study; and then, what need of Universities?'[2] Casaubon, like all students of *belles lettres*, had regarded the study of ancient literature—philosophy, history, poetry, oratory—as an intrinsic part of any form of knowledge of the world and our place in it. Gibbon sensed that, by the 1750s, the era of *belles lettres* as the dominant form of learning and understanding was coming to an end.

Gibbon himself was one of the first to attempt a sustained analysis of the fundamental transformation of intellectual values of his era. This transformation was to become even more radical and complex over the next hundred years, and it has a strong claim to being the single most fundamental feature of the modern era. The West's sense of itself, its relation to its past, and its sense of its future were all profoundly altered as cognitive values generally came to be shaped around scientific ones. The issue is not just that science brought a new set of such values to the task of understanding the world and our place in it, but rather that it completely transformed the task, redefining the goals of enquiry. The redefinition begins with attempts by seventeenth-century natural philosophers to establish the legitimacy of science, or natural philosophy, as it was then.[3] The means by which this legitimacy was established involved a fundamental appeal to objectivity and non-partisanship,

---

[1] Lat. *bonae litterae*: humane learning, by contrast with logic, metaphysics, and theology.

[2] Meric Casaubon, *Of Credulity and Incredulity in Things Natural, Civill and Divine* (London, 1668), 25–6.

[3] 'Natural philosophy' designates a group of disciplines that includes, among other things, what we would distinguish as physics, chemistry/alchemy, biology, and physiology, and excludes some disciplines that we might include under 'science', such as mathematics and medicine. Aristotle defined its domain as covering those things that are independent of us and undergo change. This field undergoes some changes with the rejection of Aristotelian natural philosophy from the seventeenth century onwards, but these do not compromise our use of the term (although some qualifications will have to be made later, e.g. on the question of whether 'experimental philosophy' can be treated, for terminological purposes, as a type of natural philosophy, rather than an alternative to it, in the seventeenth century: similarly for 'rational mechanics' in the eighteenth century). Aristotle's own term derives from *phusis*—'nature'—and is usually translated as 'physics', but since it is quite different from what we understand as 'physics' I have generally preferred the term 'natural philosophy'. Similarly with the seventeenth-century term 'physiology', which refers to

what later became the idea that science should be value-free. But how can something that is value-free realize human ideals and aspirations? The answer is that it cannot, and what in fact happens instead is that scientific, technological, and economic goals replace—rather than realize—more traditional political, social, and cultural ones. Jawaharlal Nehru, the first prime minister of independent India, provides a typical example of what is at issue in a speech in 1960, where he spelled out how he understood the implications of science for India in these terms:

It is science alone that can solve the problems of hunger and poverty, of insanitation and illiteracy, of superstition and deadening custom and tradition, of vast resources running to waste, of a rich country inhabited by starving people.... Who indeed could afford to ignore science today? At every turn we seek its aid.... The future belongs to science and to those who make friends with science.[4]

At stake here is not merely an issue of how a third-world country might model itself on and catch up with the West, but rather something that goes to the core of the way in which the West conceives of how its future will be determined, and what values and goals this future will embody. As John Gray reminds us:

Today, faith in political action is practically dead, and it is technology that expresses the dream of the transformed world. Few people any longer look forward to a world in which hunger and poverty are eradicated by a better distribution of the wealth that already exists. Instead, governments look to science to create ever more wealth. Intensive agriculture and genetically modified crops will feed the hungry; economic growth will reduce and eventually remove poverty. Though it is often politicians who espouse these policies most vociferously, the clear implication of such technical fixes is that we might as well forget about political change. Rather than struggling against arbitrary power, we should wait for the benign effects of growing prosperity.[5]

---

natural philosophy, not what we would now term physiology. The terms 'science' (in its modern meaning) and 'scientist' were introduced in the nineteenth century, the former denoting a form of what is usually a professional activity, and is quite different from the Latin term *scientia*, which denotes a form of wisdom that derives from the systematic organization of material, at least in the Aristotelian tradition. Nevertheless, I have, where necessary, used the terms 'science' and 'scientific' in a very broad generic sense to include a range of cognitive activities covering, for example, classical antiquity, medieval China, and modern science proper.

[4] Quoted in Tom Sorell, *Scientism: Philosophy and the Infatuation with Science* (London, 1991), 2. This statement mirrors the view of the report of Vannevar Bush commissioned by President Roosevelt at the end of 1945, in which proposals as to how science can be turned from warfare to curing disease, development of scientific talent in American youth, fuller and more fruitful employment, and a more fulfilling life, are called for. In his report—*Science, the Endless Frontier* (Washington, 1946)—Bush writes that 'scientific progress is one essential key to our security as a nation, to our better health, to more jobs, to a higher standard of living, and to our cultural progress': quoted in Gerald Holton, *Einstein, History and Other Passions* (Cambridge, Mass., 1996), 5–6.

[5] John Gray, *Heresies* (London, 2004), 50–1. Cf. the 1993 remarks by the chairman of the US Congress Committee on Science, Space, and Technology, George E. Brown Jr.: 'Global leadership in science and technology has not translated into leadership in infant health, life expectancy, rates of literacy, equality of opportunity, productivity of workers, or efficiency of resource consumption. Neither has it overcome failing education systems, decaying cities, environmental degradation, unaffordable health care, and the largest national debt in history.': quoted in Holton, *Einstein, History and Other Passions*, 6.

My concern in this book is with the early stages of the redefinition of the nature and goals of enquiry. It is the first volume of a projected larger study of the transformation of cognitive and intellectual values in the modern era, in which I have set out to write a conceptual and cultural history of the emergence of a scientific culture in the West from the early-modern era to the present. The study treats science in the modern period as a particular kind of cognitive practice, and as a particular kind of cultural product, and my aim is to show that if we explore the connections between these two, we can learn something about the concerns and values of modern thought that we could not learn from either of them taken separately.

Part I offers a general introduction to the whole project, identifying some of the issues that drive it. Its central concern is with the assimilation of all cognitive values to scientific ones and with how this came about. From the end of the nineteenth century, what were identified as the fundamental values of the sciences came to be seen by many scientists, philosophers, and others as providing a new basis for morality, politics, religion, and philosophy. It was widely believed that new aims and rationales for these practices and disciplines had emerged, and that the new model of cognitive enquiry supplied by the sciences could establish them on a legitimate basis, and guide their projects more fruitfully. I shall be arguing that this phenomenon requires explanation, and that we need to ask how it arose. In particular, I have set out to clear the ground by showing that the reasons commonly adduced for the success of a scientific culture in the West in the wake of the Scientific Revolution[6]—its use of adversarial non-dogmatic argument, its ability to dissociate itself from religion, its technological benefits—are mistaken and cannot explain this success. Indeed, a distinctive feature of the Scientific Revolution is that, unlike other earlier scientific programmes and cultures, it is driven, often explicitly, by religious considerations: Christianity set the agenda for natural philosophy in many respects and projected it forward in a way quite different from that of any other scientific culture. Moreover, when the standing of religion as a source of knowledge about the world, and cognitive values generally, came to be threatened, it was not science that posed the threat but history. From the sixteenth century onwards, it was historical methods

---

[6] There is a huge literature on whether there ever was *the* Scientific Revolution. As Shapin puts it, 'Many historians are now no longer satisfied that there was any singular and discrete event, localized in time and space, that can be pointed to as "the" Scientific Revolution. Such historians now reject even the notion that there was any single coherent cultural entity called "science" in the seventeenth century to undergo revolutionary change. There was, rather, a diverse array of cultural practices aimed at understanding, explaining, and controlling the natural world, each with different characteristics and each experiencing different modes of change. We are now much more dubious of claims that there is anything like a "scientific method"—a coherent, universal, and efficacious set of procedures for making scientific knowledge—and still more sceptical of stories that locate its origin in the seventeenth century, from which time it has been unproblematically passed on to us.' Steven Shapin, *The Scientific Revolution* (Chicago, 1996), 3–4. In my discussion of the 'Enlightenment Interpretation', in Ch. 1, I shall be criticizing the assumptions that, as Shapin points out, many historians of science now reject. In common with everyone else, I shall continue to use the term, however. On the historiography of the Scientific Revolution, see the thorough and nuanced account in H. Floris Cohen, *The Scientific Revolution: A Historiographical Inquiry* (Chicago, 1994).

of investigation that provided the radical cutting edge for those who questioned the legitimacy of established religions.

Part II focuses on the earlier developments that shaped the questions that will be at issue in the understanding of natural philosophy in the early-modern period. In Chapter 2, I argue that natural philosophy changes status from a marginal enterprise to one that forms the principal point of entry into our understanding of the world not with the seventeenth-century Scientific Revolution but in the thirteenth century. Moreover, this fundamental transformation of Western intellectual culture raised questions that remained unresolved, coming to a head at the beginning of the sixteenth century in the Pomponazzi affair, where the need for Aristotelian natural philosophy in underpinning a systematic theology collides head on with the impossibility of reconciling Christian teaching with Aristotelian natural philosophy, a problem compounded as competing forms of natural philosophy now begin to emerge in an uncontrolled way. The early stages of this emergence, and the responses to it, all of them manifest failures, are the subject of Chapter 3, where I look at the two principal alternatives to the Thomist programme for reconciliation of Aristotelian natural philosophy and Christian teaching, namely the fifteenth-century Platonist revival and sixteenth-century naturalism,[7] and at the late sixteenth-century scholastic response. The kind of natural philosophy dealt with in these two chapters is above all matter theory, but there is also another tradition of understanding the natural world, natural history, which, from the Patristic periods onwards, follows a very different path, that of an allegorical interpretation of nature guided by scripture. In Chapter 4, I look at how, under the influence of developments in legal and bibical philology, this tradition undergoes a radical change. Notions of objectivity and impartiality are brought to the fore, but equally important is the new construal of natural-historical enquiry as something that enables us to uncover God's intentions for his creation. The incorporation of these features into natural philosophy more generally, in Boyle and others in the second half of the seventeenth century, provides a distinctive vindication of the natural-philosophical enterprise, one in which it takes over certain roles from religion. Both Christianity and natural philosophy are transformed into something quite new in the process.

Part III deals with the replacement of the traditional Aristotelian understanding of natural philosophy at a methodological level (Ch. 5), in terms of the reform of the natural philosopher (Ch. 6), and in terms of its general implications for understanding of the aims of natural-philosophical enquiry (Ch. 7). In the course of the sixteenth century, Aristotelian understandings of methods of discovery and presentation underwent a gradual collapse. At first they were reworked, but by the end of the sixteenth century they had begun to be replaced by a variety of new

---

[7] Renaissance naturalism is different from what is referred to as naturalism in contemporary philosophy. The former is the view that areas that had traditionally been believed to require supernatural explanation in fact require natural explanation, but this is usually on the understanding that a number of capacities and powers for which contemporary naturalists would have no place have been incorporated into nature. Modern naturalism is closer to the more reductionist forms of corpuscularianism that emerged only with Hobbes in the seventeenth century.

approaches, the more radical of which offered a completely different understanding of the point of the natural-philosophical exercise. One of the spurs to reworking was the attempt to draw out the natural-philosophical significance of developments in the practical-mathematical disciplines, initially in astronomy and then in mechanics. The issues in the case of astronomy turn on the hypothetical standing of the mathematical devices used to reconcile observations of celestial motions, and we shall see that the particularly intractable nature of the problems here has the result that trying to deal with them in a systematic way (Kepler) is initially far less successful than a piecemeal approach (Galileo). In Chapter 6, I look at a set of issues that complement the methodological disputes and are crucial to their resolution, but have been largely ignored, namely, those questions surrounding the *persona* of the natural philosopher. This issue is the key to understanding how natural philosophy becomes inserted into European culture in the sixteenth and seventeenth centuries. Notions of truth and justification, I argue, turn just as much on conceptions of intellectual honesty as they do on notions of method, and in this regard I look at the standing of the natural philosopher in Bacon, Galileo, Descartes, and Royal Society apologists, focusing on claims that the natural philosopher requires a kind of intellectual honesty lacking in scholastic natural philosophy. This is closely tied in with one of the distinctive features of early-modern natural philosophy, that questions that had earlier been seen in terms of truth are now discussed instead in terms of impartiality and objectivity. In Chapter 7, I draw out some of the consequences of the rethinking of the natural-philosophical project examined in the two preceding chapters. I begin by asking what had traditionally been expected from natural-philosophical enquiry, looking in particular at how the identity of philosophy generally emerged from various contrasts between the philosopher and the sophist. For Aristotle, the identity of natural philosophy lay in its search for the intrinsic principles underlying natural phenomena, and this conception excludes a number of cognitive disciplines—practical mathematics (above all mechanics, optics, and astronomy), medicine, and natural history—on the grounds that these are either not concerned with natural phenomena or do not pursue their enquiry in terms of underlying principles. By raising the questions of just what kind of understanding they do provide, how their general aims differ from natural philosophy, and what kind of connection there can be between these enterprises and natural philosophy, we can open up the issue of the aims of enquiry, and gain some insight into the realignment of disciplines that emerges in the seventeenth century, which is our concern in Part IV.

Part IV deals with three seventeenth-century forms of natural-philosophical practice. The first is the mechanist systems of Beeckman, Gassendi, Hobbes, and Descartes, examined in Chapter 8. Such systems are developed as successors to Aristotelian natural philosophy, and they stay in some respects within the Aristotelian fold, above all in their construal of natural philosophy as being fundamentally matter theory, even though this matter theory is radically rethought in terms of considerations derived from (an idealized conception of) mechanics. These systems developed an elaborate set of micro-corpuscularian first principles and these principles then operated as the *explanans* by which macroscopic natural phenomena were accounted for. We can distinguish two kinds of programme in the pursuit of mechanism: Gassendi's is a legitimatory programme that focuses on matter theory, for example, whereas Beeckman's approach seems to come directly out of mechanics, which it attempts to transform into natural philosophy by fleshing it out in micro-corpuscularian terms. The crucial stage in mechanism comes with the rise of concerted attempts to integrate mechanics and matter theory into a consistent whole, at the same time offering the mechanism so devised as a complete theory of the cosmos, and it is the approaches of Hobbes, whose closest affinities are with Gassendi, and Descartes, whose closest affinities are with Beeckman, that bring out most clearly what is at issue here. In Chapter 9, I focus on mechanism as a legitimatory programme in natural philosophy. In particular, I look at the issues arising from the fact that the *explanandum* had to be tailored and radically reduced to accommodate the minimal explanatory resources allowed in mechanism. Moreover, unprecedented problems arise once we move to the organic realm, and I look at Cartesian biomechanics, especially the problems it faces in its account of foetal development, and at the disputes over the inclusion of medicine within natural philosophy.

A very different kind of approach from mechanism, explored in Chapter 10, is one that attempted to incorporate considerations drawn from natural history, traditionally excluded from natural philosophy in the Aristotelian sense, into natural philosophy proper. Here we witness a rejection of the foundationalist approach of what are deemed 'speculative' natural-philosophical systems, and the development of an 'experimental' natural philosophy in their place. A fruitful way to think of what is at issue, I argue, is in terms of the *explanans* being accommodated to the *explanandum*. Points of contact between this approach and that of systematic mechanist natural philosophy are surprisingly rare, and both highly overdetermined and contentious when they occur. This is something that we shall be looking at in some detail. I examine Gilbert on the magnet and at Bacon's criticisms of the idea that the study of the magnet has general implications for natural philosophy, but the focus is primarily on Boyle's account of pneumatics, by contrast with Hobbes' traditional natural-philosophical approach, and on Newton's account of the spectrum, by contrast with Descartes' attempt to move from geometrical to physical optics by providing a micro-corpuscularian account of the underpinnings of light. One of the distinctive features of the last is that Newton is able to keep it as part of an exercise in geometrical optics, thus ensuring that we do not leave the quantitative realm. The phenomena can thus be connected mathematically, rather than in terms of a matter-theoretical account of underlying physical processes that was a *sine qua non* of traditional natural philosophy. The questions at stake here are taken up in detail in Chapter 11, which looks at attempts to quantify natural phenomena and, in particular, forces. Early efforts along these lines—notably by Galileo and Descartes—tried to extrapolate from statics to dynamics, whereas later in the century kinematics, as pioneered by Galileo, was taken as the model, albeit in rather different ways, by Huygens and Newton. Building on Hooke's suggestion that planetary orbits were not a given and unquestionable feature of the cosmos, but should be treated as resultants of tangential rectilinear motion and attractive accelerating forces, Newton was able to show how such orbits were generated, and to clarify the dynamics needed to account for the processes involved. In this way, mechanics, traditionally excluded from natural philosophy in the Aristotelian sense, is transformed not only into a natural-philosophical discipline, but into what was in many respects the natural-philosophical discipline *par excellence*.

In Part V, I look at the questions of the unity of natural philosophy, and the unity of knowledge more generally. These questions, which are at the core of subsequent attempts to model all cognitive values on scientific ones, are complex and my treatment is selective, identifying and focusing on a number of issues that prove to be decisive. The question of the unity of natural philosophy is considered in the context of two traditional understandings of natural philosophy and three new ones. The two traditional understandings are the Aristotelian notion of the unity of *scientia*, whereby the ultimate form of understanding of natural processes was one in which the essential principles underlying the behaviour of things were understood in a systematic way; and the Christian idea of a universe designed and created *ex nihilo* by a single God as an abode for human beings, so that the world was the product of design, and it was only through understanding the design of the world that we had any fundamental knowledge of it. The new understandings of natural philosophy, embodied in mechanism, experimental philosophy, and 'physico-mathematics' respectively, offer quite different accounts of what the purview of natural philosophy is and just what it can achieve. One dominant idea underlying mechanism, namely that there is a microscopic level of common causation, turns out to be highly speculative, supported neither by empirical evidence nor microscopy. I broach the more general question of the unity of knowledge by contrasting traditional physico-theology with the Spinozean subsumption of a mechanist natural philosophy under politico-theology. In antiquity, and to some extent in the Renaissance, the rationale for pursuing knowledge and learning had been seen in terms of the interrelated goals of wisdom and happiness. But wisdom and happiness had in many respects been transferred to the afterlife as part of the medieval rethinking of philosophy, and they had become unlikely contenders as the aims of natural philosophy by the beginning of the seventeenth century, being replaced by the goals of truth and use, which were not intrinsically connected. The response of Spinoza is to undermine the claims of Christianity to supply the requisite notion of wisdom, and to develop a novel account of how a mechanized natural philosophy can lead to wisdom and happiness. The general unqualified rejection of the Spinozean model by natural philosophers does not mean that, in a struggle between legitimacy, which the Spinozean conception effectively abandoned, and autonomy, which it established beyond doubt, they favoured legitimacy over autonomy. They wanted both, and the Christian notion of a designed cosmos, examined by means of a form of natural philosophy modelled on natural history, which provided a unique form of understanding of God and which guided scriptural interpretation rather than being guided by it, quickly became the preferred context within which to view natural-philosophical enquiry. In this connection, I look at the attempts by English natural philosophers and theologians to accommodate the account in Genesis to natural-philosophical accounts of the formation of the earth. What emerges from these attempts, I argue, is a fundamental shift from the traditional Thomist view that natural philosophy, conceived as dealing with justification and demonstration, and revelation, conceived as uncovering divine truth, must somehow be bridged by metaphysics, to a view of revelation and natural philosophy as being mutually reinforcing, where there is a process of 'triangulation', as it were, towards the shared truth of revelation and natural philosophy. In this way, the nature of the natural-philosophical exercise is transformed and provided with a unique vindication and legitimacy, one that lies at the basis of its subsequent standing.

# PART I

# 1

# Science and Modernity

What is the significance of science viewed as a symptom of life? . . . Is the resolve
to be so scientific about everything perhaps a kind of fear of, and escape from,
pessimism? A subtle last resort against—truth? and, morally speaking, a sort of
cowardice and falseness?

Friedrich Nietzsche, *Die Geburt der Tragödie*[1]

One of the most distinctive features of the emergence of a scientific culture in modern
Europe is the gradual assimilation of all cognitive values to scientific ones. This is not
merely a distinctive feature of Western scientific practice, it is a distinctive feature of
Western modernity: a particular image of the role and aims of scientific understanding is tied up in a fundamental fashion with the self-image of modernity. A striking
illustration of this is the way that the West's sense of what its superiority consisted in
shifted seamlessly, in the early decades of the nineteenth century, from its religion to
its science.[2] As late as 1949, Herbert Butterfield, in his influential *The Origins of Modern Science*, could argue that civilized ideals, which had previously been transmitted
by Christianity, were now transmitted by science, and that Christianity had evolved
into a new secular science of faith.[3] While what is at issue would perhaps no longer
be put in quite these terms, it remains the case that, over the last fifty years, a particular image of the role and aims of scientific understanding has been promoted by
the West, and internalized by its recipients, as an essential element in the process of
modernization.

A crucial ingredient in the plausibility and success of this notion has been the idea
that science, by contrast with religion for example, appeals solely to reason and experience, and is as a consequence untinged by historical or cultural factors, which can
therefore be ignored, making science something that in essence has no context, historical or otherwise. Science is thereby protected in advance from the historicization
and contextualization that, coming to a head in the middle of the nineteenth century,

---

[1] Friedrich Nietzsche, *Basic Writings of Nietzsche*, trans. and ed. Walter Kaufman (New York,
1968), 18.

[2] See Michael Adas, *Machines as the Measure of Man: Science, Technology, and Ideologies of Western
Dominance* (Ithaca, NY, 1989). Cf. Lewis Pyenson, *Cultural Imperialism and Exact Sciences: German
Expansion Overseas, 1900–1930* (New York, 1985); idem, *Empire of Reason: Exact Sciences in
Indonesia, 1840–1940* (Leiden, 1989); idem, *Civilizing Missions: Exact Sciences and French Overseas
Expansion, 1830–1940* (Baltimore, 1993).

[3] See the discussion in Regis Cabral, 'Herbert Butterfield (1900–79) as a Christian Historian of
Science', *Studies in History and Philosophy of Science* 27 (1996), 547–64.

eventually undermined Christianity's claims to *sui generis* legitimacy. The problem is magnified by the cultural standing that science has taken on in virtue of this image. In particular, the notion of science as something answerable to nothing but reason and experience has done much to encourage the otherwise somewhat unlikely association between scientific values, morality, and democracy.

This association began in earnest with the Darwinism debates of the late nineteenth century, and it became a dominant cultural theme in the twentieth century. In the Anglophone world, this development starts with Herbert Spencer, who set out explicitly to derive ethical principles from scientific ones,[4] and from the late ninteteenth century onwards there have been recurrent attempts to guide morality scientifically. In 1916, for instance, Richard Gregory, the editor of *Nature*, singled out the scientific values of selflessness and love of truth to act as the basis for morality.[5] He was followed in 1923 by the contributors to the volume *Science and Civilization*, who called for moral values based upon science to replace those based on religion, with Julian Huxley's contribution identifying the next great task of science as the creation of a new religion.[6] By 1931, the science columnist John Langdon-Davies was taking up the defence of the moral values of science with an attack on the use by religion of emotionally loaded words to describe abstract concepts.[7] At the same time, the Vienna Circle had decided that the best people to do philosophy were not philosophers but scientists. Reminiscing about his time with the Circle in 1926–31, Carnap tells us:

The task of fruitful collaboration, often so difficult among philosophers, was facilitated in our Circle by the fact that all members had a first-hand acquaintance with some field of science, either mathematics, physics or social science. This led to a higher standard of clarity and responsibility than is usually found in philosophical groups, particularly in Germany. . . . The common spirit was one of co-operation rather than competition. The common purpose was to work together in the struggle for clarification and insight.[8]

That such an approach is not restricted to an outdated positivism is clear, for example, from Barrow and Tipler's more recent announcement that:

[4] See e.g. Herbert Spencer, *The Principles of Ethics* (2 vols, New York, 1892), i, pp. xv–xvi.

[5] Richard Gregory, *Discovery: Or the Spirit and Service of Science* (London, 1916). Gregory was assistant editor of *Nature* from 1893 and editor 1919–39. See the discussion in Peter J. Bowler, *Reconciling Science and Religion: The Debate in Early Twentieth-Century Britain* (Chicago, 2001), 68–70.

[6] Julian Huxley, 'Science and Religion', in F. S. Marvin, ed., *Science and Civilization* (Oxford, 1923), 279–329: 279. See the discussion in Bowler, *Reconciling Science and Religion*, 68–75, from which I draw the examples here.

[7] See John Langdon-Davies, 'Science and God', *The Spectator*, 31 January 1931, 137–8.

[8] Rudolph Carnap, 'Intellectual Autobiography', in Paul Arthur Schilpp, ed., *The Philosophy of Rudolph Carnap* (La Salle, Ill., 1963), 3–84: 21. On the Logical Positivist approach to ethics, see Moritz Schlick, *Problems of Ethics* (New York, 1939). The earliest statement of the idea that scientists (in this case mathematicians) were best placed to pursue the humanities and *belles lettres* is Fontenelle's 1699 claim, in the Preface to his *Histoire de renouvellement de l'Académie Royale des Sciences en mdcxcix*: 'The geometrical spirit is not so attached to geometry that it cannot be taken and applied to other knowledge. A work of morals, politics, and criticism, perhaps even of rhetoric, would be improved, other things being equal, if written by a geometer': Bernard le Bovier de Fontenelle, *Œuvres de Monsieur de Fontenelle . . . nouvelle édition* (10 vols, Paris, 1762), v. 12.

Whereas many philosophers and theologians appear to possess an emotional attachment to their theories and ideas which requires them to believe them, scientists tend to regard their ideas differently. They are interested in formulating many logically consistent possibilities, leaving any judgement regarding their truth to observation.[9]

There is a moral dimension to this view of the standing of science. In the USA during the 1930s and 1940s, for example, scientific values were contrasted with those of facism, communism, Catholicism, and McCarthyism in particular. While Charles Morris was identifying the strength of pragmatism as lying in the fact that 'it is essentially the marriage of the scientific habit of mind with the moral ideal of democracy',[10] Robert Merton was explicitly setting out to establish the correspondence between scientific ideals and those of democracy,[11] and the Yale social scientist Mark A. May was proposing a 'morality of science' as a basis for world culture, whereby everyone would eventually live by the code of the scientist, which consisted in a devotion to honest, free, critical, evidence-based enquiry.[12] It is worth reminding ourselves that at the time that May was writing, many scientists were not only failing to show themselves as more moral than anyone else in the population, but being a good deal less moral, willing and occasionally enthusiastic collaborators in barbaric atrocities.[13] Yet this did not prevent an uncritical idea of the 'morality of science' being taken up again after the Second World War by Richard Hofstadter and Walter Metzger, in their 1955 attack on McCarthyism, as the theoretical foundation of academic freedom for all disciplines, including the humanities.[14] In 1957 we find a member of the Mental Health Research Institute at the University of Michigan arguing that 'the ethical system derived from scientific behaviour is qualitatively different from other ethical systems—is, indeed, a "superior" ethical system'.[15]

But the connections between scientific and ethical progress are in fact at best fragile, a fragility manifest in a revealing way in the development of a 'scientific', i.e. laboratory-based, medicine. In the 1940s, two great successes

---

[9] John D. Barrow and Frank J. Tipler, *The Anthropic Cosmological Principle* (Oxford, 1986), 15.

[10] Charles Morris, *Pragmatism and the Crisis of Democracy* (Chicago, 1934), 8.

[11] See his essay 'The Normative Structure of Science' (originally entitled 'A Note on Science and Democracy') in Robert Merton, *The Sociology of Science*, ed. N. Storer (Chicago, 1973). See the discussion in David A. Hollinger, 'The Defense of Democracy and Robert K. Merton's Formulation of the Scientific Ethos', *Knowledge and Society* 4 (1983), 1–15.

[12] See David A. Holliger, 'Science as a Weapon in *Kulturkämpfe* in the United States During and After World War II', *Isis* 86 (1995), 440–54: 442.

[13] See e.g. Benno Müller-Hill, *Murderous Science: Elimination by Scientific Selection of Jews, Gypsies, and Others, Germany 1933–1945* (Oxford, 1988); John Cornwall, *Hitler's Scientists: Science, War, and the Devil's Pact* (New York, 2003); Daniel Barenblatt, *A Plague upon Humanity: The Hidden History of Japan's Biological Warfare Program* (New York, 2005). Cf. Edwin Black, *War Against the Weak: Eugenics and America's Campaign to Create a Master Race* (New York, 2001).

[14] Richard Hofstadter and Walter Metzger, *The Development of Academic Freedom in the United States* (New York, 1955). See the discussion in Holliger, 'Science as a Weapon in *Kulturkämpfe*', 447.

[15] Anatol Rapoport, 'Scientific Approach to Ethics', *Science* 150 (1957), 796–9: 797. The call for a 'scientific ethics' may have diminished since the 1950s, but it has certainly not disappeared: see e.g. Michael Ruse and Edward O. Wilson, 'Moral Philosophy as Applied Science', *Philosophy* 61 (1986), 173–92, and the reply by Antony Duff, 'Moral Philosophy as Applied Science?', *Philosophy* 63 (1988), 105–10.

in pharmaceuticals—the discoveries of penicillin and cortisone—helped fuel an enthusiasm for scientific medicine. In some respects this was ironic, because neither of these was the outcome of any scientific programme: they were 'gifts of nature', discovered wholly by accident under highly contingent and unlikely circumstances.[16] Nevertheless, there were clearly fundamental consequences for medicine. Penicillin, a naturally occurring non-toxic compound, along with the other antibiotics that followed in its wake, cured many lethal and chronic infections at a stroke, and suggested limitless possibilities for medicine pursued in the laboratory.[17] In the wake of these developments, various attempts were made to put medicine on a 'scientific' footing. From the 1960s onwards, clinical trials were well funded, and they dominated the field: when they failed, as they routinely did, for example in the attempts to extend chemotherapy to a wide range of cancers, researchers told themselves they had not got the mix quite right, and tried again on a new set of patients, only to fail again. As Le Fanu notes, 'the results were predictably appalling, with those receiving chemotherapy dying more rapidly and with much worse quality of life than those receiving no therapy'.[18] The divide between clinical and scientific approaches to medicine became an issue of public concern with the publication in 1967 of Maurice Pappworth's *Human Guinea Pigs*, in which Pappworth—the author of a standard clinical textbook and a defender of the diagnostic superiority of clinical skills over the tests and trials pursued by proponents of scientific medicine—while not doubting the huge advances that had been made in synthetic chemistry over the previous thirty years, convicts the medical profession of ruthless, cruel, dangerous, and often purposeless experiments on infants, pregnant women, the mentally ill, prisoners, and the old and dying, subjecting them to what is in effect a form of torture.[19] It is not possible to dismiss this episode as one concerning the misuse of science, rather than being about science itself, for the procedures followed not only were those prescribed by the most conservative canons of scientific

[16] See James Le Fanu, *The Rise and Fall of Modern Medicine* (London, 1999), Pt I.

[17] In fact, not only did hopes that the drug might be synthesized chemically turn out to be unfounded (despite a huge amount of well-funded research) but no understanding of how antibiotics work has been developed. The commonly accepted explanation that they are 'chemical weapons' produced by bacteria to maximize their chances of survival is quite false, and Selman Waksman, who was awarded the Nobel prize for his discovery of streptomycin, concluded that they were a 'purely fortuitous phenomenon', that 'there is no purposeness behind them', and that 'the only conclusion that can be drawn from these facts is that these microbiological products are accidental': quoted ibid. 15.

[18] Ibid. 156. He continues: 'The blindness of oncologists to what they were doing is well exemplified by a 1983 report claiming that chemo was no more toxic to the elderly than to the young, so they should receive chemo at maximum doses. Curiously the author of this report . . . felt it unnecessary to make any reference to the results of treatment, where only 20% of elderly patients have any response to treatment. . . . In Britain Tim McElwain of London's Royal Marsden Hospital commented on "the confusion of busyness with progress . . . with nasty drugs being thrown at unfortunate patients with very little evidence of gain".'

[19] See ibid. 204–5. Cf. the report of Peter Medawar's view that the real science in medicine is the thorough understanding of the medical problem that comes from talking to the patient and performing a physical examination, from which it is possible to infer what is wrong in 90% of cases, by contrast with 'the technological gizmos and the arcane tests that pass for the "science" of medicine, which are frequently wrong' (ibid. 253).

method, but also yielded benefits in some cases. The episode effectively put an end
to any notion of some intrinsic, superior 'scientific morality',[20] but it also raises the
issue of the appropriateness of exporting procedures from one discipline to another,
and indicates that the appropriateness in question can be complex, involving ethical
as well as technical issues, and highlighting concerns about how we compare very
different kinds of scientific practice each of which might be successful in some areas
but not others.

One lesson to be learned from the 'scientific medicine' episode is that the question
of the unity of science is highly overdetermined, and any attempt to pose it as if it
were a purely abstract question is going to be fruitless.[21] The issues are not confined
to medicine, and open up the contentious question of the extra-scientific sources of
and motivation behind the notion of the unity of science. In mid-nineteenth century
Germany, for example, scientists such as Virchow, DuBois Reymond, and Helmoltz
explicitly saw the unification of science and the unification of the German state as
being indissolubly linked, and nearly a century later Dewey was talking of the unity
of science in political terms as a bulwark against intolerance.[22] This is an issue that
has a very significant practical dimension for, just as in medicine, the future funding
of a range of scientific disciplines depends on decisions made about the unity of science: the debates over the building of an extremely expensive supercollider in the USA
in the 1990s rested in part on whether condensed matter physics was, as its advocates argued, autonomous from the guiding principles of particle physics, or whether
all physics in some way follows from the fundamental laws of particle physics, which
should therefore be given priority (in this case something approaching carte blanche)
in funding.[23] The fundamental question of the 'unity of science' is one that we shall
be turning to in a number of contexts. Its primary importance for us lies in the fact
that any attempted assimilation of cognitive values generally to scientific ones works
on the assumption that science is unified.[24] If science is simply a loose grouping of

---

[20] Ethics committees to oversee scientific and medical research, committees that included
members from outside science and medicine, were finally established around this time.

[21] See Ian Hacking, 'The Disunities of the Sciences', in Peter Galison and David J. Stump, eds,
*The Disunity of Science* (Stanford, 1996), 37–74; and Philip Kitcher, 'The Ends of the Sciences', in
Brian Leiter, ed., *The Future for Philosophy* (Oxford, 2004), 208–29.

[22] See Peter Galison, 'Introduction: The Context of Disunity', in Peter Galison and David J.
Stump, eds., *The Disunity of Science* (Stanford, 1996), 1–33: 1–8. On the German case, see e.g.
Timothy Lenoir, 'Social Interests and the Organic Physics of 1847', in Edna Ullmann-Margalit,
ed., *Science in Reflection* (Dordrecht, 1988), 169–81. In the case of Dewey, see his 'Unity of Science
as a Social Problem', in Otto Neurath, Rudolph Carnap, and Charles Morris, eds, *Foundations of
the Unity of Science* (2 vols, Chicago, 1970), i. 32–3.

[23] Galison, 'Introduction: The Context of Disunity', 2.

[24] In the last century, this has been most explicit and most marked in the writings of the
Logical Positivists. The flavour of the project is well captured in Otto Neurath, 'Unified Science as
Encyclopedic Integration' (first published 1938), in Otto Neurath, Rudolph Carnap, and Charles
Morris, eds, *Foundations of the Unity of Science* (2 vols, Chicago, 1970), i. 1–27. Even this
unification project was not straighforward, however: see Richard Creath, 'The Unity of Science:
Carnap, Neurath, and Beyond', and Jordi Cat, Nancy Cartwright, and Hasok Chang, 'Otto Neurath:
Politics and the Unity of Science', both in Peter Galison and David J. Stump, eds., *The Disunity
of Science* (Stanford, 1996), 158–69 and 347–69 respectively. On the cultural transformation of

disciplines with different subject matters and different methods, tied in various ways each of which work for some purposes but not for others,[25] then there can be no modelling of cognitive values generally on scientific ones. As James Clerk Maxwell—with Newton the greatest unifier of physical theory that physics has known—remarked in an 1856 paper:

Perhaps the 'book', as it has been called, of nature is regularly paged; if so, no doubt the introductory parts will explain those that follow, and the methods taught in the first chapters will be taken for granted and used as illustrations in the more advanced parts of the course; but if it is not a 'book' at all, but a magazine, nothing is more foolish to suppose than that one part can throw light on another.[26]

A century later, one of the other great unifiers of physical theory, Paul Dirac, suggested that the appropriate goal in making fundamental connections between disciplines in physics was that of removing inconsistencies, not attempting to unite theories that were previously disjoint. The former, he argued, led to brilliant successes, as in Maxwell's investigation of an inconsistency in the electromagnetic equations, Planck's resolution of inconsistencies in the theory of black-body radiation, Einstein's resolution of inconsistencies between his theory of special relativity and the Newtonian theory of gravitation. By contrast, the top down method of attempting to unify physical theories that were previously disjoint had produced nothing of significance.[27]

Since the assumption of the unity of science underlies not only reductionist programmes, but the assimilation of cognitive disciplines to science, and/or their modelling on science, it inevitably plays a key role in understanding how science has taken on a particular foundational standing. My aim in what follows is to examine the origins of—and examine the rationale for—a self-image of science whereby it purports to serve as a model for all forms of purposive behaviour, providing cognitive norms for everything from morality to philosophical dispute,[28] from

Logical Positivism from a model of a culturally and socially engaged philosophy (in which the unity of science plays an absolutely central role) to a model of philosophy as a narrow technical theory of induction, inference, and semantics see the comprehensive and intriguing account of the development of Logical Positivism in George A. Reisch, *How the Cold War Transformed Philosophy of Science: To the Icy Slopes of Logic* (Cambridge, 2005). Reisch's book builds in part on the picture sketched in Peter Galison, 'Aufbau/Bauhaus: Logical Positivism and Architectual Modernism', *Critical Inquiry* 16 (1990), 709–52.

[25] For an account of how this works in contemporary microphysics, see Peter Galison, *Image and Logic: A Material Culture of Microphysics* (Chicago, 1997).

[26] James Clerk Maxwell, 'Are There Real Analogies in Nature?', in Lewis Campbell and William Garnett, *The Life of James Clerk Maxwell, with a Selection from his Correspondence and Occasional Writings and a Sketch of his Contributions to Science* (London, 1882), 235–44: 243.

[27] Quoted in Hacking, 'The Disunities of the Sciences', 54.

[28] See e.g. Hans Reichenbach, *The Rise of Scientific Philosophy* (Berkeley, 1951), and the discussion in Ronald N. Giere, 'From *wissenschaftliche Philosophie* to Philosophy of Science', in idem, *Science Without Laws* (Chicago, 1999), 217–36.

political organization[29] to religion,[30] and even being considered part of the process whereby we progress to the next stage of evolution.[31] We shall see that these origins were forged in the debates over the purpose and standing of natural philosophy in the early-modern era, although we cannot understand the novel developments of the late sixteenth and early seventeenth centuries unless we understand the profound transformation of Western philosophical culture of the thirteenth century. In particular, we shall see that the distinctive feature of the Aristotelianism that was introduced then was that it made natural philosophy the point of entry into the whole philosophical enterprise. This included the role of providing foundations for a systematic theology, thereby giving natural philosophy a cognitive priority that was to become one of the central features of early-modern scientific culture. In sum, from the thirteenth century onwards in the West, the understanding of natural philosophy was transformed from a wholly marginal enterprise into the unique model for cognitive enquiry generally. It is with this phenomenon, on which hinge some of the central questions of modernity, that we shall be concerned. Our first task will be to reflect on what exactly needs explaining and why.

## THE ENLIGHTENMENT INTERPRETATION

Since classical antiquity, there have been a number of civilizations that have witnessed a form of 'scientific revolution': rich, productive scientific cultures in which fundamental and especially intractable mathematical, physical, medical, astronomical, or other problems are opened up and dealt with in an innovative and concerted fashion, producing cumulative results over several generations. Among these,[32] we can

---

[29] See e.g. J. D. Bernal, *The Social Function of Science* (London, 1939) and, at the other end of the political spectrum, Karl R. Popper, *The Open Society and its Enemies* (2 vols, London, 1945), and *The Poverty of Historicism* (London, 1957).

[30] See e.g. Julian Huxley, *Religion without Revelation* (London, 1927). The idea of a scientific basis for religion underwent many transformations in the twentieth century. Note Paul Davies' claim that 'science offers a surer path to God than religion . . . science has actually advanced to a point where what were formerly religious questions can be seriously tackled' (*God and the New Physics* (Harmondsworth, 1983), p. ix) and Stephen Hawking's claim that he expects cosmological theory to tell us 'why it is that we and the universe exist. If we find the answer to that, it would be the ultimate triumph of human reason—for then we would know the mind of God' (*A Brief History of Time* (London, 1988), 175). The view that the new physics made a religious view of the world possible goes back as far as Eddington: see Bowler, *Reconciling Science and Religion*, ch. 3. There is competition from biology, however: see Richard Dawkins' claim that, with the advent of modern biology, 'we no longer have to resort to superstition when faced with the deep problems; Is there a meaning to life; What are we for? What is man?' (*The Selfish Gene* (London, 1978), 1).

[31] Popper maintained that the evolution of the argumentative function of language, because 'it has led to the evolution of science', 'has created what is perhaps the most powerful tool for biological adaption which has ever emerged in the course of organic evolution': Karl Popper, *Objective Knowledge* (London, 1972), 237.

[32] Cases where there were significant scientific developments, but where one might question whether there was something that could be identified as a scientific revolution include Mesopotamia, Egypt, India, Japan, and Mayan civilization. On these see the topical essays in vol. xv of Charles Coulton Gillespie, ed., *Dictionary of Scientific Biography* (New York, 1981), especially: David Pingree, 'History of Mathematical Astronomy in India', 533–633; B. L. van der Waerden,

include classical Greece and the Hellenistic Greek diaspora;[33] Arab-Islamic North Africa/Near East/Iberian peninsula in the ninth, tenth, and eleventh centuries;[34] thirteenth- and fourteenth-century Paris and Oxford;[35] and China from the twelfth to the fourteenth century.[36]

The scientific revolution with which we shall be concerned—*the* Scientific Revolution—is quite different from these. It is sometimes asked why the Scientific Revolution occurred in the West in the modern era and not, say, in China, or medieval Islam, or medieval Paris or Oxford. But it is the Scientific Revolution that requires explanation, not these developments: what is peculiar and exceptional is the nature of scientific development in the West in the modern era.[37] Scientific developments in the classical and Hellenistic worlds, China, the medieval Islamic world, and medieval Paris and Oxford, share a distinctive feature. They each exhibit a pattern of slow, irregular, intermittent growth, alternating with substantial periods of stagnation, in which interest shifts to political, economic, technological, moral, or other questions. Science is just one of a number of activities in the culture, and attention devoted to it changes in the same way attention devoted to the other features may change, with the result that there is competition for intellectual resources within an overall balance of interests in the culture.

The 'Scientific Revolution' of the early-modern West breaks with the boom/bust pattern of all other scientific cultures, and what emerges is the uninterrupted and cumulative growth that constitutes the general rule for scientific development in the West since that time. The traditional balance of interests is replaced by a dominance of scientific concerns, while science itself experiences a rate of growth that is pathological by the standards of earlier cultures, but is ultimately legitimated by the cognitive standing that it takes on. This form of scientific development is exceptional and anomalous. The question is, then, not why the Scientific Revolution didn't occur in any of the other cases of rich, innovative scientific cultures, but why it occurred in the West. The core issue here is this: how was scientific practice in the West so

'Mathematics and Astronomy in Mesopotamia', 667–80; Richard A. Parker, 'Egyptian Astronomy, Astrology, and Calendrical Reckoning', 706–27; Shigeru Nakayama, 'Japanese Scientific Thought', 728–58; Floyd G. Lounsbury, 'Maya Numeration, Computation, and Calendrical Astronomy', 759–818.

[33] See G. E. R. Lloyd, *The Revolutions of Wisdom* (Berkeley, 1987).

[34] See Roshdi Rashed, ed., *Encyclopedia of the History of Arabic Science* (3 vols, London, 1996).

[35] See Marshall Clagett, *The Science of Mechanics in the Middle Ages* (Madison, 1959).

[36] See Joseph Needham, *Science and Civilisation in China* (7 vols in 50 sections, Cambridge, in progress, 1954– ).

[37] This was first pointed out in Joseph Ben-David, *The Scientist's Role in Society* (Chicago, 1984). See also Nathan Sivin, 'Why the Scientific Revolution Did Not Take Place in China—Or Didn't It?' in E. Mendelsohn, ed., *Transformation and Tradition in the Sciences* (Cambridge, 1984), 531–54. Similar considerations hold in the case of technological development: intensive bursts of technological innovations are both rare and isolated, and there is no reason to suppose that technological innovation will continue if unimpeded. In this case, what needs explaining is the peculiarity of the Industrial Revolution of the late eighteenth/early nineteenth century in Western Europe: see Joel Mokyr, *The Lever of Riches: Technological Creativity and Economic Progress* (New York, 1990).

transformed in the course of the modern era that it was able to establish cognitive priority for itself, so that it was able to shape other cognitive values around its own?

To help orientate ourselves, it is worth noting that, in one sense, this mode of development is compatible with Kuhn's model of scientific development in terms of the emergence of new paradigms, which usher in periods of intense scientific activity.[38] But in another sense, it is antithetical to Kuhn's account, for what it suggests is that the development of science in the West since the sixteenth century follows a pattern wholly different from that of any other scientific culture. I know of no concerted attempt to investigate this phenomenon. But since such an investigation is precisely what we shall be setting out to provide, it will be helpful, in understanding the approach that I shall be taking, to have some alternative account with which to contrast it. I suggest such an alternative account is to be found in an implicit general thesis underlying much traditional writing in the history of science and in the philosophy of science which, if it were an accurate account of what was at stake, would explain the peculiarity of scientific development in the West. The core claim of the thesis, as I shall reconstruct it, is that science in the early-modern era was so spectacularly successful that not only could it displace competing accounts, but it was able to extrapolate from the method by which it achieved these fundamental results to all cognitive domains. The first thing to do is to flesh this thesis out a little, and in the process give some account of why it has been thought to have such a plausible ring to it.

Let us start with some historiographical flesh, for it is from this that a good deal of the plausibility of the thesis derives. From the point of view of understanding science as a cultural product, the two most formative scientific events of the modern era have generally been taken to be Copernicanism and Darwinism, the first marking the beginning of this era more decisively than any other scientific development, the latter marking the transition from one cultural idiom to another—very different—cultural idiom. The triumphs of Copernicanism and Darwinism, as they are usually construed, were twofold. In the first place they were successful in the face of fierce opposition from established religion. In the second, they replaced firmly held philosophical views that had persisted since antiquity, and which had the authority of two millennia. If we think of Copernicanism as marking the beginning of the struggle with non-scientific disciplines, and Darwinism marking the start of the final stage of this struggle, then it is tempting to think of their triumphs as indicating the *sui generis* nature of scientific values. That is, what they seem to indicate is that, unlike the cognitive values and norms of theology or the humanities, basic scientific values and norms are open to no refutation from outside.

A fundamental question arises here. If there is something unique about the Scientific Revolution that marks it out from other transformations of scientific cultures,

---

[38] See Thomas Kuhn, *The Structure of Scientific Revolutions* (2nd edn, Chicago, 1962). This kind of approach had been anticipated independently by Ludwig Fleck, *Entstehung und Entwicklung einer wissenschaftlichen Tatsache* (Basle, 1935) and by Gaston Bachelard in *Le Nouvel Esprit scientifique* (Paris, 1934) and *La Formation de l'esprit scientifique* (Paris, 1938). On Bachelard see Stephen Gaukroger, 'Bachelard and the Problem of Epistemological Analysis', *Studies in History and Philosophy of Science* 7 (1976), 189–244.

is this because its practitioners hit upon the only really successful way of pursuing science, or is it that, owing to a variety of contingent reasons, it was able to present its own model of scientific practice (or perhaps an idealized version of it) as the only viable one? I shall use the term 'the Enlightenment Interpretation' for the view that holds that what marks the Scientific Revolution out from other transformations of scientific cultures is that its practitioners hit upon a uniquely successful way of pursuing science, and that the scientific practice that was produced in the Scientific Revolution represents the only way in which scientific practice could have developed with any long-term viability.[39] On the Enlightenment Interpretation, there are two features of scientific development since the Scientific Revolution that are identified as distinctive, and mark it out from other scientific programmes, especially its medieval predecessors. These are its autonomy and its method.

In its most straightforward form, the claim with respect to autonomy is that, unlike medieval natural philosophy, for example, seventeenth-century science gradually breaks free of religious considerations and follows an autonomous path. The claim with respect to method is that the distinctive feature of this autonomous path is a method of investigation that is quantitative and empirical, as a result of which it is able to produce results of lasting value in a way that its medieval predecessors were not. This twofold process of securing autonomy from manifestly inappropriate considerations that are independent of physical evidence, and the establishment of an appropriate and viable method of producing reliable results, then opens up the way for a consolidation of scientific results which marks the scientific enterprise out from other forms of enquiry. This gives us another feature of the Enlightenment Interpretation: that it is not just its remarkable consolidation of results, but the very fact that it is capable of such consolidation, that marks modern scientific practice out from other enterprises and sets new standards of cognitive success by which disciplines that purport to make advances in our knowledge must be judged.

In reflecting on the adequacy of this view, it is crucial that we begin by distinguishing clearly between the kind of factors that might have played a part in the emergence of the Scientific Revolution, and those that might have played a part in its consolidation. In the Enlightenment Interpretation, there is an implicit assumption that a satisfactory account of the former is a satisfactory account of the latter, that the story about the establishment of Copernicanism from Kepler and Galileo onwards, culminating in Newton's *Principia*, for example, explains the subsequent consolidation of science, because these developments finally point us in the right direction—in

---

[39] We shall be dealing with some specific versions, and specific claims, of the Enlightenment Interpretation, but as a general indication of its role as the default position, at least before the influence of Kuhn began to be felt, some of the following general histories may be taken as indicative: Edwin Arthur Burtt, *The Metaphysical Origins of Modern Physical Science: A Historical and Critical Essay* (London, 1924); Butterfield, *The Origins of Modern Science* [1949]; E. J. Dijksterhuis, *The Mechanization of the World Picture* (Oxford, 1961 [orig. pub. 1950]); Charles Singer, *A Short History of Scientific Ideas to 1900* (Oxford, 1959). The Enlightenment Interpretation is still current in some popular histories of science—e.g. John Gribbin, *Science: A History 1543–2001* (London, 2002)—as well as in more specialized ones—e.g. Julian B. Barbour, *Absolute or Relative Motion: A Study from a Machian Point of View of the Discovery and the Structure of Dynamical Theories* (Cambridge, 1989).

the direction of truth—whereas earlier developments, or developments outside the West, were less successful in this respect. The sign of this assumption, where it is only implicit, is the absence of any serious consideration of how the Scientific Revolution was consolidated, as if explaining how it came to be established is *ipso facto* an explanation of its consolidation.[40] But once we consider the question of consolidation seriously, then a moment's reflection shows that such developments could not possibly explain how the Scientific Revolution subsequently came to be consolidated, if only because of the sheer contingency involved in consolidation. Very significant scientific advances, in optics, astronomy, the theory of machines, medical advances, and technological advances had been made in earlier cultures, yet after a period of relatively intense scientific activity things had come to a stop in all these cases.

One can perhaps think of these as mini-scientific revolutions, but what we cannot do is to think of them as failed scientific revolutions. What distinguishes them from *the* Scientific Revolution is their apparent failure to consolidate scientific gains. By consolidation here I do not mean the ability to build up and strengthen particular scientific results or theories or even programmes of research (for they clearly had the ability to do that), but rather to consolidate the scientific enterprise as such. The latter is a legitimatory venture: its concern is with the credentials and standing of a particular kind of activity. Such consolidation aims to establish science as a model of cognitive activity. We should not assume that large-scale consolidation of this type was ever part of the programmes of Alexandrian, Arab-Islamic, or Chinese science, for example. Quite the contrary, the evidence indicates that the solution of a limited range of specific problems seems to have been the rule, and success in this enterprise usually brought an end to significant attention paid to scientific problems. The idea of large-scale consolidation is not something inherent in the scientific enterprise as such, but it is inherent in the scientific enterprise after the Scientific Revolution. Without this kind of consolidation, we would simply not have had the Scientific Revolution: we would have had a development on a par with what happened in early medieval Baghdad or Andalusia, or in Sung and Ming dynasty China. Successful consolidation, of a kind that aims at the promotion of the cognitive claims of science and builds a legitimatory scientific culture around them, is the characteristic feature of the Scientific Revolution. But such consolidation is not simply a question of success, it is a question of success in achieving an aim, an aim absent from earlier scientific cultures, and from those outside the West.

Why and how this aim was generated in the Scientific Revolution is a question at least as worthy of our attention as that of how it was successfully achieved. If large-scale legitimatory consolidation had never played a significant role in scientific

---

[40] The failure to distinguish between the emergence of modern science and the emergence of a scientific culture which legitimates that science also lies at the heart of much of the kind of criticism of science that began with Max Horkheimer's statement in 1946 that 'the collapse of a large part of the intellectual foundation of our civilization is to a certain extent the result of technical and scientific progress': 'Reason Against Itself: Some Remarks on Enlightenment', in James Schmidt, ed., *What is Enlightenment? Eighteenth-Century Answers and Twentieth-Century Questions* (Berkeley, 1996), 359–67: 359. Cf. Stephen Toulmin, *Cosmopolis: The Hidden Agenda of Modernity* (New York, 1990).

programmes, and if their aims had, with some rare exceptions, been largely dictated from outside, how did it come about that an internally generated programme of consolidation developed, and when and under what conditions did this happen? Two key issues here are ones that we have identified in setting out the Enlightenment Interpretation: could the autonomy of science—with respect to religion—and the methodology of science explain the ability of science in the wake of the Scientific Revolution to shape a culture in which it gradually came to provide the models and norms for cognitive enquiry generally?

## SCIENTIFIC AUTONOMY

Consider the autonomy claim first, that is, the view that the success of Western science lay, at least in part, in its ability to dissociate itself from religion.[41] It is certainly true that the relations between religion and natural philosophy shifted quite radically in the sixteenth and seventeenth centuries, but, as we shall see in some detail in the chapters that follow, these shifts are by no means straightforward, and the outcome is by no means a turn away from religion, but rather in many respects a turn towards it. We must remember here that the sixteenth and seventeenth centuries were the most intensely religious centuries Europe has known. A range of exacting moral standards, accompanied by demands for self-vigilance, which had been the preserve of monastic culture throughout the Middle Ages, were transferred wholesale to the general populace in the course of the Reformation and Counter-Reformation.[42] Religious

[41] This is something more characteristic of nineteenth-century and early twentieth-century treatments. See e.g. J. W. Draper, *History of the Conflict between Religion and Science* (London, 1875); A. D. White, *A History of the Warfare of Science and Theology in Christendom* (2 vols, New York, 1896). David S. Landes, in *The Wealth and Poverty of Nations*, esp. ch. 14, is careful to talk of 'organised religion' rather than religion *simpliciter*, and this has been the general view, at least since Robert Merton's *Science, Technology and Society in Seventeenth-Century England* (New York, 1970, first published 1938). The trouble is that this claim is compatible with, yet masks, all kinds of assumptions. At one extreme 'organised religion' might effectively be acting as a euphemism for Roman Catholicism, so that a Weberian Protestant ethic might be assumed to be projecting science forwards (Draper's *History* offered a trenchant criticism of Catholicism but saw a significant role for Protestantism in the early development of science). At the other extreme, it might be being assumed that early-modern natural philosophy is an essentially secular enterprise and is inhibited significantly by organized religion, but not significantly by religion that is not of a centralized authoritative form, perhaps on the assumption that organized religion places constraints on scientific enquiry which religion that is not organized does not. Before we can even begin to ask in what sense (if any) it is true that the success of Western science lay, at least in part, in its ability to dissociate itself from organized religion, we need to ask what form of guidance or constraint organized religion provided that is absent in enquiry not motivated in this way. These are questions to which we shall be devoting considerable attention.

[42] For details see Jean Delumeau's tetralogy, *La Peur en occident (XIV^e–XVIII^e siècles): Une cité assiégée* (Paris, 1978); *Le Péché et la peur: La culpabilisation en occident, XIII^e–XVIII^e siècles* (Paris, 1983); *Rassurer et protéger: Le sentiment de sécuritée dans l'occident d'autrefois* (Paris, 1989); *L'Aveu et le pardon* (Paris, 1992). See also idem, *Le Catholicisme entre Luther et Voltaire* (Paris, 1971); R. Po-Chia Hsia, *Social Discipline in the Reformation* (London, 1989); Gerhard Oestreich, *Neostoicism and the Early Modern State* (Cambridge, 1982), ch. 11; Phillipe Ariès, *Religion populaire et réforme liturgique* (Paris, 1975); and Lucien Febvre, *The Problem of Unbelief in the Sixteenth Century: The Religion of Rabelais* (Cambridge, Mass., 1982).

sensibilities in the secular population were deep and intense in the early-modern era, as deep and intense as anything in monastic culture, and—a crucial point for our concerns—these religious sensibilities motivated a great deal of natural-philosophical enquiry well into the nineteenth century.

We shall see that a good part of the distinctive success at the level of legitimation and consolidation of the scientific enterprise in the early-modern West derives not from any separation of religion and natural philosophy, but rather from the fact that natural philosophy could be accommodated to projects in natural theology: what made natural philosophy attractive to so many in the seventeenth and eighteenth centuries were the prospects it offered for the renewal of natural theology. Far from science breaking free of religion in the early-modern era, its consolidation depended crucially on religion being in the driving seat: Christianity took over natural philosophy in the seventeenth century, setting its agenda and projecting it forward in a way quite different from that of any other scientific culture, and in the end establishing it as something in part constructed in the image of religion. We shall be investigating the complex processes by which this accommodation occurred, and how both natural philosophy and theology were transformed in the process. By the nineteenth century the two had started to come apart, but the intellectual causes of this phenomenon do not lie in any conflict or incompatibility between natural philosophy and theology. Quite the contrary, materialistically inclined atheists (at least before Diderot) were forced to ignore recent developments in natural philosophy, and reverted to the radical naturalistic conceptions that were prevalent immediately prior to the Scientific Revolution.[43]

The case of nineteenth-century Anglicanism is instructive here. The causes of Anglicanism's decline in authority from the 1840s onwards are complex, but the reasons given by those who had 'lost their faith' in Victorian England hardly ever included advances in science.[44] Rather, at least some of the difficulties for Christianity arose because of the emergence, from the seventeenth century onwards, of a historical understanding of, first, the Bible, and then Christianity as a whole, a development that gradually undermined the credentials of Christianity, as it was historicized and then relativized, from Bacon through to Hume and Gibbon. The final blow in the British Isles came with the publication of *Essays and Criticisms* in 1860, where the contributors, predominantly Anglican clergymen, urged the replacement of an inspirational reading of the Bible with a historical one, arguing that the Bible had to be read like any other book.[45] It was primarily biblical criticism and history rather than science that were the external causes of the intellectual rethinking of religious

[43] See Winfried Schröder, *Ursprünge des Atheismus: Untersuchungen zur Metaphysik- und Religionskritik des 17. und 18. Jahrhunderts* (Stuttgart-Bad Cannstatt, 1998).

[44] See the detailed discussion in Susan Budd, *Varieties of Unbelief: Atheists and Unbelievers in English Society 1850–1960* (London, 1977), 104–23.

[45] Victor Shea and William Whitla, eds., *Essays and Reviews: The 1860 Text and Its Reading* (Charlottesville, 2000). See also Ieuan Ellis, *Seven Against Christ: A Study of Essays and Reviews* (Leiden, 1980); and Peter Hinchcliff, *Benjamin Jowett and the Christian Religion* (Oxford, 1987), ch. 4.

sensibilities and sources of authority.[46] As Owen Chadwick points out, in the 1860s 'theologians were busier with the consequences of Biblical criticism than with the consequences of the natural sciences', and after that 'their new historical knowledge made them shrink away from basing the revelation of God upon documents which without doubt contained historical truth but no one could yet say how much truth'.[47]

However, as science sloughed off the religious ideologies that gave it its rationale, it took upon itself the mantle of religion in many respects, while at the same time trying to forge a new rationale for itself. In a lecture in 1853, the most influential advocate of applied science in his time, Lyon Playfair, declared that 'science is a religion and its philosophers are priests of nature', and Huxley referred to his own lectures on science as 'lay sermons'.[48] Beatrice Webb, reflecting on what she refers to as the 'religion of science' of her adolescence in the 1870s, defined it as 'an implicit faith that by the methods of physical science, and by these methods alone, could be solved all the problems arising out of the relation of man to man and of man towards the universe'.[49] 'Who will deny', she asked,

that the men of science were the leading British intellectuals of that period; that it was they who stood out as men of genius with international reputations; that it was they who were routing the theologians, confounding the mystics, imposing their theories on philosophers, their investments on capitalists, and their discoveries on medical men; whilst they were at the same time snubbing the artists, ignoring the poets, and even casting doubts on the capacity of the politicians?[50]

In 1875 Francis Galton was calling for 'a scientific priesthood' to tend to the health and welfare of the nation,[51] and in 1889 the French Darwinian Alfred Giard was claiming that 'among the most happy public expressions of opinion toward the end of this century must be counted the tendency of science to replace gradually the role hitherto enjoyed by religion',[52] an assessment confirmed by the view of the English historian Alfred Benn, who writes in 1906 that 'a great part of the reverence once given to priests and to their stories of an unseen universe has been transferred to the

---

[46] On the impact of German biblical criticism in England in the nineteenth century see John Rogerson, *Old Testament Criticism in the Nineteenth Century* (London, 1984).

[47] Owen Chadwick, 'Evolution and the Churches', in C. A. Russell, *Science and Religious Belief: A Selection of Recent Historical Studies* (London, 1973), 282–93: 288 and 289 respectively.

[48] Quoted in John Hedley Brooke, *Science and Religion* (Cambridge, 1991), 31.

[49] Beatrice Webb, *My Apprenticeship* (London, 1926), 83.

[50] Ibid. 130–1.

[51] Francis Galton, *English Men of Science: Their Nature and Nurture* (New York, 1875), 195. The idea of a secular version of religion had effectively begun with Comte's idea of 'the religion of humanity', fostered by a Comtean 'Positivist Society' founded by Littré and others in the late 1840s, where the idea of a secular religion was promoted. See Frank Manuel and Fritzie Manuel, *Utopian Thought in the Western World* (Cambridge, Mass., 1979), ch. 30; and Leslek Kotakowski, *Positivist Philosophy from Hume to the Vienna Circle* (Harmondsworth, 1972), ch. 3. What we are concerned with here is very different from the idea of a 'scientific priesthood' which might be associated—e.g. in H. Fisch, 'The Scientist as Priest: A Note on Robert Boyle's Natural Theology', *Isis* 44 (1953), 252–65—with those natural philosophers who saw natural philosophy as a way of pursuing natural theology.

[52] Quoted in Brooke, *Science and Religion*, 298.

astronomer, the geologist, the physician, and the engineer'.[53] The trend to see scientists as having a religious standing had begun with Newton's sanctification by his hagiographer John Conduitt, who describes Newton as 'a Saint & his discoveries might well pass for miracles'.[54] Nor was the symbolism of Newton's supposed discovery of the law of universal gravitation by means of a falling apple lost on Newton's admirers. As Patricia Fara points out,

In religious iconography, the infant's apple indicates that Christ, the Second Adam, will redeem humanity. For Bacon's followers, Newton became the new Adam who would uncover God's mathematical laws of nature. [James] Thompson presented him as the saviour who would explain the cosmos to 'erring Man', the fallen human race, and such scriptural metaphors were still widely prevalent in Regency England.[55]

The phenomenon was certainly not confined to England, and it showed no sign of abating over the next two centuries. At the end of the nineteenth century, the great German physicist and physiologist Helmholtz could reflect, autobiographically, on his life in science as being something 'everlastingly sacred', and the work of the scientist as being 'sanctified'.[56]

Internal factors also caused a rethinking of religious sensibilities and sources of authority, however, and if we fail to understand the role of these from the outset we may find ourselves advocating a view of the emergence of a scientific culture which, because of a mistaken understanding of just what we are being called upon to explain, tries to account for local and contingent developments as if they were the logical outcome of large-scale historical forces. Since this is a misunderstanding to which the kind of project in which we shall be engaged is especially susceptible, an example may serve to warn us of the dangers. We shall come across a number of such cases in the course of our investigation of the early-modern development of natural philosophy,

---

[53] Alfred W. Benn, *The History of English Rationalism in the Nineteenth Century* (2 vols., London, 1906), i. 198.

[54] Quoted in Rob Iliffe', "Is He Like Other Men?" The Meaning of the *Principia Mathematica* and the Author as Idol', in Gerald Maclean, ed., *Culture and Society in the Stuart Restoration* (Cambridge, 1995), 159–76: 176.

[55] Patricia Fara, *Newton: The Making of Genius* (London, 2002), 199.

[56] *Science and Culture: Popular and Philosophical Essays*, ed. D. Cahan (Chicago, 1995), 392. See also David Cahan, 'Helmholtz and the Civilizing Power of Science', in David Cahan, ed., *Hermann von Helmholtz and the Foundations of Nineteenth-Century Science* (Berkeley, 1993), 559–601; and Irmline Veit-Brause, 'The Making of Modern Scientific Personae: The Scientist as a Moral Person? Emil du Bois-Reymond and His Friends', *History of the Human Sciences* 15 (2002), 19–50. At the end of the nineteenth century, there was a circle in Germany (the *Monistenbund*) that fostered the idea of a 'religion of science', led by Ernst Haeckel and Friedrich Wilhelm Ostwald, with Ostwald telling us that 'we expect from science the highest that mankind can produce and win on this earth ... Everything that mankind, in terms of its wishes and hopes, its aims and ideals, combines in the concept God, is fulfilled by science': Friedrich Wilhelm Ostwald, *Monism as the Goal of Civilization* (Hamburg, 1913), 37. See the account in H. Schipperges, *Weltbild und Wissenschaft: Eröffnungsreden zu den Naturforscherversammlungen 1822 bis 1972* (Hildesheim, 1976). The movement was represented in the USA by Paul Carus in his *The Religion of Science* (Chicago, 1893) and numerous later books. On the religious image of the scientist in the twentieth century, see Gerhard Sonnert, *Einstein and Culture* (Amherst, 2005), 144–83.

but the best example—one deeply ingrained in popular culture—is the case of the nineteenth-century abandonment of religion in favour of science in England.

The simultaneous combination of the decline in the fortunes of religion and the increase in the fortunes of science has often encouraged the assumption that the abandonment of religion in favour of science was the inevitable outcome of the progress of science, finally bringing to a head and settling a question over the relative authority of science and religion that had been simmering since the condemnations of Copernicanism. But to suppose this is to make assumptions about the role of intellectual factors in the abandonment of Christianity that are wholly unjustified. The well-attested 'crisis of faith' in England from the 1840s onwards was provoked not by the success of science but rather by a complex combination of contingent events, paramount among which are political reaction to the French Revolution, denominational rivalry, and evangelicalism.[57] In the first case, Burke's polemic against the French Revolution had identified atheism and materialism as the main contributing factors, and his work linked resistance to the Revolution with the protection of religion.[58] This certainly led to a deep suspicion of science on the part of some in England, with Patrick Colquhoun, magistrate and police reformer, encouraging elementary education in morals but making it clear that 'science and learning, if universally diffused, would speedily overturn the best constituted government on earth'.[59] Significant resistance to universal scientific education, even on the part of scientists, is clear from the opposition to the Parochial Schools Bill of 1807.[60] On the other hand there was also a sudden explosion of publications expounding natural religion, and two strategies were in operation: clergymen appealed to natural theology to refute the atheism and materialism of radical religious, philosophical, and scientific writers; and scientists (many of whom were clergymen) set out to show that science and rational thought did not lead to atheism and materialism, but to reverence for God and the existing political and social structure.[61] Second, the Anglican Church gradually lost its religious-political

---

[57] For a good summary of the issues, to which I am indebted here, see Frank M. Turner, 'The Victorian Crisis of Faith and the Faith That was Lost', in Richard J. Helmstadter and Bernard Lightman, eds, *Victorian Faith in Crisis: Essays on Continuity and Change in Nineteenth-Century Religious Belief* (London, 1990), 9–38.

[58] See Ursula Henriques, *Religious Toleration in England, 1787–1833* (London, 1961) and V. Kiernan, 'Evangelicalism and the French Revolution', *Past and Present* 1 (1952), 44–56.

[59] Patrick Colquhoun, *A Treatise on Indigence* (London, 1806), 148–9.

[60] See D. S. L. Cardwell, *The Organisation of Science in England* (London, 1972), 38.

[61] Turner, 'The Victorian Crisis', 12–13. The most famous nineteenth-century works in this genre are William Paley, *Natural Theology: or, Evidences of the Existence and Attributes of the Deity, collected from the Appearances of Nature* (London, 1802) and *The Bridgewater Treatises, on the Power, Wisdom, and Goodness of God as Manifested in the Creation*, which appeared between 1834 and 1837. The Bridgewater Treatises covered everything from geology and anatomy to astronomy and the 'moral and intellectual constitution of man'. By the middle of the nineteenth century, evangelical writers in Britain had begun to move away from natural theology back to scriptural sources: see David W. Bebbington, 'Science and Evangelical Theology in Britain from Wesley to Orr', in David N. Livingstone, D. G. Hart, and Mark A. Noll, eds, *Evangelicals and Science in Historical Perspective* (Oxford, 1999), 120–41; and Aileen Fyfe, 'The Reception of William Paley's *Natural Theology* in the University of Cambridge', *British Journal for the History of Science* 30 (1997), 35–59.

monopoly from the end of the eighteenth century—the Catholic emancipation of 1829 came about largely because Parliament no longer believed that the Established Church had any unique claims to precedence on religious matters—and this provoked a very significant increase in theological controversy.[62] Third, with the rise of the evangelical movement from the late eighteenth century, we enter a period of sharp and intense public criticism of ecclesiastical institutions on moral, intellectual, and spiritual grounds. But the aim is to re-Christianize these institutions, not to replace them with something non-Christian. As Turner points out, 'Victorian faith entered crisis not in the midst of any attack on religion but rather during the period of the most fervent crusade that the British nation had known since the seventeenth century, indeed during the last great effort on the part of all denominations to Christianise Britain.'[63]

These developments belie the notion of a gradual but inevitable process of secularization, in which Western culture moves inexorably from Christian to secular. How the relations between science and religion were played out varied, often radically, from country to country, and there was no general movement of inevitable secularization brought about by science. While in France science had gradually been deployed by the *philosophes* in favour of atheism and materialism from the middle of the eighteenth century, in England there was a move in the opposite direction, as science was marshalled in defence of Christianity. The contrast between eighteenth-century England and France is particularly striking here. Priestley, at the radical cutting edge of dissenting thought in England, records his experience of a dinner in France:

When I was dining at . . . Turget's table, M. de Chatellux . . . said the two gentlemen opposite me were the Bishop of Aix and the Archbishop of Toulouse, 'but,' said he, 'they are no more believers than you or I.' I assured him that I was a believer; but he would not believe me.[64]

Even Hume, often regarded as the archetypical British atheist of the eighteenth century, found himself in a similar position when dining with d'Holbach and others in Paris. Hume wondered whether there were in fact any atheists at all in the world, and remarked that he had never actually met one, only to be informed by d'Holbach that he was surrounded by fourteen of them.[65] By contrast, far from associating science and atheism, most British readers had learned what they knew about science from the new religious magazines that sprang up at the end of the eighteenth century, magazines that set out to incorporate scientific reading into the practice of Christian

---

[62] See in particular Jeffrey Cox, *The English Churches in a Secular Society: Lambeth, 1870–1930* (Oxford, 1982); P. T. Marsh, *The Victorian Church in Decline* (London, 1969); and Frank M. Turner, *Between Science and Religion: The Reaction to Scientific Naturalism in Late Victorian England* (New Haven, 1974).

[63] Turner, 'The Victorian Crisis', 11. See also Kenneth Hylson-Smith, *Evangelicals in the Church of England 1734–1984* (Edinburgh, 1989), and Michael R. Watts, *The Dissenters*, ii. *The Expansion of Evangelical Nonconformity* (Oxford, 1995).

[64] Quoted in Brooke', *Science and Religion*, 180.

[65] Interview with Boswell, dated 3 March 1777; the journal entry is given in David Hume, *Dialogues concerning Natural Religion*, ed. and introd. Norman Kemp Smith (Indianapolis, 1947), 76–9. There were actually seventeen at the table, other than Hume himself, but the three remaining had yet to make up their minds on the question.

piety.[66] Similar developments in the USA had quite different effects, as a free market in religious ideas encouraged a proliferation of evangelical sects which continues to this day:[67] despite the constitutional separation of church and state in the First Amendment, the teaching of natural selection theory in state schools could be seriously questioned in the courts, in the second half of the twentieth century, because it conflicted with a literal reading of the Old Testament, and indeed the Kansas Board of Education dropped the teaching of evolution from the state's science curriculum in 1999.[68] Yet at the same time scientific research, including evolutionary biology, has flourished in the USA. The one does not seem to have significantly impeded the other.[69] Early nineteenth-century England was very different from this: there, Christianity had significant difficulty in reorganizing itself to meet a number of challenges that came not from science, but primarily as a consequence of an intensified religious life, provoked in part by the rise of evangelical sects, in which science generally played a supportive role.[70]

Such local factors acted to induce an intensified religious culture in Victorian England, one in which new options were opened up, and choices forced.[71] The intense criticism that we witness in the mid-nineteenth century did not result in a consolidation and renewal of religious belief, however, but rather in a more general search for something that would meet these new moral, spiritual, and intellectual demands. The intensified religious context ruled out complacency in these matters, but it was

---

[66] See John Brooke and Geoffrey Cantor, *Reconstructing Nature: The Engagement of Science and Religion* (Oxford, 1998); Bernard Lightman', "The Voices of Nature": Popularising Victorian Science', in Bernard Lightman, ed., *Victorian Science in Context* (Chicago, 1997), 187–211; idem, 'The Story of Nature: Victorian Popularizers and Scientific Narrative', *Victorian Review* 25 (1999), 1–29; Jonathan R. Topham, 'The *Wesleyan-Methodist* Magazine and Religious Monthlies in Early Nineteenth-Century Britain', in Geoffrey Cantor et al., *Science in the Nineteenth-Century Periodical: Reading the Magazine of Nature* (Cambridge, 2004), 67–90; Aileen Fyfe, *Science and Salvation: Evangelical Popular Science Publishing in Victorian Britain* (Chicago, 2004).

[67] See George M. Marsden, *Fundamentalism and American Culture: The Shaping of Twentieth Century Evangelicalism, 1870–1925* (Oxford, 1980).

[68] The decision was overturned in 2001. The issue is not confined to Kansas, and has if anything been compounded in recent years. A November 2004 CBS poll found that 65% of Americans favoured teaching of creationism in science classes; 37% believed that natural selection should not be taught at all. Fifty-five percent of respondents believed that human beings were not the product of evolution but had been created in their present form. On 2 August 2005, President George W. Bush was reported in the newspapers as publicly supporting the teaching of a version of creationism—'intelligent design'—alongside natural selection in science classes in schools in the USA. There is a useful overview of American fundamentalism in Michael Ruse, *The Evolution-Creation Struggle* (Cambridge, Mass., 2005), chs. 8 and 12.

[69] This may change, however. At the time of writing, it does appears that stem-cell research may in fact be impeded in the USA, for example, on grounds that bear only very tangentially on genuine ethical issues and seem to be driven primarily by political and religious considerations. More generally, on the subordination of science to a political agenda by some conservatives in the USA, see Chris Mooney, *The Republican War on Science* (New York, 2005).

[70] In England, the development of a free market in religious ideas beginning with the repeal of the Tests Act had the opposite effect to that in the USA: see Cox, *The English Churches*.

[71] Cf. Matthew Arnold: 'Two things about the Christian religion must surely be clear to anyone with eyes in his head. One is, that men cannot do without it; the other that they cannot do with it as it is.' *God and the Bible* (New York, 1893), p. xi.

less successful in dictating the range of possible solutions. This left scope for science, which had played a crucial role in the debates against atheism and materialism, to be seen as something that might meet these new moral, spiritual, and intellectual demands. It is worth noting here that in his *A Survey of the Wisdom of God in the Creation* (1763), John Wesley, the writer to whom the evangelical movement owed most, had both pursued and recommended the study of nature on the grounds that it inspired awe and humility in the face of the marvellous organization in the created order. He saw the wonderful fit between the functional anatomy of animals and plants and their environment as a pious alternative to the arrogance of theologians.[72] The move to science for those disillusioned with traditional forms of Christianity was by no means a radical one. As Turner notes,

The activities of the advocates of scientific naturalism during the third quarter of the century in particular illustrate the actions of engaged laymen criticising the adequacy of religion in a manner reminiscent of evangelicalism. Their attack pitted what they regarded as real religion, honest in thought and morally beneficent in action, against the nominal religion of the Anglican Church. . . . Anglican clerical scientists and other interested clergy had claimed to resist the inroads of materialism, which was regarded as a political and social as well as a spiritual danger, through their . . . advocacy and support of natural theology. The scientists and scientifically-minded philosophers associated with scientific naturalism sought to beat the Church of England at its own cultural game. Like the evangelicals of an earlier day, the honest doubters and advocates of scientific naturalism demanded a truer and more genuine religion that was not an intellectual, political, and moral scandal.[73]

It is in this context that Huxley's invention of the notion of 'agnosticism' plays a key role in marking out his group from atheists and materialists, while at the same time offering an evolutionary form of natural religion.[74] The 'agnostics' could present themselves on the one hand as opponents of immoderate religious movements and on the other as opponents of Catholicism, at a time when factions within the established Church were prevaricating.

But, of course, this scientific movement had features that marked it out from religious movements. One of Huxley's inner circle, the mathematician T. A. Hirst, wrote of their 'X Club' founded in 1864, that its aim was 'devotion to science, pure and free, untrammeled by religious dogmas. Amongst ourselves there is perfect outspokenness.'[75] The new scientific movement was committed to a new ideology—unfettered

---

[72] John Wesley, *A Survey of the Wisdom of God in the Creation: or a Compendium of Natural Philosophy* (2 vols, London, 1827).

[73] Turner, 'The Victorian Crisis', 17–18. It is worth remembering, nevertheless, that in Galton's 1874 survey of English scientists, 70% of them regarded themselves as Anglicans: *English Men of Science*, 126–7.

[74] In fact, Huxley was not successful in controlling the term, which came to be associated with Spenser's philosophy of the 'unknowable': see Bernard Lightman, 'Huxley and Scientific Agnosticism: The Strange History of a Failed Rhetorical Strategy', *British Journal for the History of Science* 35 (2002), 271–89.

[75] Cited in Lightman, 'Huxley and Scientific Agnosticism', 272. See also Roy MacLeod, 'A Victorian Scientific Network: The X-Club', *Notes and Records of the Royal Society* 24 (1969), 305–22; and J. Vernon Jensen, 'The X Club: Fraternity of Victorian Scientists', *British Journal for the History of Science* 5 (1970/1), 63–72.

adversarial engagement—and with this came a distinctive kind of concern with scientific method. Method was not seen as something that one might devise to help one in particular scientific investigations, as it had been in the sixteenth and seventeenth centuries, but as a *post facto* rationalization of the success of science, in the work of Whewell, Mill, and others. This tied science into a new adversarial and democratic culture, which by virtue of these qualities was also meritocratic. The new theories of method combined the demands of quasi-religious authority, whereby there was a single authorized road to truth, and the demands of a meritocratic adversarial basis for science. It was these new theories of method that were considered to be what it was that provided science with its unique road to success. As Huxley put it in 1866:

If these ideas be destined, as I believe they are, to be more and more firmly established as the world grows older; if that spirit be fated, as I believe it is, to extend itself into all departments of human thought, and to become co-extensive with the range of knowledge; if, as our race approaches its maturity, it discovers, as I believe it will, that there is but one kind of knowledge and but one method of acquiring it; then we, who are still children, may justly feel it our highest duty to recognise the advisableness of improving natural knowledge, and so aid ourselves and our successors in our course towards the noble goal which lies before mankind.[76]

A modern version of this project can be found in the work of Karl Popper. Popper also drew the connections between science and a democratic culture explicitly,[77] and he tied this in with the idea that the aim of the scientific enterprise is to try to falsify theories.[78] In Popper's account, the 'scientist as hero' reaches his apogee, taking on the role of the ascetic by a form of intellectual self-deprivation. Fighting his natural inclinations, the scientist must himself try to show the theories he has nurtured to be false. In compensation, however, he attains to a form of intellectual morality of a profound kind to which no one else can reasonably aspire: the scientist becomes the only truly intellectually honest person, for only the scientist is so concerned for truth that he works on the assumption that his own theories are false.[79] The parallels with the ascetic monk who considers himself permanently unworthy are too obvious to be pressed.

[76] T. H. Huxley, *Collected Essays* (9 vols, New York, 1893–4) i. 41.

[77] Popper, *The Open Society*, and *The Poverty of Historicism*. The theme goes back to John Stuart Mill, *On Liberty* (London, 1859). Paul Feyerabend, in his *Against Method* (London, 1975), took a more Millian view of modern liberal democracy than Popper, seeing its strongest feature as its pluralism, and he devised his scientific method accordingly, under the slogan of 'anything goes'.

[78] Karl R. Popper, *The Logic of Scientific Discovery* (rev. edn, London, 1968).

[79] Imre Lakatos, in his very influential paper 'Falsification and the Methodology of Scientific Research Programmes', in Imre Lakatos and Alan Musgrave, eds, *Criticism and the Growth of Knowledge* (Cambridge, 1970), 91–196, which set the agenda for a whole generation of post-Popperian thinking, is even more explicit. He writes: '*Sophisticated methodological falsificationism* offers new standards for intellectual honesty. Justificationist honesty demanded the acceptance of only what was proven and the rejection of everything unproven. Neojustificationist honesty demanded the specification of the probability of any hypothesis in the light of the available empirical evidence. The honesty of naïve falsificationism demanded the testing of the falsifiable and the rejection of the unfalsifiable and the falsified. Finally, the honesty of sophisticated falsificationism demanded that one should try to look at things from different points of view, to put forward new theories which anticipate novel facts, and to reject theories which have been superseded by more powerful ones' (122).

## METHOD AND LEGITIMATION

It might seem that Popper has overplayed his hand here, but two points are worth noting. First, the idea that the natural philosopher must be someone who has personal qualities that enable him to act as a paradigm of intellectual honesty pervades early-modern natural philosophy, and can be found set out explicitly as least as early as Descartes.[80] It is one of the constitutive ingredients in the early-modern construction of the *persona* of the natural philosopher. Popper is simply one of the most recent to try to articulate—through his notion of falsification—just what is involved in this idea of intellectual honesty. Second, the claims of the Enlightenment Interpretation for the cognitive standing of science over religion thrive on the idea of the intellectual honesty of science, on its uncompromising probing of the evidence unhindered by dogma. If one wanted to defend the Enlightenment Interpretation on this question, Popper's programme offers a way of engaging the issues. Nevertheless, it soon becomes clear that this route is not a productive one. Questions of intellectual honesty do play an important role in the legitimation of the scientific enterprise from the early-modern era onwards, and they are crucial to the notion of scientific authority, but they are complex questions that go to the heart of what we might term the moral psychology of the natural philosopher, not the kinds of things that can simply be reduced to commitment to a particular methodology. Methodological questions are in any case highly overdetermined, and the connection between what drives the early development of the Scientific Revolution and what drives its consolidation as a model for cognitive enquiry is particularly problematic. Some of the problems here can be highlighted by considering the role of adversarial procedures in scientific enquiry.

In comparisons of the development of natural philosophy in the early-modern West with other cultures that initiated and supported successful scientific developments, two things have traditionally been claimed as the basis for its comparative success: its ability to dissociate itself from religion, and its independent adversarial approach. David Landes, for example, argues that economic and social progress in the modern world are due to Western civilization and its dissemination, and he identifies science as one of the crucial ingredients in Europe's economic growth. Science in the West, he argues, developed as an autonomous method of intellectual enquiry that successfully disengaged itself from the social constraints of organized religion and from the political constraints of centralized authority, and that, although Europe lacked a political centre, its scholars benefited from the use of a single vehicle of communication, Latin, which facilitated adversarial discourse in which new ideas about the physical world could be tested, demonstrated, and then accepted across the continent and eventually across the world.[81]

To give consideration of adversarial methods more substance, we need to add another dimension to the discussion, going beyond individual commitment to

[80] See Stephen Gaukroger, *Descartes' System of Natural Philosophy* (Cambridge, 2002), 239–44.
[81] David S. Landes, *The Wealth and Poverty of Nations: Why Some are So Rich and Some are So Poor* (New York, 1999), esp. ch. 14.

method. We need to consider the large-scale social and institutional context that shapes the possibility of an adversarial approach, as a number of writers in the Weberian tradition, notably Nelson and Huff,[82] have done. The Weberian approach takes its bearings from Weber's discovery that, in the East, a number of the pre-industrial cultures possessed the necessary technology and structures for the development of capitalism, yet (as he saw it) lacked the kinds of motives and sanctions needed to encourage the abandonment of traditional values. This raises the question of what provided these motives and sanctions in the West. In a comparison of Arab-Islamic, Chinese, and early-modern European scientific cultures, for example, Huff locates successful adversarial practice as occupying a central point between what we might characterize as an atomistic intellectual culture, namely that of Arab Islam, in which adversarial argument is possible but in which there is no network for following up the outcome of such argument, and the holist intellectual culture typical of Sung- and Ming-dynasty China, where there is an extensive network for the communication of results, but little role for adversarial argument. Islam had no corporate entities, China had only one, but the West had many, and this, Huff argues, enables the West to establish 'neutral zones of free enquiry' which both allow and encourage innovation, and grant science a measure of autonomy without which it could not survive in a hostile climate.[83]

On this account, Arab-Islamic science had two distinctive features. The first is that there was no institutional support available for scientific work that was not motiv-ated by extra-scientific concerns; but mathematical astronomy, for example, received strong institutional support at centres such as the Marāgha observatory, because of the importance of determining the direction of Mecca at different locations if one was to face Mecca while praying. Islamic law did not recognize—indeed refused on religious grounds to recognize—corporate entities, with the consequence that no autonomous status groups, whether professional groups (with some qualifications in the case of medicine) or institutions such as universities were able to develop. And in the absence of such an institutional setting in a society in which daily life was regulated in a com-prehensive way by religion, not only theories at variance with religious doctrine, but even those with no bearing on religious doctrine, were discouraged. Even though the teaching methods were adversarial, as a student one's interaction was limited to one's mullah. Innovation was at best frowned upon and at worst treated as a form of heresy. Second, the way in which the achievements of Greek philosophers, and Greek and Alexandrian mathematicians, were 'naturalized' in Arab-Islamic culture is distinct-ive. They were domesticated, incorporated into an indigenous cultural and philo-sophical system, rather than being institutionalized in such a way that they carried 'their own specific gravity of autonomy and legitimacy, independent of the moral and

---

[82] Benjamin Nelson, *On the Roads to Modernity: Conscience, Science, and Civilizations* (Towota, NJ, 1981), chs. 7, 8, and 9; and Toby E. Huff, *The Rise of Early Modern Science* (Cambridge, 1993).

[83] In some respects, this idea has affinities with Gibbon's typically Enlightenment view that the political pluralism of modern Europe allowed freedom of thought by preventing a return to the intellectual tyrannies of the Roman Empire and Christianity.

religious scruples of the surrounding culture'.[84] The consequence of these two institutional features of Arab-Islamic civilization is that while it was occasionally possible for innovations to be made in astronomy, optics, and even metaphysics, there was no way in which they could be followed up in a systematic manner.

The case of China is almost the reverse. If Arab-Islamic culture could initiate scientific developments but not follow them up, China had an extensive network of communications and this acted in such a way as to foster scientific and technological developments. In the Sung and Ming dynasties we find inventions such as mechanical clocks, movable type, and seismographs that predate developments in the West by at least a couple of centuries; and we find significant advances in observational astronomy and medicine, as well as an understanding and employment of a variety of products and devices from explosives to magnets. Yet there were serious obstacles to innovation that was not practically oriented. The bureaucratic structure of Chinese society is a crucial factor here. Not only was the office of emperor increasingly sacralized in the Ming dynasty, traditions of philosophical disputation are relatively marginal in Chinese intellectual culture.[85] Adherence to tradition plays a crucial role in all artistic and intellectual pursuits to a far greater extent than was ever the case in Arab-Islamic culture or the Christian West, with the result that there is a strong sense that scholarship rather than innovation is the path to wisdom. This was reinforced by the Confucian tendency to self-effacement and avoidance of contentiousness, as well as a strong commitment to outward obedience to public authorities.

The contrast between Arab-Islamic, Chinese, and Western culture in these respects is strikingly evident in the very different ways in which the legal process functions in these cultures, and Huff considers differences here to lie at the root of many of the others. Islam and the West both had adversarial systems of sorts, and legal reasoning, with its highly developed notions of proof and evidence, had an important effect on reasoning in general, particularly in the West. This is completely lacking in China. There were no private lawyers in China: the very idea of having someone help argue one's case before the authorities was alien to the whole system and in the rare cases where it happened it was punished severely.[86] As G. E. R. Lloyd notes,

So far from positively delighting in litigation, as many Greeks seem to have done, so far from developing a taste for confrontational argument in that context and becoming quite expert

---

[84] Huff, *The Rise of Early Modern Science*, 63. This aspect of Islamic learning is contrasted with that of the West in Remi Brague, *Eccentric Culture: A Theory of Western Civilization* (South Bend, Ind., 2002), ch. 5.

[85] On this see Nathan Sivin, 'On the Word "Taoist" as a Source of Perplexity. With Special Reference to the Relations of Science and Religion in Traditional China', *History of Religions* 17 (1978), 303–30; and idem, 'Ruminations on the Dao and its Disputers', *Philosophy East and West* 42 (1992), 21–9. See also the discussion in G. E. R. Lloyd, *Adversaries and Authorities: Investigations into Ancient Greek and Chinese Science* (Cambridge, 1996), 26–41.

[86] Huff notes such behaviour was tantamount to challenging the word of a public authority and was an unforgivable sign of disrespect and dissension, 'the ultimate betrayal of filial piety, of family and clan, and, above all, the betrayal of the principle of *jang*, yieldingness'. *The Rise of Early Modern Science*, 269.

in its evaluation, the Chinese avoided any brush with the law as far as they possibly could. Disputes that could not be resolved by arbitration were felt to be a breakdown of due order and as such reflected unfavourably on *both* parties, whoever was in the right.[87]

This lack of an adversarial model shaped the way in which scientific practice was pursued in China, and Chinese respect for authority formed a sharp contrast with the Greek model of confrontational debate.[88] The situation in Islam was totally different. The judge of religious law—the *qadi*—was not in a position to innovate, but merely to interpret the law. Because this law had been handed down from God, interpretations could vary. There was no individual could decide between genuine, conscientious, and properly intentioned judgements, no mere mortal who could speak on behalf of God. Consequently, there was scope for shopping around—'forum shopping' as lawyers call it—for judgements, and one could then follow that more favourable to one's case. There are parallels in education here. In China, only the State could ever certify a student's competence. No individual could have this power, no matter what his skills or standing. In Islam, only an individual teacher could ever certify a student's competence. In neither case was there a corporate body of expertise—a professional body, a university, or whatever—to which those with special skills could make a contribution, and which could provide certification of competence. And in neither case was there a system that could provide group support for those who questioned tradition, or had heterodox views.

   This, on Huff's account, is the essential difference between China, Arab Islam, and the West. What lies at its source is the Investiture Controversy (1050–1122), in which the Church was effectively formed as a corporation, declaring itself legally autonomous from the secular order. In the wake of this, Gratian's codification of canon law around 1140 began the construction of a new system of law. This not only harmonized various legal traditions but provided new foundations for the law, creating a new science of law which became a model of intellectual achievement, and establishing a principle of authority and legitimacy over discordant authorities. What this legal revolution did, Huff argues, was to create a 'neutral space for enquiry', and this is what allowed innovation to occur. Moreover, by instituting corporate bodies—towns, cities, guilds, universities, professional groups—on its own model, it brought about a kind of decentralization of responsibilities and expertise which created the kind of protected climate in which such innovations could flourish.

   I offer this account as an illustration of how we might achieve a good deal more insight once we lift questions of method outside the realm of pure epistemology, and we can learn vital lessons from it. But the lessons lie in appreciating the value of the extra dimensions of analysis, and it soon becomes evident that we must go

---

[87] Lloyd, *Adversaries and Authorities*, 220. It seems to have been the Greeks who were exceptional in this respect, not the Chinese. As Lloyd notes elsewhere, 'The extant remains of Egyptian and Babylonian medicine, mathematics and astronomy can be combed in vain for a single example of a text where an individual author explicitly distances himself from, and criticises, the received tradition in order to claim originality for himself, whereas our Greek sources repeatedly do that' (*The Revolutions of Wisdom*, 57).

[88] See Lloyd, *Adversaries and Authorities*, ch. 2.

beyond what turns out to be the somewhat formulaic contrasts offered in this kind of Weberian approach. If we confine our attention to two issues—the existence of a neutral space for enquiry, and the role of an adversarial culture—we can glimpse the extent of the challenge.

First, the appropriateness of the idea of 'neutral spaces for enquiry'—and the idea of corporate entities such as universities providing such neutral spaces—is questionable. If there were any 'neutral spaces' in the first half of the seventeenth century, for example, they were not much in evidence in the universities.[89] Rather we must turn to the patronage of figures such as the Medici (Galileo), Maurice of Nassau (Stevin), Peiresc (Gassendi), the Earl of Northumberland (the circle that included Harriot, Hues, and Warner) and the Marquis of Newcastle (Digby and Hobbes), or to the use of private means (Descartes and Boyle), or some form of professional employment (Charleton) or public employment (Bacon) which left time to pursue natural philosophy. None of these were unique to the West. Moreover, even if the universities had provided the requisite neutral spaces, the new generation of natural philosophers could have learned little from them because they were teaching the wrong things. Neither Galileo nor Descartes, for example, was able to pick up the mathematical skills he so desperately needed during the course of his university education. Galileo had initially studied medicine at Pisa but left before completing his degree, and in 1583 started learning mathematics at his father's house from the Florentine court instructor Ostilio Ricci, who taught military fortification, mechanics, architecture, and perspective.[90] Descartes similarly learned his mathematics in a practical context: having studied law at Poitiers, he picked up and refined his mathematical skills in the armies of Prince Maurice of Nassau and Maximilian I, to which he was attached from 1618 to 1620.[91] More generally, it is far from clear that what we should be doing is trying to identify a single 'neutral space of enquiry'. Natural philosophy was not a uniform field, and the kind of conditions under which one might fruitfully pursue ballistics or mineral extraction, for example, are likely to be very different from those under which one might fruitfully pursue questions about the formation and age of the earth. Moreover, we shall see that some areas of natural philosophy were pursued in a way that was closely guided by natural-theological considerations, flourishing—and quite possibly only able to flourish—in an environment that was far from 'neutral'.

---

[89] John Gascoigne gives a figure of 42% for university-educated natural philosophers born between 1551 and 1650 holding career university posts who were sufficiently noteworthy to be included in the *Dictionary of Scientific Biography*: 'A Reappraisal of the Role of the Universities in the Scientific Revolution', in David C. Lindberg and Robert S. Westman, eds, *Reappraisals of the Scientific Revolution* (Cambridge, 1990), 207–60: 209.

[90] See Stillman Drake, *Galileo at Work* (Chicago, 1978), ch. 1; Thomas B. Settle, 'Ostilio Ricci, A Bridge Between Alberti and Galileo', *Actes du XIIᵉ Congrès International d'Histoire des Sciences* (Paris, 1971), 121–6; and Mario Biagioli, *Galileo Courtier, The Practice of Science in the Culture of Absolutism* (Chicago, 1993), 6–8.

[91] See Stephen Gaukroger, *Descartes, An Intellectual Biography* (Oxford, 1995), 62–7. More generally, see Geoffrey Parker, *The Army of Flanders and the Spanish Road, 1567–1659: The Logistics of Spanish Victory and Defeat in the Low Countries' Wars* (Oxford, 1972); and specifically on the professionalization of armies at this time, see Philippe Contamine, *Guerre, État et société à la fin du moyen âge* (Paris, 1972), 536–46.

   This prompts a more general question, about whether it might be unhelpfully anachronistic to think about a 'neutral space of enquiry' in the early-modern era. Talk of a neutral space makes sense when we think of science primarily in terms of truth, because what such a space provides is a way of following arguments through to their conclusions without hindrance from prejudice or dogma. But although early-modern natural philosophers were of course concerned with truth, public discussion of the value of natural philosophy tended to turn on its usefulness rather than its truth.[92] This is important if we are to understand the disputes over the legitimacy of the natural-philosophical enterprise. The ultimately successful form taken by the development of early-modern natural philosophy was in no way determined from the outset. Quite the contrary, even the image of natural philosophy as an inherently worthwhile enterprise is not something that was secure in the Scientific Revolution. Within three years of receiving its charter, the newly formed Royal Society almost collapsed through lack of attendance at meetings and lack of funds.[93] While in seventeenth-century Italy, for example, one would be hard pressed to find a Tuscan prince and nobleman who did not at least feign an interest in natural philosophy, in Britain the Royal Society and its members were the subject of a great amount of sharp criticism and ridicule.[94] In a sermon preached at Westminster Abbey in 1667, the Public Orator of the University of Oxford, Robert South, refers to the Fellows of the Royal Society as 'the profane, atheistical, epicurean rabble, whom the nation so rings of, and who have lived so much to the defiance of God'. They are

a company of lewd, shallow-brained huffs making atheism and contempt of religion, the sole badge and character of wit, gallentry, and true discretion; and then over their pots and pipes, claiming and engrossing all these wholly to themselves; magisterially censuring the wisdom of all antiquity, scoffing at all piety, and, as it were, new modelling the whole world.... The truth is, the persons here reflected upon are of such a peculiar stamp of impiety, that they seem to be a set of fellows got together, and formed into a kind of diabolical society, for the finding out new experiments in vice.[95]

King Charles II, the patron of the Royal Society, referred to the Fellows as 'my fer-rets', and is reported by Pepys as laughing at Sir William Petty and others on a visit

---

[92] This is true of Renaissance conceptions as well, except that for Renaissance thinkers the utility of knowledge lay in its capacity to make us wiser and happier, whereas in the early-modern era there is a shift to seeing usefulness in terms of the improvement of our material conditions through increased control over nature.

[93] Contrary to its initial expectations, the Royal Society failed to secure an endowment from the King. This made it almost wholly dependent upon the joining fees and subscriptions of its Fellows, which explains why, by contrast with its continental counterparts, its membership consisted predominantly of men of wealth and high status, whose contribution to natural philosophy was often very small. See Michael Hunter, *The Royal Society and its Fellows 1660–1700* (2nd edn, Oxford, 1994), ch. 2.

[94] Satire and ridicule were not confined to the anti-Royal Society ranks, however. Sprat and Dryden dished it out from the Royal Society side and later Mandeville joined their ranks, and the Royal Society does not seem to have suffered more than its opponents. See Michael Hunter, *Science and the Shape of Orthodoxy: Intellectual Change in Late Seventeenth-Century Britain* (Woodbridge, 1995).

[95] Robert South, *Sermons preached upon Several Occasions* (7 vols., Oxford, 1823), i. 373–5.

to the Royal Society in 1664, 'for spending time only in weighing of ayre, and doing nothing else since they sat'.[96] Oldenberg wrote to Boyle in 1666 that Wren's plans for the rebuilding of London in the wake of the Great Fire should have been put to greater propaganda use since

such a modell, contrived by him, and received and approved by ye R. Society, or a Committee thereoff, before it had come to the view of his Majesty, would have given the Society a name, and made it popular, and availed not a litle to silence those, who aske continually, What have they done?[97]

The concern was still being echoed by Evelyn thirteen years later. ''Tis impossible to conceive', he writes, 'how so honest, and worthy a *design* should have found so few *Promoters*, and so cold a welcome in a *Nation* whose *eyes* are so wide open.'[98]

When Thomas Shadwell's comedy *The Virtuoso* was staged in London in 1676 (it was so popular it ran, on and off, for the next twenty years), natural philosophers were cruelly and publicly lampooned, and Hooke was singled out for special attention in the person of Sir Nicholas Gimcrack, 'who has broken his brains about the nature of maggots; who has studi'd these twenty years to find out the several sorts of Spiders, and never cares for understanding Mankind'.[99] Gimcrack remarks that ''tis below a Virtuoso, to trouble himself with Men and Manners. I study Insects.' At one point, on being discovered imitating the movements of a frog in order to learn how to swim, he declares that he contents himself with the speculative part of swimming, not the practical part, since knowledge, and not use, is his ultimate end.[100] Hooke was severely embarrassed on attending the play, recording in his diary: 'Damned dogs. *Vindica me deus* [God grant me revenge]. People almost pointed.'[101]

In 1709, William King published parodies of the Royal Society's *Philosophical Transactions* in which instructions were included on how to write unintelligibly.[102] Nine years earlier, he had attacked the editor of the *Transactions*, Sir Hans Sloane,

---

[96] Cited in Lisa Jardine, *On A Grander Scale: The Outstanding Career of Christopher Wren* (London, 2002), 185.

[97] Oldenburg to Boyle, 18 Sept, 1666: Henry Oldenburg, *The Correspondence of Henry Oldenburg*, ed. A. Rupert Hall and Marie Boas Hall (13 vols., Madison, 1965–75), iii. 231.

[98] John Evelyn, *Sylva; or, A Discourse of Forest-Trees, and the Propagation of Timber in His Majesties Dominions* (London, 1679), sig. A3v.

[99] Thomas Shadwell, 'The Virtuoso', in *Complete Works*, ed. Montague Summers (5 vols, London, 1927), iii. 113. Compare Meric Casaubon's comment on the Royal Society, eight years earlier: 'They therefore that would reduce all learning to natural experiments...how well they provide for Religion, the peace and tranquillity of publick Estates, the maintenance of truth, whether in matters Civil or Ecclesiastical; and what will be the end of such attempts...though such men cannot, or will not yet all wise men may easily foresee' (*Of Credulity and Incredulity in Things Natural, Civill and Divine*, 136).

[100] Richard Baxter, in an undated letter to Boyle, refers to his experimental philosophy as 'recreations', unlike card-playing, but recreations none the less: *The Works of the Honourable Robert Boyle* ed. Thomas Birch (6 vols, London, 1772), vi. 516.

[101] Robert Hooke, *Diary, 1672–80*, ed. H. W. Robinson and W. Adams (London, 1935), 235.

[102] William King, *The Original Works of William King, LL.D.* (3 vols, London, 1776), ii. 57–178.

telling his readers that Sloane,

hath not so much as neglected an Ear-pick or a Rusty Razor, for he values any thing that comes
from the Indies or China at a high rate; for were it but a Pebble, or a Cockle-shell from thence,
he'd soon write a Comment upon it, and perpetuate its Memory upon a Coper-plate . . . there
is not an odd coloured or an ill shapen pebble in the Kingdom, but the Secretary will manage
it so as to make it contribute to the general heap of Transactions.[103]

Magnetism was a particular source of amusement, with the journalist Ned Ward
in 1700 dismissing magnets along with the other 'Philosophical Toys' at 'Maggot-
mongers Hall' (the Royal Society). His contemporary Thomas Brown describes how
physicians, trying to cure a boy who had accidentally swallowed a knife, decided
upon a 'more Philosophical' remedy, 'and therefore better approv'd; and that was,
to apply a *Loadstone* to his *Arse*, and so draw it out by a *Magnetick* Attraction'.[104]
Perhaps the best-known caricature of the Royal Society, however, is the Academy of
Lagado on the island of Laputa ('whore' in Italian)—a caricature of Bacon's *New
Atlantis*—in Jonathan Swift's *Gulliver's Travels*, first published in 1726.[105] Here the
cranks of unworkable machines are turned, and attempts are made to store sunbeams
in cucumbers, to be opened on cold days to provide heating. This hostility towards
natural philosophy, which continued well into the nineteenth century,[106] was never
confined to Great Britain. In 1740, Linnaeus wrote:

one question is always asked, one objection always made to those who show curiosity about
nature, when ill-educated people see natural philosophers examining its products. They ask,
often with contempuous laughter, 'What use is it?' . . . Such people think that natural philosophy is just about the gratification of curiosity, just an amusement to pass the time for lazy
and thoughtless people.[107]

---

[103] *William King, The Original Works of William King, LL. D.* i. 14–16. Cf. Alexander Pope's
lines in the *Dunciad*: 'Impale a Glow-worm, or Vertu profess | Shine in the dignity of F.R.S.' King
is not completely off-target on the interest in pebbles, and stones more generally. See the letter
from Hooke to Boyle, 5 June 1663 in R. T. Gunther, *Early Science in Oxford* (15 vols, Oxford,
1923–67), vii. 132–3.

[104] Both quoted in Patricia Fara, *Sympathetic Attractions: Magnetic Practices, Beliefs, and Symbolism
in Eighteenth-Century England* (Princeton, 1996), 159–60. It is just possible that Brown may have
known of the Swiss physician Wilhelm Fabricius von Hilden, who, some time in the early decades
of the seventeenth century, used a magnet to remove an iron splinter.

[105] The 'High Tory' satirical reaction to science in the eighteenth century is usefully summarized
in Richard G. Olson, 'Tory-High Church Opposition to Science and Scientism in the Eighteenth
Century: The Works of John Arbuthnot, Jonathan Swift, and Samuel Johnson', in John G. Burke,
*The Uses of Science in the Age of Newton* (Berkeley, Calif., 1983), 171–204.

[106] The change in the fortunes of science in *Punch*, from a satirical attitude in the 1840s to a
more respectful one as the the century progressed, is traced in Richard Noakes, '*Punch* and Comic
Journalism in Mid-Victorian Britain', in Cantor et al., *Science in the Nineteenth-Century Periodical*,
91–122.

[107] Charles Linnaeus, *L'Équilibre de la nature*, trans. B. Jasmin, introd. C. Limoges (Paris, 1972).
145–6. Such 'lazy and thoughtless' people could, however, occasionally be awakened from their
slumbers by natural-philosophical spectacles. A report in the *Gentleman's Magazine* for 1745 (vol.
15, p. 194) notes that demonstrations of electrical phenomena were 'so surprising as to awaken
the indolent curiosity of the public, the ladies and people of quality, who never regard natural
philosophy but when it works miracles'.

Likewise on the other side of the dispute: what defenders of the value of natural philosophy from Francis Bacon onwards defended and promoted was its usefulness. Indeed, it was these defences of the usefulness of natural philosophy that came first, and they set the terms on which questions of its value were disputed. Bacon tell us in *Novum Organum* that 'the true and lawful goal of the sciences is none other than this: that human life be endowed with new discoveries and powers'.[108] Christopher Wren takes up the theme in his draft of the Royal Society's charter:

The Way to so happy a Government, we are sensible is in no manner more facilitated than by the promoting of useful Arts and Sciences, which, upon mature Inspection, are found to be the basis of civil Communities, and free Governments, and which gather multitudes, by an *Orphean* Charm, into Cities, and connect them in *Companies*; that so, by laying in a Stock, as it were, of several Arts, and Methods of Industry, the whole body may be supplied by a mutual Commerce of each others peculiar faculties; and consequently that the various Miseries and toils of this frail Life, may, by the Wealth and Plenty be diffused in just Proportion to every one's Industry, that is, to every one's Deserts.[109]

This theme also forms the core of Sprat's vindication of the Royal Society, set out in detail in Part 3 of his *History of the Royal-Society* (1657).[110] The title page of Glanvill's *Plus Ultra* (1668) contrasts the 'practical, useful learning' of the new natural philosophers with 'the notional way'.[111] It continues throughout the seventeenth and eighteenth centuries, with Priestley, one of the great spokesmen for the value of science, writing in 1768 that

all knowledge will be subdivided and extended; and knowledge, as Lord Bacon observes, being power, the human powers will, in fact, be increased; nature, including both its materials, and its laws, will be more at our command; men will make their situation in this world abundantly more easy and comfortable; they will probably prolong their existence in it, and will grow daily more happy, each in himself, and more able (and, I believe, more disposed) to communicate happiness to others.[112]

Even Huxley's defence of science, a century later, still turns on it usefulness. He talks of a 'new nature' created by science and manifested 'in every mechanical artifice, every chemically pure substance employed by manufacture, every abnormally fertile race of

---

[108] Francis Bacon, *The Works of Francis Bacon* ed. James Spedding, Robert Leslie Ellis, and Douglas Denon Heath (14 vols, London, 1857–74), iii. 79.

[109] Text as given in Stephen Wren, *Parentalia: or, memoirs of the Family of the Wrens; viz. Of Mathew Bishop of Ely, Christopher Dean of Windsor, &c. but chiefly of Sir Christopher Wren, late Surveyor-General of the Royal Buildings, President of the Royal Society, &c. &c.* (London, 1750), 196–7.

[110] Thomas Sprat, *The History of the Royal-Society of London for the Improving of Natural Knowledge* (London, 1657).

[111] This contrast drove Meric Casaubon to write his *A Letter to Pierre Moulin . . . Concerning natural experimental Philosophie* (Cambridge, 1669), and to ask: 'What is it that these account *useful*, and *useless*?' (5).

[112] Joseph Priestley, *An Essay on the First Principles of Government* (London, 1768), 6. On this whole question of the usefulness of science in the eighteenth century, see Larry Stewart, *The Rise of Public Science* (Cambridge, 1992).

plants, or rapidly growing and fattening breed of animals'. This new nature, we are told, is

the foundation of our wealth and the condition of our safety from submergence by another flood of barbarous hordes; it is the bond which unites into a solid political whole, regions larger than any empire of antiquity; it secures us from the recurrence of pestilences and famines of former times; it is the source of endless comforts and conveniences, which are not mere luxuries, but conduce to physical and moral well-being.[113]

To the extent to which the discussion of the value of science turns primarily on usefulness, the idea of a 'neutral space for enquiry' is irrelevant.

The second question is that of the role of an adversarial culture. This turns out to be a very complex issue, as we shall see in the chapters that follow, but the crux of what is at stake can be set out succinctly. Huff's argument is that for scientific innovation one needs an adversarial culture. However, when we start to look at how early-modern natural philosophers describe the circumstances needed to foster innovation, the first thing they criticize is an adversarial culture. If Huff's analysis is correct, the combination of a staunchly adversarial culture within a relatively autonomous corporate structure, the university, should characterize early-modern natural philosophy. But it does not. Rather, it characterizes the far less fruitful, radically adversarial, scholastic natural philosophy of the universities of Paris and Oxford in the thirteenth and fourteenth centuries. There can be no doubt this was an innovative natural-philosophical culture, but it was one that was not consolidated, ultimately following the standard boom/bust pattern. When natural philosophy was revived in sixteenth-century Europe, it was nurtured in a very different kind of culture, and predominantly outside scholasticism. Indeed, its distinguishing feature was an unqualified wholesale rejection of an adversarial approach, which was almost universally seen, outside scholastic circles, as characteristic of sterile, unproductive dispute for its own sake, without regard to use or truth. Far from encouraging innovation, key early-modern natural philosophers such as Bacon, Descartes, and Boyle explicitly saw adversarial method as representative of an especially fruitless form of argument which cut any progress and innovation off at its roots. Bacon sums up the situation nicely in his criticism of Aristotle in Book 2 of the *Advancement of Learning*:

And herein I cannot a little marvel at the philosopher Aristotle, that did proceed in such a spirit of difference and contradiction toward all antiquity; undertaking not only to frame new words of science at pleasure, but to confound and extinguish all ancient wisdom; inasmuch as he never nameth or mentioneth an ancient author or opinion, but to confute and reprove.[114]

Glanvill, pre-eminent Royal Society apologist, puts the point even more dramatically. 'Peripatetick Philosophy', he tells us, 'is *litigious*, the very spawn of *disputations* and *controversies* as undecisive as needless. This is the natural result of the former: *Storms* are the products of *vapours*.'[115] Bacon's own recommended approach is in marked contrast with what he considers to be the Aristotelian one:

---

[113] Huxley, *Collected Essays*, i. 51.       [114] Bacon, *Works*, iii. 352.
[115] Joseph Glanvill, *Scepsis Scientifica: or, Confest Ignorance, the way to Science; in an Essay of The Vanity of Dogmatizing, and Confident Opinion* (London, 1665), 118.

I like better that entry of truth which cometh peaceably with chalk to mark up those minds which are capable to lodge and harbour it, than that which cometh with pugnacity and contention.[116]

It would certainly be an exaggeration to say that adversarial culture plays no part at all in early-modern natural philosophy—Galileo's *Dialogo* employs adversarial techniques, for example, and not just at the dramatic level—but its role is so far from being straightforward that it is an unlikely candidate for one of the characterizing features of early-modern natural philosophy.

The gradual consolidation of a scientific culture in the early-modern era, to the extent to which it occurred before the second half of the nineteenth century, was, then, not due an adversarial approach, or to the existence of some neutral space for enquiry, or to an enthusiasm for science on the part of the public or an educated elite. Nor, it should be noted, was it due to any practical benefits. Unlike science in China, for example, where the practical benefits were often immediate,[117] or medieval Islam, where they were at least direct if not immediate, the Scientific Revolution produced very little of any practical benefit for a long time. Ballistics and reliable clock mechanisms were the outcome of work in kinematics,[118] but generally speaking where there was some practical pay-off, in military and public architecture and ship design for example, it was hardly ever the new mathematical physics that produced the goods but developments in traditional Alexandrian disciplines such as statics and hydrostatics.[119] Furthermore, the pioneers were rarely scientists. As Peter Mathias notes in connection with the Industrial Revolution in England, the country where the changes first became apparent:

by and large, innovations were not the result of the formal application of applied science, nor the product of the formal educational system of the country.... Most innovations were the products of inspired amateurs, or brilliant artisans trained as clockmakers, millwrights, blacksmiths or in the Birmingham trades.... They were mainly local men, empirically trained, with local horizons, often very interested in things scientific, aware men, responding directly to a

---

[116] Bacon, *Works*, iii. 363. It is worth pointing out, however, that there is sometimes a gap between his recommended and his actual approach: see Stephen Gaukroger, *Francis Bacon and the Transformation of Early Modern Culture* (Cambridge, 2001), 105–14.

[117] See Mokyr, *The Lever of Riches*, ch. 9.

[118] Nevertheless, the importance of scientific advances to early ballistics should not be overestimated. John F. Guilmartin, *Gunpowder and Galleys: Changing Technology and Mediterranean Warfare at Sea in the Sixteenth Century* (Cambridge, 1974), points out that gunners would have had little use for instruments such as quadrants, preferring their own experience in the field. It should also be noted that it was only in the nineteenth century that weapons manufacturers explored the implications of seventeenth-century ballistics in a systematic way: see A. Rupert Hall, *Ballistics in the Seventeenth Century: A Study of the Relations between Science and War with Reference Particularly to England* (Cambridge, 1952), 158. See also idem, 'Gunnery, Science, and the Royal Society', in John G. Burke, ed., *The Uses of Science in the Age of Newton* (Berkeley, 1983), 111–42.

[119] In the case of public architecture see James A. Bennett, *The Mathematical Science of Christopher Wren* (Cambridge, 1982) and Lisa Jardine, *On A Grander Scale*. Shipbuilders in the seventeenth and eighteenth centuries were highly skilled but had little formal education, and certainly little use for new developments in natural philosophy: see Larrie D. Ferreiro, *Ships and Science: The Birth of Naval Architecture in the Scientific Revolution, 1600–1800* (Cambridge, Mass., 2006), ch. 2.

particular problem. Up to the mid-nineteenth century this tradition was still dominant in British manufacturing industry. It was no accident that the Crystal Palace in 1851, a miracle of cast iron and glass like the great railway stations of the nineteenth century, was the conception of the head gardener of the Duke of Devonshire. He knew about greenhouses.[120]

Indeed, it is not just that scientists were not the innovators behind the Industrial Revolution, but that for much of its early years advances in science had little bearing on technological advances. As Mokyr has pointed out, 'most of the devices invented between 1750 and 1830 tended to be a type in which mechanically talented amateurs could excel. In many cases British inventors appear simply to have been lucky... When, after 1850, deeper scientific analysis was needed, German and French inventors gradually took the lead.'[121] It is also worth remembering in this context that machines, which began to be introduced in a limited way in areas such as mining and cotton manufacturing from the eighteenth century,[122] were so slow until the use of the steam turbine, the internal-combustion engine, and the electric motor, that engineers used statics to describe the action of machines before the 1880s.[123] The other significant developments—such as the mass production of fertilizers and glass, light engineering, the use of thermometers (two hundred years after their invention) by physicians, and the use of anesthetics, not to mention fundamental domestic

---

[120] Peter Mathias, *The First Industrial Nation: An Economic History of Britain, 1700–1914* (London, 1983), 124–5. See also A. Rupert Hall, 'What Did the Industrial Revolution in Britain Owe to Science?', in Neil McKenrick, ed., *Historical Perspectives: Studies in English Thought and Society in Honour of J. H. Plumb* (London, 1974), 129–51. A parallel point is made in the context of the Royal Society in the seventeenth century in Marie Boas Hall, 'Oldenburg, The *Philosophical Transactions*, and Technology', in John G. Burke, ed., *The Uses of Science in the Age of Newton* (Berkeley, 1983), 21–47. Cf. Thomas Kuhn, *The Essential Tension* (Chicago, 1977), who notes what he terms the backwardness of science in Britain around the time of the Industrial Revolution, concluding that it played an insignificant role in the technological changes (141–5). See also Neil McKendrick, 'The Role of Science in the Industrial Revolution: A Study of Josiah Wedgwood as a Scientist and Industrial Chemist', in M. Teich and R. Porter, eds., *Changing Perspectives in the History of Science* (London, 1973), 274–319.

[121] Mokyr, *The Lever of Riches*, 244.

[122] Such machines often had very limited purposes before the nineteenth century. Newcomen's engine, for example, was devised in 1714, but was confined to pumping water, which was of limited value until a coal economy took off in Britain in the nineteenth century, where (with the aid of steam power from the end of the eighteenth century) it became crucial in enabling the working of deeper shafts. Note also that there was often a significant gap between the invention of a machine and its full mechanization. Samuel Crompton's 'Spinning Jenny' was invented in 1775, and although it had an immediate impact, it was not fully mechanized until the mid-1830s. Still, the 1820s are the key period in mechanization, with the extensive introduction of power looms throughout textile manufacturing. On the 'industrial revolution' generally see chs. 2 to 4 of David S. Landes, *The Unbound Prometheus: Technological Change and Industrial Development in Western Europe from 1750 to the Present* (2nd. edn, Cambridge, 2003), and, for a broader perspective, Mokyr, *The Lever of Riches*. One important issue at stake in understanding the eighteenth- and early nineteenth-century development of capitalism is the relative importance and priority of organization of work practices rather than technological developments as such (in Marxist terms, relative priority of relations of production over forces of production): see Keith Tribe, *Genealogies of Capitalism* (London, 1981). It is of interest here that the great eighteenth- and early nineteenth-century political economists—Smith, Malthus, and Ricardo—think of production almost exclusively in terms of agricultural, not industrial, production.

[123] J. P. Den Hartog, *Mechanics* (New York, 1961), 2.

improvements such as piped water, underground sewage, better food, softer clothing, warmer homes, and street lighting—are likewise developments dating from the third decade of the nineteenth century at the earliest. Despite the claims of its advocates for the usefulness of natural philosophy, these were at best promissory notes before then.

To what, then, was the gradual consolidation of a scientific culture in the West due? It is to this nexus of questions—for, as we shall see, there are a number of fundamental questions involved—that we now turn, and we shall begin by looking at the basis on which natural philosophy came to occupy a central place in medieval and then early-modern culture.

# PART II

# 2

# Augustinian Synthesis to Aristotelian Amalgam

In the thirteenth century, natural philosophy was transformed from a marginal enterprise into one that was to provide the principal point of entry into understanding the natural world and our place in it. This transformation was fundamental to the grasp of what kind of enterprise natural philosophy was and how it complemented, reinforced, or undermined other forms of natural understanding, particularly those provided by theology but also, at times, those provided by disciplines such as optics and mechanics. The engine of transformation was Aristotelianism. Aristotelian natural philosophy marginalized other forms of natural philosophy from the thirteenth to the sixteenth centuries, yet its introduction into the West was far from smooth, and its project remained disputed, coming to a head on the issue of whether Aristotelian natural philosophy could be reconciled with the Christian doctrine of the personal immortality of the soul at the beginning of the sixteenth century.

The depth and extent of the hostility to Aristotelianism in the thirteenth century was such that it is at first difficult to see how it could possibly have survived. In 1210, the University of Paris banned all public and private teaching of Aristotle's natural philosophy in the Arts Faculty, under penalty of excommunication. The ban, imposed by the Parisian synod, was renewed in 1215 by the papal legate, Robert of Courçon, in the official sanctioning of the statutes, again in 1228 and in the 1231 bull *Parens scientiarum* by Pope Gregory IX.[1] The bans did not automatically hold outside Paris,[2] but there were around 3,000 to 4,000 students in Paris by 1200, about a tenth of the population of the city, and about 150 masters, making it the leading intellectual

---

[1] The texts of the various condemnations are given in vol. i. of H. Denifle and E. Châtelain, eds, *Chartularium Universitatis Parisiensis* (4 vols, Paris, 1889–97). See Roland Hisette, *Enquête sur les 219 articles condamnés à Paris le 12 Mars 1277* (Louvain/Paris, 1977); idem, 'Etienne Tempier et ses condemnations', *Recherches de théologie ancienne et médiévale* 47 (1980), 231–70; Gordon Leff, 'The *Trivium* and the Three Philosophies', in Hilde de Ridder-Symoens, ed., *A History of the University in Europe*, i. *Universities in the Middle Ages* (Cambridge, 1992), 307–36: 320–1; Étienne Gilson, *History of Christian Philosophy in the Middle Ages* (London, 1955), 244–6; and John F. Wippel, 'The Condemnations of 1270 and 1277', *Journal of Medieval and Renaissance Studies* 7 (1977), 169–201. Gregory appointed a commission—which produced nothing, possibly because its chairman, William of Auxerre, died in the same year—to investigate whether Aristotle's works might be revised so that they could be taught.

[2] The University of Toulouse, founded in 1229, initially advertised the fact that it taught Aristotle, for example, but in 1245 the Paris prohibitions were extended to Toulouse.

centre of Europe, and indeed every thirteenth-century scholastic theologian of note taught or studied at Paris.[3] The Paris bans effectively stopped serious research on Aristotle before about 1240, when the Dominican Albertus Magnus moved to the Paris Faculty. He was accompanied by his amanuensis,[4] Thomas Aquinas, who had studied Aristotle's natural-philosophical works, and probably his metaphysics, at the Naples *studium* (which was unaffected by the Paris bans[5]), from which he had matriculated in 1239. Aquinas, who joined the Dominicans in 1244, began his large-scale project of reconciling Christian theology with Aristotelian metaphysics and natural philosophy in the early 1250s, continuing to teach in Paris until 1259. Things were eased considerably in 1255 with the legalisation of the study of the known works of Aristotle, but this period of tolerance lasted little more than ten years, and in 1267 Bonaventure began a series of attacks on Averroistic Aristotelianism, followed in 1270 by Aegidius Romanus' stinging rebuke of the 'errors of the philosophers', amongst whom he includes Aristotle, Averroes, Avicenna, al-Ghazali, al-Kindi, and Maimonides. Within a year of Aquinas returning to Paris in 1269, a new ban was placed on the teaching of Aristotle by the Bishop of Paris, Étienne Tempier, who condemned thirteen philosophical propositions associated with Aristotelianism. Although it initially had little effect, the ban was renewed in 1277 in a blanket condemnation of 40 theological and 179 philosophical propositions. The 1277 Condemnation was an entirely different matter from the earlier bans.[6] It had the encouragement and support of Pope John XXI, who had taught in the Paris Faculty thirty years earlier, and it shaped the intellectual landscape of western Europe over the next 350 years.

This was not because it put an end to the study and teaching of Aristotle, for Aristotle provided a basic philosophical framework for almost all work in natural philosophy up until the second half of the sixteenth century. Indeed, Aristotelianism was not just the dominant interpretation of natural philosophy during this time, it was in

---

[3] The only figure we cannot be completely sure about in this respect is Grosseteste, but on balance the evidence indicates that he did study in Paris: see James McEvoy, *The Philosophy of Robert Grosseteste* (Oxford, 1986), 6–8.

[4] It is likely that amenuenses would have been needed above all because of eyesight problems. One commentator has suggested that the invention of eyeglasses, by 1280 at the latest, meant that officials who would earlier have had to retire in their forties and fifties because of failing eyesight could now remain in office, resulting in a significant shift in the age of officials by the fourteenth century: Svante Lindquist, 'A Wagnerian Theme in the History of Science: Scientific Glassblowing and the Role of Instrumentation', in Tore Frängsmayr, ed., *Solomon's House Revisited* (Canton, Mass., 1990), 160–83: 160.

[5] The emperor Frederick II had set up the Naples *studium* in 1224 to train the ruling class of the Kingdom of Sicily, and his aim was to deprive Bologna of its primacy and make Naples the leading centre for the study of law in the empire. As Nardi points out, 'the main difference between Frederick's *studium* and the most important seats of learning in Europe was that in Naples the eccesiastical authorities had no authority to recruit teachers, award the *licentia docendi*, or exercise jurisdictional powers': Paolo Nardi, 'Relations with Authority', in Hilde de Ridder-Symoens, ed., *A History of the University in Europe*, i. *Universities in the Middle Ages* (Cambridge, 1992), 77–107: 87.

[6] On the practical effects of the ban, see Luca Bianchi, 'Censure, liberté et progrès intellectuel à l'Université de Paris au XIIIe siècle', *Archives d'histoire doctrinale et littéraire du Moyen Âge* 63 (1996), 45–93.

effect constitutive of natural philosophy: it provided the problems that natural philosophy dealt with, the means of solving them, and criteria for what counted as a satisfactory explanation. What the 1277 Condemnation did was to draw into the open a number of fundamental ambiguities about just what the relative standing of theology, metaphysics, and natural philosophy was, and it was instrumental in establishing or reinforcing a set of constraints on how questions were decided as being metaphysical or natural-philosophical questions, constraints that would be widely contested in the course of the next three and a half centuries, but, at least until the early decades of the sixteenth century, contested within a framework that was established in the thirteenth century.

In order to understand why Aristotle was taken up so wholeheartedly by a number of thirteenth-century philosophers and theologians, and why this movement encountered such a hostile reception from others, our first task must be to understand what the Aristotelian philosophy/Christian theology amalgam replaced.

## THE AUGUSTINIAN SYNTHESIS

'What can there be in common between Athens and Jerusalem, between the Academy and the Church, between heretics and Christians?' asks Tertullian, the early third-century founder of Latin theology, rhetorically. 'We have no need for curiosity since Jesus Christ', he tells us, 'nor for enquiry since the Evangelist.'[7] Tertullian's hostility to classical learning derives from what he identifies as the use to which it had been put by heretics: the Gnostics derive their doctrine of eons from the Platonists, Marcion derives his doctrine of God from the Stoics, the identification of God with matter derives from Zeno, with fire from Heraclitus, the notion of the annihilation of the soul derives from the Epicureans, and so on. In other words, it is classical philosophers who are the source of all these false doctrines.[8] Tertullian's aim is to establish a single source of authority, a single route to truth, namely Christian teaching, at a time when there were moves in the eastern parts of the Roman Empire towards forms of religious pluralism, and when there was an upsurge in theological speculation.[9] When

---

[7] *De praescriptionibus haereticorum*, Book 7. Cf. *Apologeticum* 46: 'What is there in common between the philosopher and the Christian, the pupil of Hellas and the pupil of Heaven, the worker for reputation and for salvation, the manufacturer of words and of deeds, the destroyer and the builder, the interpolator of error and the artificer of truth, the thief of truth and its custodian?' However, Tertullian is sometimes more nuanced in his view of the merits of classical learning, and famously nominated Seneca as 'one of us'. The opposition between Athens and Jerusalem derives from Paul's contrast between Greek and Jew: Romans 1: 16, 3: 9, 10: 12; 1 Corinthians 1: 24, 10: 32, 12: 13; Galatians 3: 28; Colossians 3: 11. Paul's hostility may have derived from the bemused reception he received from the Epicurean and Stoic philosophers whom he met in Athens, who were singularly unimpressed by his performance, calling him a babbler and ridiculing his claims about the resurrection of the dead. See Peter Harrison, *The Bible, Protestantism, and the Rise of Natural Science* (Cambridge, 1998), 11–12.

[8] Apologists for this view would doubtless have received succour from Cicero's remark that there is no doctrine so absurd that some philosopher has not advocated it (*De divinatione* 2. 58. 119).

[9] See the discussion of Tertullian in ch. 6 of Charles Norris Cochrane, *Christianity and Classical Culture* (rev. edn, Oxford, 1944).

Tertullian tells us that 'secular wisdom rashly undertakes to explain the nature and dispensation of God' and that 'heretics and philosophers deal with the same material, and their arguments are largely the same', he identifies a problem that is going to hound Christian thought. Christianity was offering doctrines on questions on which there had been a great deal of philosophical thought, and in writers such as Tertullian it is offering these doctrines not initially on the basis of engagement and criticism of earlier views (in the way that Aristotle set out to refute and replace Plato's doctrines, for example) but on the basis of a theologically motivated system of belief that runs along a completely different trajectory. Yet many early Christians, Tertullian included, had been converted from Neoplatonism. That is, they had moved from a philosophical system—even if one with explicitly theological overtones—to a theological one. They had abandoned a philosophical search for the truth for a theological one. If these two routes conflicted then there were a number of possible options open, along a spectrum running from abandonment to assimilation. Tertullian, preoccupied with the perils of worldliness, sees an irreconcilable opposition between Christian and worldly values in every domain,[10] and the abandonment of Graeco-Roman culture is by far the predominant tendency in his thinking.

Even though as late as 398 we find the Council of Carthage prohibiting the reading of pagan books, by the fourth century it was assimilation that was proving the more attractive path for those seeking to covert pagans and others to Christianity. In the Patristic period, we witness the gradual 'Christianization' of philosophy (primarily metaphysics, natural philosophy, and ethics), begun by the early Latin Fathers and brought to completion by Marius Victorinus and Augustine. In its early stages, the project is that of nurturing what is worthwhile in pagan thought in the nourishing atmosphere of Christian teaching, with Tertullian's Latin contemporary Clement of Alexandria, for example, presenting himself as Christ's gardener, cutting twigs from the rank, dried-back, and brittle bushes of pagan literature, and grafting them onto the stock of Christ's truth.[11] In its later development, especially in the writings of Augustine, the project amounts to nothing short of a total translation of all philosophy into Christian terms. Christianity is conceived of as the final form of philosophy. Using the language of the classical philosophers to formulate his theology, Augustine attempts to show that Christianity is able to answer all the questions of classical metaphysics.[12] In general terms, not only does Christianity supplement classical philosophy here, it appropriates the teachings of this philosophy, denying that they were ever the property of the ancients in the first place. It not only construes every philosophical question in terms of Christian teaching, but initiates a widespread rejection of the moral and other qualities that marked out the ancient philosopher as the embodiment of wisdom and virtue.[13]

---

[10] For examples, see ibid. 227.

[11] Peter Brown, *The Body and Society* (London, 1989), 124.

[12] Cf. Aquinas, *Summa theologica*, II-II q. 9a. 2; 1a 1. 6.

[13] See Juliusz Domanski, *La Philosophie, théorie ou manière de vivre?: Les Controverses de l'Antiquité à la Renaissance* (Fribourg/Paris, 1996), 23–9.

This appropriation of earlier thought by Christianity made it possible for it to present itself as the final answer to what earlier philosophers were striving for, and we should not underestimate just how successful it was in this respect. The main schools of Hellenistic philosophy had each sought to present a philosophy that transcended the flux and disorder of life and achieved peace of mind (*ataraxia* or *apatheia*). The Stoics had argued that this was to be achieved by grasping the underlying reality of things in terms of their general principles. The Epicureans had maintained that knowledge of the principles governing things was a means to an end: we understand things so that we need no longer fear them, with fear of death being paramount amongst those forms of fear we must overcome. The Pyrrhonists and later Academics—using the image of the painter Apelles, who failed to create the effect of the foam on the horse's mouth, gave up, and flinging his sponge at the wall, accidentally hit the painting in such a way that it produced the required effect—had argued that peace of mind came when one realized that no understanding was possible: the tranquillity we seek comes to us, as if by chance, once we stop searching for it. The Christian version of the search for peace of mind and tranquillity associates it with a state not fully achievable in this life—although monastic culture cultivated the idea of the power to be constant amid the flux and disorder of life, this was in the context of an attempt to separate oneself from the world through asceticism[14]—but which is a reward for what one does in this life, and which relies as much upon sacramental as upon intellectual enlightenment. It translates it from a philosophical project into something that meshes philosophical and religious concerns together[15] into a synthesis whose phenomenal success indicates that it offered far more than any of the available religious or philosophical systems taken in their own right.

Clement had claimed that philosophy served the same function for the Greeks as the Torah did for the Jews, foreshadowing the coming of Christ, but the key figure in this development is Augustine.[16] Drawing on a long tradition of thinking about the prehistory of Christianity, he sets out the basis for a reconciliation between Christian and classical thought. 'What is now called Christian religion,' he writes, 'has existed among the ancients, and was not absent from the beginning of the human race until Christ came in the flesh; from which time true religion, which existed already,

---

[14] See, in particular, Antoine Guillaumont, 'Le dépaysement comme forme d'ascèse dans la monachisme ancien', in idem, *Aux origines du monachisme chrétien: Pour une phénoménologie du monachisme* (Bégrolles-en-Mauge, 1979), 89–116; and Jean Leclercq, *L'Amour des lettres et le désir de Dieu: Initiation aux auteurs monastiques du moyen âge* (Paris, 1957). See also Catherine Walker Bynum, *Jesus as Mother: Studies in Spirituality of the High Middle Ages* (Berkeley, Calif., 1982), ch. 1.

[15] It would be a mistake to think that the Christian version 'theologizes' a purely philosophical account, however, for the Middle Platonists had argued that the process is aided by the power of God's love.

[16] Even in the fifteenth and sixteenth centuries, after Aquinas' Christianized Aristotelianism had taken hold, Augustine was extremely influential: see Diarmaid MacCulloch, *Reformation: Europe's House Divided, 1490–1700* (London, 2003), 106–23. Augustine's works were the first to appear in print after the Bible, with *De civitate dei* appearing in full as early as 1467. The influence of his works on Luther (who started his career in the Erfurt house of the strict order of Augustinian Eremites) was immense.

began to be called Christian'.[17] In other words, Christianity had, in some way, always existed, even before the Incarnation. In fact, for Augustine, both the true religion and the true philosophy existed from the beginning of the time.[18] In his discussion of Plato in Books 8 to 10 of the *De civitate dei*, a work written in the aftermath of Alaric's sack of Rome and very much with pagan refugees from Rome in mind, he speculates whether Plato could have had some knowledge of the Hebrew scriptures,[19] and he suggests that the God of the Platonists (i.e. the Neoplatonists) is the same as that of Christianity,[20] and even that they speak, albeit in a confused way, of the Trinity.[21] Yet, he tells us, these same Platonists cannot know God. They mistakenly believe that they can reach him by purely intellectual means, whereas in fact he can only be reached through the sacraments, which were instituted with the Incarnation of Christ. For Augustine, the superiority of Christianity over ancient philosophies and over the contemporary rivals of Christianity lay in the institution of the sacraments. Augustine's claim is not that Christianity is ancient philosophy plus the sacraments; it is that ancient philosophy is Christianity minus the sacraments. This is why Augustine can project back on to the source all the confusions that his appropriation of Neoplatonism engenders: he treats Plotinus' talk of God giving rise to 'emanations' as confused talk of creation, he treats his postulation of three divine Hypostases as confused talk about the Trinity, and he translates his account of the fall of the world soul into the fall of individual souls, although here, interestingly, the 'original sin' that affects these individual souls is very much a species sin rather than a sum of individual sins, which brings it very close to the Neoplatonic conception.[22] In sum, for Augustine, Christianity is the culmination of all previous philosophical reflection and religious belief, something that can be glimpsed by the appropriate allegorical readings of the ancient philosophers and sages just as much as it can by the allegorical reading of the Old Testament.[23]

[17] *Retractions* 1. 13.

[18] See Wilhelm Schmidt-Biggemann, *Philosophia Perennis: Historical Outlines of Western Spirituality in Ancient, Medieval and Early Modern Thought* (Dordrecht, 2005), 412–16.

[19] There was a widespread view amongst early Christian theologians that the Greeks had stolen their wisdom from the Hebrews, but distorted it: see, e.g. Clement of Alexandria, *Stromateis* 1. 81. 4.

[20] Seven centuries later, Abelard will argue that the Platonists were vouchsafed a special revelation of the Trinity before and outside the Christian dispensation, and it is notable that this was not one of the doctrines for which he was condemned, which, since he was condemned for just about everything else, gives a good indication of the continued theological standing of Plato in the twelfth century.

[21] The Christian notion of the Trinity was no doubt helped upon its way by the existence of a long pagan tradition of worshipping gods in threes: see G. W. Bowersock, *Hellenism in Late Antiquity* (Ann Arbor, 1990), 17–19.

[22] It can, however, be argued that the doctrine of original sin had been implicit in the Christian practice of infant baptism. Peter Harrison has pointed out to me that it is also regarded as being implicit in Paul's teaching that in Adam all sinned (Romans 5: 12, 19).

[23] See James S. Preus, *From Shadow to Promise: Old Testament Interpretation from Augustine to the Young Luther* (Cambridge, Mass., 1969), 9–23; Gerhard Ebeling, *Evangelische Evangelienauslegung* (Munich, 1942), 110–26; and Allan A. Gilmore, 'Augustine and the Critical Method', *Harvard Theological Review* 39 (1946), 141–63.

The idea that Christianity pervaded the whole of the pre-Christian era was a common assumption, and the thought and beliefs of the pre-Christian era were subjected to a kind of allegorical reading in order to yield or reveal what were often marvellous anticipations of Christianity.[24] There were non-Christian precedents for this: there is evidence to suggest that Homer was being read allegorically as early as Plato's time, and the third-century Neoplatonists Porphyry and Plotinus developed this into an art form, subjecting Homer's works to a detailed allegorical reading that enabled them to present him as a sage with revealed knowledge of the fate of souls and the mystical structure of the universe.[25] They used this allegorical reading to attack Christianity, and it is not surprising that the Church Fathers should reply in kind: and with a vengeance, for the Patristic project was a far more ambitious and all-encompassing one than that of the Neoplatonists.

The real challenge for theologians such as Augustine was not paganism, however, but rival movements within Christianity: his aim is to establish Nicene orthodoxy. The idea of the presence of Christianity in the pre-Christian era has a doctrinal cutting edge, and the claim that Christianity is not something new is crucial to the version of Christianity that Augustine managed to establish. The issue on which everything turned was the vexed one of the relation between Christianity and its religious forebear, pre-Christian Judaism. In some ways the problem can be traced back to the different agendas of the two key figures in early Christianity, Jesus and Paul. Whereas Jesus seems to have been concerned to fulfill the Law, for Paul, Christ replaces the Law.[26] In the early centuries of Christianity, there was for a while a close contest between those who, like Tertullian, saw Christianity as the true development of the religious precepts contained in the 'Old' Testament—as Christians came to designate it—and those who saw the two as completely opposed. The Manichaeans and Gnostics had held that the Old Testament had been abrogated by the coming of Christ, and that as a consequence it should be discarded. The second-century Gnostic, Marcion, in his *Antitheus*, had set out the moral and theological discrepancies between the Old Testament and the Gospels, and argued that the former was the record of the Jewish God of Hate, something which was now superseded by the message of the God of Love in the Gospels. Allegorical reading of the Old Testament was explicitly ruled out by Marcion as an attempt to save something which was in fact wholly alien to Christian tradition: Christianity, for Marcion, began with the Incarnation, which was a wholly novel and unprecedented event.[27] The God of the Old Testament was still accepted as divine, however, with

---

[24] See the discussion in Hans Blumenberg, *The Legitimacy of the Modern Age* (Cambridge, Mass., 1983), 63–75.

[25] See Robert Lamberton, *Homer the Theologian* (Berkeley, 1986).

[26] See Charles Freeman, *The Closing of the Western Mind: The Rise of Faith and the Fall of Reason* (London, 2003), 115, and more generally chs. 8 and 9 on the relation between Jesus and Paul.

[27] On Manichaeism see Adolf von Harnack, *Marcion: das Evangelium vom fremden Gott* (Leipzig, 1921); Hans Jonas, *The Gnostic Religion*, 2nd edn. (Boston, 1963), chs. 2 and 3; and Blumenberg, *The Legitimacy of the Modern Age*, part II. On the general background to these questions see F. E. Peters, *The Harvest of Hellenism* (New York, 1970), ch. 13. Manichaeism survived in the East, and there are traces of it from the seventh century onwards in the West. In the twelfth and thirteenth

the result that two independent realms of evil and good were postulated, with independent Gods ruling over these.

Augustine had himself been a Manichaean in his early twenties,[28] but later became one of its fiercest critics. It is not too difficult to understand the basis for his change of heart, for Manichaeism did harbour some deep theological inconsistencies. Its association of the material world and the realm of evil, for example, is difficult to reconcile with its view of the Incarnation as a turning point, for the Incarnation could not be understood as a real event on the Manichaean account, because this good God would then have to have immersed himself in the realm of evil and become part of it. Nor is it clear what sense could be made of Redemption, for Christ could not literally have died on the cross on the Manichaean account. It was crucial to Christianity, as Augustine was to construe it, that there was only one God, and that this God was the God of the Old Testament as well as the New. Indeed, Christianity received the Old Testment in a very different way from post-Christian Judaism, retaining elements that were archaic for Jewish culture. As Rémi Brague has noted,

the sacrificial dimension of the Covenant lost its pertinence for Judaism after the destruction of the Second Temple; it survived in the Christian sacraments. Davidic royalty had disappeared under foreign domination; it resurged in the sacerdotal mission of the Christian emperors and the kings of the west. Prophecy had disappeared, and Judaism had taken notice of this disappearance, which it explained in diverse ways; in Christianity, it continued in the role of the Saints, and in particular, with the founders of orders.[29]

Augustine's sources were certainly not purely biblical, however. In shifting from Manichaeism to his mature position, his principal influence was Neoplatonism,[30] with its conception of the 'One' as incorporeal, immutable, infinite, and the source of all things: a conception that completely contradicts the Manichaean/Gnostic idea that there could be a God who was vengeful and spiteful.[31] Indeed, here Augustine uses the work of a pagan philosopher—Plotinus' *Against the Gnostics, or against those who say that the Creator of the World is Evil and that the World is Evil* (*Enneads*, II. bk. 9)—against a version of Christianity.

Christianity's appropriation of all earlier thought meant four things. First, it meant that it had no external competition. No system of thought was alien to it, not even

centuries it witnessed a significant revival and was associated with such heretical groups as the Cathars. See ch. 8 of Jeffrey Burton Russell, *Dissent and Reform in the Early Middle Ages* (Berkeley, 1965).

[28] On Augustine's early Manichaeism, see ch. 5 of Peter Brown, *Augustine of Hippo* (London, 1967).

[29] Rémi Brague, *Eccentric Culture*, 52.

[30] In the *Confessions*, he tells us that he was 'led towards Christianity by reading the books of the Platonists', though he was familiar only with the Latin versions (7. 9): in the case of Plotinus this would have been the Latin translation of Victorinus. His familiarity with the philosophical tradition was in fact very limited, and seems to have been confined to Cicero, Porphyry, and Plotinus.

[31] Note, however, that the Gnostics also drew on Plato, specifically on his idea of a demiurge who is not necessarily good. See Jaap Mansfeld, 'Bad World and Demiurge: A "Gnostic" Motif from Parmenides and Empedocles to Lucretius and Philo', in R. van den Broeck, ed., *Studies in Gnosticism and Hellenistic Religions* (Leiden, 1981), 261–314.

paganism, because it had effectively appropriated all other intellectual systems and made them its own, and in the strongest possible way: by providing something which it considered they all lacked.[32] Second, it had assimilated a sophisticated body of philosophical doctrine, derived above all from Stoicism and Neoplatonism, which, with the decline of speculative philosophical schools at the end of the Hellenistic era, meant that it assumed an intellectual leadership. Third, it meant that philosophy—in which one should primarily include moral philosophy, metaphysics, and natural philosophy—could not threaten theology because philosophy was evaluated with respect to the contribution it made to the whole, a whole that was ultimately governed by revealed religion. This did not mean that the reconciliation of various philosophical systems—or more usually selected ingredients from various philosophical systems—with revelation and Christian dogma was not contested during the Patristic era,[33] but Christian natural theology was shaped within what was very much a shared framework. Finally, it meant there were no irreconcilable truths: there was one truth, one reality, that of Christianity.

The intellectual superiority of the Christian synthesis was only really tested in its confrontation with Islam. During the later decades of the twelfth century, in particular, the constraints on natural theology changed somewhat with the expansion of Europe into the territories surrounding the Mediterranean basin, and the beginning of a push to convert various pagan groups such as Tartars, and more importantly Muslims and Jews, who had built up a body of quite sophisticated philosophical and theological doctrine. This required a rethinking of the role of natural theology. Since the authority of revealed theology was primary for the Church Fathers and Augustine, natural theology traditionally occupied only an auxiliary role, elucidating and supporting the deliverances of scripture, and Origen, the one Church Father who had given natural theology a formative role, had quickly fallen into heterodoxy. But revealed theology is useless in converting those who do not share the same sacred texts, and it is therefore at this juncture that we witness the beginnings of attempts to develop a natural theology.[34]

What we might term the first-wave response of Christian philosophers to the challenge posed by Judaism and Islam can be illustrated by the case of Anselm

---

[32] The model of theocratic self-containment that the Church Fathers and Augustine aimed at was never really achieved in the Christian West. But it was realized in Arab-Islamic culture, which collapsed into the profound parochialism that one might expect from a theocracy after the Middle Ages: see Bernard Lewis, *The Muslim Discovery of Europe* (London, 2000).

[33] For a detailed—albeit occasionally somewhat opaque and convoluted—account of these developments, see Jaroslav Pelikan, *Christianity and Classical Culture* (New Haven, Conn., 1993).

[34] The term 'natural theology' is often reserved for developments in the seventeenth, eighteenth, and nineteenth centuries, but the discipline was pursued in a way that was to become canonical for many later writers in Cicero's *De natura deorum*, and the term was used in Roman encyclopedist Varro. In *De civitate dei*, Augustine discusses Varro's threefold division of theology into mythical (i.e. poetic), political (i.e. relating to state functions), and natural, arguing that the third was the only truthful form of Gentile theology. See Werner Jaeger, *The Theology of the Early Greek Philosophers* (Oxford, 1947), 2–4. There are very significant differences between the kind (and aims) of natural theology at issue here and that we find pursued in the eighteenth century, for example, but this should not blind us to the fact that it formed a distinct stream in Christian thought at an early stage in its development.

of Canterbury, writing in the second half of the eleventh century. Anselm draws upon the resources of an earlier kind of unified model of theology and philosophy developed by the Church Fathers and particularly Augustine. He sees metaphysics as a doctrine about the nature of God, and believes that there should be a way of starting from fundamental metaphysical premisses to which everyone, whether Christian, Jew, or Muslim, could agree, and from which one could demonstrate the basic attributes of a Christian God.

Anselm offers two such starting points. In the *Monologion*—a deeply Augustinian work whose Preface tells us there is nothing in the text not in absolute harmony with the writings of Augustine—the argument of the early chapters works in terms of the Platonic idea that we can find various degrees of perfection in the world, and that such degrees presuppose a standard of perfection, which Anselm goes on to identify with God. Later, in the *Proslogion*, Anselm replaced this with the ontological argument, as being a more economical and effective way of achieving his end:

I began to ask myself whether there might be found a single argument which would require no other for its proof than itself alone; and alone would suffice to demonstrate that God truly exists, and that there is a supreme good requiring nothing else, which all other things require for their existence and well-being; and whatever we believe regarding the divine Being.[35]

The crucial phrase here is the last one, for the 'single' argument that Anselm seeks is designed to secure not only the self-sufficient existence of God, but also 'whatever we believe regarding the divine Being'. The idea is not to convince someone who does not believe in God that there is a God, but to show that there is an argument for the existence of God that shows God to be the God of Christianity. And the *Monologion* makes it clear that the key doctrines here are those of the Trinity, the Incarnation, and Redemption, indicating that it is Judaic and Muslim notions of God, as well as Arian, monophysite, or other heretical views, rather than the existence of God as such, that are at issue. Having shown that God has no cause, Anselm goes on in the *Monologion* to show that he is the cause of everything else (chs. 7–14), and that, amongst other characteristics, he is omnipresent and eternal, transcending substance (chs. 15–27); and finally that this single God, in expressing himself through his Word, is a father whose son is the Word, and the love between the two is the Holy Spirit (chs. 28–79). The bulk of the argument, about two-thirds of it, is concerned to establish the doctrine of the Trinity on the basis of the understanding of God's nature arrived at in the earlier chapters.

Two centuries later, Ramón Lull, writing in Majorca—which was distinctive in that it was a commercial centre in which Christians, Muslims (who still made up half the population in the second half of the thirteenth century), and Jews interacted—advances a programme of natural theology that again sets out the doctrines of the Trinity and the Incarnation in a way designed to convince Muslims and Jews. In the case of the Incarnation for example, Lull argues that God, having created human beings, must will the union of the divine and human natures in the person of Christ,

---

[35] Anselm, *Basic Writings*, trans. S. N. Deane (2nd edn, La Salle, Ill., 1962), 1.

as this is the only way to achieve harmony between the creator and his creation.[36] Lull advocated a programme of *reductio artium ad theologiam*[37] so that philosophy generally was just a form of theology. His starting point is in some ways similar to a version of the Platonic arguments from degrees of perfection that Anselm had advocated in the *Monologion*, but Lull offers a distinctive twist: we are to progress by considering divine 'names' (i.e. attributes of God such as power, wisdom, virtue, truth, glory, etc.), which he believes are common to all religions, and which he refers to as axioms, and as we progress through combinations of these names we will converge on a shared understanding of God, which will, of course, turn out to be the Christian one.[38]

Neither Anselm's nor Lull's work had any effect on the Muslims whom they had hoped to convert: Lull, towards the end of his life, apparently despairing of the effectiveness of this method, or at least seeing the need for it to be supplemented in a more practical way, advocated armed crusades to deal with Islam. And the view from the other side did not reflect any intellectual superiority on the part of Christianity. Quite the contrary. The Muslim scholar Sā'id al-Andalusī specifically excluded Europeans from his 1068 list of nations that had an interest in science or learning, and they are dismissed as being little more than animals.[39] And it is indeed true that the transmission of the writings of Plato, Aristotle, and the Alexandrian mathematicians and astronomers to Islamic countries via Byzantium had put Islam intellectually far in advance of the Christian West at this time.

As far as *scientia*—science or learning—was concerned, there were two things that had given Islamic thinkers the edge: Aristotelian natural philosophy and the practical-mathematical disciplines that they had inherited from the Alexandrians. And they had not simply inherited these, but had built on them, developing Aristotelian natural philosophy in a sophisticated way,[40] and developing areas such as positional astronomy to a very high degree of refinement.[41] Although Islamic intellectual culture had become largely moribund by the end of the twelfth century, its achievements, and the writings of Aristotle on metaphysics and natural philosophy which had been of such help in raising the level of intellectual sophistication of this culture, became known in the West in the course of the twelfth century. From the middle of the twelfth century, almost as quickly as the texts of Aristotle were being translated into Latin for the first

---

[36] See Charles H. Lohr, 'Metaphysics', in Charles B. Schmitt, Quentin Skinner, and Eckhard Kessler, eds, *The Cambridge History of Renaissance Philosophy* (Cambridge, 1988), 537–638: 549.

[37] See Mark D. Johnston, *The Evangelical Rhetoric of Ramón Llull* (New York, 1996), 17–20.

[38] See Schmidt-Biggemann, *Philosophia Perennis*, 81–92.

[39] Sā'id al-Andalusī, *Book of the Category of Nations*, trans. & ed. Sema'an I. Salem and Alok Kumar (Austin, 1991), 7.

[40] See e.g. Paul Lettinck, *Aristotle's Physics and its Reception in the Arabic World* (Leiden, 1994). On the two main figures in Arabic natural philosophy, Avicenna and Averroes, see respectively Lenn Goodman, *Avicenna* (London, 1992), and Dominique Urvoy, *Ibn Rushd* (London, 1991). Avicenna's core natural-philosophical writings are conveniently available in French translation as *Le Livre de Science*, trans. Mohammad Achena and Henri Massé (2 vols Paris, 1955). Various of Averroes' commentaries on Aristotle's natural-philosophical writings are to be found in English translation in S. Harvey, 'Averroes on the Principles of Nature: the Middle Commentary on Aristotle's Physics, I, II', unpub. Ph.D. thesis, Harvard University, 1977.

[41] See Roshdi Rashed, ed., *Encyclopedia of the History of Arabic Science*.

time, a series of commentaries began to be produced at the University of Salerno,[42] and these and other sources made Aristotle's work available to theologians and philosophers at centres such as Paris for the first time in the Christian West around the beginning of the thirteenth century.[43]

In sum, the situation holding before the thirteenth-century disputes over Aristotelianism is that, from the Patristic era and, above all, from Augustine onwards, there is a conception of the unity of philosophy and theology in which metaphysics is effectively a science of God. Christian theology is conceived as an indispensable ingredient in any viable metaphysics, and it is this that marks out Christian metaphysics from the metaphysical systems of pagan philosophers, which are, nevertheless, unknowingly engaged in the same project, while lacking the key to the problem that Christianity provides. This somewhat ecumenical view of the continuity of ancient philosophy and Christian natural theology is reflected in the later responses to non-Christian systems, where the problem is identified as being resolved by a kind of philosophical reflection on the nature of God which must lead anyone, whether Christian, Muslim, or Jew, to the orthodox Christian conception. Although the classical and Hellenistic sources of Christian philosophy—whether that of Plato (the only work of Plato's that had been transmitted through the Middle Ages was the *Timaeus*,[44] which is his one contribution to natural philosophy), or Aristotle, or that of Neoplatonists or Stoics or Epicureans—had always been concerned with the structure of the world, natural philosophy figures in this conception only in a rather marginal way, and is effectively subsumed under metaphysics. Moreover, it must be remembered, in the context of natural philosophy, that there was a Christian tradition of rejection of natural philosophy as an appropriate topic of study for Christians. In Deuteronomy 4: 9, we are warned to beware 'lest you lift your eyes up to heaven, and when you see the sun and the moon and the stars, all the host of heaven, you will be drawn away and worship and serve them'. Augustine's mentor, Ambrose of Milan, explained the absence of discussion of scientific matters in the Scriptures on the grounds that 'there is no place in the words of the Holy Scripture for the vanity of perishable knowledge which deceives and deludes us in our attempt to explain the unexplainable',[45] and Augustine himself took a similar approach:

When it is asked what we ought to believe in matters of religion, the answer is not to be sought in the exploration of the nature of things, after the manner of those whom the Greeks called 'physicists'. . . . For the Christian, it is enough to believe that the cause of all created things,

[42] See Danielle Jacquart, 'Aristotelian thought in Salerno', in Peter Dronke, ed., *A History of Twelfth-Century Western Philosophy* (Cambridge, 1988), 407–28.

[43] On the history of Latin translation of Aristotle see Bernard Dod, 'Aristoteles Latinus', in N. Kretzman, Anthony Kenny, and Jan Pinborg, eds, *The Cambridge History of Later Medieval Philosophy* (Cambridge, 1982), 45–79.

[44] The *Timaeus* was known through partial Latin translations of Cicero and Chalcidius. There are twelfth-century Latin translations of the *Meno* and *Phaedo*, but these had a very restricted circulation.

[45] Ambrose, *Hexameron*, 6. 28.

whether in heaven or on earth, whether visible or invisible, is nothing other than the goodness of the Creator.[46]

This attitude is also confirmed in his views on astronomy, where he takes the point that the motions of celestial bodies are hardly mentioned in the Scriptures to indicate that they needlessly burden the mind, and that one should desist from astronomy altogether.[47]

This complacency about areas of philosophy outside theology, not least natural philosophy, is undermined with the introduction of Aristotelianism into centres such as Paris in the thirteenth century, as Western Christendom transformed itself from an intellectual backwater into something that was to surpass Islamic and Byzantine cultures.[48] The introduction of Aristotelianism was not simply a matter of rediscovery of texts however. There are two developments that shape the context into which it was introduced. The first is the project of providing philosophical foundations for a systematic theology, a project to which Aristotelianism seemed, to a growing number of theologians, to provide the key. The second is the changed institutional circumstances under which theology and philosophy were pursued, circumstances which, at least initially, hampered the introduction of Aristotelianism.

## THE TRANSITION TO A SCHOLASTIC CULTURE

The establishment of a Christianized Aristotelianism in the thirteenth century is associated above all with Albertus Magnus and Aquinas. Whatever philosophical virtues Aristotelianism may have had over its rivals, we can be sure than neither Albertus nor Aquinas would have been attracted to Aristotelianism simply in virtue of its philosophical merits. They were first of all theologians, and it was clear that the introduction of a new philosophical system into theology would have significant and perhaps unforseen consequences. If we are to understand why Aristotelianism was taken up and developed by scholastic philosophers and theologians from the mid-thirteenth century onwards, we need to understand what its theological benefits were perceived to be, for this was what its acceptance ultimately turned on.

One of the earliest features of the revival of an intellectual culture in Europe was the attempt to establish a systematic theology on a philosophical basis. John Scotus

---

[46] Augustine, *Enchiridion*, 3. 9.

[47] *De doctrina christiana* 2. 29. 46. Although this hostility to astronomy has biblical precedents, it is possible that questions of authority and power were involved here as well, because of the close relation between astronomy and astrology. In the third and fourth centuries, both the Church and the Roman emperors began to claim absolute power and to deny that the stars exercised influence over them (though they accepted that the stars influenced everyone else), contrary to earlier astrological practices: see Marie Theres Fögen, *Die Enteignung der Wahrsager* (Frankfurt, 1993). On Augustine's attitude to astrology, see Lynn Thorndike, *A History of Magic and Experimental Science* (8 vols, New York, 1923–58), i. 504–22.

[48] It should be said that the decline of Byzantium was in part due to the very hostile attitude of the Latin West to the Eastern Orthodox Christians. As MacCulloch has noted, the fourth Crusade of 1204 'had turned into a Venetian expedition to wreck and exploit Constantinople, a disaster from which the eastern Empire never fully recovered': *Reformation*, 55.

Erigena, in the ninth century, was a pioneer in this kind of activity, but the context in which such questions could come to the fore emerged only with the Investiture Controversy, beginning around 1050 and coming to a head with Pope Gregory VII's 1075 decree *Dictatus Papae*,[49] in which he asserted papal supremacy over the entire Western church and declared its independence from secular control.[50] In the wake of a protracted war with Henry IV and then Henry V of Saxony, a concordat was signed in Worms in 1122, and in the process, the church achieved a legal identity independent of emperors, kings, and feudal lords, with a hierarchy of ecclesiastical courts being established, which culminated in the papal curia. This required a wholly new approach to law, as Berman has pointed out:

The dualism of the ecclesiastical and secular legal systems led in turn to a pluralism of secular legal systems within the ecclesiastical legal order and, more specifically, to concurrent jurisdiction of ecclesiastical and secular courts. Further, the systematization and rationalization of law were necessary in order to maintain the complex equilibrium of plural competing legal systems. Finally, the right order of things introduced by the Papal Revolution signified a kind of systematization and rationalization of law that would permit reconciliation of conflicting authorities on the basis of synthesizing principles: wherever possible, the contradictions were to be resolved without destruction of the elements they comprised.[51]

There is an exact parallel between these efforts to reconcile secular and ecclesiastical law and the attempts to establish a systematic theology on a philosophical basis, attempts which begin in earnest at the same time as the beginnings of the Investiture Controversy, in the middle of the eleventh century, with Berengar of Tours and Lanfranc, Archbishop of Canterbury under William the Conqueror, and above all with Lanfranc's pupil, Anselm, who probably began his philosophical writings in the 1060s. Anselm, as we have seen, believed that a philosophically based systematic theology would be not only a bulwark against heresy but also a means to convincing Muslims and others of the truth of the basic tenets of Christianity, above all the distinctive Christian doctrines of the Trinity and the Incarnation. In the process, the hope was that it might help to clarify such central doctrines for the benefit of the orthodox.

Theologically, Anselm was opening up a hornets' nest, but this was an area in which Islamic and Jewish philosophers had traditionally seen a fundamental incoherence in Christianity, so if a rational and compelling case for the truth of Christianity were to be mounted, it had to be dealt with directly. The Gospels had presented the life of Jesus in the Messianic and eschatological terms that one

---

[49] The *Dictatus* consists of 27 propositions, which were probably designed as a table of contents for a fuller treatment that was never written. The text is given in Karl Hofmann, *Der Dictatus Papae Gregors VII* (Paderborn, 1933), 11; and an English translation in Brian Tierney, *The Crisis of Church and State, 1050–1300, with Selected Documents* (Englewood Cliffs, NJ, 1964), 49–50.

[50] This was not the first time such rights had been asserted. Pope Nicholas I (856–67) had made a similar assertion, to no effect: indeed, it came at the beginning of two centuries of steep decline in papal power.

[51] Harold J. Berman, *Law and Revolution: The Formation of the Western Legal Tradition* (Cambridge, Mass., 1983), 118.

associates with the Palestinian Judaic tradition,[52] but the generation of Paul and John had introduced a Hellenized form of Judaism into the picture, speaking of Jesus as *Kyrios* or *Logos*, as dwelling in the Father 'in the beginning' and then 'becoming flesh'.[53] It was left to subsequent generations of Christian theologians to reconcile this with Christian teachings and beliefs, and to make rational sense of the claim. Justin, a second-century pagan convert to Christianity, approached the question from a philosophical—in fact Stoic—understanding of reason (*logos*) as something shared by everyone, including the classical Greek philosophers, who had profound access to the truth; but Christ was the ultimate *Logos*, the 'word' of God, and so only with his coming was the entire truth accessible. This was little more than a play on words, and it left all kinds of questions about the nature of God, and the relation between Jesus and the Father, wide open. It took four councils—Nicaea (325), Constantinople (381), Ephesus (431), and Chalcedon (451)—to come to an agreement on definitions of the Trinity and the Incarnation,[54] namely that there were three persons in God sharing one nature, and that in Jesus there was one person with two natures. Leaving to one side the question of how this God could be identical with the God of the Old Testament, and the standing of the third person of the Trinity,[55] the question asked was how, if Jesus had two natures, one of which he did not share with the Father, he could be said to be God in the same way that, or to the same degree that, the Father was God. Between the extremes of tritheism, which distinguished three separate natures in the Trinity, and monophysitism, which maintained that there was only one nature in Jesus, which he shared with the other persons of the Trinity, some middle path had to be traced. One such middle path was Arianism, which seemed both to allow for the single nature of the persons of the Trinity and to allow two natures to Jesus, but only by giving the Father a certain

[52] On the understanding of Jesus among his earliest followers see Robert Eisenman, *James the Brother of Jesus* (New York, 1998), and Ekkehard W. Stegemann and Wolfgang Stegemann, *The Jesus Movement: A Social History of its First Century* (Edinburgh, 1999).

[53] See Peters, *The Harvest of Hellenism*, 690; Pierre Hadot, *What is Ancient Philosophy?* (Cambridge, Mass., 2002), ch. 10. On the complex relations between Hellenism and Judaism see Arnaldo Momigliano, *Alien Wisdom: The Limits of Hellenization* (Cambridge, 1971), 74–96. Generally, on the early attempts to reconcile Christian theology and Greek philosophy see Pelikan, *Christianity and Classical Culture*.

[54] The Council of Chalcedon settled these doctrinal questions in the Latin Church but their Christology caused a schism with the Eastern Church: see Jean Meyendorff, *Le Christ dans la théologie byzantine* (Paris, 1969), chs. 1 and 2. Part of the problem was linguistic. The Latin theologians of the Council of Nicaea translated the Greek term *ousia* (substance) as *substantia*, affirming the doctrine of *una substantia*, one substance in the Trinity. But the Greeks translated the Latin term *substantia* as *hupostatis*, which is more like 'personality', and consequently it looked to them as though what was being claimed was the heretical view that there was only one person in the Trinity.

[55] The Council of Toledo (589) inserted a '*filioque*' clause into the Nicene creed asserting the 'procession' of the Holy Spirit from the Father *and* the Son, and not just from the Father, thus distinguishing it from the 'generation' of the Son from the Father. The clause tied the Holy Spirit in with the Incarnation as well as creation, helping turn the focus to the immanence of God in the world. The *filioque* question remained a source of bitter dispute between the Eastern and Western churches.

priority over the other persons of the Trinity.[56] Since Jesus shares in the human nature as well as the divine nature, Arians argued that he is partly human and partly divine, and so cannot be on a par with a being that has a uniquely divine nature. But he can hardly have lost his equality with the Father only at the Incarnation, and so must have been inferior to the Father from the beginning. Arius' position was not without precedents, and indeed was an elaboration of that of Origen, who, basing himself in developments in Platonic theology, had argued that the *Logos* is the 'image' of the Father, and so in some way at a lower order of reality, like the lower hypostases of Platonic theology, although this *Logos* was outside time and wholly divine like the Father. Arius simply drops the qualifying and guarded language that Origen had used, talking of the Father not as 'begetting' *Logos* but as 'creating' it. Jesus was a creation of the Father, and his existence was therefore temporal, something consonant with the Gospels' terminology of the 'son of God'.

Augustine had given a considered exposition of the orthodox doctrine of the Trinity in *De trinitate*, setting it out in terms of the philosophical vocabulary of *substantia* and *persona*, and Boethius, with the benefit of Aristotle's logical writings—which he had translated into Latin, a translation that was available in the West in the eleventh century—had offered a more elaborate version.[57] The persons of the Trinity lack *differentia* by which they might be marked out as being of different species or genera, for example, and hence they can be compared to mathematical points which can be placed on one another, as opposed to points that are distinguished by *differentia*, for instance by being placed along a line. Boethius' writings were virtually the single conduit to ancient thought in the tenth and eleventh centuries, and he introduced the basic Aristotelian notions of prime matter, which he thought of as a condition for Christ's human nature, and of the distinction between matter and God's pure form.[58] These provided some of the basic vocabulary in which Christological and Trinitarian issues were thought through.

These issues hinged largely on the philosophical question of universals, and what was at stake in the disputes over universals was which account of universals best accommodated orthodox theology on the complex questions of the Trinity and the Incarnation. The 1092 dispute between Anselm and Roscelin over the nature of the Trinity, for example, turned on the question of whether species and genera have a reality of their own. Anselm, taking a traditional Platonist view, assumed that they do, but Roscelin, following Aristotle's doctrine in the *Categories* (available in Boethius' Latin translation), maintained that only individuals exist. Roscelin made a move that was indicative of the direction the debate would take.[59] In commenting on Aristotle's

---

[56] On the theological credentials of Arianism see Richard Hanson, *The Search for the Christian Doctrine of God* (Edinburgh, 1988); Maurice Wiles, *Archetypal Heresy: Arianism through the Centuries* (Oxford, 1996); and Daniel H. Williams, *Ambrose of Milan and the End of Nicene–Arian Conflicts* (Oxford, 1995).

[57] See G. R. Evans, *Philosophy and Theology in the Middle Ages* (London, 1993), 60–2.

[58] See Anthony Levi, *Renaissance and Reformation* (New Haven, Conn., 2002), 35.

[59] See the accounts of these questions in Marcia Colish, *Medieval Foundations of the Western Intellectual Tradition, 400–1400* (New Haven, Conn., 1997), chs. 11 and 21, and Evans, *Philosophy and Theology*, ch. 4, to which I am indebted here.

logical works, Boethius had contrasted two positions one might take on logical or semantic grounds: one is to assert the analytical priority of abstract ideas or universals, the other is to assert their analytical posteriority. Roscelin applied the distinction to metaphysics, arguing that individual things and the concepts signifying them are more real than the universal things. He then drew theological consequences from this metaphysical position. The Father, the Son, and the Holy Spirit are indeed true deities and their names meaningful. The term 'God', by contrast, which signifies the divine nature possessed by all three persons of the Trinity, is a meaningless abstraction. Roscelin was charged with tritheism at the Council of Soisson in 1092, one of his principal accusers being Anselm. Anselm's own position had been that just as when one says of someone that he is 'white', 'just', and 'literate', one does not thereby mean he is three separate entities, so when one uses the terms 'Father', 'Son', and 'Spirit' of God one does not mean he is three entities. Roscelin subsequently replied that Anselm's view committed him either to the claim that the Trinity is like three souls or three angels, or to the claim that the Trinity is not three things, in which case the Father and the Holy Spirit were incarnate with the Son. Anselm's response was to point to his limited intentions in making the distinction in the first place. The aim was simply to use an analogy to illustrate how the terms 'God', 'Son', and 'Spirit' could be predicated of God without generating three Gods. It was not to suggest the identity of the Father and the Son, a view that Anselm insisted he did not hold.[60] Far from resolving the issues, the upshot of this dispute was that far more work on the question of universals would be needed before any philosophical defence of the orthodoxy could be mounted.

Nor were questions of the Trinity and the Incarnation the only philosophically problematic questions. Forty years before the dispute between Roscelin and Abelard, Berengar had argued that accidents cannot subsist without a substance for them to inhere in. Applying this metaphysical doctrine to the sacrament of the eucharist, he pointed out that the accidents of bread remain after the consecration, so its substance must remain. What actually happens, on Berengar's view, is that a new substance is added to that of the bread. In opposition to this view, Lanfranc argued that the substance of the bread is transformed into the 'true body' of Christ: this means that, unlike all other sacraments, it requires no participants other than the priest,[61] a radical view but one officially adopted by the Fourth Lateran Council in 1215. Lanfranc's case depended crucially on the Aristotelian vocabulary of substance and accident, which he had learned from Boethius' translations of Aristotle's logical writings, but it was clear that without considerable refinement of the philosophical discussion of substances and their properties or accidents, little progress could be made on these contentious issues.

---

[60] Anselm of Canterbury, *Opera Omnia*, ed. F. S. Schmitt (2 vols, Stuttgart, 1968), i. 282.

[61] See Aquinas, the greatest defender of the doctrine of transubstantiation, as it was then coming to be known, *Summa theologica*, III q. 80 a. 12, reply to obj. 2, where he notes that 'the perfection of the sacrament does not lie in the participation of the faithful but in the consecration of the elements', and he points out that this distinguishes it from the other sacraments (III q. 73 a. 1).

Such progress was the aim of Abelard's attempt, in the twelfth century, to devise a philosophically grounded systematic theology. Abelard introduced a significant tightening up of philosophical resources. He distanced himself from Roscelin, his teacher, by arguing that questions of whether universals are prior or posterior are logical questions and not questions about the degree of reality or being of those things designated by universal concepts. Quite the contrary, ideas of particulars and ideas of universals are, he insisted, both less real than what they refer to, for concepts derive from what they refer to, which are independent of the concept in the sense that they can exist without anyone having a concept of them. But some concepts are more derivative than others. We acquire ideas of individual things first, forming a concept of these things and giving them a name which we can use in the absence of the thing itself, and Abelard insisted that logicians deal only with these names, not with the essence or existence of the thing named. The concept that we form of a thing by acquaintance with that thing is a concept that has a concrete significance. We can also proceed to abstract common traits from our concepts of similar things, and in this way form a concept that has an abstract significance. Abelard's move from knowledge of individual things, to knowledge of their concepts, was knowledge of abstract concepts, is in sharp contrast to the Platonist tradition, where knowledge of the most general and abstract formed the starting point for all knowledge, whether such knowledge be seen in terms of pure intellectual reflection on essences (as in Anselm's proofs of the existence of a Christian God which start, in the case of the ontological argument for example, with a reflection on the essence of God) or in terms of divine illumination.

Abelard's attempt to move from his understanding of the nature of universals and how we come by knowledge of them to theological questions was, it has to be said, not a success if the defence and vindication of orthodoxy was the aim, and his doctrines were condemned at the Councils of Soisson (1121) and Sens (*c*.1140). His application of the semantic theory that nouns and verbs have a univocal signification, irrespective of their case endings, to theological questions led him to argue that verbs in propositions stating the goodness of God are univocal with those in propositions stating his creative activity, and he concludes that God could not have done differently from what he has done. His application of the theory of names to the persons of the Trinity led him to assert that the terms 'power', 'wisdom', and 'goodness' are attributable pre-eminently to the Father, Son, and Holy Spirit respectively as proper names, but this suggests, amongst other things, that the Father does not intrinsically—that is, by his very nature—possess wisdom and goodness, that the Son does not intrinsically possess power and goodness, and that the Holy Spirit does not intrinsically possess power and wisdom.

Yet despite his problematic incursions into theology, Abelard made two crucial moves. First, he shows what is wrong with reading degrees of reality off from logical distinctions, revealing how logical distinctions might be more fruitfully employed at a fundamental level. Second, having rethought the role of logic in this way, he is able to engage the question of universals in a far more methodical way than any of the other thinkers, from Erigena onwards, who had tried to establish a systematic theology on a philosophical basis. The basic dichotomy that emerged from his account was that between knowledge via abstraction and knowledge via descent from abstract universals, and despite the heterodoxy of some of Abelard's conclusions, the former, abstractive knowledge, seemed to provide something whose logical and epistemological credentials were both more thorough and more coherent than those of the Platonist alternatives. The question was whether an abstractive epistemology could be adjusted to give an orthodox account of fundamental theological questions.

The rediscovery of the Aristotelian corpus, with its elaborate defence of abstractive knowledge, provided what seemed, to an increasing number of theologians and philosophers in the course of the thirteenth century, exactly the right resources with which to develop a fundamental philosophical vindication of those key theological issues—such as the Trinity, the Incarnation, and transubstantiation—that required a particularly sophisticated account of substance and its properties, and the relation between particulars and universals. In this way, Aristotelianism seemed to hold the key to a set of fundamental theological questions, and this, above all, is what would secure its philosophical primacy over traditional Platonism.

If this was the sum total of what was at stake, however, we might expect a relatively smooth transition from the pre-Aristotelian scholasticism of Abelard and his contemporaries to the Aristotelian scholasticism of Albertus, Aquinas, and their successors. But what actually happened was quite different. Aristotelian scholasticism was introduced in the face of massive resistance and condemnation from theologians. A crucial determining factor here is the role of natural philosophy. The doctrinal differences between Platonist and Aristotelian systems have very significant consequences for how philosophy is pursued, and the distinctive thing about following the Aristotelian route in abstractive epistemology is that you must start from sense perception, which in terms of the Aristotelian division of areas of philosophical enquiry means you must start from natural philosophy. This transforms the nature of philosophical enquiry in a number of ways, not least in that it makes the entry into the philosophical foundations of systematic theology something that is largely independent of the kinds of areas in which theologians, and the clergy generally, had taken an interest.

To understand why the introduction of Aristotelianism was so bitterly opposed and condemned in the thirteenth century, we must appreciate that the issues went beyond any straightforward doctrinal question. They went right to the heart of the Church's authority, and to help us to understand how this happened, we need to focus on just how the authority structure of the Church had changed by the thirteenth century.

In the eleventh and twelfth centuries, as we have seen, the Church underwent a momentous and irreversible transformation, in which it lost certain rights and powers and gained others. The period of Caesaro-Papism, which had begun in the fourth century under the rule of Constantine, and in which the Emperor had taken upon himself the role of arbitrator in doctrinal disputes and exercised spiritual leadership of the Church (and in which, reciprocally, the Pope had exercised significant authority over the appointment and deposition of emperors),[62] finally came to an end in the

---

[62] On the high point of this period, see Robert Holtzmann, *Geschichte der sächsischen Kaiserzeit (900–1024)* (Munich, 1941).

West.[63] The Church lost its secular powers, but became an imperial power in its own domain.[64] It was effectively formed as a corporation, declaring itself legally autonomous from the secular order, and claiming for itself all spiritual authority. This process was a protracted one, but in 1215 the Fourth Lateran Council formalized both Church doctrine and administrative organization. In the former case, for example, heresy was defined carefully in legal terms, and was declared in 1199 by Innocent III—who furthered the work of his predecessor Lucius III in centralizing the recently formed episcopal Inquisitions into a papal Inquisition[65]—to be on a par with high treason, with the pope's powers over matters of Church doctrine and administrative organization attracting the kind of draconian sanctions held by the emperor in the secular realm.[66] The separation of secular and spiritual powers was, however, a fluid business. In the eleventh century, the monastic reformer Peter Damian had seen the separation of powers as a ground for rejecting the claims of reason to interpret revelation,[67] arguing that God's powers transcended human logic, even the principle of non-contradiction, yet at the political level he was no defender of two realms, strongly supporting Henry III's use of his imperial powers to promote reform within the Church and the papacy.[68] And new uncloistered orders of friars often saw themselves as choosing spiritual over secular learning, yet it was the Dominicans who, in spite of the fact that they were forbidden through their constitution of 1228 'to study the books of pagans and philosophers, though they

[63] This did not prevent there remaining a significant degree of ecclesiastical autonomy in national churches. The Pragmatic Sanction of Bourges of 1438 made the French king the supreme head of the church in all but doctrinal matters, and the concordat negotiated with German princes in 1447 conferred the same kind of role on them. At the end of the fifteenth century, papal bulls and decrees required royal consent in France and Spain, and by the 1490s control of the Spanish church (and, it should be noted, the Spanish Inquisition) was firmly in state hands, albeit with the support of most of the clergy. See Levi, *Renaissance and Reformation*, 4–5, 286–7.

[64] There is a good narrative of the events making up the Investiture Controversy and its aftermath in Stephen Ozment, *The Age of Reform, 1250–1550* (New Haven, Conn., 1980), 138–81. On the complex political prehistory of the Controversy, see Friedrich Heer, *The Holy Roman Empire* (London, 1968). On its politico-legal legacy see R. W. Carlyle and A. J. Carlyle, *A History of Medieval Political Theory in the West* (6 vols, Edinburgh, 1970), iv. On the administrative and authority structure of the Church that resulted, see the discussion of ordination of priests in J. Turmel, *Histoire des Dogmas* (6 vols, Paris, 1931–6), vi. 491–543. On the complex swapping of images of pope and secular emperor, see Ernst Kantorowicz, *The King's Two Bodies* (Princeton, 1957). The divide between secular and sacred jurisdictions held to a large extent but it should be noted that it was not in principle watertight, and in the early 1500s, the Emperor Maximilian I could contemplate realizing his political ambitions by having himself made pope, uniting in the one person both jurisdictions.

[65] This Inquisition should not be confused with 'the' Inquisition, which was primarily a Dominican affair begun by Gregory IX in 1227 in Florence.

[66] See Walter Ullmann, *A Short History of the Papacy in the Middle Ages* (London, 1972), 219–26, and, more generally, Robert I. Moore, *The Formation of a Persecuting Society: Power and Deviance in Western Europe 950–1250* (Oxford, 1981). It should be noted that secular authorities occasionally took action against heretics when they saw them as a source of social disorder: see Richard Kieckhefer, *Repression of Heresy in Medieval Germany* (Philadelphia, 1979), 75–82.

[67] See Gordon Leff, *Medieval Thought* (Harmondsworth, 1958), 91.

[68] John B. Morrall, *Political Thought in Medieval Times* (Toronto, 1980), 25–6.

might give them a passing glance',[69] provided the leaders of the move to reconcile pagan and Christian thought in the 1250s.

The problem of authority was complicated by the fact that it had been resolved by the formation of the Church as a corporation, yet the Church was not the only such corporation formed in the wake of the Investiture Controversy. Several different kinds of entities were forming themselves into autonomous or quasi-autonomous bodies, not least the universities.[70] Around the end of the twelfth century, for example, the law students of the *studium* at Bologna formed themselves into a corporation, a 'university' (the Latin term *universitas* simply means a legally defined corporation), to secure exemption from municipal tribunals and set up their own, to secure freedom from municipal taxation, to secure the right to fix prices for lodging etc., and to secure rights over teaching, and they exercised these rights with relish, fining professors who began or finished their classes late.[71] But the Law 'university' and other Faculties at Bologna were separate, and as well as significant national variations,[72] the kind of autonomy that a Law or a Medicine Faculty could secure for itself was different from the kind of regulation to which an Arts or Theology Faculty was subject. The new Arts Faculties were staffed by a new kind of *magister* who, while still a cleric, was very different from the monk,[73] and who now not only

[69] Denifle and Châtelain, eds., *Chartularium Universitatis Parisiensis*, ii. 222.

[70] On the general questions of just what counts as a university, in what senses Bologna or Paris might be claimed to be the first medieval university, and whether educational institutions before the twelfth century (e.g. in medieval Arab cultures) are in any sense universities, see Walter Rüegg, 'Themes', and Jacques Verger, 'Patterns', in Hilde de Ridder-Symoens, ed., *A History of the University in Europe*, i. *Universities in the Middle Ages* (Cambridge, 1992), 3–34 and 35–74 respectively. See also Jacques Le Goff, 'The Universities and the Public Authorities in the Middle Ages and the Renaissance', in idem, *Time, Work, and Culture in the Middle Ages* (Chicago, 1980), 135–49.

[71] See David Knowles, *The Evolution of Medieval Thought* (London, 1962), 159–63. The process was a protracted one, with the commune of Bologna opposing the formation of a cosmopolitan body in its midst which had a jurisdiction parallel to its own, and in 1211 the city enacted legislation prohibiting the formation of groups whose members swore to lend each other mutual aid and support. Although the Pope came down on the side of the students, matters continued to fester throughout the rest of the decade. See Nardi, 'Relations with Authority', 84–5.

[72] The two main models were those of Paris and Bologna. Paris was divided into the four Faculties—arts, law, medicine, and theology—and both teachers and students were members of these Faculties. Other divisions, such as the *nationes* for students of different geographical origins, were strictly subordinate to these. Bologna was more complex (see Berman, *Law and Revolution*, 123–31). It consisted of a *studium generale* which comprised a cluster of universities, each for students of only one discipline and divided into two *nationes* (students from Bologna needed no separate 'nation'). Although strictly speaking the university consisted only of students, the teachers being hired annually, the latter quickly formed their own separate corporation—the *collegium doctorum*—which was distinct from the students' corporation. In the Iberian peninsula, southern France, and Eastern Europe, universities were a mixture of these two models. See Aleksander Gieysztor, 'Management and Resources', Hilde de Ridder-Symoens, ed., *A History of the University in Europe*, i. *Universities in the Middle Ages* (Cambridge, 1992), 108–43.

[73] Teaching outside the monasteries was introduced in the early ninth century by Charlemagne, who oversaw the setting up of cathedral schools for the training of the clergy, where the liberal arts, as well as theology, were taught. But these schools developed in a haphazard way before the twelfth century. On the training of the new university masters see Jacques Verger, 'Teachers', in Hilde de Ridder-Symoens, ed., *A History of the University in Europe*, i. *Universities in the Middle*

immersed himself in secular learning, particularly the liberal arts, but saw this very much as part of his identity, by contrast with the monk, for whom such learning was very marginal to how he conceived his role.[74] While these Arts Faculties gained some administrative autonomy, at Paris for example, what resulted from the setting out of the Church's responsibilities and powers by the Lateran Council was a focus on questions of metaphysics and natural theology of a degree previously unknown, as the Church took responsibility for its newly defined domain with a heightened vigilance. Aristotle's texts on metaphysics and natural philosophy were introduced at just the time that this new focus was consolidated, so that they were subjected to a scrutiny of a wholly new intensity, by a clergy who had a new sense of their rights and authority on such matters.

The conflict between what the Church regarded as its areas of authority, and the sensibilities of those teaching this material, came to a head quickly. With the introduction of Aristotle's natural philosophy texts and their Arab commentaries, something became evident that had for all intents and purposes remained hidden since the Patristic era, namely the realization that there may be more than one legitimate way of dealing with certain basic questions—such as whether the soul could persist after the death and corruption of the body, whether the world had, or could have, existed forever—and that different ways of arriving at a conclusion on a question might generate different conclusions. One of these Arab commentators, Averroes, had maintained that theology and Aristotelian natural philosophy were each wholly autonomous disciplines that could generate conflicting and irreconcilable doctrines. Averroism undermined the separation of powers that gave the Church its legitimacy, by raising the possibility that, in the intellectual realm, these powers might overlap or compete.

When Aristotelianism was officially accepted by the University of Paris in 1255, the Arts Faculty in effect became a Philosophy Faculty, something administratively on a par with the Theology Faculty, and right from the start there was one pressing question on which they were at odds, whether the Christian virtue of humility or the Aristotelian one of magnanimity should take precedence. In his *Quaestiones morales* (*c.*1272), Siger of Brabant subordinates the moral to the intellectual virtues, and takes seriously the possibility that humility is not a virtue at all. The Averroist Boethius of Dacia goes further, arguing in his *De summo bono* (*c.*1275) that the highest possible good is to be found in the operation of the intellectual virtues, and that as a consequence it is easier for a philosopher to be virtuous than anyone else, and that whoever does not live the life of a philosopher does not live rightly or virtuously.[75] The 1277 Condemnation explicitly rejected such claims, singling out for condemnation the statements that 'the most excellent way of life is the philosophical one'

*Ages* (Cambridge, 1992), 144–68. See also Ugo Gualazzini, *Ricerche sulle scuole pre-universitarie del medioevo: contributo di indagini sul sorgere delle università* (Milan, 1943).

[74] See Jacques Le Goff, *Les Intellectuels au moyen âge* (Paris, 1957), and Peter Godman, *The Silent Masters: Latin Literature and Censors in the High Middle Ages* (Princeton, NJ, 2000).

[75] Boethius of Dacia, *On the Supreme Good*, ed. and trans. J. F. Wippel (Toronto, 1987), 32–5. See C. H. Lohr, 'The Medieval Interpretation of Aristotle', and Georg Wieland, 'The Reception and Interpretation of Aristotle's *Ethics*', both in Norman Kretzmann, Anthony Kenny, and Jan Pinborg, eds., *The Cambridge History of Later Medieval Philosophy* (Cambridge, 1982).

(prop. 40), 'the highest human good consists in the intellectual virtues' (prop. 144), 'philosophers alone are the wise men of the world' (prop. 154). The issues were, then, not just over fine points of doctrine, but raised the whole question of the nature of philosophy and its relation to revelation, as well as the question of the shift in standing from the monk to the philosopher as paradigm bearer of wisdom.

For the thirteenth-century opponents of Averroism, if the 1277 Condemnation can be taken as indicative, what was at issue was the doctrine of 'two truths', that is, the doctrine that theology and Aristotelian natural philosophy were each a wholly autonomous source of truth that could generate truths that conflicted with the other. But, as Charles Lohr has pointed out, the Paris Faculty of Arts masters who envisaged philosophy as an autonomous discipline did not conceive theology and philosophy to be doing the same kind of thing.[76] They saw themselves as different from theologians, and their model was Aristotle, subservient to no authority and free of dogmatism. Theology was conceived to be an unveiling of the truth concealed in the words of sacred texts, and so is essentially a form of interpretation.[77] Philosophy, by contrast, was not conceived as the uncovering of the truth that lay hidden in a unique authority: there was no hidden truth in a philosophy text, but rather it was one source among many, which may contain errors that should be exposed. Such a mode of reading does not require texts to be reconciled with theology because it is not engaged in uncovering truths which can then be opposed to different truths which have been uncovered by different means. The aim of philosophy is the examination of opposing opinions by philological and ratiocinative investigation: it worked in the realm of opinions, and judged these opinions by assessing their strengths and weaknesses and contrasting them with other opinions. The method is most strikingly exemplified in the work of Nicholas of Autrecourt, whose treatise *Exigit ordo executionis*, composed around 1340,[78] advocated atomism, the existence of a void, the eternity of all things, and (against the Averroists) the plurality of intellects, as well as offering corpuscularian accounts of both transubstantiation and the resurrection of the body. Nicholas' claim is not that these are true doctrines, however, only that they are more probable than alternative opinions. Nicholas clearly sees himself as working in a domain of enquiry quite distinct from that of theology, where questions that could never even be raised in a theological context can be pursued in some detail in a purely hypothetical way.

It might seem that this is a weaker claim than the doctrine of 'double truth', but in some respects it is more radical, for it is postulating the existence of two completely different kinds of enterprise, which engage some of the same questions, but in completely different ways. It is not potentially conflicting results that matter, so much as how one goes about thinking through complex fundamental questions in the first place. On the other hand, nor is it surprising that those who see the issue as being one

---

[76] Lohr, 'The Medieval Interpretation of Aristotle', 88–91, to which I am indebted in what follows. Cf. Bruno Nardi, *Saggi sull'aristotelismo padovano dal secolo XIV al XVI* (Florence, 1958).

[77] On the disputes over the aims of such interpretation see Ozment, *The Age of Reform*, 63–72.

[78] This work, also known as *Tractatus universalis*, was ordered to be publicly burned in 1346, but a manuscript copy has survived, edited and published by J. R. O'Donnell in 1939. It is available in English translation in Leonard Kennedy, Richard Arnold, and Arthur Millward, *The Universal Treatise of Nicholas of Autrecourt* (Milwaukee, 1971).

of uncovering a pre-given but concealed truth should in consequence think of the threat of Averroism as lying in its generation of heterodoxy. But the real threat lies not in conflicting discourses but rather in the emergence of parallel discourses with different aims and concerns: it lies in the issue of the range of ways in which one can engage particular questions, as much as in the conclusions one comes to.

## THE CONDEMNATIONS OF ARISTOTLE

The 1210 Paris condemnation was directed towards three things: the question of theological works written in the vernacular; the circulation of the first Latin translations of Aristotle's writings on natural philosophy with commentaries by David of Dinant, as well as some Arabic commentaries that had begun circulating in Latin;[79] and the Amalrician heresy. The solution to the first was to hand such works in to the bishops of individual dioceses. The solution to the second was to hand in the books by David to the Bishop of Paris for burning.[80] The solution to the third was remove the body of Amalric from the graveyard (he had died in 1206) and cast it on unhallowed ground, and to condemn his followers to death at the stake or life imprisonment.

David argued that God, matter, and soul must ultimately be the same thing, whereas Amalric's contention was that God was ultimately identical with the physical world. These two positions were associated in the minds of those who condemned them. A contemporary anonymous writer tells us that 'Master Amalric and other heretics of that time absorbed David's error',[81] and William the Breton writes that:

During those days certain short writings, said to be by Aristotle and teaching metaphysics, were being read in Paris, having been recently brought from Constantinople and translated from Greek into Latin. These writings provided an opportunity not only for the subtle doctrines of the Amalrician heresy but also for other doctrines which had not yet been invented, and it was therefore decreed that they should all be burnt. Moreover it was laid down in the same Council that no one should henceforth dare to transcribe or read those books.[82]

Amalric advocated the doctrine that God is ubiquitous and immanent in the world: Christ is physically present in the universe in just the same way that he is present in eucharist, and the Holy Spirit dwells in human souls. In other words, there is a basic denial of God's transcendence. We do not know what the sources of this doctrine were, and David of Dinant may in fact not have been one of them. In a contemporary

---

[79] David may in fact have been expounding/defending Averroes' commentaries rather than offering something original: see Enzo Maccagnolo, 'David of Dinant and the Beginnings of Aristotelianism in Paris', in Peter Dronke, ed., *A History of Twelfth-Century Western Philosophy* (Cambridge, 1988), 429–42.

[80] This had the desired result, David's work effectively being lost to posterity, although a few texts were recovered in the twentieth century, and are published in *Davidis de Dinanto Quaternulorum Fragmenta*, ed. M. Kurdziałek (Warsaw, 1963).

[81] Quoted in Maccagnolo, 'David of Dinant and the Beginnings of Aristotelianism in Paris', 430.

[82] Quoted ibid. 431.

commentary on Peter Lombard's *Sententiae*, Alexander of Hales, writing in Paris, criticizes Anselm's claim that 'things created in God are the very essence of God', telling us that 'this is very close to that heresy according to which "all things are in God" '.[83] Alexander is quite right, and the doctrine is one that we might expect to arise in a theology that relied so heavily on Neoplatonic philosophy. Although Plotinus' God is actually more transcendent than the orthodox Christian one,[84] Books 4 and 5 of the Sixth *Ennead* are devoted to showing that 'The one identical essence is everywhere entirely present', and one can see how, once translated into Christian terms, this might suggest pantheism. Moreover, the very idea of degrees of perfection by which Anselm establishes the existence of God in the *Monologion* suggests a lack of a qualitative distinction between God and the rest of existence.[85] In other words, Amalric's effective denial of God's transcendence is easily generated within orthodox Augustinian Christian thought: Aristotelianism is not needed for it.

David of Dinant, so far as we can tell from reconstructed sources, thought of metaphysics as Augustine and Anselm did, as a general science of God, but he puts a number of distinctive glosses upon it.[86] First, he defines metaphysics as the science of being, and divides all forms of being into three subspecies—God, mind, and matter—arguing that God and mind, both being immaterial, can be equated. But he also seems to have argued, contrary to the claim that God is one of the divisions of being, that God and matter can be equated because both evade all categories, matter evading categories because, prior to the imposition of form, matter is undifferentiated. Neither of these doctrines is uniquely Aristotelian. The conception of matter as a propertyless substratum on which the equation of God and matter rests could have been drawn either from Plato's account of original matter in the *Timaeus* or from Aristotle's account of 'prime matter'. The equation of God and mind could be defended in Neoplatonic terms, but it was also a doctrine associated with Aristotle's Arab commentators, where it was defended in Aristotelian terms, roughly along the lines that while mind can have an identity in its own right to the extent to which it is instantiated in a particular body, without such instantiation it cannot have its own identity, so all disembodied mind is one and the same. The works of Averroes, with whom we associate the distinctive doctrine of the 'unity of the intellect', did not appear in Latin translations until the 1220s, but the Arabic

---

[83] Quoted ibid. 431.

[84] As A. H. Armstrong points out in *The Architecture of the Intelligible Universe in the Philosophy of Plotinus* (Cambridge, 1940), Plotinus uses elements derived from both Plato and Aristotle in his construction of God (56), and the more transcendent aspects in fact derive from the latter (3). It might also be noted here that one of the greatest obstacles to the complete assimilation of Neoplatonism was Arianism, which fitted the Neoplatonic single God perfectly but the consubstantial Christian Trinity poorly.

[85] The ontological argument of the *Proslogion* is more ambiguous in this respect. Spinoza, in the *Ethica*, notoriously uses the ontological argument to establish his pantheism, by interpreting it as showing that only one substance exists, but Descartes uses the ontological argument to establish the transcendence of God: see Stephen Gaukroger, 'The Role of the Ontological Argument', *Indian Philosophical Quarterly* 23 (1996), 169–80.

[86] See the discussion in Colish, *Medieval Foundations*, 246–7.

tradition on these questions was familiar as early as the mid-twelfth century,[87] and the association of Aristotle with Averroism, which was to dog the acceptance of Aristotelianism,[88] may well have begun with the introduction of Aristotle into the West, although the very earliest Aristotelians do not seem to have been directly influenced by the Arab commentators—Averroes' works were not known in Paris until the 1230s, when William of Auvergne first discussed them in his *De universo* and *De anima*—but rather independently drew many of the same radical conclusions from Aristotle.[89]

Matters came to a head with the condemnation of 1277, in which the 'errors' of Aristotelianism/Averroism were finally set out in detail. Tempier's list made no distinction between the three main forms of Aristotelianism, and although it included predominantly Averroist or 'naturalist' propositions, there were also some doctrines we associate with Avicenna, and up to 20 of the 219 condemned propositions were doctrines advocated by Aquinas, most notably the individuation of the soul by the body, the theory of the relation between the reason and the intellect, and the Aristotelian proof of the uniqueness of the world.[90]

Avicenna in the eleventh century, Averroes in the twelfth, and Aquinas in the thirteenth each attempted to reconstruct a unified system which accommodated both theological and natural-philosophical considerations in the wake of the introduction of Aristotelian natural philosophy and metaphysics. Tempier sees no need for any accommodation.[91] For him, philosophy was a dependent and subordinate part of theology, as it had been for Augustine and the whole tradition of Christian thinking

---

[87] See Jacques Jolivet, 'The Arabic Inheritance', in Peter Dronke, ed., *A History of Twelfth-Century Western Philosophy* (Cambridge, 1988), 113–48.

[88] The introduction of Aristotelianism had also been opposed in the Muslim world in the eleventh and twelfth centuries, on the grounds of its irreconcilability with Islamic belief, most notably in al-Ghazali's *The Incoherence of Philosophers*, which accuses philosophers (i.e. Aristotelian philosophers) of three counts of infidelity and seventeen counts of heresy. Averroes replied in detail: see Averroes, *Tahāfut al-Tahāfut: The Incoherence of the Incoherence*, trans. from the Arabic, with introd. and notes by Simon van den Bergh (London, 1954). Even though Averroes' work was treated far more seriously in the West than it was in the Islamic world, he was banished from the city, had his books burned, and was forced to emigrate to Morocco towards the end of his life.

[89] See F. van Steenberghen, *Aristotle and the West* (Louvain, 1955), 219–29.

[90] In the numbering of P. Mandonnet, *Siger de Brabant et l'averroïsme latin au XIII^me siècle, 2^me partie: Textes inédits* (2nd edn, Louvain, 1908), 175–91, these propositions are 42–3, 50, 53–5, 110, 115–16 (individuation of the soul); 46, 162–3 (reason and intellect); and 27 (uniqueness). It is easy to assume that these condemnations were largely forgotten in the wake of the de facto establishment of Thomism as the official philosophy of the Church in the fifteenth century, but the condemnations of Aristotle were mentioned in the widely read and repeatedly reprinted text of the Professor of Philosophy at Paris in the mid-seventeenth century, Jean de Launoy, *De varia Aristotelis in Academia Parisiensi Fortuna* (Paris, 1653).

[91] He had very significant support in this respect. There is a good statement of the traditionalist position in a letter of John Pecham to the Bishop of Lincoln, 1 June 1285, where he complains that the authority of Augustine and traditional, orthodox Christianity has been challenged by 'irreverent innovations in language, introduced within the last twenty years into the depths of theology against philosophical truth, and to the detriment of the Fathers whose positions are distained and openly held in contempt': quoted in James A. Weisheipl, 'Albertus Magnus and Universal Hylomorphism: Avicebron', in Francis J. Kovas and Robert W. Shahan, eds, *Albert the Great: Commemorative Essays* (Norman, 1980), 239–60: 239. The irony is that, as Weisheipl shows, what the traditionalists

up to the thirteenth century, and metaphysics was a 'science of God'. Peter of Spain, who, as Pope John XXI, gave his authority to the 1277 Condemnation, was one of staunchest advocates of this tradition in the thirteenth century.[92] But the trouble is that the pieces no longer fit together as they did in Augustine's synthesis, for elements of genuinely different traditions are being juxtaposed. Augustine's relatively narrow range of philosophical interests and sources helps hold together his account under philosophically artificial conditions. With the reintroduction of Aristotle's texts, these artificial conditions are exposed for what they are, and the old Augustinian unity of doctrine is no longer attainable. Peter of Spain's response falls apart: as Gilson puts it, 'one has the uncomfortable impression of meeting already-known formulas, which have come from elsewhere and have lost their meaning during the journey'.[93] And this is no less true of the thought of the greatest representative of this tradition in the thirteenth century, Bonaventure, whose philosophy is in many respects an unreconciled mixture of elements taken from Augustine, Neoplatonists, and Aristotle as well as Arab Aristotle commentators.[94]

On the other hand, when one looks at the positions of Avicenna and Averroes, one can appreciate the dilemma facing Tempier and Peter of Spain. Avicenna's response had been to attempt to weld together theology and Aristotelian philosophy, to rework theology in terms of Aristotelian metaphysics.[95] His work had a great influence on figures as diverse as Aquinas and Peter of Spain himself, but it led in the direction of an Aristotelian rationalization of God, and a naturalistic conception of the universe as ruled by laws that were intelligible and necessary.[96] Consequently, in spite of his influence on thirteenth-century Christian thinking about the relation between metaphysics and theology, what he offered was not only something that a Christian philosopher could not accept, but was a lesson in the dire consequences of going down the Aristotelian path. Averroes, by contrast, made a strict separation between philosophy and theology, envisaging them as two wholly separate kinds of enterprise, each legitimate in its own right. The problem is that there are questions on which they come into conflict, and in such cases the two act as different and possibly irreconcilable sources of truth. Nevertheless, as I have indicated, it was the idea of an autonomous philosophical practice rather than 'double truth' as such that was at issue for those associated with Averroism in the thirteenth century. And in the early fourteenth century, while there were some opponents of the papacy based at the court of Louis of

---

invoked were not pure Augustinian doctrines but doctrines that had been revised radically by Arab commentators such as Averroes and Avicebron. Weisheipl's conclusion is that 'Avicebron rather than Augustine is the source of what appeared to the vast majority of thirteenth-century theologians as the traditional and sound doctrine' (241).

[92] See Gilson, *History*, 319–32.      [93] Ibid. 321.

[94] See Étienne Gilson, *La Philosophie de St. Bonaventure* (Paris, 1945).

[95] See Goodman, *Avicenna*, ch. 2.

[96] Note, however, that these are laws externally imposed by God, not intrinsic to nature. Avicenna is opposed to the Aristotelian view that there is agency in nature and he criticizes the Christian school of philosophers in Baghdad on these grounds. See H. V. B. Brown, 'Avicenna and the Christian Philosophers in Baghdad', in S. M. Stern, Albert Hourani, and Vivian Brown, eds, *Islamic Philosophy and the Classical Tradition* (Columbia, SC, 1972), 35–48.

Bavaria, such as John of Jandun and Marsilius of Padua, who are often associated with Averroism, their aim was the curbing of papal authority by means of a reaffirmation of the division of secular and ecclesiastical powers that resulted from the Investiture Controversy,[97] and they did not advocate double truth as a response to possible conflicts between ecclesiastical and secular authorities.

Whatever the actual support for Averroism, however, advocates of the traditional view tended to associate any form of Aristotelianism with Averroism, which they took as an advocacy of 'double truth'. The perceived threat from Averroism was the possibility that revealed theology might have competition from Aristotelian natural philosophy. The basic problem identified in the various thirteenth-century condemnations of Aristotelianism that came to a head in 1277 was that Aristotelian natural philosophy had embraced doctrines in clear and indisputable conflict with Christian teaching, doctrines such as the eternity of the world, and the denial of the possibility of creation *ex nihilo*. But Tempier's response, decisive as it might have seemed, was not only ineffectual: it actually compounded the problems in many ways.

This can be illustrated by the issue of God's omnipotence, one of the central concerns of the 1277 condemnation. Tempier objected to Aristotelian natural philosophy on the grounds that it rules out the ability of God to create more than one world, and he explicitly condemned the view that 'the first cause cannot make many worlds'. Tempier was not, of course, advocating the idea that God had in fact created a world other than the geocentric one, but his criticism, rather than putting an end to natural-philosophical speculation, as he might have hoped, actually provoked it, for if it were possible for God to have created such a world, then there is a legitimate natural-philosophical question about what its physical characteristics would have been. Such natural-philosophical questioning had to be couched completely hypothetically, of course, as indeed it was in those fourteenth-century natural philosophers such as Buridan, Nicholas of Autrecourt, and Oresme who pursued these questions.[98] But there is no doubt that they believed they were dealing with real physical possibilities which their natural-philosophical resources had to account for satisfactorily. Oresme, for example, concluded that God could have made several worlds distinct from our own, even though he in fact only created one, and he established this by looking at what physical characteristics such other worlds might have:

For the truth is that in this world a part of the earth does not tend towards one centre and another part to another centre, but all heavy bodies in this world tend to be united in one mass such that the centre of the weight of this mass is at the centre of this world, and all the parts constitute one body numerically speaking. Therefore, they have one single place. And if some part of the earth in the other world were in this world, it would tend towards the centre

---

[97] See Gilson, *History*, 521–7, and Alan Gewirth's introduction to Marsilius of Padua, *Defensor Pacis* (Toronto, 1980).

[98] A far more radical hypothetical approach can be found in Ockham, who points out that God could have chosen to save people in ways that seem absurd and blasphemous, and could, for example, have incarnated himself as a stone or an ass. See Ozment, *The Age of Reform*, 37–42; and Erwin Iserloh, *Gnade und Eucharistie in der philosophischen Theologie des Wilhelm von Ockham* (Wiesbaden, 1956), 77 and 179–80.

of this world and become united with the mass, and conversely. But it does not follow that the portions of earth or of the heavy bodies of the other world, were it to exist, would tend to the centre of this world because in their world they would form a single mass possessed of a single place and would be arranged in up and down order, as we have indicated, just like the mass of heavy bodies in this world.[99]

Once the question of what natural philosophy investigates is opened up in this way, that is, once the question of what would happen in various physically possible situations is considered a core part of the natural-philosophical exercise, other hypothetical questions can be raised in a purely natural-philosophical fashion. Oresme devotes a whole chapter of *Le Livre du ciel et du monde*,[100] for example, to the question whether the earth moves or is at rest, that is, whether the motion of the celestial orb can be accounted for by a diurnal motion of the earth or by an actual rotation of the orb, concluding that the information in astronomical tables could be accounted for either way, but that there is no compelling reason to accept that the earth undergoes a diurnal rotation:

Everyone maintains, and I myself believe, that it is the heavens that move and not the earth: for God has established an immobile earth, in spite of arguments to the contrary which are not conclusively persuasive. However, after considering all that has been said, one could still believe that the earth moves and not the heavens, for nor is the opposite clearly evident. But, prima facie, this seems as contrary to natural reason as, or more contrary to natural reason than, all or many of the articles of our faith. What I have said by way of diversion or intellectual exercise can in this manner serve as a valuable means of refuting and checking those who offer arguments that would impugn our faith.[101]

The argument here is revealing of just what deep and difficult waters Tempier's approach gets one into. Tempier's intention had presumably been to show the severe limitations of Aristotelian natural philosophy when compared to what the omnipotent God of Christianity was capable of: Aristotle's natural philosophy worked with a limited understanding of what was possible, which led it to deny things that were in fact deemed possible for a Christian God.

In an important sense, albeit one that is going to turn out to be problematic, Oresme's approach is in line with Tempier's concerns on this question. The Aristotelian procedure was to work from observed events and processes to underlying principles, and then, starting from these underlying principles, to provide an account of the various forms of physical behaviour that one wanted to explain. Now not everything one derived from one's underlying principles was going to be a realized possibility. An account of how things actually behave is not exhaustive of how they might have behaved under any physically characterizable circumstances, and this is after all a good part of the rationale for our seeking underlying principles in the first place: in Aristotelian terms, the aim is to provide an account not just of how things actually behave, but of how they would behave in a range of circumstances,

---

[99] Nicole Oresme, *Le Livre du ciel et du monde*, ed. Albert D. Menut and Alexander J. Denomy, trans. and introd. Albert D. Menut (Madison, 1968), 174 (text)/175 (trans.), (fo. 38a-b).

[100] Ibid. 518–39, (fo. 137c–144c).

[101] Ibid. 536–8 (text)/537–9 (trans.), (fo. 144b-c).

thereby transcending local contingencies and focusing on those features of the behaviour of bodies that derive from their essential structure. The second part of the process, the derivation of physical behaviour from these underlying principles, is what the medieval philosophers termed *scientia*,[102] and knowledge consisted in this, not in the discovery of principles, which was a prelude to or precondition for knowledge.[103] In pursuing *scientia*, one works from underlying principles in order to provide an account of various possible physical situations, some of which may be unrealized. How one decides which of these are realized and which are not is not always a straightforward matter, however. In the cases of other possible worlds and the diurnal rotation of the earth, for example, purely natural-philosophical considerations—within which we include any observational evidence, such as that contained in astronomical tables—do not decide the question one way or another in Oresme's view. Christian belief does enable us to decide, however. Of course, if this happened universally, the question of 'double truth' would not be an issue. The physical and cosmological questions that Oresme dealt with are in areas where he could make a case that natural philosophy provides possible alternatives but no way of determining which of them is actual. But note that the decision is possible on Oresme's account because the rejected explanation is in each case 'as contrary to natural reason, or more contrary to natural reason, than all or many of the articles of our faith'. Here it is natural reason that enables us to decide between what natural philosophy identifies as the options: one of them coheres with 'the articles of our faith' and the other doesn't. The use of 'the articles of our faith' is sanctioned by natural reason. The implication of Oresme's argument is that if the doctrine of the existence of other worlds, for example, were not more contrary to reason than the articles of faith, then the articles of faith would not then provide a criterion for deciding between the two possible explanations. What we would be envisaging here would in effect be the kind of situation Averroes raises and since, from what Oresme says, there is no a priori reason why 'the articles of our faith' should override natural philosophy, we may indeed have a situation in which natural reason faces a stalemate, or where we may prefer natural philosophy.

This is, of course, hardly the kind of outcome that Tempier envisaged: it is even worse than what he set out to oppose. Nor is it clear that the abandonment of natural philosophy is really an option, in the way that it might have been for Augustine, for with the rise to prominence of Aristotelianism, natural philosophy became the entry point into philosophy generally, including philosophical theology,

---

[102] Aquinas actually defines *scientia* as the state of mind one is in when one has successfully engaged in this process—see e.g. Aquinas, *Summa theologica*, II-II, q. 49 a. 1, and q. 50 a. 3—but it seems, by extension, to cover the process itself. The move from *scientia* as a state of mind, in fact as a virtue, to *scientia* as exclusively a body of knowledge, particularly in Lutheran conceptions, is emphasized in Peter Harrison, 'The Natural Philosopher and the Virtues', in Conal Condren, Stephen Gaukroger, and Ian Hunter, eds, *The Philosopher in Early Modern Europe: The Nature of a Contested Identity* (Cambridge, 2006) 202–28.

[103] See Charles H. Lohr, 'Metaphysics and Natural Philosophy as Sciences: The Catholic and Protestant Views in the Sixteenth and Seventeenth Centuries', in Constance Blackwell and Sachiko Kusukawa, eds, *Philosophy in the Sixteenth and Seventeenth Centuries* (Aldershot, 1999), 280–95.

so to abandon natural philosophy would be in effect to abandon control over the project of providing philosophical foundations for a systematic theology. Such control was exactly what the Church had been guaranteed through the division of responsibilities codified by the Fourth Lateran Council. It could hardly relinquish it. Here the Thomist solution, which allowed two separate sources of knowledge but introduced a complex and subtle metaphysics for mediating them, shows its mettle. Aquinas' project rested on a radical rethinking of the role of metaphysics, however, and the success or failure of the project would depend on how well this rethinking measured up to the task.

## THE ARISTOTELIAN AMALGAM

As did Averroes, Aquinas recognised philosophy and theology as autonomous disciplines. The difference is that whereas for Averroists these disciplines might proceed in quite different directions and might remain unreconciled, for Aquinas they must ultimately be bridged. But the solution did not lie in a synthesis of an Augustinian kind. That was no longer an option outside the Platonist tradition: Augustinian theology was formulated within Neoplatonic terms, taking a Neoplatonic conception of the divinity and 'Christianizing' it, whereas Christianized Aristotelian metaphysics had to start with a Neoplatonically formulated Christianity and reshape it as best it could. It was a mixture, or at best an amalgam, with an internal balance that was much more delicate than anything needed in the Augustinian synthesis. But it also had a flexibility that the Augustinian synthesis lacked, and it was this flexibility that enabled it to adapt as natural-philosophical questions came to the centre of the philosophical enterprise.

Aquinas' mentor, Albertus Magnus, offered a conception of philosophy as a discipline that achieved something different from theology, since philosophy is concerned with natural truths and theology with supernatural ones, and he defended the idea of philosophy as something which, within theologically determined limits, could be pursued for its own sake. This formed the basis for Aquinas' attempt to keep separate foundations and sources for Aristotelian philosophy and Christian theology, but, given this, to attempt then to reconcile them in the form of an Aristotelian/Christian amalgam. There was some precedent for this. A century earlier, Peter Lombard in his classic theology textbook, the *Sententiae*, had collected conflicting passages from Patristic authorities on theological and philosophical matters and tried to reconcile them, although this exercise was essentially a semantic one,[104] whereas Aquinas' task was far more demanding, and the key lay in the understanding of metaphysics.

---

[104] Nevertheless it was singled out for criticism by later opponents of scholasticism in terms that were reminiscient of thirteenth-century opponents of Aristotelianism. Thomasius, for example, in the Foreword to the first German translation of Grotius' *De Jure Belli ac Pacis* (1707) writes: 'It is likely that in these four books Lombard attempted to unite the doctrines of Augustine and Aristotle; [for] the whole work contains a mish-mash of theology and philosophy. The Holy Scriptures are explained in accordance with the principles of pagan philosophy.' Quoted in Ian Hunter, *Rival Enlightenments* (Cambridge, 2001), 63.

As we have seen, the understanding of metaphysics since Augustine had been premissed on the idea that ancient metaphysics lacked something crucial to its success, something that only Christianity could provide. There could be no complete non-Christian metaphysics, for Christianity was integral to any successful metaphysics. Aquinas moved away from this understanding of metaphysics to one in which it was a general science that was able to provide an architectonic for forms of knowledge with different sources. For Aquinas, natural philosophy was not and could not be an intrinsically Christian enterprise: it proceeded from sensation, which is common to Christians and pagans.[105] There are two distinct sources of knowledge, sensation and revelation, and since knowledge is unitary, there must be some way of bridging these. The only thing that could bridge them is something that covers the natural and the supernatural, and the only thing that satisfies this description is metaphysics. The project is one of reconciling natural philosophy to Christian belief, rather than vice versa, but the very notion of metaphysics as a medium of reconciliation requires that metaphysics have some degree of independence from either of these enterprises. The idea is not that metaphysics underlies natural philosophy or theology: it cannot do this, since the only sources of knowledge are revelation and sense perception, and these do not underlie metaphysics but the disciplines it seeks to reconcile. Rather, metaphysics underlies the connection between the two, by providing an account (the theory of analogy) of the various kinds of being and the kinds of knowledge appropriate to them. In this sense, metaphysics is not an inherently Christian enterprise, any more than natural philosophy is. It is true that, because revelation is regarded as secure in a way that knowledge derived from sensation could never be, reconciliation will tend to be unidirectional in favour of theology, but the crucial point is that this is not a feature of metaphysics as such; rather, it is a feature of the disciplines that metaphysics seeks to reconcile.

This independence of metaphysics is evident in Aquinas' treatment of Anselm's ontological argument in the *Summa contra Gentiles,* where he rejects the argument because its first premiss, the existence of a being with every perfection, is something that, while he accepted it without reservation, would not naturally be accepted by everyone. Not everyone understands by God 'that than which no greater can be thought', and many ancient thinkers maintained 'that the world is God'.[106] Aquinas is directing the argument here to the classical Greek philosophers rather than his Christian contemporaries, and this is indicative of his whole approach to what makes a metaphysical argument compelling.

This is a radical departure from the traditional understanding of role and nature of metaphysics. To understand what was at issue here we need to look at Aristotle's threefold classification of the 'sciences' into the practical sciences, which concern themselves with those variable, contingent, and relative goods that are involved in

---

[105] See Aquinas, *Summa theologica,* I qq. 84–8.

[106] Aquinas, *Summa contra Gentiles,* I, 11. Cf. 1. 2, where he notes that we must choose our weapons appropriately: against the Jews one must use the Old Testament because that is all they accept, against heretics the New Testament because that is all they accept, and against pagans, 'it is necessary to return to natural reason, with which all are compelled to agree'.

living well; the productive sciences, which enable us to do or make things; and the theoretical sciences, which are concerned with understanding how things are and why they are as they are. The division of the theoretical sciences works in terms of two variables: whether the phenomena falling under the science are changing or unchanging, and whether their being or existence is dependent or independent.[107] Since there is nothing amenable to 'scientific' understanding that falls under the description of something that changes and has a dependent existence, this gives us three actual combinations:

|  | *Independent existence* | *Dependent existence* |
|---|---|---|
| *Unchanging* | first philosophy | mathematics |
| *Changing* | physics | — |

The first is 'first philosophy', later called metaphysics and sometimes theology, and there is only one thing that falls under it, namely God, for God is independent of us, that is to say, he is not a product of our minds or our thought, and, being beyond natural processes, he (or rather 'it': Aristotle's God is genuinely impersonal) is unchanging. Nothing else has both these attributes. In the second category comes mathematics, which deals with those things that are unchanging but have dependent existence. For Aristotle, the objects of mathematics are mere human abstractions, having no existence in their own right. Here he is directly contradicting Plato's account, which allows numbers a transcendent existence as pure Forms.[108] God is the only pure form in Aristotle's account. Finally, physics or natural philosophy deals with whatever has independent existence and changes. It is a given of Greek thought that the natural realm is characterized by constant change, and the difference between the celestial realm, with its regular circular motions and fixed stars, and the constant and apparently chaotic change on earth, is constantly stressed. This makes the natural realm one that includes all material objects and processes.[109]

Our present concern lies not with the vexed question of the autonomy of physics or natural philosophy with respect to mathematics (we shall turn to that question in Ch. 11), but with its autonomy with respect to metaphysics. The issues here are more complicated than in the case of mathematics because of the fact that Aristotelian metaphysics straddles theology on the one side and natural philosophy on

---

[107] See Aristotle, *Metaphysics*, Book ε. Strictly speaking, the Greeks do not seem to have had a concept of existence: *to be* is never just simply *to be* (exist) but *to be an x*, or *to be a y*, etc. See Charles H. Kahn, *The Verb 'Be' in Ancient Greek* (Dordrecht, 1973). Nothing hinges on this for our very limited purposes.

[108] See the discussions in Stephen Gaukroger, 'Aristotle on Intelligible Matter', *Phronesis* 25 (1980), 187–97, and idem, 'The One and the Many: Aristotle on the Individuation of Numbers', *Classical Quarterly* 32 (1982), 312–22.

[109] Note that the terminology of medieval classifications may not correspond with Aristotle's. A manuscript manual for arts students at Paris, 1230–40, divides philosophy into 'rational', 'natural', and 'practical', and under natural philosophy includes metaphysics, physics, and mathematics: see C. H. Lohr, 'The Medieval Interpretation of Aristotle'. There is nothing to suggest this different classification has intended implications for how we conceive of these disciplines however.

the other. On the one hand, since metaphysics deals with whatever is unchanging and independent, and natural philosophy with whatever is changing and independent, we seem to have straightforwardly distinct domains. But Aristotelian metaphysics in its Christianized version includes under its rubric both uncreated or infinite being, and created or finite being, so that topics such as the nature of the soul, which could be seen as straightforwardly natural-philosophical issues, could also be seen to fall under rational theology qua metaphysics.[110]

In Aquinas, it is theology and natural philosophy that have their own distinctive contents. Metaphysics stands above them because it is an abstraction from them, and as an abstraction it enables us to discern the distinctive features of the two domains. Aquinas uses it as a way of connecting theology and natural philosophy, and the skill comes in trying to develop these two in their own directions while keeping them consonant with one another.

## COMPETING CONCEPTIONS OF METAPHYSICS

One problem that Aristotelian philosophers faced in abandoning the Augustinian account was to provide some philosophical understanding of God. This had not been a problem in the Augustinian synthesis of Neoplatonic metaphysics and Christianity, for there Christianity provided the key to metaphysics, as we have seen, and what Augustine considered the manifest failure of earlier metaphysical systems was induced by the lack of this essential ingredient. By contrast, Aristotelian metaphysics was not intrinsically Christian. But nor did its adherents consider it inherently pagan, in spite of its origins: it was a purely abstract rational discourse that could be used to articulate and clarify the fundamental principles of a Christian theology. It was generally agreed that the vehicle for a philosophical account of God was metaphysics, but the Thomist idea of metaphysics as bridging theology and natural philosophy seemed to many in the fourteenth century a poor instrument for providing rational foundations for theology.

Aquinas' bridge was in effect threefold. First, there were a small number of theological truths considered to be philosophically demonstrable, such as the existence of God as first cause. Second, there was an ordering of natural and supernatural truths, which revealed their relations at a general abstract level. Third, there was the discovery of natural analogies to transcendent truths. It was this third that was most characteristically Thomist, and which was what his scholastic opponents questioned. In separating theology and natural philosophy, Aquinas developed the doctrine that the sense of 'being' when we are talking about the supernatural, and its sense in a natural context, are different: the concept of 'being' is equivocal. This means that anything we can say about God by starting from his creation—that is, in moving from effect back to first cause—would always be equivocal. Rational theology would be effectively impossible on this basis, as Aquinas realized. Reflecting on the nature of

---

[110] This was encouraged by Aristotle's discussion of being at *Metaphysics* 1026$^a$ 29–33, where the study of being *qua* being is a *scientia* which is superior to all others, including natural philosophy.

causation, however, he noted that even if the cause and the effect are completely different in kind, nevertheless the effect always bears traces of its cause in some way, even if we cannot specify what these are in particular cases, and he attempted to fill this out in terms of the doctrine of analogy. We cannot attain knowledge of divine things by use of our sensory and cognitive faculties, but the successful exercise of those faculties yields something that bears some relation to the divine, and that we can capture in terms of analogy.[111]

Duns Scotus rejected this kind of account. If metaphysics was a general theory of being, he reasoned, if it encompassed both finite and infinite being, then it must be a discipline whose subject matter was being-qua-being, as Aristotle had maintained. One could hardly distinguish infinite being from finite being in the first place unless they were both forms of being. Consequently, there must be some unified notion of being, provided by metaphysics, and through this metaphysics we have access to some understanding of divine being.[112] Yet this access turns out to be very limited, for rather than having a more direct relation than analogy, we seem to have a less direct one. Scotus drew the contrast between God and his creation in terms of a distinction between finite and infinite being, and what is created and finite cannot in any way determine what is uncreated and infinite on Scotus' account.[113] God's relation to anything else must always be absolutely free, contingent, and unconditioned. The core of Scotus' criticism of Aquinas was that his approach tied God in too closely with the institutions of priests, sacraments, accidental forms of grace, etc., losing sight of the gulf between God's will and the finite and contingent means by which this will is effected, means that are not any indication of intrinsic merit.[114] But Scotus' own approach had the drawback of separating God and his creation so radically that they not only had properties at least as fundamentally different as was the case in Aquinas, but infinite being was hardly accessible at all, and Scotus not only could not find a conclusive argument for the immortality of the soul, for example, but argued that belief in resurrection and eternal life could not be rationally established and were matters of faith alone.[115] In effect, Scotus opened up a gulf between God and his creation, and it was left to Ockham to develop fully this distancing of the supernatural and

[111] See the discussions in Étienne Gilson, *The Christian Philosophy of St. Thomas Aquinas* (London, 1961), 103–10, and Marcia L. Colish, *The Mirror of Language* (New Haven, Conn., 1968), 208–23. A less contentious use of analogy is in the opposite direction. We have no access to the mental states of animals in the way that we do to the mental states of human beings, and in attempting to grasp their mental states, extrapolation from our own states, no matter how inadequate this procedure might be, is often the only means available to us.

[112] See the detailed discussion of the ramifications of this understanding in Jean-Luc Marion, *Sur la théologie blanche de Descartes* (Paris, 1981).

[113] See Werner Dettloff, *Die Entwicklung der Akzeptations- und Verdienstlehre von Duns Scotus bis Luther* (Münster, 1963).

[114] See Wolfhart Pannenberg, *Die Prädestinationslehre des Duns Skotus* (Göttingen, 1954), 39–42.

[115] See Paul Oskar Kristeller, *Renaissance Thought and Its Sources* (New York, 1979), 186, and, for a detailed discussion, Sophia Vanni Rovighi, *L'immortalita dell'anima nei maestri francescani del secolo XIII* (Milan, 1936), 197–233.

the natural.[116] Ockham, emphasizing the contingent character of churches, priests, sacraments, and habits of grace, maintained that the moral order was an arbitrary enactment of the Divine will, and hence lacking in inherent rationality, and he denied the possibility of any rational knowledge of God.[117]

In line with this approach, treatments of metaphysics in the fourteenth century moved from the exploration of the relation between theology and metaphysics, which had been the staple of Christian philosophy up to this point, to that between metaphysics and natural philosophy.[118] This was a source of concern, and by the fifteenth century theologians such as Jean Gerson, Chancellor of the University of Paris, were becoming worried by the divisions that had opened up between metaphysics as a science of being and metaphysics as a science of God, and above all with the 'rationalist' way in which natural philosophy was being pursued, where reconciliation with revealed theology was no longer paramount.[119] Indeed, not only was this not a *desideratum* but the differences between the philosophical schools took over the theological agenda: conflict between Thomist, Scotist, and Ockhamist factions in his own Theology Faculty prompted Gerson to threaten resignation in 1400, as he tried to put an end to endless theological speculation.[120]

The Church's solution to the problem did not lie in Gerson's proposals for the reform of the theology curriculum, however, but the establishment of Thomism as the official Church philosophy. With the failure of the Council of Basel (1431–49) and the restoration of the supremacy of the papacy,[121] there was a renewed interest in the Thomist programme, with its distinction between truths of reason and truths of revelation, and its attempted balance between the claims of theology, metaphysics, and natural philosophy. By the early sixteenth century, systematic theology was beginning to be taught in the universities through commentary no longer on Peter Lombard's *Sententiae* but on Aquinas' *Summa theologicae*.[122] The institutional attractiveness of Thomism, particularly at the all-important University of Paris, cannot be overestimated. As far as the Theology Faculty was concerned, Aquinas' epistemology, with its Aristotelian stress on sense perception as the basis for knowledge, left open a space for revelation, because God necessarily transcends

[116] On Ockham's conception of God's divine powers, see Marilyn McCord Adams, *William Ockham* (2 vols, Notre Dame, Ind., 1987), ii. 1198–231. Ockham denies that theology can be a *scientia* in the Aristotelian/Thomist sense: see Alfred J. Freddoso, 'Ockham on Faith and Reason', in Paul Spade, ed., *Cambridge Companion to Ockham* (Cambridge, 1999), 326–49: 345–6.

[117] On Ockham's view, God can directly put beliefs in our minds which in fact correspond to nothing: see Quodlibet 5 q. 5: William Ockham, *Quodlibetal Questions*, trans. A. J. Freddoso and F. E. Kelley (2 vols, New Haven, Conn., 1991), ii. 416. See the discussion in Gordon Leff, *William of Ockham: The Metamorphosis of Scholastic Discourse* (Manchester, 1975), ch. 5.

[118] Lohr, 'Metaphysics', 591.

[119] See ibid., 596–7.

[120] On Gerson see Ozment, *The Age of Reform*, 73–80. It is worth noting here that one of the great obstacles that Greek Orthodox prelates found to union with the Roman Church in the mid-fifteenth century was the use of Aristotelian dialectic in arguing theological points: see James Hankins, *Plato in the Italian Renaissance* (Leiden, 1994), 221–2.

[121] On the failure of the Council of Basel and its aftermath, see Francis Oakley, *The Western Church in the Middle Ages* (Ithaca, NY, 1979), 71–80, and Ullmann, *Short History*, ch. 13.

[122] See Michael J. Buckley, *At the Origins of Modern Atheism* (New Haven, Conn., 1987), 43.

human faculties. In particular, Aquinas' denial of some higher intellectual knowledge which allows one to penetrate revealed religion (a doctrine dear to Neoplatonists) retained a unique role for the clergy in interpreting revelation. The Thomist solution thereby showed its mettle at the institutional level, offering a compromise that benefited both the Church and the secular Arts programme. As Lohr has pointed out, 'the idea of a philosophy autonomous in its own realm, but guided both positively and negatively by revelation, represented a kind of pragmatic sanction, defining the powers of the clergy in its relation to science. . . . Just as the papacy had to recognise the authority of secular rulers in the temporal sphere, so also the clergy—whose function had traditionally been that of teaching—had to admit the self-sufficiency of the secular sciences and to concede the limitation of its role to that of surveillance.'[123]

This finely balanced compromise was not to last very long, however, and the beginning of the end of the Thomist project comes in the early decades of the sixteenth century. If the 1277 Condemnation marks the failure of an Augustinian synthesis of Christian revelation and a Neoplatonic philosophy and theology, and the beginning of a reconciliation between a (Neoplatonically formulated) Christian theology and an Aristotelian metaphysics and natural philosophy, then the Fifth Lateran Council (1512–17) marks the beginning of the end of this reconciliation, as a wedge is driven between theology and natural philosophy.

The wedge came with the revival of the Averroist doctrine of the unity of the intellect in the northern Italian universities. There had in fact been a tradition of Averroism of one kind or another in the northern Italian universities, which comprised medical rather than theology Faculties, from the thirteenth century onwards.[124] Padua was always at the forefront of this movement and matters came to head in the early decades of the sixteenth century, when Pomponazzi, by that time in Bologna but still very much associated with the Padua Faculty, defended Alexander of Aphrodisias' account of Aristotle's doctrine of the soul against that of Averroes.

The doctrine of the personal immortality of the soul derived from Paul at the earliest and above all from the early Church Fathers. Its origins are a little obscure. Although there is no commitment to an afterlife in Judaism as such, Paul was a Pharisee before his conversion to Christianity, and the Pharisees did believe in the afterlife; moreover much of his language and eschatology is reminiscent of the radical Jewish sect of Essenes, who believed that the soul—but *not* the body—enjoyed an afterlife. Since there is no evidence that Jesus held such a view, it is likely that it was one or both of these that provided Paul's source.[125] Its standard medieval formulation derived from Augustine, as presented in his *De immortalitate animae* and

[123] Lohr, 'Metaphysics', 600.

[124] See Gilson, *History*, 521–7. The medical curriculum included a significant amount of natural philosophy: see Jerome J. Bylebyl, 'Medicine, Philosophy and Humanism in Renaissance Italy', in John W. Shirley and F. David Hoeniger, eds, *Science and the Arts in the Renaissance* (Washington, 1986), 27–49.

[125] For details, see Richard Heinzmann, *Die Unsterblick der Seele und die Auferstehung des Leibes* (Münster, 1965). The first discussion to trace Jesus back to the Essenes was the manuscript 'De Primordiis Christianae religionis' (first version 1703) by Johann Georg Wachter, which had a significant impact on early eighteenth-century religious thought, numbering amongst its supporters

*De quantitate animae.* In its Augustinian form, it is in effect the Neoplatonic doctrine of immortality stripped of those ingredients he believed to be incompatible with Christianity, namely the transmigration of souls and their pre-existence (a doctrine accepted by earlier theologians such as Origen).[126] Personal immortality was tied in with Aristotelian natural philosophy in an explicit way in 1311 when the Council of Vienne declared the Aristotelian definition of the soul as the form of the body to be an article of faith.[127] It is important to note, however, that the Council was not in fact concerned with the question of immortality as such but with Christological questions. Pierre Olivi and other thirteenth-century Franciscans had denied that the soul could be the form of the body because immersion in matter would deprive it of a separate existence, but this had highly heterodox consequences for the doctrine of the Incarnation, and the Council of Vienne rejected it on these Christological grounds.[128] More generally, the doctrine of personal immortality was not an issue for thirteenth-century scholastic philosophers: Scotus was at best pessimistic about the chances of its rational demonstration, and Aquinas, though he defended the soul's incorruptibility in his rejection of the Averroist doctrine of the unity of the intellect,[129] was silent about personal immortality as such. It is not Thomists, Scotists, Averroists, or any other movement within scholasticism that put the question of immortality at centre stage, but the Platonist movement.[130] There was a tradition of humanist treatises on immortality from early in the fifteenth century, crowned in the 1460s and 1470s with the publication of Ficino's *Theologia Platonica de immortalitate animae*, the most comprehensive Neoplatonist account of this question. Drawing principally on Plato, Plotinus, and Augustine, and set in the context of a detailed discussion of the attributes of God, levels of being, and the hierarchy of souls, Ficino's defence of the immortality of the soul was above all an attempt to recapture the original Augustinian synthesis of theology and philosophy.[131] The treatment of philosophy is radically anti-Aristotelian, in that it was crucial for Ficino's conception of the philosopher that he be able to ascend through contemplation to a direct (if only fleeting) spiritual vision of God, by contrast with the Aristotelian and above all Thomist view that human cognitive life is restricted to what we can know on the

Voltaire and Frederick the Great: see Jonathan I. Israel, *Radical Enlightenment: Philosophy and the Making of Modernity 1650–1750* (Oxford, 2001), 650–2.

[126] See the discussion in Kristeller, *Renaissance Thought and Its Sources*, ch. 11. One of Augustine's main arguments for the immortality of the soul, in the *Soliloquies*, derives from Plato's *Phaedo*: see Étienne Gilson, *The Christian Philosophy of Saint Augustine* (London, 1961), 51–5.

[127] See N. P. Tanner, ed., *Decrees of the Ecumenical Councils* (2 vols, London, 1990), i. 361.

[128] Generally on these questions see Colin F. Fowler, *Descartes on the Human Soul: Philosophy and the Demands of Christian Doctrine* (Dordrecht, 1999).

[129] For example in *Summa theologica*, I q. 57 a. 6, and *On the Unity of the Intellect Against the Averroists*, trans. Beatriz H. Zedler (Milwaukee, 1968).

[130] See Kristeller, *Renaissance Thought and its Sources*, 187–96. See also Giovanni Di Napoli, *L'immortalità dell'anima nel Rinascimento* (Turin, 1963).

[131] As Anthony Levi notes (*Renaissance and Reformation*, 396 n. 9), Ficino's borrowings from Augustine are taken from his early and middle writings, when he was still very much under the influence of Plotinus, and he hardly even mentions the later writings.

basis of abstraction from sensation, supplemented only by revelation.[132] For Ficino the separation of theology and philosophy destroys the contemplative life to which the philosopher/theologian aspires, and to which human beings are naturally fitted, something he argued was evident from our ability to grasp incorporeal entities such as God and ideas. It is the striving to understand God that ultimately provides a rationale for immortality, for God has provided us with such a desire, and since it can be manifested without hindrance only once we are freed of our bodies, immortality is given to us in order that we might realize this desire.

In other words, Ficino ties the defence of the personal immortality of the soul to a return to the Augustinian synthesis, one that depends crucially on a commitment to Neoplatonism. Yet as we have seen, the Church had already moved philosophically in the other direction some 170 years earlier at the Council of Vienne, effectively stipulating that any understanding of these questions had to be couched in Aristotelian terms, in which the soul is the form of the body. This was reinforced by the Fifth Lateran Council in 1513, where the doctrine of personal immortality was established as a dogma, albeit one whose philosophical defence was acknowledged to be problematic.[133] The Council's response was to instruct theologians and philosophers to reconcile philosophy with theology on this issue. 'Philosophy' here means Aristotelian natural philosophy: as the fifteenth-century scholastic Alonso de Cartagena put it, 'since Aristotle's rationality is not grounded on his authority, but authority is derived from his rationality, we can regard anything that is consonant with reason as having been taught by Aristotle'.[134]

This is the challenge that Thomism had to meet, but within three years of the challenge being raised, the very doctrines that the Council had condemned as the source of problems about the immortality of the soul, and which Thomism was supposed to have answered decisively, were given an articulate and powerful airing which showed that they were far from having been laid to rest. In his *De immortalitate animae*, published in 1516, Pomponazzi offered an argument that engaged Platonist, Thomist, and Averroist positions on the nature of the soul. He argued against the Platonists (he was clearly responding to Ficino) and in agreement with Averroists and Aquinas, that philosophically speaking the soul was the form of the body. There could be no cognition except through the body, and this ruled out the kind of knowledge of pure intelligibles that Ficino and other Platonists had postulated. In this connection he also supported the Aristotelian view that there is no such thing as an uninstantiated form. But if this is the case, he argued, then the death and corruption of the body result in the disappearance of the soul. On the other hand, he accepted the Church teaching

---

[132] See the discussion in Kristeller, *Renaissance Thought and Its Sources*, 189–90.

[133] See Étienne Gilson, 'Autour de Pomponazzi: problématique de l'immortalité de l'âme en Italie au début du XVIᵉ siècle', *Archives d'histoire doctrinale et littéraire du moyen âge* 18 (1961), 163–279; Fowler, *Descartes on the Human Soul, passim*; and Emily Michael and Fred S. Michael, 'Two Early Modern Concepts of Mind: Reflecting Substance vs. Thinking Substance', *Journal of the History of Philosophy* 27 (1989), 29–48.

[134] Cited in Eckhard Kessler, 'The Transformation of Aristotelianism During the Renaissance,' in John Henry and Sarah Hutton, eds, *New Perspectives in Renaissance Thought* (London, 1990), 137–47: 137.

of the personal immortality of the soul, and he argued that Aquinas decisively refuted Averroes' view that there cannot be individual souls in his doctrine that the human soul is not a form that arises from matter but is the object of a special creation by God. But he also contended that, in terms of Aristotelian metaphysics/natural philosophy, Aquinas' own proposal was not decisive.

Pomponazzi's dilemma was that two completely different lines of thought, each of which he has every reason to believe to be completely compelling and neither of which he was prepared to renounce, led to incompatible conclusions. Somehow one must embrace both. Note, however, that Pomponazzi was not claiming that both are true. He clearly held the truth of the doctrine of personal immortality—it is 'true and most certain in itself' as he puts it in the Preface to *De immortalitate*[135]—and the falsity of its denial. But in pointing out, in the same sentence, that this doctrine 'is in complete disagreement with what Aristotle says', he did not oppose the truth of what Aristotle says: he simply did not discuss Aristotle's doctrine in terms of truth. This is why the characterization of the position in terms of 'double truth' is misleading. What he was drawing attention to is the fact that there are two quite different but completely legitimate ways of pursuing the question, and the radical twist is that there is no metaphysics that can reconcile these.

This was the problem we started with in the 1277 Condemnation. We have come around full circle, with much the same cast: Aquinas, Averroists, and Neoplatonists who aspired to a version of the original Augustinian synthesis. But in the intervening centuries, the doctrine of personal immortality has become more pressing because it has been explicitly tied to Aristotelian natural philosophy (1311) and explicitly made a dogma of the Church (1513), and this is the issue on which the question of the relations between theology, metaphysics, and natural philosophy will rest. The new complicating element is that each of theology, metaphysics, and natural philosophy will be contested in the course of the sixteenth and early seventeenth centuries: fundamental theological controversies will break out in the Reformation, fundamentally new natural philosophies will vie for attention with Aristotelian natural philosophy, and there will begin to be a questioning of the role of metaphysics in relation to natural philosophy that goes far beyond any of the disputes between Aristotelians and Neoplatonists. These sixteenth-century disputes will not complete another circle, but will rather begin to move in completely new directions, as the number of contentious natural-philosophical issues gradually begins to expand in an uncontrolled way.

---

[135] The passage is translated in Ernst Cassirer, Paul Oskar Kristeller, and John Herman Randall Jr., *The Renaissance Philosophy of Man* (Chicago, 1948), 281.

# 3
# Renaissance Natural Philosophies

The revival of Averroism was not an exclusively sixteenth-century matter. Petrarch, the fourteenth-century founder of what became the humanist movement, saw his project explicitly as an alternative to Averroism,[1] and the Italian Neoplatonist movement associated Aristotelianism with Averroism from its beginnings in the mid-fifteenth century. Indeed, it was Ficino's questioning of the ability of Aristotelianism to provide a philosophical basis for Christian doctrine that led to the focus on the dogma of personal immortality, which, he argued, could be accounted for straightforwardly in Neoplatonist terms but not at all in Aristotelian ones. By contrast, the Averroist strain in Renaissance natural philosophy, also predominantly an Italian phenomenon, offers a variety of forms of naturalism, even though some of its sources derive from Neoplatonism. In fact it draws on both Aristotle and Neoplatonism in some respects, but also on Stoic, Epicurean, and Presocratic sources, generally eschewing forms of any kind but in compensation, as it were, endowing matter directly with inherent active principles that shape the behaviour of the natural realm. Against both of these, there is a revival of Aristotelian orthodoxy, captured in the late scholastic textbooks of the mid-sixteenth to the early seventeenth centuries. Of the participants in these disputes, the Neoplatonists are exceptional in denying that natural philosophy is the point of entry into philosophical enquiry generally. Both scholastics and naturalists, and the corpuscularians who had little impact in the sixteenth century but quickly became dominant in the seventeenth, all took this as given, and this has the consequence of making philosophical disputes turn on natural-philosophical questions, further propelling natural philosophy into the centre of controversy.

None of these three dominant Renaissance natural philosophies survives unscathed into the seventeenth century. The reasons why, while they differ in each case, as we shall see, nevertheless have to do primarily with their inability to reconcile natural-philosophical and orthodox Christian thinking, and this is crucial for understanding the success of the natural-philosophical systems that replace them.

---

[1] Petrarch to Boccaccio, 28 August 1364: *Opera* (Basle, 1554), 880; trans. in Cassirer et al., *The Renaissance Philosophy of Man*, 140–1. Nevertheless, this did not prevent Averroist strains in some Aristotelian humanists of the sixteenth century: see Charles B. Schmitt, *Aristotle in the Renaissance* (Cambridge, Mass., 1983).

## PLATONISM AS AN ALTERNATIVE TO SCHOLASTICISM

In Neoplatonic thought, metaphysics and natural philosophy had always been part of the same enterprise. This had traditionally been much to the cost of natural philosophy and, with the exception of the work of the sixth-century Platonist natural philosopher Johannes Philoponus,[2] the subordination had been sealed with Augustine's appropriation of Neoplatonism as the philosophy of Christianity. The introduction of Aristotelianism had changed this, but the critical use of Platonic ideas never entirely died out in medieval natural philosophy. In the thirteenth century, Grosseteste invoked a Neoplatonist metaphysics in setting out a theory of light, as we shall see below. A good example in the fourteenth century is Oresme, who uses a number of traditional Platonist objections to Aristotle, as well as a number of Platonically inspired new ideas, to criticize details of Aristotelian natural philosophy, while remaining firmly within an Aristotelian natural-philosophical framework.[3] In the fifteenth century, Nicholas of Cusa used resources derived from Platonism to break out of Aristotelian natural philosophy at certain crucial points.[4] In the sixteenth century, a number of natural philosophers used Philoponus to make critical points against Aristotelianism.[5] If reconciliation between a Neoplatonically conceived Christian theology and an Aristotelian natural philosophy was a central constraint, then it is not surprising that it would be considered that deficiencies in the latter should be made good by the former.

Genuine Platonist and Neoplatonist ideas were not transmitted through the Augustinian tradition, however, any more than they were through the writings of Cicero, even though he was the other key traditional source for Plato. Islamic philosophy in the tenth and eleventh centuries had witnessed a revival of interest in Neoplatonism, which dealt in an encyclopedic way with a wide range of issues, including natural-philosophical questions,[6] but this tradition was marginal in Islamic culture—testified to by the fact that whereas almost everything of Aristotle's was translated into Arabic, only a few of Plato's works were available in translation[7]—and

---

[2] See Richard Sorabji, 'John Philoponus', Michael Wolff, 'Philoponus and the Rise of Pre-Classical Dynamics', and David Sedley, 'Philoponus' Conception of Space', all in Richard Sorabji, ed., *Philoponus and the Rejection of Aristotelian Science* (London, 1987).

[3] Note also Oresme's comment at the end of Book 1 of *Le Livre du ciel et du monde*: 'Although Aristotle was an excellent philosopher, nevertheless it is clear from what Eustrathios says concerning the First Book of the *Nicomachean Ethics* that Aristotle was sometimes unduly harsh in his criticisms of Plato, whose opinion he hated unreasonably. As we have said many times, he was here arguing against Plato, who St. Augustine prefers and recommends above all others, along with Plato's followers in philosophy, in the eighth and ninth books of *The City of God*, and he holds that their teachings are more congruous and more in harmony with Catholic faith than those of other philosophers' (fo. 62d; 260–2 [text]/261–3 [trans.]).

[4] See Ernst Cassirer, *The Individual and the Cosmos in Renaissance Philosophy* (Philadelphia, 1963); and Blumenberg, *The Legitimacy of the Modern Age*, 483–547.

[5] See Charles Schmitt, 'Philoponus' Commentary on Aristotle's Physics in the Sixteenth Century', in Richard Sorabji, ed., *Philoponus and the Rejection of Aristotelian Science* (London, 1987).

[6] See Ian Richard Netton, *Muslim Neoplatonists: An Introduction to the Thought of the Brethren of Purity* (London, 1982).

[7] Plato's works were known primarily through Galen's summaries.

was never transmitted to the West. Albertus Magnus' knowledge of Plato was such that he classified his predecessors into Epicureans, Stoics, and Peripatetics, with Socrates and Plato being put in the category of Stoics, along with Pythagoras and Hermes Trismegistus, as well more recognizable candidates for this nomenclature.[8] Plato's texts began to appear in Latin translation only in the fifteenth century, beginning with the *Republic* in 1420, and it was from the Eastern Orthodox Church that the Christian West, in the mid-fifteenth century, encountered a fully fledged Platonist system in which Aristotle was accommodated to Plato, rather than the other way around.[9]

There had always been a presumption in favour of Platonism in the Orthodox Churches, and in the eleventh century Michael Psellus had set out to form a comprehensive philosophico-theological system by combining Neoplatonism with the *Chaldaic Oracles* and the *Corpus Hermeticum*. Towards the end of the fourteenth century, Plethon began to combine Psellus and Proclus (who had actually been Psellus' main source), seeking to reconstruct the ancient theology of which he believed Pythagoras and Plato to be representatives. Arriving in 1438 as philosophical adviser to the Greek Orthodox delegation to the Council of Florence (1439–40), Plethon offered a comprehensive Platonist system that seemed to some in the West to have the potential to rival the dominant Christianized Aristotelian system. The northern Italian states were more susceptible to this influence than elsewhere. The Venetian Republic had extensive trade with a huge region covering Anatolia, the Steppes, and the Black Sea, and acted as a mediator between East and West in the fifteenth century; moreover within its orbit was Padua, where humanism had gained a foothold early in the fifteenth century (albeit not in the rigidly Aristotelian Arts Faculty). There had been a wave of new translations of Plato beginning with the rough draft of the *Republic* completed in 1402 by Chrysoloras, a Byzantine scholar who arrived in Florence to teach in 1397, and Uberto Decembrio, whose son was to revise and publish the translation in 1420, and Bruni had started producing his influential translations of the dialogues in the early decades of the century.[10] But translations were not the only way in which the ground was prepared. Petrarch believed that Plato's work was very close to revelation, and, following Augustine's lead, he found close parallels between the *Timeaus* and the Gospel of St John. Plato's works were not considered alien interlopers like those of Aristotle, which had to be accommodated to Christian doctrine: they were taken to be the philosophical key to Christian doctrine, part and parcel of the same enterprise, an enterprise in which the aim was the *de facto* obliteration of the divide between

---

[8] Albertus Magnus, *De causis et processu universitatis* 1. 1. 1. *Opera omnia*, ed. Augustus Borgnet (38 vols., Paris, 1890–9), x. 361b. The classification presumably derives in part from the prologue to Diogenes Laertius' *Lives of Eminent Philosophers* 1.13–16.

[9] See Raymond Klibansky, *The Continuity of the Platonic Tradition During the Middle Ages* (London, 1950), and Paul Shorey, *Platonism Ancient and Modern* (Berkeley, 1938).

[10] On Latin translations of Plato between 1400 and 1600, in both manuscript and printed editions, see the lists in Hankins, *Plato*, 669–796.

natural and revealed theology.[11] This project began to look realizable with the textual and intellectual resources that Plethon introduced and, mainly through his disciple Bessarion, Platonism became a formative influence on later fifteenth-century Italian thought.[12]

Although concerned to some extent with reconciling Christianity and Platonism, Plethon was not a Christian but a Platonist, and he could with some plausibility be seen as advocating a return to Greek paganism.[13] The point was not lost either on his critics, such as George of Trebizond, or his followers such as Bessarian. Bessarian, who converted to the Roman church and was made a cardinal in 1439, put a more ortho-dox Christian gloss on Plato's writings than had his master.[14] The question was how much this was a mere gloss and how much it revealed a real union between Plato and Christianity. The issues at stake here were fundamental and had been problematic since the overtly allegorical readings of the Old Testament of Origen and Augustine, which had the effect of stripping it of historical meaning, and raised the general ques-tion whether the past had value only to the extent that it prefigured Christianity.[15] The Old Testament had been transformed into a Christian book, and there was now danger of works such as the *Timeaus* being given a virtually similar standing.[16]

George of Trebizond, who saw himself, as Hankins puts it, as a prophet sent to warn the West against a revival of paganism orchestrated by a conspiracy of Platon-ists,[17] had no doubt that the union between Plato and Christianity was a sham. In his *Comparatio philosophorum Platonis et Aristotelis* (1458) he sets out a stinging attack on Plato and Platonism, distinctive not so much for the fervour of its invective (not uncommon in humanist circles) but for the extent of his knowledge of Plato, which far outstripped that of earlier defenders of Aristotle, and indeed he translated more Plato into Latin than anyone before Ficino. George sees a line of descent from the first Plato, through the second (Mohammed), to the third, Plethon, who he believed was trying to incorporate a Byzantine philosophy into the Roman Church, in the pro-cess undermining its chief intellectual bulwark, Aristotelian scholasticism, precluding the union of the Eastern and Western churches and thereby preventing the salvation of the Eastern Church from the Turk. On George's account, it was Platonism, not Aristotelianism, that was the source of schisms, heresies, and the like, and the Roman church had escaped destruction only by protecting itself with the armour of Aris-totelian scholasticism.

---

[11] Note in this respect the later sanctification of Socrates and Plato, begun by Bessarion: see Raymond Marcel, ' "Saint" Socrate, patron de l'humanisme', *Revue internationale de philosophie* 5 (1951), 135–43.

[12] On Plethon and Bessarion, see Hankins, *Plato*, 161–263, and on the question of Plethon's influence, 436–40.

[13] Plethon, who was born around 1355, began as a Zoroastrian, and was expelled from Constantinople for heresy. By 1409 he was based at Mistra, which he proposed turning into a state modelled on Plato's *Republic* and *Laws*.

[14] See Hankins, *Plato*, 255–61      [15] See Ozment, *The Age of Reform*, 64–72.

[16] This kind of reading of the *Timaeus* goes back to Philo of Alexandria, and can be found explicitly, e.g. in Kepler: Johannes Kepler, *The Harmony of the World*, trans. with introd. and notes by E. J. Aiton, A. M. Duncan, and J. V. Field (Philadelphia, 1997), 301 (Book 6, ch. 1).

[17] Hankins, *Plato*, 167.

Bessarion responds to the *Comparatio* in *In calumniatorem Platonis* (1469), and takes George to task on a number of fronts, not least his translations of Plato, in an attempt to show that he knows nothing of philosophy in general and of Plato in particular, and on his knowledge of Aristotle, where he uses Albertus Magnus, Aquinas, Scotus, and others to show that George's version of Aristotelianism is idiosyncratic and unreliable. But there is a distinctive approach in the text which was to be influential in the subsequent development of a specifically Latin Platonism. This is the contrast he draws between the kind of discursive reasoning we find in scholastic authors, which is appropriate to the temporal and material world, the world of politics and of constant flux, and the superior form of divine intuition that an intellectual elite can have of the divine. The latter is knowledge of the cause, whereas the former is knowledge only of effects, and he urges that we do not try to use language and argument appropriate to sensible things to capture divine things. As Hankins points out, there are two crucial and influential moves in Bessarion's approach.[18] First, he uses a Neoplatonic understanding of biblical and Patristic exegesis to undercut the possibility of a science of theology based on Aristotelian dialectic. This denies any legitimacy to the scholastic enterprise. Second, what he is in effect advocating is the replacement of scholastic theology with a kind of intuitive knowledge or wisdom which is a form of contemplative understanding. This undercuts an indirect approach based on analogy. In one respect, this idea of interpretation for contemplation is reminiscent of the pre-scholastic monastic tradition in the West, which was close to what had been advocated at the turn of the century by theologians such as Gerson, who were trying to find a way to counter the disputatious character that theology had taken on under the influence of scholasticism. In the monastic tradition, reading had provoked not question, answer, and disputation, but prayer and contemplation.

But Bessarion's Platonist successors were not advocating a return to monasticism, and their idea of contemplation of the divine was an intellectual not a spiritual form of contemplation, whatever their protestations to the contrary. What drove them was the combination of philology, as opposed to dialectic, and direct contemplation of the divine, rather than an indirect analogical grasp whose success could in any case not be guaranteed. The precocious Giovanni Pico Della Mirandola planned the definitive work of Platonic synthesis[19] but completed little more than a preface—'on being and the one'—to his encyclopedic project, and it did not replace Ficino's *Theologia Platonica*, which appeared between 1469 and 1474, and remains the high point of the metaphysical stream of Renaissance Platonism. From the point of view of natural philosophy, this stream culminated in a distinctively Platonic natural philosophy in Patrizi's *Nova de universis philosophia* of 1591. In what follows, I shall take these two to represent the scope and limits of Platonism's attempt to replace scholastic Aristotelianism as the system that unites theology, metaphysics, and natural philosophy.

In the Preface to his translation of and commentary on Plotinus (1492), Ficino writes:

[18]  Ibid. 225.
[19]  As the 1491 proemium to *De ente et uno* makes clear, however, his was a synthesis in which Aristotle plays a role at least equal to that of Plato, by contrast with Ficino's approach.

Almost the entire world is occupied and divided between two sects of Peripatetics, the Alexandrians and the Averroists. The first think our intellect is mortal, the second that it is one in number. Both schools are equally destructive of religion, especially as they seem to deny that men are subject to divine providence, and in both cases they seem to have been failed by their Aristotle. Today few men except our sublime fellow-Platonist Pico seem to understand Aristotle's mind with that sense of piety with which formerly Theophrastus, Themistius, Porphyry, Simplicius, Avicenna, and recently Plethon interpreted him.[20]

The point about approaching these questions with a sense of piety is crucial.[21] Ficino is opposed to the scholastic procedure, which he associates particularly with the Averroists, who formed the dominant schools in the Padua and Bologna Faculties, of identifying the best exegetes of a text—those who give the best arguments for an opinion—without regard to whether they provided interpretations that were edifying of Christian faith and morals. The issue is that which bedevilled thirteenth-century disputes over Averroism, under the guise of the misleadingly named doctrine of 'double truth', whereby the theological mode, which interprets sacred texts so as to reveal the underlying truth, is opposed to the philosophical mode, which seeks to be free of all dogmas and concentrates solely on which opinions are best supported by the arguments. What Ficino wants to do is to shift philosophy into a theological mode, since the theological mode is the only one that directs itself to truth, and to do this requires a move from an Aristotelian to a Platonic model. Indeed, in a sense, Platonic philosophy will replace traditional theology, virtually becoming a special esoteric form of Christianity for an intellect elite,[22] just as it had in effect for Bessarion.

Platonism and Christianity are not the only ingredients in Ficino's project however. Ficino was employed by Cosimo de' Medici to translate Plato's works. He began learning Greek in 1456, and received his first manuscript from Cosimo in 1462, but in that year Cosimo also managed to procure the Greek text of the first fourteen books of the *Corpus Hermeticum*, and Ficino completed the translation of this a year later under the title of *Pimander*, actually the name of the first of the books of the *Corpus*.[23] Although in fact dating from the late second century CE, the *Corpus* was believed to be the work of a Hermes Trismegistus, supposed to have lived just after the time of Moses, and it was taken to represent a tradition of ancient pagan theology which mirrored and complemented the revealed truth of scripture, with its Egyptian provenance throwing light on stories of Plato's travels in Egypt.[24] As I have indicated, Psellus had incorporated parts of the *Chaldaic Oracles* and the *Hermetica*, which were known to Byzantine writers in the eleventh century, into his original Neoplatonic

[20] Ficino, *Opera Omnia* (2 vols, Basle, 1576), 1438, cited in Hankins, *Plato*, 274.

[21] See ibid. 275–6.          [22] Ibid. 287.

[23] See Brian Copenhaver and Charles B. Schmitt, *Renaissance Philosophy* (Oxford, 1992), 146–9, to which my account here is indebted.

[24] On the *Corpus Hermeticum* see the Introduction to Brian Copenhaver, *Hermetica: The Greek Corpus Hermeticum and the Latin Asclepius in a New English Translation, with Notes and Introduction* (Cambridge, 1992). Frances A. Yates, *Giordano Bruno and the Hermetic Tradition* (Chicago, 1964), while a mine of information on many points, is curiously evasive on the dating of the Hermetic texts, apparently assuming that whatever the dates of the particular texts that have come down to us, they reflect material from remote antiquity. Such a reading is not consistent with the evidence.

synthesis, and no one before the seventeenth century doubted their great antiquity. Lactantius and Augustine had both considered Trismegistus as a writer from remote antiquity, and although Augustine had condemned the idolatry in the Hermetic texts, Lactantius had used Trismegistus as an ally, as a pagan source in support of the truth of Christianity, noting in particular that he spoke of 'God and Father'. The Hermetic texts were considered to offer a *prisca theologia*, an ancient or original theology, supplementing the revelations given to Moses on Mount Sinai.

In his *Theologia Platonica*,[25] Ficino welded together Christian, Hermetic, and Neoplatonic sources into a syncretic treatise on philosophical theology which offered the first developed alternative to the Aristotelian system. The seemingly marvellous anticipations of Christianity evident in the Hermetic corpus, all the more remarkable in the light of its supposed great antiquity, and the marvellous and natural coherence between Platonism and both the Hermetic doctrines and Christian revelation, seemed to Ficino, as they had seemed to earlier thinkers in the Eastern Church, to suggest the key to the understanding of the link between God and his creation. What put Ficino ahead of his predecessors is the fact that his account drew not just on these sources but also on a whole body of Patristic and scholastic argument, and he deployed Augustine and Aquinas almost as readily as he did Plato, Plotinus, and Proclus. The aim was not to use Platonism to take pot-shots at Aristotelianism, as some scholastic writers had done, nor was it just setting out a Platonic system without regard to the kinds of questions that Aristotelianism had engaged, as Eastern Platonists had done. It was the setting out of a new synthesis which was presented as the answer to problems that Christian Platonists and Aristotelians shared, and it forced to the centre a question that the scholastic tradition had certainly taken seriously, but only as one of a number of issues. Ficino made the doctrine of the personal immortality of the soul the question on which the whole enterprise stood or fell.

The theme is set out in the first Book of the *Theologia*, where Ficino argues that the yearning for immortality which is characteristic of human beings would violate our understanding of God's behaviour if we were not allowed that immortality that we seek: for God not to allow immortality would frustrate the very nature of his most illustrious creation. Much of Ficino's account of the faculties of the soul and the attributes of God follows traditional scholastic accounts, but his argument for the soul's indissolubility is a resolutely Neoplatonic one and follows from its place in the ontological order. Perhaps the most distinctive feature of Neoplatonic conceptions is the hierarchical structure of the universe. Ficino's universe is typical in this regard, but his structuring goes beyond the traditional Neoplatonic hierarchy in two respects.[26] First the categories of being are determined by the five basic kinds of substance: God,

[25] A new edition of the Latin text of the *Theologia* with full English translation is gradually appearing: Marsilio Ficino, *Platonic Theology*, ed. James Hankins and William Bowen, trans. Michael J. B. Allen and John Warden (6 vols, Cambridge, Mass., 2001– ).

[26] See the discussion in Paul Oscar Kristeller, *Eight Philosophers of the Renaissance* (Stanford, 1964), 43–7. For a full exposition of the doctrines and a detailed discussion see Kristeller, *The Philosophy of Marsilio Ficino* (New York, 1943), who deals with Ficino's metaphysics at 35–200, and with his account of the spiritual or contemplative life at 206–401.

the angelic mind, the rational soul, quality, and body. God has the highest degree of being and the highest degree of goodness: body, by contrast, is simply a negation of this, having no being or goodness in its own right. This is a revision of Plotinus' scheme, replacing his vegetative and sensitive souls, and a development of that of Proclus, introducing the single category of quality and putting the human mind at the centre of a symmetrical classification. Second, Ficino conceives the hierarchy to be dynamic rather than static, the various parts and degrees being held together by active forces, the central one of which, following Plato's *Symposium*, he identifies with love. To provide some medium for the active forces he resurrects the Neoplatonic world soul, and gives astrology a central role in a natural system of mutual influences.[27] Having established this tightly structured hierarchy, Ficino then goes on to establish the soul's indissolubility on the basis of its central place in the ontological order: it plays a key role in holding the hierarchy together.

Ficino puts the earth at the physical centre of the universe and the rational soul at the ontological centre, so that the human being is doubly at the centre of things, and the focus of creation. As Copenhaver and Schmitt note, in this schema, 'macrocosm and microcosm, world-soul and human soul, affect one another through symmetries of psychic correspondence and mutually sustain an optimistic view of man's ability to fulfill an immortal destiny in a cosmos divinely ordered for human ends'.[28] One charge that this approach faced, a charge that George of Trebizond had laid against Bessarion, was that of introducing a host of redundant middle deities between God and his creation. Whatever the merits of the hierarchical scheme as a complete picture of the ways in which the various degrees of being interact, just how those who took an independent interest in natural philosophy might articulate their results in terms of the Neoplatonic scheme is not easy to conceive. Deriving physical principles from the metaphysical hierarchy would seem an impossible task, and it is certainly one that Ficino does not attempt. On the other hand, nor is it clear how one might incorporate physical principles into the system, because it is completely obscure how the system works at a physical level. The reliance on active principles connecting various parts of being, for example, is very problematic. In the sixteenth century, there will be a number of philosophers who will use 'active principles' to explain phenomena such as magnetism, which appears to act without a physical intermediary between the magnet and the magnetically attracted body. But when such claims come to be examined in early seventeenth-century writers such as Mersenne and Descartes, it turns out that the purported 'explanations' are little more than an exercise in labelling. One can invoke active principles to account for anything, but in invoking them it is far from clear that one has understood something that one did not understand before

[27] Astrology, which had been widely condemned by the Church in the thirteenth and early fourteenth centuries, witnessed a revival in the wake of the Black Death, in the middle of the fourteenth century, after which time it was the norm to find astrologers attached to royal courts. It is noteworthy that the members of the Paris Medical Faculty explained to the king that the cause of the plague had been astrological, and hence beyond their power: Roger French, *Medicine Before Science: The Rational and Learned Doctor from the Middle Ages to the Enlightenment* (Cambridge, 2003), 130.

[28] Copenhaver and Schmitt, *Renaissance Philosophy*, 151.

invoking the active principle. The question therefore arises whether they can perform any genuine explanatory work. If they cannot, then Ficino's metaphysical system loses its attachment to any substantive natural-philosophical content.

After the era of Ficino and Pico, Platonism became a more eclectic discipline, as authors such as Steuco and Mazzoni attempted to reconcile Aristotelianism and Platonism into a 'perennial' system, as Steuco termed it.[29] Patrizi, by contrast, who converted to Platonism on reading Ficino's *Theologia Platonica*, was very hostile to Aristotelianism, marking him out from Steuco and the more syncretic tradition of sixteenth-century Platonism.[30] Nevertheless, his attempt to ground a natural philosophy in Neoplatonic metaphysics was such that the nature of the task required that his system was a hybrid one even by the rather eclectic standards of Renaissance Platonism. *Nova de universis philosophia*, which first appeared in 1591, was intended by Patrizi not merely as a summation of the Platonic system,[31] but as an explicit alternative to Aristotle. In the Dedication, he explains to Pope Gregory XIV that there have been only four pious philosophers—Zoroaster, Hermes, Plato, and Patrizi himself—and he asks the Pope to abandon the Aristotelian system taught in the schools and colleges and to replace it with his.[32] The full title of the book gives an good indication of its structure. It rises to the first cause, we are told, not by the standard natural-philosophical route of motion or change, but by means of *lux* (light) and *lumen* (brightness).[33] Second, by a 'new and special method' all divinity comes into view. Third, the universe is derived by the Platonic method from God. We shall look at these in turn, but first we need to understand the role that theories of light play, for it is through an intimate attachment to optics that sixteenth-century Neoplatonism takes the form of a natural philosophy.

It is in the Arab optical tradition, in the *De Prospectibus* of al-Kindi in the ninth century, that we find the first statement of the principle that luminous rays issue in all directions from every point on the surface of a luminous body. Al-Kindi does not restrict this principle to light, however, but considers that 'everything that has actual existence emits rays in every direction, which fill the whole world'. [34] This applies as much to fire, magnets, and words as it does light. The special significance of optics

---

[29] On this movement see Charles B. Schmitt, 'Perennial Philosophy: From Agostino Steuco to Leibniz', *Journal of the History of Ideas* 27 (1966), 505–32.

[30] Patrizzi had argued in his translation of the work known as 'Aristotle's Theology' that this was a genuine work, and he used it to discredit other (genuine) doctrines of Aristotle's in an attempt to bring Aristotle into the Platonist camp. This was disingenuous in the extreme, as he had already argued that the work was spurious in his *Discussiones peripateticae* of 1571: it was in fact an apocryphal Arabic work based on Plotinus.

[31] The work subsequently appeared in a revised version in 1593, and it incorporated revised versions of a number of his earlier natural-philosophical writings. On Patrizi see Kristeller, *Eight Philosophers*, 111–126, and the literature cited in Copenhaver and Schmitt, *Renaissance Philosophy*, 187 n. 65.

[32] Copenhaver and Schmitt, *Renaissance Philosophy*, 190.

[33] Cf. James 1: 17: 'Every best gift and every perfect present is from above, coming down from the Father of lights'; and Paul to the Ephesians 5: 13: 'All that is made manifest is light'.

[34] Al-Kindi, *De Prospectibus*, prop. 7, cited in David C. Lindberg, *Theories of Vision from al-Kindi to Kepler* (Chicago, 1976), 19.

derives from the fact that it is concerned with the radiation of power, which al-Kindi considered the most fundamental natural phenomenon.[35] Al-Kindi offered an extra-mission theory of light, following Euclid and Ptolemy, whereby vision is effected by means of a 'power' proceeding from the eye to the sensible thing.[36] His successor in optics, Alhazen, offered an intromission theory, whereby vision is effected by the eye being struck by light rays which are emitted from or reflected off the object seen.[37] Alhazen was the first to integrate anatomical, physical, and geometrical considera-tions into a unified theory of vision, and he presented the first plausible solution to the problem of how large images can enter the pupil of the eye, which was one of the most serious problems for intromission theory. On Alhazen's physico-physiological theory, an external agent—*lumen*—is posited which is capable of stimulating the sense of vision. The luminous quality or brightness of a body is *lux*, and it is by means of *lumen* that *lux* is able to act on vision. The *lux/lumen* distinction became the staple of sub-sequent Arab and Western optics, undergoing a number of revisions and refinements, and the origins of the distinction in a consideration of the transmission of powers is important.

When Arab optics reached the West in the thirteenth century, in the work of Robert Grosseteste—who, though not a Franciscan himself, was closely associated with the English Franciscans—we find it immediately being given a very explicit metaphysical gloss, as part of the theology of creation.[38] Grosseteste incorporated optics into an account which had three other ingredients. The first is the Augustinian doctrine of divine illumination. In the *Soliloquia*, Augustine had argued that just as objects must be made visible by being illuminated before they can be seen, so too must truths be made intelligible by a kind of light before they can be known, and just as the sun is the source of physical light, so God is the source of spiritual light or truth. In his *De veritate* and in the commentary on the *Posterior Analytics*, Grosseteste explicitly took up this doctrine, drawing intimate parallels between optics and the power of God. These parallels were able to be so close because of the second ingredient in his account, a light cosmogony deriving from the Neoplatonic doctrine of emanation, known in the Middle Ages primarily through a compendium

[35] On al-Kindi's metaphysics, which is a mixture of (primarily) Neoplatonism and Aristotelian-ism, see Thorndike, *A History of Magic and Experimental Science*, i. 642–7; and Alfred L. Ivry, 'Al-Kindi as Philosopher: The Aristotelian and Neoplatonic Dimensions', in S. M. Stern, Albert Hourani, and Vivian Brown, eds, *Islamic Philosophy and the Classical Tradition* (Columbia, SC, 1972), 117–40.

[36] See Lindberg, *Theories of Vision*, 18–32, on al-Kindi's optics. Al-Kindi defended the extra-mission theory on anatomical grounds—were the eye a receptacle we would expect it to be shaped like the ear, which is a receptacle and so is hollow, whereas the eye is spherical—and on optical grounds—above all why acuity depends on position in the visual field. There are also epistemological considerations: we see objects out there in the world not in the head, which is where vision takes place on the intromission theory.

[37] See Lindberg, *Theories of Vision*, 58–86, on Alhazen's optics.

[38] See A. C. Crombie, *Robert Grosseteste and the Origins of Experimental Science, 1100–1700* (Oxford, 1971), ch. 6; McEvoy, *The Philosophy of Robert Grosseteste*, part III; and Steven P. Marrone, *William of Auvergne and Robert Grosseteste: New Ideas of Truth in the Early Thirteenth Century* (Princeton, 1983), pt II.

of passages from Plotinus and Proclus, misleadingly entitled *Theologia Aristotelia*. Here light was construed as the 'first corporeal form', with the material universe itself evolving from a primordial point of light.[39] Hence the study of 'physical' light was a prerequisite to the understanding of the origins and structure of the material universe. Finally, the third ingredient in his account was the Neoplatonic idea that all causation in the material universe operates on the analogy of the radiation of light. A crucial source here was pseudo-Dionysius the Aeropagite,[40] who was wrongly identified (by some right up to the nineteenth century) with the first-century Dionysius whom Paul converted in Athens.[41] His writings, which date from some time between the second half of the second century and the beginning of the sixth, had an immense authority because of his assumed closeness to the origins of Christianity, and to its founder, Paul, and Dionysius played the same role in Franciscan philosophy, from Bonaventure onwards, that Aristotle played in that of the Dominicans.[42] Dionysius was the author of *Coelistis Hierarchia* and *Ecclesiastica Hierarchia*, in which an extremely elaborate hierarchy of heavenly and terrestrial beings was set out. The hierarchy worked via degrees of illumination deriving from God himself—the creation of the world was explicitly identified with the appearance of light in the darkness, with the emergence of a spatial universe from a purely spiritual one[43]—and physical illumination and spiritual enlightenment were effectively identified. The basic distinction was between the intelligible realm and the visible realm, and one of Dionysius' aims was to show how the intelligible is veiled in the visible and how it can be unveiled through illumination.[44] To study light on this view, was to study the emanations of God.[45]

Grosseteste's Dionysian 'metaphysics of light', in which light was the substance underlying all physical change in the cosmos, provided a rationale for the study of optics, a rationale supplemented with a new element in the attempt of the Franciscan Roger Bacon to elucidate theological truths in terms of light metaphors. His *Opus Maius* (1267) takes its starting point from the phrase 'Guard us, O Lord, as the pupil of thine eye.' This phrase, he argued, like many others in the Bible, cannot properly be understood without a knowledge of how the mechanism of 'corporeal' vision corresponds to physical enlightenment, and he proceeded to construct an analogical

[39] On the history of this light cosmogony prior to Grosseteste, see Schmidt-Biggemann, *Philosophia Perennis*, 138–42, 273–83.

[40] See Roger French and Andrew Cunningham, *'Before Science: The Invention of the Friars' Natural Philosophy* (London, 1996), chs. 9 and 10.

[41] See Joseph Stiglmyr, *Das Aufkommen der pseudo-dionysischen Schriften und ihr Eindringen in die christliche Literatur* (Bonn, 1895).

[42] See French and Cunningham, *Before Science*, 218–24. Dionysius also exercised a considerable influence on the Dominicans: see J. Durantel, *Saint Thomas et le Pseudo-Denis* (Paris, 1919).

[43] See Schmidt-Biggemann, *Philosophia Perennis*, 275.

[44] See René Roques, *L'Univers dionysien: structure hiérarchique du monde selon le Pseudo-Denys* (Paris, 1983).

[45] See French and Cunningham, *Before Science*, ch. 10, and, more generally on the importance of a light metaphysics, Klaus Hedwig, *Sphaera Lucis: Studien zur Intelligibilität des Seienden im Kontext der mittelalterlichen Lichtspekulation* (Münster, 1980).

account of epistemology in which God has direct spiritual vision, angels have refracted spiritual vision, and human beings have reflected spiritual vision, that is, the ability to see spiritual truths as they are mirrored in earthly creation.[46] The theme was developed further in the Platonic revival, with Ficino devoting a short treatise, *De sole et lumine* (1493),[47] to the question of the relation between corporeal and incorporeal light. This is the context in which we need to examine Patrizi's use of light metaphors, for, eccentric as it might first seem, these are not unprecedented, and in fact have a substantial Neoplatonic tradition behind them.

The first part of *Nova de universis philosophia*, entitled *Panaugia* ('all-splendour'), treats an incorporeal correlate of light as an intermediary between the spiritual and the material levels of being, and is devoted to exploring the physical and metaphysical properties of light, and by extension, its incorporeal analogue. Knowledge of the properties and behaviour of physical light is the key to knowledge of the properties and behaviour of its incorporeal analogue, and this incorporeal analogue is what links God to his creation. Corporeal light is taken in a very broad sense here, and Patrizi's discussion is as concerned with its life-giving qualities as much as with optics. It also has a cosmological aspect, for outside the visible universe lies the empyrean (the place of the saints in the Christian cosmos), which is an infinite region of pure light. This light is corporeal but derives from incorporeal, divine things—namely souls, intellects, angels, and God, although God is the ultimate source of incorporeal and, by extension, corporeal light. At this point (Book 10), the *lux/lumen* distinction is given an explicitly incorporeal reading, as we are told that God, as the *lux prima*, is the source of incorporeal light—a view that goes back to one of the earliest Christian cosmologies, that of Basil in the fourth century[48]—and from him proceeds *lumen*, diffused light, which is found first in his Son, and then in incorporeal creatures. Light, in its incorporeal version, serves not simply to unify the cosmos throughout each level of being, but to secure the immediacy of divine action at each level. This unity prepares the way for the metaphysics set out in the second part, *Panarchia* (all the principles), in which we are given a detailed account of the hierarchy of being, drawing on Plotinus, Proclus, and Ficino, and adding an extra level of being—form—between Ficino's qualities and matter. One of the more novel innovations of Patrizi's treatment here is his rejection of Plotinus' transcendent God and a move to an immanent God who includes all things and is not separate from his creation. As we shall see, this kind of immanent view, which comes close to pantheism, will be singled out by Mersenne as indicative of the dangers of this whole programme. The dangers are especially apparent in one of the linchpins of Patrizi's approach, indeed one of the linchpins of his view of the integrated structure of the universe, namely the world soul, which takes on a number of roles that might traditionally have been reserved for the supernatural, and Part 3 is devoted to an account of how the relation of the

---

[46] See the discussion in Carolly Erickson, *The Medieval Vision: Essays in History and Perception* (New York, 1976), 42–4.

[47] Ficino, *Opera*, i. 965–86.

[48] See W. G. L. Randles, *The Unmaking of the Medieval Christian Cosmos, 1500–1760: From Solid Heavens to Boundless Æther* (Aldershot, 1999), 3–5.

world soul to the cosmos as a whole is analogous to that of the relation between the individual soul and the body.

In the final part of *Nova de universis philosophia*, suitably named *Pancosmia* (all the cosmos), Patrizi introduces the four fundamental principles of the physical world: space, light, heat, and fluidity or humid air.[49] His treatment of space mirrors the analogies between the corporeal and the incorporeal that dominated Part 1. In Books 1 to 3, he sets out how incorporeal space gives rise to corporeal space. The former is the space of geometry, and contains points rather than bodies, the distinctive feature of which is that they exhibit resistance. How exactly incorporeal space can 'give rise' to corporeal space is not spelled out, but the process seems like one of creation rather than straightforward causation. The first thing to fill corporeal space, however, is, in deference to Genesis, not matter but light (Book 4). Indeed it is light that initially gives rise to the corporeal world, for a formal and active principle, namely heat, derives from light, and in combination with a passive and material principle, fluidity, material bodies are formed with different degrees of density, depending on the combination of heat and fluidity. Having established this theory of the constitution of matter, Patrizi can move finally to the large-scale structure of the cosmos in terms of the kinds of corporeal and incorporeal constituents that make up the three layers: the empyrean, the region that lies beyond the stars and is filled with light (Book 9), the ether, which fills the region between the stars and the moon and through which they move (Book 10), and the sublunary realm. Patrizi's treatment of the ethereal realm was of some influence because he rejected the idea that the celestial bodies were carried around on crystalline orbs and instead postulated a fluid medium, the ether, in which they moved[50]—they 'fly within a liquid sky'—and he explained the diurnal motion of the earth in terms of its movement from west to east, rather than in terms of the motion of the celestial orb from east to west. It is worth noting, however, that the rejection of the crystalline orbs was not based on optical or astronomical evidence. Jean Péna had argued in 1557 that crystalline orbs would produce anomalous refractions of the light from celestial bodies and that the orbs must therefore be treated as abstractions,[51] and Tycho Brahe had rejected their existence as being incompatible with the path of the comet observed in 1577, as well as with the appearance of a new star in 1572. Patrizi, however, was oblivious to such considerations. In Patrizi's system, it is the nature of matter that determines cosmological structure, and if the basic

[49] The term is *fluor*, lit. flow. The idea that the firmament consists of a fluid or humid air had been advocated in Francesco Giorgio, *De harmonia mundi totius cantica tria* (Venice, 1525), a work of Neoplatonic and Hermetic inspiration, although it ultimately goes back to Basil in the fourth century. See Randles, *The Unmaking of the Medieval Christian Cosmos*, 32–4.

[50] The idea was not without precedent: some advocates of the Ptolemaic system had construed the planetary orbs not as crystalline shells but as different regions of a fluid heavens which have differential rates of rotation around a terrestrial centre. Robertus Anglicus had offered an account of fluid shells in the thirteenth century, Andalo di Negro had done so in the fourteenth, and Giovanni Pontano in the fifteenth. See James M. Lattis, *Between Copernicus and Galileo: Christoph Clavius and the Collapse of Ptolemaic Cosmology* (Chicago, 1994), 94–6.

[51] Jean Péna, *Euclidis optica et catoptrica* (Paris, 1557), Preface. See Peter Barker, 'The Optical Theory of Comets from Apian to Kepler', *Physis* 30 (1993), 1–25.

building blocks of our universe at the superlunary level are light, heat, and space, then there is simply no material from which crystalline orbs can be formed.[52]

Patrizi's cosmological ideas were not without influence with his contemporaries and immediate successors. Gassendi explicitly acknowledged his indebtedness to Patrizi on the question of the nature of space, for example,[53] and Bacon's cosmology was very much in the tradition of speculative cosmology and derived celestial motions from matter theory,[54] and the scheme he set out owed a good deal to Patrizi.[55] Kepler, by contrast, although he considered Patrizi as the founder of a cosmological system—while at the same time implicitly accusing him of seeking novelty for its own sake[56]—singled him out for criticism in the *Apologia pro Tychone contra Ursum* for his rejection of astronomical hypotheses, something that was consonant with Patrizi's reliance on a general theory of matter to provide the groundwork for an investigation of the structure of the cosmos. Kepler's approach was manifestly very different from this, as his criticism of Patrizi made clear. Patrizi, he tells us,

is infuriated with astronomers for attempting to construct the apparent motions of the planets from the various circles and solid orbs and to impute to the nature of things those circles, those hypotheses, figments of their own minds. He himself asserts this about the planets. They move amongst the fixed stars in the liquid ether exactly as they appear to, free from the fetters of solid orbs, which do not exist. And exactly as appears to our eyes they truly describe with non-uniform motions spirals and lines variously contorted back and forth, never exactly repeating themselves. Nor ought we to be surprised by this diversity, because the planets are in truth animals with the faculty of reason—a view he supports with the authority of pagan philosophy—and it would not have been impossible for the divine omnipotence to create creatures with enough wisdom to perform those ordained motions until the end of the world.[57]

As we shall see below, there are Platonic elements in Kepler's systematic astronomy, but they function in a very different way from anything we find in Patrizi. Rather than astronomy and cosmology being shaped around the matter theory that issues from a Neoplatonic metaphysics, for Kepler it is the former that do the work: any metaphysics must be accommodated to them. For Patrizi, who does not hide his contempt for astronomers in *Nova de universis philosophia*, this is to get things completely the wrong way around. Instead of asking how the cosmos is structured and what it is

---

[52] See Edward Grant, *Planets, Stars, and Orbs: The Medieval Cosmos, 1200–1687* (Cambridge, 1996), 349.

[53] Pierre Gassendi, *Opera Omnia* (6 vols, Lyon, 1658), i. 246.

[54] See ch. 5.

[55] See Francis Bacon, *The Oxford Francis Bacon*, vi. *Philosophical Studies c.1611-c.1619*, ed., introd., notes, and comm. by Graham Rees (Oxford, 1996), pp. xlii–xliv and 158–60.

[56] *Epitome Astronomiae Copernicanae*, in *Johannis Kepler Astronomi Opera Omnia*, ed. C. Frisch (8 vols, Frankfurt, 1858–71), vi. 306; 'Epitome of Copernican Astronomy, Books 4 and 5', trans. C. G. Wallis, in *Britannica Great Books* 16 (Chicago, 1952), 843–1004: 850. Compare Kepler's *New Astronomy*, trans. William H. Donahue (Cambridge, 1992), 117, where a similar complaint is made against Patrizi.

[57] Translation quoted from Nicholas Jardine, *The Birth of History and Philosophy of Science: Kepler's 'A Defence of Tycho against Ursus' with Essays on Its Provenance and Significance* (Cambridge, 1988), 154. As Jardine points out in his discussion of the significance of the *Apologia*, Kepler misrepresents Patrizi on the question of real and apparent motion: 234–5.

made from, and then proceeding to investigate how and why its constituents move in the way that they do, they carry out observations and calculations and devise ridiculous hypotheses to account for them. He accuses Copernicus and (unaccountably) Tycho, for example, of thinking of the stars as being fixed to the heavens like knots or nails in a plank,[58] whereas, he believes, it is clear from reflection on the ultimate constituents of the material from which the region between the stars and the moon is constructed that they must be moving through a fluid. If scholasticism, by comparison with Patrizi's system, could only come up with a piecemeal account of cosmology, the astronomers are even worse, giving priority to observational minutiae and devising geometrically motivated hypotheses which are oblivious to any understanding of the large-scale physical structure of the cosmos.

In 1592, Pope Clement VIII called Patrizi to Rome as Professor of Platonic Philosophy at La Sapienza University, where he lectured on the *Timaeus*. But his call for his system to replace the Christianized Aristotelianism of the scholastics came to nothing, as it met the fate awaiting any novel comprehensive system. The Inquisition found it contained a number of doctrinal errors, and it was placed on the *Index expurgatorius*, along with many of the texts whose orthodoxy it had questioned.[59]

## NATURALISM AND THE SCOPE OF NATURAL PHILOSOPHY

Heterodoxy was not by any means the preserve of Neoplatonism in the sixteenth century. A far more significant generator of heterodoxy was a form of Aristotelianism, associated principally with the University of Padua, in which Pomponazzi was a leading figure. In the late fifteenth and early sixteenth centuries there was a revival of interest in Averroes in the northern Italian Universities, accompanied by a spate of translations of his Aristotle commentaries.[60] The term 'Averroism' is generally used to pick out two distinct doctrines held by Averroes. One is a doctrine about the autonomy of natural philosophy, the other a distinctive natural-philosophical doctrine about the fate of the soul when it leaves the body at death, namely the doctrine of the unity of the intellect. The doctrines are connected indirectly, but crucially. That of the unity of the intellect is clearly contrary to orthodox Christian teaching, and hence was held to be untrue, yet because it is a natural-philosophical doctrine, and not a theological one, its natural-philosophical credentials were not necessarily undermined by this. Its natural-philosophical inadequacy could be demonstrated only in natural-philosophical terms, and the real dilemmas arise when no natural-philosophical inadequacy can be shown. These problems come to a

---

[58] *Nova de universis philosophia*: *Pancosmia*, fo. 106r col. 2 and fo. 92v col. 1. See Jardine, *Birth*, 155.

[59] The Indices had begun to appear in 1561, but the first Roman Index was not issued until 1590. For details of how the Index system worked, see George H. Putnam, *The Censorship of the Church of Rome and its Influence on the Production and Distribution of Literature* (2 vols., New York, 1906–7).

[60] See Schmitt, *Aristotle in the Renaissance*, 22–3. A key figure was Johannes Argyropulos, whose 1460 lectures on the *De anima* resurrected the question of the Averroist doctrine of one mind, introducing it to a new generation.

head in Pomponazzi, and it is clear from the beginning that there are really two connected basic determinants. One is the purview of natural philosophy, the other is its autonomy. Pomponazzi pushes natural-philosophical explanation into areas where it would traditionally have been thought inappropriate: in particular, into areas in which effects seem to be produced via divine or supernatural activity, rather than natural processes. This exacerbates the problems significantly, and forces the question of the autonomy of natural philosophy to the fore.

There was a measure of eclecticism in Pomponazzi's thinking, and he was certainly not free of Stoic and Neoplatonic influences, but his aim was to uncover Aristotle's doctrines, compare them with Church teaching, and try to draw conclusions as to what it was reasonable to hold. He opens the Preface to *De immortalitate* with a request to him from a friend, couched in these terms:

> Beloved teacher, in former days when you were expounding the first book of *De caelo* to us and had come to that place in which Aristotle tries to show by many arguments that the ungenerated and the incorruptible are convertible, you set forth the position of St Thomas Aquinas on the immortality of the soul. Although you were in no doubt that it was true and certain in itself, yet you judged that it is in complete disagreement with what Aristotle says. Therefore, unless it is too much trouble for you, I should very much like to know two things from you. First, leaving aside revelation and miracles, and remaining entirely within natural limits, what do you yourself think in this matter? And, second, what do you judge was Aristotle's opinion on the same question?[61]

Two years later, in 1518, Pomponazzi defended his philosophical conclusions on the grounds that it was his duty to interpret Aristotle and therefore not to deviate from what Aristotle thought.[62] This conservative gloss on his project should not mask the radicalness of what he is proposing: what Pomponazzi does is to open up the whole question of whether Aristotelian natural philosophy—accepted, in its Christianized version, as orthodoxy in the scholastic tradition—can in fact serve in the role of a philosophical foundation for a systematic theology. The credentials of Aristotelian natural philosophy had been secured in the thirteenth century, as we have seen, in its treatment of the Trinity, the nature of Christ, and transubstantiation, but less attention had been devoted to the question of the personal immortality of the soul. If, as Aristotelian natural philosophy required, the soul was the substantial form of the body, how could it survive the death and corruption of the body? Aquinas had dealt with several issues, including Averroist conceptions of the disembodied soul as one in number, but there was little doubt that this was one area in which the original Platonist conception of the soul as an intermediary between sense perception and the realm of Forms, and having no essential relation to the body, fitted rather more easily with Christian teaching. This had, of course, been the thrust of the attack on Aristotle by Ficino.

What had now happened was that Pomponazzi had unravelled a little of the careful work done by Aquinas, and in the course of opposing both Neoplatonist and

---

[61]  Translated in Cassirer et al., *Renaissance Philosophy of Man*, 281.

[62]  Pietro Pomponazzi, *Tractatus acutissimi utillimi et mere peripatetici* (Venice, 1525), 104r–v.

Averroist accounts of the soul he had treated them purely in philosophical terms, only to find that, in purely philosophical terms, the conclusion drawn was at variance with Aquinas' Aristotelian defence of Christian teaching on the issue. Aquinas had separated lower functions of the soul, such as growth and sense perception, which he considered do indeed end with the death and corruption of the body, from higher cognitive and intellective functions, which do not. But it is crucial on his Aristotelian account that, for human beings, the activities characteristic of the higher functions, in particular the grasp of universals, must start from sense perception, that is, from something intrinsically corporeal. In particular, all knowledge works from sensory images. In advocating this doctrine, however, Aquinas distinguished between the kind of intuitive grasp of truth characteristic of the intellect, and the reasoning processes that underlie and accompany sensation. All knowledge starts from sensation, but once the intellect is engaged and has done the work of abstraction, sensory images are no longer needed.[63] This is where Pomponazzi's difficulties with the Thomist account began, for the idea of a form of cognition that does not involve a representation of the object cognized is just not cognition for Pomponazzi, and the representation can hardly be pure form for no Aristotelian account of cognition could countenance pure forms. Consequently, the mind cannot act in cognition without corporeal representations, that is, without the body. As Pomponazzi realised, this left the question of immortality wide open:

keeping the saner view, we must say that the question of the immortality of the soul is a neutral problem, like that of the eternity of the world. For it seems to me that no natural reasons can be brought forth proving that the soul is immortal, and still less any proving that the soul is mortal, as very many scholars who hold it immortal declare.[64]

Philosophically, Pomponazzi advocated the view that the soul is the 'highest form'—and it is interesting how even Pomponazzi had to resort to Neoplatonic notions at this point—but philosophy cannot establish its immortality.

The implications of this failure of Aristotelian natural philosophy to supply appropriate philosophical support for a core doctrine go beyond the issue of personal immortality. At the most fundamental level, what is at stake is the failure of Aristotelian natural philosophy to provide a philosophical basis for a systematic theology. By the early to middle decades of the sixteenth century, such a failure had become deeply problematic, because the need for a philosophical basis was greater than ever, and the need for it to take the form of Aristotelian natural philosophy was also greater than ever. The magnitude and ramifications of the failure are evident on the issue of transubstantiation, and the radical nature of the responses to the failure is evident in the rise of naturalism.

In Anselm's elaboration of a systematic theology, particularly in his *Cur Deus Homo*, the eucharist had been raised to the primary sacrament: it was the only

---

[63] See Stephen Gaukroger, *Cartesian Logic: An Essay on Descartes's Conception of Inference* (Oxford, 1989), 38–47; and Julien Peghaire, *Intellectus et ratio selon S. Thomas d'Aquin* (Paris and Ottawa, 1936), *passim*.

[64] Translated in Cassirer et al., *Renaissance Philosophy of Man*, 377.

occasion in which one was in the real presence of the crucified Christ. This view became central to the Western church (as opposed to the Eastern church, for which the crucifixion had no significance apart from the resurrection).[65] This understanding of the eucharist turned on the question of transubstantiation, which became the issue on which everything hinged in the theological disputes of the 1520s onwards. On it rested the whole question of an ecclesiastical hierarchy, the central issue at stake in the Protestant break with Catholicism. While the Catholics insisted on the need for a priesthood and a clerical hierarchy, Luther rejected the notion that the spiritual estate was superior to the temporal estates, the aristocracy and the laity, regarding the clerical office as one calling among others: all vocations, on this view, were equally spiritual (something crucial for the development of physico-theology, as we shall see in the next chapter). Levi has noted that Catholic theologians in the 1520s were well aware that baptism could be conferred by anyone, that sins could be forgiven in the case of genuine contrition without priestly forgiveness, and that marriage partners conferred the sacrament on one another. Consequently, as he points out, without transubstantiation,

there was no need for a hierarchical priesthood validly empowered to celebrate the mass, and without the church's need for a hierarchical priesthood, it would have been difficult to establish the need for any hierarchy consisting of more than administrative officers. . . . In the west, after the nation states had assumed responsibility for civil administration, only the unbroken apostolic continuity of a sacramental priesthood, founded by Jesus in his lifetime and essential for the valid transformation of the eucharistic elements in the central act of worship, made the hierarchical church necessary.[66]

Transubstantiation was a doctrine that had traditionally been formulated and defended in Aristotelian terms,[67] and it would seem that it is impossible to capture the doctrine in a satisfactory way in any other philosophical terms.[68] Never was the defence of Aristotelianism, both in its own right and in terms of its credentials as a foundation for a systematic theology, so necessary, yet it no longer seemed that these roles were reconcilable. More generally, the questions now had to be raised, first, whether it was at all viable to think one could provide philosophical foundations for theology at all, something fideists were to deny; second, if it were viable, whether a philosophy completely different from Aristotle's might fit the bill, as Gassendi, for example, will suggest in his efforts to revive ancient atomism; or, third, whether, instead of trying to shape one's natural-philosophical foundations to a pre-given theology, one might explore the consequences of one's natural philosophy and (within limits) develop a

---

[65] See Miri Rubin, *Corpus Christi: The Eucharist in Late Medieval Culture* (Cambridge, 1991) and Sarah Beckwirth, *Christ's Body: Identity, Culture and Society in Late Medieval Writings* (London, 1993).

[66] Levi, *Renaissance and Reformation*, 353. See Gary Macy, 'The Doctrine of Transubstantiation in the Middle Ages', *Journal of Ecclesiastical History* 45 (1994), 11–44.

[67] It became the official doctrine of the Church with the Fourth Lateran Council of 1215, and in the third quarter of the century Aquinas provided its Aristotelian formulation.

[68] This is evident in the problems inherent in Descartes' attempt to think through transubstantiation in mechanist terms. See Jean-Robert Armogathe, *Theologia cartesiana: l'explication physique de l'Eucharistie chez Descartes et Dom Desgabets* (The Hague, 1977).

natural theology on this basis, something we begin to find in seventeenth-century English natural philosophy.

The question whether Aristotelian natural philosophy provides a satisfactory basis for Christian doctrine prompts the question whether this is an appropriate test of the adequacy of a natural philosophy. The attacks on the doctrine of 'double truth' had centred on the idea that natural philosophy and Christian teaching had provided different competing accounts, but there was a further question, whether particular phenomena had been mischaracterized as being supernatural and hence falling under Christian teaching, or whether they were in fact matters more appropriately explained in natural-philosophical terms.[69] We can find evidence of this line of reasoning in two posthumously published treatises by Pomponazzi, *De incantationibus* and *De fato*, both written around 1520.[70] *De incantationibus* deals with a range of phenomena that had traditionally been construed in terms of supernatural causation, arguing that these phenomena had been mischaracterized, that they were in effect wholly explicable in natural terms. In the process he excludes not only explanations in terms of demons and spirits, but also those in terms of miracles. His natural explanations depend on two distinctive features: the importance of planetary influences and what we might describe as the psychological state of the subject of these phenomena. The former, as the first two books of *De fato* make clear, is part of a thoroughgoing form of physical determinism of a Stoic kind, and indeed the traditional arguments against astrology had focused on its perceived determinism. The latter suggests that any devotional and miraculous phenomena can be explained naturalistically through the action of material spirits produced by or accompanying particular psychological states.

Pomponazzi is not carving out completely new ground here, for Ficino had paved the way in his holistic spiritual magic, in which astrological and psychological explanations are employed to provide non-supernatural accounts of questions that had traditionally been thought to be outside the realm of natural explanation.[71] Ficino's motivation and that of Pomponazzi differ radically, however. Ficino's aim was the construction of a transcendental Platonic system, Pomponazzi's is the elaboration of a naturalist Aristotelian one. What Pomponazzi effectively does is to begin to reformulate and expand the domain of natural philosophy by questioning the extent to which it is ever in need of supplementation by supernatural explanations, even in cases of miraculous apparitions and prayer. In the case of prayer, for example, he distinguishes two aims: obtaining some external benefit and making oneself more pious. Because God's will has been immutably fixed from eternity and

[69] The question is not restricted to natural-philosophical explanation. We can also find a naturalistic approach to sexual activity, which is treated in the Italian Galenic tradition as being one of the passions of the soul and as a result something not encumbered by theological edicts: see Ian Maclean, *Logic, Signs and Nature in the Renaissance: The Case of Learned Medicine* (Cambridge, 2002), 88–9, 252–3.

[70] Pietro Pomponazzi, *De naturalium effectuum causis sive de incantationibus* (Basle, 1556), and *De fato* (Basle, 1567).

[71] The classic treatment of these questions, to which I am indebted here, is Daniel P. Walker, *Spiritual and Demonic Magic from Ficino to Campanella* (London, 1969).

guides the movement of the heavens, prayer is unable to alter these. However, prayer does indeed make us more pious, and can be effective if the prayers

come from the depths of the heart and be fervent; for thus are the spirits more strongly affected and more powerful in their effect on matter—not in order that they may prevail upon the intelligences [viz. the powers that move the celestial spheres] (for these are entirely immutable), but in order that they may be more moved.[72]

What we have here is a combination of the psychological reduction of prayer, plus a theory of the material effects of psychological states whereby psychological states of sufficient intensity make the subject of the state more receptive to various kinds of spiritual influence. Even more radical, his psychological reduction of prayer is matched by an implicit astrological account of the success of Christianity, whereby the stars were favourable to the growth of Christianity at the time it developed by giving power to its symbols (such as the name of Jesus and the sign of the cross) to produce miracles so that Christianity might spread,[73] but this is something distinctive of the era, and an era that produced other planetary conjunctions might not be one in which Christianity would have flourished. Of course, it is God who, in His providential wisdom, produces the sequence of planetary conjunctions in the first place, so it is He who makes these conducive to the spread of Christianity through the efficacy of its symbols, but the efficacy of the Christian symbols is something natural, not supernatural, and is to be understood in terms of a combination of psychological states producing material effects through their release or rearrangement of spirits, and particular conjunctions of celestial bodies producing the material medium in which these spirits act.

The philosophical resources that Pomponazzi employed were eclectic, but his motivation derived from a particular naturalistic construal of Aristotle, and he sought to ground his project in Aristotelianism. There were more thoroughgoing forms of naturalism than that of Aristotle, however, and the kind of naturalist project that Pomponazzi advocated was subsequently pursued with more tailored resources. From among the host of naturalist writings that appeared from the mid- to the late sixteenth century—whose authors included figures such as Cardano, Paracelsus, Fracastro, Servetus, Stellato, Porzio, and Campanella—I shall take the work of Telesio and Bruno as representative. Both followed the programme of pushing natural philosophy in a naturalistic direction and both undermined the boundary between the natural and the supernatural. Rejecting the kind of commitment to Aristotle that we find in Pomponazzi, however, they made free use of Presocratic and Hellenistic natural philosophy, mixing it with elements taken from Neoplatonism and Aristotelianism as they saw fit.

The natural philosophy of antiquity was concerned with the problem of change. Parmenides had denied that knowledge of something that was changing was possible, and since nature is constantly changing, this meant that knowledge of nature is

---

[72] *De incantationibus*, 255. Translation quoted from Walker, *Spiritual and Demonic Magic*, 108: see the discussion at 107–111.

[73] *De incantationibus*, 302–10.

impossible. Plato responded to this problem by positing a world of unchanging Forms beyond the sensible realm of nature. Accepting Parmenides' dictum, he argued that the real objects of knowledge are the Forms, of which nature is merely an imperfect copy. What one must aim to know is the unchanging prototype, not the changing copy. Aristotle countered with the argument that the Forms did not constitute a realm separate from that of the sensible world, but rather underlay the sensible world. The form of something was actually part of it, just like its matter. Indeed, it was even more a part of it, since it constituted its essence. But, as Aristotle's Hellenistic successors realized, he never completely shook off his Platonic and Parmenidean legacy.[74] His thought still had room for a transcendental God who was linked in its activity with the system's only other transcendental being, the human intellect. Although in the first two books of *De anima* Aristotle had defined, described, and analysed the human soul in terms of its functioning in a natural relationship with the body, elsewhere he hinted that it might be immortal and separable from the body. This ambivalence did not survive Aristotle long, however. At about the time that Plato's successors in the Academy were discarding the Forms, their contemporaries in the Lyceum were purging Aristotelianism of any supernatural elements.

The cosmos of Zeno of Citium, the founder of Stoicism, was essentially that of Aristotle cleansed of its last traces of transcendentalism, and pushed even further back towards the dynamism of the pre-Parmenidean philosophers. Despite the fact that Aristotle had relocated the Platonic forms within material beings, they were still forms, principles of structure. By contrast, all vestiges of forms are gone from Zeno. He saw both being in general and the universe of individual beings as an immense physical organism and so was led by the analogy with living beings to an internal principle that had already been discussed in fifth-century medical circles, the *pneuma* or vital spirit. For both Plato and Aristotle the human soul was one of the transcendentals, in whole or in part capable of escaping the body and so enjoying immortality. The Stoics conceded that people were different from animals, but only in degree, not in kind. The human soul was like that in animals in that it was nothing more than a certain tension in the pneumatic system of the organism, and death was in effect simply a dissolution of the system. More generally, the Stoics offered a biological model of the universe which suggested that the cosmic system was controlled, that the control was rational, as in human beings, and that there was a close connection between corporeal, psychic, and ethical functions in both human beings and the universe. In other words, their naturalism is a decidedly holistic naturalism.

The other great natural philosophy of the Hellenistic era, Epicurean atomism, was similarly naturalistic. For Plato, unchanging reality lay beyond the sensible changing world, whereas for Aristotle it lay behind this sensible world. Epicurus takes the view that unchanging reality lies in the world, at the microscopic level. There is a level of the sensible world itself which provides a reference point for understanding

[74] On Hellenistic philosophy, see the texts and commentaries in A. A. Long and D. N. Sedley, *The Hellenistic Philosophers* (2 vols, Cambridge, 1987).

its changes. Moreover, although not overtly holist in the way that Stoicism is, Epicureanism fostered a view of the cosmos as an interconnected whole, in which ethics, logic, and natural philosophy have interrelated places.

Stoicism and Epicureanism were assimilated to some extent in the sixteenth century,[75] and if we think of their characteristic features not in terms of whether they see the world at the most fundamental level as compromising atoms and empty space, or a continuum, but in terms of their relation to Platonism and the more transcendent readings of Aristotle, then we can perhaps see how the typically naturalistic Hellenistic philosophies might be contrasted with the more typically dualist philosophies of classical antiquity.[76] But if the contrast is that between transcendence and naturalism, then we must not only include those Aristotelians who offered a naturalistic reading of Aristotle, such as Pomponazzi, but also recognize that the Neoplatonic doctrine of the world soul might be, and was, assimilated to the naturalist cause, despite the fact that its origins lay in the idea that such a soul was needed to unite a wholly transcendent God with the natural world.[77]

While both Stoics and Epicureans were naturalists in a broad sense, their positions differ in a way that is significant for sixteenth- and seventeenth-century natural philosophy, in that the Epicureans conceived of the fundamental constituents of the world as being inert corpuscles, whereas Stoic holism and the tendency to model the cosmos on analogy with a living organism precludes any constituents being called inert. There is an important division for our purposes between a programme of reduction of the natural world to inert atoms, and a programme that sees the ultimate constituents of the natural world in terms of immanent powers or principles. I propose to reserve the term 'corpuscularianism' for the former and 'naturalism' for the latter.[78] Corpuscularianism, which plays very little role in the sixteenth century but a dominant one in the seventeenth, takes a variety of forms, depending on whether those properties of the corpuscles that do the explanatory work are restricted

[75] See Louise Fothergill-Payne, 'Seneca's Role in Popularizing Epicurus in the Sixteenth Century', in Margaret J. Osler, ed., *Atoms, Pneuma, and Tranquillity: Epicurean and Stoic Themes in European Thought* (Cambridge, 1991), 115–34. On the Epicurean tradition from the Hellenistic era to the seventeenth century, see Howard Jones, *The Epicurean Tradition* (London, 1989). There is no similarly compact treatment of the history of Stoicism. On Stoicism in antiquity see J. M. Rist, *Stoic Philosophy* (Cambridge, 1969); on its pre-early-modern development see Marcia Colish, *The Stoic Tradition from Antiquity to the Early Middle Ages* (2 vols, Leiden, 1985); on its importance for sixteenth-and seventeenth-century moral and political thought see Oestreich, *Neostoicism and the Early Modern State*; and on its role in early modern natural philosophy, see Peter Barker, 'Stoic Contributions to Early Modern Science', in Osler, ed., *Atoms, Pneuma, and Tranquillity*, 135–54.

[76] We are not concerned with dualism in the Cartesian sense here, a doctrine not to be found before Plotinus at the earliest. See the succinct and conclusive discussion of the issues in Eyjólfur Kjalar Emilsson, *Plotinus on Sense-Perception: A Philosophical Study* (Cambridge, 1988), 145–8.

[77] The most perceptive discussion of naturalism remains Robert Lenoble, *Mersenne ou la naissance de la mécanique* (2nd edn, Paris, 1971), 83–167.

[78] My distinction between naturalism and corpuscularianism corresponds at least in outline to what Ralph Cudworth refers to as hylozoic atheism and atomistic atheism respectively: see *The True Intellectual System of the Universe* (2nd edn, 2 vols, London, 1743), i. 144.

to mechanical properties such as speed/velocity and size/weight (as in Beeckman), or whether they have macroscopically modelled properties such as shape, which are invoked in explaining macroscopic effects such as taste, as in traditional Epicureanism (a tradition Gassendi follows to some extent). There is also the question of whether such corpuscularian conceptions subsume the mental and the supernatural under the natural realm, that is, whether a fully reductionist corpuscularianism is being advocated. Hobbes, for example, was accused of this, and some of his followers, such as Margaret Cavendish[79], as well as the Leveller Richard Overton[80] and John Milton,[81] may have advocated a particularly strong form of reductionism, but this kind of reductionism was very rare, if it really existed at all, before the eighteenth century.[82]

In the case of naturalism properly speaking, we find parallel considerations, although the situation is more complicated. There are varieties of naturalism depending on whether the primary motivation is naturalistic Aristotelianism, Stoicism, or some form of Epicureanism, but whereas Pomponazzi and Nifo, for example, were explicitly taking their bearings from an Aristotelian understanding of natural processes,[83] the distinctions are often difficult to make, and natural philosophers such as Telesio and Bruno are far harder to characterize. Moreover, whereas a reductionist programme is rarely pressed beyond physical phenomena by corpuscularians (Descartes' account of *bêtes machines* being the most famous exception), naturalism can offer a far more plausible reductionist programme in this regard: the problem of the nature of soul being a case in point, as naturalized Aristotelianism has the resources to provide a sophisticated account of this in purely natural-philosophical terms. But the problems are compounded by the assimilation of what had been traditionally considered to be supernatural phenomena to the natural realm. The driving force behind such assimilation was the postulation of immanent

[79] Margaret Cavendish, Duchess of Newcastle, *Observations upon Experimental Philosophy to which is added The Description of a New Blazing World* (London, 1666). However, Emma Wilkins has pointed out to me that although Cavendish believed the 'corporeal soul' was material, she also believed that we have supernatural souls: she explicitly did not discuss supernatural souls in her natural philosophy on the grounds that religion and natural philosophy did not mix.

[80] Richard Overton, *Man's Mortallitie* (Amsterdam, 1643). Despite the fact that 'Amsterdam' is given as the place of publication, the work was in fact printed in London on a secret private press.

[81] See Christopher Hill, *Milton and the English Revolution* (London, 1977), chs. 25 and 26 on Milton's mortalism and materialism respectively.

[82] See John W. Yolton, *Thinking Matter: Materialism in Eighteenth-Century Britain* (Oxford, 1983). Reductionism generally implies mortalism, but not vice versa. While reductionism was a rare doctrine, mortalism of one kind of another seems to have been not uncommon in England in the sixteenth and seventeenth centuries: see Norman T. Burns, *Christian Mortalism from Tyndale to Milton* (Cambridge, Mass., 1972).

[83] The complexity of the varieties of the eclecticism among the Paduans is illustrated by the fact that, in rejecting Pomponazzi's naturalism on the soul in his *De immortalitate animae libellum* of 1518, Nifo will defend a view based on the Neoplatonist commentary on Aristotle's *De anima* traditionally ascribed to Simplicius: see Simplicius, *On Aristotle On the Soul 1.1–2.4*, trans. J. O. Urmson, notes by Peter Lautner (London, 1995).

powers or principles. Such powers and principles came in a range of strengths, as it were, starting from Aristotelian potentialities and being gradually reinforced by Stoic and Neoplatonic additions. The doctrine of the world soul was of great significance in the latter. Although there was nothing heterodox in the doctrine itself—it was a traditional doctrine, ascribed to by Augustine, for example—as an immanent principle it could be credited with a great deal of responsibility for the regulation of terrestrial events, and given the extreme transcendence of the Neoplatonic God (compared to the Christian God), it had been given a great deal to do in the regulation of natural events in writers such as Plotinus. The danger it posed to orthodoxy was that, in the hands of natural philosophers such as Telesio and Bruno, it both contracted the realm of those phenomena requiring supernatural explanation, and at the same time blurred the distinction between the natural and the supernatural.

Telesio provided the first significant version of the naturalist project with tailored resources, thereby moving from the question whether Neoplatonism or Aristotelianism can provide the resources for a thoroughgoing naturalism, to that of how we might build up the resources for a thoroughgoing naturalism from scratch.[84] The natural philosophy on which Telesio chose to ground his project proved to be influential in the late sixteenth century, not least for Bacon, but even more important was the general approach of setting one's natural-philosophical aims and then seeking the natural philosophy that best realized those aims, for it is in this way that various corpuscularian natural philosophies would be established in the seventeenth century.

Telesio offered a natural philosophy based on Presocratic and Stoic sources, stripped down to its bare essentials. In his *De rerum natura*, the first two books of which appeared in 1565,[85] he begins by eschewing any natural-philosophical assumptions, starting from sense experience. The reader is warned not to expect any philosophical subtlety from his account, for the work follows nothing, he tells us, but our observations, sense experience, and natural powers.[86] This is not a statement of empiricism in any modern sense: Telesio's account is as speculative as that of any of his Aristotelian or Platonist contemporaries. Rather, although he accuses Aristotle's system of being at variance with sensation and with scripture, I suggest we take the claim as indicating that he is not concerned to reconcile natural philosophy with Christian doctrine, via metaphysical or any other means, but will rather pursue it as an autonomous discipline—'from its own principles' (*iuxta propria principia*) as the full title of the work tells us—just as it was pursued in antiquity. Moreover, he construes natural philosophy as having a very wide purview: Telesio's default position is, in effect, that something needs a supernatural explanation only when it has been established that it cannot be explained naturally.

---

[84] Telesio's natural philosophy is discussed in detail in Martin Muslow, *Frühneuzeitliche Selbsterhaltung: Telesio und die Naturphilosophie der Renaissance* (Tübingen, 1998).

[85] *De rerum natura* was underwent constant revision through Telesio's life and appeared in three significantly different editions. The most convenient edition, and one I shall cite, is the third and final one: Bernardinus Telesio, *De Rerum Natura Iuxta Propria Principia Libri IX* (Naples, 1586: repr. with introd. by Cesare Vasoli, Hildersheim, 1971).

[86] *De rerum natura*, Prooemium.

Telesio's naturalism does away not only with Platonic dualism, but even with the residual dualism of Aristotle,[87] offering a single pair of principles, hot and cold. Just as philosophy began in the West with speculation on the basic elements or 'principles' (*archai*) of the physical world—water (Thales), air (Anaximenes), fire (Heraclitus)—so we find a return to basic elements or principles in those sixteenth-century thinkers seeking to lay new foundations for natural philosophy. Some reduce the number of fundamental elements or principles—Cardano dispenses with the element of fire for example—and some add to them—the alchemical tradition, followed by Paracelsus for example, added sulphur and mercury. What is at issue here are basic 'principles', designated by the names of common substances it is true, but it is not a matter of simply choosing common substances and designating them as elementary. Nevertheless there is some obscurity in Telesio's account as to the standing of these basic principles of hot and cold. On the one hand, they are imposed on a 'receptive nature', which is in effect a propertyless substratum, much like Aristotle's prime matter or the 'receptacle' of Plato's *Timeaus*, and so are analogous to the imposition of form on matter, but on the other hand he describes the action of heat and cold as dilating and contracting matter, which suggests that the principles vary the properties of matter rather than providing them with properties in the first place. Still, what Telesio is rejecting is clear: Aristotelian forms are supposedly already always there in matter in a potential form, but Telesio finds this incompatible with the generation and corruption of properties in matter. Whatever the exact way in which heat and cold act on matter, the principal effect is to determine their state of motion or rest, and this plays a crucial role in his cosmology, in the theory that the coldness of the earth is the cause of its immobility, whereas the great heat of the sun causes its rapid motion through the heavens.[88]

Everything is explained in terms of the contrast between hot and cold, not least sentience, which Telesio ascribes to everything in one degree or another. This is because everything strives to conserve itself and in order to do this it must be able to distinguish those things that help preserve it from those that threaten it (Book 7). The ability of things to make such distinctions is due to the fact that they possess *spiritus*, a subtle fluid with Hellenistic precedents in the Epicurean *anima* and the Stoic *pneuma*, as well as in the spirits postulated by physicians,[89] which is enclosed within the body: it is akin to Aristotelian forms except that it is a separate material substance rather than an immaterial principle. *Spiritus* is acted upon by external things and undergoes a physical change as a result, and this is how Telesio accounts for sensation,

---

[87] Just how residual is this dualism is a matter of dispute. For a very naturalistic reading of Aristotle's account of the soul, in which heat plays a central role, see Gad Freudenthal, *Aristotle's Theory of Material Substance: Heat and Pneuma, Form and Soul* (Oxford, 1995).

[88] *De rerum natura*, Book 1 chs. 1–5.

[89] The three authors that Telesio quotes at length are Aristotle, Hippocrates, and Galen, and Walker points out that Telesio 'uses medical spirits, which were traditionally hot and rarefied, and therefore, according to his own principles, especially sentient and active' (*Spiritual and Demonic Magic*, 190). See also his 'Medical Spirits in Philosophy and Theology from Ficino to Newton', in D. P. Walker, *Music, Spirit and Language in the Renaissance*, ed. Penelope Gouk (London, 1985), ch. 11.

although the only change possible in *spiritus* is expansion or contraction. At this point (Book 8), Telesio extends his discussion to the vexed question of universals and abstractive knowledge. In sensation, he maintains, *spiritus* is able to perceive things as being either the same or different, and it is able to compare these things with what is stored in the memory: similarity as perceived by the senses is, in this way, the basis of all knowledge, even geometry, and this is something we share with animals.

Telesio recognizes only one limit or exception to the explanatory power of the principles of hot and cold. Were these the only principles, he tells us (Book 5, ch. 2), we would expect human beings, like everything else in the universe, to strive only for self-preservation. But human beings are always anxiously, restlessly, looking for something beyond mere self-preservation and pleasure: they look for useless knowledge, for God, for eternity, and for this we must introduce a higher soul, which is transcendent and immortal.

There are striking parallels with Pomponazzi here. There is nothing in Pomponazzi or Telesio to suggest that their commitment to the immortality of the soul was disingenuous, advocated only because of worries about orthodoxy. The consideration of human aspirations that Telesio appeals to, and which he finds to be incompatible with a purely corporeal *spiritus*, is one that Pomponazzi would certainly have shared. And their concerns are perfectly reasonable and acceptable, so long as one thinks that an account of the nature of the mind is the relevant domain of explanation in accounting for these phenomena. It is on this last point that I think they are profoundly mistaken, and the project a doomed one. A hundred years later Spinoza will spell out a form of naturalism highly reminiscent of Telesio's, but in which a radically different kind of monism is offered, one that is able to raise questions of moral, aesthetic, religious, and other forms of intellectual aspiration in a way that does not construe the relevant question as being whether these are to be explained by something material or whether they require the postulation of an immaterial soul. But for Pomponazzi and Telesio this is precisely the question, and it is irresolvable: just as Pomponazzi, at the end of *De immortalitate*, advocates the view, reminiscent of Platonism, that the soul is the 'highest form', so Telesio finds himself obliged to go beyond *spiritus* to account for certain aspects of human behaviour.

But just as Pomponazzi, whatever his qualms about what Aristotelian natural philosophy can tell us about the human soul, pushes the claims of naturalistic explanation into realms which had previously been the preserve of religion, so Telesio, whatever his qualms about what his own monist natural philosophy can tell us about the human soul, pushes his naturalism into very contentious areas. In Book 8 of *De rerum natura*, for example, he applies his basic principles of hot and cold to moral psychology, maintaining that differences in moral character arise from differences in people's *spiritus* with respect to warmth, purity, and subtlety (chs. 35–6). In spite of Telesio's commitment to free will, he makes it clear that our passions and emotions simply reflect the changes to which our *spiritus* is exposed: moderate emotions constitute virtue because they are conducive to the conservation of *spiritus*, whereas immoderate ones correspond to harmful impulses (Book 9, ch. 3).

Pomponazzi and Telesio, in different ways, pursue the theme of the autonomy of natural philosophy, and this is in part what drives the naturalist programme, but the thinker who really brings out how radical the naturalist programme is, and how radical the claim of the autonomy of natural philosophy can be, is Bruno. Although Bruno attacks Patrizi ('pedant scum') for substituting one useless system for another and praises Telesio in his *De una causa*,[90] his programme is, in its sheer ambition, more a development of Patrizi than Telesio, taking over Patrizi's Neoplatonist holism and transforming it into a thoroughgoing pantheism. The move is the archetypical naturalist one in which the domain of natural-philosophical explanation is extended into areas traditionally thought to require divine or supernatural explanation. The distinctive feature of Bruno's account is that his extension of the scope of natural philosophy effectively means there is nothing that natural-philosophical reflection cannot explain. The charges against him laid by the Venetian and Roman Inquisitors included: heterodox views on the Trinity, the divinity of Christ and the Incarnation, on Jesus' life and death, on transubstantiation and the mass, on the virginity of Mary, on hell, on Cain and Abel, on prayer to the saints, on holy relics, and on metempsychosis; and that he asserted the eternity of the universe and the existence of a plurality of worlds similar to our own, that he asserted that the earth is animate and possesses a rational soul, that the Holy Spirit can be identified with the world soul, that human beings existed prior to Adam, that he depicted the pope as a pig in his *Cantus Ciraeus*; and that he questioned the doctrine of the immortality of the soul, and asserted that the earth moves.[91] Bruno rejected many of these charges (that of denying Mary's virginity for example) as false, and maintained that others (such as the doctrine of the Trinity) were private worries that he had not espoused publicly, but many others had a textual basis in his writings. And although Bruno had studied theology,[92] much of the basis for his arguments seems to depend on natural-philosophical questions, although his Neoplatonically inspired synthesis meshes natural-philosophical, metaphysical, and theological questions in a way that makes separation difficult, and there can be no doubt that he regarded Christianity as a corruption of an earlier undefiled religion, which he associated with Hermes Trismegistus.[93] Nevertheless, Bruno makes it clear at the beginning of his *De triplici minimo* that all philosophical questions—and this is very much an all-inclusive category—must be decided by the light of reason.[94]

---

[90] Giordano Bruno, *Cause, Principle and Unity*, trans. Richard J. Blackwell and Robert de Lucca (Cambridge, 1998), 54.

[91] See Luigi Firpi, *Il processo di Giordano Bruno* (Rome, 1993) and Maurice A. Finocchiaro, 'Philosophy versus Religion and Science versus Religion: The Trials of Bruno and Galileo', in Hilary Gatti, ed., *Giordano Bruno: Philosopher of the Renaissance* (Aldershot, 2002), 51–96. The case of Campanella has many parallels to that of Bruno: see John M. Headley, *Tommaso Campanella and the Transformation of the World* (Princeton, 1997).

[92] On Bruno's education see Ingrid Rowland, 'Giordano Bruno and Neapolitan Neoplatonism', in Hilary Gatti, ed., *Giordano Bruno: Philosopher of the Renaissance* (Aldershot, 2002), 97–119.

[93] These aspects of Bruno's thought are dealt with in Yates, *Giordano Bruno and the Hermetic Tradition*.

[94] Giordano Bruno, *De triplici minimo* (Frankfurt, 1591), Book 1, ch. 1.

Bruno had a great interest in Lull, and it was for his development of Lull's 'art of memory' that he initially gained fame.[95] His interest in the causes of religious wars led him to investigate the origin of theological disputes, and like Lull before him, to offer something that would put an end to them. Whereas Lull offered something that was designed to secure Christian orthodoxy, however, Bruno's holistic, animistic, magical, and pantheist metaphysics effectively lost contact with Christianity from an early stage. Bruno's holism derived from a core thesis of his metaphysics, namely that substance is both unitary and divine. He set out the essentials of this doctrine in *De la causa* in these terms:

Have we not seen that the Peripatetics, like the Platonists, divide substance by the specific difference of corporeal and incorporeal? Just as these specific differences are reduced to the potency of a single genus, so the forms must be of two kinds: some are transcendent, that is, higher than genus, and are called principles, such as 'entity', 'unity', 'one', 'thing', 'something', and their like; other forms belong to a given insofar as it is distinct from another genus, such as 'substantiality' and 'accidentality'. The forms of the first sort do not distinguish matter or make matter here one thing, there another, but, as absolutely universal terms embracing corporeal as well as incorporeal substances, they signify the absolutely universal, absolutely common and undivided matter of both. . . . Again, if everything that exists (beginning with the supreme and sovereign being) possesses a certain order and constitutes a hierarchy, a ladder where one climbs from the composite to the simple things, and from those to the most simple and absolute things, by means of proportional and copulative middle terms which participate in the nature of the one and the other extreme, yet possess their own, independent value, there is no order which does not involve a certain participation, nor participation which does not involve a certain union, nor union which does not involve a certain participation. It is therefore necessary that there be a single principle of subsistence for all existing things.[96]

Bruno draws both metaphysical and cosmological conclusions from his conception of substance. Metaphysically, he conceives of God as being included in the infinite unitary substance that makes up the totality of things—'the universe is in none and all of its parts, which occasions an excellent contemplation of divinity'[97]—and an internal world soul drives changes in this substance so that we have something more like an internally generated unfolding of events rather than a universe in which independent things interact. Indeed, the world soul is best thought of as an underlying active principle in accord with which things in the universe act, and here it is part of Bruno's polemic against Aristotle that we have to distinguish real changes, which occur as a result of this action, from merely superficial changes in the forms of individual things.

God does not transcend his creation on this picture, if indeed one can speak of creation at all, since he does not create *ex nihilo*—matter is simply absolute possibility or potency, and is coeternal with God, who has to realize himself through his action in

---

[95] On Bruno's art of memory see Frances A. Yates, *The Art of Memory* (London, 1978), chs. 9–14; and Stephen Clucas, '*Simulacra et Signacula*: Memory, Magic and Metaphysics in Brunian Mnemonics', in Hilary Gatti, ed., *Giordano Bruno: Philosophy of the Renaissance* (Aldershot, 2002), 273–97. Bruno's publications on this question came later in his career.

[96] Giordano Bruno, *De la causa, principio et uno* (London, 1584) translated in Bruno, *Cause, Principle and Unity*, 74–5.

[97] *Cause, Principle and Unity*, 8.

the world. One of the issues that was made clear in Bruno's trial for heresy was that he believed that God needs the material world just as much as it needs him.[98] No mediation, and hence no Christology, was necessary in Bruno's theology. Indeed, in his *Eroici furori*, contemplation of the divine explicitly takes place through the medium of contemplation of nature. This is a view reinforced in his cosmology,[99] which does away with any residual notion of the empyrean, and thus any physical location where God and the blessed might exist. In *La cena de le Ceneri*, the philosopher is led on a journey across the heavens only to discover not only that there are no such things as the crystalline orbs, but that there is no end to the journey as we begin to traverse infinite space. Not only are there other universes or worlds, but each of them is infused with divinity, just as ours is.

After Bruno, the naturalist tradition collapsed in natural philosophy, not so much because of the dreadful death inflicted upon him by the Roman Inquisition in 1600, but because he cut natural philosophy loose from virtually all its traditional bearings, while offering little more than promissory notes, especially when compared to the newly developing 'physico-mathematical' and corpuscularian movements. His defence of the earth's diurnal motion, for example, was simply that it rotates on its axis in order to partake of the sun's light and heat, and it revolves around the sun so that it can partake in the seasons.[100] This hardly engaged the natural-philosophical or astronomical issues seriously, and could not possibly have furthered the cause of Copernicanism. The threat that Bruno posed lay not in his Copernicanism but the way in which his naturalism was able to generate or support just about every conceivable heterodoxy. In his 800-page attack on naturalists and others, *L'Impiété des Déistes, Athées et Libertins de ce Temps*, Mersenne considered Bruno to be 'the most dangerous thinker of deists, atheists or free-thinkers', and singled him out for attack, along with Cardano and Charron.[101] The core error of naturalism, on Mersenne's view, is that it blurs the distinction between the natural and the supernatural.[102]

---

[98]  See Angelo Mercati, *Il Sommario de processo di G. Bruno* (Vatican City, 1942), 79.

[99]  Bruno's cosmology is developed primarily in his *La cena de le Ceneri* (London, 1584)—translated as *The Ash Wednesday Supper*, trans. S. Jaki (The Hague, 1975)—and *De l'infinito universo et mondi* (London, 1585)—translated in Dorothea Waley Singer, *Giordano Bruno, His Life and Thought: With Annotated Translation of his Work, On Infinite Universe and Worlds* (New York, 1968). *La cena* presents a critical account of Ptolemaic and Aristotelian cosmology, presenting Copernicanism as an alternative and then revising the Copernican account to establish the infinity of the world, while *De l'infinito* pursues much the same ends by means of a detailed refutation of Aristotle's *De caelo*.

[100]  See Finocchiaro, 'Philosophy versus Religion', 80.

[101]  Marin Mersenne, *L'Impiete des Deistes, Athees et Libertins de ce temps, combatuë, & renuersee de point en point par raisons tirees de la Philosophie, & de la Theologie* (Paris, 1624). See Lenoble, *Mersenne*, 259–64; and more generally Keith Hutchison, 'Supernaturalism and the Mechanical Philosophy', *History of Science* 21 (1983), 297–333.

[102]  These questions are dealt with in his *Quaestiones celeberrimae in Genesim* (Paris, 1623) as well as in *L'Impiete des Deistes*. They are also pursued in François Garasse, *La Doctrine curieuse des beaux esprits de ce temps, ou prétendus tels* (2 vols., Paris, 1623), i. 1–98. An earlier criticism of naturalism along the lines that it ascribes to nature qualities that can only be divine can be found in Laurent Pollot, *Dialogues contre la pluralité des religions et l'athéism* (La Rochelle, 1595), 104v-118v. Later in the seventeenth century, Henry More will offer the same kind of diagnosis of 'enthusiasm', as being

This can result either in a tendency to deny the very existence of the supernatural, as in naturalism proper, or to mistake the natural for the supernatural, as in theories of natural magic. In both cases, the root problem derives from a tendency to see nature as being full of all kinds of powers, and in both cases it results in the truly supernatural being effectively left out of the picture. Naturalism, broadly defined, is the doctrine that the truly supernatural (God alone) does not need to be invoked to explain a whole range of events in which it was traditionally thought to be required. Whether the explanations offered in place of traditional ones are naturalistic or quasi-supernatural was not the key issue for Mersenne: the key issue was the exclusion of the (genuinely) supernatural. This was the characteristic feature of naturalism for him, and it was this that made it a threat to established religion, and hence something to be opposed as strongly as possible.

## LATE SCHOLASTICISM

One of the effects of the failure to reconcile the Eastern and Western Churches in the mid-fifteenth century was a revival of Thomism, which quickly became established as the official philosophy of the Western Church. In this climate, the Neoplatonic revival, which had taken its initial inspiration from thinkers of the Greek Orthodox Church, was not the default position, despite its greater closeness to the Augustinian philosophy that lay at the core of Christian theology. Neoplatonism did raise a number of difficulties for Thomism, however. One particularly pressing difficulty, as we have seen, was the doctrine of personal immortality. Ficino had offered an account of this designed to show how it followed from the fundamental principles of his Neoplatonic metaphysics. Aristotle, by contrast, had offered a naturalistic account of the 'soul' in the first two books of *De anima*, and one more (but not wholly) consonant with Christian teaching in the *Metaphysics* and the third book of *De anima*, and there was dispute among Aristotelians on what the philosophically defensible and consistent position is on what happens to the soul upon the death and corruption of the body. One view, associated with Alexander of Aphrodisias, was that since the soul is defined by Aristotle functionally, as the organizing principle of the body, without the body there can be no soul, so the soul cannot enjoy immortality. Another was the view associated with Averroes, that the soul is not subject to corruption so cannot perish, but it cannot be individuated in separation from the body—it no longer has the sensations, memories, affective states, etc. that make it *my* soul—so, in a disembodied state, we can only talk of one soul or one mind, and this is identical with God, in so far as we conceive of God to be a purely spiritual entity. In other words, we have immortality, but not personal immortality. In contrast with both of these, we have what was by this stage—that is, from the middle of the fifteenth century onwards—the orthodox Thomist position, that the soul is the form of the body and that it enjoys personal immortality.

---

caused by the failure of Aristotelians to distinguish between material and immaterial substances: *Observations on Anthroposophia Theomagica and Anima Magica Abscondita* ([London], 1650), 7–8, and *Enthusiasmus Triumphatus* (London, 1656), 48–9.

In other words, Aristotelian natural philosophy gave no decisive guidance on this question, which is why the Thomist project of devising a metaphysics that could resolve and unify the differing considerations was needed. And this was indeed the thrust of the Fifth Lateran Council's instruction to philosophers and theologians, as we have seen. But for the opponents of scholasticism, the metaphysics was needed only because of an inherent fragmentation in Christianized Aristotelianism, a fragmentation which they believed reflected a deep flaw in the whole project of Christianized Aristotelianism. It must be remembered that competing philosophies—which by the sixteenth century included not just Neoplatonism but also philosophies based upon Stoicism and Epicureanism—each constituted a total world-view, however philosophically impoverished these world-views might have been by the standards of Aristotelianism. In the case where world-views were at stake, a clear internal consistency, constrained by a clear internal hierarchy, was of very great significance. Fragmentation was a high price to pay for the great philosophical subtlety and depth that was characteristic of scholastic Aristotelianism in comparison with its competitors.

Late scholasticism offered a concerted response to this problem. The late scholastic textbooks are a bastion of orthodoxy, and we can identify three phases in the movement. The 'first wave' of this textbook tradition, beginning in the work of Francisco Toletus in the 1560s and culminating in the Coimbra commentaries later in the century,[103] was by and large Thomist, at least on the issues that bore crucially on the relation between theology, metaphysics, and natural philosophy, although there are significant elements of Scotism in key commentators such as Suárez. It comprises primarily the textbooks of the Jesuit commentators based at Coimbra, the Jesuit commentators based at the Collegio Romano, and Antonio Rubius, who compiled textbooks both during his twenty-five years in Mexico and then at the Jesuit College at Alcalá. These were the three main sources of Jesuit textbooks in the late sixteenth and early seventeenth centuries, and it is from these that Descartes, for example, learned his philosophy.[104] The second wave of textbooks—such as the *Corps de Philosophie* (1603–10) of Scipion Dupleix, the *Summa philosophiae* (1610) of Eustachius a Sancto Paulo, and the *Totius philosophiae* (1629) of Abra de Raconis—while following the Coimbra commentaries, often to the point of *verbatim* repetition, nevertheless differ from them in a number of crucial respects, and by 1630 had displaced them. They are no longer commentaries on Aristotle but condensations of his thought, which is quite a radical shift of genre.[105] Moreover these condensations laid a far greater emphasis on natural philosophy than the older

---

[103] Confining our attention to commentaries on natural-philosophical texts, the *Parva naturalia*, the *Meteorology*, the *De anima*, the *Physics*, and the *De caelo* commentaries appeared between 1692 and 1698. On these commentaries see Dennis Des Chene, *Physiologia: Natural Philosophy in Late Aristotelian and Cartesian Thought* (Ithaca, NY, 1996). Note that these commentaries occasionally took an independent route, without offering a systematic interpretation of the text of Aristotle.

[104] See Gaukroger, *Descartes, An Intellectual Biography*, ch. 2.

[105] See Laurence W. B. Brockliss, 'Rapports de structure et de contenu entre les *Principia* et les cours de philosophie des collèges', in Jean-Robert Armogathe and Giulia Belgioioso, eds, *Descartes: Principia Philosophiae, 1644–1994* (Naples, 1996), 491–516.

commentaries had done.[106] It is also of interest that they are less orthodox, and on the crucial question of our knowledge of God all follow the transcendentalist doctrine of Scotus.[107] Finally, there was a third wave of textbooks, which took the form of a conservative reaction to the Jesuit textbooks, but it was a retreat into dogmatism and, philosophically speaking, an admission of failure, and it never had any impact outside Catholic clerical circles.[108]

The explicit aim of the first wave textbooks was the systematic reconstruction of Aristotle's metaphysics and natural philosophy from first principles, rearranging material in Aristotle as necessary.[109] It should be noted that, despite their general advocacy of Thomism, not only did these commentaries set out to supplant Aquinas but in many ways they were meant to supplant Aristotle as well.[110] They recast the whole Aristotelian tradition with two main aims: to show how the truths of a Christianized Aristotelianism could be derived from first principles, and to show how this was a single, coherent, comprehensive system. The project traded on a traditional feature of Aristotelianism, whereby understanding ultimately took the form of *scientia*. Research or discovery was not part of *scientia* as such, as we have already seen, but rather a prerequisite for *scientia*, which was constituted by the derivation of true and certain conclusions from first principles that were both evident and indemonstrable: that is, neither in need of, nor capable of, further demonstration. *Scientia* is built up and consolidated as more and more conclusions are drawn from the basic principles, and the ultimate aim is a wholly exhaustive and encyclopedic account of theoretical knowledge, that is, knowledge concerned with understanding how things are and why they are as they are.[111]

---

[106] See Charles B. Schmitt, 'The Rise of the Philosophical Textbook', in Charles B. Schmitt, Quentin Skinner, and Eckhard Kessler, eds, *The Cambridge History of Renaissance Philosophy* (Cambridge, 1988), 792–804: 803.

[107] See Roger Ariew, *Descartes and the Last Scholastics* (Ithaca, NY, 1999), ch. 2.

[108] This third wave comprises the ultra-Thomist commentaries of the Complutenses, based at the Philosophical College of the Discalced Carmelites at Alcalá (Lat. *complutum*), and Salmanticenses, based at the Theological College at Salamanca. The Complutenses commentaries began with the logic commentary of Diego de Jesus, which was first published in 1608, and they appeared in a definitive five-volume version in 1670. Although they dealt with natural-philosophical questions, they seem to have had no influence on natural-philosophical disputes outside Catholic clerical circles. The Salamancan commentaries, which began to appear in 1630, were primarily concerned with theology rather than natural philosophy, and similarly had no impact outside Catholic clerical circles, where they formed the epitome of orthodoxy.

[109] See the discussion in Charles H. Lohr, 'The Sixteenth Century Transformation of the Aristotelian Division of the Speculative Sciences', in D. Kelley and R. Popkin, eds, *The Shapes of Knowledge from the Renaissance to the Enlightenment* (Dordrecht, 1991), 49–58; and idem, 'Jesuit Aristotelianism and Sixteenth-Century Metaphysics', in G. Fletcher and M. B. Scheute, eds, *Paradosis* (New York, 1976), 203–20. See also Thorndike, *A History of Magic*, vii. 372–425.

[110] See Joaquim F. Gomez, 'Pedro da Fonseca: Sixteenth Century Portuguese Philosopher', *International Philosophical Quarterly* 6 (1966), 632–44: 633–4. The later Carmelite Complutenses commentaries set out to reverse this trend.

[111] There is a good account of these questions in Lohr, 'Metaphysics and Natural Philosophy'. See also L. W. B. Brockliss, 'The Scientific Revolution in France', in Roy Porter and Mikulas Teich, eds, *The Scientific Revolution in National Context* (Cambridge, 1992), 55–89: 56–7.

The encyclopedic *scientia* approach set out to meet the requirements of a unified system, something lacking in later scholasticism when compared with Neoplatonism. But in attempting to do this, it failed in a different respect, a respect in which it had previously manifested great strengths. For with systematization came a closing-off of scholasticism to new developments within natural philosophy. The Neoplatonist systems had willingly sacrificed innovation in natural philosophy for an overall hierarchical coherence, above all because, with Ficino, such a coherence had secured and, indeed, guaranteed personal immortality for the soul, an area where Aristotelian natural philosophy had failed to deliver. Neoplatonists had denied any legitimacy to independent natural-philosophical investigation: natural philosophy was ultimately an outcome of the metaphysics that generated an understanding of every aspect of the cosmos, and it was at best a matter of detail. Sixteenth- and early seventeenth-century scholastics were not quite so ambitious, or reckless: for them, the point of the exercise was to show how Aristotelian natural philosophy and a Christian philosophical theology could be reconciled, in the process throwing new light on both domains. What the controversies over natural philosophy, and particularly over the immortality of the soul, had shown them was that they needed a tighter, more systematic framework within which to achieve these.

Among the problems they encountered in attempting to realize this project, there are two to which I want to draw attention. The first is that the natural philosophy that they were trying to reconcile was no longer something generated internally within scholasticism but increasingly from outside. The second is that the project of reconciliation depended on a Thomist understanding of metaphysics as a bridge between natural philosophy and a Christian philosophical theology, but the Thomist conception was intrinsically problematic, and the late scholastic textbooks in fact move closer and closer to a Scotist conception of metaphysics, which made it completely inappropriate as an instrument of reconciliation.

Up to the sixteenth century, natural philosophy, no matter how unorthodox, had been pursued largely within the confines of scholasticism by scholastics who, whatever qualms they may have had about the details, or even some of the basic assumptions, of Aristotle's natural philosophy, pursued their project within the broadly Aristotelian framework of the kind developed in the thirteenth century. This changed in the course of the sixteenth century, as natural-philosophical developments increasingly fell outside its own control. It was these developments that scholasticism had to reconcile with its Christian philosophical theology, but they were increasingly unable to do this. It is true that not all questions were of this kind, and indeed the most pressing questions identified by the Fifth Lateran Council—the immortality of the soul, the unity of the intellect, and free will—were dealt with in a way that integrated the different kinds of consideration into an amalgam of some philosophical sophistication.[112] But these were areas where the issues were settled in the sense that there was agreement on what exactly had to be established and why it mattered. Once one moved outside this area of consensus, severe problems arose.

---

[112] See Dennis Des Chene, *Life's Form: Late Aristotelian Conceptions of the Soul* (Ithaca, NY, 2000).

The most problematic such area was cosmology, and a particularly pressing question was that of the cause of the rotation of the heavens: were celestial bodies attached to crystalline orbs, or did they move through some kind of fluid matter, an ether? The question turned out to be far from straightforward, however, raising the complex issue of just what had to be reconciled with what in dealing with these kinds of issue. Three potential areas of relevance were: astronomical observations of the motions of celestial bodies, a physical or cosmological theory of the nature of the celestial regions, and revelation. Each of these was problematic. Indeed, even the question of whether reconciliation was needed in the first place was contentious.

The immediate upshot of the defences of heliocentrism by Copernicus and Rheticus was not an upsurge of interest in the natural-philosophical consequences of astronomical systems but a move in the opposite direction, a stress on the autonomy of mathematical models in saving the phenomena.[113] This was reinforced by a view developed in the early sixteenth century by Jacopo Zabarella and Archangelus Mercenarius. In itself the view—that celestial matter and form were completely unlike their terrestrial counter parts—might seem innocuous enough, having been held by Aquinas for example, but Zabarella and Mercanarius were from the Averroist stronghold of Padua, and the distinction between terrestrial and celestial matter in effect rules out any understanding of the cosmos based on natural philosophy, which depends on, and derives from, observation of terrestrial events.[114] The view was developed further by Benito Pereira, a colleague of Clavius at the Collegio Romano. Pereira's most influential and popular work was a commentary on Genesis,[115] which exemplifies the kind of theological cosmogony that concerned him most. Because we have no knowledge of the nature of celestial matter, he argues, astronomers are obliged to employ what he considers to be physical absurdities, such as epicycles and eccentrics. Here mathematical astronomy becomes something like an especially impoverished form of natural philosophy, something not concerned with truth, except that instead of assessing opinions on the strength of arguments, as natural philosophy does, the astronomer is engaged simply in the exercise of how best to save the appearances.[116]

This approach was consonant with Aristotle's view of the relation between physical and mathematical enquiry, even if he would not have drawn exactly the same

---

[113] See Nicholas Jardine, 'The Significance of the Celestial Orbs,' *Journal of the History of Astronomy* 13 (1982), 168–94.

[114] Cf. Giovanni Pontano: 'If we seek in heaven things which relate to our eyes and ears, why should we not then seek what relates to our noses'. *De rebus coelestibus libri XIIII* (Basle, 1556), 2113. Cited in Jardine, *The Birth of History and Philosophy of Science*, 233: see the discussion there.

[115] Benedictus Pereira, *Prior tomus Commentariorum et Disputationem in Genesim* (Lyon, 1590).

[116] Peter Barker and Bernard Goldstein, in their 'Realism and Instrumentalism in Sixteenth-Century Astronomy: A Reappraisal', *Perspectives on Science* 6 (1998), 232–58, argue that no sixteenth-century writers on astronomy have a fictionalist reading of astronomy: they simply hold that causal knowledge is an ideal which is unattainable. If for 'writers on astronomy' we substitute 'astronomers', Barker and Goldstein are right. But scholastic critics of astronomy, such as Pereira, *do* seem to think that astronomy is simply not in the game of providing causal explanations.

conclusions from it. The traditional rationale of astronomy was the construction of tables for the purpose of calculating the positions of celestial objects. It was a mathematical discipline and on the dominant Aristotelian way of thinking about mathematical disciplines, it allowed deduction of the positions of the planets from purely mathematical considerations, rather than from the physical constitution of the planets or the nature of the orb or fluid or internal motive force by which they moved. On such a conception, there is a stark contrast between a mathematical understanding of motion and a physical understanding, and the one cannot be used to elucidate the other. The clearest presentation of this issue is given in Pereira, who sets out six differences between natural philosophy and mathematical astronomy.[117] The first two identify areas central to natural philosophy which are of no concern to astronomers. Natural philosophy attempts to discover the nature of the substance of celestial bodies—whether it comprises some combination of the four elements, for example, or whether celestial bodies are made up from a fifth kind of matter—and it seeks the various kinds of causes of their motion, the function of the celestial realm, and so on. The third area of difference concerns the 'accidents' of the celestial realm. Astronomers confine their attention to size, shape, and motion, whereas the natural philosopher deals with the full range of accidents, and understands them in terms of the nature of the heavens, in terms of its substance, what role the motions of celestial bodies play, and how they are related to sensation. Fourth, the astronomer, unlike the natural philosopher, is not concerned to establish the true causes of things, which derive from the natures of those things, but with causes that are merely sufficient for saving the phenomena. Fifth, in natural philosophy one will generally demonstrate celestial phenomena a priori, whereas the astronomer will only demonstrate them a posteriori. Finally, the natural philosopher will explain a property of the cosmos by deriving it from its nature, whereas the astronomer will simply provide a mathematical characterization. The natural philosopher will explain the spherical shape of the cosmos, for example, by saying that it is neither heavy nor light but is designed to be moved in an orb, whereas the astronomer will say that it is round because every part of it is equidistant from its centre, the earth.

Because, on this conception, astronomical hypotheses are designed to reconcile sets of observations, not to reveal the structure of the cosmos, there is no impediment to using such hypotheses even in cases where one believes that the literal physical interpretation of the hypothesis is false. So, for example, tables based on Copernicus' *De revolutionibus* came into general use from 1551 with the appearance of the *Prutenic Tables*, but the attraction of *De revolutionibus* was that it was believed to offer a simpler and more accurate means of calculation in many respects, not because it was thought to provide a physically accurate account of the motions of celestial bodies: Rheticus was the only astronomer we know of, other than Copernicus himself, who

---

[117] Pereira, *De communibus omnium rerum naturalium principiis et affectionibus* (Rome, 1576), 47D–48B. Note that Pereira refers to 'astrologers', but in fact he is concerned with mathematical astronomy. See also William H. Donahue, *The Dissolution of the Celestial Spheres* (New York, 1981), 28–30.

believed that the Copernican system actually represented the physical structure of the cosmos before the 1580s.[118]

The trouble was that physical questions could not be divorced from astronomical ones so easily, because the latter always contain some assumptions about physical structure. For example, Copernicus was a staunch advocate of the rigidity and impenetrability of celestial orbs, which was the default position throughout the first two-thirds of the sixteenth century.[119] The attempt to make physical sense out of the Ptolemaic model had begun with Alhazen in the eleventh century, who set out a system of concentric orbs and shells, and attempted to assign a single spherical motion to each of Ptolemy's simple motions, ultimately concluding that Ptolemy's equants failed to satisfy the requirement of uniform circular motion.[120] His treatise 'on the configuration of the world', the only one of his works that reached the West, appeared in a Latin version in the early fourteenth century, and it was a major influence on the most important fifteenth-century textbook on astronomy, Peurbach's *Theoricae novae planetarum*, first printed in 1475. Peurbach followed Alhazen in trying to offer a separate celestial orb for each component of Ptolemy's planetary motions, and by contrast with Ptolemy's *Almagest*, his illustrations are not geometrical diagrams but representations of three-dimensional solid orbs with concentric inner and outer surfaces, but whose thickness varies from point to point representing the epicycles and eccentric orbits of the sun and the planets around the earth (see Fig. 3.1). The compromise offered in the *Theoricae* between the mathematical requirements of Ptolemaic observational astronomy and the physical requirements of Aristotelian cosmology quickly became the standard physical interpretation of Ptolemaic astronomy, and it was from Peurbach's textbook, not from Ptolemy's *Almagest*, that Copernicus first learned his astronomy. Peurbach's solid illustrations made it clear to Copernicus that Ptolemy's equants required rotation around an off-centre axis, and he considered this to be something that was physically impossible if the orbs were indeed rigid.[121] Eliminating equants meant he had to look for an

[118] Robert S. Westman, 'The Astronomer's Role in the Sixteenth Century: A Preliminary Study', *History of Science* 18 (1980), 105–47, finds only ten natural philosophers in the whole of Europe prepared to accept the physical reality of the heliocentric model in 1600: Digges and Harriot in England, Bruno and Galileo in Italy, Zúñiga in Spain, Stevin in the Netherlands, and Maestlin, Rothmann, and Kepler in Germany. Zúñiga, as we shall see below, should not in fact be included in this list. See also Robert S. Westman, 'The Melanchthon Circle, Rheticus, and the Wittenberg Interpretation of the Copernican Theory', *Isis* 66 (1975), 165–93; idem, 'The Comet and the Cosmos: Kepler, Mästlin and the Copernican Hypothesis', *Studia Copernicana* 5 (1972), 7–30; Jardine, 'The Significance of the Celestial Orbs'; and Thorndike, *History of Magic*, vi. ch. 31.

[119] The situation changed as the century progressed and by the end of the sixteenth century there was a strong view in favour of fluid heavens: see William H. Donahue, 'The Solid Planetary Spheres in Post-Copernican Natural Philosophy', in Robert S. Westman, ed., *The Copernican Achievement* (Berkeley, 1975), 244–75.

[120] See Owen Gingerich, 'Islamic Astronomy', in idem, *The Great Copernicus Chase and Other Adventures in Astronomical History* (Cambridge, 1992), 43–56.

[121] See Noel M. Swerdlow, '*Pseudodoxia Copernicana*: Or, Enquiries into Very Many Received Tenets and Commonly Presumed Truths, Mostly Concerning Spheres', *Archives internationales d'histoire des sciences* 26 (1976), 108–58.

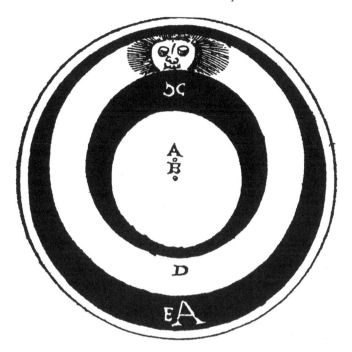

**Figure 3.1**

alternative mechanism, and substituting epicycles for equants pointed him in the direction of a system in which the sun, rather than the earth, was at the centre.[122]

Copernicus was certainly not the only person to reject Ptolemaic astronomy on physical grounds. A rather different—and, for most of the sixteenth century, much more prominent—approach followed that which had been pursued four centuries earlier by Averroes, who had offered a very influential rebuttal of the Ptolemaic system in his commentary on the *Metaphysics*:

The astronomer must, therefore, construct an astronomical system such that the celestial motions are yielded by it and that nothing that is from the standpoint of physics impossible is implied.... Ptolemy was unable to see astronomy on its true foundations.... The epicycle and the eccentric are impossible. We must, therefore, apply ourselves to a new investigation concerning that genuine astronomy whose foundations are principles of physics.... Actually, in our time astronomy is nonexistent; what we have is something that fits calculation but does not agree with what is.[123]

---

[122] See Noel M. Swerdlow, 'The Derivation and First Draft of Copernicus' Planetary Theory: A Translation of the *Commentariolus* with Commentary,' *Proceedings of the American Philosophical Society* 117 (1973), 423–512.

[123] Averroes, *Metaphysics*, Bv. 12, summae secundae ch. 4, comm. 45. Quoted in Pierre Duhem, *To Save the Phenomena* (Chicago, 1969), 31.

Averroes had hoped to complete this study himself,[124] but it was left to his contemporary Alpetragius, with whom he had shared a teacher (Ibn-Tofail), to carry it out. The cosmology Alpetragius took up is one in which the earth lies in the middle of a system of orbs all of whose orbits are centred upon the earth. In this homocentric system, all the planets have regular circular orbits in the same direction. It was realized at an early stage in the development of astronomy that such an account did not fit the observational data: at the most elementary level, for example, the nearer planets varied in brightness in a continuous and systematic way, indicating that they were approaching or receding from the earth during at least part of their motion.[125] Ptolemy tried to resolve the complexities of the observational data, while reconciling these with a geocentric universe, by abandoning concentric orbs and introducing epicycles and movable eccentrics. This approach allowed the data to be accounted for, but had no obvious natural-philosophical rationale: it had an air of merely 'saving the appearances', accounting for the different lengths of the seasons, for example, by making the sun's orbit eccentric, so that it now revolved not around the earth but around a point at some mathematically convenient distance from the earth.[126]

It was largely in response to such considerations that Alpetragius revived the homocentric theory, rejecting the independent movement of planets from east to west that had characterized Ptolemy's account. He realized that the theory had to be modified—for example to account for the fact that the poles of the ecliptic differed from the celestial poles, and for the fact of the variable velocities of the planets in longitude—and to do this he suggested that the poles of each planet describe small circles around their mean positions in each period of the planet, and he altered the accepted positions of the planets, putting Venus between Mars and the sun. The theory proved inadequate to account for the observational data: it could offer no convincing account of retrograde arcs, for example. But despite its inadequacies, it had an obvious natural-philosophical rationale: the earth was at the centre of the cosmos and the planets, stars, and the firmament revolved around it. This firmament consisted of nine concentric orbs placed around the earth at the centre, all moving in the same direction, and carrying the moon, the planets, and the sun, the fixed stars, with the outermost orb, which was the single 'prime mover', completing its own motion from east to west in just under one sidereal day. Although it carries the other orbs around with it, there is a lag in the motion of each orb, increased as one moves inwards from the prime mover, and there is also an increased deviation from a circular orbit as one moves inwards, with inner planets moving in what are effectively spirals. A number of

[124] See F. J. Carmody, 'The Planetary Theory of Ibn-Rushd', *Osiris* 10 (1952), 556–86.

[125] See D. Hargreave, 'Reconstructing the Planetary Motions of the Eudoxian System,' *Scripta Mathematica* 28 (1970), 335–45.

[126] Note that Ptolemy's arguments 'that the earth is in the middle of the heavens' at 1. 5 of the *Almagest*, are distinctive in that, in contrast to those of Aristotle and others, they offer no physical grounds for the centrality of the earth but exclusively astronomical arguments. Indeed, whereas for Aristotle it is crucial that the earth be literally at the physical centre of the cosmos, for Ptolemy all that matters is that the earth be at the centre 'with regard to the senses': its position can be approximate. See Liba Chaia Taub, *Ptolemy's Universe: The Natural Philosophical and Ethical Foundations of Ptolemy's Astronomy* (Chicago, 1993), 71–9.

medieval Christian thinkers, such as Albertus Magnus and Aquinas, who were either non-committal or rejected concentric orbs,[127] considered it seriously at one time or another, if only subsequently to reject it. There seems to have been a widespread sense that there was something artificial about the Ptolemaic system, and Alpetragius came closest to providing a physically satisfying geocentric model. The homocentric model underwent a revival in the early sixteenth century in the works of the Paduan natural philosophers Fracastoro and Amico, who, following Averroes, regarded the Ptolemaic system as unnatural.[128]

Copernicanism received similar treatment. Although many responses, from Peucer's *Elementa doctrinae de circulis coelestibus* (1551) to the 1633 condemnation of Galileo by the Roman Inquisition, offer a combination of biblical and natural-philosophical reasons for the unacceptability of the Copernican model as a physically true representation,[129] there were responses that focused on whether or not Copernicanism might be reconciled with Christianized Aristotelian natural philosophy. In the wake of the Inquisition's condemnation of Galileo in 1633 for example, one of the standard responses to Copernicanism in Iberian countries was to attempt to reformulate Copernicanism in terms of an Aristotelian natural philosophy, that is, within the confines of an Aristotelian theory of matter, thereby

---

[127] Aquinas, for example, was non-committal in *De trinitate* and rejected concentric orbs in his *Commentary on the Metaphysics*: see Grant, *Planets*, 281.

[128] Girolamo Fracastoro, *Homocentrica: Sive de Stellis* (Venice, 1538); Giovanni Battista Amico, *De Motibus corporum coelestium iuxta principia peripatetica sine eccentris et epicyclis* (Venice, 1536). On the sixteenth-century revival of the homocentric thesis, see Lattis, *Between Copernicus and Galileo*, 87–94.

[129] On the nature of the disputes over Copernicanism as they bore on Galileo's condemnation, see Robert S. Westman, 'The Copernicans and the Churches', and William R. Shea, 'Galileo and the Church', both in David C. Lindberg and Ronald L. Numbers, eds., *God and Nature: Historical Essays on the Encounter between Christianity and Science* (Berkeley, 1986), 76–113 and 114–35 respectively; and Olaf Pedersen, 'Galileo and the Council of Trent: The Galileo Affair Revisited', *Journal for the History of Astronomy* 14 (1983), 1–29. Although things changed very significantly in the course of the seventeenth century, it is worth noting that complete acceptance of Copernicanism took much longer, usually (but not always due) to religious factors. This reluctance to accept heliocentrism was prevalent in, but not restricted to, Catholic countries such as Spain, where resistance to Copernicanism continued at least up to the end of the eighteenth century (see David Goodman, 'Iberian Science: Navigation, Empire and Counter-Reformation', in David Goodman and Colin A. Russell, eds, *The Rise of Scientific Europe, 1500–1800* (London, 1991), 117–44: 143). As regards Protestant countries, there are late seventeenth- and early eighteenth-century English works that treat Copernicanism as a passing fad: John Edwards, *Brief Remarks upon Mr. Whiston's New Theory of the Earth* (London, 1697), 23–6, and Edward Howard, *Remarks on the New Philosophy of Descartes* (London, 1700), 207. Moreover, Blumenberg points out that Copernicanism was not accepted as being beyond dispute in Germany until 1760 (*The Genesis of the Copernican World* (Cambridge, Mass., 1987), 357). And as far as Orthodox countries were concerned, 'modern' natural philosophy replaced Aristotelianism only in the 1870s in Kiev; and in Greece we find a teacher being condemned for teaching the heliocentric theory in 1804 (Colin Chant, 'Science in Orthodox Europe', in David Goodman and Colin A. Russell, eds, *The Rise of Scientific Europe, 1500–1800* (London, 1991), 333–60: 355). For documents relating the conflict between astronomical theories generally and Scripture, there is a comprehensive collection in Pierre-Noël Mayaud, *Le Conflit entre l'Astronomie Nouvelle et l'Écriture Sainte aux XVIe et XVIIe siècles* (5 vols, Paris, 2005).

establishing its legitimacy as a physical theory in an orthodox way.[130] One of the earliest investigations along these lines had been that of the Spanish Augustinian friar Diego de Zúñiga, but it had been unsuccessful.[131] In his *Commentary on Job* of 1584, Zúñiga had argued the theological credentials of Copernicanism, namely that Holy Writ, if correctly interpreted, did not deny the assertion of Solomon in the *Ecclesiastics* that 'the earth is fixed forever'. What this means, he argued, is that the earth is always the same, and not that it does not move at all, and he adds that Copernicus' hypothesis gives a better account of planetary motions than any of its competitors. But thirteen years later, in his *Philosophiae prima pars*, Zúñiga offered a purely natural-philosophical examination of Copernicanism, failing to reconcile it with Aristotelian natural philosophy and concluding that Copernicus' system was physically impossible: as indeed it proved to be, in the context of Aristotelian natural philosophy.

Rejecting Ptolemaic and Copernican systems on physical grounds was of course quite a different matter from devising something more satisfactory. Here was the greatest weakness of the late scholastic movement. The systematization that is crucial to its project takes up all its resources, so to speak, so that the kind of innovation that we find in natural philosophy in the fourteenth century, for example, is wholly missing from the sixteenth and early seventeenth centuries. Reconciliation of doctrines is paramount, or where this is not possible, gathering of arguments for competing opinions: the Coimbra Commentators had difficulty reconciling the biblical view that the empyrean consisted of water with the Aristotelian view that it was a fifth element, for example, and in true scholastic style found themselves 'compelled by an ambiguity of opinion to accommodate themselves to both points of view'.[132] This approach would not have been so bad if it were a way of accommodating new developments, registering them as problems that future scholars might deal with. But this was not at all what happened: quite the contrary, the way in which the systematization was pursued closed off receptivity to new developments. Yet there can be little doubt that the time had come for scholasticism to redeem the promissory notes of three centuries, and systematization was the only way in which it could do this. Lohr gives a sense of what was at issue in his discussion of

---

[130] See Beatriz Helena Domingues, *Tradição na Modernidade e Modernidade na Tradição: A Modernidade Ibérica e a Revolução Copernicana* (Rio de Janeiro, 1996), and her summary in 'Spain and the Dawn of Modern Science', *Metascience* 7 (1998), 298–312. More generally, on attempts to accommodate Aristotelianism to the new natural philosophies, see Christia Mercer, 'The Vitality and Importance of Early Modern Aristotelianism', in Tom Sorell, ed., *The Rise of Modern Philosophy* (Oxford, 1993), 33–67: 57–66.

[131] See Víctor Navarro Brotóns, 'The Reception of Copernicus in Sixteenth-Century Spain: The Case of Diego de Zúñiga', *Isis* 86 (1995), 52–78. More generally on the reception of Copernicanism in Spain see idem, 'Contribución a la Historia del Copernicanismo en España', *Cuadernos Hispanoamericanos* 283 (1974), 3–24; and José María López Piñero, *Ciencia y Técnica en la Sociedad Española de los Siglos XVI y XVII* (Barcelona, 1979), 178–96.

[132] *In quattuor libros De coelo*, 1. 2. q. VI, a. III. The author of this commentary is Emmanuel de Goes.

Pereira's programme at the Collegio Romano, the Jesuit powerhouse of late scholastic systematization:

Aristotle himself had regarded the opinions of his predecessors as stuttering attempts to express his own ideas and sought by the use of dialectics to discover among their theories the true principles of a question under discussion. In the same way the professors of the Collegio Romano were to seek the true principles of Aristotelian philosophy, not only the first principles of being, but also the axioms on which Aristotle's conception of science was founded. With these epistemological first principles in hand Aristotle could be reinterpreted or even rewritten to agree with the true principles of philosophy, that is, those which lead to Catholic doctrine. It was in accordance with this hermeneutic that Pereira defined 'first philosophy' not only as the science of being, but also as the science of science itself. Conscious of the fact that the basic problem with which scholasticism was confronted was that of maintaining the fundamental principles of its worldview, he held that metaphysics as the first philosophy also had the task of expounding and defending its *principia generali naturali lumine manifesta* in the face of the doubts and uncertainty which secular Aristotelianism had called forth.[133]

On the original Thomist conception of metaphysics, it acts as a bridge between Aristotelian natural philosophy and Christian theology, and it was such bridging that the systematization and synthesis were designed to achieve. But the kind of systematization and synthesis that Pereira envisages closes off any avenue for an independent natural philosophy, with the result that metaphysics acts not as a bridge but as a foundation. This is in keeping with Pereira's own conception of how cosmology should be pursued, which, as we saw above, leaves little scope for any natural-philosophical treatment of this subject. The approach he takes may have Paduan precedents, but what drives the sharp division he draws between the terrestrial and the celestial is reminiscent of the sharp division that Scotus drew between the natural and the supernatural, as is the way in which he conceives of metaphysics as a science of being. Pereira's approach is one that was to become standard. The first generation of scholastic textbooks had been of mixed orthodoxy, those issuing from Coimbra being Thomist on basic metaphysical issues, but the textbooks of Suárez,[134] as well as the influential works of otherwise Thomist philosophers such as Cajetan, take up a Scotist position on the nature of metaphysics, treating it as a general science of being. For Suárez, as for Scotus, there must be some unified notion of being, provided by metaphysics, and through this metaphysics we have access to some understanding of divine being: metaphysics does not unify knowledge from disparate sources, it stands over and regulates knowledge. The drift to Scotism is consolidated in the second wave of textbooks, those of Eustachius, Abra de Raconis, and Dupleix, who assume Scotism as a matter of course. This undermines the very finely balanced notion of metaphysics that is so crucial to the Thomist programme, and its upshot is

---

[133] Lohr, 'Metaphysics', 608.

[134] The most important textbook is Fransisco Suárez, *Metaphysicarum disputationem, in quibus, & universa theologia ordinatè traditor, & quaestiones ad amnes duodecim Aristotelis libros pertinentes, accuratè dispuntatur* (Salamanca, 1597).

to lock scholasticism out of any new developments in natural philosophy. One can only agree with Alan Gabbey, when he points out that 'the scholastics believed their explanatory schemes and ontological categories coped adequately with the universal range of natural phenomena, and one gets the impression in reading their treatises that no empirical discovery or philosophical upheaval, present or future (or indeed from their recent past) could lead to a revision or displacement of that scheme.'[135]

---

[135] Alan Gabbey, 'The *Principia Philosophiae* as a Treatise in Natural Philosophy', in Jean-Robert Armogathe and Giulia Belgioiso, eds, *Descartes: Principia Philosophiae, 1644–1994* (Naples, 1996), 517–29: 524–5. Cf. Montaigne's statement that he knew in Pisa 'a good man, but such an Aristotelian that the most sweeping of his dogmas is this: that the touchstone and measure of all serious speculations and of all truth is conformity with the teaching of Aristotle, for outside these everything is chimera and inane; and that Aristotle saw everything and said everything'. Michel de Montaigne, *Essais*, ed. Rat (2 vols Paris, 1965), i. 161 (Essay I. 26).

# 4

# The Interpretation of Nature and the Origins of Physico-Theology

Understood in its broadest seventeenth-century sense, as enquiry into natural phenomena, natural philosophy forms a spectrum. At the opposite poles of this spectrum are what we can designate as matter theory and natural history. The two had been pursued alongside one another from antiquity,[1] but the contrast between a canonical work of natural history such as Pliny's *Natural History* and a canonical work of natural philosophy *qua* matter theory, such as Aristotle's *Physics* or *De caelo*, is immense.[2] Natural history is not even a 'theoretical' enterprise in the Aristotelian sense, and therefore cannot be included in his understanding of 'physics' or natural philosophy proper. The divergence between the two is compounded as we move from classical to Patristic culture, where we find a radical reassessment of what natural enquiry reveals and what procedures are the appropriate ones for it to follow. Natural history is transformed into/replaced by (both describe different features of what occurs) a form of allegorical interpretation of nature in which guidance is scriptural rather than empirical. This enterprise effectively displaced matter theory until the rise of scholasticism, when the Aristotelian natural-philosophical project was revived.

From the discussion of the last two chapters, it might seem that the Aristotelian understanding of natural philosophy completely displaced the natural-historical one, but this is not quite what occured. There is another dimension to the question, which is the subject of this chapter. Aristotelian matter theory was certainly the dominant understanding of the form that a *scientia* of natural processes would take, but Christianized Aristotelianism did not in fact answer to all the needs of Christian natural theology. The former was complemented by a form of interpretation of nature that was driven primarily by scriptural considerations, but which had a genealogical relation to natural history, and which was to evolve in the seventeenth century into something closely resembling ancient natural history, but motivated largely by explicitly natural-theological concerns. By the second half of the seventeenth century, in an attempt to provide direction for the post-Aristotelian natural philosophies that had now moved to centre stage, we witness natural

---

[1] See Roger French, *Ancient Natural History* (London, 1994).

[2] Note, however, that Aristotle himself pursued natural history in works such as *Historium animalium*, and his immediate successor at the Lyceum, Theophrastus, devoted the bulk of his time to botany, a paradigmatic natural-historical field.

philosophy being modelled by some natural philosophers around such natural-historical considerations, alien as these are to the traditional understanding of natural philosophy fostered, for example, by mechanists such as Descartes and Hobbes.

## FIRST CAUSES

In Chapter 2 we saw how Aquinas dealt with the problem of Averroism, which suggested that theology and natural philosophy might follow autonomous paths and as a result may yield conflicting conclusions on certain fundamental issues. Aquinas' response, I have argued, was to revise the understanding of metaphysics so that it acted as a bridge between natural philosophy and theology. Metaphysics becomes as theologically neutral as natural philosophy on this conception. This was a problematic and disputed understanding of metaphysics, but even if it had been unproblematic and had yielded a satisfactory reconciliation of Aristotelian natural philosophy and Christian teaching, for example on the most contentious question, that of the personal immortality of the soul, it would not thereby have consolidated the union of Aristotelian natural philosophy and Christian theology as a complete form of understanding of the natural realm, nor even the sole form of understanding of the natural realm. Indeed, Aquinas himself operated with another autonomous form of such understanding. The problems here mirror those raised by Averroism in certain respects, but they cannot be resolved in the way that Aquinas resolved those of Averroism, and they point us in a completely different direction.

When dealing with natural processes in a straightforwardly natural-philosophical context, Aquinas' approach is resolutely Aristotelian, invoking internal principles to explain the natural behaviour of bodies. But when he turns to providing proofs for the existence of God, he embraces a very different and much more traditional Christian conception of nature, one that is anything but theologically neutral. In his 'Five Ways', his five proofs for the existence of God in *Summa theologica*,[3] his target is not Averroism, but the radical dualist doctrines originally associated with the Manichaeans, and advocated in the twelfth and thirteenth century by groups such as the Cathars.[4] On such a view, a sharp distinction is drawn between the material and spiritual realms, with God's responsibility being confined to the latter, either because, in the process of creation, he had delegated the creation of material things to lesser spiritual entities, or because the creation of the material world was considered to be the work of the Devil.

The new target brought with it a completely different conception of natural processes on Aquinas' part. By contrast with the Aristotelian conception of nature as an autonomous and independent realm, the Bible portrayed nature as completely dependent on the will of God, and it is this dichotomy with which Aquinas now had to come to terms. The first proof for the existence of God, for example, is, despite

[3] *Summa theologica*, I q. 2 a. 3.
[4] See Steven Runciman, *The Medieval Manichee: A Study of the Christian Dualist Heresy* (Cambridge, 1982).

its Aristotelian gloss, in fact quite un-Aristotelian in what it assumes.[5] It is crucial to Aristotelian natural philosophy that change generally and motion in particular are due to the realization of a potentiality in the thing undergoing the change, and when discussing physical change Aquinas assumes that things have this power, and that it is not contrary to Christian doctrine to maintain that in creating things God created them with potentialities or self-active powers. Yet the first demonstration of God's existence takes a completely different and contrary path, arguing that every moving thing is moved by some other thing, that is, by something other than itself, and that there must be one first mover, itself unmoved. The second argument reinforces the point that a body's behaviour must be traced to God rather than to something intrinsic to the body, arguing that nothing can be its own efficient cause, because that would mean it was prior to itself, which is impossible. Its efficient cause must therefore lie outside it, giving rise to a chain of such causation, which must ultimately lead back to a first cause which is itself uncaused. It is not that such an understanding of causation is irredeemably incompatible with the Aristotelian idea of change being caused by the internal principles, for it is possible that some gloss could be put on these internal principles such that their ultimate source is God.[6] Rather, it is that two very different kinds of story are being told here. One of these is distinctively Aristotelian, and it is this that is called upon to provide the requisite categories for the discussion of the Trinity, the nature of Christ, and transubstantiation, by contrast with the Neoplatonic and Augustinian notions that the scholastic tradition rejects as inadequate for this purpose. The other turns on precisely these Neoplatonic and Augustinian notions, preferring what is a more typically Stoic conception of chains of causes to the Aristotelian idea of internal principles, offering in the process a view of nature which, even if one were able show that there is no strict incompatibility with the internal principle view, offers a very different understanding of the natural realm.

The fifth proof is instructive in this respect. It in effect deduces divine providence from the presence of harmony, order, and above all benevolent purpose in the world. There are two ways in which one might think of this demonstration. One might start from a general abstract harmony, the kind of thing presupposed in Neoplatonic systems, and deduce the existence of something that imposes the harmony from this. Or, one might start from the individual natures of things, conceived along Aristotelian lines, and try to show that they individually and collectively manifest harmony, order, and benevolent purpose. The first approach is clearly question-begging, its hierarchical conception of the cosmos effectively assuming what has to be shown. The second,

---

[5] See French and Cunningham, *Before Science*, 185–97.

[6] Shifting backwards and forwards between internal principles of one kind or another and single divine causation was inevitable in Christian natural history. In Book 3, ch. 8 of *De trinitate*, for example, Augustine advocates a doctrine whereby plants and animals develop from pre-existing seeds, telling us that 'certain seeds of all the things which are generated in a corporeal and visible fashion lie hidden in the corporeal elements of this world'. Aquinas himself held the view that in the case where divine and natural causation acted one could not apportion partial causal responsibility but, rather, the causes must act concurrently. See A. J. Freddoso, 'God's Concurrence with Secondary Causes: Why Conservation is Not Enough', *Philosophical Perspectives* 5 (1991), 553–85; and idem, 'God's General Concurrence with Secondary Causes: Pitfalls and Prospects', *American Catholic Philosophical Quarterly* 67 (1994), 131–56.

by contrast, looks a good deal more compelling, showing, rather than just asserting, that natural phenomena collectively have something in common that requires explanation. Yet there is every indication that Aquinas' approach is the former. His way of thinking through the question is evident in the fourth proof, which is crucial for his account of evil as a privation, in opposition to the Manichaean arguments revived by the Cathars, whereby evil was something independent of and separate from God. The proof sets out to demonstrate supreme perfection from degrees of perfection, working very much with the idea of incomplete perfections being just incomplete instantiations of a supreme perfection. What is doing the work here is manifestly a general, abstract notion of perfection, not something that originates at the level of individual things, and it is hard to avoid the conclusion that the same kind of understanding underlies the fifth 'Way'.

In the course of the seventeenth century, we will witness a non-Aristotelian development of the fifth Way that does genuinely argue from something like individual characteristics (if not natures) to an understanding of divine purpose in nature. But what will be at issue here are final causes, not efficient causes, and the development will occur in the context of a problematic bifurcation of understandings of nature, one that is manifest in Aquinas' treatment, but has much earlier origins. The bifurcation, as it bears on our concerns, might be expressed as that between natural philosophy and natural history, but, by contrast with the way in which the disciplines were pursued in antiquity, in the seventeenth century natural history was very much part of natural philosophy in the broadest sense. A better way to draw the distinction for the early-modern era, therefore, is between systematic matter theory and natural history.

In the sixteenth century, the principles of scriptural interpretation from which natural history borrowed so much themselves began to be transformed, and this had profound ramifications in natural history, which was at the same time also being challenged by details of New World flora and fauna that defied traditional forms of natural-historical classification. The new natural history that emerged from this was one that had a number of distinctive features: it increasingly displaced scriptural interpretation as a way of discovering God's purposes in his creation, and it replaced allegorical interpretation by instituting criteria of objectivity of reporting in natural-historical enquiry that matched the new criteria of philological and historical accuracy that were being demanded by biblical hermeneutics. This development was sometimes independent of those in matter theory and mechanics, while at other times—for example in the development of 'experimental philosophy', which we shall be looking at in Chapter 10—it was integrated with them to produce a new and powerful form of natural philosophy. Even more crucially, it offered a form of legitimation for the natural-philosophical enterprise, broadly construed, which would be embraced with enthusiasm by many natural philosophers, particularly in England from the middle of the seventeenth century.

The legitimatory problems faced by natural philosophy in its Aristotelian form and those faced by natural history were quite different. In the former, the most problematic question was how Aristotelian matter theory and Christian theology were to be accommodated to one another. The issues in the case of natural history turn on a very different kind of question, namely that of what kind of information about the world is provided by scripture. Here scripture is treated as something intrinsically reliable, but reliable only if interpreted in the right way, so the problem now becomes: under what interpretation is scripture reliable? This reconnects with the first set of issues, about the relation between natural philosophy and theology, in a spectacular way in the trial of Galileo in the early 1630s, but the combination of the two has even more far-reaching consequences for how natural philosophy, in a broad sense, comes to be pursued in the seventeenth and eighteenth centuries, for it was widely believed to provide a striking vindication of the worth and power of natural philosophy in its ability to uncover the most fundamental level underlying natural processes, a level at which God's intentions for his creation can be discerned clearly, in a way that transcends any confessional differences, and which guides, rather than being guided by, scriptural interpretation. In short, natural history came to be grounded in, and legitimated by, the belief that such enquiry provided access to an understanding of God's purposes in his creation. When these concerns came to guide natural philosophy generally, beginning in the second half of the seventeenth century, they provided it with a quasi-religious standing that was is going to be a key part of its overall legitimation.

## INTERPRETATION OF NATURE

Aristotelian natural philosophy did not just replace other natural philosophies, it also put forward natural philosophy as a systematic way of understanding natural phenomena which tended to displace alternative ways of accounting for these natural phenomena. But these alternatives never completely disappeared. We have already glimpsed traces of them in the Renaissance, in the contemplative procedures recommended in the Neoplatonist natural philosophies and in the occult connections postulated in some versions of naturalism, but there were also traces in orthodox scholastic Aristotelians, in Pereira for example, whose most influential and popular work was his elaborate commentary on Genesis published in 1590.

Pereira's commentary cannot simply be relegated to the theological side of his interests. Commentaries on Genesis, in their sixteenth-century versions, are a genre in which the prime concern is knowledge of nature, cosmology in particular. What they offer is not something that Aristotelian natural philosophy, no matter how successful and comprehensive, could wholly supersede. Cosmology had played a role in Christian theology from its earliest stages, and early Christian commentators on Genesis devoted much attention to the question of the position of the second heaven or firmament created on the second day in relation to the first heaven of the first day, as well as to the question of the nature of the material barrier formed by the firmament dividing 'the waters which were below it from those that were above it'. In response, competing cosmological models were proposed in the fourth century by the author of the pseudo-Clementine *Retractiones* and by Basil, and in the seventh century by Isidore of Seville.[7] Albertus Magnus and Aquinas had both

---

[7] See Randles, *The Unmaking of the Medieval Christian Cosmos*, ch. 1, and Schmidt-Biggemann, *Philosophia Perennis*, 237–44.

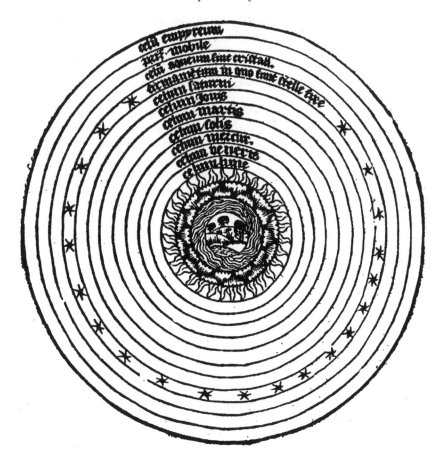

**Figure 4.1**

offered views on the nature of the empyrean in their commentaries on the second book of Peter Lombard's *Sententiae*, each treating it as being a distinct physical location—as indeed it was represented in textbooks, such as Juan de Celeya's 1518 *Exposito de celo & mundi Aristotelia* (see Fig. 4.1)—and enquiring whether and how each of the sensory faculties would function in this region, Aquinas following Aristotle in regarding the firmament and the crystalline heaven as being composed of a distinct non-terrestrial fifth element.[8] The kinds of account being offered here

[8] Aquinas, *Scriptorum super libros sententiarum*, ed. R. P. Mandonnet and Maria Fabianus Moos (3 vols., Paris 1929–33), ii. 350 (2. 14. q. 1 a. 1); cf. *Summa theologica*, I q. 68. See Thomas Litt, *Les Corps celestes dans l'univers de Saint Thomas d'Aquin* (Louvain, 1963).

are very different from a cosmology developed within a natural-philosophical system such as that of Aristotle or the Stoics, or even that of Patrizi. They are part of a set of disciplines that have a clearly Neoplatonic organization, and which mirror and reinforce the Neoplatonic foundations for Christian theology devised by the Church Fathers. But they work in quite a different way and on a different level, and can persist in spite of the thirteenth-century abandonment of Neoplatonism in favour of Aristotelianism.

The understanding of the physical world fostered in the Church Fathers was one in which an explanation of physical phenomena took the form of an account of what those phenomena signified. Origen, Basil, and Ambrose, for example, all make it explicit that the physical world was designed to minister to human needs, and what is important is not what causes physical things to behave in the way they do, but what they signify. Origen in particular maintained that both the world and scripture were symbolic through and through, and that a method of interpretation was required for the former just as much as it was for the latter.[9] Inevitably, interpretation of the world was modelled on the comparatively well-developed interpretation of scripture, and as a consequence the world was interpreted as if it were a book containing unique but hidden spiritual truths. The task of interpretation was to penetrate beyond literal meanings and mundane uses to these underlying spiritual truths.

In the case of scriptural interpretation, Origen's tripartite division into literal interpretation, moral interpretation (where lessons on how to live could be gleaned), and allegorical interpretation (in which the underlying spiritual truths were revealed), was crucial. Passages that seemed to convey something contradictory or nonsensical when read in a literal way were endowed with meaning, thereby providing a means by which scripture could be shown to be authoritative in every detail, for nothing in it was now false, superfluous, or meaningless, and at the same time the possible meanings of scripture are inexhaustible.[10] Applied to the natural world, the existence of moral and allegorical levels of interpretation enabled one to overcome the problems posed for a literal reading of the natural world as meeting man's needs by the existence of parasites and predators. Natural objects for which no mundane purpose could be found were invested with symbolic meaning: for Basil, poisonous animals represent the wicked, for example, and for Augustine winged creatures represented believers who were able to soar into the heavens. The standard text on these questions was the *Physiologus* compiled by Origen (or one of his immediate disciples), where an elaborate system of allegorical meanings was set out. But it was Augustine, in *De doctrina Christiana*, who established the interpretative principles themselves. He added an extra level of interpretation, aetiology or (in later medieval versions) anagogy, which interprets the text or the world in its relation to theological truths,

---

[9] Origen, *The Song of Songs, Commentary and Homilies*, trans. R. P. Lawson (London, 1957), 223.

[10] Harrison, *The Bible, Protestantism and the Rise of Natural Science*, 19. I have followed Harrison's discussion on a number of points in what follows.

but it is in his account of the nature of signs that he exerted the greatest influence for medieval theories of interpretation. Origen's view had been that the multiplicity of meanings was due to the fact that the words of scripture are equivocal, whereas Augustine argued that the words used in scripture have univocal meanings, and this provided a constraint on possible interpretations.[11] Scripture does contain a multiplicity of meanings, nevertheless, but this is because the things the words refer to have multiple meanings, and it is in this that the spiritual meaning of scripture lies. The true meaning of natural things lies in their spiritual significance, and this is provided by scripture. To confine one's attention to natural objects alone is to be a slave to the sign, and such literal reading of nature is tantamount to idolatry.[12] Moreover, physical things were commonly treated as if they had no meaning in their own right, only in what they signified spiritually, so one had to look beyond the sensory manifestation of things to their spiritual meaning.[13]

Resemblances between physical things themselves play no role in this conception: all relations are, in true Neoplatonist fashion, between physical things and the 'higher' spiritual truths they signify. But with the development of scholastic thought, from Anselm onwards, and particularly once scholasticism took on an Aristotelian form in the thirteenth century, relations between things began to take on significance in their own right,[14] and started to act as systematizing principles upon which knowledge of the natural world is based. William of Conches had advocated a systematic literal reading of nature in the twelfth century, and he was accused of treating nature as an autonomous principle and of Manichaeism.[15] At the same time, Hugh of St Victor was arguing that things could be a source of illumination in their own right.[16] Unless this were possible, of course, an Aristotelian natural philosophy of the kind advocated by Albertus Magnus and Aquinas would not be possible. But the new search for intrinsic connections between physical things did not by any means displace their interpretation in terms of spiritual truths. In the Aristotelian scholastic tradition, the two complemented each other in crucial respects, and encouraged the notion that nature could be read as a book. On the one hand, this further reinforced the idea that methods employed in interpreting scripture might be the appropriate model for natural interpretation, and it is striking how natural philosophy was pursued on exclusively textual lines in the scholastic tradition: nature was something that one learned about from the writings of past masters, which were treated as repositories of truth, even if occasional revisions had to be made in the light of experience. On the

[11] Harrison, *The Bible, Protestantism and the Rise of Natural Science*, 28.

[12] Augustine, *De doctrina Christiana*, 3. 7. Note, however, that in his *De Genesi ad literam*, Augustine does offer a literal interpretation of Genesis, possibly because his interest in this stems from a concern to refute the Manichaeans (*De Genesi contra Manichaeos libri duo*), who, as I have indicated, rejected allegorical interpretation, forcing Augustine to offer a literal reading in this case.

[13] See the definitive treatment in Eric Auerbach, *Mimesis* (Princeton, 1968).

[14] See Harrison, *The Bible, Protestantism and the Rise of Natural Science*, chs. 2 and 3.

[15] See French and Cunningham, *Before Science*, 76–9.

[16] As Harrison notes, this approach was in fact implicit in the liberal arts curriculum of the medieval schools: the *trivium* (grammar, rhetoric, and dialectic) illuminated the meanings of words whereas the *quadrivium* (arithmetic, geometry, astronomy, harmonics) illuminated the meanings of things referred to by words: *The Bible, Protestantism and the Rise of Natural Science*, 57.

other hand, the study of the natural world now assumed a new standing that put it on a par with the study of scripture, as it took on a new religious significance, for both now were indispensible routes to understanding of the divine.

A good example of this approach in the sixteenth century is emblematics, which combines religious, natural-historical, literary, and more general cultural concerns into a series of concentrated images. Consider Conrad Gesner's *Historia animalium*, the first four volumes of which appeared in the 1550s.[17] Edward Topsell's 1607 English version of Gesner proudly describes on its title page the kind of approach offered:

> The story of euery beast is amplified with Narrations out of Scriptures, Fathers, Philosophers, Physicians, and Poets: wherein are declared various Hyeroglyphicks, Emblems, Epigrams, and other good Historics.[18]

The chapters in Gesner's *Historium* deal with particular animals, and are generally divided into eight sections. He gives us accounts of the various names in different languages for the animal, regional differences in appearance, daily habits, cries and calls, its relationship with other animals, sources of food, and so forth. The accounts are taken largely from classical sources, and are exhaustively referenced in characteristic humanist style. The last section, invariably the longest, is devoted to epithets, icons, proverbs, and emblems. Ashworth points out that in the extensive final section of the entry on the fox, for example, we find fox epithets (crafty, sly, deceitful, cunning), a lexicon of the meanings of 'foxy', fox metaphors (such as that Christ called Herod a fox because of the guile he displayed), fox omens ('it is bad luck to encounter a new-born fox on the path'), a list of appearances of foxes in scripture, several pages of fox proverbs and fox associations, and then, without a word of explanation, the following enigmatic conclusion:

> Mind is worth more than beauty. A fox, entering the workshop of a stage-manager, came upon a smoothly polished mask of a human head, so elegantly fashioned that although it lacked breath, it appeared to be alive in other respects. When the fox took the mask in its paws it said: What a fine head this is, but it has no brain. Alciati, in his Emblemata.[19]

The reference here to Alciati provides the key to the exercise. Alciati's *Emblem-ata*—first published in 1531 and subsequently passing through numerous editions

---

[17]  Conrad Gesner, *Historia animalium* (5 vols., Zurich, 1551–87). On Gesner, see William B. Ashworth Jr., 'Emblematic Natural History of the Renaissance', in N. Jardine, J. A. Secord, and E. C. Spary, eds., *Cultures of Natural History* (Cambridge, 1996), 17–37, to which I am particularly indebted here, and Caroline Aleid Gmelig-Nijboer, *Conrad Gesner's Historia Animalium: An Inventory of Renaissance Zoology* (Meppel, 1977). More generally see William B. Ashworth Jr., 'Natural History and the Emblematic World View', in David C. Lindberg and Robert S. Westman, eds, *Reappraisals of the Scientific Revolution* (Cambridge, 1990), 303–32. A key work in the recognition of the shift from an emblematic view in the seventeenth century was Michel Foucault, *Les Mots et les choses* (Paris, 1966). On the genre of animal parables in antiquity see French, *Ancient Natural History*, ch. 6.

[18]  Edward Topsell, *The historie of fovre-footed beastes. . . . collected out of all the volumes of Conradvs Gesner, and all other writers to this present day* (London, 1607).

[19]  See Ashworth, 'Emblematic Natural History of the Renaissance', 20–1.

in many languages[20]—started a genre that continued until the middle of the seventeenth century. The emblem comprises a motto, an image, and an explanatory epigrammatic poem. These are designed to embody, in a highly compressed form, a wealth of detail, bringing that detail into focus around key features of the entity in question.

It is important to appreciate the extent to which the emblematic tradition remained part of the culture within which early seventeenth-century natural philosophers worked. Bacon, Galileo, and Descartes each had contact with this tradition in one way or another, for example. Bacon brought out a collection of apophthegms—expressions that present very condensed information in a striking (usually witty) manner—in 1624, in which he included contributions from Pericles, Cicero, Alexander, Laud, and his father Nicholas Bacon. The importance of presenting information in a non-literal way becomes clear in his defence of a distinctive role for aphorisms, for example in the Preface to his *Maxims of Law*:

Whereas I could have digested these rules into a certain method or order, which, I know, would have been more admired, as that which would have made every particular rule, through this coherence and relation into other rules, seem more cunning and more deep; yet I have avoided to do this, because this delivering of knowledge in distinct and disjointed aphorisms doth leave the wit of man more free to turn and toss, and to make use of that which is so delivered to more several purposes and applications.[21]

Proverbs and other forms of concentrating information also played a crucial role in his thinking.[22] One virtue of such devices was that they were easily memorized, but they also had a richness which enabled the person grasping them to go beyond the words themselves to the store of knowledge that they compressed. As for Descartes, the Jesuit culture in which he was educated was even more preoccupied with emblems and symbols. There was a strong current of concern with the educational value of emblems, and the solution of enigmas and interpretation of emblems and symbols was recommended as an exercise in the manual of rules governing teaching in Jesuit schools, the *Ratio Studorium*.[23] The Jesuits devoted a huge literature to sacred icons

[20] The work is conveniently available as Andrea Alciati, *Emblemata cum commentarijs amplistimis* (Padua, 1621: facsimile copy New York, 1976). On Alciati and the emblematic tradition, see John Manning, *The Emblem* (London, 2002).

[21] *Maxims of Law*, Preface; *Works*, vii. 321. See also his remark in the *Parasceve* that 'too much method produces iterations and proxility' (*Works*, i. 395/iv. 253). Cf. *Valerius Terminus*, where Bacon speaks approvingly of 'publishing in a manner whereby it shall not be to the capacity nor taste of all, but shall as it were single and adopt his reader' (*Works*, iii. 248). There were a number of classical precedents for rejecting any fixed order, the most important being Caesellius Vindex (works now lost), who was followed in antiquity by writers such as Aulus Gellius, and in the sixteenth century by writers such as Caelius Rhodiginus. See Ann Blair, *The Theater of Nature* (Princeton, 1997), 38–9.

[22] See Lisa Jardine, *Francis Bacon: Discovery and the Art of Discourse* (Cambridge, 1974), chs. 9–11.

[23] See Aldo Scaglione, *The Liberal Arts and the Jesuit College System* (Amsterdam, 1986), 89.

and symbols,[24] to the extent that it was the core of their literary activity.[25] Finally, as for Galileo, emblematics not only figured prominently in the court culture in which he worked, but he himself devised an emblem for Cosimo de' Medici. In 1608, he tied natural philosophy in with princely power, by devising an emblem for Cosimo that reconciled the naturalness of princely rule on the one hand with his coercive powers on the other, in the form of a lodestone (the Medici power) which exercised sympathetic attraction selectively on iron filings (the subjects) who were voluntarily drawn to the lodestone, in contrast with non-ferrous materials (those who were not subjects of the Medici), which were unaffected.[26]

Nevertheless, despite its cultural resilience, emblematics was coming to an end as a model for natural history at the beginning of the seventeenth century. To understand why, however, it is not to developments in natural history itself to which we must turn, but rather to developments in biblical hermeneutics. The intimate connection between interpretation of Scripture and interpretation of nature, and the modelling of techniques of natural interpretation upon techniques of scriptural interpretation, meant that fundamental changes in the latter had direct consequences for the former.

## HERMENEUTICS

Questions of textual interpretation were the core of the humanist enterprise, and in two areas they were particularly problematic: law and the Bible. There were common problems in the two cases, which first came to be entangled explicitly in Valla's work in the 1440s. This work remained unknown until the beginning of the sixteenth century, however, by which time others were coming to use similar general procedures for textual authentication in both areas. What was at issue for biblical hermeneutics was a radical reassessment of the authority of the Bible, something that turned into a pressing problem in the course of the seventeenth century. This posed a far more fundamental challenge to the traditional Christian understanding of the world and our place in it than natural-philosophical developments did, or could have done. It opened up areas of concern that, from around the 1670s in particular, resulted in a reshaping of Northern European culture, a reshaping in which natural philosophy,

---

[24] The tradition includes: Jeronimo Nadal, *Adnotationes et Meditationes in Evangelia* (Anvers, 1594), Blaide de Vigenère's translation of Philostratus, *Images ou Tableaux de Platte Peinture des deux Philostrates sophistes grecs* (Paris, 1614); Melchior de La Cerda, *Usus et exercitatio demonstrationis* (Cologne, 1617); Pierre Coton, *Sermons sur les principales et plus difficiles matieres de la fay* (Paris, 1617); Nicolas Caussin, *Electorum symbolorum et parabolarum historicarum syntagmata* (Paris, 1618); Etienne Binet, *Essay des merveilles de nature et des plus nobles artifices* (Rouen, 1621); Nicolas Caussin, *Eloquentiae sacrae et humanae parallela* (Paris, 1624); idem, *La Cour sainte ou l'institution chrétienne des Grands* (Paris, 1624); Francisco de Mendoça, *Viridarium sacrae et profanae eruditionis* (Lyon, 1635); Pierre Le Moyne, *Les Peintures Morales* (Paris, 1640); Gérard Pelletier, *Palatium reginae eloquentiae* (Paris, 1641).

[25] The definitive account of this tradition is Marc Fumaroli, *L'Age de l'eloquence: Rhétorique et 'res literaria' de la Renaissance au seuil de l'époque classique* (Geneva, 1980).

[26] See Biagioli, *Galileo Courtier*, 120–7.

although it did not initiate these developments, came to play an important role in their resolution, as questions in natural theology came to the fore.

Let us look first at the two streams that come together in Valla, starting with biblical questions. It was a fundamental tenet of the humanist tradition that no translation of a literary work could replace the original. There was one area where application of this principle was highly contentious however, namely the Bible. Even though Jerome had himself advocated this principle, his Latin translation became the single basis for scholastic knowledge of the Bible. But at the beginning of the sixteenth century, the Latin translations began to be perceived as inadequate, as scholars such as Reuchlin started work on the Hebrew texts, and Erasmus began editing the Greek text of the New Testament. This was very unsettling for a number of reasons. For one thing, whole traditions of theology could be threatened by retranslation of a single word. In his translation of the Gospel of John, for example, Erasmus, reflecting on the meaning of the Greek term *logos*, changed the translation of the opening words from 'In principio erat verbum . . . ' to 'In principio erat sermo . . . ', thereby challenging a long tradition of theological enquiry into the 'word'.[27] More generally, the coming of the Reformation polarized the question of Latin. Latin was the language of the Catholic Church, which saw European nations as being a single family under the headship of the pope, and Latin as the common language of this family.[28] Its status was effectively that of a sacred language, and the diversity of languages was regarded as an effect of sin,[29] suggesting that there was something morally dangerous in the use of the vernacular. As well as this, the vernacular translations offered scope for rewordings that were motivated by theological views in opposition to that of the Catholic Church: Tyndale's English translation of the New Testament, for example, changes, along Lutheran lines, 'charity' to 'love', 'priest' to 'senior', and 'church' to 'congregation'.

These developments should be seen against the background of the notion of 'inspired interpretation', according to which God's direct intercession is needed to interpret his words as revealed in the Bible, and once such an inspired version exists, it cannot be revised or emended.[30] The idea of an 'inspired' Latin or vernacular version of the Bible is in direct conflict with the philological tradition. The origins of the idea

---

[27] Werner Schwarz, *Principles and Problems of Biblical Translation: Some Reformation Controversies and Their Background* (Cambridge, 1955), 13–14. On Erasmus' theology see Manfred Hoffmann, *Erkenntnis und Verwirklichung der wahren Theologie nach Erasmus von Rotterdam* (Tübingen, 1972).

[28] The Council of Trent decreed that the Latin version of Jerome, together with works of the Church Fathers, was to be the final authority in matters of faith and discipline, although it should be noted that this was only after prolonged debate between the Vulgate faction and that favouring use of the Hebrew and Greek texts in interpreting problematic passages. On these debates see Salvador Muños Iglesias, 'El decreto tridentino sobre la Vulgata y su interpretación por los teólogos des siglio XVI', *Estudios biblicos* 5 (1946), 145–69. All translations of the Bible into the vernacular were placed on the first edition of the *Index* in 1559: see the comprehensive account in Heinrich Reusch, *Die 'Indices Librorum Prohibitorum' des sechzehnten Jahrhunderts* (Nieuwkoop, 1961), 176–208.

[29] See François de Dainville, *La Naissance de l'humanisme moderne* (Paris, 1940), 64. More generally on the question of Latin, see Françoise Waquet, *Le Latin ou l'empire d'un signe* (Paris, 1999).

[30] Schwarz, *Principles and Problems*, 15–16.

of an inspired version came with Philo, in the middle of the first century, who treated the Septuagint, the Greek version of the Hebrew Old Testament, in these terms, as a final version which cannot be changed. Three centuries later, Jerome, in the course of translating the Old Testament, discovered fundamental disprepancies between the Hebrew text and the Septuagint, arguing that the Hebrew text was in accord with the New Testament, and at odds with the Septuagint, on such questions as the coming of Christ. Jerome abandoned the idea of an inspirational reading, preferring what later came to be known as philological methods, and in this he was opposed by Augustine, a staunch advocate of the inspirational basis of the Septuagint, not because he was unaware of the discrepancies between the two versions, but because this was outweighed by fears of potential schisms over which version should be accepted.[31] Yet in the sixteenth century, when these questions became disputed again, it was Jerome's Latin version that was put in the position of 'inspired interpretation', by contrast with the new Protestant vernacular translations from the Greek and Hebrew.

It is instructive, for example, that Reuchlin's translation of the Old Testment from the Hebrew is guided purely by philological principles, and he does not deal with theological or philosophical questions.[32] Establishing the authentic text is prior to such activity, and he is highly critical of the Vulgate on these grounds, but this of course undermines not only the authority of the Vulgate but threatens the traditions of Christian interpretation. The situation was exacerbated with the publication of Erasmus' translation of the New Testament in 1516. In comparing the Greek texts of the Psalms with the Vulgate, Erasmus had noted as early as 1501 that Jerome's literal translation of words introduced discrepancies between the texts, so that the Vulgate could be understood only if it was compared with the Greek original. Erasmus refuses to draw any distinction between sacred and profane literature in this respect—the methods of investigation and study are the same—and this is reinforced by his discovery in 1504 of the manuscript of Valla's 1449 treatise on the interpretation of the New Testament.[33] Here Valla had set out rules for translation, insisting that differences in the Greek should be mirrored exactly by differences in the Latin, and that linguistic guidance is to be sought in contemporary pagan authors and not in later Christian ones. Erasmus follows these procedures, and defends himself against criticisms from advocates of inspirational readings on the grounds that 'it is one thing to be a prophet and another to be a translator; in one case the Spirit foretells future events, in the other sentences are understood and translated by erudition and command of language'.[34]

There were parallel developments in the study of law. Valla had inaugurated a philological-historical approach to Roman law,[35] in which his aim was to separate

---

[31] Ibid. 39–44.

[32] Nevertheless, it should be noted that Reuchlin's work was inspired by the idea of deepening understanding of Christianity through study of the kabbalah. See Lewis W. Spitz, *The Religious Renaissance of the German Humanists* (Cambridge, Mass., 1963), ch. 4.

[33] Laurentius Valla, *In Latinam Novi Testamenti Interpretationem ex Collatione Graecorum Exemplarium Adnotationes* (Paris, 1505).

[34] Quoted in Schwarz, *Principles and Problems*, 136.

[35] See Donald R. Kelley, *The Foundations of Modern Historical Scholarship: Language, Law, and History in the French Renaissance* (New York, 1970), 19–51; and Lisa Jardine and Donald R.

out the literal meaning of legal texts from figurative constructions that had been placed on these. He saw the greatest culprit in the latter respect being the *Glossa ordinaria*, a compilation of glosses written on the Digest of Justinian from that of the first Western Romanist, Irnerius, at the end of the eleventh century, up to the appearance of the *Glossa* in 1250. The *Glossa* spawned a tradition of 'post-glossators', such as the fourteenth-century lawyer Bartolus of Sassoferrato, whose concern was with what underlay the divergent opinions of the earlier glossators, and with how such divergences might be reconciled so that application of the law to particular cases might be clarified.[36] Valla, by contrast, was not a lawyer but a classical scholar, and his interest was in recapturing the original meanings of the words in the authentic texts. He knew that the Digest itself was a corrupt text, and he pointed out that in the course of its compilation, classical texts had been abridged and altered without acknowledgement by compilers who, lacking the appropriate skills, had introduced anachronisms and contradictions. It had later been transmitted through Byzantine compilers who had added to the confusion, mixing Greek and Latin terms, and finally by scholastic interpreters who were ignorant of ancient Rome, the origins of Roman law, and who, by Valla's reckoning, devoted themselves to prolix discussions of trivial questions in an ill-informed and inelegant way.

Lawyers generally had not been concerned with questions of reconciliation of texts because individual topics were considered from a casuistic perspective.[37] Valla, by contrast, rejected any attempt to give priority to the applicability of legal principles to cases, because the weight of accretions had in his view obscured the original meanings of the laws to such an extent that application was not viable until the original laws and their meanings had been uncovered. This required the restoration of a large number of ancient texts, exposing distortions and forgeries. Indeed, in effectively establishing the increasingly held view that the Donation of Constantine was a forgery,[38] he undermined canon law and much of the ground on which papal supremacy rested. As far as Roman law was concerned, the upshot of his attacks on the glossators, and Bartolus in particular, was that of a diminishing of the authoritative standing of Roman law and of the glossators' commentaries. Lawyers had dealt with Roman law as if it were an expression of a single unchanging code of ideals, and some glossators had

Kelley, 'Lorenzo Valla and the Intellectual Origins of Humanist Dialectic', *Journal of the History of Philosophy* 15 (1977), 143–64. See also Harold J. Berman, *Law and Revolution ii. The Impact of the Protestant Reformations on the Western Legal Tradition* (Cambridge, Mass., 2003), ch. 3.

[36] On this tradition see Peter Stein, *Regulae Iuris: From Juristic Rules to Legal Maxims* (Edinburgh, 1966).

[37] See Roderich Stintzing, *Geschichte der deutschen Rechtswissenschaft*, (Munich/Leipzig, 1880), i. 123–4.

[38] The Donation, which was forged in the late eighth/early ninth century, purported to be a fourth-century grant by which the Emperor Constantine had conferred extensive privileges and lands on the pope and his successors 'to the end of time'. The Holy Roman Emperor Otto III had rejected the Donation as a forgery at the end of the tenth century because he wanted Rome as his own seat, but despite scepticism as to its authenticity, especially among Renaissance scholars, the forgery was not demonstrated to be such until the middle of the fifteenth century, independently by Nicholas of Cusa, Reginald Pecock, and Valla, who were able to show that the style of the document precluded its being from the fourth century.

treated it as having a divine source.[39] Valla and his successors completely rejected such an approach, undermining the very idea of Roman law as a coherent body of legal principles, showing it to be a collection of mutually contradictory laws deriving from different periods with different aims and concerns. In particular, it was positive law arising from contingent political edicts and decisions, not a body of natural law. In setting out to correct this, the legal humanists argued that the different historical layers had to be separated and put into context, so that the aims and meanings of legal principles could be discovered. It was in this vein that Valla began a serious philological study of the Bible, maintaining the importance of grammatical principles over theological ones, and the new procedures of legal textual criticism that Valla inaugurated were continued in Budé's critical and largely negative analysis of the Pandects of Justinian in 1508, where the themes of the historicity and contingency of the legal principles were emphasized, and in a more positive vein, in Baudouin's 1561 attempt to set out the principles that must guide historical scholarship generally.[40]

There were, then, developments in legal and biblical philology that in the course of the sixteenth century transformed the study of these areas. But the principles developed there were extended outside law and scriptural interpretation, and they went to the heart of a number of areas that bore on the standing of natural philosophy. Consider, for example, the question of the authority of the Catholic Church in what it conceived to be doctrinal matters, which covered a number of questions also dealt with independently in natural philosophy. In the 1550s, the Dominican theologian Melchior Cano had been working on a project to set out rules for the assessment of authorities on doctrinal matters, and the concerns and solutions are strikingly similar to those developed within biblical and legal interpretation. This is hardly surprising, for it was Gratian's codification of canon law in the wake of the Investiture Controversy that provided the model for a systematic approach to law, establishing a principle of authority and legitimacy over discordant authorities.[41] Cano's posthumously published *De locis theologicis* (1563) was designed to provide the Catholic Church with a set of systematic procedures establishing grounds of, and degrees of, authority in response to the Protestant questioning of this authority, as well as to humanist criticisms of its misuse of sources. Cano identified both intrinsic and extrinsic sources of authority. The former include, among other things, the gospels, pronouncements of the Church whether as a whole or in council, and some opinions of the Fathers and scholastics. Extrinsic sources include natural philosophy and philosophy more generally, as well as history, which now becomes a separate source of authority.[42] Just what degree of authority historical arguments can have in

[39] See Walter Ullmann, *The Medieval Idea of Law, as Represented by Lucas de Penna: A Study in Fourteenth-Century Legal Scholarship* (London, 1946), 75–6.

[40] Guillaume Budé, *Annotationes ... in quatuor et viginti Pandectarum libros* (Paris, 1535), and François Baudouin, *De institvtione historiae vniuersae et eivs cum iurisprvdentia coniunctione*, ΠΡΟΛΕΓΟΜΕΝΩΝ *libri II* (Paris, 1561). On Budé see Kelley, *Foundations of Modern Historical Scholarship*, ch. 3. On Baudouin see ibid. ch. 5, and Julian Franklin, *Jean Bodin and the Sixteenth Century Revolution in the Methodology of Law and History* (New York, 1963), ch. 8.

[41] See Berman, *Law and Revolution, passim.*

[42] See Franklin, *Jean Bodin*, 106–15, which I rely on here.

resolving questions of religious dogma depends on our assessment of such matters as the reliability of historical authors, and this in turn depends on familiarity with the full range of historical sources. However, since such sources will yield only probable beliefs, not certain knowledge, reasonable doubt is sometimes appropriate, and to meet such doubt we need to balance a number of factors, above all the reliability of the author and the intrinsic plausibility of what is claimed. *De locis* was to play a pivotal role in the adjudication of natural-philosophical disputes. Both sides in Galileo's trial, for example, took it as authoritative, even though they were unable to agree on which sections were relevant to the dispute.[43]

On the Protestant side, the approach was rather different. A core ingredient in Lutheran theology was the doctrine of the 'real presence' of the saviour in the host during communion. By contrast with the Catholic doctrine, that real presence occurred only in communion as a result of a miraculous transformation—transubstantiation—and with the Calvinist view that there was no real presence at all, merely a symbolic one,[44] Lutherans argued that Christ was ubiquitious. As Luther put it, Christ is 'substantially present everywhere, in and through all creatures, in all their parts and places',[45] and the universal ubiquity of a providential deity meant that his design or plan could be known through the study of nature.[46] On this interpretation, it was not a question of establishing by what authority natural-philosophical questions could be adjudicated, but rather of using the kinds of considerations that emerged from legal and biblical interpretation to place natural history on a firm foundation, both at the level of procedure and at that of motivation.

The key contribution here is Bodin's *Methodus ad facilem historiarum cognitionem* of 1566. For Bodin, Roman law manifestly does not provide a coherent set of

---

[43] See Richard J. Blackwell, *Galileo, Bellarmine, and the Bible* (Notre Dame, 1991).

[44] The Calvinist view, as represented e.g. by Keckermann, was that accidents such as whiteness and heavyness were simply properties of substances that were incapable of independent existence. Hence it was impossible for the properties of Christ's divine nature to be 'communicated' to those of his human nature, which in turn meant that the Lutheran doctrine that Christ was corporeally present everywhere must be false. It also followed that the properties of the eucharist could not change while its substance remained. See Batholomew Keckermann, *Gymnasium logicum, id est, De usu & exercitatione logicae artis absolutiori & pleniori, libri tres* (London, 1606). On these questions generally, see Walter Sparn, *Wiederkehr der Metaphysik: Die ontologische Frage in der lutherischen Theologie des frühen 17. Jahrhunderts* (Stuttgart, 1976).

[45] Quoted in Peter Barker, 'The Role of Religion in the Lutheran Response to Copernicus', in Margaret J. Osler, ed., *Rethinking the Scientific Revolution* (Cambridge, 2000), 59–88: 62. Baker presents an important reassessment of the role of Lutheranism in the transmission of Copernican ideas.

[46] At least, it meant this to Lutherans. Calvin (who did not in any case accept the premiss) would not have accepted this inference for, although he certainly thought that natural creation manifested the work of the creator, he held the view that human reason is so impaired by sin that natural philosophy cannot be of use to us. Nevertheless, there was a form of Calvinist physico-theology, as represented for example in the work of Alsted. On this see Wilhelm Schmidt-Biggemann, 'Apokalyptische Universalwissenschaft: Johann Heinrich Alsteds *Diatribe de mille annis apocalypticis*', *Pietismus und Neuzeit* 14 (1988), 50–71.

principles of natural law, so we must ask how we might go about providing such principles. One thing that was needed was a detailed systematic historical study of how laws had come into existence, so that fundamental legal principles that transcended the particular contingent formulations in which they were embodied might be discovered. For this, procedures were needed to assess the reliability of records of historical events. In the *Methodus*, Bodin sets out to steer a middle path between the glossators' view that the task is to extract legal principles from what, in effect, they had treated as the God-given system of Roman law, and the sceptical view that we cannot aspire to any historical or legal principles because the sources are always at best uncertain and at worst conflicting.[47] The way to achieve this is to set out some generally agreed procedures for establishing reliability in the records and reports one works with, and Bodin sets out principles by which such assessments could be made.[48] He points out, for example, that the historian should prefer eyewitness accounts over second-hand reports, and should test these against other available sources of evidence. Moreover, there is the general question of the reliability of the source: we should prefer reports from those who have had administrative experience, and we should take account of whether our sources were praised or criticized by their contemporaries or immediate successors.

When Bodin turns to natural history, we find the same kinds of concern evident, and the lessons are drawn in an explicit fashion. A factor of utmost importance in motivating the new natural histories was the idea that contemplation of the natural world led one to contemplate its creator. The study of nature was religiously and morally edifying, a theme that had pervaded the whole range of sixteenth-century natural histories.[49] Emblematics had certainly engaged the question of moral edification in its own distinctive way, but it was just one way of achieving this, and not always the most appropriate one. A good deal depended upon what exactly one saw as being at issue. It might seem that moral and religious edification were ends in themselves which required no further explanation, but by the late sixteenth century in France we begin to find a more precise threat identified in such treatises, a threat to which their natural-theological messages are a response. At the beginning of his *Universae naturae theatrum* (1596), Bodin targets the 'impious' in the following terms:

---

[47] See George Huppert, *The Idea of Perfect History* (Urbana, 1970), ch. 6.

[48] See ibid. ch. 9.

[49] See e.g. Blair, *The Theater of Nature*, 28–30. Melanchthon is an interesting case here because of the way in which he made natural philosophy a central part of the defence of Lutheranism. His first published work, *Commentarius de anima* (Wittenberg, 1540) repeatedly draws attention to the skill of God in creating different parts of the body for different uses, and he claims that (Galenist) anatomy is both the beginning of theology and the path to faith-driven knowledge (*agnitio*) of God. See Sachiko Kusukawa, *The Transformation of Natural Philosophy: The Case of Philip Melanchthon* (Cambridge, 1995), 100–14. Note also Calvin's claim, in his commentary on Genesis, that the study of astronomy 'is not to be reprobated', for 'astronomy is not only very pleasant, but also very useful to be known: it cannot be denied that this art unfolds the admirable wisdom of God'. John Calvin, *Commentaries on the First Book of Moses Called Genesis*, trans. John King (2 vols, Edinburgh, 1847–50), i. 86–7.

How valuable is it that those who cannot be dragged by any precepts of divine laws or oracles of the prophets from their ingrained folly or led to the worship of the true deity, are forced by the most certain demonstrations of this science, as if under the application of torture and questioning, to reject all impiety and to adore one and the same eternal deity! . . . But because often we must dispute with those who have no taste of true piety, they must be constrained by natural science, whose power is so great that it alone can wrest, even from those who are unwilling, clear assent about the state and origin of the world and the infinite power of one eternal God, through the effects and continuous series of causes.[50]

Ann Blair has pointed out that the target here may well have included those who took advantage of the wars of religion to reject traditional Christian teaching altogether. The Calvinist minister Pierre Viret, for example, noted as early as 1564, two years after the outbreak of the religious wars in France, that this group presented greater difficulties than the 'superstitious and idolatrous' Catholics, and he accused them of having abused 'the liberty that is given to them to follow either one or the other of the two religions in conflict'.[51] This group was identified as 'atheists', but the term was used very loosely, and among those that might be included were Renaissance naturalists, and those otherwise labelled enthusiasts, who claimed to have direct divine inspiration without the mediation of any authority.

There is clearly a significant difference between the kind of view advocated here in Bodin, which was based in natural history, and the traditional Thomist approach. On the former, natural philosophy, particularly at the natural-historical end of the spectrum, can be directed so that it reveals fundamental Christian truths about the intentions of the Creator. On the latter, by contrast, there is not and could not be anything intrinsically Christian about natural philosophy, and it is the task of metaphysics, as Aquinas construed it, to reconcile Aristotelian natural philosophy and Christian theology, although, as we have seen, Aquinas also advocated another doctrine in a different context, in the 'five Ways' effectively operating with an understanding of nature that, while still far from Bodin's, was closer to it than it was to the traditional Aristotelian idea of individual natures.

As in the cases of biblical and legal interpretation, and that of the establishment of the Church's authority on doctrinal matters, what mattered above all in natural history was reliability. The problem was exacerbated by the inability of traditional classifications of flora and fauna to cover New World discoveries. The first natural histories of the New World, which began with L'Ecluse's *Exotica* (1605), and were firmly established by the time of George Markgraf's *Historia naturalis Brasiliencis* (1648), introduced animals and plants that had no known similitudes, affinities, antipathies: as Ashworth puts it, 'they came to the Old World naked, without emblematic significance'.[52] This spelled the end of emblematic zoology and botany. But it also forced a

[50] Jean Bodin, *Universae naturae theatrum* (Lyons, 1596), sigs. 3r–v.: trans. in Blair, *The Theater of Nature*, 22.

[51] Pierre Viret, *Instruction chrestienne* (2 vols, Geneva, 1564), vol. ii, sig. Cvi recto: trans. in Blair, *The Theater of Nature*, 22.

[52] See Ashworth, 'Natural History and the Emblematic World View', 318. See also Karen Reeds, *Botany in Medieval and Renaissance Universities* (New York, 1991). More generally, see

rethinking of just what natural history consisted in. The ground for such a rethinking was in fact already being cleared in other areas of natural history. Outside zoology and botany, the emblematic model had never had quite the same purchase in the sixteenth century. Much natural history from the mid-sixteenth century onwards was compiled as a response to perceived gaps in the traditional Aristotelian and didactic classific-ations of knowledge, but the emblematic view—as its demise in the face of New World flora and fauna indicates—tended to work with domains that were essentially closed, and hence was of little use in this genre. Cardano's *De subtilitate* (1550) and *De varietate* (1557), for example, cover natural philosophy and various secrets of the trades and medicine, as well as acrostics, poems hidden in poems, and mathematical conundrums. Johann Jakob Wecker's *De secretis* (1582) moves from the metaphysical and natural-philosophical implications of creation to how to counterfeit coins and gems, and how to catch fish. Della Porta's *Magia naturalis* (1589) deals with many categories usually excluded from classifications of knowledge either because they were considered too ephemeral (the art of beautifying women) or because they cover 'mar-vels' (optical tricks, invisible writing, etc.), but he also dealt with practical questions in metallurgy and optics which, if they had been covered in other classifications, were covered inadequately.[53] What lay behind this extension of what was to be included in knowledge was not just the opportunity to challenge the exclusiveness of traditional classifications, but also the opportunity to make clear how far modern knowledge had passed beyond Aristotle. In Book 17 of *De subtilitate*, for example, Cardano notes that there are so many inventions unknown to the ancients—such as domestic furnaces, church bells, stirrups on saddles, counterweights in clocks—that it would take more than a book to list them fully.

The traditional way of dealing with natural-historical, and natural-philosophical questions more generally, had been to compile a commentary on a text of Aristotle.[54] But this was only possible on the assumption that one's domain of enquiry was essen-tially closed or fixed by the text commented on, whereas this was not a viable assump-tion in the case of New World flora and fauna. New World natural history showed up the 'toadstools of philosophers' who had used sophistry to 'deny what ordinary experience teaches', as the geographer André Thevet put it in 1588,[55] but it worked under constraints that its European version did not. As Anthony Pagden notes,

the authority of the 'I' that was Aristotle, Aquinas or Jerome, derived not, as did that of the American observer, from privileged access to information and experience. As Hobbes had noted, it derived precisely from a cultural standing which was believed to confer authority. Aquinas and Jerome had been favoured by God, Aristotle by membership of a past society

---

Stephen Greenblatt, *Marvelous Possessions: The Wonder of the New World* (Chicago, 1991), Anthony Grafton, *New World, Ancient Texts: The Power of Tradition and the Shock of Discovery* (Cambridge, Mass., 1992), and Anthony Pagden, *European Encounters with the New World: From Renaissance to Romanticism* (New Haven, 1993).

[53] On the culture in which della Porta worked see Nicola Badaloni, 'I fratelli Della Porta e la cultura magica a Napoli nel'500', *Studi Storici* 1 (1959–60), 677–715.

[54] See Edward Grant, 'Aristotelianism and the Longevity of the Medieval World View', *History of Science* 16 (1978), 93–106.

[55] Quoted in Pagden, *European Encounters with the New World*, 90.

which was believed, more contentiously, to have had a unique understanding of the natural world, and whose works had been sanctioned by Aquinas. The observers of the American world, whose authority rested solely on their status *as* observers, had, therefore, to raise themselves as authors (and with them the texts that they had written) to a level which, if it was not directly comparable with that occupied by either the Church Fathers or the Bible, was, nevertheless, as distinctive and authoritative as the scientific works of antiquity.[56]

The response was a move away from the notion that observation and experiment simply confirm or refute some natural-philosophical view, towards the idea that the particularity of an experience endows it with a legitimacy.[57] This is a move that had precedents in biblical and legal hermeneutics. As we have seen, the new approach to biblical interpretation was one that bypassed allegorical reading in favour of a reconstruction of a text with a clear literal meaning. Just as in the case of legal humanism, this historicized the text: one was no longer reading something that, through the application of higher levels of interpretation, transcended the time and place in which it was written to reveal timeless truths, so that the intentions of the human author were entirely subservient to the truth of the text. Rather, one was now reading accounts of events that occurred in the distant past, accounts whose veracity had to be not only beyond question, but had to form the paradigm of historical authenticity: the transformation of Moses into 'a sacred historian', 'the father of history', and author of a factual account of the first stages of the formation of the earth was a striking example of these developments. Moreover, information about the authors and their intended audience now became relevant.[58] In this way, the gap between scripture and both historical and natural-historical texts narrowed, for scripture conveyed historical and geographical information. The Garden of Eden and the Flood no longer signified deeper spiritual truths whose meaning could be grasped through allegorical interpretation: the geographical location of the Garden of Eden and the actual extent of the Flood now became empirical questions, to be pursued not by reading more scripture but through historical and natural-historical scholarship and physical exploration. Correlatively, allegorical interpretation came to be regarded as obscuring the historical, geographical, and natural-philosophical truths contained in the Bible.

---

[56] Pagden, European Encounters with the New World, 55–6. See also A. D. Momigliano, *Studies in Historiography* (New York, 1966) ch. 8 on the precedents in Herodotus for New World historians.

[57] One of the most detailed and most important treatments of this question is to be found in Peter Dear, *Discipline and Experience* (Chicago, 1995). The context in which Dear discusses these questions is very different from that in which I shall raise them, however. Dear is concerned with the connection between natural philosophy *qua* matter theory and the 'mixed mathematical' disciplines, which he sees, in its Jesuit version, as a route to a viable quantitative natural philosophy. As my discussion of mixed mathematics in Ch. 11, will make clear, I do not believe that mixed mathematics could possibly have played this role. Moreover, questions of particularity of experience first emerge not through attempts to quantify natural phenomena but through natural history. The connection with quantification comes relatively late, in Newton's account of the spectrum, which we shall be looking at in Ch. 10.

[58] See the exemplary account in Harrison, *The Bible, Protestantism and the Rise of Natural Science*, ch. 4.

## DIVINE TRANSCENDENTALISM VERSUS
## PHYSICO-THEOLOGY

In broad terms, we can distinguish two polar opposites in the early to mid-seventeenth century on the question of what significance natural philosophy has for an understanding of divine intentions. One is exemplified in Descartes' view that God is both wholly transcendent and wholly inscrutable, and consequently we can learn nothing about him from natural philosophy. By contrast with the traditional Christianized Aristotelian stance that we have the sense organs we do because God gave them to us so that we might understand his creation, for example, Descartes and Cartesians generally take the view that we have been given sense organs so that we might protect our bodies from harm, and that their exercise does not yield any knowledge in its own right. The other view is that associated most strongly with Boyle, for whom natural philosophy is a non-sectarian way of understanding God's creation, on a par with scripture.

The Cartesian position is best seen as a response to the failure of Thomism. Outside (and even to some extent within) scholastic circles, the Thomist idea of a reconciliatory metaphysics was generally regarded to have failed by the beginning of the seventeenth century, but just as there are new versions of the natural-historical enterprise, so too are there new versions of the attempt to reconcile natural philosophy *qua* matter theory with theology. The most comprehensive version of the latter is that of Descartes. Descartes' view is distinctive in that he argues that God wholly transcends our knowledge, and so cannot be reached by any form of natural reasoning, because what we are able to imagine or conceive of cannot impose any limit on the powers of an omnipotent and omniscient God.[59] Clearly, on such a view, natural philosophy could, by means of its own resources, generate nothing that would match divinely instituted truths. Descartes' very strong reading of divine transcendence seems to exacerbate rather than resolve the Pomponazzi problem, in effect allowing a gap between what is true for us and what is true for God.[60] But in forcing open this gulf, what Descartes emphasizes is the fact that it cannot be bridged, but must be closed in some other way. Metaphysics is not sufficient, or even appropriate, for only something divinely guided could play this role. Descartes' candidate for the role is the doctrine of clear and distinct ideas, which he transforms from a rhetorical doctrine, in which we amplify some emotion or belief by presenting that belief clearly and distinctly to ourselves, into a cognitive doctrine, in which we assess the

---

[59] The question of just what it was possible for an omnipotent God to do had a long history in medieval thought. The problem seems to have begun with Jerome's statement that 'although God can do all things, he cannot raise up a virgin after she has fallen': see Francis Oakley, *Omnipotence, Covenant and Order* (Ithaca, NY, 1984), ch. 2. The discussion later turned on paradoxes of omnipotence, such as whether an omnipotent God could create something so heavy that he could not lift it: see Amos Funkenstein, *Theology and Scientific Imagination from the Middle Ages to the Seventeenth Century* (Princeton, 1986), ch. 3. Montaigne held that God's power was such that we could not even be sure that 2 x 10 = 20: *Essais*, Book 2, ch. 12 (Apologie de Raimond Sebond): *Essais*, ed. Rat, i. 588.

[60] See Gaukroger, *Cartesian Logic*, 60–71.

truth or falsity of an idea by presenting it to ourselves clearly and distinctly.[61] On the Cartesian view, clarity and distinctness is a faculty (somewhat like conscience in the case of morality) with which God has provided us so that we might assess purported truths independently of whatever authority they might claim. But because of the radical gulf between God's cognitive concerns and powers, and human cognitive concerns and powers, God is required to guarantee that our use of this faculty will genuinely generate truths.

On this conception, there is no way at all in which we could discern God's purposes in nature. God is, and remains, completely inscrutable, no matter how successful our inquiries into nature.[62] But it is not just God's inscrutability that prevents us gaining knowledge of him through natural enquiry. One thing that Descartes, under the influence of Mersenne, had been particularly concerned to refute was the Renaissance naturalist tendency to make God part of his creation. Descartes' God is completely transcendent and is not present in his creation. Consequently, even if he were not inscrutable, natural enquiry would not reveal him, for there are no discernible traces of him in his creation.

Such an understanding stands in direct opposition to a long tradition of religious natural speculation, which can be traced back as far as Paul: 'For the invisible things of him, from the creation of the world, are clearly seen, being understood by the things that are made; his eternal power also, and his divinity' (Romans 1: 20). Here, natural philosophy, especially in its natural history form, becomes in effect a type of natural theology. This is a far more widespread view than the Cartesian one, and we can find it clearly set out in Gassendi, for example. He admonishes Descartes for failing, in Meditation III, to follow the 'royal path' of philosophizing:

First, as I said before, you have strayed from the royal path, which is open and level, and which leads to the knowledge of God's existence, power, wisdom, goodness, and other qualities: namely, the excellent work of this universe, which exalts its author through its immensity, its divisions, its variety, its order, its beauty, its constancy, and its other attributes.[63]

The path Descartes has abandoned is, in short, that which leads to the discovery of design and purpose in nature. In forging this path for himself in his *Syntagma*, Gassendi collapses metaphysics into natural philosophy,[64] rejecting the idea of metaphysics (which he calls 'theology') as a discipline separate from natural philosophy, a separation he traces back to Plato. Instead, he follows the Hellenistic division of philosophy into logic, natural philosophy, and ethics:

---

[61] See Gaukroger, *Descartes, An Intellectual Biography*, 115–24.

[62] That is to say, we have no access to God through nature, or through anything else. Unmediated or direct knowledge of God is not ruled out, however: see Marion, *Sur la théologie blanche de Descartes*, 140–59, and Laurence Devillairs, *Descartes et la connaissance de dieu* (Paris, 2004), *passim*.

[63] Pierre Gassendi, *Opera Omnia* (6 vols., Lyon, 1658), iii. 337 col. 2. Note that this passage does not appear in the original set of objections that was appended to Descartes' *Meditationes,* but in the much expanded version, *Disquisitio Metaphysica*. The project is pursued in detail by Gassendi's British follower, Walter Charleton, in his *The Darknes of Atheism Dispelled by the Light of Nature. A Physico-Theological Treatise* (London, 1652).

[64] Generally, see Olivier Bloch, *La Philosophie de Gassendi* (The Hague, 1971), and Barry Brundell, *Pierre Gassendi: From Aristotelianism to a New Natural Philosophy* (Dordrecht, 1987).

The Stoics, Epicureans, and others combined theology with physics. Since the task of theology is to contemplate the natures of things, these philosophers considered that the contemplation of the divine nature and of the other immortal beings was included, especially since the divine nature reveals itself in the creation and government of the universe.[65]

Gassendi's idea was that, in pursuing natural philosophy, one automatically pursues questions about the nature of God because one finds abundant evidence of divine purpose, and hence of the nature of divine causation. Note that this approach does not require Gassendi to deny God's transcendence, and he does not identify God with his creation, any more than any other advocate of physico-theology does. The construal of God as immanent in nature remains the preserve of naturalism, and only Spinoza will defend such a view in the seventeenth century. Gassendi, by contrast, wants to revive and Christianize Epicurean atomism, and it is crucial for this that he be able to purge it of its naturalistic elements.[66]

It is Boyle, however, rather than Gassendi, who provides the best example of the form taken by physico-theology in the middle of the seventeenth century. Around 1649, and while under the influence of the Protestant reformer Samuel Hartlib, he began to consider natural philosophy as the path to natural theology, and this shaped his approach to natural philosophy throughout his career.[67] In *A Disquisition about the Final Causes of Natural Things*, composed in the mid-1670s, Boyle identifies 'two chief sects of modern philosophizers' who deny

that the naturalist ought at all to trouble to busy himself about final causes. For *Epicurus*, and most of his followers (for I except some late ones, especially the learned *Gassendus*) banish the considerations of the ends of things; because the world being, according to them, made by chance, no ends of any thing can be supposed to have been intended. And on the contrary, Monsieur *des Cartes*, and most of his followers, suppose all the ends of God in things corporeal to be so sublime, that it were presumption in man to think his reason can extend to discover them.[68]

But for Boyle the whole point of pursuing natural philosophy in the first place is that it reveals to us the handiwork and purposes of God in a way that goes deeper than anything else we can achieve by use of natural reason:

For the works of God are not like the tricks of jugglers, or the pageants, that entertain princes, where concealment is requisite to wonder; but the knowledge of the works of God proportions our admiration of them, they participating and disclosing so much of the inexhausted perfections of their author, that the further we contemplate them, the more foot-steps and impressions we discover of the perfections of their Creator; and our utmost science can but give us a juster veneration of his omniscience. And as when some country fellow looks upon a

---

[65] Gassendi, *Opera Omnia*, i. 27 col. 1.

[66] See Margaret J. Osler, 'Fortune, Fate, and Divination: Gassendi's Voluntarist Theology and the Baptism of Epicureanism', in Margaret J. Osler, ed., *Atoms, Pneuma, and Tranquillity: Epicurean and Stoic Themes in European Thought* (Cambridge, 1991), 155–74.

[67] On the early move from religious and moral interests to natural-philosophical ones, see Michael Hunter, *Robert Boyle (1627–91): Scrupulosity and Science* (Woodbridge, 2002), ch. 2.

[68] Boyle, *Works*, v. 393. See Timothy Shanahan, 'Teleological Reasoning in Boyle's *Final Causes*', in Michael Hunter, ed., *Robert Boyle Reconsidered* (Cambridge, 1994), 177–92.

curious watch, though he may be hugely taken with the rich enamel of the case, and perhaps with some pretty landskip that adorns the dial-plate; yet will not his ignorance permit him so advantageous a notion of the exquisite maker's skill, as that little engine will form in some curious artist, who besides that obvious workmanship, that first entertains the eye, considers the exactness, and knows the use of every wheel, takes notice of their proportion, contrivance, and adaptation all together, and of the hidden springs, that move them all: so in the world, though every peruser may read the existence of a Deity, and be in his degree affected with what he sees, yet he is utterly unable to descry there those subtler characters and flourishes of omniscience, which true philosophers are sharp-sighted enough to discern.[69]

Indeed, Boyle notes, philosophers of almost all religions 'have been, by the contemplation of the world, moved to consider it under the notion of a temple',[70] and 'if the world be a temple, man sure must be the priest, ordained (by being qualified) to celebrate divine service not only in, but for it'.[71] The natural philosopher has become not only religiously motivated but religiously empowered. He accepts that science may be used by the libertine, who attempts to 'misemploy it to impugne the grounds, or discredit the practice of, religion', but the more one studies natural philosophy the more one comes to reject the libertine hypothesis that the world is produced by 'so incompetent and pitiful a cause as blind chance or the tumultuous joslings of atomical portions of senseless matter'.[72] Pagan philosophers had made natural philosophy the basis for their moral philosophy and the study of nature had been traditionally regarded by many Christian philosophers as either a distraction or idolatrous. Boyle's response, accentuating a feature of the religious natural history tradition, is to transform natural enquiry into what is in effect a form of worship, the natural philosopher being singled out by the skills that enable him to search deep into the nature of things, to see what others have missed in God's creation. Against those English divines who 'out of a holy jealousy (as they think) for religion, labour to deter men from addicting themselves to serious and thoughtful inquiries into nature, as from a study unsafe for a Christian, and likely to end in atheism',[73] he replies that

Provided the information be such, as a man has just cause to believe, and perceives, that he clearly understands, it will not alter the case, whether we have it by reason, as that is taken for the faculty furnished but with its inbred notions, or by experiments purposely devised, or by

---

[69] *The Usefulness of Natural Philosophy*, Essay III: Boyle, *Works*, ii. 30. Cf. the statement of an earlier chemist/alchemist: 'Every creature in this ample Machine of the World, in which the Invisible Creator exhibits himself to us to be seen, heard, tasted, smelt, and handled, is nothing else but the shadow of God': Oswald Croll, *Basilica chymica* (London, 1635), Preface.

[70] Ibid. Essay III; *Works*, ii. 31.

[71] Ibid. Essay III; *Works*, ii. 32. Boyle's imagery of temples and high priests is not by any means idiosyncratic. Compare, for example, Matthew Hale: 'The Glorious God therefore seems to have placed Man in this goodly Temple of the World, endued him with Knowledge, Understanding, and Will, laid before him these glorious Works of his Power and Wisdom; that he might be the common Procurator, the vicarious Representative, the common High Priest of the inanimate and irrational World': *The Primitive Origination of Mankind, Considered and Examined According to the Light of Nature* (London, 1677), 372.

[72] *Christian Virtuoso*; *Works*, v. 514.

[73] *The Usefulness of Natural Philosophy*, Essay II; *Works*, ii. 15.

testimony human or divine, which last we call revelation. For all these are but differing ways of informing the understanding, and of signifying to it the same thing.[74]

Such an understanding of natural philosophers is possible only on the basis of a wholly new conception of the enterprise, and a wholly new conception of those who command the requisite authority to undertake it. It is to these questions that we now turn.

[74] Ibid. Essay III; *Works*, ii. 31.

# PART III

# 5

# Reconstructing Natural Philosophy

To understand what is at issue in the question of the legitimacy of natural philosophy in the early-modern era, we need to look at the origins of philosophical enquiry in more general terms, and it is helpful to take our bearings from the Pomponazzi question. I have identified Pomponazzi's dilemma on the standing of natural-philosophical enquiry vis-à-vis Christian teaching as a dilemma that encapsulates problems that will motivate early-modern worries about the appropriate way to pursue enquiry into the natural realm. Let us begin, then, by recalling the problem facing Pomponazzi and his contemporaries. It was that there were two different ways of arriving at certain core doctrines: a natural-philosophical route and a theological one. The two were connected because, as we saw in Chapter 2, from the end of the eleventh century there was a concerted project of establishing the credentials of orthodox Christianity both in order to avoid heresy and in order to convince non-Christians of the superiority of Christianity. What was shared with this latter audience was a pagan philosophical culture which provided a metaphysical apparatus for discussing theological questions. This metaphysical apparatus was disputed in both Christian and Islamic cultures, but in both cases Aristotelianism eventually triumphed over Platonism. In the Christian West, this occurred because making philosophical sense of a number of aspects of Christian theology required the development of a conception of abstractive knowledge, and Aristotelianism was the only comprehensive philosophical system able to provide adequate resources for this. But the adoption of Aristotelianism meant that the point of entry into a philosophically grounded theology was natural philosophy, tying the fate of Christian theology to natural philosophy in an unprecedented way.[1] The lack of fit between the two was evident to many theologians in the thirteenth century, as we have seen, but their attempt to return to what by this time was a philosophically impoverished Augustinian model failed to match the advances in thinking through philosophical and theological questions driven by the Christianized Aristotelianism that had

---

[1] Cf. Buckley, *At the Origins of Modern Atheism*, who, reflecting on nineteenth-century developments, laments that 'Religion abandoned the justification intrinsic to its own nature and experience, and insisted that its vindication would be found in philosophy, become natural philosophy, become mechanics' (359). Note, however, that if the argument of the last three chapters holds, then this form of justification is in fact an intrinsic part of medieval and modern Christianity, not some later accretion, and above all not something that can be removed without a fundamental reshaping of Christianity, in which its standing vis-à-vis (as well as its ability to engage with) other religions and secular movements is radically altered.

been developed and refined by Aquinas. The problems of the irreconcilability of Aristotelian natural philosophy and Christian theology came to a head again in the sixteenth century for, despite the efforts of the late sixteenth-century scholastics, no metaphysical bridge could be established between natural philosophy on the one hand, and Christian revelation and theology on the other.

Pomponazzi, as we have seen, did not deny divine providence or divine activity generally, but argued that this activity takes a physical form that must be described and explained purely in natural-philosophical terms. These natural-philosophical explanations then replaced the traditional supernatural ones, and in the process repositioned a range of issues in the natural-philosophical realm. But what is the upshot of such repositioning? Remember that, in the case of personal immortality, he contrasted what he took to be a satisfactory natural-philosophical understanding of the question with Christian teaching on the subject, maintaining that the latter was 'true and most certain in itself'. The problem, as we have seen, is that there seem to be two quite different but completely legitimate ways of pursuing the question, with no metaphysics that can reconcile them. Yet if we are to prefer the one to the other, the choice seems straightforward, for only one of them even purports to offer us truth. How could it be maintained that a natural-philosophical doctrine was satisfactory if it was in conflict with a doctrine one accepted as true? Pomponazzi was not being disingenuous—he was not committed to mortalism but felt he had to disguise this by affirming his commitment to Christian doctrine. Every scholastic philosopher from Aquinas onwards was aware that there was a discrepancy between Aristotelian natural philosophy and Christian teaching on this matter, and it was source of puzzlement and concern. Thomists assumed that some form of metaphysical reconciliation was possible. Pomponazzi offered philosophical arguments to show that such reconciliation is actually impossible, prompting the question of what exactly one should do in these circumstances. Were we to confine ourselves to *De immortalitate*, we might conclude that Pomponazzi's answer was that there is nothing we can do: the immortality of the soul, like the question of the eternity of the world, is a 'neutral' issue, that is, there is no philosophical way of establishing its truth one way or the other.[2] Yet this did not deter him from preferring very contentious natural-philosophical explanations to supernatural ones in *De fato* and *De incantationibus*. Somehow, natural-philosophical explanations were not automatically trumped by other kinds of explanation, despite the fact that he did not see them as establishing the truth of the matter. This is not merely an oddity of Pomponazzi's account, but raises the whole question of the standing, and particularly the autonomy, of natural philosophy.

The issues raised by the autonomy of natural philosophy are deep ones, and proved beyond the resources of medieval and Renaissance philosophical cultures.

---

[2] This seems to have been a set Lutheran response to such issues. As Roger French notes, 'When Daniel Sennert wanted reassurance on whether animals had souls he wrote to a number of German theology faculties, some of which replied that it was a matter of philosophy only, for Luther had not pronounced on the topic': *Medicine before Science*, 169 n. 42.

They appeared in the West with the introduction of Aristotelianism in the twelfth century, coming to a head again at the beginning of the sixteenth century in the Fifth Lateran Council's deliberations on the philosophical standing of the doctrine of the immortality of the soul. The Thomist attempt at resolution had failed, as was becoming increasingly clear in the course of the sixteenth century, and attempts to replace it with something different were very radical at first, as in the work of Telesio and Bruno, showing little regard for reconciliation or orthodoxy. This situation changed in the early seventeenth century, as natural philosophers began to forge links between natural philosophy and Christian teaching in a wholly new ways. The issues raised by the autonomy of natural philosophy hinge directly on the question of the aims of cognitive enquiry, however, and unless we can uncover the sources of this especially intractable problem, we will not be able to appreciate fully the magnitude of the difficulties facing seventeenth-century natural philosophers.

I want to argue that, underlying these changes, there is a complex shift in the relations between truth and justification, relations that shape the context within which both natural philosophy and religious thought are pursued, and bear directly on the questions of legitimation that came to affect both natural philosophy and religion in the seventeenth and eighteenth centuries. I begin by looking at the sixteenth- and early seventeenth-century theories of natural-philosophical method, in particular at what exactly it was that was identified as the source of the problems in the case of scholastic natural philosophy, and Aristotelian natural philosophy more generally. We have already seen that, by the late sixteenth century, scholasticism was increasingly coming to be thought of as a form of sterile disputation. The problem was diagnosed as methodological: Aristotelian natural philosophy was committed to a mode of enquiry that could not possibly constitute a method of discovery. Consequently the search began for something that would genuinely constitute such a method, and I shall focus on Bacon in this regard. Finally, I turn to one of the dominating natural-philosophical problems of the early seventeenth century, that of the appropriate form of enquiry in the case of astronomy, focusing on the extent to which this could be considered a hypothetical enterprise. In the Pomponazzi case, there had been an apparent conflict between natural-philosophical reasoning and a Christian belief which seems to have been accepted by everyone (except perhaps Bruno). The Copernican question was different in that the conflict was not between Aristotelian natural philosophy and Christian teaching, but arose because of perceived inadequacies in Aristotelian natural philosophy, so that, now, what was at issue was a conflict between Christian teaching and new astronomical theories which, once they left the realm of hypothetical claims, were of dubious natural-philosophical standing. It is in establishing the natural-philosophical standing of these claims that the tasks of natural philosophy came to be realigned and above all connected with practical-mathematical disciplines which had been deemed to have no relevance to natural philosophy in the Aristotelian tradition. This raises the question of what skills and qualities the natural philosopher must bring to the discipline, a question that will concern us in the next chapter.

## THE PROBLEM OF DISCOVERY

One of the pre-eminent questions for sixteenth-century natural philosophers was whether there was a method of discovery that could be relied upon to guide one's research in natural philosophy. In his earlier writings such as the *Topics*, Aristotle had elaborated procedures for the 'discovery of knowledge'. These procedures were designed to guide one in uncovering the appropriate evidence, discovering the most fruitful questions to ask, and so on, and they did this by providing devices or strategies for classifying or characterizing problems so that they could be posed and solved using set techniques. In his later works such as the *Prior* and *Posterior Analytics*, however, there was a marked change of emphasis. Aristotle now pursued the question of the presentation of results, as his interests shifted to the validity of the reasoning used to establish conclusions on the basis of accepted premises: syllogistic. In other words, his concerns shifted from questions of discovery to questions of demonstration. What happened in the sixteenth-century development of the Aristotelian account of method turned in large part on a basic confusion about the method of discovery, in that Aristotle's original method of discovery, the topics, became lost, at least in the context of scientific discovery, and his method of demonstration—syllogistic—came to be construed as method per se, that is, as a method of discovery as well as a method of presentation.

In the sixteenth century, this gave rise to two opposing tendencies. Defenders of Aristotle tried to understand how syllogistic could be construed so that it could be used as, or at least be part of, a method of discovery. Critics of Aristotle, by contrast, argued that syllogistic could not possibly be part of a method of discovery, and that many of the problems in Aristotle's account of a whole range of natural-philosophical matters could be traced to his having attempted to employ this useless method. These critics sought a genuine method of discovery in rhetoric, which was the area in which the study of the topics had been developed after the death of Aristotle, principally by those Roman thinkers who stood at the foundations of early-modern rhetoric, Cicero and Quintilian. There were both conservative and radical advocates of this approach; the conservatives, such as Ramus, saw a method of discovery as being a guide to the storehouse of knowledge built up since antiquity, and the radicals, such as Bacon, saw it as offering an opportunity to replace traditional learning with something completely new.

As an example of the defenders of Aristotle, we can take those early sixteenth-century Paduan Aristotelians such as Zabarella and Nifo who developed an account of the demonstrative syllogism as a method of discovery known as *regressus* theory. The basic issue to which *regressus* theory was directed was the informativeness of the procedure of building up knowledge syllogistically, and, although this was not clearly recognized at the time, there was in effect a double problem.[3] First, Aristotle's procedure seemed to require that one started from sense perception, abstracting more and more general principles from what was observed, and then deducing

---

[3] See Gaukroger, *Cartesian Logic*, ch. 1.

one's observations from those basic principles, a procedure that seemed circular and uninformative. Second, there was the question of how a purely formal device such as the syllogism could yield new information, how it could go beyond the information contained in the premises.

The first of these is the key to understanding how the syllogism can be informative for the *regressus* theorists. Their core argument is that, while it is true that one starts with observations, proceeds to general principles, and then shows how the observations can be deduced from these general principles, nevertheless the grasp of the observations that one has at the end of the process is very different from what one has at the beginning. One starts by grasping *that* something happens, but at the end of the process one grasps *why* that same thing happens. On this reading, the syllogism is not a discovery of new facts so much as a discovery of the reasons underlying the facts. It is a way of articulating the facts in terms of the principles underlying them, rather than a means for discovery of the facts. For Aristotle, the epistemic and the consequential directions in demonstrative syllogisms run in the opposite direction. That is to say, it is knowing the premises from which the conclusion is to be deduced that is the important thing as far as providing a deeper scientific understanding is concerned, not discovering what conclusions follow from given premises. The demonstrative syllogism was simply a means of presentation of results in a systematic way, one suitable for conveying these to students.[4] The conclusions of the syllogisms were known in advance, and what the syllogism provided was a means of relating those conclusions to premises that would explain them.

*Regressus* theory incorporates this kind of understanding into a larger theory of scientific demonstration.[5] *Regressus* combines an inference from an observed effect to its proximate cause with an inference from a proximate cause to an observed effect, and it is this combination that produces the knowledge required. The most usual scheme employed is a fourfold one, although there are a number of variants.[6] First, one obtains 'accidental' knowledge of an effect through observation; second, through induction and demonstration of the fact, one obtains 'accidental' knowledge of the cause of the fact; third, via a form of reflection referred to as *negotiatio*, one grasps the necessary connection between the proximate cause and its effect; and finally, fourth, one demonstrates the fact from the cause that necessitates it.

*Regressus* theory was subject to a number of problems. One of these derives from Aristotle, namely that of distinguishing demonstrative from non-demonstrative syllogisms. For Aristotle, scientific demonstrations proceed syllogistically, and he argued

---

[4] See Jonathan Barnes, 'Aristotle's Theory of Demonstration', in Jonathan Barnes, Malcolm Schofield, and Richard Sorabji, eds, *Articles on Aristotle, i. Science* (London, 1975), 65–87.

[5] For general accounts of this development, see Nicholas Jardine, 'Galileo's Road to Truth and the Demonstrative Regress', *Studies in History of Science* 7 (1976), 277–318; idem, 'Epistemology of the Sciences', in Charles Schmitt, Quentin Skinner, and Eckhard Kessler, eds, *The Cambridge History of Renaissance Philosophy* (Cambridge, 1988), 685–711; Neal W. Gilbert, *Renaissance Concepts of Method* (New York, 1960); John H. Randall, *The School of Padua and the Emergence of Modern Science* (Padua, 1961); and Heikki Mikkeli, *An Aristotelian Response to Humanism: Jacopo Zabarella on the Nature of Arts and Sciences* (Helsinki, 1992).

[6] See Jardine, 'Epistemology of the Sciences', 687 ff.

that some forms of demonstration provide explanations or causes whereas others do not. This may occur even where the syllogisms are formally identical. Consider, for example, these two syllogisms:

The planets do not twinkle
That which does not twinkle is near

---

The planets are near

The planets are near
That which is near does not twinkle

---

The planets do not twinkle

In Aristotle's discussion of these syllogisms in his *Posterior Analytics*, he argues that the first is only a demonstration 'of fact', whereas the second is a demonstration of 'why', or a scientific explanation. In the latter we are provided with a reason, or cause, or explanation of the conclusion: the reason why the planets do not twinkle is that they are near. In the former, we have a valid argument but not a demonstrative one, since the planets' not twinkling is not a cause or explanation of their being near. So the first syllogism is in some way uninformative compared to the second: the latter produces understanding, the former does not. Now the two syllogisms are formally identical: both are in Barbara mode, which means that the way in which the conclusion is deduced from (or generated by) the premisses is identical. The fact that one of the syllogisms gives us a cause of the effect is not therefore something due to a formal difference, and in any case there are other kinds of syllogism in which cause is related to effect. Aristotle himself refers us to a form of intellectual insight (*nous*) by which we distinguish the difference between demonstrative and non-demonstrative syllogisms, but he does not give us an account of what difference it is that we are supposed to recognize. Nevertheless, what he was trying to achieve is clear enough. He was seeking some way of identifying those forms of deductive inference that resulted in epistemic advance, that furthered one's understanding. Realizing that no purely logical criterion would suffice, he attempted to show that epistemic advance depended on some non-logical but nevertheless internal or structural feature which some deductive inferences possess. But he was unable to provide any account of just what gave rise to this feature.

The *regressus* account has a related problem. In the crucial third stage of the *regressus*, we are supposed to grasp the necessary connection between cause and effect through a *negotiatio*. In contrast to Zabarella and to his own account in his early publications, Nifo, in his later writings, began to show some scepticism about *negotiatio*, suggesting that the best one can hope for in some cases is conjectural knowledge.[7] And indeed *negotiatio* does remain a mysterious process, although the idea of inspecting the contents of one's mental states for guidance as to the truth or certainty of a proposition is something that reappears in Descartes, even though its source is very different.

---

[7] See the discussion in Jardine, 'Galileo's Road to Truth and the Demonstrative Regress'.

Those who rejected the idea that the syllogism could play any role in scientific understanding, tended to assume (along with many supporters of Aristotle) that, for Aristotle, the demonstrative syllogism was a method of discovery, a means of deducing novel conclusions from accepted premisses. Conceived as a tool of discovery, there is some justice in the claim that the demonstrative syllogism looks trivial, but this was never its purpose for Aristotle: discovery was something to be guided by the topics, which were procedures for classifying or characterizing problems so that they could be solved using set techniques. More specifically, they were designed to provide the distinctions needed if one was to be able to formulate problems properly, as well as supplying devices enabling one to determine what has to be shown if the conclusion one desires is to be reached. Now the topics were not confined to scientific enquiry, but had an application in ethics, political argument, rhetoric, and so on, and indeed they were meant to apply to any area of enquiry. The problem was that, during the Middle Ages, the topics came to be associated very closely and exclusively with rhetoric, principally through the texts of Cicero and Quintilian, and their relevance to scientific discovery became at first obscured and then completely lost. The upshot of this was that, for all intents and purposes, the results of Aristotelian natural philosophy lost all contact with the procedures of discovery which produced them. While these results remained unchallenged, the problem was not particularly apparent. But when they came to be challenged in a serious and systematic way, as they were from the sixteenth century onwards, they began to take on the appearance of mere dogmas, backed up by circular reasoning. It is this strong connection between Aristotle's supposed method of discovery and the unsatisfactoriness not only of his particular results but also of his overall natural philosophy that provoked the intense concern with method in the seventeenth century.

The first stage of this revision took the form of what might be termed a humanist backlash. If the defenders of Aristotle had ignored (because they misrecognized) his method of discovery, humanists such as Ramus ignored his method of presentation. The topics had been pursued with vigour and refined in rhetoric and law in the Renaissance, and served there as the means of discovery or 'invention'. The humanist critics of Aristotle held up the topics as constitutive not just of discovery but of the whole process of cognitive understanding.

The *regressus* theorists had believed that we cannot simply demonstrate an effect through its proximate cause since, although causes are better known 'in nature', effects are better known 'in us', because our knowledge always starts from sensation. This distinction was crucial to orthodox Aristotelianism. It draws a sharp line between what is 'better known to us', which is a function of our limited experience, and what is 'better known in nature', that is to say, the most general precepts underlying the discipline under consideration, precepts which enable us to grasp the universal principles around which the discipline is structured. This distinction motivates Aristotelian accounts of pedagogy, invention or discovery, and judgement, the idea being that we must start from what is better known to us and work towards, or—in the all-important case of the pedagogical context—be guided towards, what is better known in nature. This guidance takes the form of the methods of resolution (analysis of a problem into its elements) and composition (construction of a solution out of these elements), all this being done in the context of a syllogistic formulation of all knowledge. Disputes between Aristotelians and their opponents on question of scientific demonstration in the sixteenth century generally took place in a pedagogical context. Ramus thinks of knowledge in exclusively pedagogic terms, transforming the topics into a system of pedagogic classification of knowledge: the point of the exercise is to enable us to refer any question back to the storehouse of ancient wisdom, the role of the topics being to provide us with points of entry into this storehouse.[8] Ramus' approach had no monopoly in attempts to deal with this question, but it did manage to engage a very broad range of questions—about the relative standing of various disciplines, the aims of pedagogy, and the nature of knowledge—which had become problematic in the course of the sixteenth century. An important ingredient in this response is an outright rejection of the distinction between 'better known to us' and 'better known in nature': one kind of knowledge can be said to be prior to another only if the one is needed to explain the other, and such priority resides resolutely with the most general precepts. Instead of trying to combine them, Ramists prized apart discovery and demonstration, maintaining that the former had nothing to do with the syllogistically motivated procedures of resolution and composition, but depended simply on observation and inferences from such observation. Demonstration is irrelevant to how knowledge is acquired on this view: all that matters is how it is best conveyed and this will be the same in all pedagogic circumstances, for it will always consist in the move from the more general to the less general.

## SPECULATIVE VERSUS PRODUCTIVE DISCIPLINES

The idea that there is no independent method of presentation of results, only a method of discovery, encouraged the view that the only effective way of demonstrating something was to reproduce how it was discovered. This proved to be a very powerful idea, not least because the presentation of material in such a way that the procedure used by the investigator was explicit and open to assessment allowed the reader potentially to share in the witnessing of the phenomena, thereby removing the need for an appeal to the intrinsic authority of the investigator. Combined with an attack on the sterile nature of scholastic book-learning, the idea fostered a renewed concern with methods of discovery, a concern that was to be at the forefront of philosophy in the seventeenth century. One of the key figures in this development was Bacon, and his concern was above all to make natural philosophy a practical, productive discipline.[9] Following the Roman rhetorical tradition, he thought of epistemology in psychological terms, and his methodological project has two main parts: one aims to rid the mind of preconceptions, while the other aims to guide the mind in a productive direction. These components are interconnected, for until we understand the

---

[8] See the discussion in Walter J. Ong, *Ramus, Method and the Decay of Dialogue* (Cambridge, Mass., 1983).

[9] For a detailed discussion of Bacon on these questions see Gaukroger, *Francis Bacon and the Transformation of Early Modern Philosopy*; Peter Urbach, *Francis Bacon's Philosophy of Science* (La Salle, Ill., 1987); and Francis Anderson, *The Philosophy of Francis Bacon* (New York, 1971).

nature of the mind's preconceptions, we do not know in which direction we need to lead its thinking.

Bacon's radical view is that various natural inclinations of the mind must be purged before the new procedure can be set in place. His approach here is genuinely different from that of his predecessors, as he realizes. Logic or method in themselves cannot simply be introduced to replace bad habits of thought, which Bacon identifies as 'idols', because it is not simply a question of replacement. The simple application of logic to one's mental processes is insufficient.[10] In the first instance, what is needed is a purging of those features of the mind that lead us astray. Only once we have achieved this, or at least have made some significant advances along these lines, can we pursue his method of discovery. What he is seeking from this method of discovery is the discovery of causes which are both necessary and sufficient for their effects. Showing his Aristotelian heritage, what Bacon is looking for are the ultimate explanations of things, and it is natural to assume that ultimate explanations are unique. Bacon's method is designed to provide a route to such explanations, and the route takes us through a number of proposed causal accounts, which are refined at each stage. The procedure he elaborates, eliminative induction, is one in which various possibly contributory factors are isolated and examined in turn, to see whether they do in fact make a contribution to the effect. Those that do not are rejected and the result is a convergence on those factors that are truly relevant. The kind of 'relevance' that Bacon is after is, in effect, necessary conditions: the procedure is supposed to enable us to weed out those factors that are not necessary for the production of the effect, so that we are left only with those that are necessary.

This is not the end of the matter, however, for the requirements that Bacon places on something if it is to be a truth are even stronger. In *Valerius Terminus*, he goes through a number of what he considers to be inadequate criteria that have been used to establish truth. He begins by setting out a number of criteria that he finds unsatisfactory—reliance on antiquity and authority, upon commonly accepted notions, on the natural assent of the mind, and so on—on the grounds that none of them are 'absolute and infallible evidence of truth, and bring no security sufficient for effects and operations'. The criterion he advocates ties in evidence for the truth of a theory and its usefulness in a very intimate and somewhat surprising way:

That the discovery of new works and active directions not known before, is the only trial to be accepted of; and yet not that neither, in case where one particular giveth light to another; but where particulars induce an axiom or observation, which axiom found out discovereth and designeth new particulars. That the nature of this trial is not only upon the point, whether the knowledge be profitable or no; not because you may always conclude that the Axiom which discovereth new instances be true, but contrariwise you may safely conclude that if it discover not any new instance it is in vain and untrue.[11]

---

[10] This is contrary to the view of contemporary scholastic writers on logic. These include Chrystostomus Cabero, *Brevis summularum recapitulatio* (Valladolid, 1623), who offers the idea that logic is morally binding on thought, and Raphael Aversa, *Logica* (Rome, 1623), who uses a medical analogy to suggest that logic remedies the natural weaknesses of reasoning by establishing rules for inference.

[11] Bacon, *Works*, iii. 242.

It looks here as if Bacon is maintaining that something can be true only if it is useful. This is hardly plausible. Not only are there useless truths, but there are falsehoods which have practical application: approximations, for example, are sometimes more useful than the truths of which they are the approximation. Nevertheless, what Bacon is seeking is not just truths but informative truths, and his claim is that the only way in which we can judge whether something is informatively true is to determine whether it is productive, whether it yields something tangible and useful. And if something does consistently yield results which are tangible and useful, then it is informatively true. In some respects Bacon's concerns mirror those of his predecessors here, but he is ultimately after something different, for the aim of the natural philosopher, on Bacon's view, is not merely to discover truths but to produce new works. This is something that goes beyond the idea that truths simply be informative: they must also be productive.

The issue of productive truths highlights a question prominent among those raised in thinking through the causes of the failure of scholastic natural philosophy, namely that of the kinds of aim that natural philosophy should foster. These concerns were generally motivated by specific humanist considerations about what philosophy generally should aim to achieve, and they contrast contemplative but sterile forms of understanding with forms of understanding that induce one to behave differently. Such arguments have their original home in a moral context, but Bacon will shift them into a natural-philosophical context. It is important that we be attentive to this shift, for it enables us to understand that the standing that natural philosophy came to have in the seventeenth century was by no means *sui generis*. Quite the contrary, the discipline had to be fundamentally reshaped, and one important strand in this reshaping was the remodelling of natural philosophy along the lines of moral philosophy.

We have seen that Aristotle was criticized by Petrarch and others for claiming that the point of ethics was not to gain knowledge but to make one behave better, while at the same time offering nothing that might move one to act more virtuously.[12] By the Renaissance, this kind of demand had become widespread, to the extent that, in late sixteenth-century England, for example, Sidney and his Areopagus circle were arguing that the traditional aims of philosophy, as construed by humanists, were better served by poetry than philosophy.[13] When Bacon attempted to reform philosophical practice in response to these kinds of criticisms, he continued to see practical outcome as proof of the worth of the philosophical enterprise, even though he wanted to argue that natural philosophy, and not moral philosophy, was the paradigm philosophical activity. The underlying idea is that just as ethics manifests its worth in making people behave more virtuously, and medicine manifests it worth in making people more healthy, so natural philosophy manifests its worth in enabling us to secure control over our natural environment.

---

[12] Petrarch has a more general concern with usefulness, unfavourably comparing medicine, which he sees as largely useless, with a useful art such as agriculture: *Invectivarum contra medicum libri IV*, Book 1, ch. 5, and Book 2, ch. 18.

[13] This forms a theme in French humanism also, with Peiresc and La Mothe le Vayer defending it in the seventeenth century.

In his *Cogitationes de natura rerum*, Bacon criticizes Aristotle's distinction between natural motions (rectilinear motions in the case of terrestrial bodies, circular motions in the case of celestial ones) and violent motions. Aristotle had distinguished between natural objects and processes on the one hand, and artefacts and unnatural or constrained or violent processes on the other. Natural philosophy was concerned to explain the properties of things in terms of their essences. What lies at the basis of this conception is the distinction between those things that have an intrinsic principle of change, and those things that have an extrinsic principle of change. An acorn, which has within itself the power to change its state, namely into an oak tree, and a stone raised above the ground, which has the power to change its position, namely to fall to the ground, both come in the first category. In neither case is anything external required for the change/motion to occur. For Aristotle, we explain and understand things by understanding their natures, and to grasp the nature of something is to grasp the source of all its natural properties. If we ask why a stone falls, the answer is that stones are heavy and heavy things fall: that is all there is to it. If we are asked why this tree puts out broad flat leaves in spring and keeps them through the summer, we may reply that it does this because it is a beech. In other words, it is not necessary to look outside the thing to account for its behaviour. And wherever the behaviour of something can be explained without looking outside the thing, that behaviour, and the feature that the thing acquires or retains, is natural. It is natural for stones to fall, it is the nature of beeches to have broad flat leaves. Such explanations are explanations of unconstrained, internally generated natural processes, and explanations of this kind lie at the core of Aristotle's natural philosophy.[14] Natural philosophy is a *scientia* of natural processes: it tells us why and how they occur. By contrast, there can be no *scientia* of unnatural or constrained or 'violent' states and processes, which might be caused by any number of extrinsic events. Natural philosophy cannot be expected to account for these: a stone falling to the ground when released from constraints has a single explanation which refers us to an intrinsic cause, whereas the causes of a stone rising from the ground do not have anything to do with anything essential to the stone, but rather arise from some purely contingent circumstances.

Bacon argues that this way of approaching natural philosophy is fundamentally mistaken. It is 'violent' motions, he argues, not natural motions, that should be the subject of natural-philosophical enquiry. These include those unnatural processes produced by mechanical devices such as levers, pulleys, and screws; those strategic unnatural placements of stones that hold buildings up; those unnatural motions of bodies produced by artillery, and so on. These are 'the life and soul of artillery, engines, and the whole enterprise of mechanics'.[15] Note that Bacon is not concerned with the truth or otherwise of Aristotle's account here. His argument is that the whole

---

[14] There is a good discussion of these issues in William Charlton's introduction and notes to his translation of the *Physics*: *Aristotle's Physics I, II* (Oxford, 1970), from which I have taken the example here. For a more comprehensive treatment, see Wolfgang Wieland, *Die aristotelische Physik* (Göttingen, 1970), and Helen S. Lang, *The Order of Nature in Aristotle's Physics* (Cambridge, 1998).

[15] Bacon, *Works*, iii. 29 [text]/v. 433 [trans].

investigation is beside the point, so questions of whether it is true or not are simply irrelevant.

Crucial to this approach is his distinction between practical, active enquiry and philosophical contemplation.[16] At the most basic level, what is wrong with Aristotle's approach to natural philosophy for Bacon is that it is directed towards seeking a contemplative understanding of natural phenomena.[17] But if one is guided by a concern to pursue natural philosophy with a view to transforming nature for our benefit, it will be wholly inadequate, because it will not deal, or will deal only peripherally, with those natural-philosophical questions than give natural philosophy its legitimacy as a worthwhile area of enquiry in the first place. Bacon distinguishes between understanding, on the one hand, how things are made up and what they consist of—an exercise he associates with disputatious scholastics—and, on the other, by what force and in what manner they come together, and how they are transformed. It is the latter that we must seek to understand, he argues, for this is what leads to the augmentation and amplification of human powers. To restrict ourselves to the former is to approach nature as if we were examining 'the anatomy of a corpse'. We must not concern ourselves with the classification of motions as being natural or violent, as Aristotle did, but investigate instead those 'appetites and inclinations and things by which all of the many effects and mutations that are evident in the works of nature and art are made up and brought about'.[18] In this way, we will discover and distinguish the different kinds of motion, and then we will be able to hasten or arrest these, and by doing this change and transform matter.

The value of natural philosophy on Bacon's conception is manifest in what it can achieve, not in any claim to truth as such. The problem with Aristotelian natural philosophy is not that it is untrue, but rather that it is looking for the wrong things. This kind of consideration was certainly not limited to Bacon but was widespread in the early seventeenth century, especially among those who, unlike Bacon, will take up the physico-mathematical route. Isaac Beeckman, for example, was completely

---

[16] See Gaukroger, *Francis Bacon*, 44–57.

[17] The questions here are not as straightforward as they may seem. In the opening paragraphs of the *Metaphysics* (981$^b$17–20), Aristotle seems to take uselessness as a sign of worth: 'But as more arts were invented, and some were directed to the necessities of life, others to recreation, the inventors of the latter were naturally always regarded as wiser than the inventors of the former, because their branches of knowledge did not aim at utility'. Nevertheless, as Lloyd notes, 'The picture of Greek intellectuals as being profoundly unconcerned with the practical applications of their ideas stems largely from texts that belong to a particular, Platonist, tradition.' G. E. R. Lloyd, *The Ambitions of Curiosity* (Cambridge, 2002), 70. Note also the dissenting position taken by John Wilkins, one of the main moving forces behind the establishment of the Royal Society, who sees Aristotle as defending practical against speculative knowledge: 'And whereas the Mathematicians of those former ages, did possess all their learning, as covetous men doe their wealth, only in thought and notion; the judicious *Aristotle*, like a wise Steward, did lay it out to particular use and improvement, rightly preferring the reality and substance of publicke benefit, before the shadows of some retired speculation, or vulgar opinion': *Mathematicall Magick* (London, 1648), 7.

[18] Bacon, *Works*, iii. 20 [text]/v. 425 [trans]. Bacon is not alone in this approach. There are similar sentiments expressed, e.g. in the preface to Guido Ubaldo del Monte, *Mechanicorum Liber* (Pesaro, 1577), translated in Stillman Drake and I. E. Drabkin, ed. and trans., *Mechanics in Sixteenth-Century Italy* (Madison, 1969), 241–7.

opposed to Aristotelian procedure of invoking essential principles different in kind from the properties they purportedly explained, insisting that macroscopic processes had to be explained in terms of microscopic mechanical processes which were essentially similar to them.[19] Beeckman came to natural philosophy not through scholasticism or humanism but from a practical engineering background, including laying water conduits for breweries, and one thing that this experience had made clear to him was that if you wanted to understand how a machine worked you needed to grasp the structure of the machine and the interaction between its parts. Machines operate by means of pressures and motions producing other pressures and motions, and to understand how the machine functions one needs to be able to picture the connections between the parts and how they move.[20] Beeckman is taking a step beyond Bacon here, however. For all his references to the importance of machines, Bacon is still working within the idea of natural philosophy as matter theory,[21] whereas Beeckman has begun to assimilate the requirements of mechanical explanation. The kinds of methodological concerns that will drive Beeckman's project are most clearly revealed—and revealed in their most general form—not in mechanics as such, however, but in astronomy.

## HYPOTHESES AND THE PHYSICAL STANDING OF ASTRONOMY

In Book II of *The Advancement of Learning*, Bacon tells us that 'the same phenomena in astronomy are satisfied by the received astronomy of the diurnal motion and proper motions of the planets, and likewise by the theory of Copernicus who supposed the earth to move; and the calculations are indifferently agreeable to both.'[22] The situation is a stalemate, which astronomers cannot, and should not be expected to, resolve, for by contrast with matter theory, such an approach could not possibly inform us about what the physical reality was. This was a widespread view in the sixteenth and early seventeenth centuries, and it received an articulate rationale in Peirera, as we have seen. When he criticized astronomers' models of the cosmos, the thrust of Peirera's argument was not that such models were not on a par with revelation but that they were not even on a par with natural philosophy. They were concerned merely with saving the appearances, even if this meant employing what he regards as physical absurdities, such as epicycles and eccentrics. We can distinguish three levels of investigation here: revelation, natural philosophy, and astronomy and

[19] See Beeckman to Mersenne, 1 Oct. 1629, in Marin Mersenne, *Correspondance du P. Marin Mersenne, religieux minime*, ed. Cornelius de Waard, R. Pintard, B. Rochot, and A. Baelieu (17 vols, Paris, 1932–88), i. 283.

[20] John Schuster sums up Beeckman's approach nicely in his *Descartes and the Scientific Revolution, 1618–1634* (2 vols, Ann Arbor, 1977), i. 59–60. See also Klaas van Berkel, *Isaac Beeckman (1588–1637) en de mechanisierung van het wereldbeeld* (Amsterdam, 1983), 155–216.

[21] See Stephen Gaukroger, 'The Role of Matter Theory in Baconian and Cartesian Cosmologies', *Perspectives on Science* 8 (2000), 201–22.

[22] Bacon, *Works*, iii. 365.

the practical-mathematical disciplines generally. Schematically, there are three forms of outcome which these yield: truth, establishment of the best explanation on the basis of argument and evidence, and saving the appearances. If natural philosophy is deemed unsatisfactory as a way of uncovering the real structure of the natural realm, then the practical-mathematical disciplines are even less equipped to achieve this, since they do not even concern themselves with explanation on this conception.

This is an issue of fundamental importance, because one of the most pressing questions in the move to develop a quantitative natural philosophy in the first half of the seventeenth century was that of the physical relevance of the practical-mathematical disciplines. A traditional reproach was that these disciplines, particularly astronomy, were able to generate hypotheses but could offer no procedures for deciding between them. A different criticism that came to the fore in the early seventeenth century, particularly in the case of kinematics, was that they dealt only with mathematical idealizations that tell us nothing about reality. These are two different kinds of criticism, but they converge on the claim that the practical-mathematical disciplines do not engage the physical realm, and hence are not physically informative. The prospects for a quantitative natural philosophy hinged on the ability of natural philosophers to meet these criticisms, and the first half of the seventeenth century was a watershed (although criticisms of Newton's *Principia* on these grounds would continue well into the eighteenth century[23]), and what resulted was a radical reordering of the discipline.

There are a number of kinds of response to the general problem of physical relevance, and I shall be looking at some of these in subsequent chapters, but for the present I want to focus discussion on the attempt to establish the physical standing of Copernicanism. I shall be looking, in the first instance, at two very different kinds of approach, that of Kepler and that of Galileo. Kepler sought a geometrical archetype that underlies the structure of the cosmos, and constrains the motion of celestial bodies accordingly. Galileo had a far more piecemeal approach, comparing the physical consequences of the Ptolemaic and Copernican models and arguing that the latter makes more physical sense than the former.

Tied up in this question are issues of hypotheses, idealizations, truth, justification, objectivity, and legitimation. Rather than separate these out and attempt to treat them independently, I want to keep them contextualized, for in this way we shall see that there is no timeless right answer to the question of what kind of enquiry natural philosophy engages in and what standing its results have. To proceed otherwise could only be on the assumption that these issues are *sui generis*, that the aims and goals of natural philosophy are generated internally. We have seen that this was not the case in the medieval and Renaissance development of natural philosophy, and our discussion in this and succeeding chapters will show that it was not the case in the seventeenth or eighteenth centuries either. The aims and goals of natural philosophy are shaped by how best they can respond to the various tasks that they engage in, aims and goals

---

[23] The criticism begins with an anonymous review of the *Principia* in the *Journal des savants* of 2 August 1688, in which it is characterized as mechanics as opposed to a natural-philosophical 'system of the world': see Paul Mouy, *Le Développement de la physique cartésienne 1646–1712* (Paris, 1934), 256–8.

that natural philosophers take as crucial to the success of their project, and that might vary significantly at the level of detail. It is not at all helpful to see these tasks as being imposed from outside, any more than it is helpful to see solutions to Christological concerns being imposed from outside on the philosophical question of universals in the eleventh and twelfth centuries: it is these Christological questions that motivated the medieval discussion of universals in the first place, and generated a philosophical tradition that takes these as core metaphysical questions. Moreover, the autonomy of natural philosophy, a pressing question for its exponents in the sixteenth and seventeenth centuries, does not hinge on a neat separation of internal and external questions but on a complex understanding of priorities and relevance. I shall be working on the assumption that these are not a priori questions, that there may be a number of dimensions to them, and that they may be illuminated significantly by a historical analysis of how they emerge from an interplay of what turns out to be a complex network of factors. The aim is to investigate, for example, how questions of realism in natural philosophy are generated, rather than simply taking them as given and seeking to resolve them without consideration of why we might be asking such questions in the first place.

We saw earlier that there was a tradition of interpreting and representing Ptolemaic astronomy in physical terms from Peurbach's 1475 textbook onwards. Copernicanism had generally been interpreted as false as a physical description of the cosmos before the last decades of the sixteenth century. However, in the wake of Tycho's observations of a new star and of the path of a comet in the 1570s, the physical credentials of the Ptolemaic/Aristotelian model as presented by writers such as Peurbach were undermined, and the question of the physical standing of alternative models began to be pursued with increasing vigour. Astronomical questions, such as shapes of orbits and placing of celestial bodies, were involved here. But so too were physical questions, such as the kind of medium through which—or by means of which—celestial bodies moved, whether there was a single central celestial system or many such systems, and what forces or devices kept the planets in stable orbits, with everything from systems of celestial levers, magnetic attraction, and immersion in a rotating celestial fluid being postulated to replace the crystalline spheres.[24] These difficulties were exacerbated because of a lack of agreement on the relative priorities of physical, observational, and mathematical questions. Such physical concerns are not to be resolved by simply translating one's astronomical model into solid-shell form, as Peurbach did with Ptolemy. As one commentator has remarked, the solid sphere planetary models were not so much a celestial physics as a reason why no one had developed a celestial physics.[25]

The two attempts to establish the physical standing of a heliocentric system that I shall be looking at in what follows operate at different ends of what for present

---

[24] A system of celestial levers is postulated in Nathaneal Torporley, *Diclides Coelemetricae seu valuae Astronomicae Vniuersales* (London, 1602), in which each planet is placed at the extremity of a lever, with a moving force (*magade*) at the other extremity. Among the advocates of magnetic forces we shall be concentrating on Kepler, and among the advocates of celestial fluids, Descartes.

[25] Bruce Stephenson, *Kepler's Physical Astronomy* (Princeton, 1994), 26.

purposes I shall treat as a spectrum, with the notion of truth as something revealed, exemplified in Kepler's *Mysterium cosmographicum* of 1596, at one end and truth as what survives the process of refutation, exemplified in Galileo's *Dialogo sopre i due massimi sistemi del mondo* of 1632, at the other. Before Kepler and Galileo, there is no difficulty in identifying scholastics and Neoplatonists who pursued natural philosophy at either pole of the spectrum. It is a measure of the greatly increased sophistication in thinking about the physical standing of these questions that neither Kepler nor Galileo can be placed unequivocally at either pole. Kepler in some ways realized a radically revised Neoplatonist agenda, but his route to it was via a consideration of how to establish the merits of competing hypotheses. Galileo's procedure, by contrast, was to sort through various theories, all of which he treated as hypotheses, showing how one of these, Copernicanism, survives criticism better than the others. He used an adversarial dialogue form, but the way in which he set about establishing his own theories, as we shall see later when we come to look at his treatment of kinematics in his *Discorsi* (1637), used novel procedures for establishing the physical standing of these theories, procedures that lifted them out of the hypothetical realm.

Kepler's project was an extremely ambitious one: his aim was to show that the Copernican system was the only possible astronomical model because it was the only one that could be realized in the geometry that was inherent in the divine archetype that he believed he had discovered.[26] But Kepler convinced no one that he had discovered this, and his cosmological system had no other adherents.[27] Galileo's more piecemeal approach, by contrast, was both far less ambitious, in that it was not concerned to develop a cosmological model, and far more compelling, turning the tide in favour of Copernicanism very dramatically.[28]

Let us begin with Kepler, whom I have placed in a Neoplatonist tradition. Within scholastic Aristotelianism, what had distinguished natural philosophy from revealed theology was that the latter was understood to take us beyond the natural world to some understanding of the rationale for physical events and human affairs. In the Neoplatonist tradition, by contrast, natural philosophy and theology blend into one another. But, as we have seen, this is at the expense of natural philosophy, which, even in Patrizi, is not pursued as an independent form of enquiry but rather emerges as a by-product of Neoplatonist metaphysics, which is itself ultimately subservient to Neoplatonic theology. Kepler, while working broadly within this tradition, used its resources in a radical and unprecedented way. The tradition had held astronomy in contempt, dealing with all celestial matters in terms of Neoplatonic cosmology. Kepler short-circuited the chain of connections between astronomy, natural philosophy, metaphysics, and theology, making a direct link

---

[26] On the long and complex history of cosmic archetypes up to Kepler, see Schmidt-Biggemann, *Philosophia Perennis*, ch. 5.

[27] See Wilbur Applebaum, 'Keplerian Astronomy after Kepler: Researches and Problems', *History of Science* 34 (1996), 451–504.

[28] See e.g. Jean Dietz Moss, *Novelties in the Heavens: Rhetoric and Science in the Copernican Controversy* (Chicago, 1993). Critics of heliocentrism came to identify it with Galileo rather than Copernicus, as, e.g., Alexander Ross, *The new planet no planet, or, The earth no wandring star, except in the wandring heads of Galileans* (London, 1646).

between astronomy and theology—the latter being a Christianized version of Plato's *Timaeus*—in the first instance, and then coming back to natural philosophy to fix the details; although, unlike his Neoplatonic predecessors, he was concerned to account for very fine-tuned astronomical details in a physically precise way.

The *Timaeus* was not treated in the Christian Neoplatonist tradition in the same way that the scholastics treated Aristotle's *Physics* or *Metaphysics*, as a work outside the Christian canon, but rather as an integral part of that canon. Kepler himself described the *Timaeus* in a marginal note in *Harmonices mundi* as 'beyond all hazard of a doubt a kind of commentary on the first chapter of Genesis, or the first book of Moses, converting it to the Pythagorean philosophy, as is readily apparent to the attentive reader, who compares the actual words of Moses in detail'.[29] While it is unclear just how literally we should take this statement,[30] there can be no doubt that the *Timaeus* had the status of a sacred text for Kepler. In virtue of such a standing, it played a role very different from that of Aristotle's writings. It didn't help provide a rational framework for, and point of entry into, a systematic theology, but was rather a source of truths about God's plans for the cosmos. This was the role it played in Kepler's first work, *Mysterium cosmographium*, where a mathematical model of the motions of celestial bodies was directly mapped onto an archetypal structure of the cosmos based on the cosmogony of the *Timaeus* and taken directly to express the nature of the creator. In the Preface he writes:

It is my intention in this small treatise to show that the almighty and infinitely merciful God, when he created our moving world and determined the order of the celestial bodies, took as the basis for his construction the five regular solids which have enjoyed such great distinction from the time of Pythagoras and Plato down to our own days; and that he co-ordinated in accordance with their properties the number and proportion of the celestial bodies, as well as their relationship between the various celestial motions.[31]

The aim was to provide a unique physical interpretation for the Copernican system. This is, of course, what generations of natural philosophers had denied was possible, and Kepler's procedure in meeting this was twofold. In the first place, he built on a body of thinking by those of his predecessors and contemporaries who had considered that there must be some way of deciding between such hypotheses. But then he attempted to trump these efforts by arguing that the astronomical model he was

---

[29] Kepler, *The Harmony of the World*, 301. The mention of Pythagoreanism is interesting in that A. E. Taylor has argued that the *Timaeus* sets out not Plato's own views but those of fifth-century Italian Pythagoreanism (*A Commentary on Plato's Timaeus* (Oxford, 1928), 11). This reading was challenged by Francis Cornford in his *Plato's Cosmology* (London, 1937), pp. vii–xi.

[30] See J. V. Field, *Kepler's Geometrical Cosmology* (London, 1988), 1. However, nor is it clear that we should take the *Timaeus* itself absolutely literally since Plato himself describes his account of the physical world there as 'a likely story' (29C–D), and some of the doctrines proposed such as the generation of the universe and the self-motion of the soul are not internally consistent and are not consistent with doctrines to be found in other dialogues: see Gregory Vlastos, 'The Disorderly Motion in the *Timaeus*', and 'Creation in the *Timaeus*: Is it a Fiction?', in R. E. Allen, ed., *Studies in Plato's Metaphysics* (London, 1965), 379–99 and 401–19 respectively.

[31] Kepler, *Gesammelte Werke*, i. 9. Translation (slightly altered) from Alexandre Koyré, *The Astronomical Revolution* (Paris/London/Ithaca, 1973), 128.

advocating—Copernicanism—was uniquely manifested in a particular cosmological structure, drawing attention to an apparently remarkable convergence between a mathematical model that fits the astronomical observations better than any other, and a Platonic theory about the kind of archetype that God might have employed in creating the cosmos, given that it has the structure it does.

The central question in respect to hypotheses in the *Mysterium* is that of the possibility of deriving true conclusions from false premises. Since the same observations could often be deduced from different, conflicting astronomical models, the very fact of a true conclusion couldn't guarantee the truth of any model, Copernicanism included. The point goes back to Averroes, and is set out explicitly in Nifo:

> One should understand that a sound demonstration is one in which the *causa* is necessary for the effect. Now it is granted that when eccentrics and epicycles are posited the appearances follow and can be saved. But the converse is not true. When the appearances are posited, epicycles and eccentrics do not have to be [posited], except for the time being until another and better *causa* is discovered which is necessary [for the appearances]. The proponents of epicycles and eccentrics are therefore in error, because they argue from a posit having several *causa*s for the truth of one of them. But these appearances can be saved both in this way and in others which have not yet been discovered.[32]

Kepler argued that there were in fact ways of distinguishing between such models, by going beyond the cases from which the model was deduced to new cases. There was a range of procedures here. One might be simply extending the traditional *regula falsi*—whereby one solves a problem iteratively by assuming a value for an unknown quantity, computing the other values and seeing whether a contradiction is generated—to the case of competing hypotheses, trying to generate contradictions between them and new data. On the other hand, hypotheses might be matched against natural-philosophical assumptions. Although the latter was an unusual procedure, and Maestlin questioned Kepler's use of natural philosophy to support astronomical hypotheses for example,[33] it was not completely unprecedented, for as Jardine points out, Copernicus, Tycho, Rothmann, and Ursus had all used arguments from natural philosophy to defend their astronomical models.[34] Kepler went even further, showing in *Astronomia nova* that his model, which makes physical assumptions that Copernicus and Tycho did not—in that it uses the true sun rather than the mathematically convenient but physically irrelevant mean sun (the centre of the earth's orbit in the Copernican account)[35]—gave as good a fit to Tycho's very precise data as did Tycho's own

[32] Nifo, *In Aristotelis libros de coelo et mundo* (Naples, 1517), f. 82. Translation taken from Jardine, *The Birth of History and Philosophy of Science*, 232.

[33] See Rhonda Martens, *Kepler's Philosophy and the New Astronomy* (Princeton, 2000), 59.

[34] Jardine, *The Birth of History and Philosophy of Science*, 248.

[35] See Kepler, *New Astronomy*, 54–5, on the inappropriateness of thinking one can account for the motion of physical bodies in terms of rotation around geometrical centres. The empirical inadequacy of mean-sun models was not evident because they were always constructed and assessed with respect to acronychal observations, that is, observations made when the earth is directly on a line between the sun and the body being observed, so that the observed direction to the body is also the direction from the sun to that body. The discrepancy is apparent from nonacronychal

mean sun model.[36] Moreover, procedures for choosing between hypotheses had been employed both in historical investigation and in the general vindication of history in the sixteenth century by writers such as Baudouin and Bodin, who often adapted procedures used to ascertain reliability in law, such as reinforcing testimonies, to establish reliability and degrees of probability,[37] and cognate problems had occupied medical writers.[38] Finally, Kepler wanted a set of procedures that one could go through to establish the credentials of one proposed explanation over others, but he also wanted the explanation to reveal the essence of the phenomenon. In this respect, what he was seeking was something far stronger than other astronomers had been looking for. One might put the project by saying that, although the procedures for weeding out hypotheses initially treat them as being on a par, the true explanation is in fact different in kind from the false ones because it reflects or captures God's intentions, which are unambiguous and the only thing that can make sense of the world. There is a qualitative difference between this and an explanation or hypothesis being more or less accurate than others, or being more or less likely than others. Kepler's project was not merely to establish the natural-philosophical legitimacy of his model but to capture God's intentions in constructing the cosmos.

In the *Mysterium*, we are urged to compare hypotheses that are devised to account for a set of observations, but which fail when applied to other observations, with the heliocentric model. Once we place the sun at the centre of the cosmos, he tells us, 'we will be able to demonstrate any of the phenomena that appear in the sky, being able to go forwards and backwards in time, deducing one phenomenon from another, and thus how they are intimately connected; and the most complex demonstrations will always lead us back to the same initial hypotheses.'[39] In other words, we test available astronomical hypotheses by seeing how they fit not only current observations, but past ones also, and we can predict future positions and thereby decide between different hypotheses. But there is a further consideration: one of these hypotheses, as well as saving the observed phenomena, might reveal their underlying cause. The revealing of such a cause requires a different kind of demonstration, however:

I have no hesitation in asserting that everything that Copernicus has demonstrated a posteriori and on the basis of observations interpreted geometrically, may be demonstrated a priori without any logical subtleties.[40]

The a priori demonstration Kepler has in mind here is one that connects the astronomical model directly to a cosmological archetype. Among the concerns that

observations, as Kepler makes clear in ch. 6 of *Astronomia Nova*. Kepler's insistence that celestial bodies must revolve around physical bodies, not geometrical points, was vindicated by Galileo's discovery of four of Jupiter's moons in January 1610.

[36] See Stephenson, *Kepler's Physical Astronomy*, 44.

[37] See Julian Franklin, *Methodology of Law and History* (New York, 1963), Ian Maclean, *Interpretation and Meaning in the Renaissance: The Case of Law* (Cambridge, 1992), and Peter Burke, *The Renaissance Sense of the Past* (London, 1969). For a detailed case study where these questions were at issue, see Hendrik J. Erasmus, *The Origins of Rome in Historiography from Petrarch to Perizonius* (Assen, 1962).

[38] See Maclean, *Logic, Signs and Nature in the Renaissance*.

[39] Kepler, *Gesammelte Werke*, i. 15.     [40] Ibid. 16.

he has in the *Mysterium* are whether the sun is at the centre of the universe, why there are six planets, no more no less,[41] and why the orbits of these planets are spaced in the way they are. Astronomers in the Ptolemaic tradition had not attempted to establish the order or size of the planetary orbs:[42] instead, there was general agreement that the order of the planets was reflected in the decreasing sidereal periods as one worked inwards from the orb of the fixed stars. Copernicus, by contrast, makes it clear in the dedicatory letter to *De revolutionibus* that 'the orders and sizes of the stars, and all their orbs, and the heaven itself are so connected that nothing can be altered in any part of it without bringing confusion to all the remaining parts and to the whole universe'.[43] This is a very strong statement, and not only does Copernicus not attempt to back it up, but his representation of the cosmos in *De revolutionibus* (Fig. 5.1) is highly geometricized, not only showing the orbs either as circles, or (depending on how one interprets the figure) as orbs having uniform thickness with no gap between each of them,[44] but also representing them so that the planets look as if they are all much the same distance from adjacent planets, even though they are not, on the Copernican model. The representation of the planetary orbs in the Copernican system in Maestlin's 1596 edition of Rheticus' *Narratio prima* (Fig. 5.2) corrects the first, and Kepler's representation of the Copernican system (Fig. 5.3) corrects the second, depicting actual distances. Kepler had initially sought some numerical pattern in the distances between one planet and another but, failing

---

[41] In the Ptolemaic system, which included the sun and the moon (but not of course the earth) among the planets, there were seven planets. The fact that there were six planets in the Copernican system was not remarked upon by Copernicus, but Rheticus, in his *Narratio prima* of 1540, offered a numerological defence: 'Who could have chosen a more suitable and more appropriate number than six? By what number could anyone more easily have persuaded mankind that the whole universe was divided into spheres by God the Author and Translator of the world? For the number six is honoured above all others in the sacred prophecies of God and by the Pythagoreans and the other philosophers. What is more agreeable to God's handiwork than that this first and most perfect work should be summed up in the first and most perfect number?' (Trans. in Edward Rosen, *Three Copernican Treatises* (New York, 1971), 147.) On reading Galileo's *Sidereus Nuncius* (Venice, 1610), Kepler was faced with an increase in the number of celestial bodies, but he accommodates these as satellites, rather than planets, in his *Dissertatio cum Nuncio Sidereo* (Prague, 1610). The criteria for something's being, or not being, a planet here cannot include size, for the two outer Galilean satellites, Ganymede and Callisto, are in fact the size of Mercury.

[42] Ptolemy had in fact attempted to discover orbital radii, though sixteenth-century astronomers were not aware of this. See Bernard Goldstein, 'The Arabic Version of Ptolemy's *Planetary Hypotheses*', *Transactions of the American Philosophical Society*, 57/4 (1967), 3–55.

[43] Copernicus, *De revolutionibus*, iiii recto. Copernicus can, at least in principle, calculate the size of orbits. The circles that formed the deferents of the superior planets in the geocentric system now become the true orbits and those that were the epicycles simply reflect the earth's orbital motion; in the case of inferior planets this is reversed, the deferents becoming the orbit of the earth and the epicycles becoming the true orbits. From the fact that the ratios of the radii of the epicycles to the radii of the deferents can be calculated from observations, we can calculate the size of the orbits.

[44] In this case we must take the labels for Mercury and Venus to lie within their spheres, and the labels for Mars, Jupiter, and Saturn, as well as the fixed stars, as lying on top of their spheres. The sphere of the earth contains a middle circle which shows its orbit in a sphere which must also accommodate the moon.

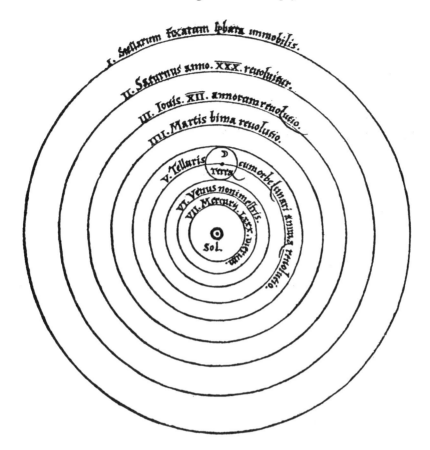

**Figure 5.1**

to find this, he explored geometrical patterns, and hit upon nested Platonic solids.[45] These are convex regular polyhedra: their faces are regular polygons of the same shape and they meet in the same way at the vertex of the solid. There are only five such polyhedra[46]—the tetrahedron (four triangular faces), the cube (six square faces), the octahedron (eight triangular faces), the dodecahedron (twelve pentagonal faces), and the icosahedron (twenty triangular faces)—and the ratios of the largest spheres that can be fitted inside them (their incircles) and the smallest spheres that enclose them (their circumcircles) are such that, when these polyhedra are nested, the distances

---

[45] On the polyhedral theory, see Bruce Stephenson, *The Music of the Heavens: Kepler's Harmonic Astronomy* (Princeton, 1994), ch. 4.

[46] This had been proved by Euclid, *Elements*, Book 13, scholium to prop. 19. Descartes will offer an algebraic proof in his early *De solidorum elementis*: *Œuvres de Descartes*, ed. Charles Adam and Paul Tannery (2nd edn, 11 vols, Paris, 1974–86), x. 269–76.

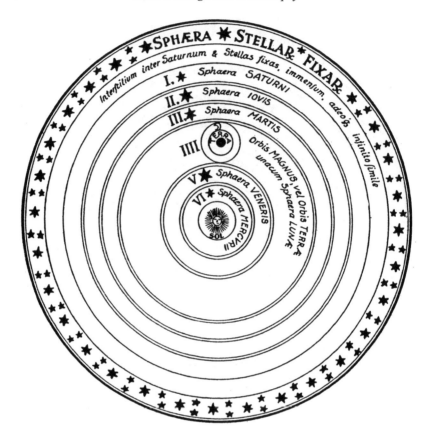

**Figure 5.2**

between them are in proportion to the distances between the orbs of the planets. For example, if a cube is inscribed in the inner surface of the orb of Saturn then its insphere will be the outer surface of the orb of Jupiter, and if a tetrahedron is inscribed in the inner surface of the orb of Jupiter then its insphere will be the outer surface of the orb of Mars, and so on (see Fig. 5.4).[47]

Kepler's geometrical-cosmological version of the Copernican model accounts for both the number of planets and distances between their orbits. On his argument, there must be six and only six planets because there are five and only five regular polyhedra, and on the question of distances between the planets, the model fitted observational data extremely well.[48] But Kepler's account completely ignored physical

[47] See E. J. Aiton, 'Johannes Kepler and the *Mysterium Cosmographicum*', *Sudhoffs Archiv* 62 (1977), 174–94.

[48] See Field, *Kepler's Geometrical Cosmology*, 38.

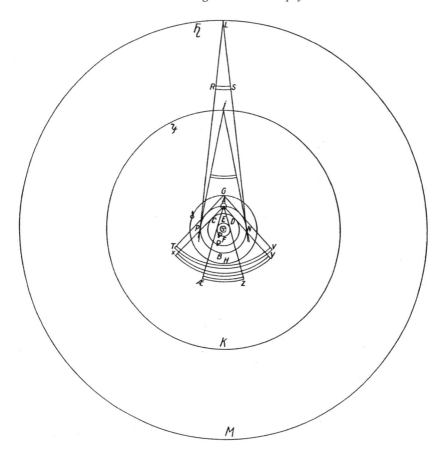

**Figure 5.3**

questions such as the size of planets and the density of the medium through which they move. These can hardly be dismissed as possible contributory factors to the size of orbits, unless one literally thinks of the planets being carried around on crystalline orbs, which Kepler does not. And this is what is odd about his procedure. In one sense he is in the tradition of those who wish to establish the natural-philosophical standing of astronomy. But God's intentions were expressed in a cosmological archetype that, Kepler believed, was realized in the form of a Copernican astronomical model, and God's intentions were not physical either in nature or in his cosmological archetype: only the bodies occupying the prescribed spatial locations could properly be considered physical. What made them occupy these spatial locations, however, was not the physical relations in which they stood to one another, but something geometrical. Moreover, as Book IV of the *Harmonice mundi* makes clear, both the cosmological archetype and the astronomical model mediated what was fundamentally

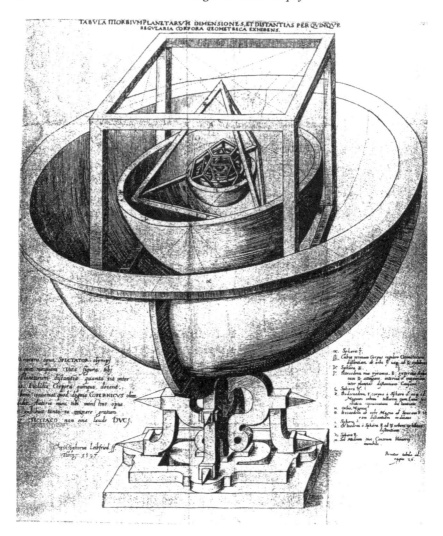

**Figure 5.4**

a meeting of minds: a relation between our understanding of harmony and simplicity, and God's.[49]

To complement this picture in a fully Neoplatonic way, Kepler had urged, in the *Mysterium*, that the motion of planets was due to individual souls in each

---

[49] Kepler was influenced by Proclus' view that the mind was created with the imprint of mathematical ideas. See Martens, *Kepler's Philosophy and the New Astronomy*, 34–5.

planet,[50] but on reading Gilbert's *De magnete* in 1602, he largely translated these souls—which, as Aristotle had argued, were immaterial because they had to act throughout eternity—into a solar magnetic influence, something wholly physical and susceptible to geometrical analysis, enabling him to give a precise quantitative account of planetary orbits.[51] Gilbert himself had attempted to explain the earth's diurnal rotation in terms of its magnetic power, as we shall see, but had retained planetary souls to account for the orbital motion of the planets, and Stevin had gone beyond this in his treatise on celestial motions, *De hemelloop*, written in the early 1600s,[52] deriving a cosmic magnetism from the fixed stars to regulate a system of rigid crystalline spheres that rotated around the sun.[53] Kepler had been convinced by Tycho's 1577 observations of the comet that one could not call upon solid spheres to do this kind of work, which meant that there must be more to the motion of the planets than just geometry.

In his *Astronomia nova* of 1609, and again in Book 4 of his *Epitome* of 1620, he spelled out his own system of magnetic influences, in which the sun, rather than the fixed stars, provides the impelling and guiding force for the rotation of the planets. Unlike the systems of Copernicus and Tycho, in which the sun sat at the centre but had no physical role other than illumination, Kepler gave the sun's central position a physical purpose. The sun alone had an animal soul and it acted on the animal faculty of rotation in each planet. The means by which this was performed was decidedly physical, however. Kepler postulated a rotation in the sun, which results in a radial emission of a quasi-magnetic force, and this moves the planets in circular orbits,[54] its power decreasing in direct proportion to its distance from the sun. Magnetism has the advantage that it acts at a distance and that it is directional: the earth's magnetism directs compass needles in a particular direction for example. Note, however, that the solar force is not exactly magnetic, for it neither attracts nor repulses the planets but impels them in a certain direction. So far, this is highly qualitative, but Kepler

[50] A similar theory had been proposed by Ptolemy in chs. 7 and 8 of his *Planetary Hypotheses*: see 'The Arabic Version of Ptolemy's *Planetary Hypotheses*', ed. Goldstein. See also the discussion in Taub, *Ptolemy's Universe*, 117–18.

[51] See Stephen Pumfrey, 'Magnetical Philosophy and Astronomy, 1600–1650', in René Taton and Curtis Wilson, eds, *Planetary Astronomy from the Renaissance to the Rise of Astrophysics, Part A: Tycho Brahe to Newton* (Cambridge, 1989), 45–53, to which I am indebted here.

[52] The astronomical writings are collected in vol. iii of Simon Stevin, *The Principal Works of Simon Stevin*, ed. Ernst Cronie et al. (5 vols, Amsterdam, 1955–66). Copernicanism received a favourable reception in the Netherlands among the small circle of astronomers and mathematicians familiar with it: see R. H. Vermij, 'Het copernicanisme in de Republiek', *Tijdschrift voor Geschiedenis* 106 (1993), 349–67: 357–62.

[53] Another early 'magnetic' defence of Copernicanism—in this case influenced directly by Gilbert—is Nicholas Hill, *Philosophia Epicurea, Democritiana, Theophrastica, proposita simpliciter, non edocta* (Paris, 1601). By the second decade of the seventeenth century, there were a number of such 'magnetic' defences in England: a typical example is Mark Ridley, *A Short Treatise of Magneticall Bodies and Motions* (London, 1613).

[54] As Martens notes (*Kepler's Philosophy*, 183 n. 26) even after he had established that planetary orbits were elliptical, the circle is still prior—corresponding to the archetypal geometrical arrangement of the cosmos—because the sun pushes the planets in circular orbits: it is the planets that disrupt this circular motion with their librations.

is working with a very finely tuned astronomical model, and the adequacy of his account is tested against what kind of explanation it can give of the fine tuning. In the first place, he has to account for the eccentricity of orbits. The planets each have magnetic poles of different polarities—directed toward those fixed stars under which lie the limits of each planet's latitudinal motion—which maintain their direction in the solar system, and as a result they resist being attracted into alignment with the sun.[55] This causes a net attraction to the sun when the planet's unlike pole faces the sun, and a net repulsion when its like pole faces it. It is the oscillating magnetic axis that results in the advance and retreat of the planet, a result that was particularly important for his treatment of the varying speed and distance of Mars. Second, there was the problem of the inclination of each orbital plane with the ecliptic, and this is explained on the same model: the planet is forced above the ecliptic in one half of the orbit and below it in the other because of the deflection of the magnetic threads making up the poles of the planet.

If one grants Kepler his two crucial assumptions—the existence of a divine archetype which uses the five regular solids as a model for the cosmos, and the existence of magnetic forces emanating from the sun which are able to move planets, which in turn are themselves able to modify the effects of this action in complex ways depending on their own magnetic alignments—then his account is compelling not just at the level of grand design but also at the level of detail. Not only does the nesting of regular solids give a very good fit with planetary distances, but in the crucial case of Mars, where the variations are particularly significant, Kepler can present a coherent account of both the eccentricity of the orbit, and the inclination of the orbital plane with the ecliptic, which meets his own very exacting standards. Nor is it simply a case of Kepler saying that if we accept his premises, we get the right outcome, for as we have seen, he is well aware that false premises can generate a true conclusion. But his procedures for deciding between hypotheses that yield true conclusions in particular cases are not procedures that enable us to assess his archetypal and physical principles, which are not hypothetical and which have no observable consequences in the way that astronomical hypotheses do.

How then are we to assess such principles? The assessment of fundamental physical principles is different from both that of archetypal principles and that of the assessment of astronomical hypotheses. Physical principles are complex and layered in a way that astronomical hypotheses are not. Kepler makes it clear in the *Apologia* that astronomical hypotheses must be distinguished from geometrical hypotheses: we can construct an orbit using either a concentric with an epicycle, or an eccentric, but if these represent the same planetary motion then they are astronomically indistinguishable. The difference lies in the geometrical means of constructing the orbit, not in the orbit itself,[56] and hence, by contrast with astronomically distinct hypotheses, they will not have different empirical consequences. In the case of astronomical hypotheses, the ultimate claim—at least in the simplest case, where there is agreement on

[55] Stephenson, *Kepler's Physical Astronomy*, 130–7, gives a good account of some of the complexities here.

[56] Jardine, *The Birth of History and Philosophy of Science*, 142–3.

the absolute and relative nature of particular motions—is that one arrangement or ordering of the planets mirrors or matches the actual arrangement and ordering of the planets, including their motions. But in *Astronomia nova* Kepler makes it clear that, on the basis of Tycho's data, he can devise different astronomical hypotheses to fit the data:[57] in this case, the only solution is to go one step further, to physical considerations, to decide the issue:

Indeed, all things are so interconnected, involved, and intertwined with one another that after trying many different approaches to the reform of astronomical calculations, some well trodden by the ancients and others constructed in emulation of them and by their example, none other could succeed than the one founded upon the motions' physical causes themselves, which I establish in this work.[58]

The trouble is that the move into the physical realm brings with it unprecedented difficulties. In the case of claims about a force that moves the planets in particular orbits, what is being postulated is some mechanism by which a particular arrangement and ordering is produced and maintained. This is necessarily a complex mechanism, involving, in the present case, a number of different kinds of consideration: the existence of a solar magnetic force, its effect on magnetized bodies under its influence, the existence of magnetic poles on all planets (and their satellites), and the interaction between the solar magnetic force and the planetary magnetic alignments; the assumptions that a body needs to be maintained in any state of motion, and that the cosmos is finite and is contained in a sphere and so has a single centre; assumptions about how the force varies with distance, and whether it is affected by intervening media; as well as basic unanswered (and unasked) questions about how such a force could be generated in the first place, and what its physical means of transmission are; and finally what exactly this force is, since it behaves in some ways, but not in others, like magnetism, and might seem to leave more unexplained than it explains. It is worth remembering here that magnetism by itself does not secure heliocentrism, and can just as easily be put to use in defending geocentrism. Niccolò Cabeo, in his *Philosophia magnetica* of 1629, set out to show in detail that magnetism actually held the earth in place in a geocentric system, and his work was taken up and developed in the 1640s in Athanasius Kircher's *Magnes sive de arte magnetica* (1641), Jacques Grandami's *Nova demonstratio immobilitatis terrae petita ex virtute magnetica* (1645), and Nicolo Zucchi's *Nova de machinis philosophia* (1649).[59]

Questions about evidence and demonstration are raised here that go well beyond the issues surrounding the assessment of astronomical hypotheses. A number of Kepler's conclusions are not compatible with Aristotelian physical theory, yet he has nothing to put in its place. His Neoplatonism is highly modified and has little in common with the top-down metaphysical systems of Ficino, Patrizi, and his contemporary and antagonist Robert Fludd.[60] None of the traditional systems of

---

[57] See Stephenson, *Kepler's Physical Astronomy*, 2.

[58] Kepler, *New Astronomy*, 48.

[59] See Stephen Pumfrey, 'Neo-Aristotelianism and the Magnetic Philosophy', in John Henry and Sarah Hutton, eds, *New Perspectives on Renaissance Thought* (London, 1990), 177–89.

[60] On Kepler's disputes with Fludd see Field, *Kepler's Geometrical Cosmology*, 179–87.

natural philosophy are able to provide him with what he needs, not even with a viable way of organizing problems in physical theory.

The most fundamental problems in physical theory as far as the establishment of a Copernican system was concerned centred on the nature of motion: how we distinguish apparent from real motions, and what the motion of the planets is due to. These questions inhabited the intersection of the spaces of natural philosophy and astronomy, and the two traditional sources, Aristotle and Ptolemy, in dealing with these and similarly basic questions, tended to treat them differently: as physical questions in Aristotle and as astronomical questions in Ptolemy.[61] In Book 1 of the *Almagest*,[62] for example, Ptolemy sets out six basic hypotheses[63] on which his enterprise rests, and Copernicus and Kepler both discuss these briefly in the introductory sections of *De revolutionibus* and *Astronomia nova* respectively.[64] The first of these is that 'the heavens move spherically'. Ptolemy's arguments here are predominantly astronomical, contrasting how things appear with how they would appear were the stars to move linearly, for example, drawing attention to the fact that they reappear each day, and that they do not diminish in size, although he does add a brief argument about the homogeneous nature of the parts of the celestial ether requiring that it be spherical because the sphere is the only homogeneous solid body. Aristotle, by contrast, approaches the question exclusively via physical arguments from the impossibility of continued rectilinear motion.[65] It is of interest to note that Copernicus also introduced the sphericity of the cosmos as an assumption of his system, mixing mathematical and physical considerations:

The world is shaped like a globe, in part because this shape, being an integral whole, needs no joints, and so is the most perfect of all figures; in part because this shape has the greatest volume and is thus best suited to contain and hold all things; in part because all the discrete parts of the world—the sun, the moon, and the stars—have this shape; and in part because everything in the world tends to take on this shape, as for example in the case of drops of water and other liquids, when they take on a shape by themselves.[66]

Kepler not only concurs, but it is his sense of the order and harmony in the cosmos that requires sphericity rather than something physical, as is clear from his responses to Bruno and others who argue for the infinity of the cosmos.[67]

[61] Taub, *Ptolemy's Universe*, ch. 3, looks at the differences in detail.

[62] Ptolemy, *The Almagest*, trans. R. Cateby Taliaferro, in *Britannica Great Books*, 16 (Chicago, 1952), 1–465: 7–14.

[63] The Greek term *hupothesis* means literally a basis on which something else is constructed, rather than something tentative, and this is how the term should be understood in Ptolemy: see Taub, *Ptolemy's Universe*, 41.

[64] Nicolaus Copernicus, *On the Revolution of the Heavenly Spheres* trans. C. G. Wallis, in *Britannica Great Books*, 16 (Chicago, 1952), 501–838: 511–21; and Kepler, *New Astronomy*, 54–9 (via Tycho and Copernicus).

[65] e.g. *De caelo*, 277$^a$12–27.

[66] *On the Revolution of the Heavenly Spheres*, 511.

[67] See Koyré, *From the Closed World to the Infinite Universe*, 58–87. Galileo shared this view: see *Dialogue Concerning the Two Chief World Systems—Ptolemaic and Copernican*, trans. Stillman Drake (Berkeley, 1953), 19, where Salviati tells us that the universe must necessarily be 'the most

Ptolemy's second basic hypothesis is that the earth is 'sensibly' spherical, as opposed to flat, cylindrical, or some other shape, and again the arguments are observational, ranging from the timing of dawn and dusk, the times of sighting of eclipses, and the ways in which the stars appear. Copernicus and Kepler likewise rely on similar observational arguments. Aristotle, by contrast, wants to prove that the earth is spherical, rather than just appealing to observation, and while he does use observational evidence, he relies predominantly on physical arguments, particularly his notion of natural place.[68]

In defence of his third hypothesis, that the earth is at the centre of the cosmos, Ptolemy uses astronomical evidence alone, whereas Aristotle's extensive argument in the first two books of *De caelo* is resolutely physical, showing first that the cosmos must have a centre and then that the earth must occupy that centre, and moreover that the peculiar properties of the earth, such as the fact that bodies tend towards its centre, are due to its being at the centre of the cosmos, rather than to some feature of the earth itself. Copernicus' response is wholly astronomical, although he clearly has physical reasons—for example, to do with the centre of rotation of the celestial orbs—for advocating a heliocentric astronomy. Kepler, as we have seen, presses a detailed astronomical argument, but he bolsters it with both geometrical-archetypal arguments, and with a physical account of how the planets are kept in directed orbits around the sun. Likewise with what is—in Ptolemy's ordering—the sixth hypothesis, 'that there are two different primary motions in the heavens', namely a diurnal motion which carries everything from east to west, and the motion of the planets (including the sun and the moon) along the ecliptic from west to east. This is closely tied to Ptolemy's astronomical model, and stands or falls with it on astronomical grounds.

The fourth hypothesis, that the earth has 'the ratio of a point relative to the heavens' was, qualitatively speaking, not in contention since all parties agreed to that, Aristotle merely noting that the earth must be of small size,[69] and the arguments are exclusively astronomical. The heliocentric theory, however, required the distance to the fixed stars to be so large as to be almost inconceivable in the view of many of its critics, and certainly several degrees of magnitude greater than what was required in the geocentric theory.[70] By contrast, the fifth hypothesis, 'that the earth makes no motion involving change of place' was one defended by both Aristotle and Ptolemy on natural-philosophical grounds, from the direction of the fall of bodies to their behaviour on the surface of the earth, with Ptolemy offering only one astronomical argument, namely that the kind of phenomena we would experience if the earth moved would be similar to those that we would experience if the earth were not centrally located, and they would be different from those we do in fact experience.

---

orderly, having its parts disposed in the highest and most perfect order among themselves', and Galileo adds in a marginal note, 'The author assumes the universe to be perfectly ordered.'

[68] e.g. *De caelo*, 297$^a$8 –$^b$ 35.
[69] *De caelo*, 297$^b$31–298$^a$21.
[70] See e.g. *On the Revolution of the Heavenly Spheres*, 516.

Copernicus has no difficulty arguing that if the earth were moving, celestial phenomena would appear in the same way as if we suppose the heavens to rotate around a stationary earth:

For every apparent change in place occurs on account of the movement either of the thing seen or of the spectator, or on account of the necessarily unequal movement of both. For no movement is perceptible relative to things moved equally in the same directions—I mean relatively to the thing seen and to the spectator. Now it is from the earth that the celestial circuit is beheld and presented to our sight. Therefore, if some movement should belong to the earth it will appear, in the parts of the universe which are outside, as the same movement but in the opposite direction, as though the things outside were passing over.[71]

The physical questions presented greater obstacles however. To Ptolemy's objection that a diurnal rotation of the earth would require such a great speed that bodies on its surface would be flung off, Copernicus replies by distinguishing natural and violent motions. 'Things to which force of violence is applied get broken up and are unable to subsist for a long time,' he tells us, 'but things which are caused by nature are in the right condition and are kept in their best organisation.'[72] The point is partly *ad hominem*, in that advocates of a geocentric model assume that the planets and the fixed stars revolve at a great rate around a central body—a rate which is certainly greater than that of the diurnal rotation of the earth—yet remain perfectly intact. But it must also be stressed that Copernicus shares with his opponents a commitment to the Aristotelian dynamics which underlies the doctrine of natural and violent motions. The trouble is that this is an absolute distinction, because it depends on whether or not the source of the motion derives from the nature of the thing undergoing the motion, and motions cannot be designated natural or violent relative to something. Yet it is exactly the latter than Copernicus needs when he compares the effects of being on a moving earth with someone travelling on a moving ship:

And things are as Aeneas says in Virgil: 'We sail out of the harbour, and the land and the cities move away.' As a matter of fact, when a ship floats on over a tranquil sea, all the things outside seem to voyagers to be moving in a movement which is the image of their own, and they think on the contrary that they themselves and all the things with them are at rest. So it could easily happen in the case of the movement of the earth that the whole world should be believed to be moving in a circle.[73]

Making physical sense out of this claim in terms of Aristotelian dynamics is impossible. Even less satisfactory is Copernicus' response to Ptolemy's claim that bodies thrown upwards would not fall back to the same spot on earth if it were moving. He treats such bodies as combining a natural motion, which is circular and which the body has in virtue of being part of the whole (the earth), and a violent motion, which is rectilinear and is temporary, while 'the body is not conformed in its nature'.[74] At first sight, it looks as if what Copernicus is claiming here is that the rectilinear motion takes the body back to 'its own place', construed not as the surface of the earth generally but as the specific spot from which it

---

[71] See e.g. *On the Revolution of the Heavenly Spheres*, 514–15.       [72] Ibid. 518.
[73] Ibid. 519.       [74] Ibid. 520.

was projected in the first place. But to treat the exact spot from which a body is projected as 'its own place' makes a nonsense of the doctrine of natural place. It is therefore more likely that the claim is that the body remains directly over the spot from which it was projected, throughout the upward and downward motions, because it is this circular motion—which the body shares with the rotating earth because it is part of the earth—that keeps the body aligned with the spot on the ground. If the body did not share this circular motion, its rectilinear motion alone would not bring it back to the same spot. One can think of this approach as treating the earth as being like any other celestial body, and therefore as having a natural circular motion, but Aristotle distinguishes sharply between circular motions, which are characteristic of the celestial realm, and rectilinear motions, which are characteristic of the terrestrial realm. Rectilinear motion is directed towards its own annihilation, because an unconstrained body undergoes rectilinear motion only when it is returning to its natural place, and on reaching its natural place the end towards which the motion is directed is achieved and the body comes to rest. Circular motion by contrast continues indefinitely. Copernicus' idea seems to be that somehow one can combine the two, something for which there are no precedents in Aristotelian natural philosophy, where a body must undergo one kind of motion or another. This is because circular motion and rectilinear motion express the natures of different kinds of body. The outcome of a rectilinear motion that returns a body to its natural place, for example, is rest, which is an absolute state in Aristotelian natural philosophy. If the body fell back on to a rotating object, any circular motion must be violent: it could not be a motion that derived from the essence of the body, as the rectilinear motion was. What Copernicus is proposing is entirely in line with the standard and indeed indispensable astronomical procedure of superposing simple motions to generate observed motions, but in the present case this just does not make physical sense in Aristotelian terms.

Kepler's problems in reconciling the observational consequences of a revolving and rotating earth are no less profound. He is prepared to renounce some aspects of Aristotelian natural philosophy, but as a result is left with an account which in many respects is quite ad hoc. In the Introduction to *Astronomia Nova* he deals directly with Ptolemy's claim about objects projected vertically upwards. He concedes that a stone projected upwards to a distance which was significant compared with the earth's diameter would not follow the earth's motion, 'but its forces of resistance would mingle with the earth's forces of attraction, and it would thus detach itself somewhat from the earth's grasp.' But in fact projectiles are separated from the surface by distances which are insignificant compared with the earth's diameter. In this case, the body's natural inclination to rest can do nothing to impede the earth's grasp, 'for the earth cannot be pulled out from under it, since the earth carries with it anything sailing through the air, linked to it by the magnetic force no less firmly than if those bodies were actually in contact with it.'[75] But Kepler's example of a projectile is a stone, not a lodestone or magnetized body, and a stone is hardly drawn to the earth by magnetism.

<hr />

[75] *New Astronomy*, 58.

Ptolemy's physical objections to the earth's motion can be met at a number of levels, and Copernicus and Kepler both invoke a mixture of astronomical and natural-philosophical considerations. In astronomical terms, straightforward geocentrism was in rapid decline in the early decades of the seventeenth century, and the dispute was really between various forms of heliocentric system, whether it be Copernicanism or Tycho's geoheliocentric model (Fig. 5.5). Tycho's model was difficult to fault in purely astronomical terms, whereas the Copernican model had the disadvantage that the annual motion of the earth required a stellar parallax (stars should appear to shift slightly as the earth moves—e.g. between January and June—from one side of the sun to the other, with closer stars undergoing a greater apparent displacement), but such a parallax had never been observed. The Tychonic model was preferred by Jesuit astronomers from 1620 onwards, and in the wake of the 1633 condemnation of Galileo's Copernicanism and the increasingly obvious problems with the Ptolemaic

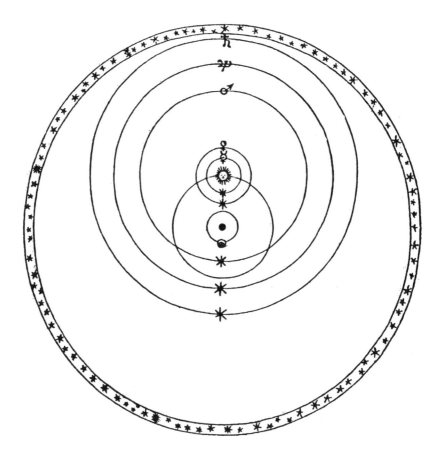

Figure 5.5

model it became the orthodoxy for Jesuits and more widely. Riccioli tried to show, in his *Amalgestum novum* of 1651, how modifications to the Tychonic system enabled it at least to equal the predictive power of the Copernican system. In 1691 Pardies noted that the Tychonic system was the generally accepted astronomical model, a claim repeated as late as 1728, and indeed the Tychonic system was being taught in French *collèges* up to lifting of the bans on teaching Copernicanism in 1757.[76] In natural-philosophical terms, by contrast, the Ptolemaic model made sense, whereas the Tychonic system seemed to have no natural-philosophical rationale at all, and Copernicanism was not supportable in terms of any well-developed natural philosophy. In the absence of a fully developed natural philosophy which could provide a comprehensive physical basis for Copernicanism, the key to its defence lay in identifying the level at which one's natural-philosophical resources might be able to supply at least something of what was needed, and developing these resources accordingly. The most ingenious attempts along these lines were those of Galileo, in his *Dialogo* of 1632.

Galileo had no doubts, on astronomical grounds, that the earth rotates daily on its axis and revolves annually around the sun. His telescopic discovery of the phases of Venus was a decisive blow against the Ptolemaic system[77] but did not decide between the Copernican and the Tychonic systems. However, he had no time for astronomical models that made no appeal to physical questions. Just as Rothmann rejected the Tychonic system because it only showed the 'how' of retrograde motion and not the 'why',[78] so Galileo was dismissive of Tycho's system,[79] and it is of interest that although the *Dialogo* claims to deal with the 'two chief world systems:

---

[76] See Christine Schofield, 'The Tychonic and Semi-Tychonic World Systems,' in René Taton and Curtis Wilson, eds, *Planetary Astronomy from the Renaissance to the Rise of Astrophysics, Part A: Tycho Brahe to Newton* (Cambridge, 1989), 33–44: 41. See also Laurence W. B. Brockliss, 'Copernicus in the University: The French Experience', in John Henry and Sarah Hutton, eds, *New Perspectives on Renaissance Thought* (London, 1990), 190–213. The Ptolemaic, Tychonic, and Copernican systems were being treated on a par in elementary texts in England, such as in the third edition of Joseph Moxon, *A Tutor to Astronomy and Geography* (London, 1686). In his *An Essay at the Mechanism of the Macrocosm* (London, 1707), Conyers Purshall, a product of pre-Newtonian Oxford, was defending a revised version of the Tychonic system in which planetary orbits and periods were brought into numerical harmony with Kepler's laws.

[77] On the Copernican model, Venus ought to appear much larger at perigee than at apogee, and on the assumption it does not generate its own light but reflects that of the sun, it ought to exhibit the full range of phases, just as the moon does, whereas on the Ptolemaic system it ought to be permanently crescent-shaped, the only changes being increase and decrease in size and a change in the direction in which the tips of the crescent point. Despite problems in observing Venus because of its great brightness, which disproportionately exacerbates the problem of chromatic aberration, Galileo was able to establish decisively in 1610 that the former, and not the latter, was what careful observation established.

[78] See Richard A. Jarrell, 'The Contemporaries of Tycho Brahe', in René Taton and Curtis Wilson, eds, *Planetary Astronomy from the Renaissance to the Rise of Astrophysics, Part A: Tycho Brahe to Newton* (Cambridge, 1989), 22–32: 31.

[79] 'I have never set much store by Tycho's verbosity': Galileo, *Dialogue Concerning the Two Chief World Systems*, 52. Tycho defended an Aristotelian natural philosophy in his dispute with Rothmann, and it was he who proposed the case of the cannon ball fired vertically upwards, which we shall examine below. See Alexandre Koyré, *Galileo Studies* (Hassocks, 1978), 141–3.

the Ptolemaic and the Copernican', not only had the Ptolemaic system been replaced by the Tychonic by this time, but his contemporaries identified Galileo's target either as the Ptolemaic and the Tychonic systems, or just the Tychonic system.[80] His key discussion in Day 2 is resolutely physical, the astronomical discussion of Day 3 merely bolstering Copernicanism with his telescopic observations, but ignoring Kepler's pathbreaking work on the orbit of Mars for example, and the defence of the earth's annual motion in Day 4 is pursued in terms of a theory of the tides, that is, a physical theory.

One of the central questions in establishing the motion of the earth on physical grounds was how to account for the fact that bodies on the surface of the earth seemed to behave like bodies on stationary surfaces, not as we would expect bodies on rotating surfaces and moving surfaces to behave. Galileo's genius was to subject these expectations to detailed scrutiny, analysing them into component assumptions, discarding or revising some of these component assumptions, and then putting the components back together and showing that, once our expectations have been corrected, bodies on the surface of the earth behave exactly as we should expect bodies on rotating and moving surfaces to behave. His physical discussion focuses on the earth's diurnal motion—the subject of the 'Second Day' of the *Dialogo*—and the justification for this is offered at the beginning of his discussion:

Then let the beginning of our reflections be the consideration that whatever motion comes to be attributed to the earth must necessarily remain imperceptible to us and as if nonexistent, so long as we look only at terrestrial objects; for as inhabitants of the earth, we consequently participate in the same motion. But on the other hand, it is indeed just as necessary that it display itself very generally in all other visible bodies and objects which, being separated from the earth, do not take part in this movement. So the true method of investigating whether any motion can be attributed to the earth, and if so what it may be, is to observe and consider whether bodies separated from the earth exhibit some appearance of motion which belongs equally to all. For any motion which is perceived only, for example, in the moon, and which does not affect Venus or Jupiter or other stars, cannot be in any way the earth's or anything but the moon's. Now there is one motion which is most general and supreme over all, and it is that by which the sun, moon, and all the other planets, and fixed stars—in short, the whole universe the earth alone excepted—appear to be moved as a unit from east to west in the space of twenty-four hours. This, in so far as first appearances are concerned, may just as logically belong either to the earth alone as to the rest of the universe, since the same appearances would prevail as much in the one situation as in the other. Thus it is that Aristotle and Ptolemy, who thoroughly understood this consideration, in their attempt to prove the earth immovable, do not argue against any other motion than this diurnal one.[81]

Galileo deals with a number of traditional objections to the earth's motion, amongst which are: first, bodies projected vertically upwards would not fall back

---

[80] Schofield, 'The Tychonic and Semi-Tychonic World Systems', 41. See also Howard Margolis, 'Tycho's System and Galileo's Dialogue', *Studies in History and Philosophy of Science* 22 (1991), 259–75.

[81] Galileo, *Dialogue Concerning the Two Chief World Systems*, 114.

to the same spot on a rotating earth; second, bodies such as cannon balls projected westwards would have a greater range from bodies projected eastwards; third, bodies that are some distance from the earth's surface, such as birds, would be left behind by the earth's motion; and fourth, bodies would be extruded from the surface of a rapidly rotating earth. The *Dialogo* broke new ground on these questions, for neither Copernicus, Kepler, nor any other defender of heliocentrism had provided a satisfactory answer to them.

The first three objections cover the relation between bodies and moving surfaces, and are dealt with together. The motion of the earth in these three cases can be assumed to be rectilinear, whereas in the case of the fourth objection, centrifugal effects are invoked, so circular motion is needed. Galileo tells us that the first objection, which ultimately derives from Aristotle, is regarded as the strongest, and he treats the second as a variant of it. A rock falling from the top of a tower takes some time to reach the ground, but during that time, if the earth underwent a diurnal rotation it would have moved a very significant distance to the east, so the rock would fall not directly to the bottom of the tower but instead to the west of the tower at a distance equal to that which the earth had travelled during the fall.[82] Proponents of this view, Galileo tells us, argue that it is confirmed by an experiment in which a rock is dropped from the top of the mast onto a stationary boat, and then on to a moving boat. In the first case, the stone falls vertically downwards to the base of the mast, whereas in the second case it falls into the water behind the boat, because in the time the ball has taken to fall the boat has moved on. The same consideration holds in the case of a cannon ball shot vertically upwards: it lands at the same location as the cannon, not far to the west.

The most convincing ingredient in Galileo's answer turns on his re-examination of the case of what happens when a ball is dropped from a mast.[83] Consider two situations in which a lead ball is dropped from the top of the mast of a moving ship towards the deck of the ship. If we imagine the ship to be passing under a high bridge, in the first situation we let the ball be held at the top of the mast and released as soon as the ship has passed under the bridge. In the second situation we imagine the ball to be suspended over the side of the bridge at exactly the height of the first ball so that as the ship emerges from the bridge and the two balls meet, they are released simultaneously. What actually happens, Galileo points out, is not that both fall some distance behind the ship: only the second ball does this, while the first falls directly to the base of the mast.[84] In both cases the ball is dropped from the same point, yet their behaviour during fall is different. The reason for this, Galileo argues, is that the second ball starts from rest (relative to the situation described), so that when it is released, the only motion it has is one vertically downwards. The first ball, by contrast, has been

---

[82] Ibid. 126.     [83] Ibid. 138–45.

[84] Galileo never actually performed an experiment to confirm this. The first such experiment was performed by Gassendi on a rapidly moving ship in Marseilles around June 1641, and reported in the opening pages of his *De motu impresso a motore translato*: Gassendi, *Opera*, iii. 478–81.

moving with the ship, it does not suddenly lose this motion when released. Because of this, the motion it undergoes during the fall is actually a resultant of two component motions, a horizontal motion in the same direction as the ship and a vertically downwards motion. We do not notice the horizontal motion because we take our bearings from the ship in this case, but if the ship suddenly disappeared, we would be alerted to this component of the motion.

The same reasoning can be applied to the ball falling from the tower. Because the ball shares in the motion of the earth, its motion actually has two components, only one of which we notice because we share in the other—namely the motion of the earth—with the falling body. What, then, one might ask, keeps the clouds and birds aligned with locations on the surface of the earth? Here Galileo invokes the movement of the air as it is carried around with the rotation of the earth, treating it in effect as a fluid carrying along with it any bodies immersed in it. But birds, which can move through the air in various directions, seem more of a problem:

I am easily convinced that the air can take the clouds along with it, they being of material that is very tractable by reason of its lightness and its lack of any contrary tendency; indeed, they are of a material that shares in the properties and qualities of the earth. But birds, being animate, can also move contrary to the diurnal motion; and that the air can restore this to them once they have interrupted it seems to be problematical to me, especially since they are solid and heavy bodies.[85]

The answer Galileo gives forms one of his most explicit statements of kinematic relativity. We are asked to imagine ourselves shut up below the decks on a large ship. We have with us some flies and butterflies, a large bowl of water with some fish in it, and a bottle which empties into a large container drop by drop:

With the ship standing still, observe carefully how the little animals fly with equal speed to all sides of the cabin. The fish swim indifferently in all directions; the drops fall into the vessel beneath; and, in throwing something to your friend, you need throw it no more strongly in one direction than another, the distances being equal; jumping with your feet together, you pass equal spaces in every direction. When you have observed all these things carefully (though there is no doubt that when the ship is standing still everything must happen in this way), have the ship proceed with any speed you like, so long as the motion is uniform and not fluctuating this way and that. You will discover not the least change in all the effects named, nor could you tell whether the ship was moving or standing still.[86]

Although this account takes us beyond mere optical relativity to a claim about our inability to distinguish motions in which we share, Galileo is certainly not advocating wholesale relativity in the *Dialogo*. He makes it clear that 'between motion and rest, which are contradictories, there is no middle ground (as if one might say the earth neither moves nor stands still; the sun and stars do not move and do not stand still)'.[87] Moreover, his theory of the tides, set out in detail in Day 4, depends on showing how a combination of the earth's diurnal and annual motions produces accelerations and decelerations which in turn cause the seas to surge and retreat periodically.

---

[85] Galileo, *Dialogue*, 184.     [86] Ibid. 186–7.     [87] Ibid. 130.

The fourth objection, which raises the question of the tendency of a rapidly rotating earth to cause bodies on its surface to be extruded, shows that he does indeed recognize that certain motions have distinctive physical effects, although in this case he must mitigate these effects, for we experience none of the effects that we would normally expect from being placed on the surface of a rotating object. While the surrounding air may be invoked to keep things aligned with the surface, it cannot explain why bodies are not 'extruded and scattered' from a rotating surface.

Galileo makes it clear that there is indeed a force by which bodies are extruded from the centre, and he notes that when an open bottle of water is swung around on a sling, no matter whether it is swung horizontally or vertically, the water remains in the bottle, and one can feel the sling being tugged by the bottle. The swirling produces an *impetus* in the bottle which causes it to continue in a motion at a tangent to the circle in which it is constrained by the sling, even though the bottle has a natural tendency towards the centre of the earth.[88] There are two tendencies or forces in play here: the tendency or *impetus* of the body to move away at a tangent, and the natural tendency to move to the centre, which is due to its *gravità* (heaviness). Galileo realizes that the former can only be opposed by the latter, so that if he is to account for the fact that a body on the surface of a rotating earth is not extruded, what he has to show is that the former is balanced by the latter.[89] This prompts him to note that the distance between a body extruded along a tangent and the surface of the earth is greater by an ever-increasing ratio the further away it is from its original point of contact with the spherical surface of the earth. Were the earth's surface flat, the distance from the surface would be simply proportional to its distance from the point at which it was extruded from the surface, because the angle between the surface and the trajectory would be constant. But the surface is curved, and the angle between the surface and the tangent increases as a result. Now the pull of the body's weight decreases as the body becomes further removed from the surface of the earth. In terms of the forces or tendencies acting, this means that a constantly decreasing *gravità* is pitted against a constant *impetus*. But the angle that the tangent makes with the surface (a so-called 'horn' angle, because of its shape) is extremely small at first, and at this earliest stage in the tangential motion, the body has as yet very little *impetus*, while at the same time being under the full effect of *gravità*, with the result that it is drawn back into a circular motion. This effect is magnified in the case of the earth, whose surface is so large that its curvature is extremely slight, with the result that the horn angle is undetectably small. This makes sure that the body remains under the compensatory influence of its *gravità* long enough to counter any tangential tendencies.[90]

This argument cannot plausibly be taken as providing an independent argument for the earth's rotation. Rather, Galileo's strategy seems to be this. He is convinced on independent astronomical grounds that the earth is rotating, and it is common

---

[88] Ibid. 190.    [89] Ibid. 192–6.

[90] See the helpful accounts of these arguments in Maurice Clavelin, *The Natural Philosophy of Galileo* (Cambridge, Mass., 1974) ch. 5, and D. K. Hill, 'The Projection Argument in Galileo and Copernicus: Rhetorical Strategy in the Defence of the New System', *Annals of Science* 41 (1984), 109–33.

ground that objects are not extruded from its surface. The only thing that could prevent such extrusion, he argues, is a force which compensates for the tendency of bodies on rotating surfaces to be extruded at a tangent. Since this force is the *gravità* of the body, and since *gravità* is stronger the closer the body is to the earth, it must therefore act while the body is not too far removed from the surface. But Galileo has not actually looked at how the forces balance out: he has just said they must, otherwise things wouldn't happen as they do. He is unable to establish that the compensatory influence of *gravità* actually compensates by the right amount. And in fact the arguments he presents indicate that it overcompensates, for they have the consequence that no body would ever be extruded from a rotating body the size of the earth, for the faster the spin of the earth the harder it would be to eject the body.[91]

Virtually all the resources that Galileo brings to bear in Day 2 of the *Dialogo* are underdeveloped, but they are remarkably effective as a first-line physical defence of Copernicanism,[92] in a way that the physical defences of Copernicus and Kepler were not, and they point the way to how more highly developed resources might be pursued, above all in the attempt to go beyond optical relativity and provide some basis for establishing the conditions under which motions are detectable; and in the analysis of motion provided, where circular motion is resolved into two forces rather than just being treated as natural. Yet by contrast with Kepler, Galileo's project seems extremely modest, and while it identified a number of misunderstandings to which the Aristotelian and Ptolemaic systems were subject, misunderstandings that fundamentally undermined their credibility, it offered no new systematic natural philosophy. His approach was a piecemeal rather than a systematic one, and this was the source of its success. But Descartes, for one, saw this as a failing of Galileo's work, telling Mersenne that Galileo 'has not examined things in order and that, without considering the first causes of nature, he has only sought to account for some particular effects, and thus that he has built without foundation'.[93] Indeed, it was the Cartesian cosmological system, which Descartes first formulated at the same time that Galileo was preparing his *Dialogo* for publication, that was to provide the alternative to all the ancient and medieval natural-philosophical systems.

The question of providing fundamentally different natural-philosophical systems raises the problem of just what kind of enquiry natural philosophy was, whether one should be trying to replace the Aristotelian system in the first place or providing something quite different, whether one should even be pursuing natural philosophy in the

---

[91] See the discussion in Joella G. Yoder, *Unrolling Time: Christiaan Huygens and the Mathematization of Nature* (Cambridge, 1988), 35–8.

[92] In England, e.g., the arguments of the *Dialogo* were taken up by John Wilkins in his *The Discovery of a New World* (London, 1638), and *A Discourse Concerning a New Planet* (London, 1640), which were formative texts in the establishment of Copernicanism in England. See Barbara J. Shapiro, *John Wilkins, 1614–1672: An Intellectual Biography* (Berkeley, 1969), ch. 2.

[93] Descartes to Mersenne, 11 October 1638. Descartes, *Œuvres*, ii. 380. Gassendi, in his *De motu*, will also stress the need for an account of the causes underlying the phenomena Galileo describes (see Paolo Galluzzi, 'Gassendi and *l'Affaire Galilée* of the Laws of Motion', *Science in Context* 13 (2000), 509–45). Cf. Kenelm Digby, *Two Treatises* (Paris, 1644), 310, who also sees Galileo's project as lacking a causal account.

traditional sense. These were all issues that were now up for renewed discussion and they directly engage questions about the point of pursuing natural philosophy, its legitimacy, and the standing of its practitioners. This last question, to which we now turn, has been largely neglected, but it is a crucial one, for it is the key to understanding how the new natural philosophies become inserted into European culture in the sixteenth and seventeenth centuries.

# 6

# Reconstructing the Natural Philosopher

In the first half of the seventeenth century, Bacon, Galileo, and Descartes each set out to construct the *persona* of the new natural philosopher, someone with very different commitments from, and indeed a wholly different mentality to, the traditional natural philosopher, reflecting the radical change in the requirements of the discipline. The aims of, and skills required for, the envisaged new natural philosophies were such that the clerical scholastic natural philosopher was simply not the kind of person who could undertake such an enterprise successfully, raising the question of who was the kind of person best suited to natural philosophy, and what the best environment for its pursuit was.

The importance of this question is nowhere more evident than in the fate of scholasticism, for the criticisms of scholasticism that we begin to encounter with increasing frequency in the course of the sixteenth century focus less and less on doctrinal points as on the question of what is appropriate to the office of the philosopher. The kind of autonomy that the Arts masters had secured for themselves from the thirteenth century onwards had been modelled on the idea of the philosopher as someone who, by contrast with the master of the Theology Faculty, aimed not to uncover hidden truths but to dispute questions fearlessly and free of any dogma. It might reasonably have been expected that this new breed of philosopher, epitomized in the sixteenth century in Pomponazzi and his colleagues at Padua and Bologna, might have formed the model for the philosopher by contrast with the theologian or Platonist. But this philosophical *persona* was in fact among the earliest casualties of the sixteenth century, as what scholastic philosophers had considered their distinctive approach, and their greatest strength, came increasingly to be considered as their most damning feature: sterile argument for its own sake, without regard to any productive outcome, and specifically without regard to truth.

## SPECULATIVE VERSUS PRODUCTIVE PHILOSOPHERS

The question of what it means to be a philosopher goes back to the origins of the understanding of what philosophy is, which we can trace to Plato and the immediate Platonist tradition.[1] This tradition was not a disinterested one. Its concern was

---

[1] On the question of the origins of the terms 'philosophy' and 'philosopher' see Bruno Snell, *Die Ausdrücke für den Begriff des Wissens in der vorplatonischen Philosophie* (Berlin, 1924); Anne Marie Malingrey, *Philosophia: Étude d'un groupe des mots dans la littérature grecque, des Présocratiques au*

not to discover what had been meant by 'philosophy'—the Presocratics had in fact designated what they were doing as *historia* (enquiry)—but to carve out and shape a particular kind of discourse for its own purposes, providing it with a genealogy and characterizing it in a way that marginalized its competitors.[2] It did this in a particularly successful manner, to the extent that it is difficult for us even to reconstruct what the alternatives might have been.[3] But there are residual problems in the way that it conceived of the philosophical project, and these residual problems are of concern to us because they came to a head in the medieval and Renaissance rediscovery of philosophical discourse.

There were two sets of contrasts at work in Plato and the Platonist tradition. The first was that between philosophical discourse and earlier forms of thought that made no claim to the title of 'philosophy'; the second was that between competing conceptions of what philosophy consists in. In the latter respect, Plato's concern was to mark out what he took to be the philosophical enterprise from the activities of the sophists. The image of the sophist that stood out is that of someone willing to teach anyone who is prepared to pay, to devise arguments to win a case, including making weak arguments appear better than strong ones. In short, the failing of the sophist is ultimately not an intellectual but a moral failing, and this is the question on which I want to focus.

The tendency to see philosophical failings along the lines of moral ones will have a long history and was particularly prevalent in the seventeenth century. This was especially marked in the case of those philosophers associated with atheism (often a routine charge against one's philosophical opponents), for it was an almost universal view among early-modern theologians that atheism was motivated solely by the need for those who lived immoral lives to believe that there was no God who would judge and punish them, and conversely atheism was regularly inferred from immoral behaviour.[4] In *La Doctrine curieuse* of 1623, Garasse identifies as atheists, along with Luther and Calvin and their followers, all 'sodomites'.[5] In England, it was Hobbes

---

*IVe siècle après J.-C.* (Paris, 1961); Hadot, *What is Ancient Philosophy?*; and specifically on Plato's use of the term, Monique Dixsaut, *Le Naturel Philosophe* (Paris, 1985). Understanding of the origins of philosophy have changed radically, and the modern idea that it can be traced back to Thales—as opposed to Pythagoras, or Adam, or the Egyptians, or Chaldeans, for example—is a mid-eighteenth century notion: see Constance Blackwell, 'Thales Philosophus: The Beginning of Philosophy as a Discipline', in Donald R. Kelley, ed., *History and the Disciplines: The Reclassification of Knowledge in Early-Modern Europe* (Rochester, 1997), 61–82.

[2] See Walter Burkert, 'Platon oder Pythagoras? Zum Ursprung des Wortes "Philosophie"', *Hermes* 88 (1960), 159–77, who shows that the crucial etymology of *philosophos* given in Diogenes Laertius, *Lives of Eminent Philosophers*, 1. 12–13, for example, cannot go back further than Plato and is rooted in Platonic thought. By contrast, the word *sophistes*, in the broad sense of 'master of technique' can be found as early as Pindar. Pierre Chantraine, *Dictionnaire étymologique de la langue grecque, histoire des mots* (4 vols, Paris, 1968–80), is an invaluable source on etymologies. See also Hadot, *What is Ancient Philosophy?*, ch. 2.

[3] See Antonio Capizzi, *The Cosmic Republic: Notes for a Non-Peripapetic History of the Birth of Philosophy in Greece* (Amsterdam, 1990), *passim*.

[4] See Alan Charles Kors, *Atheism in France, 1650–1729*, i.*The Orthodox Sources of Disbelief* (Princeton, 1990), 19.

[5] See ibid. 29–30.

and his followers who were regularly accused of immorality. An anonymous pamphlet of 1675 written against 'town-gallants' associates them with Hobbesians. The three cardinal virtues of the town-gallant, we are told, are

> *Swearing, Wenching*, and *Drinking*; and if other mens lives may be compared to a *Play*, his is certainly but a *Farce*, which is acted only on three *Scenes*, The *Ordinary*, the *Play-house*, and the *Tavern*. His Religion (for now and then he will be pratling of that too) is pretendedly *Hobbian*: And he Swears the *Leviathan* may supply all the lost leaves of *Solomon . . .* [6]

But the link between philosophical and moral failings was not restricted either to atheists or to contemporaries. Ancient philosophers were equally the subject of attack, and the condemnation of Aristotle by Joseph Glanvill, one of the most prominent apologists for the Royal Society, brings out the flavour of the issues at stake:

> And that *Aristotle* dealt so invidiously with the Philosophers that were before him, will not need much proof to one, that is but indifferently acquainted with his writings. The great Lord *Bacon* hath particularly charged him with this unworthiness in his excellent *Advancement of Learning*, wherein he says, that '*Aristotle* as though he had been of the race of *Ottomans*, thought he could not reign, except that the first thing he did, he kill'd all his Brethren.' And elsewhere in the same discourse 'I cannot a little marvel at the Philosopher *Aristotle*, that proceeded in such a spirit of difference and contradiction to all *Antiquity*, undertaking not only to frame new words of Science at pleasure, but to confound and extinguish all the *antient Wisdom*, inasmuch as he never names any *Antient* Author, but to confute or reprove him' consonant whereunto are the observations of *Patricius* that he carpes at the *Antients* by name in more than 250 places, and without name in more than 1000. [H]e reprehends 46 *Philosophers* of worth, besides *Poets* and *Rhetoricians*, and most of all spent his spleen upon his excellent and venerable Master *Plato*, whom in above 60 places by name he hath contradicted. And as *Plato* opposed all the *Sophisters*, and but two *Philosophers*, viz. *Anaxagoras* and *Heraclitus*; so *Aristotle* that he might be opposite to him in, *this* also, oppos'd all the *Philosophers,* and but two *Sophisters* viz, *Protagoras* and *Gorgias*. Yea, and not only *assaulted* them with his arguments, but *persecuted* them by his *reproaches*, calling the *Philosophy* of *Empedocles*, and all the Antients *Stuttering*; *Xenocrates,* and *Melissus, Rusticks*; *Anaxagoras, simple* and *inconsiderate;* yea, and all of them in a heap, as *Patricius* testifies, *gross Ignorants, Fools* and *Madmen*.[7]

Glanvill's use of Bacon here is pivotal. A crucial part of Bacon's project for the reform of natural philosophy was a reform of its practitioners. One ingredient in this was the elaboration of a new image of the natural philosopher, an image that conveyed the fact that the natural philosopher was no longer an individual seeker after the arcane mysteries of the natural world, employing an esoteric language and protecting his discoveries from others, but a public figure in the service of the public good, that is, the crown.[8]

---

[6] Anon, *The Character of a Town-Gallant; exposing the extravagant fopperies of som vain self-conceited pretenders to gentility and good breeding* (London, 1675). On the association of Hobbes with libertinage, see Samuel I. Mintz, *The Hunting of Leviathan* (Cambridge, 1962), ch. 7.

[7] Joseph Glanvill, *A Letter to a Friend Concerning Aristotle*, appended to *Scire/i Tuum Nihil Est; or, the Author's Defence of the Vanity of Dogmatising* (London, 1665), 84–5. The reference to Patrizi is to his *Discussionum Peripateticarum*.

[8] This forms one of the central themes of Gaukroger, *Francis Bacon*: see esp. chs. 2 and 4.

The idea that philosophers prefer useless learning to virtue goes back to Petrarch, and indeed was one of the mainstays of Petrarchian humanism.[9] Renaissance humanists raised the question of the responsibilities appropriate to the humanist, in particular whether the life of activity in affairs of state (*negotium*) should be preferred to that of detachment and contemplation (*otium*).[10] The answer almost invariably given[11]—not least by Bacon himself, in the seventh Book of *De dignitate*[12]—was that *negotium* should be preferred to *otium*. Once this question had been decided, the issue then became not just the appropriate learning but also, given the practical nature of the programme, the appropriate behaviour for such a practical humanist. The choice, in the first instance, was between the active or practical life and the contemplative life, where philosophers had traditionally fallen in the latter category.[13] The explicit shift to the defence of the active or practical life placed new requirements on philosophy, for philosophers now had to show that they were able to live up to the aims of the active or practical life. What Bacon effectively did was to transform philosophy into something that came within the realm of *negotium*. This was completely at odds with the conceptions of philosophy of classical antiquity and the Christian Middle Ages.[14] Promoted through the rhetorical unity of *honestas* and *utilitas*, Bacon presented philosophy as something good and useful, and thus as intrinsic to the active

[9] See Neal W. Gilbert, 'The Early Italian Humanists and Disputation', in A. Molho and J. Tedeschi, eds, *Renaissance Studies in Honor of Hans Baron* (Florence, 1971), 203–36.

[10] The antithesis between a quiet life of contemplation and public life can be traced back to Euripides' *Antiope*. It was introduced into the Christian tradition by Origen, as a development of a distinction in Philo, then developed by Augustine and Gregory the Great. Gregory's defence of the superiority of the contemplative life subsequently became a central trope of medieval culture. On this development, see Mary E. Mason, *Active Life and Contemplative Life: A Study of the Concepts from Plato to the Present* (Milwaukee, 1961); and Edward C. Butler, *Western Mysticism: The Teaching of Augustine, Gregory and Bernard on Contemplation and the Contemplative Life* (New York, 1966).

[11] Among the more important exceptions are Lipsius, who, in his *De Constantia* (Leiden, 1584), advocated avoidance in public affairs, and Thomas More, who though serving as ambassador, under-treasurer of the Exchequer, and Lord Chancellor, longed for the contemplative life throughout his career. In the course of the seventeenth century in France, there was a widespread move away from the ideals of civic humanism towards those of the private life: see Nannerl Keohane, *Philosophy and the State in France: The Renaissance to the Enlightenment* (Princeton, 1980). Gassendi was a stauch defender of the contemplative life: see Lisa Tunick Sarasohn, 'Epicureanism and the Creation of a Privatist Ethic in early Seventeenth-Century France', in Margaret J. Osler, ed., *Atoms, Pneuma, and Tranquillity: Epicurean and Stoic Themes in European Thought* (Cambridge, 1991), 175–96.

[12] Bacon, *Works*, i. 713–44 [text]/v. 3–30 [trans.]. See Brian Vickers, 'Bacon's So-Called "Utilitarianism": Sources and Influence', in Marta Fattori, ed., *Francis Bacon, Terminologia e fortuna nel XVII secolo* (Rome, 1984), 281–313.

[13] The *locus classicus* for the defence of the contemplative life is Book 10 of the *Nicomachean Ethics*, where Aristotle argues that the contemplation of truth is the single activity that is pursued for its own sake and hence the sole endeavour in which true happiness is to be found: $1177^a11$–17.

[14] It was also completely contrary to the view taken by the Roman Catholic Church in the seventeenth century, which was particularly critical of what it saw as Bacon's espousal of 'Machiavellian' principles, which left no room for theology or the guidance of the Church in natural-philosophical enquiry. See Marta Fattori, '"Vafer Baconus": la storia della censura del *De augmentis scientiarum*', *Nouvelles de la République des lettres* (2000), 97–130; idem, 'Altri documenti inediti dell'Archivio del Sant'Uffizio sulla censura del *De augmentis scientiarum* di Francis Bacon', *Nouvelles de la République des lettres* (2001), 121–30; idem, 'Sir Francis Bacon and the Holy Office', *British Journal for the History of Philosophy* 13 (2005), 21–49.

life. Indeed, it started to become a paradigmatic form of *negotium*, and in this way, it could usurp the claims made for poetry by writers such as Sidney, who argued that poetry can move one to act virtuously, whereas philosophy cannot.

In the humanist thought that made up the source from which Bacon derived much of his inspiration, moral philosophy figured predominantly. Petrarch had made it clear that philosophy should be concerned primarily with ethics, and he complained that Aristotle, while telling us in the *Nicomachean Ethics* (1094$^b$23–1095$^a$6) that the aim of the study of ethics is not to gain knowledge but to behave more virtuously, did not in fact tell us anything that moves us to act virtuously.[15] For that, Petrarch argued, we must turn above all to Cicero and Seneca. The notion that ethics was the centrepiece of philosophy was something that had been fostered particularly in Roman philosophy, where, with the exception of Lucretius, there had been an almost exclusive concern with moral, political, and legal questions.[16] The connection between being a philosopher and being moral was also the theme of Boethius' *De consolatione philosophiae* (528), which was to provide the West in the tenth and eleventh centuries with virtually their only connection with the metaphysical thought of antiquity.[17] But it also captured an underlying theme in classical and Hellenistic philosophy, where the idea of the philosophical sage was very much that of someone who, through philosophical training, had reached a state of moral excellence.[18] It was in fact an integral part of the humanist project that the philosopher aspire to a form of humanity and morality. It should be remembered here that human happiness had been the concern of philosophers in Greek and Roman antiquity, and it was to them that one turned for guidance on how life was to be lived. Philosophers had a distinctive grasp of these questions, for, as Cicero put it, 'since

[15] Petrarch, *De sui ipsus et multorum ignorantia*, trans. in Cassirer et al., *The Renaissance Philosophy of Man*, 103. This conception of philosophy as essentially devoted to moral questions was by no means an exclusively humanist notion, however, and can be found in Petrarch's scholastic contemporary Nicholas of Autrecourt, for example, who criticized Aristotle on similar grounds: *The Universal Treatise of Nicholas of Autrecourt*, 31–2.

[16] See e.g. vol. i. of Colish, *The Stoic Tradition*. Note also that the Latin Fathers were not Romans but North Africans right up to the time of Augustine.

[17] For a sketch of the influence of Boethius in this period see H. Liebeschütz, 'The Debate on Philosophical Learning During the Transition Period (900–1018)' A. H. Armstrong, ed., *The Cambridge History of Later Greek and Early Medieval Philosophy* (Cambridge, 1970), ch. 37. A comprehensive account can be found in Pierre-Paul Courcelle, *La Consolation de Philosophie dans la tradition littéraire. Antécédents et postérité de Boèce* (Paris, 1967).

[18] This theme is pursued in detail in a number of relatively recent writings of which these are representative: Julia Annas, *The Morality of Happiness* (Oxford, 1993); Peter Brown, *The Body and Society*; idem, *Power and Persuasion in Late Antiquity: Towards a Christian Empire* (Madison, 1988); Juliusz Domanski, *La Philosophie*; Ilsetraut Hadot, *Seneca und die griechisch-römische Tradition der Seeleneitlung* (Berlin, 1969); Pierre Hadot, *Philosophy as a Way of Life: Spiritual Exercises from Socrates to Foucault* (Oxford, 1995); idem, *Plotinus or the Simplicity of Vision* (Chicago, 1998); idem, *What Is Ancient Philosophy?*; Dorothee Kimmich, *Epikureische Aufklärungen: Philosophische und poetische Konzepte der Selbstsorge* (Darmstadt, 1993); Malingrey, *Philosophia;* Martha Nussbaum, *The Therapy of Desire: Theory and Practice in Hellenistic Ethics* (Princeton, 1994); Jackie Pigeaud, *La Maladie de l'âme: Étude sur la relation de l'âme et du corps dans la tradition médico-philosophique antique* (Paris, 1981); Paul Rabbow, *Seelenführung: Methodik der Exerzitien in der Antike* (Munich, 1954); André-Jean Voelke, *La Philosophie comme thérapie de l'âme* (Paris, 1993).

the ultimate aim is to live in conformity and harmony with nature, it necessarily follows that those possessed of philosophical wisdom live their lives in a state of happiness, perfection, and good fortune, without any restriction, hindrance, or need'.[19] The notion that Cicero was articulating here is the Stoic one of indifference to calamity and misfortune. Achieving this goal was not easy, however, and it required philosophers to undergo training to prepare themselves for a life quite different from that of their fellows. What was required was set out by Philo of Alexandria, at the end of the Hellenistic era, when he examined how the *persona* of the philosopher or sage is to be formed:

Every person—whether Greek or Barbarian—who is in training for wisdom, leading a blameless, irreproachable life, chooses neither to commit injustice nor return it unto others, but to avoid the company of busybodies and hold in contempt the places where they spend their time—courts, councils, marketplaces, assemblies—in short, every kind of meeting or reunion of thoughtless people. As their goal is a life of peace and serenity, they contemplate nature and everything found within her. ... Thus, filled with every excellence, they are accustomed no longer to take account of physical discomforts or exterior evils, and they train themselves to be indifferent to indifferent things; they are armed against both pleasures and desires, and in short, they always strive to keep themselves above passions.[20]

We must not forget that these were questions that were paramount throughout antiquity, and at least from Socrates onwards the philosopher took on or fostered a distinct *persona* and attitude, depending on the philosophical doctrine or school. For the Socrates of the *Phaedo*, philosophy fitted one for death, which is associated with the attainment of true knowledge.[21] For the Plato of the *Republic*, the *persona* of the philosopher—someone who is 'noble, gracious, the friend of truth, justice, courage, temperance' (487ª)—fitted him for kingship.[22] For Diogenes the Cynic, by contrast, it fitted him to the life of a beggar or a slave, and this was by no means something one merely fell into: it required an *askesis*, a pattern of living, which involved indifference to hardship and suffering (*apatheia*), self-sufficiency and a refusal to engage in the responsibilities of civil society (*autarkeia*), complete and blunt freedom of speech (*parrhēsia*), and lack of shame in performing bodily functions (*anaideia*).[23] Aristotle used a different trope, that of the comparison of philosophy and medicine, maintaining that just as listening attentively to a physician but neglecting to act on the advice given is useless, so too most people mistakenly

---

[19] *De finibus* 3. 7.     [20] Quoted in Hadot, *Philosophy as a Way of Life*, 264.

[21] The theme was to be an important one in Christian philosophy, but the chief philosophical source was not Plato but the extended discussion in Book 1 of Cicero's *Tusculan Disputations*.

[22] See Plato, *Republic* 484ᵇ: 'If philosophers have the capacity to grasp the eternal and immutable, while those who have no such capacity are not philosophers and are lost in multiplicity and change, which of the two should be in charge of a state?' Note, however, there is a case to be made that by the time of the *Laws*, Plato has moved to an image of a community where all citizens—philosophers and non-philosophers alike—can aspire to a life of virtue: see Christopher Bobonich, *Plato's Utopia Recast* (Oxford, 2002).

[23] See H. D. Rankin, *Sophists, Socratics and Cynics* (London, 1983), ch. 13. John Chrysostom will take Diogenes the Cynic as his main example of the inappropriateness of philosophical values for the Christian life: see Domanski, *La Philosophie*, 28–9.

'take refuge in theory and think that they are being philosophers, and will become good in this way'.[24]

This fostering of a philosophical *persona* is particularly marked in the Hellenistic era, where *ataraxia*, peace of mind, was explicitly the aim of all the major schools, and where regulation of the passions played a major role for Epicureans and Stoics alike in attaining the state of mind, and corresponding behaviour, worthy of or appropriate to a member of their philosophical school. Indeed, as Pierre Hadot has remarked, it is love of wisdom, 'which is foreign to the world, that makes the philosopher a stranger to it. So each school will elaborate its rational depiction of this state of perfection in the person of a sage, and each will make an effort to portray him.'[25] This philosophical self-fashioning was pursued in a different way in the Christian era. We have already looked at the claim of Boethius of Dacia that it is easier for the philosopher to be virtuous than for anyone else, and we have seen that this was singled out for criticism in the 1277 Condemnation. No less striking is the idea of philosophical self-fashioning that pervaded Renaissance thought, with Pico Della Mirandola's eulogy on 'the dignity of man' being in fact an attempt to redefine the office of the philosopher as the paradigm sage, and to set out a programme for the attainment of this goal.[26]

In general terms, philosophers in antiquity, in the Middle Ages, and in the early-modern era, were able, with varying degrees of success, to construct images of themselves as paradigmatic bearers of moral, aesthetic, and intellectual responsibility. Whatever deep philosophical quarrels they may have had among themselves, it was important to establish that the philosophical view was not simply one kind of opinion among others. What was required to establish this was the construction of a philosophical *persona* capable of bearing and displaying this authority: an authority which was very different from that borne and displayed by theologians and statesmen, for example, whose claims on moral, natural-philosophical, and other questions may have overlapped with, and perhaps competed with, those of philosophers. The question raised here is one about the relation between philosophy and the behaviour appropriate for the philosopher, or at least the philosophically educated: what kind of *persona* philosophy does or should shape or encourage.

There are two respects in which the model of moral philosophy was important for early-modern thinkers. First, philosophical self-fashioning had always turned on the moral question of the understanding and regulation of the passions, and because of this they have a peculiar centrality, for they have not merely been one object of study among others for philosophers, but something that had to be understood if one were to be 'philosophical' in the first place. Mastery of the passions was, in one form or another, not only a theme in philosophy but a distinctive feature of the philosophical *persona* from Socrates onwards, and Renaissance and early-modern philosophers pursued the theme of self-control with no less vigour than had the philosophers of antiquity. This is the model around which Bacon wished to shape

---

[24] *Eth. Nic.* 1105[b]12–15.        [25] Hadot, *Philosophy as a Way of Life*, 57.
[26] See William G. Craven, *Giovanni Della Mirandola, Symbol of His Age* (Geneva, 1981), ch. 2.

his new practitioner of natural philosophy.[27] It was a model inappropriate to the artisan, and it gave the new practitioner a dignity and standing that the collective nature of his work would not otherwise suggest. Second, in a humanist dimension, being virtuous and acting virtuously are the same thing: there is no separate practical dimension to morality. Indeed, this forms the basis for much humanist criticism of traditional moral philosophy: Sidney, for example, in stressing the superiority of the active, practical life over the contemplative one, drew what he took to be the consequences for moral thought, namely that teaching the nature of virtue is not the same thing as, and indeed is no substitute for, moving people to practice virtue, and that all philosophy has managed is the former.[28] Sidney and Bacon both wanted to overcome the distinction between knowing what is moral and acting morally. Moreover, it is interesting to note here that Bacon stresses in the *Advancement of Learning* that moral philosophy is a cognitive enterprise, one in which the practical outcome is constitutive of the discipline.[29] If, as I am suggesting, we see natural philosophy as being in some respects modelled on moral philosophy, something which is natural enough in a humanist context, and which is reinforced in the shift from *otium* to *negotium*, then we may be able to delve a little more deeply into why Bacon claims that the aim of the natural philosopher is not merely to discover truths, even informative ones, but to produce new works.

The moral basis of his conception is evident, I suggest, in his discussion of the classical philosophers in *Redargutio philosophiarum*. We are told there that there are three classes of philosopher.[30] First, there are the sophists, who claimed to know everything and travelled around teaching for a fee. Second, there are those philosophers who, having a more exalted sense of their own importance, opened schools which taught a fixed system of beliefs, in which category Bacon includes Plato, Aristotle, Zeno of Citium, and Epicurus. Third, there were those who devoted themselves to the search for truth and the study of nature without fuss, without charging fees, and without setting up a school, such as Empedocles, Heraclitus, Democritus, Anaxagoras, and Parmenides. Regarding philosophers of the second category as no better than those of the first, he proceeds to look at individuals, namely Plato and Aristotle, not entering into controversy on points of doctrine but judging them by 'signs',[31] that is, those distinctive characteristics of a doctrine (including the character of those who propound it and what its effects are). What follows is a reflection on the personalities of Aristotle and Plato, in effect a reflection on their personal worth. In the case of Aristotle,

---

[27] This is particularly evident in Bacon's account of his scientific utopia, *New Atlantis*, where self-respect, self-control, and internalized moral authority are central.

[28] Sidney, *An Apology for Poetry*, ed. Geoffrey Shepherd (London, 1965), 112. Compare Bacon's assessment in *De augmentis*: 'Moral philosophers have chosen for themselves a certain glittering and lustrous mass of matter, wherein they may principally glorify themselves for the point of their wit, or power of their eloquence; but those which are of the most use for practice, seeing that they cannot be so clothed with rhetorical ornaments, they have for the most part passed over.' (*Works*, i. 715 [text]/v.4–5 [trans.]).

[29] Book 2: *Works* iii. 432–4.

[30] Bacon, *Works*, iii. 565. For more detail see Gaukroger, *Francis Bacon*, ch. 4, which I draw on here.

[31] Ibid. 566.

the exercise could be mistaken for one in character assassination: Aristotle was, we are told, impatient, intolerant, ingenious in raising objections, perpetually concerned to contradict, hostile to and contemptuous of earlier thinkers, and purposely obscure. We need to ask what the point of these personal criticisms was. It is not as if Bacon did not have specific objections to the content of Aristotle's philosophy. He mentions some of the major points on which he disagrees with Aristotle here in *Redargutio philosophiarum*: Aristotle mistakenly constructed the world from categories, and no less mistakenly dealt with the distinctions between matter and void, and rarity and density, in terms of a distinction between act and potency. The personal attack on Aristotle seems both unnecessary to make his point, and counterproductive.

But I think that to see matters thus is to miss Bacon's point. The personal criticism is not an added extra: it is integral to his project. He explicitly tells us he is going to judge not by content of particular doctrines but by signs. Why, then, is the personal criticism so central to what he wants to do? The answer is that the natural philosopher is not simply someone with a particular expertise for Bacon, but someone with a particular kind of standing, a quasi-moral standing, which results from the replacement of the idea of the sage as a moral philosopher by the idea of the sage as a natural philosopher. We expect the moral philosopher to act in a particular way, like a sage, and this is an indication of the worth of his moral philosophy. The shift from moral philosopher to natural philosopher as the paradigmatic sage means that the natural philosopher now takes on this quality. The worth of a natural philosophy is reflected in its practitioners, just as the worth of a moral philosophy is reflected in its practitioners: or, perhaps, one should say embodied in its practitioners.

In his discussion of moral philosophy in Book 2 of the *Advancement of Learning*, Bacon remarks on the various ways in which reason can be affected:

For we see Reason is disturbed in the administration thereof by three means; by Illaqueation or Sophism, which pertains to Logic; by Imagination or Impression, which pertains to Rhetoric; and by Passion or Affection, which pertains to Morality. And as in negotiation with others men are wrought by cunning, by importunity, and by vehemency; so in this negotiation with ourselves men are undermined by Inconsequences, solicited and importuned by Impressions or Observations, and transported by Passions. Neither is the nature of man so unfortunately built, as that these powers and arts should have the force to disturb reason, and not to establish and advance it: for the end of Logic is to teach a form of argument to secure reason, and not to entrap it; the end of Morality is to procure the affections to obey reason, and not to invade it; the end of Rhetoric is to fill the imagination to second reason, and not to oppress it: for these abuses of arts come in but *ex obliquo*, for caution.[32]

The ultimate aim of moral philosophy, in Bacon's view, is to get people to behave morally; to discourse on the nature of the good, or to dispute whether 'moral virtues are in the mind of man by habit and not by nature', will not secure this end in their own right. What moral philosophy does not provide, and what needs to be

---

[32] Bacon, *Works*, iii. 409–10.

provided, are the means of educating the mind so that it might aspire to and attain what is good:

The main and primitive division of moral knowledge seemeth to be into the Exemplar or Platform of Good, and the Regimen or Culture of the Mind; the one describing the nature of good, the other prescribing rules how to subdue, apply, and accommodate the will of man thereunto.[33]

The first question, on the nature of the good, is divided into discussions of the various kinds of goods, and the various degrees of good. We can distinguish something that is good in itself, for example, from something that is good as part of a greater whole, and the latter should have priority over the former: 'the conservation of duty to the public ought to be much more precious than the conservation of life and being.' It is on this basis that Bacon rejects Aristotle's claims for the value of the contemplative life over the active life, for all the arguments Aristotle gives for the contemplative life 'are private, and respecting the pleasure and dignity of man's self', where of course the contemplative life is pre-eminent, and he gives examples of the social harm that can come from ignoring civil life and using one's own happiness as a criterion. On the question of the relative merits of active and passive good—actively to propagate or to conserve—Bacon comes down firmly on the side of the former.[34] On the question of how to inculcate morality,[35] Bacon refers to 'the Culture and Regimen of the Mind.' He quotes Aristotle's remark that we want to know what virtue is and how to be virtuous: they are part of the same package, as it were. But he also points to Cicero's praise of Cato the younger, who took up philosophy not that he might dispute like a philosopher, but that he might live like one. It is not just the parallel between the moral life and the philosophical life that is of interest here, but the fact that there is a particular *persona* associated with morality and with philosophy: it is not simply a question of having a particular expertise. What we must understand from the outset is what is within our power and what is not. We are limited in what we can do by the nature of the mind, and we need to 'set down sound and true distributions and descriptions of the several characters and tempers of men's natures and dispositions, specially having regard to those differences which are most radical in being the fountains and causes of the rest, or most frequent in concurrence or comixture'. In understanding these, we are discovering 'the divers complexions and constitutions' of the mind, but we also need to discover 'secondly, the diseases, and lastly the cures'. The 'diseases' are the 'perturbations and distempers of the affections' that disturb the mind. The cure consists in setting before oneself 'honest and good ends', and being 'resolute, constant, and true unto them'. The diseases and cure here have an importance that goes far beyond the moral realm, however, and Bacon's detailed account of the nature of the diseases and the regimen required for their cure is developed not in the context of moral philosophy, but in that of natural philosophy.

This takes us to the question how one becomes such a sage in the Baconian sense. In the most general terms, at least one ingredient in the answer is a very traditional

---

[33] Ibid. 419.          [34] Ibid. 424–8.          [35] Ibid. 432–42.

one: the purging of the emotions. But Bacon puts a distinctive gloss on this. The sage for Bacon must purge not just affective states but cognitive ones as well. This is the core of his doctrine of the 'idols' of the mind, the need for which he spells out in the Preface to *Novum organum*:

My plan is as easy to describe as it is difficult to effect. For it is to establish degrees of certainty, take care of the sense by a kind of reduction, but to reject for the most part the work of the mind that follows upon sense; in fact I mean to open up and lay down a new and certain pathway from the perceptions of the senses themselves to the mind. Now this was doubtless seen by those who have attached so much importance to dialectic—whence it is clear that they were looking for props in the intellect, distrusting the mind's inborn and spontaneous movements. But this remedy comes too late to a cause already lost once the mind has been invaded by the habits, hearsay and depraved doctrines of daily life, and beset by the emptiest of *Idols*. Thus (as I have said) the art of dialectic bolts the stable door too late and cannot recapture the horse, and does more to entrench errors than to reveal truths. There remains but one way to health and sanity: to do the whole work of the mind all over again, and from the very outset to stop the mind being left to itself but to keep it under control, and make the matter run like clockwork.[36]

This provides the platform for setting out, in Book 1 of *Novum organum*, an account of the systematic forms of error to which the mind is subject, and here the question is raised of what psychological or cognitive state we must be in to be able to pursue natural philosophy in the first place. Bacon believes an understanding of nature of a kind that had never been achieved since the Fall is possible in his own time because the distinctive obstacles that have held up all previous attempts have been identified, in what is in many respects a novel theory of what might traditionally have been treated under a theory of the passions, one directed specifically at natural-philosophical practice.

Bacon argues that there are identifiable obstacles to cognition arising from innate tendencies of the mind (idols of the tribe), from inherited or idiosyncratic features of individual minds (idols of the cave), from the nature of the language that we must use to communicate results (idols of the market-place), or from the education and upbringing we receive (idols of the theatre). Because of these, we pursue natural philosophy with seriously deficient natural faculties, we operate with a severely inadequate means of communication, and we rely on a hopelessly corrupt philosophical culture. In many respects, these are a result of the Fall and are beyond remedy. The practitioners of natural philosophy certainly need to reform their behaviour, overcome their natural inclinations and passions etc., but not so that, in doing this, they might aspire to a natural, prelapsarian state in which they might know things as they are with an unmediated knowledge. This they will never achieve. Rather, the reform of behaviour is a discipline to which they must subject themselves if they are to be able to follow a procedure which is in many respects quite contrary to their natural inclinations. In short, the reform of one's *persona* is needed because of the Fall: after the Fall it is lacking in crucial ways. Whereas earlier philosophers had assumed that a certain kind of philosophical training would shape the requisite kind of character, Bacon argues that

---

[36] *The Oxford Francis Bacon*, xi. 52–4 [text]/53–5 [trans.].

we need to start further back as it were, with a radical purging of our natural characters, in order to shape something wholly new.

## OFFICIIS PHILOSOPHIAE

One of the great failures of Bacon's project, in his own lifetime, was his inability to find an audience for his work. The transformation of the natural philosopher is necessary for the transformation of natural philosophy, but who was this new natural philosophy written for? After all, if the qualities required by the new natural philosopher were so radically different from those of the old, surely these needs would be paralleled in the readers, but these could no more be the traditional readers than the writers were the traditional writers. If the new natural philosophers were not simply to write for one another, it was crucial that a new kind of audience be constructed for the new kind of natural philosophy.

Bacon, who showed no knowledge of or interest in centres of natural-philosophical research (not even the leading such institution of the day, Gresham College, which had been set up from an endowment from Bacon's own uncle's will), and who engaged in no correspondence on natural-philosophical questions, saw the audience for his natural philosophy as being the monarch, although neither Elizabeth nor James showed any interest in his expensive grandiose schemes.[37] Descartes, by contrast, wrote several letters on natural-philosophical topics each day in his maturity, maintaining extensive contact with the natural-philosophical community through the circle of Mersenne, he designed his *Principia Philosophiae* along the model of late scholastic textbooks as something for use in colleges and universities, and in the last weeks of his life he was busy drawing up a plan for an Academy at Stockholm.[38] Descartes certainly had a better sense than did Bacon of the importance of an audience able to respond to the new work in the appropriate way, and the textbooks of followers such as Regius had a considerable impact, but his writings were subject to significant censorship in the second half of the seventeenth century,[39] whereas Bacon's quite suddenly began to receive an enthusiastic reception, in England and in continental Europe, in the years immediately after his death.[40] As a result, it was

---

[37] See Gaukroger, *Francis Bacon*, 130–1, 160–5.

[38] 'Project d'une Académie à Stockholm', 1 Feb. 1650, in Descartes, *Œuvres*, xi. 663–5.

[39] In the two relevant absolutist regimes, the Catholic Church and France, bans were imposed on Cartesianism in 1663 and 1671 respectively. See Trevor McClaughlin, 'Censorship and Defenders of the Cartesian Faith in France (1640–1720)', *Journal of the History of Ideas* 40 (1979), 563–81; Nicholas Jolley, 'The Reception of Descartes' Philosophy', in John Cottingham, ed., *The Cambridge Companion to Descartes* (Cambridge, 1992), 393–423; Tad M. Schmaltz, 'What has Cartesianism to do with Jansenism?', *Journal of the History of Ideas* 60 (1999), 37–56; and Israel, *Radical Enlightenment*, 23–58. For details of publication of Descartes' works in the seventeenth century, see Matthijs van Otegem, *A Bibliography of the Works of Descartes (1637–1704)* (2 vols, Utrecht, 2002).

[40] For a summary view of his reception see Gaukroger, *Francis Bacon*, 1–5. For more details, see Antonio Pérez-Ramos, *Francis Bacon's Idea of Science and the Maker's Knowledge Tradition* (Oxford, 1988), ch. 2, and Theodore M. Brown, 'The Rise of Baconianism in Seventeenth-Century England: A Perspective on Science and Society during the Scientific Revolution', in *Science and*

Bacon, rather than Descartes, who provided the ideology behind the new scientific academies, even in intensely nationalistic France, where Cartesians were excluded from membership of the Académie des Sciences, which was founded by Colbert, chief minister to Louis XIV, 'in the manner suggested by Veralum [Bacon]'.

But it is the case of Galileo that is the most interesting one in this respect, for here we can discern a process whereby an audience is shaped and the natural-philosophical enterprise legitimated. Galileo was a mathematician, a profession associated with the mechanical arts and with a particularly lowly standing in the ranking of university disciplines. His own education in the subject had come not from his university training—following his father's wishes he had trained in medicine at Pisa, although he left before taking his degree—but from the Florentine court instructor Ostilio Ricci, who taught military fortification, mechanics, architecture, and perspective, and whom Galileo had invited to his father's house to provide instruction.[41] When Galileo took up a university teaching post in mathematics, at Pisa (1589) and then at Padua (1591), the fact that he was able to do this without having completed a degree indicates that he was teaching not in a philosophical discipline but in a technical one, which was learned through apprenticeship rather than training, and the salary was correspondingly less: about one-sixth to one-eighth that of a philosophy professor.[42] Mathematics was crucial to Galileo's understanding of natural philosophy, which, as we shall see in subsequent chapters, took its starting point from the practical-mathematical disciplines, above all mechanics. There was very little Galileo could do within the university system to further his approach to natural philosophy, or even to build up an audience for it.[43]

The patronage system, by contrast, was structured in an totally different way, with an entirely different ranking of priorities. Its attraction was not that it had a more sympathetic approach to the practical-mathematical disciplines than the universities, for it didn't, but that there was no inherent fixed ranking of disciplines. The main clients of the Florentine patrons—painters, sculptors, architects, and others—had attempted, throughout the sixteenth century, to enhance their social status by developing explicit theories grounded in the liberal arts, attempting to transform their standing as mere artisans into that of artists, thereby setting a model

---

*History: Studies in Honor of Edward Rosen*, Studia Copernica 16 (Wroctaw, 1978), 501–22. On his posthumous reception in England see Charles Webster, *The Great Instauration: Science, Medicine and Reform (1626–1660)* (London, 1975). For details of publication of Bacon's works in the seventeenth century, see R. W. Gibson, *Francis Bacon: A Bibliography of his Works and of Baconiana, to the Year 1750* (Oxford, 1950).

[41] See Thomas B. Settle, 'Ostilio Ricci, A Bridge Between Alberti and Galileo'.

[42] Mario Biagioli, 'The Social Status of Italian Mathematicians', *History of Science* 27 (1989), 41–95: 53.

[43] This is generally true of university education although there was a small amount of flexibility. See, e.g. on various national systems, Klaas van Berkel, 'A Note on Rudolphus Snellius and the Early History of Mathematics in Leiden', in C. Hay, ed., *Mathematics from Manuscript to Print, 1300–1600* (Oxford, 1988), 156–61; Mordechai Feingold, *The Mathematicians' Apprenticeship: Science, Universities and Society in England, 1560–1640* (Cambridge, 1984); and Thomas B. Settle, 'Egnazio Danti and Mathematical Education in Late Sixteenth-Century Florence', in John Henry and Sarah Hutton, eds, *New Perspectives on Renaissance Thought* (London, 1990), 24–37.

for natural philosophers.[44] The overriding factor in the patron–client relationship was the enhancement of the reputation of the patron, and in the realm of natural philosophy, natural-philosophical discoveries played a key role.[45] Just as in painting, architecture, music, and verse, the client was expected, ideally, to produce something that would dazzle the patron's competitors, so too in natural philosophy what was to be preferred was some dazzling new discovery. Here we have something which in many ways realized Bacon's picture of a successful natural-philosophical practice, in that it was directed towards manifest and concrete results, and had no place for merely contemplative natural philosophy. Moreover, the princes to whom Galileo dedicated his discoveries have for many purposes the same absolutist powers as had the sovereign whom Bacon wished to oversee his 'great instauration'. Patronage provided a powerful system of legitimation outside the university system, with its own standards of social status and credibility, but one in which the patrons needed the clients as much as the clients needed the patrons, and as a result the natural-philosophical agenda—as long as it produced the goods—could be shaped to a large extent by the client natural philosophers, since the patrons themselves were considered to be above the details, to which their characteristic attitude was one of disinterestedness.[46] In this way, natural philosophy made a move from the clerical to the civil terrain. The price to be paid, as Biagioli points out, is that 'within court patronage one could gain legitimation as a scientific author only by effacing one's individual authorial voice. To be a legitimate author meant to represent oneself as an "agent" . . . of the prince'.[47] When Kepler and Galileo communicated, for example, it was as clients of Rudolph II and Cosimo II respectively, not in their own right: Galileo gave Cosimo a copy of *Sidereus Nuncius*, which Cosimo sent to Rudolph, which Rudolph then passed on to Kepler for his opinion. Moreover, although the patron did not dictate the natural-philosophical programme of research, the client was there to respond to queries from the patron, or to comment on reports of discoveries passed on to him by the patron. Biagioli has shown how Galileo's interests, once he was in (or had one foot in) the patronage network, were shaped by this mode: he addressed himself to topical debates, invariably engineered by patrons, on such questions as buoyancy, the Bologna stone, and sunspots, or to accidental events

---

[44] See Peter Burke, *The Italian Renaissance: Culture and Society in Italy* (Princeton, 1986), ch. 3. Biagioli notes that Galileo felt similarly obliged to immerse himself in literary and artistic disputes—on Dante's *Inferno*, on the relative priorities of Ariosto and Tasso, on the relative merits of painting and sculpture—to prove his competence with courtly and academic culture: *Galileo Courtier*, 118–19.

[45] See Jay Tribby, 'Dante's Restaurant: The Cultural Work of Experiment in Early-Modern Tuscany', in A. Bermingham and J. Brewer, eds, *The Consumption of Culture, 1600–1800* (London, 1991), 319–37.

[46] There are variations here, and, as the seventeenth century progressed, some patrons did begin to take a more active role in experiments. Prince Leopoldo de' Medici took such an especially active role in the Accademia del Cimento (1657–1667), for example. On the Accademia de Cimento, see W. E. Knowles Middleton, *The Experimenters: A Study of the Accademia del Cimento* (Baltimore, 1971); and Paolo Galluzzi, 'L'Accademia de Cimento: Gusti' del Principe, Filosofia e Ideologia dell'Esperimento', *Quaderni Storici* 48 (1981), 788–844.

[47] Biagioli, *Galileo Courtier*, 53.

such as the new star of 1604 or the comets of 1618, where he was asked specific questions such as 'what are comets?', 'why does ice float on water?', 'why is Saturn three-bodied?', 'why does the Bologna stone shine of its own light?', and 'what are sunspots?'[48]

The main difference between the patronage model and that advocated by Bacon was that, in Bacon's scheme, gentlemanly behaviour required rejection of adversarial dispute characteristic of scholasticism, since this was considered as ungentlemanly and fruitless, whereas, in the patronage system of the northern Italian states, patrons initiated and managed natural-philosophical disputes to enhance their image. They were part of a social economy of honour and status, much as duels had been, and like duels they had sharply defined rules of etiquette, constraining who should dispute with whom: attacks on Galileo's work on buoyancy derived from someone of lower social standing, for example, and he was advised to have them answered by 'someone young' so that his opponent could be shamed and 'taught a lesson'.[49] It was also crucial that clients of other patrons did not get any advantage. So, for example, when Kepler finally received a copy of *Sidereus nuncius*, the first thing he requested was Galileo's telescope—Galileo had produced a number of telescopes for Cosimo to circulate—but Galileo kept putting him off, maintaining he did not have a spare one, for fear that Kepler might use it to make discoveries that could eclipse the great success of Galileo and his patron.[50] What resulted from the patronage model was a radically adversarial mode of dispute, although it functioned in a significantly different way from scholastic dispute. In the first place, the whole adversarial style was different. Galileo criticized those who 'would like to see philosophical doctrines compressed into the most limited space, and would like people always to use that stiff and concise manner, that manner bare of any grace or adornment typical of pure geometricians who would not even use one word that was not absolutely necessary.'[51] Galileo's attacks on the spokesman for Aristotelianism in his dialogues, Simplicio, was, as Biagioli notes, 'not only Galileo's straw man but also a representative of what court culture perceived itself to be rejecting',[52] and we should remember here that court culture included senior clerics, such as cardinals, who were very different from the scholastic representatives of religious orders.[53] Second, scholastic dispute was

[48] Biagioli, *Galileo Courtier*, 159–209.       [49] See ibid. 62, and more generally 60–73.

[50] Mario Biagioli, 'Replication or Monopoly? The Economies of Invention and Discovery in Galileo's Observations of 1610', in Jürgen Renn, ed., *Galileo in Context* (Cambridge, 2001), 277–320. Galileo was able to retain his pre-eminent position as the leading observational astronomer until the observation of three comets in the second half of 1618 by Jesuits associated with the Collegio Romano.

[51] Galileo to Prince Leopold of Tuscany, quoted in Biagioli, *Galileo Courtier*, 114–15. The gulf between Italian patronage culture and later Royal Society culture could not be greater here. Compare Sprat's instruction to adopt 'a close, naked, natural way of speaking; positive expressions; clear senses; a native easiness, bringing all things as near to mathematical plainness as they can; and preferring the language of Artisans, Countrymen, and merchants, before that of Wits, and Scholars'. *History of the Royal-Society*, 113.

[52] Biagioli, *Galileo Courtier*, 115–16.

[53] Biagioli notes that Pope Urban VIII, who was behind the 1633 condemnation of Galileo, was not an orthodox Aristotelian at all but held a position closer to Ockhamism (ibid. 351).

above all part of a method of discovery, whereas that was not the case here. Rather, what seemed to be at issue in the case of patronage-directed disputes is that they acted as a means of defending the dignity, and expanding the standing, of the patron: in the process, they acted to legitimate the natural-philosophical programmes pursued under the umbrella of the patronage.

Entry into the upper echelons of the patronage system, namely gaining the patronage of a major prince, was not straightforward. Galileo's attempts began in the early 1600s, when he refined the sector or proportional compass, a device using repeated fixed proportions to solve arithmetical and geometrical problems. Noting the difficulty that many gentlemen had in performing such operations as calculating compound interest, arranging armies with unequal fronts and flanks, using sighting devices on cannons, and calculating the height of distant buildings, Galileo explained the uses of his own improved proportional compass in *Le Operazioni del compasso geometrico et militare* (1606), dedicated to the 'most serene Prince Cosimo de' Medici'. Gentlemen falter and abandon their undertaking, he tells us, because they are 'occupied and distracted with many other affairs' and so 'cannot exercise in this the assiduous patience that would be required of them', so he offers them instruction in his pamphlet which 'will enable them to resolve instantly the most difficult of arithmetical operations; of which however I describe only those that occur most frequently in civil and military affairs'.[54] Cardinal Gonzaga and Cosimo de' Medici responded favourably to presents of the compass and the pamphlet, but they failed to gain him the patronage he sought.

The spectacular development that finally projected Galileo into the public arena, and quickly secured him the patronage of the Grand Duke of Tuscany, came in 1609. In that year, Galileo put to one side his pathbreaking work on mechanics, to which he had devoted most of the past twenty years, and to which he returned in a serious way only in the 1630s, to concentrate on the development of his telescope, the implications of which were to occupy him over the next twenty years.[55] The first public record of the telescope is from September 1608, when the Dutch spectacle maker Hans Lipperhay applied for a patent for a device 'by which things at a very great distance can be seen as if they were nearby'. On hearing of the invention in May 1609, Galileo immediately bought spectacle lenses and reproduced the telescope, and set about improving the instrument, offering it, on the basis of its great military potential, to the doge of Venice. By November he had developed a telescope with a magnifying power of twenty times, and on 30 November he began to use it to study the moon, finding a rough, uneven surface marked with large craters and mountains, and the drawings that accompany *Sidereus Nuncius* emphasize and indeed exaggerate these very earthlike surface features (Fig. 6.1). This is in contrast with the traditional

---

[54] Galileo Galilei, *Operations of the Geometric and Military Compass 1606*, ed. and trans. Stillman Drake (Washington DC, 1978), 41.

[55] On Galileo's development of the telescope see Albert van Helden's introduction to Galileo Galilei, *Sidereus nuncius or The Sidereal Messenger*, trans. and introd. Albert van Helden (Chicago, 1989), 1–24. For further discussion, see Albert van Helden, 'Galileo and the Telescope', in Paolo Galluzi, ed., *Novità celesti e crisi del sapere* (Florence, 1984), 150–7; Mary Winkler and Albert van Helden, 'Representing the Heavens: Galileo and Visual Astronomy', *Isis* 83 (1992), 195–217.

**Figure 6.1**

Aristotelian conception of the moon's surface as perfectly smooth,[56] where its apparent surface patterns, for example, are taken to be a reflection of the earth's oceans.[57] By January 1610 Galileo had resolved the Milky Way into clusters of stars, and had noted the peculiar behaviour of three stars, normally obscured by the brightness of Jupiter, which he soon realized, on analysing their behaviour, must be satellites of Jupiter; by this time he had discovered a fourth satellite, and he named them collectively 'the Medicean stars', a tribute which appears in block capitals on the title page of the work. *Sidereus nuncius* appeared within nine weeks—distributed via the patronage network, copies being sent to ambassadors, princes, and cardinals, and from there passed on the mathematicians and astronomers—and it catapulted Galileo to fame.

The novelty value of the work was not lost on contemporary audiences, which for discoveries of this magnitude were immense, for the concern with novelties was not restricted to the patronage system. The Jesuits paid extensive attention to novel scientific discoveries in their teaching in their colleges, to the extent that some critics of the Jesuit teaching system have suggested that the Jesuit masters had little genuine

[56] See Samuel Y. Edgerton, *The Heritage of Giotto's Geometry: Art and Science on the Eve of the Scientific Revolution* (Ithaca, NY, 1991), ch. 7.

[57] See e.g. the discussion in 'On the Face of the Orb of the Moon', Plutarch, *Moralia* (Loeb edn.: 15 vols, Cambridge, Mass., 1927–69), xii.

scientific interest, but were concerned rather with novelties.[58] In 1611, on the first anniversary of the death of it founder, Henri IV, the *collège* at La Flèche—where Mersenne, Descartes, and Descartes' later collaborator in optics, Claude Mydorge, were all students—engaged in elaborate celebrations.[59] Among the sonnets presented to commemorate the king was one describing how God had made Henri into a celestial body to serve as 'a heavenly torch for mortals'; it is entitled 'On the death of King Henri the Great and on the discovery of some new planets or stars moving around Jupiter, made this year by Galileo, celebrated mathematician of the Grand Duke of Florence'.[60] Galileo's discovery of the moons of Jupiter was indeed widely celebrated,[61] and the Collegio Romano had supported theses defending Galileo in the same year,[62] although they had incorporated the discovery into a Tychonic framework, not a Copernican one. There can be no doubt that the Jesuits encouraged a fascination with novelties in their students, and Descartes was to be no exception. In a manuscript dating from 1621,[63] he describes with evident fascination how to create various optical illusions deriving from della Porta's *Magia naturalis*—a textbook of natural-philosophical illusions, remedies, novelties and much else—which first appeared in 1589, and which he was almost certainly familiar with from his days at La Flèche. In short, the concern with novelty that was so central to the patronage of natural philosophy was not unique to it, but pervaded European culture more widely. And of course it stands to reason that if what the patronage system had prized had attracted no interest and had no appeal outside that system, then it would hardly be able to further the interests and influence of patrons, or display their grandeur and magnanimity. Indeed, to a large extent the patronage system was able to present itself both as a source of natural-philosophical novelties, and of the no less remarkable and ingenious taming of these novelties by court natural philosophers, fuelling a kind of interest in natural philosophy which was quite different from the increasingly limited appeal of scholastic textbook natural philosophy.

The same concern to shape a new kind of natural philosopher is evident in Descartes, although the questions were approached differently from both Bacon and Galileo. That Descartes should be concerned with such questions might at first seem somewhat surprising, especially when compared with Bacon. Bacon's purging was targeted very precisely in his doctrine of idols, and his understanding of what was needed to build on the newly cleared foundations was not abstract

---

[58] See e.g. Gabriel Compayré, *Histoire critique des doctrines de l'éducation en Frances* (2 vols, Paris, 1879), i. 194.

[59] Theatre and public spectacle were an important ingredient in Jesuit culture: see Per Bjurstrom, 'Baroque Theater and the Jesuits', in Rudolph Wittkower and Orma B. Jaffe, eds, *Baroque Art: The Jesuit Contribution* (New York, 1972), 99–110.

[60] See Camille de Rochemonteix, *Un Collège des jesuits au XVIIᵉ et au XVIIIᵉ siècles* (4 vols, Le Mans, 1889), i. 147.

[61] On its impact in England, where Harriot and his circle had been observing the moon with a telescope at the same time as Galileo, see Francis J. Johnson, *Astronomical Thought in Renaissance England* (Baltimore, 1937), ch. 7.

[62] Biagioli points out that the Jesuits also supported Galileo's anti-Aristotelian work on buoyancy, and were unhappy with the 1616 condemnation of Copernicanism (*Galileo Courtier*, 296–7).

[63] Descartes, *Œuvres*, x. 215–16.

and metaphysical but something psychological and practical: in keeping with his conception of the reformed philosophical enterprise. It might seem that Descartes could not countenance a project of this kind, since he had such a rarefied notion of philosophical activity: after all, the *Meditationes* ask us to begin our search for knowledge by imagining that there is no natural world, and that we have no bodies. In his *Disquisitio metaphysica*, Gassendi makes exactly these criticisms of Descartes. Gassendi had been one of those asked by Mersenne to set out a set of objections to Descartes' *Meditationes*, which were published with Descartes' replies, and dissatisfied with the response, he had elaborated on his own objections, and responded to Descartes' replies at length.[64] Descartes attacked Gassendi for raising objections that were not those that a philosopher would raise,[65] thereby opening up the question of what it is to be a philosopher. Among other things, he charged Gassendi with using debating skills rather than philosophical argument; with being concerned with matters of the flesh rather than those of the mind; and with failing to recognize the importance of clearing the mind of preconceived ideas. The dispute pitted Descartes, the advocate of a complete purging of the mind, against Gassendi, the defender of legitimate learning. But in fact matters were not quite so simple and, in the broad outlines of what it sought to achieve, Descartes' aims were similar to those of both Bacon and Galileo.

To understand how, it is crucial that we distinguish between two kinds of enterprise. The first, which is largely legitimatory, is set out in the *Meditationes* and in *Principia Philosophiae*,[66] and the route it follows is that of a radical purging of the mind of anything that can conceivably be doubted, establishing clarity and distinctness (manifested paradigmatically in the *cogito*) as the only criterion by which to establish the veridicality of our ideas, and then, having established that our understanding of the natural world must begin with quantitatively and mechanistically formulated ideas, building up a novel cosmology. This is the way to establish the truth of Cartesian natural philosophy, but the important thing to note is that Descartes does not claim that it is the way to pursue this natural philosophy: Gassendi conflates the two and is understandably shocked at the claim. What is offered in these works is the route to be followed by someone who wishes to be convinced of the truth of Cartesian natural philosophy, but it is not the path of discovery to be followed by the natural philosopher. This latter path, and the requisite state of mind and character of the natural philosopher who wishes to pursue it, are formulated in quite different terms, ones that involve psychological and moral considerations as much as epistemological ones.[67]

Descartes' discussion of this path occurs in *La Recherche de la verité par la lumière naturelle*, which contrasts the fitness for natural philosophy of three characters: Epistemon, someone well versed in scholasticism; Eudoxe, a man of moderate

---

[64] Pierre Gassendi, *Opera Omnia*, iii. 269–410. Descartes himself wrote a counter-reply, which appeared in the French translation of the *Meditationes*: Descartes *Œuvres*, ixA. 198–217.

[65] Descartes, *OEuvres*, vii. 348–9.

[66] For a detailed discussion see Gaukroger, *Descartes' System of Natural Philosophy*, chs. 1 and 3. We shall return to these questions later.

[67] See, ibid. 239–46.

intelligence who has not been corrupted by false beliefs; and Poliandre, who has never studied but is a man of action, a courtier, and a soldier (as Descartes himself had been). Epistemon and Poliandre are taken over the territory of sceptical doubt and foundational questions by Eudoxe, but in a way that shows Poliandre's preparedness for, or capacity for, natural philosophy, and Epistemon's lack of preparedness. Preparedness here is in effect preparedness for receiving instruction in Cartesian natural philosophy. The *honnête homme*, Descartes tells us,

came ignorant into the world, and since the knowledge of his early years rested solely on the weak foundation of the senses and the authority of his teachers, it was close to inevitable that his imagination should have been filled with innumerable false thoughts before his reason could guide his conduct. So later on, he needs to have either very great natural talent or the instruction of a very wise teacher, to lay the foundations for a solid science.[68]

The thrust of Descartes' discussion is that Poliandre has not had his mind significantly corrupted, because, in his role as an *honnête homme*, he has not spent too much time on book-learning, which 'would be a kind of defect in his education'. The implication is that Epistemon has been corrupted in this way, and so is not trainable as the kind of natural philosopher that Descartes seeks. It is only the *honnête homme* who can be trained, and it is Poliandre whom Eudoxe sets out to coax into the fold of Cartesian natural philosophy, not Epistemon. It is true that we might think of the procedure of radical doubt and the purging that results as a way of transforming everyone into an *honnête homme*, and to some extent it is, although in his account of the passions Descartes makes it clear that, once we leave the programmatic level, ridding ourselves of prejudices and preconceived ideas is not so simple, and it requires the cultivation of a particular mentality, which is really what we witness in *La Recherche*.

In *La Recherche*, the *honnête homme* alone is identified as the kind of person who uses his natural faculty of forming clear and distinct ideas to the highest degree: or, at least, it is he who, when called upon, uses it to the highest degree. This does not mean that the *honnête homme* alone is able to put himself through the rigours of hyperbolic doubt and discover the true foundations of knowledge: in theory everyone is able to do that, scholastics included. After all, hyperbolic doubt erases our beliefs—everyone's beliefs—to such an extent that everyone becomes a natural-philosophical *tabula rasa*:

An examination of the nature of many different minds has led me to observe that there are almost none at all so dull and slow as to be incapable of forming sound opinions or indeed of

---

[68] Descartes, *Œuvres*, x. 496. On *La Recherche* see Alberto Guillermo Ranea, 'A "Science for *honnêtes hommes*": *La Recherche de la Vérité* and the Deconstruction of Experimental Knowledge', in Stephen Gaukroger, John Schuster, and John Sutton, eds, *Descartes' Natural Philosophy* (London, 2000), 313–29. More generally, see Ettore Lojacono, 'Socrate e l'honnête homme nells cultura dell'autunno del Rinascimento francese e in René Descartes', in Ettore Lojacono, ed., *Socrate in Occidente* (Florence, 2004), 103–46. The standard contemporary account of the *honnête homme* and how he should make his way in the world is Nicolas Faret, *L'Honneste Homme. Ov l'Art de plaire a la court* (Paris, 1630). This immensely popular work was reprinted five times in the 1630s alone, and within two years of its first publication had appeared in English as *The Honest Man: or, the Art to Please in Court* (London, 1632).

grasping all the most advanced sciences, provided they receive proper guidance. And this may be proved by reason. For since the principles in question [namely, those of the *Principia*] are clear, and nothing is permitted to be deduced from them except by very evident reasoning, everyone has enough intelligence to understand the things that depend upon them.[69]

But if the aim is to develop and refine natural-philosophical skills as one progresses, then we require something different:

As for the individual, it is not only beneficial to live with those who apply themselves to [the study of philosophy]; it is incomparably better to undertake it oneself. For by the same token it is undoubtedly much better to use one's eyes to get about, but also to enjoy the colours of beauty and light, than to close one's eyes and be led around by someone else. Yet even the latter is much better than keeping one's eyes closed and having no guide but oneself.[70]

'Using one's eyes to get about' is not something that everyone finds equally easy, however. What Descartes is seeking are those who can develop his system to completion:

The majority of truths remaining to be discovered depend on various particular observations/ experiments which we can never happen upon by chance but which must be sought out with care and expense by very intelligent people. It will not easily come about that the same people who have the capacity to make good use of these observations will have the means to make them. What is more, the majority of the best minds have formed such a poor opinion of the whole of philosophy that has been current up until now, that they certainly will not apply themselves to look for a better one.[71]

We must recognize that some are more fitted than others to follow the path of instruction/enlightenment in natural philosophy. And in the *Recherche*, Descartes realizes, practically, that people come to natural philosophy not with a *tabula rasa* but with different sets of highly developed beliefs which are motivated in different ways and developed to different degrees. These rest upon various things, and this is what leads him, in *La Recherche*, to construct an image of the *honnête homme* as a model in which the moral sage and the natural philosopher meet,[72] for, as he puts it in the Prefatory Letter to the French translation of the *Principia*, 'the study of philosophy is more necessary for the regulation of our morals and our conduct in this life than is the use of our eyes to guide our steps'.[73]

In the *Principia*, Descartes set out to reform philosophy in its entirety, but he does not see the project as establishing the kind of stagnant system that scholasticism had become, where what has caused the decline of the system was clearly in large part due, in his view, to the slavish adherence of its proponents to Aristotle. In this respect, Descartes is not in the slightest interested in winning over scholastic philosophers to his system: they are simply not the kind of people who can develop it, and would only lead it to the kind of stagnation to which they have led Aristotelianism. A fortiori, they cannot act as paradigm philosophers, as sages whose wisdom can guide the rest.

---

[69] Descartes, *Œuvres*, ixB. 12.    [70] Ibid. ixB. 3.    [71] Ibid. ixB. 20.

[72] There can be little doubt that this was a radical move, especially in view of the association of the *honnête homme* with a 'scorn for religion', as one contemporary put it: see René Pintard, *Le Libertinage érudit dans la première moitié du XVII$^e$ siècle* (2 vols, Paris, 1943), i. 15.

[73] Descartes, *Œuvres*, ixB, 3–4.

This role falls instead to those who, reflecting upon the current state of philosophy, have formed a low opinion of it, and have avoided taking it up. This low opinion, wholly merited, is what makes them *honnêtes hommes*, and it is precisely these whom Descartes sees as being potentially the new paradigm philosophers, marked by an intellectual honesty that rescues philosophy from the intellectual disgrace into which it has fallen. Note also that these *honnêtes hommes* are invited to engage in co-operative work. Descartes's vision of natural philosophy as a co-operative enterprise reflects, just as does Bacon's, the idea that natural philosophy increases the public good, thus fulfilling what is in effect a moral imperative. In this way, the contrast with useless scholastic natural philosophy shows that a secular enterprise does something morally fulfilling in a way that the scholastic enterprise does not.

Not only the concern with the usefulness of philosophy, but also that of intellectual honesty, overlaps very significantly with those of Bacon and Galileo, and what underlies it is above all the rejection of the idea of coming to natural philosophy with preconceived ideas. Bacon's doctrine of idols is dedicated to removing such preconceived ideas, and this informs the whole outlook of the Royal Society. Robert Hooke, in his Preface to Robert Knox's history of Ceylon, for example, describes to the reader the qualities required in the ideal reporter: 'I conceive him to be no ways prejudiced or byassed by Interest, affection, hatred, fear or hopes, or the vain-glory of telling strange Things, so as to make him swarve from the truth of Matter of Fact.'[74] In his history of the Royal Society, Sprat stresses that the 'histories' collected by the Royal Society 'have fetch'd their Intelligence from the constant and unerring use of *experienc'd Men* of the most unaffected, and most unartificial kinds of life'[75] and that:

If we cannot have sufficient choice of those that are skill'd in all *Divine* and *human* things (which was the antient definition of a Philosopher) it suffices, if many of them be plain, diligent, and laborious observers: such, who, though they bring not much knowledg, yet bring their hands, and their eyes uncorrupted: such as have not their Brains infected by false Images; and can honestly assist in the *examining*, and *Registring* what the others represent to their view.[76]

Galileo uses the charge that his opponents have preconceived ideas as a rhetorical ploy, and he links this with their failure to control their passions. This is clear in his attacks on Grassi in *Il Saggiatore*,[77] where Grassi's failure to appreciate the novel hypotheses on the nature of comets that Galileo presents to him is taken as 'a sign of a soul altered by some passion'.[78] Preconceived ideas are construed here as a form of

[74] Robert Knox, *An Historical Relation of the Island Ceylon, in the East-Indies* (London, 1681): Preface, P. xlvii.

[75] Sprat, *History of the Royal-Society*, 257.  [76] Ibid. 72–3.

[77] Galileo Galilei, *Il Saggiatore* (Rome, 1623), trans. in Stillman Drake, *The Controversy on the Comets of 1618* (Philadelphia, 1960), 151–336. There is an excellent discussion of the controversy in Biagioli, *Galileo Courtier*, ch. 5. As Biagioli notes, the situation is complicated, for Galileo's argument in *Il Saggiatore* is not anti-system per se, but rather a response to the 1616 condemnation of the Copernicani system. Worried that the Tychonic system might replace the condemned Copernican one (as indeed it was doing among Jesuit astronomers), Galileo responds by trying to put the whole question of astronomical reality on hold, denying validity to any system.

[78] Cited in Biagioli, *Galileo Courtier*, 308. See also the discussion in Dear, *Discipline and Experience*, 85–92.

vested interests, and Grassi, as a supporter of Aristotelianism, is presented as someone with an axe to grind, someone who is unable to argue a case on its merits and so has to rely on a philosophical system, which is treated as a form of intellectual dishonesty and a lack of objectivity. In fact, Galileo is far from being entirely fair to Grassi, and, twelve years earlier, he had done exactly what he is now accusing Grassi of doing. In a dispute with della Colombe over buoyancy that began in 1611, it was Galileo who, when faced with recalcitrant evidence, tried (ultimately with success) to turn the dispute away from particular observations to systems of natural philosophy.[79] In this case, Galileo had maintained that whether a body floats on the surface of water or sinks depends on the specific weight of the body and not its shape. Delle Colombe was able to show, however, that whereas a sphere of ebony sank to the bottom of a container of water, a shaving of ebony floated on the surface. Galileo enveloped the questions in basic hydrostatics, trying to turn the focus away from delle Colombe's experiment, and arguing for its irrelevance when seen in the context of the larger theory.

Whatever the rights and wrongs of the dispute, however, the crucial point is that, whereas earlier disputes in natural philosophy automatically involved competing systems (for that was what was ultimately at stake), there was now a new ingredient in the brew, as charges of intellectual dishonesty were brought against those who argued from the standpoint of a purported systematic understanding. This anti-system view would take a variety of forms. One would be the kind of radical stand against system-building that we find defended in the eighteenth century in such writers as Voltaire, Condillac, Diderot, and Hume. Another, which has a more direct bearing on our present concerns, would be eclecticism. Lipsius, who was one of the first to use the term 'eclecticism' in the modern era, took Seneca as his model, and advised that we should 'not strictly adhere to one man, nor indeed one sect' and that the only sect we should follow 'is the Eclectic (let me translate it "Elective") which was founded by one Potamo of Alexandria'.[80] The English natural philosopher Walter Charleton spelt out his debt to this 'school' in no uncertain terms, telling us that eclectics

adore no Authority, pay a reverend esteem, but no implicite Adherence to Antiquity, nor erect any Fabrick of Natural Science upon Foundations of their own laying: but, reading all with the same constant Indifference, and aequanimity, select out of each of the other sects, whatever of Method, Principles, Positions, Maxims, Examples, &c. seems in their impartial judgements, most consentaneous to *Verity*; and on the contrary, refute, and, as occasion requires, elenchically refute what will not endure the Test of either right *Reason*, or faithful *Experiment*. . . . Here

---

[79] On this dispute see Drake, *Galileo Studies*, ch. 8, and Biagioli, *Galileo Courtier*, ch. 3.

[80] Justus Lipsius, *Manducationis ad Stoicam philosophiam libri tres* (Antwerp, 1604), 10; cited in C. W. T. Blackwell, 'The Case of Honoré Fabri and the Historiography of Sixteenth and Seventeenth Century Jesuit Aristotelianism in Protestant History of Philosophy: Sturm, Morhof and Brucker', *Nouvelles de la Republique des Lettres* (1995), 49–77: 53. Potamo[n] was an Alexandrian living at the end of the first century BCE, who attempted to reconcile the doctrines of Plato, Aristotle and the Stoics. On the history of eclecticism in the early-modern era, see Michael Albrecht, *Eklektik. Eine Begriffsgeschichte mit Hinweisen auf die Philosophie- und Wissenschaftsgeschichte* (Stuttgart/Bad Canstatt, 1994).

to declare ourselves of this Order, though it be no dishonour, may yet be censured as superfluous: since not only those Exercises of our Pen, which have formerly dispersed themselves into the hands of the Learned, have already proclaimed as much.[81]

Boyle set out his preference for a form of syncretism in a no less explicit way, telling us approvingly that eclectics do 'not confine themselves to the notions and dictates of any one sect, but in a manner include them all, by selecting and picking out of each that which seemed most consonant to truth and reason, and leaving the rest to their particular authors and abettors'.[82] Even Boyle's antagonist Hobbes, not an advocate of any kind of syncretism, or indeed any attempt at philosophical reconciliation, was nevertheless resolutely opposed to what he considered needless philosophical controversy, telling us in his *Six Lessons to the Savilian Professors of the Mathematics,* that his enthusiasm for Euclid had been due to the fact that there were no sects in mathematics.[83]

The connection between the character of eclecticism and the character of the philosopher was if anything reinforced in the eighteenth century, and is spelled out particularly clearly in d'Alembert's entry on eclecticism in the *Encyclopèdie*:

The eclectic is a philosopher who, riding roughshod over prejudice, tradition, antiquity, universal consent, authority, in a word, everything that subjugates the mass of minds, dares to think for himself, goes back to the most clear and general principles, examines them, discusses them, allowing only that which can be demonstrated from his experience and his reason; and having analyzed all philosophical systems without any deference or partiality, he constructs a personal and domestic one that belongs to him. I say *a personal and domestic philosophy* because the ambition of the eclectic is not so much to be the instructor of the human race as its disciple; not so much to reform others as to reform himself; to know the truth rather than to teach the truth. He is not a man who plants and sows; he is a man who reaps and sifts. . . . The sectarian is a man who embraces the doctrine of a philosopher; the eclectic, on the contrary, is a man who recognises no master.[84]

This is a distinctively Enlightenment statement of the values of eclecticism, but the way in which it focuses on the dignity of the philosopher captures a good deal of what was at stake in the seventeenth-century sense of what it meant to be a natural philosopher.

In sum, the figures we have focused on—Bacon, Galileo, and Descartes—each saw philosophy as being in desperate need of radical reform, and each of them saw this reform as being carried out by a quite new kind of person: a philosopher wholly

---

[81] Walter Charleton, *Physiologia Epicuro-Gassendo-Charltoniana: or A Fabrick of Science Natural, upon the Hypothesis of Atoms* (London, 1654), 4. See the discussion of Charleton's complex identity as a natural-philosophical physician in Emily Booth, *'A Subtle and Mysterious Machine': The Medical World of Walter Charleton (1619–1670)* (Dordrecht, 2005), chs. 3 and 5.

[82] *Appendix to the Christian Virtuoso,* in *The Works of the Honourable Robert Boyle*, vi. 700.

[83] Thomas Hobbes, *The English Works of Thomas Hobbes*, ed. William Molesworth (11 vols, London, 1839–1845), vii. 346.

[84] Denis Diderot, *Encyclopèdie ou Dictionnaire Raisonné des Sciences, des Arts et des Métiers* (17 vols, Paris, 1751–65), v. 270 cols 1–2. The article on eclecticism runs from 270 col. 1 to 293 col. 2, and the treatment is comprehensive.

unlike the clerical scholastics who wrote and taught philosophy. These new kinds of philosopher were not simply people who carried out investigations in a different way from their predecessors: they had, and needed to have, a totally different *persona*. The techniques of self-examination and self-investigation encouraged both by the whole-sale attempt to transfer monastic religious values to the population at large, and by the sense that one was responsible for the minute details of one's daily life in the form of new norms of appropriate behaviour, opened up the possibility of a new understand-ing of one's psychology, motivation, and sense of responsibility, and shaped one's per-sonal, moral, and intellectual bearing.[85] Bacon, Galileo, and Descartes used this—in rather different ways, but with the same broad aims—to transform our understand-ing of what qualities, including personal qualities, one needs to be a philosopher.

## THE NATURAL PHILOSOPHER VERSUS THE ENTHUSIAST

One of the issues on which a good deal of dispute about the nature of the *persona* of the natural philosopher turned was that of enthusiasm, which was closely tied up with the rise of radical Puritanism in the last decades of the sixteenth century. It was tar-geted by Bacon in *An Advertisement touching the Controversies of the Church of England* of 1589, where he attacks the substitution of enthusiasm or zealotry for learning.[86] Most zealots, he tells us in his *Advertisement*, are 'men of young years and superficial understanding, carried away with partial respect of persons', and their contentions 'either violate truth, sobriety, or peace'.[87] They 'leap from ignorance to a prejudicate opinion, and never take a sound judgement in their way'.[88] They are, in short, incap-able of assessing and making sound judgements on the cases they consider, and yet they not only come to conclusions on such cases, but do not consider their lack of learning a handicap. It is for these reasons that Bacon insists that 'the people is no meet judge nor arbitrator, but rather the quiet, moderate, and private assemblies of the learned'.[89]

Bacon was not alone among natural philosophers in perceiving the danger. In the preface to *De magnete*, Gilbert complains of the 'Ocean of Books' published in his time,

through which very foolish productions the world and unreasoning men are intoxicated, and puffed up, rave and create literary broils, and while professing to be philosophers, physicians, mathematicians, and astrologers, neglect and despise men of learning.[90]

---

[85] For a detailed account of how this worked in the case of one small section of society—the French aristocracy between the late sixteenth century and the beginning of the eighteenth cen-tury—see Jonathan Detwald, *Aristocratic Experience and the Origins of Modern Culture: France, 1570–1715* (Berkeley, 1993).

[86] See the excellent discussion in Julian Martin, *Francis Bacon, the State, and the Reform of Natural Philosophy* (Cambridge, 1992), 42 ff.

[87] *Advertisement*, in Bacon, *Works*, viii. 82.     [88] Ibid. 82–3.     [89] Ibid. 94.

[90] Gilbert, *On the Magnet*, trans. Silvanus P. Thompson (New York, 1958), Preface, sig. *ijr. Stephen Pumfrey, 'William Gilbert's Magnetic Philosophy, 1580–1684: The Creation and Dissolution of a Discipline', Ph.D. thesis (The Warburg Institute, London, 1987), argues in detail (14–73) that one of the main aims of publishing *De magnete* was to reclaim magnetism for natural

It was not just that there was a movement afoot which had eschewed learning in favour of some special form of insight to which Puritans had claimed access. There was also an extensive undergrowth of literature, in the form of self-help and self-improvement books—some of it based on the *problemata* model of frequently asked questions with answers, following prototypes traditionally ascribed to Aristotle, Alexander of Aphrodisias, and Plutarch, and some of it apparently *sui generis*—which was beginning to replace traditional learning.

The phenomenon was not restricted to Puritans, however, and later in the century Descartes' *Meditationes* and *Principia* were identified in England with enthusiasm.[91] Indeed, the association between enthusiasm and the idea that one could rely on internal criteria in cognitive judgements seems to have been a natural one for English natural philosophers in the second half of the seventeenth century, judging from their reaction to Descartes. Meric Casaubon, writing in 1668, tells us:

But for his *Method*: I tooke him for one, whom excessive pride and self-conceit (which doth happen unto many) had absolutely bereaved of his witts. I could not believe that such stuffe, soe ridiculous, soe blasphemous (as I apprehended it, and doe still) could proceed from a sober man. A cracked brain man, an Enthusiast . . .[92]

The theme is elaborated on in his discussion of the *Meditationes*,

What a mysterie doth he make of his *Ego sum: ego cogito*, to attaine to the excellencie whereof, a man must first strip himselfe of all that he hath ever knowne, or beleeved. He must renounce to his natural reason, and to his senses; nothing but caves and solitude will serve the turne for such deep meditation, such profound matter: rare inventions to raise the expectations of the credulous, and in the end to send them away pure Quacks, or arrand Quakers.[93]

Thirty years later, John Sergeant repeats the same charges, if with qualifications:

I much value your good Opinion, and I perceived I was in danger of losing it, by a hint you gave me, with a Dis-relishing Air, that I call'd Cartesius a Fanatick; which you thought very harsh. In answer, I deny the charge. 'Tis one thing to say, that when Cartesius was laying his *Method to Science*, by denying all his senses and devesting himself of all his former Knowledges, which . . . was no less than to *Unman himself, he fell for some few Days*, into a *Spice of Enthusiasm*; nay, was *brim-full of it*; and fancy'd he had *Visions and Revelations*, so that he seem'd *Crack-brain'd*, or to have drunk *a Cup too much* . . . And 'tis another Thing to say, he was *habitually* a Fanatick, or Enthusiast all his life, and in every Action he did, or Book he writ; the former of which can neither be *deny'd* with *Truth*, nor the Later *objected* with any Degree of *Modesty*.[94]

---

philosophy from unlicensed magical writers. More generally on the threat of printing in England at this time, see Adrian Johns, *The Nature of the Book* (Chicago, 1998), esp. ch. 2.

[91] Although I shall concentrate on England in what follows, this interpretation can also be found in the Netherlands, for example in the anonymously published work of Martinus Schoock, *Admiranda methodus novae philosophiae Renati Descartes* (Utrecht, 1643), 255–61.

[92] 'On Learning', transcribed in Michael R. G. Spiller, *'Concerning Natural Philosophy': Meric Casaubon and the Royal Society* (The Hague, 1980), 195–214: 203.

[93] Ibid. 205.

[94] John Sergeant, *Non Ultra, or, a Letter to a Learned Cartesian* (London, 1698), 108–9.

What lies behind this form of criticism is not only the idea that, if one starts from one's own resources, without explicit guidance, one can easily go astray, but also the idea that there are many who will take advantage of this to give implicit and indeed pernicious guidance. Many in England in the second half of the seventeenth century, for example, believed that Roman Catholics had infiltrated the various Protestant sects, with Glanvill, for instance, warning that Roman Catholics 'put themselves into all shapes and disguises among our sects'.[95] Casaubon accuses Descartes of taking

the same course with his disciples, as many Jesuited Puritans doe with theirs; which is, first to cast them downe to the lowest pitt of despaire, and then, with such engines of persuasion they are commonly well stored with, to rayse them up againe to the highest pitch of confidence; but soe that they leave themselfes a power still to caste down and rayse againe, when they see cause; which must needs oblige the credulous disciple, as he hath found the horrour of the one, and the comfort (whether reale or imaginarie) of the other, to a great dependencie. Soe Descartes, after he hath obliged his disciples to forgett and foregoe all former praecognitions and progresses of eyther senses or sciences, then he thinks he hath them sure: they must adheare to him tooth and nayle, or acknowledge themselfes to have beene fooled.[96]

There can be no doubt that starting from some 'internal' criterion is fraught with dangers. No one seems to have doubted that such a criterion was open to abuse: in the wrong hands, it no longer embodied a standard of objectivity but rather allowed one to legitimate anything. And we must remember here that as often as not the decision as to whether the criterion had been used appropriately, or by the appropriate person, turns on the doctrines that it is used to generate. Although some relatively conservative figures such as Cudworth will use similar means to reconstruct the history of philosophy and natural theology, there will also be those such as Hobbes and Spinoza who will employ such an 'internal' criterion to formulate uncompromisingly heterodox systems: and in the latter case one which derives directly from a reflection on the Cartesian criterion of clarity and distinctness.[97]

The reaction of Royal Society apologists to what they took to be the phenomenon of enthusiasm went beyond just criticism, however, and had its more constructive aspects. There was an attempt to harness the energies and novel practical skills produced within the radical Protestant movement, for example, by incorporating elements of the project into a tightly-controlled natural-philosophical programme. Glanvill, in his defence of the Royal Society in 1668, gives us an idea of how this project was conceived, distinguishing the kind of chemistry pursued there from that of Paracelsians and others, for example, telling us that:

its late *Cultivators*, and particularly the Royal Society, have refined it from its *dross*, and made it *honest, sober*, and *intelligible*, an excellent *Interpreter* to *Philosophy*, and *help* to *common Life*. For *they* have laid aside the *Chrysopoietick*, the *delusory Designs*, and *vain Transmutations*, and

---

[95] Joseph Glanvill, *The Zealous and Impartial Protestant* (London, 1681), 26.

[96] 'On Learning', in Spiller, '*Concerning Natural Philosophy*', 205.

[97] See Richard H. Popkin, 'Cartesianism and Biblical Criticism', in Thomas Lennon et al., eds, *Problems of Cartesianism* (Kingston and Montel, 1982), 61–82.

*Rosicrucian vapours, Magical Charms* and *superstitious Suggestions*, and formed it into an *Instrument* to know the *depths* and *efficacies* of Nature.[98]

Such sentiments played a crucial role in the natural-philosophical programme that emerged in England in the seventeenth century, which was somewhat different from that which we find in France, Italy, or the Netherlands. For one thing, it retains a very practical view of what it is to do natural philosophy, compared, for example, with early seventeenth-century France. But it also involved the transformation of a disorganized, highly individualistic, practically oriented form of natural-philosophical practice into something in which enthusiast excesses could be reshaped or curbed.

Tudor and Elizabethan England had raised practical above theoretical learning,[99] and practical knowledge was very much part of the attack on scholasticism. By the 1590s it has taken a distinctly strident form in writers such as Thomas Blundeville, most noted for his writings on horsemanship and horsebreeding, in his *Exercises* on cosmography, astronomy, geography, and the art of navigation (London, 1594),[100] by William Barlow, in his *The Navigator's Supply* (London, 1597),[101] but most of all in *The newe Attractiue* (1581) of Robert Norman, seaman turned instrument-maker, who attacks those who seek knowledge from Latin and Greek texts—they are referred to as pedants who promise much and perform little—and offers an empirically based, as opposed to a textually based, procedure:

I meane not to vse barely tedious coniectures or imaginations, but briefly as I maie to passe it ouer, foundyng my arguements only vpon experience, reason, and demonstration, whiche are the groundes of Artes.[102]

The first attempt to harness this kind of approach and incorporate it into a broad natural-philosophical programme was that of Bacon, who contrasted contemplation of natural processes with the invention of artificial means of establishing dominion over nature and making it more productive. The project was given a new direction in Boyle's emphasis on uncovering facts and providing nothing but the lowest level theories—he was, as he put it himself, 'no admirer of the theoretical part of [the chemists'] art'[103]—and his insistence on the collective witnessing of experiments,[104]

---

[98] Joseph Glanvill, *Plus Ultra* (London, 1668).

[99] See Gaukroger, *Francis Bacon*, 14–18.

[100] In the Preface to his *Theoriques of the seven Planets* (London, 1602), Blundeville suggests that the main audience for his *Exercises* had been 'Gentlemen of the Innes of Court' (sig. A3r).

[101] See the discussion in J. A. Bennett, 'The Challenge of Practical Mathematics', in Stephen Pumfrey, Paolo L. Rossi, and Maurice Slawinski, eds., *Science, Culture and Popular Belief in Renaissance Europe* (Manchester, 1991), 186–9.

[102] I have used the 1614 edition: Robert Norman, *The nevve, attractive shewing the nature, propertie, and manifold vertues of the loadston* (London, 1614), 'To the Reader', sig. A1r.

[103] Boyle, *Works*, i. 463

[104] These aspects of Boyle's programme are discussed in detail in Steven Shapin and Simon Schaffer, *Leviathan and the Air Pump: Hobbes, Boyle, and the Experimental Life* (Princeton, 1985), and Steven Shapin, *A Social History of Truth: Civility and Science in Seventeenth Century England* (Chicago, 1994). But see Barbara J. Shapiro, *A Culture of Fact: England, 1550–1720* (Ithaca, NY, 2000), for a corrective to many aspects of these accounts, especially the latter. See also Lawrence M. Principe, *The Aspiring Adept: Robert Boyle and his Alchemical Quest* (Princeton, 2000), 71–3.

helping to undermine the possibility of drawing contentious natural-theological consequences from natural philosophy by making that natural philosophy as uncontentious as possible.[105] This does not mean that it removes as much as possible from the natural realm, deferring to the supernatural. Quite the contrary, such a move is taken as characteristic of the enthusiast, who confuses the private and the public, the natural and the supernatural. In the latter case, the threat comes not from the collapsing of the supernatural into the natural, as with the naturalists, but with the mistaking of the natural for the supernatural, with the result, as Sprat points out, that the enthusiast 'goes neer to bring down the price of the True and Primitive Miracles, by such a vast, and such a negligent augmenting of their number'.[106]

Sprat makes it an issue of intellectual morality and intellectual honesty. Natural philosophy, as practised by the Royal Society, far from harming Christian values, he tells us, reinforces them,

seeing many duties of which it is compos'd, do bear some resemblance to the qualifications that are requisite in *Experimental Philosophers*. The spiritual *Repentance* is a careful survay of our former Errors, and a resolution of amendment. The spiritual *Humility* is an observation of our Defects, and a lowly sense of our own weaknesses. And the *Experimenter* for his part must have some Qualities that answer to these: he must judge aright of himself, he must misdoubt the best of his own thoughts; he must be sensible of his own ignorance, if ever he will attempt to purge and renew his Reason . . . it may well be concluded, that the doubtful, the scrupulous, the diligent *Observer of Nature*, is neerer to make a modest, a severe, a meek, an humble *Christian*, than the man of *Speculative Science*, who has better thoughts of himself and his own *Knowledge*.[107]

The point is echoed in Glanvill, who tells us that 'the *Philosophy* of the *Virtuosi*' deals 'with the *plain Objects* of *Sense*, in which, if any where, there is *Certainty*; and teacheth *suspension* of *Assent* till what is *proposed*, is well proved; and so is equally an Adversary to *Scepticism* and *Credulity*'.[108]

The Royal Society to a large extent institutionalized this approach in its early years, as least as far as presentation of results was concerned, and Sprat, presenting the case

---

[105] Spiller quotes a passage from Addison that is of interest here, which suggests a basis for the concern with lack of contention that is far stronger than anything I am claiming, and goes well beyond the evidence. Addison writes, in issue 262 of the *Spectator* (31 Dec. 1711) that: 'Among the advantages which the Publick may reap from this Paper it is not the least, that it draws Mens Minds off from the Bitterness of Party, and furnishes them with Subjects of Discourse that may be treated without warmth or Passion. This is said to have been the first design of those Gentlemen who set foot on the Royal Society, and had then a very good Effect, as it turned many of the greatest Genius's of that Age to the Disquisitions of natural Knowledge, who, if they had engaged in Politicks with the same Parts and Applications, might have set their Country in a Flame. The Air-Pump, the barometer, the Quadrant, and the like Inventions, were thrown out to those busy Spirits, as Tubs and barrels are to a Whale that he may let the Ship sail on without Disturbances, whilst he diverts himself with those innocent amusements.' As Spiller notes— '*Concerning Natural Experimental Philosophie*', 30—this account of the origins of the Royal Society is implausible, and seems to derive from a careless recollection of remarks of Sprat and Stubbe.

[106] Sprat, *History of the Royal-Society*, 362. Cf. Glanvill, *Philosophia Pia* (London, 1671), 55–85.

[107] Ibid., 367.

[108] Joseph Glanvill, *A Praefatory Answer to Mr. Henry Stubbe* (London, 1671), 143–4.

that it provides a firm foundation for the social order,[109] made no secret of its power to curb enthusiasm:

So that it is now the fittest season for *Experiments* to arise, to teach us Wisdome, which springs from the depths of *Knowledge*, to shake off the shadows, and scatter the mists, which fill the minds of men with a vain consternation. This is a *work* well-becoming the most *Christian Profession*. For the most apparent effect, which attended the passion of *Christ*, was the putting of an eternal silence, on all the false oracles, and dissembled inspirations of *Antient Times*.[110]

Indeed, not only is it able to curb enthusiasm, it is able to harness it as well, in the form of natural philosophy, irrespective of the religion of the participants. If enthusiasm was manifested in private interpretations of scripture, then the antidote lay in a public, co-operative, and universally valid enterprise.[111] Since it operates via a procedure that avoids disputes, it offers a means of 'abolishing or restraining the fury of *Enthusiasme*'.[112] The Royal Society:

freely admitted men of different Religions, Countries, and Professions of Life . . . For they openly profess, not to lay the Foundation of an *English*, *Scotch*, *Irish*, *Popish*, or *Protestant* Philosophy; but a Philosophy of *Mankind*.[113]

This was a radical claim, and some critics of the Royal Society such as Meric Casaubon and Henry Stubbe believed that it had not only misunderstood and underestimated the threat of enthusiasm, but had become a centre for it.[114] The problem was in fact twofold: if the Royal Society apologists denied any connection between their natural or 'experimental' philosophy and the divine then they were open to the charge of atheism, whereas if they stressed such a connection, they were open to the charge of enthusiasm.[115] Sprat struggled with the challenge. In response to a possible charge of atheism and materialism, he pointed out that it was true that the experimental philosopher dealt only with material things,

But this is so far from drawing him to oppose invisible *Beings*, that it rather puts his thought into an excellent good capacity to believe them. In every *work* of *Nature* that he handles, he knows that there is not only a gross substance, which presents itself to all mens eies; but an infinit subtility of *parts*, which come not into the sharpest sense. So that what the Scripture relates of the Purity of *God*, of the Spirituality of his *Nature*, and that of *Angels*, and the *Souls* of men, cannot seem incredible to him, when he perceives the numberless particles that move

---

[109] See P. B. Wood, 'Methodology and Apologetics: Thomas Sprat's *History of the Royal Society*', *British Journal for the History of Science* 13 (1980), 1–26.

[110] Sprat, *History of the Royal-Society*, 362–3.

[111] See Michael Heyd, *'Be Sober and Reasonable': The Critique of Enthusiasm in the Seventeenth and Early Eighteenth Centuries* (Leiden, 1995), 152.

[112] Sprat, *History of the Royal-Society*, 428. [113] Ibid., 63.

[114] See Meric Casaubon, *A Treatise concerning Enthusiasme* (London, 1655). There are good accounts in Heyd, *'Be Sober and Reasonable'*, ch. 5, and Spiller, *'Concerning Natural Philosophy'*. Note that the charge of harbouring sympathy for enthusiasm was levelled by both sides. Glanvill, in turn, in the Preface to *A Praefatory Answer to Mr. Henry Stubbe*, accuses Stubbe of of opposing everything except 'Quakerism and Democracy'.

[115] See Spiller, *'Concerning Natural Philosophy'*, 113.

in every man's *Blood*, and the prodigious streams that continually flow unseen from every *Body*.[116]

Against the possible charges of enthusiasm, whether of a Puritan or a Neoplatonist variety, he moved in the other direction:

From hence he will best understand the infinit distance between himself, and his Creator, when he finds that all things were produc'd by him: whereas he by all his study, can scarce imitate the least effects, nor hasten, nor retard, the common course of *Nature*.[117]

Having thus protected himself against attacks on his flanks, Sprat tried to spell out the consequences of a properly pursued natural philosophy for a properly constructed natural theology, maintaining that the experimental natural philosopher:

will be led to admire the wonderful contrivances of the *Creation*, and so to apply and direct his *praises* aright: which *no doubt*, when they are offer'd up to *Heaven*, from the mouth of one that hath well studied what he commends, will be more suitable to the *Divine Nature,* than the blind *Applauses of the Ignorant*.[118]

Stubbe for one was not convinced, and indeed was incensed that it could be suggested that there could be a route to salvation that did not rely on the mediation of Christ. Commenting directly on this last passage in Sprat, he writes:

The former part of the passage is contrary to the *Analogy of Faith* and *Scripture*, in that it makes the acceptableness of mens prayers to depend more or less on the study of natural Philosophy. Whereas the *Apostle* suspends the *acceptableness of all Prayers unto God,* in being made unto him *in the name,* and *for the mediation of Christ Jesus,* applied by *faith*.[119]

Here we have is the nub of the issue. The Royal Society apologists were concerned to find a middle ground that enabled them to pursue natural philosophy in such a way that appropriate natural-theological consequences could be drawn from it. In this way, not only would natural philosophy and natural theology no longer stand in need of reconciliation, but radically conflicting religious beliefs would not be able to enter the picture and destroy any theological consensus before the process had even got off the ground.[120] As Glanvill, in one of his characteristically upbeat assessments, put it:

*Philosophy* gives us a sight of the *causes* of our *intellectual* diversities, and so takes us off from expecting an *agreement* in our apprehensions; whereby it discovers the *unreasonableness* of making *harmony* in opinion, the *condition* of *Charity* and *Union*; and of being *angry*, and dividing upon every *difference* of *judgment*; and hereby the *hurtful* malignitie of *disputes* are *qualified*, and the disease it self is *undermined*.[121]

---

[116] Sprat, *History*, 348. Cf. Glanville, *Philosophia Pia*, 90–1.

[117] Sprat, *History*, 349.        [118] Ibid., 349.

[119] Henry Stubbe, *A Censure upon Certain Passages contained in the History of the Royal Society* (Oxford, 1670), 36.

[120] In the mid-seventeenth century, we can find attempts to dispense with adversarial argument and start from an agreed basis, not via natural philosophy but in directly theological terms. See e.g. Thomas White, *Controversy Logick; or, The Methode to come to truth in debates of Religion* (Paris, 1659).

[121] Glanville, *Philosophia Pia*, 91–2.

Natural philosophers have become priests of nature here: obscure theological formulations are replaced by a simple theology of nature, idolatrous rites and the preaching of unintelligible dogmas are replaced by a humble reading of lessons from the book of nature, allegory and emblematics are replaced by physico-theology,[122] and sectarianism is replaced by common procedures for arriving at the truth.

---

[122] See Harrison, *The Bible, Protestantism and the Rise of Natural Science*, 197–9.

# 7

## The Aims of Enquiry

From our discussion of natural-philosophical method and the question of what qualities the natural philosopher must possess if natural-philosophical enquiry is to be pursued fruitfully, one thing that emerges unmistakably is that there are a number of strands that offer distinctive ways of dealing with the question of the aims of enquiry. Bacon's construal of truth as something essentially productive, for example, can be seen as a way of engaging the question of truth as something revealed. The difference is that whereas, on the traditional Platonist understanding, what is revealed is another realm—that of the reality underlying the appearances—Bacon shifts the whole question of truth from a contemplative to a practical exercise, so that the required result is dominion over nature. The aim of the exercise is no longer the discovery of truth conceived as the outcome of contemplation, but the discovery of relevant, informative truth, where the criteria of relevance and informativeness derive from the ability of that truth to take us beyond our present state of engagement with natural processes to one in which our degree of control over those processes is increased. A different aspect of the question is revealed in Descartes' sense that what lies beyond the justificatory procedures of natural-philosophical enquiry is an expectation about the intellectual morality of the natural philosopher. But Bacon's idea that the natural philosopher must subject himself to the dictates of an externally imposed method, and the notion we found in looking at Galileo's move from the university to the patronage system, that it is the intellectual disinterestedness of the patron that validates the work of the courtier natural philosopher, both also offer something over and above the procedures of justification that vindicate the natural-philosophical enterprise.

In this chapter, I want to explore, in more depth, those questions of truth, justification, objectivity, and legitimacy that lie at the intersection of methodological issues and concerns about the *persona* of the natural philosopher. I begin by posing the question of what was expected from natural-philosophical enquiry in the context of an investigation of the emergence of philosophy as a distinct discipline, and the philosopher as a distinct *persona*, in classical antiquity. The philosophical project was defined in Plato and Aristotle in opposition to sophistry, and took two distinct forms: the search for a transcendent truth, and the discovery of underlying principles. These represented two different models for enquiry, as was clear to thirteenth-century theologians and philosophers in the West, and their failure to connect became especially problematic from the beginning of the sixteenth century. But the new developments in natural philosophy from the late sixteenth century onwards transformed the issues significantly, and one way in which we can grasp what was at stake in this transformation is in terms of challenges to the Aristotelian idea of the 'theoretical sciences'. The Aristotelian conception excludes three cognitive disciplines—practical mathematics (above all mechanics, optics, and astronomy), medicine, and natural history—on the grounds that genuine philosophical activity consists in the discovery of principles underlying natural phenomena, and either because they are not concerned with natural phenomena (practical mathematics), or because they do not pursue their enquiry in terms of underlying principles (medicine and natural history), they do not satisfy this criterion. By raising the questions of just what kind of understanding they do provide, how their general aims differ from natural philosophy, and what kind of connection there can be between these enterprises and natural philosophy, we can open up the issue of the aims of enquiry, and gain some insight into the realignment of disciplines that emerged in the seventeenth century, which will be our concern in Part IV.

## PLATO'S CAVE VERSUS THE *ELENCHOS*

We can think of the origins of philosophy as lying in a particular kind of dispute resolution. There were a number of relatively independent developments in the transition from archaic to classical Greece that transformed the discourse by which problems were resolved from what Detienne has called 'efficacious speech' to dialogue.[1] 'Efficacious speech' had traditionally been the preserve of the poet or orator in praising the king, and of magic and religion; in both cases the words themselves are often taken to be endowed with causal powers.[2] Detienne illustrates this in the case of law. In prelegal disputes, efficacious words and gestures were directed not towards a judge for the benefit of his assessment, but towards an opponent who had to be overcome. With the emergence of the Greek *polis*, however, collective decisions gradually replaced straightforward commands, and these could be arrived at in a satisfactory way only through dialogue in which orators sought to convince through argument. Similarly in the case of law, use started to be made of witnesses who might produce proof, and judges were called upon to assess the cases made by both parties and come to a decision.[3] This is important because, as Geoffrey Lloyd has pointed out, within the *polis*, the ability to argue persuasively gradually conferred status, and this status could be transferred to other areas of intellectual activity, with the result that we find legal terminology at the root of key philosophical notions.[4]

---

[1] See Marcel Detienne, *Maîtres de vérité dans la grèce archaïque* (Paris, 1990). See also Louis Gernet, *Anthropologie de la Grèce antique* (Paris, 1968), and Pierre Vidal-Naquet, 'La raison greque et la cité', *Raison Présente* 2 (1967), 51–61.

[2] This is a phenomenon which was far more widespread than archaic Greece, and one can find traces of it in Ficino's magical account of language. There is a good general account of the phenomenon in Brian Vickers, 'Analogy versus Identity: The Rejection of Occult Symbolism, 1580–1680', in idem, ed., *Occult and Scientific Mentalities in the Renaissance* (Cambridge, 1984), 95–164.

[3] See Detienne, *Maîtres de vérité*, ch. 5; and specifically on the role of witnesses, see Douglas M. McDowell, *The Law in Classical Athens* (London, 1978), ch. 14.

[4] G. E. R. Lloyd, *Magic, Reason and Experience: Studies in the Origins and Development of Greek Science* (Cambridge, 1979), ch. 4.

There are two complementary features of the shift to dialogue: the use of argument and evidence to establish a case and, something which is a precondition of this, the refusal to accept ambiguity, trying instead to resolve conflicting accounts into contradictions between purported facts. This new approach first becomes evident in a systematic way in Thucydides' histories, where a new probing search for causes, replacing the traditional narratives, requires an explicit resolution of factual questions.[5] It is made fully explicit, however, only in Aristotle's syllogistic. Here, not only is the resolution of ambiguities—so prevalent in ordinary discourse, in drama, in poetry, in political speeches—into contradictions a precondition for translation of arguments into logical form, but the idea of contradiction lies at the core of Aristotle's understanding of logic, in the form of the justification of the principle of non-contradiction. This justification is linked closely with the nature of discursive argument, for, as he points out, anyone engaging in argument in the first place must assume the truth of the principle: if one is prepared to accept contradictions then anything follows from anything and argument is not possible.[6]

The shift to dialogue engages a new mode of dispute resolution, then, in that it gives priority to argument, and resolves ambiguities into contradictions. This is reflected in notions of cognitive grasp as we move from the archaic to the classical period, for these are features reflected in the notion of *epistēmē* (knowledge). But for *epistēmē* to become constitutive of philosophical activity, as Plato and his successors conceived of that activity, it needs more than just these two features. Plato is concerned to contrast what he considers to be genuine philosophical thought and sophistry. The sophist not only meets the criteria that philosophy be pursued in terms of arguments and that it resolve ambiguities into contradictions, but appears to meet them in a paradigm way. But the sophist is not only not a paradigm philosopher for Plato, he is not a philosopher at all.

The key question here, one that I shall argue was to have fundamental ramifications for early-modern attempts to rethink the nature of natural philosophy, is what is needed over and above a commitment to resolution of ambiguities and argument if one is to be a philosopher, as opposed to a sophist. The basic distinction between sophists and philosophers that both Plato and Aristotle draw, is that between those who use arguments simply to show off their ingenuity and thereby enhance their reputation ('sophistic' proper in Aristotle's terminology) or to seek simply to win arguments ('eristic' in Aristotle's terminology), and those who use argument to discover the truth of the matter. The early dialogues of Plato, for example, dominated as they

---

[5] Thucydides makes a sharp contrast between the real causes (*aitia*) of the Peloponnesian War, for example, and what parties to the events allege was the reason (*prophasis*) for the war. On the contrast between Herodotus and Thucydides see Arnaldo Momigliano, *The Classical Foundations of Modern Historiography* (Berkeley, Calif., 1990) and John Marincola, *Authority and Tradition in Ancient Historiography* (Cambridge, 1997).

[6] See the discussion in *Metaphysics* 1005$^b$35–1009$^b$1. See also Jonathan Lear, *Aristotle and Logical Theory* (Cambridge, 1980), ch. 6.

are by disputes with sophists, can be read as attempts to reconstrue argument as a means, not of outwitting opponents,[7] but of establishing the truth of the matter.[8]

In defence of the sophists, it might be pointed out that what they taught was not how to make the worse case appear better, but the skill of arguing both sides of a case. It was Parmenides above all to whom the early philosophical tradition was indebted for its sense of the force of probing argument, and the notion of truth that emerges from Parmenides is that of whatever survives the *elenchos*, or process of questioning and refutation.[9] Gorgias, the most famous and evidently the most formidable of the sophists, saw himself in the tradition of Parmenides, and in the *Encomium of Helen* he argues that natural philosophers each think that they alone have the secret of the universe, whereas in fact all any of them do is pit one opinion against another.[10] There can be little doubt that Plato in particular misrepresented the sophists,[11] but what I am concerned with here is not so much how the sophist option might be more accurately represented, but rather with whether there is some way in which it can be seen to present a viable and defensible response to Plato's charge. A distinctive seventeenth-century response to cognate problems, which have their origins in a context created in part by the issues that dominate the Pomponazzi affair, was to argue for a notion of

---

[7] The idea of outwitting opponents was central to the archaic understanding of cognitive grasp. The earliest accounts of cognitive enquiry indicate that the classical Greek contrast between *epistēmē* and *technē*—knowledge versus art or skills—arose from an earlier pre-classical unitary conception of cognitive grasp. This earlier conception was centred around the notion of *mētis*, cunning or ingenuity. The idea behind it is that, in overcoming an adversary, whether this be in hunting, fishing, racing, working resistant materials such as metals, or overcoming a fast-flowing river, there are only two routes open. Either the stronger will win, or, by the power of *mētis*, one reverses the natural course of events through cunning, disguise, quick-wittedness, or some cognate skill: generally speaking, some way of coming to terms with events that involves a form of understanding that enables one to overcome obstacles—including cognitive obstacles—rather than explain. An image that we find on a number of occasions is that of changing more swiftly than a rapidly changing nature. One comes to terms with something that is constantly changing by outwitting it, not by explaining it, and nature is a prototypically changing realm. See Marcel Detienne and Jean-Pierre Vernant, *Les Ruses d'intelligence: la metis des grecs* (Paris, 1974).

[8] Socrates is variously described as a sting-ray or a gadfly that constantly arouses, persuades, and reproves people; his aim, nevertheless, is not to demonstrate his ingenuity but to 'examine and search people's minds, to find out who is really wise among them, and who only thinks he is': *Apology* 41B. On Socratic argument see Gerasimos Xenophon Santas, *Socrates: Philosophy in Plato's Early Dialogues* (London, 1979).

[9] See David Furley, 'Truth as What Survives the Elenchos', in David Furley, *Cosmic Problems: Essays on Greek and Roman Philosophy of Nature* (Cambridge, 1989), ch. 4, 38–46. See also Gregory Vlastos, 'The Socratic Elenchus', *Oxford Studies in Ancient Philosophy* (1983), i. 27–58.

[10] See W. K. C. Guthrie, *The Sophists* (Cambridge, 1971), 51.

[11] It is worth remembering here that Diogenes Laertius (*Lives of Eminent Philosophers*, 1. 12) treats 'sophist' as another term for a philosopher, and that Socrates himself was caricatured by Aristophanes in the *Clouds* as a sophist who was willing to teach anyone who would pay to make weaker argument stronger and to deny the existence of the gods. On this and other contemporary images of Socrates see W. K. C. Guthrie, *Socrates* (Cambridge, 1971), 39–75. More generally, see Capizzi, *The Cosmic Republic*.

objectivity distinguished by impartiality, freedom from prejudices, lack of bias, and lack of partisanship. But this is not the kind of answer that Plato or Aristotle gave.

Consider the case of Plato. It is important to remember that Plato's early dialogues, where his notion of what it is to be a philosopher was forged, and where the basic notions of philosophical argument were elaborated, worked primarily in a moral context. The notion of truth as whatever survives the *elenchos* might be satisfactory in areas such as geometry, but in a moral context, where one wants to establish one system of values over another, it is problematic. For Plato, it was crucial in dealing with the sophists' defences of moral relativity, in particular, that the argument be directed uncompromisingly towards the true system of moral values. Not just any set of values that emerges unscathed on some particular occasion of argument will be the true system of values, and this matters because fundamental questions of morality are not the kinds of thing one can disregard, or on which one can suspend judgement. It is important to remember here that Plato draws on the wisdom and virtue of the philosopher in the *Republic* in arguing that the philosopher is the most appropriate ruler: it is particularly important in the context of the doctrine of 'philosopher kings' that philosophers consistently display certain fundamental moral qualities. The problem with Parmenides' construal of argument, however, is not that it neglected to give argument a direction, but that he explicitly denied that it could have the direction Plato required. For Parmenides, one simply could not go beyond appearances to reality. Plato's project was to show how argument could in fact do this, and he construed moral philosophy in these terms: as something that goes beyond the conventional aspects of morality—which the sophists, as Plato portrayed them, emphasized—to the underlying nature of morality.

The failing that Plato and Aristotle identified in the sophists is in an important sense a moral one. Philosophical practice can be pursued both as sophistic or as eristic, and in pursuing it in this way one is not failing at the level of argument but at the level of what motivates argument. Argument is being used for the wrong purposes, and this is due not to an intellectual deficiency so much as a moral one. On the other hand, the virtue that is lacking is not one we associate with some form of goodness but with an intellectual quality. It is a question of intellectual morality.[12] I want to distinguish two very different ways of exploring this question. There is a tradition in antiquity, usually identified as a rhetorical tradition, the principal figures in which include Isocrates, Cicero, and Quintilian,[13] which focuses on the moral qualities of the philosopher, and this way of pursuing the question is also to be found in the Hellenistic schools.[14] We encounter a revival of this approach in the Renaissance, and we saw in the last chapter that the question of the *persona* of the natural philosopher, with an explicit focus on questions of intellectual morality, was a crucial ingredient in the rethinking of the standing of natural philosophy.

Plato and Aristotle move in a different direction. The way in which they characterize the sophist clearly involves a moral condemnation, and sophistry is

---

[12] See e.g. the discussion in Book 10 of Aristotle's *Nicomachean Ethics*.

[13] See George Kennedy, *A New History of Classical Rhetoric* (Princeton, 1994).

[14] See Hadot, *Philosophy as a Way of Life*.

identified as a kind of moral failing. However, this moral failing is countered primarily in epistemological terms rather than moral ones, in the claim that justifications for particular doctrines should not only seek to convince on the basis of valid arguments and unambiguous evidence, but should also possess some extra quality that goes beyond these and indeed is independent of them. For both Plato and Aristotle, what the sophist fails to do, and what the philosopher must do, is to use argument to uncover something not normally apparent. Yet what they seek to uncover turns out to be quite different. To highlight this difference, we can say that Plato seeks to uncover transcendent truth—transcendent in the sense that it is given independently of any means by which we might establish it—whereas Aristotle seeks to uncover explanations, explanations that could not possibly be independent of the means by which we establish (or, in the limiting case, could establish) them. This difference is of crucial importance to us, because the Platonist project is that which guides Christian theology, whereas the Aristotelian project is that which guides Aristotelian natural philosophy.

The distinctive feature of genuine philosophical enquiry on the Platonist option is that it seeks the reality underlying the appearances. By engaging the world of appearances appropriately we can see through them to the world of Forms, the realm of reality. Plato's image of the cave, whereby there is a completely different world from that of shadows, to which we have access,[15] encourages such a view by suggesting parallel worlds of appearance and reality. One extreme version of this conception of truth, something found in many non-Western forms of thought, particularly Indian thought, and in more mystical varieties of Western thought, is the idea that we can transcend appearances completely and grasp reality directly. Neoplatonism comes close to this notion at times, but philosophical thought in the West generally does not encourage us to renounce appearances but to use them as a guide to reality. We see the world differently as a result of philosophical enlightenment only in a metaphorical sense, not literally. Nevertheless, despite his insistence on the idea that the path to reality is via reason, Plato's cave suggests the idea of a separate realm of truth existing independently of our cognitive life, and it is unclear why reason should provide the route to this reality. The Neoplatonist movement had a commitment to reason, but it was a reason that one ultimately transcended once one had reached reality.[16] Indeed it is striking that those who took up the Platonist option, both in late antiquity and in the Renaissance, saw their project in terms of an interpretation of nature, something that uncovers hidden truths, and is more like interpretation of a sacred text in which one seeks to uncover a hidden and unique truth than something to be pursued in terms of empirical investigation. And it is no less striking that it is such a notion that pervades Christian theology and Augustinian metaphysics, where we cannot reach a transcendent reality exclusively through rational means, but also require the sacraments.

One key difference between this and the Aristotelian option is that Plato's notion of enquiry is designed to take us to something transcendent, whereas Aristotle's

---

[15] Plato, *Republic*, 514A-517C.
[16] See, for example, J. M. Rist, *Plotinus: The Road to Reality* (Cambridge, 1967).

notion of enquiry places the outcome firmly within our cognitive world. For the Neoplatonist, if not for Plato himself, once one had transcended sensory understanding, by whatever means, the world of appearances could be left behind. On the Aristotelian conception, to the extent to which we are concerned with genuinely philosophical—as opposed to mystical or theological—investigation, it is crucial that the point of the exercise should not be seen as denying any reality to appearances. The reason why the philosophical approach retains a commitment to appearances is because that is what it sets out to explain. A successful explanation doesn't replace the *explanandum*: it reveals to us why the *explanandum* has the features it has. A project that seeks the truth per se might not take the form of attempting to provide an explanation of something at all. For Aristotle, by contrast, philosophy in general, and natural philosophy in particular, is designed to provide an account of something, an explanation or reason for it; it is concerned to identify what causes it, or what rationale or grounds can be provided for it. Like Plato, Aristotle seeks a third ingredient to mark the philosopher out from the sophist and, like Plato, he identifies the failure of the sophist as a kind of moral failing but offers an epistemological solution to the failure. But in place of Plato's search for truth, Aristotle seeks explanations. This search is systematic: it includes a formal element and a non-formal one.

The formal element is syllogistic. One thing to be noted about syllogistic is that it represents a radically adversarial procedure. The aim is to get someone to accept or believe something that they would not otherwise accept or believe, and syllogistic constrains the valid ways in which this can be done, by confining arguments to those in which the truth of the conclusion follows from the truth of the premisses. The best way to display how the syllogism works is to think of it as a process in which two people, *A* and *B*, participate.[17] *A* wants to convince *B* of something using a syllogistic form of argument. In setting out to construct the syllogism, *A* begins by working backwards. She does not seek the conclusion, because this is given in advance of the construction of the syllogism, but seeks rather the premisses that will yield that conclusion in the requisite way.[18] On finding these premisses, she presents this syllogism to *B* who, in grasping the premisses, moves inferentially from premisses to conclusion. The process described in Aristotle's definition of the syllogism—namely, that certain things (the premisses) being stated, something other than what is stated (the conclusion) follows of necessity from the truth of those things alone[19]—occurs as an intellectual process in *B*. But the syllogism itself is not identified with his mental activity: *A* and not *B* is responsible for the syllogism that *B* grasps. That syllogism is therefore in an important sense independent of *B*, who can only accept or reject it. In other words, the context of syllogistic is a thoroughly discursive one. This is true not only of the paradigmatic case of the dialectical syllogism—where *A* and *B* are opponents, and where the point of the exercise is for *A*, by employing dialectical skills, to get

[17] See Ernest Kapp, 'Syllogistic', in J. Barnes, M. Schofield, and R. Sorabji, eds, *Articles on Aristotle*, i. *Science* (London, 1975), 35–49.

[18] See Barnes, 'Aristotle's Theory of Demonstration'.

[19] *Prior Analytics*, 24$^b$18–22.

*B* to accept something contentious—but equally so of the demonstrative syllogism, on which any *scientia* must be based, where *A* and *B* are teacher and pupil respectively, the point of the exercise now being for *A* to convey information to *B* in the most effective and economic way. More generally, we can see this procedure as a particular form of dispute resolution. Resolution of a cognitive dispute through explanation is the distinctive form of philosophical practice: it shows you why you should believe something because it either follows from or underlies other things you believe.

So far, however, this process is one that characterizes not just genuinely philosophical arguments, but sophistical argument also. Like Plato, Aristotle distinguishes the sophistical from the genuinely philosophical argument in terms of going beyond what emerges from the *elenchos*, but whereas Plato introduces something external to philosophical discourse, Aristotle advocates procedures internal to it. Distinguishing sophistical knowledge from genuine knowledge he writes:

We suppose ourselves to have unqualified demonstrative knowledge of something, as opposed to knowing it in the accidental way in which the sophist knows it, when we think we know the explanation/cause [*aition*] on which it depends, as the explanation/cause of that thing and of no other, and, further, that the thing could not be other than it is.[20]

The latter identifies those truths that spring from the nature of something,[21] and these are the object of philosophy, by contrast with things that just happen to be true, but sophists are unconcerned with any distinction between the two. The task of natural-philosophical demonstration is the understanding of phenomena in terms of their causes. By contrast with Plato, Aristotle does not consider that genuinely philosophical knowledge is marked out by capturing a transcendent truth. Rather, the idea (one impossible to realize in practice, as we saw in our discussion of *regressus* theory in Ch. 5) is that we constrain our investigation internally by following a method that generates certain kinds of truths (essential ones) but not others (accidental ones).

In broad terms, then, Plato and Aristotle are each attempting to achieve the same end, namely the characterization of what it is that marks philosophical enquiry out from other forms of enquiry that reach conclusions by means of argument. The contrast in both cases turns on that between the philosopher and the sophist, and these are not mere place-holders for doctrines: the issues trade on an understanding of intellectual morality which underlies the very idea of the aims of enquiry. Plato and Aristotle argue not as if sophists have a mistaken view on the aims of enquiry, but as if they have not even raised the question, remaining content simply to enquire, and as a consequence failing to distinguish appropriate from inappropriate forms of enquiry. It is with the raising of this question that philosophy begins, and the context of moral relativism in which Plato raises it makes it clear that the failing is not a mere oversight but a personal one that prevents the sophist being the kind of person able to engage in genuine philosophical discourse. The distinction has ramifications for specifically natural-philosophical enquiry. Aristotle's attempt to make understanding in

---

[20] *Posterior Analytics*, 71$^b$8–12.
[21] This is how they are characterized at *Metaphysics* 1051$^b$13–17, for example.

terms of essences or natures the exclusive form of natural-philosophical understanding makes 'physics', as he defines it, a 'theoretical' science, by contrast with natural history, which is a 'practical' science because it generates knowledge only that something is the case rather than knowledge of why it is the case. What I want to stress here is that this distinction is not motivated wholly by the content of the disciplines, but also turns upon the question of the proper activity of the philosopher: in this case, the proper activity of the natural philosopher.

The contrast between Platonic and Aristotelian ways of securing the extra requirement for genuine philosophical discourse drives much of the Pomponazzi problem, for it is not just that there is an apparent conflict between theological and natural-philosophical conclusions, but, far more problematically, that there are two autonomous ways of proceeding, one embodying a Platonist conception of uncovering hidden truths, the other embodying the Aristotelian conception of natural-philosophical discovery of essential principles. On Pomponazzi's construal of the case of personal immortality, we know the (purported) truth in advance: we know that the soul enjoys personal immortality. The aim of philosophical argument is to provide us with valid arguments and unambiguous evidence for this truth (much as an argument in moral philosophy might be designed to establish something we are sure of in advance, such as that it is better to act virtuously). If particular natural-philosophical arguments, pursued in accord with the criteria for validity supplied by syllogistic, fail to secure this truth, then one thing we can say is that the particular natural-philosophical methods of enquiry must be mistaken. This would in effect just be the Thomist approach, and the aim would be to correct the natural-philosophical procedures until they were able to generate an understanding that accorded with Christian teaching.

An alternative view is that there are different notions of truth appropriate to theological and natural-philosophical enquiry. Consequently, what we would need to do would be to flesh out the notion of truth in different ways in different domains. Such an understanding of truth provides a basis for one version of Averroism, namely that whereby it was not that natural philosophy and theology generated different competing truths, for that is impossible, but rather that the *kinds* of truths they generated were different. To see what is at issue in general terms, consider the difference between physical and mathematical truths. One might advocate a fleshing out of truth along something like the lines of a correspondence theory in the case of statements in physical theory, on the grounds that what makes the statements of physical theory true is something about an independently existing reality, and one might think that correspondence captures such a relation. In the case of mathematics, on the other hand, one might baulk at the idea of some independently existing mathematical reality that makes the statements of pure mathematics true, and advocate a more constructivist or operationalist approach to truth. In other words, there seems to be something fundamentally different about physical and mathematical truths. Similarly with metaphysical/theological truths.

It is important that we identify where the issues arise here. We can distinguish two different notions of truth in Aristotle: a minimal one that is tied in to his understanding of validity, and a richer one that is crucial to his notion of explanation. Valid arguments preserve a particular quality between premisses and conclusion, namely truth.

Following a valid argument form guarantees that if one starts from true premisses, this truth will be preserved in the course of the argument: it will be transmitted to the conclusion. The relevant notion of truth in this logical context is a formal one: a true statement is one that 'says of what is that it is, and says of what is not that it is not'.[22] Following a valid argument form—one of Aristotle's syllogistic figures, for example—is guaranteed to take us from a premiss that says of what is that it is, and/or says of what is not that it is not, to a conclusion that says of what is that it is, and/or says of what is not that it is not. But in the context of explanation, he wants arguments to do more than preserve truth: his ultimate aim is to distinguish informative conclusions from uninformative ones. Here he appeals to a richer notion of truth, one that requires us to distinguish between truths that are relative to context and those that are true of something in an absolute way because they spring from its nature. This richer notion of truth is inappropriate in a purely logical context, because formal reasoning is designed to preserve truth without regard to how that truth might have been generated. But once we start dealing with informative truths, truths 'which spring from the nature of the thing', that is, once we move from questions of deductive validity to questions of explanation, the nature of the subject matter becomes important. It depends whether the subject matter falls within natural philosophy, mathematics, or 'first philosophy', for each has a distinctive subject matter, and distinct methods of enquiry are required, and one way in which one might flesh out this notion is to think of these three forms of 'scientific' enquiry as being directed towards fundamentally different kinds of truth.

The Averroist option, as I have construed it here, namely as maintaining that there are different kinds of truth, seems to run together the question of whether something is true, and that of how we test for or establish its truth. It seems to move from the claim that there are different ways of establishing truths to the conclusion that there are different kinds of truth. Such a move would indeed be illegitimate. How we establish truth is of course relative to the kind of theory we are working with, what kind of evidence we are drawing on, what standards of demonstration we are employing, and so on. But truth itself cannot be relative to these: something that is merely true relative to one thing, but not true relative to another, is just not true.[23] The issue is deeper than this, however. Once we distinguish Aristotle's minimal notion of truth from his richer notion, we can see that the richer notions of mathematical, theological, and physical truths are not designed to offer competing notions of truth per se, but to supplement a general minimal notion of truth that is genuinely universal.

---

[22] *Metaphysics* 1011$^b$27–8. The context is Aristotle's defence of the principle of the excluded middle. In the *Categories*, 14$^b$14–22, he points out that when we say that a man exists, the truth of the proposition is in no way the cause of/explanation for the existence of the man, but 'the fact of the man's existence does seem somehow to be the cause of/explanation for the truth of the proposition'. The context here is a discussion of 'priority'—the man's existence is prior to the truth of the proposition that he exists. Aristotle is not trying to give a metaphysical account of what makes propositions true: for that he needs a richer notion of truth which varies with the domain of enquiry, as we are about to see.

[23] See Donald Davidson, 'On the Very Idea of a Conceptual Scheme', in idem, *Inquiries into Truth and Interpretation* (Oxford, 1984), 183–98.

The problem is rather that the minimal notion does no real work once questions of explanation are engaged, for then everything hinges on the richer notions. To concede that Aristotle's minimal definition was a universal and univocal notion of truth would not change the fact that the application of the richer notion offered by him to natural philosophy, mathematics, and theology made these yield different kinds of truth in a sense centrally relevant to explanation. If these never overlapped,[24] then there would be no issue. But the Pomponazzi case hinges on apparently competing claims and their standing. This raises the problem of how these richer understandings of natural philosophy, mathematics, and theology are to be reconciled; whether the newly emerging connections between natural philosophy and mathematics, for example, show the need for a new substantial notion of truth to replace the Aristotelian one; and even whether a filling out of the notion of explanation needs a richer notion of truth at all, whether it might be achieved by bypassing (substantial) truth altogether.[25]

The problems are transformed and compounded when we move from the case of a truth that was considered to be clearly given in advance (as the doctrine of personal immortality was in the sixteenth century) to the case of a claim which, despite its theological backing, was becoming contentious, such as the earth's lack of motion. It is in this context that we can begin to understand the move from a concern with truth to concern with justification which is so characteristic of seventeenth-century natural philosophy. If a truth is not given independently, as something with which to compare our natural-philosophical conclusions, this puts justification in a very different light, for the procedures of justification our theory works with now need an internal vindication. The situation is far from simple, however.[26] On the one hand, justification, if it is to count as genuine justification in the first place, must, it seems, be driven by truth in some sense. To capture what justification is, and what we want it to do, we have to constrain what counts as a justification. It looks as if, unless we find some way of giving truth an independent role to play, some role in which it steers or guides justification, then we will not be able to distinguish between genuine justification and spurious, merely verbal, justification. After all, there are many ways in which we might attempt to justify a theory: we might point to the weight of tradition behind it, to its novelty, to its close fit with other things we believe, to its usefulness,

---

[24] This is a claim that even Aristotle does not make, something highlighted by his equivocation over whether astronomy is a physical or a mathematical discipline—cf. *Metaphysics* 989[b]33 and *Physics* 193[b]25–30.

[25] Truth in the minimal sense is not bypassed, of course, and indeed could not be bypassed in anything that purported to be a cognitive enquiry—anyone making a cognitive claim is purporting to say how things are. Moreover, since the validity of arguments is defined in terms of their preservation of truth between premises and conclusions, rational argument would not be possible without truth (or some semantic notion sufficiently close to it). Truth in a minimal sense offers an uncontentious general constraint which is not in dispute because it does not bear on any question about the nature of explanation.

[26] See Stephen Gaukroger, 'Justification, Truth, and the Development of Science', *Studies in History and Philosophy of Science* 29 (1998), 97–112.

and so on. The risk we run if we leave justification free of truth is that what counts as a justification can vary radically, and may include criteria that are not even cognitive in the requisite sense; they may require faith, the stamp of an arbitrarily instituted authority, and so on. If truth does not guide the justification we offer for a theory, how do we avoid cognitively irrelevant or inappropriate justifications? The problem is that, where we have no pre-given truth with which we must reconcile our justification, truth is completely justification-dependent. If we ask whether some theory is true, what we need to be given is the justification offered for holding that theory. We can do no more in establishing its truth than establish what its justification is, where this justification is judged against what are taken to be the standards of justification for a theory of that kind making that kind of claim. Truth is not playing a role here: justification is doing all the work, and now seems to provide our only guide to what theories we should prefer.

## TRUTH AND OBJECTIVITY

The air of paradox can be removed if we distinguish between providing a goal for argument and providing cognitive guidance for argument. Once we have made this distinction, it becomes clear that while truth cannot provide a goal for argument, individual truths, or purported truths, can provide goals for individual arguments. On the question of cognitive guidance, by contrast, individual truths are not the kind of thing that can provide this. What we want from cognitive guidance is something that makes sure that cognitively irrelevant or inappropriate considerations do not determine the direction of a justification. We have seen that truth per se looks at first sight like the right kind of thing, but it can perform this role only on pain of circularity. I shall argue that objectivity—as well as notions such as impartiality that form the cluster of concepts centring around objectivity—are where the required guidance is to be found.

The question of goals of argument can be clarified by considering the kinds of issue that arose in the seventeenth-century discussion of atheism.[27] Atheism was treated by many theologians as a problem of epidemic proportions during the sixteenth and seventeenth centuries,[28] yet it was universally agreed among them that no one could actually be an atheist. The ubiquity of atheism and its impossibility were not incompatible, however, because a distinction was made between actually being an atheist, and thinking as an atheist. The former was a function of the will, the latter a function of the intellect. It was possible to will oneself to be an atheist, and it was widely believed that the immoral were inclined to do so, in the belief that they could avoid the consequences of their immorality, by pretending that their behaviour would attract no punishment. But to think atheistically—to actually believe that there was

---

[27] See Kors, *Atheism in France*, to whose exemplary account I am indebted here.

[28] Mersenne, for example, maintained that there were 50,000 atheists in Paris alone: *Quaestiones celeberrimae in Genesim*, cols 669–74.

no God, rather than pretend that there was no God—was another matter. Not only were the demonstrations of God's existence considered to be completely compelling, but, it was argued, belief in the existence of God was unanimous in all societies, past and present, and, as Cicero had argued in this context, 'in every inquiry the unanimity of the races of the world must be regarded as a law of nature',[29] a point reinforced by the view that every major thinker of the past had believed in the existence of God. There were the odd dissenting voices on the 'argument from universal consent' in the seventeenth century, but they were few and far between before Bayle. It was considered intellectually impossible to disbelieve in the existence of God, for this was so manifest and inescapable a truth that no peoples had ever failed to recognize it, and hence such disbelief must therefore be an act of will alone. What is of interest to us in the present context is that the diagnosis of the relation between the will and the intellect in the case of atheism reflects a general model. As Kors points out,

The atheist, it was claimed, could *will* himself into being but could not truly *think* atheist-ically. In that sense, the atheist was presented as a distorted mirror image of the idealized believer. The Christian, in his own self-portrait, believing by the will in revelation . . . sought to understand, and discovered in the context of belief, to the delight of the mind, a satisfying, true knowledge of what otherwise made little or no sense. The atheist, in the Christian por-trait, disbelieving in God only by his will, sought intellectual justification for that disbelief but could go no further than ignorance and self-contradiction.[30]

We are dealing here with fundamental questions of the nature of the world and our place in it, and although the context is not explicitly natural-philosophical, it allows us to appreciate a dimension of the relation between truth and justification in a natural-philosophical context. The way in which will and the intellect are related here indicates that arguments about the existence of God are always motivated. That is to say, they aim at showing something that is given prior to the justification/ demonstration. This 'something' that they aim at showing is not 'truth' in general, but something that is held to be a particular truth. The point in the context of seventeenth-century discussions of atheism is that the 'something' that motivates the atheist's arguments is not in fact a truth, and because of this the arguments lead only to scepticism, cynicism, and doubt which has no resolution, the upshot of which is despair. Such an outcome acts as a *reductio* of the original assumption, and is sufficient to show that what motivated the argument is false.

What is at issue, then, is the idea that argument/justification/demonstration does not lead to belief, but rather that belief motivates arguments, providing them with something to demonstrate, which is their goal. One does not use argument to gen-erate beliefs; rather, argument starts from beliefs and explores their consequences to determine what degree of credence they deserve. Only once we have got the epistemic direction of argument clear can we understand that argument tests (purported) truths rather than generating them, so there is an important sense in which (purported) truths come at the beginning of the argument, not at its conclusion. Truth per se can-not motivate arguments, because it provides them with no direction. But particular

[29] Cicero, *Tusculanae disputationes*, 1. 13.
[30] Kors, *Atheism in France*, 17.

beliefs—that is, particular beliefs assumed to be true, in short particular (purported) truths—can provide such motivation, and it is these that guide argument. But they do this by providing arguments with tasks, not with guidance at the cognitive level. Consequently the kind of cognitive guidance that truth per se was supposed to provide, but is unable to provide, is not something that particular truths, considered as the goals of arguments, are able to provide either.

If neither truth per se nor particular truths can provide general cognitive guidance in natural philosophy, we must look for something outside questions of truth. The problem with truth per se is that the only way in which it can provide cognitive guidance is by offering some goal at which argument must aim, but the goal is not given prior to the argument. What we need is something that guides arguments by making sure they start and proceed in the right way, as it were, as opposed to finishing in the right way. Such guidance is provided by a newly emerging notion of objectivity, developed within a natural-historical context. Before we can examine this notion, however, we need to clarify the contrast between truth and objectivity in seventeenth-century natural-philosophical thinking.

Questions of truth and objectivity came apart in the seventeenth century, and it is important that we understand in what way they were connected before they became separated. The original connection was rooted in the scholastic theory of perceptual cognition, in particular in the theory of cognitive representation, the question on which Pomponazzi's criticism of Aquinas' defence of disembodied cognition (and hence survival) hinged. In his discussion of sense perception in Books 2 and 3 of *De anima*, Aristotle had argued that in perception, 'the mind which is actively thinking is identical with its object' ($431^b17–18$).[31] In the case of perceptual (as opposed to intellectual) cognition, where knowledge is of sensible things, this clearly cannot mean that sensible things are in the mind. Hence the importance of Aristotle's doctrine that the being or essence of something lies in its form, not in its matter, and what is in the mind is the form of the object ($431^b30$). In his elaboration of this account in the *Summa theologica*, Aquinas argues that the form of the thing known 'must of necessity be in the knower in the same manner as in the known itself' and so the sensible form 'is in one way in the thing which is external to the soul, and in another way in the senses'.[32] The intelligible species that the intellect receives from objects in sense perception are not forms produced by the mind (they are not mental representations that the mind produces to match the object known, for example) but by the thing itself, and indeed they are these things themselves in the intellect. These things really exist in the intellect, because what the thing is essentially is its form, and when the intellect takes on this form in cognition, what it takes on is the same form as the object. It is identical with the object: not with the matter of the object, which is irrelevant to its being or essence, but with its form.

Just what it was that was present to the mind in this kind of account was disputed among Aquinas' successors, particularly Duns Scotus and Suárez and

---

[31] There is a helpful account of these questions, which I have drawn on here, in John Yolton, *Perceptual Acquaintance from Descartes to Reid* (Oxford, 1984), 6–10.

[32] *Summa theologica*, I, q. 84, a. 1.

their followers.[33] By the late sixteenth century, one pressing issue was what the conformity between the object and our idea of it consisted in: what marked out a true idea of something? Two kinds of concept—a formal concept and an 'objective' concept—were postulated, and the question of true ideas was considered to lie in the relation between these.[34] The formal concept of an object was that object as it existed in the intellect, but formal concepts are not necessarily true concepts, for some of them can be mistaken. To say this is to say that they do not conform to the object of which they are the concept, but the object is a material thing: how can the idea conform to something material? The problem was added to by the fact that many scholastic writers denied that we have genuine access to essences, but they had no doubt that we had access to truth. Where could this truth derive from if not from the object itself? What was needed was something immaterial that stood in for the material thing, so that this could be compared with the formal concept. That immaterial thing is the objective concept, and it is the thing 'insofar as it is known'. Consequently, what we compare the formal concept with is not the thing itself but its objective concept. This leaves the question of what the relation between the objective concept and the thing itself is. The relation is labelled 'objective being', but what exactly this consists in is obscure. It is initially tempting to think that it is just the relation that we might have supposed to hold between the formal concept and the thing itself, had it not been for the problem of comparing entities that are unlike, in that one is corporeal and one intellectual. In a case where we routinely grasped essences in sense perception, this is indeed what the relation would be, but it is clear that sense perception is fallible, and we hardly ever—if at all—grasp essences in this way. Yet this does not mean that our formal concepts are all, or even largely, false. The tripartite formal distinction between concept, objective concept, and object opens up the possibility of introducing questions of degrees of certainty, something commonplace in the rhetorical tradition, and in the legal and historical disciplines based on university rhetorical and dialectical studies,[35] but up to this point absent from scholastic accounts of sense perception.

Peter Dear has distinguished two early stages in the development of the idea of degrees of certainty in the writings of two Jesuit natural philosophers,[36] which illuminates the issues in a helpful way, even though they go beyond scholastic philosophy. The first is the *Cursus philosophicus* (1632) of Roderigo de Arriaga, where degrees of certainty are introduced within an orthodox scholastic framework.

---

[33] For details see Gabriel Picard, 'Essai sur la connaissance sensible d'après les scolastiques', *Archives de philosophie* 4/1 (1926), 1–93; and Timothy J. Cronin, *Objective Being in Descartes and in Suárez* (Rome, 1966).

[34] See the discussion in Peter Dear, 'From Truth to Disinterestedness in the Seventeenth Century', *Social Studies of Science* 22 (1992), 619–31, and idem, *Mersenne and the Learning of the Schools* (Ithaca, NY, 1988), 49–51. See also Roland Dalbiez, 'Les sources scolastiques de la théorie cartésienne de l'être objectif', *Revue d'Histoire de la Philosophie* 3 (1929), 464–72; and Pierre Garin, *La Théorie de l'idée suivant l'école thomiste* (2 vols, Paris, 1932).

[35] See Richard W. Serjeantson, 'Testimony and Proof in Early-Modern England', *Studies in History and Philosophy of Science* 30 (1999), 195–236.

[36] Dear, 'From Truth to Disinterestedness in the Seventeenth Century', 621–4.

Arriaga distinguished between moral certainty, which holds when our beliefs are reliable, physical certainty, which holds when we are dealing with something that holds necessarily on the assumption of the normal relations of cause and effect, and metaphysical certainty, which holds in the case of such truths as those of logic. In 1646, in his *Controversiae logicae*, Honoré Fabri combined Arriaga's three degrees of certainty with the objective/formal distinction, in the process prizing open questions of truth and objectivity. Fabri distinguished two kinds of certainty in terms of the objective/formal distinction. Objective certainty encompasses the three kinds that Arriaga distinguished. Developing Aristotle's remarks in the *Nicomachean Ethics* ($1094^{b}24-5$) that different subject matters lend themselves to different kinds of demonstrations, and that we should not expect the kinds of demonstration sought in geometry, for example, to be applicable to ethics, Fabri distinguished the kind or degree of certainty appropriate to different subject matters. This is something that depends solely on the nature of the subject matter, and is objective in that sense. Formal certainty, by contrast, turns on judgements on our part: the degree of certainty we have of something in this sense is independent of the objective certainty of the subject matter, and depends rather on what evidence or reasons we have for claiming something.

In this way, theories of perceptual cognition begin to converge on traditional humanistically driven disciplines such as natural history, law, and political/civil history. Not only do truth and objectivity come apart, but this is not to the detriment of the latter, where, by contrast with what was increasingly seen as the fruitless enterprise of scholastic natural philosophy, the traditional humanistic disciplines seemed to be in good order. An enquiry is objective to the extent that it does not depend upon any features of the particular subject who studies it. An objective account is, in this sense, impartial, one that could ideally be accepted by any subject, because it does not draw on any assumptions, prejudices, or values of particular subjects.[37] Objectivity has two features that make it especially attractive as something that might regulate natural-philosophical enquiry. First, unlike truth, objectivity comes in degrees—some procedures can be more objective than others—and it is something that can be improved upon through practice. Second, the idea that natural-philosophical enquiry aims at truth might hold for what Aristotle called the theoretical sciences, but this does seem particularly inappropriate as a characterization of the aims of a discipline such as medicine, which was increasingly incorporated into natural-philosophical enquiry in the course of the sixteenth and seventeenth centuries.[38] By contrast, the idea that objectivity should regulate an area such as medical enquiry, to the extent to which it is part of a natural-philosophical

[37] This is not to deny that the extent to which full objectivity is possible, and just how objectivity should be secured, are going to be contentious in some cases, although many of the supposed problems here turn out not to be such on closer examination. See Stephen Gaukroger, 'Objectivity, History of', in N. J. Smelser and Paul B. Baltes, eds, *International Encyclopedia of the Social and Behavioural Sciences* (Oxford, 2001), xvi. 10785–9.

[38] On the Renaissance disputes over whether medicine was an art or a science see Maclean, *Logic, Signs and Nature in the Renaissance*, 70–6, and, on its problematic relationship with natural philosophy, 80–4.

enterprise, is as unproblematically appropriate as the demand that it should regulate cosmological enquiry.

The ways in which early-modern philosophers tried to reformulate the project of natural philosophy bear this out. When Bacon advocated the purging of 'idols' from the mind, when Galileo presented his arguments in the context of a patronage system that was disinterested, when Descartes argued that scholastics should be replaced by men of the world as natural philosophers, when Boyle and the members of the Royal Society attempted to present their findings in the closest way to bare 'facts', what they were all seeking, in their different fashions, was a way of securing objectivity, not a means of securing truth. Purging the mind of idols does not produce truth as such: it rids the mind of those features that would impair its objectivity. Disinterestedness does not produce truth, but manifests a form of freedom from preconceived ideas and prejudices (both of which could in fact be true). Men of the world are no more seekers after the truth than scholastic friars are, but they bring an intellectual honesty to the task because they are free from prejudice and from an education that prevents them from thinking for themselves. Presenting bare facts rather than grand theories does not produce truth but rather favours procedures that clearly manifest objectivity and impartiality. The presentation of results in terms of bare facts, for example, was not for Boyle a provisional record of research that was at a stage too early to merit systematization, but, as we shall see in detail in Chapter 10, a way of manifesting the legitimacy of his whole natural-philosophical project.

English natural philosophy, at least from the middle of the seventeenth century, is dominated by the notion of objectivity, and this is pursued not externally, in terms of truth, but internally, in terms of impartiality. The attempt to generate internal criteria of objectivity acts not as a second-best option in the absence of a means of establishing truth, but as a way of legitimating any cognitive claims a discipline might make. The procedures originate in the Renaissance models of history and law (drawn largely from training in rhetoric and dialectic), gradually becoming transferred to natural philosophy via natural history.

Both history and the law were concerned with actions or events that are not directly accessible. The aim of both was to devise procedures of enquiry whereby adequate knowledge of such actions or events could be gained. In the case of law, once competence to testify was determined by a judge, English legal procedures assumed that jurors had sufficient intellectual ability and moral probity to assess witness credibility adequately and to reach reasonable verdicts.[39] The language of the historian often mirrored that of the law, historians variously describing themselves as 'on oath' or as impartial witnesses, and they are apologetic when they are not themselves first-hand witnesses.[40] As with judges in trials, many historians sought to derive judgements from the facts that they presented, believing that history harboured lessons for those

---

[39] Shapiro, *A Culture of Fact*, 13. See also idem, *Probability and Certainty in Seventeenth-Century England: A Study of the Relationships Between Natural Science, Religion, History, Law, and Literature* (Princeton, 1983), 175–86. Note, however, that the degree of judicial direction of seventeenth-century juries far exceeds what is now the case.

[40] Shapiro, *A Culture of Fact*, 43.

participating in government. Moreover, although the usual explanation for historical events was providence, primary and secondary causes were distinguished and non-providential historical causation was explored in the case of human actions. Whatever degree of explanatory ambition was ascribed to historical investigation, however, the one thing that was seen by all as part of the historian's credentials was impartiality. This does not mean that all historians were impartial or objective of course, only that it was the virtue that one claimed for oneself and denied to one's opponents, where impartiality and objectivity mean absence of partisanship or bias, a distinctive seventeenth-century conception which stands in contrast with later conceptions of objectivity and impartiality, where the positive notion of accurate portrayal begins to replace or complement that of lack of bias.[41]

Barbara Shapiro has drawn attention to the importance of chorography—the most widely practised form of which in England was county history—in supplying a basis for natural history in seventeenth-century England. Chorographic and travel reports, which formed a large part of Royal Society reports, were couched in terms of 'matters of fact', and they drew attention to the honesty and good character of any eyewitnesses, noting their impartiality, lack of bias, and non-partisanship. Chorography combined civil and natural history, and it was this peculiar combination, as Shapiro notes, that enabled it to act as a vehicle through which 'legally derived concepts of witnessing and evaluation of testimony were transmitted from human events and actions to natural phenomena, natural events, and experiments'.[42] Sprat sums the matter up in his response to the charge that the very broad range of sources of information utilized by the Royal Society might compromise the accuracy of this information. The Royal Society, he tells us, reduces 'such matters of hearsay and information, into real, and impartial Trials, perform'd by their Experiments'.[43]

The concern with objectivity, in the form of impartiality and lack of bias, is reflected in the fact that there is at least as much concern with the character of the natural philosopher as there is with questions of method. It is not just the procedure one follows, it is the qualities that the natural philosopher brings to bear on the enterprise, just as—especially in the wake of the Reformation—it is the personal qualities of the cleric that manifest the authenticity of his religion as much as do his theological beliefs.[44]

## THE GOALS OF NATURAL PHILOSOPHY

The shift to a concern with objectivity is not something that is generated within natural philosophy, on the traditional Aristotelian conception, but within natural

---

[41] See ibid., 58.

[42] Ibid. 66. Cf. Lorraine Daston, *Classical Probability in the Enlightenment* (Princeton, 1988), ch. 1.

[43] Sprat, *History of the Royal Society*, 215.

[44] To take a very striking example, *Regulae Societatis Iesu* (Rome, 1580), instructs Jesuit priests to assume a grave and reserved manner of deportment and demeanour: 'Gestus corporis sit modestus, et in quo gravitas quaedam religiosa praecipue eluceat' (127). Cited in Dilwyn Knox, 'Ideas on Gestures and Universal Languages, *c.*1550–1650', in J. Henry and S. Hutton, eds, *New Perspectives on Renaissance Thought* (London, 1990), 101–136: 114.

history. The application of notions developed within natural history to natural philosophy makes no sense in strictly Aristotelian terms, and depends on the kind of rethinking of the aims of natural philosophy that we looked at in Bacon. It was not just the relation between natural philosophy and natural history that became an issue in the sixteenth and seventeenth centuries, however; so too was the relation between natural philosophy and the practical-mathematical disciplines, and that between natural philosophy and the medical disciplines.

The problems here go back to classical antiquity. The construal of genuine philosophical enquiry as something that enables the natural philosopher to go beyond appearances to the underlying reality or underlying principles imposes constraints on what falls under philosophical enquiry that turn out to be idiosyncratic and unproductive. Consider, for example, the exclusion of medicine and the inclusion of mathematics in Plato's idea of knowledge, and in Aristotle's classification of the theoretical sciences. In the *Gorgias*, Plato, revising normal usage, makes it clear that a *technē* is a skill that involves giving an 'account' of the thing, not a mere practical ability, and he distinguishes between a genuine *technē*, like a medical skill, and one that is not genuine but merely a 'knack' (*empeiria*), such as the ability to cook.[45] Aristotle likewise treats medicine as a *technē*. On the face of it, this makes perfectly good sense: we think of medicine in terms of prevention and healing, not in terms of underlying principles. What we seek are preventative measures and cures. But there are grounds on which it is difficult not to consider medicine as being fundamentally the same as natural philosophy in standing, and in the Hellenistic period we find disputes between the schools of medicine as to whether and how the underlying reality that is causally responsible for illness is discoverable, and whether procedures such as dissection are able to reveal such an underlying reality.[46] If the aim of the theoretical sciences is to uncover underlying principles, then medicine looks like a candidate,[47] even though for medicine such an aim is a means to an end, not an end in itself. Bacon, as we have seen, focused on exactly this issue, urging that the single most important cause of the failure of the Aristotelian conception of natural philosophy was its treatment of truth as an end in itself, something deriving from a mistakenly contemplative view of the role of natural philosophy.

By contrast, mathematics looks distinctly unpromising as a candidate, and requires significant bolstering to get it to look like something that uncovers appearances. The first step is to distinguish pure from practical mathematics. Plato, for example, maintains that calculation is for merchants and the like and is beneath the dignity

---

[45] Plato, *Gorgias*, 465A.

[46] See Michael Frede, *Essays in Ancient Philosophy* (Oxford, 1987) ch. 12 ('Philosophy and Medicine in Antiquity') and ch. 15 ('On Galen's Epistemology'). Cf. G. E. R. Lloyd, 'The Definition, Status, and Methods of the Medical *techne* in the Fifth and Fourth Centuries', in A. C. Bowen, ed., *Science and Philosophy in Classical Greece* (London, 1991), 249–60.

[47] The point was argued in detail as late as 1640 by Lazarus Riverius in his *Institutes*, which subsequently appeared as Part 1 of his *Opera medica universa* (Lyons, 1663). See the discussion in French, *Medicine before Science*, 193–5.

of mathematicians, and he disparages any form of practical mathematics.[48] The next step is then to identify just what is uncovered in mathematics so purified. The idea that mathematics might be pursued by going beyond the appearances resulted in the conception of arithmetic in Neopythagorean terms as the classification of kinds of numbers, for example in the work of Nichomachus,[49] which was hopelessly sterile.[50] This left the practical-mathematical disciplines—astronomy, optics, harmonics, and mechanics—with a very problematic place in the classification of cognitive disciplines, falling neither under mathematics nor natural philosophy. That they do not fit into the classification of knowledge offered by Aristotle is clear from the fact that in the *Metaphysics* he tells us that astronomy is a branch of mathematics for example, whereas in the *Physics* it is presented as a branch of physics.[51] Indeed the practical-mathematical disciplines were pursued exclusively outside the ancient natural-philosophical tradition. This tradition, which runs from Plato's *Timeaus*, through the comprehensive natural-philosophical works of Aristotle, and then through the Hellenistic natural-philosophical systems of the Epicureans and Stoics, to the metaphysical systems of the Neoplatonists, makes no effort—with the exception of the pseudo-Aristotelian *Mechanica*—to engage the practical-mathematical disciplines. These are pursued quite independently, along with geometry, in the Alexandrian tradition. Natural philosophy, as Plato and Aristotle construe the discipline, is matter theory: it is a search for the underlying essential principles that shape the natural behaviour of bodies. Mechanics simply has no place in this endeavour: nor, on the Aristotelian conception, does any mathematical discipline.

Rethinking these issues manifestly alters the aims of natural-philosophical enquiry. What motivates mechanism, for example, is the attempt to use mechanics, an area of practical mathematics, which on the traditional Aristotelian account had fallen outside natural philosophy altogether, as a model for natural-philosophical enquiry.

---

[48] See e.g. *Republic* 527A-B. In this respect, Plato may have been rejecting an approach that gave practical mathematics priority over theoretical mathematics, a view which Xenophon attributes to Socrates. Socrates, Xenophon tells us, 'thought that geometry should be learned so far as to enable one to receive or convey or apportion land accurately in point of measurement, or to carry out a task . . . But he depreciated the learning of geometry so far as figures difficult of comprehension. He said he didn't see the use of them . . . and that these studies were capable of wasting a man's life and preventing him from learning many other useful things.' He goes on to make the same point in the case of astronomy, concluding that Socrates dissuaded people 'from concerning themselves with the way in which God regulates the various heavenly bodies; he thought that these facts were not discoverable by human beings, and he did not consider that a man would please the gods if he pried into things that they had not chosen to reveal' (*Memorabilia* 4 ch. 7).

[49] Nichomachus of Gerasa, 'Introduction to Arithmetic', trans. Martin L. D'Ooge, in *Britannica Great Books* 11 (Chicago, 1952), 811–48.

[50] See Jacob Klein, *Greek Mathematical Thought and the Origin of Algebra* (Cambridge, Mass. 1968), ch. 4.

[51] Cf. *Metaphysics* 989$^b$33 and *Physics* 193$^b$25–30. The confusion continued throughout the Aristotelian tradition, with Valentin Nabod's popular astronomy textbook, *Astronomicarum institutionum libri III* (Venice, 1580) treating astronomy as in part falling under metaphysics because it deals with immutable celestial bodies (fos. 3–5).

This had profound consequences for the practice of natural philosophy. In antiquity, natural philosophy and the practical-mathematical disciplines such as astronomy and mechanics had been fundamentally different kinds of enterprise pursued by people with very different sets of skills and interests. By the late sixteenth century this was no longer the case, and indeed many of the problems that natural philosophy faced were generated by how one reconciled, not natural philosophy and theology, but natural philosophy and the practical–mathematical disciplines. Zúñiga, as we have seen, had no difficulty in dealing with the biblical objections to Copernicanism, but was forced to conclude that it could not possibly be true because it made no natural-philosophical sense in Aristotelian terms.

There is also a deeper concern about the aims of natural philosophy, a concern manifest in the Pomponazzi dispute. Christianized Aristotelianism cannot accept the idea that natural philosophy provides the ultimate underlying principles of natural behaviour, even in the case where these are wholly in accord with revealed truths. The shift of register between Aquinas' account of natural philosophy, where individual natures are identified as the ultimate underlying principles, and his demonstrations of God's existence from features of the natural world, where God himself is identified as the sole ultimate underlying principle, indicates some basic problems inherent in the Christianization of Aristotelian natural philosophy. There is a very fundamental shift in natural-philosophical enquiry here, and it is unprecedented. In classical and Hellenistic antiquity, natural philosophy was pursued without regard to a clearly-defined independent standard of truth that lay outside natural philosophy, a role that fundamental religious beliefs assumed at the end of the Hellenistic era. But there are no classical or Hellenistic precedents for the early-modern developments here. If one tries to dissociate natural-philosophical considerations from the biblical teaching in the case of the earth's motion, for example, the kinds of move that might make this possible—from reinterpreting biblical passages to denying that Church authorities are competent to judge such matters—are not going to work across the board. No one made analogous claims in the case of the personal immortality of the soul, for example. Biblical and religious teaching was beginning to be questioned in the course of the seventeenth century, but natural philosophy was not a significant participant in this process before the 1680s. To the extent to which there was a divergence between natural philosophy and theology, it was natural philosophers who sought to establish the theological credentials of their enterprise. Theology and natural philosophy certainly came adrift on certain issues, but few believed this was anything more than temporary, and the situation was quite different from that which held in antiquity. It is true that natural philosophy, to the extent to which it investigates the underlying intrinsic principles of things, is in itself largely neutral with respect to questions of whether the natural realm has come about by chance, whether it has been ordered by means of some internal principle in nature, or whether it has been created by a transcendent omnipotent being. And it is also true that such a conception had its supporters in the seventeenth century, particularly amongst Cartesians. Descartes envisaged his natural-philosophical project as erecting a mechanist natural-philosophical system to replace the Aristotelian system, sharing with Aristotle aims of comprehension and completeness but achieving this by radically different means. But for many natural philosophers from the end of the sixteenth to the nineteenth centuries, to account for something that has been designed without taking in to consideration the fact that it had been designed, was like studying a complex clockwork mechanism without regard to what the mechanism was built to achieve: one could not discover the reason why the parts were related in the particular way that they were related, because the very form of one's enquiry did not enable one to ask that kind of question.

It is at the natural-history end of the natural philosophy spectrum that such questions were to be posed, and this was one source of the move to force natural-historical considerations into the centre of natural philosophy. In this way, the aims of a reformed natural history, one guided by notions of objectivity and empirical enquiry rather than allegorical interpretation of nature, would be transplanted into the core of natural philosophy. But this strategy, which would take the form of 'experimental philosophy', was only one of what I want to identify as three broad directions that natural philosophy took in the mid-seventeenth century, the other two being mechanism, which treated natural philosophy as consisting in a mechanized form of matter theory, which had as little interest in natural history as did Aristotelian matter theory, and a form of practical mathematics that had been transformed into natural philosophy, which had complex connections with both mechanism and experimental philosophy.

# PART IV

# 8

# Corpuscularianism and the Rise
# of Mechanism

Mechanism is the natural philosophy that was to dominate physical theory from the 1630s up to the middle of the eighteenth century. Gassendi sets out the programme in broad terms:

There is no effect without a cause; no cause acts without motion; nothing acts on distant things except through itself or an organ or connection or transmission; nothing moves unless it is touched, whether directly or through an organ or through another body.[1]

Once one tries to fill in the detail, however, difficulties arise. In particular, mechanism should not be confused with mechanics, even though the two will often be combined, and may indeed mutually inspire one another. It is not itself a form of physical enquiry, as mechanics is, but rather something that offers a general picture of how the physical world is to be explained, what its ultimate constituents are, and what kinds of processes occur in it at the most fundamental level. In its pre-Newtonian version, which is what we shall be concerned with here, it is committed to explanation of macroscopic phenomena in terms of microscopic corpuscles which are very much a reworked version of traditional atomism. Mechanics, by contrast, makes no intrinsic distinction between the macroscopic and the microscopic, on explanatory or indeed on any other grounds. Moreover, whereas mechanics is by definition a quantitative discipline, mechanism is not. Part of its aim is to construe the corpuscles that it has identified as the ultimate constituents of physical bodies in terms of quantifiable attributes such as size, position, speed, and direction of motion. But its success as a natural philosophy, while it rests on the project of quantification to some extent, does not depend on this alone, and it is able to retain its pre-eminent position in the face of a failure to realize the programme of quantification, because of a very widespread agreement that the scholastic Aristotelianism that it replaces is hopelessly inadequate, and that any progress at the level of fundamentals could only be made within the context of corpuscularianism, of which mechanism was the best-developed form.

The virtues that have traditionally been associated with mechanism, by contrast with Aristotelianism, are a commitment to empirical enquiry and to the quantification of physical phenomena. In fact mechanism as such yields neither of these. Rather, it provides an underlying rationale that anchors various disparate projects

---

[1] Gassendi, *Opera*, i. 450.

that could not in themselves offer any claims to counter a comprehensive system such as Aristotelianism, and which would otherwise be unable to claim that they were replacing it, but which, as part of loosely co-ordinated grouping of 'new' natural-philosophical projects, can refer foundational natural-philosophical questions to this underlying rationale. Mechanism is especially suited to this role because its scope is on a par with that of Aristotelian natural philosophy. Unlike Aristotelianism, mechanism is reductionist rather than essentialist, but its reductionism can, where it is considered necessary, be vindicated in essentialist terms (in Descartes' attempt to derive mechanism from an account of matter as material extension, for example), and it certainly comes far closer to Aristotelian natural philosophy than the other two programmes that I want to distinguish. These are what came to be known as 'experimental natural philosophy', and mechanics proper.

The relation between mechanism and experimental natural philosophy was in many respects antagonistic, as we shall see in Chapter 10. The latter offered non-reductive explanations, which made no reference to micro-structure, but which its adherents treated as complete, by contrast with the mechanist commitment to micro-corpuscularian explanations as the ultimate form of explanation. It offers a way of thinking about physical problems which is quite different from mechanism, using experiment to generate the phenomena to be explained in a way that is not guided by mechanist assumptions about underlying structure. On the other hand, its adherents regarded what they were doing as broadly compatible with mechanism. The attempt to develop a quantitative natural philosophy, which will be our concern in Chapter 11, was not driven by mechanism either, and most key developments are quite neutral with respect to mechanism.

It is crucial for our concerns that the experimental and quantitative projects are treated separately from mechanism. I do not want to suggest that they are completely independent of it, only that the relation between the three is complex and shifting. In particular, I do not want to suggest that the legitimatory role of mechanism makes it redundant from the point of view of generating physical results. Quite the contrary: Descartes for one is able to produce a powerful cosmological system which is wholly driven by mechanism. But even if there were no such cases, even when the results are independent of mechanism, the important point is that it is able to play the legitimatory role it does because it is able to offer a compelling—if, within narrow limits, contested—picture of the physical universe which provides a fundamental level of understanding of the world and our place in it. It is what unifies otherwise disparate practices into something that can be seen to be part of a viable natural-philosophical programme. Indeed, the picture of the physical universe it presents, in sharp contrast with Renaissance naturalism, in almost all cases complements an orthodox theological understanding of such issues, and mechanists who raise the question are keen to argue that it complements this orthodox understanding more effectively than Aristotelianism. This is in large part why there is a general default adherence to mechanism, even where it is doing no explanatory work at the practical level. In this respect, mechanism serves a similar role to that played by Aristotelianism in carving out areas of mutual support with Christian theology, even though there may be disagreement among mechanists as to how this role is to be fulfilled. Just how mechanism can aspire to such a legitimatory role, and in particular how it can aspire to the kind of comprehensiveness required by something that purports to explain all physical phenomena, a claim that Aristotelianism had never made, is a question to which we shall return in Chapters 9 and 12. But it is important that we realize from the outset that the origins of mechanism lay in a legitimate programme as much as in anything else.

Mechanism began life in part as a way of thinking of the behaviour of macroscopic physical processes on the model of simple machines, in the work of Beeckman in the 1610s, and as a way of countering naturalism, in the work of Mersenne in the 1620s. The former, which we shall look at below, combines mechanism and mechanics in an intimate way, it is motivated in large part by the question of when purported physical explanations can be said to be genuinely explanatory, and it is radically anti-Aristotelian. The latter shares with this project a commitment to a quantitative natural philosophy, but it does this in the context of engaging the kinds of question about the relation between metaphysics, theology, and natural philosophy that had come to a head in the Pomponazzi affair.

In countering naturalism, Mersenne realized that a return to the Aristotelian conception of nature that had served medieval theologians and natural philosophers so well was not going to be successful.[2] He did not reject scholastic Aristotelianism as such, and he wished to defend a number of tenets that scholastic Aristotelianism treated as fundamental, especially the clear separation of the natural and the supernatural, the personal immortality of the soul, and the rejection of determinism. All these had been challenged in various ways by Renaissance thinkers, the first most explicitly by those who, following Neoplatonic and Stoic sources, postulated the existence of a world soul; the second most explicitly by those who who developed a strictly Aristotelian account of the mind; and the third by those who accepted the claims of astrology, which took at least some of the responsibility for human affairs away from both God and human beings themselves. The trouble with Aristotelianism was that it had simply not been able to offer an effective answer to these troublesome doctrines, some of which had been explicitly condemned by the Lateran Council in 1512, and the problem lay largely in the fact that many of these doctrines were defensible on Aristotelian grounds. The deepest challenges derived from the idea that nature, or more strictly speaking matter, was in some way essentially active. This had consequences for how nature was to be understood, and for how the human being was to be understood. On the first question, Renaissance naturalism had undermined the sharp line that medieval philosophy and theology had tried to draw between the natural and the supernatural. It encouraged a picture of nature as an essentially active realm, containing many hidden or 'occult' powers which, while they were by definition not manifest, could nevertheless be tapped and exploited, if only one could discover them. The other side of the coin was a conception of God as part of nature, as infused in nature, and not as something separate from his creation: something like a pagan 'mother nature'. This encouraged various forms of heterodoxy, from the modelling of divine powers on natural ones to the doctrine of

---

[2] See Lenoble, *Mersenne ou la naissance de la mécanique.*

pantheism. Worst of all, it opened up the very delicate question of whether apparently supernatural phenomena, such as miracles, or phenomena which offered communion with God, such as the sacraments and prayer, could perhaps be explained purely naturalistically, perhaps in psychological terms, as Telesio had been arguing. The problems were exacerbated by a correlative naturalistic thesis about the nature of human beings—mortalism—whereby the individual soul is not a separate substance but simply the 'organizing principle' of the body, that is, something wholly immanent in the matter of the body. It did not matter much whether mortalism was advocated in its Averroistic version, where the intellect is in no way personal because mind or soul, lacking any principle of individuation in its own right, cannot be apportioned one to each living human body, or whether it was advocated in its Alexandrian version, where the soul is conceived in purely functional terms: in either case, personal immortality is denied, and its source in both versions is Aristotle himself.

Mersenne saw the origin of both naturalism and mortalism as lying in the construal of matter as being in some way active, and his solution was to offer a metaphysical version of mechanism, the core doctrine of which is that matter is completely inert. The threat to established religion posed by naturalism and mortalism is a radical one which has countless ramifications, and Mersenne's solution was to cut them off at the root, by depriving them of the conception of matter on which they thrive. If there is no activity in matter then the supernatural will have to be invoked to explain any activity. In criticizing the various kinds of naturalism, Mersenne pointed to the credulity of many forms of Renaissance thought, and he extolled the virtues of mechanism for a quantitative understanding of nature, but what is fundamentally at issue is not the triumph of quantitative science over credulity but the defence of the supernatural against appropriation by the natural. This defence is undertaken by making the natural realm completely inactive, stripping it not merely of the various sympathies and occult connections postulated by naturalists, but also of the Aristotelian forms and qualities that provided much of the original inspiration for these.

It is mechanism, in one form or another, that would underlie developments in seventeenth-century natural philosophy, and the sense of the completely unacceptable nature of naturalism that Mersenne offered would be shared by seventeenth-century natural philosophers, who would see various forms of corpuscularianism as the only satisfactory alternative to scholastic natural philosophy, partly because it could be reconciled with the basic tenets of a Christian understanding of the cosmos, partly because it offered a manageable, clearly circumscribed understanding of the physical realm, and partly because it could be accommodated to and strengthened by the new quantitative approach to physical questions.[3]

In this chapter, I want to sketch four influential approaches to a corpuscularian natural philosophy in the early to mid-seventeenth century, those of Beeckman, Gassendi, Hobbes, and Descartes. Beeckman's path-breaking mechanical corpuscularianism was a direct influence on Descartes and Gassendi, but he published nothing in this area in his lifetime, and he was quickly forgotten after his death.

---

[3] This is the thrust of much of the last three books of Marin Mersenne, *La Verite des Sciences, contre les Septiqves ou Pyrrhoniens* (Paris, 1625).

Gassendi, by contrast, offered a renovated form of Epicureanism that of great influence in Académie des Sciences and the Royal Society, forming the main competitor to Cartesianism. Hobbes' motivation came in large part from his contacts with Descartes and particularly Gassendi, but what he offered was a radical version of mechanism that made no effort to mitigate the materialistic and deterministic consequences of traditional Epicureanism, with the result that it was generally taken as a lesson in the dangers of following the mechanist path. By contrast, Cartesian mechanism, though in some respects as radical as the system of Hobbes, was immensely influential, if controversial. The mature Cartesian system was astonishingly comprehensive, offering novel and often detailed mechanist accounts of everything from cosmology, optics, the formation of the earth, the tides, magnetism, the circulation of the blood, reflex action, and the development of the foetus, to animal and human psychophysiology. Of the material that appeared in Descartes' lifetime, the *Principia philosophiae* was especially important in establishing a mechanist cosmology that supplied a standard cosmological system which came under threat only with the publication of Newton's *Principia*, and even then many believed it had significant advantages over the Newtonian system well into the eighteenth century.[4]

## CORPUSCULARIANISM AND ATOMISM

Mechanism is a distinctive development within corpuscularian and atomist matter theory of the seventeenth century. It never completely displaced other forms of corpuscularianism during this period, however, and before we turn to mechanism proper, it will be helpful to sketch the variety of these other forms of corpuscularianism.

The most striking thing about corpuscularianism in the seventeenth century was its ability to adapt to virtually every form of natural philosophy. Even those natural philosophies offering active principles or active powers were available in corpuscularian versions by the early seventeenth century. Aristotelianism, for example, was assimilated to corpuscularianism by means of Aristotle's doctrine of *minima naturalia*,

---

[4] Note also that Cartesian natural philosophy, in Rohault's textbook version ( *Traité de physique*, 1671), continued to be the only natural philosophy taught at Cambridge well after the publication of Newton's *Principia*, even though it was considered to have been wholly superseded by the latter. As Newton's successor as Lucasian Professor of Mathematics, William Whiston, puts it: 'Since the Youth of the University must have, at present, some System of Natural Philosophy for their Studies and Exercises; and since the true System of Sir Isaac Newton was not yet made easy enough for the Purpose, it was not improper, for their Sakes, yet to translate and use the System of Rohault.' (*Historical Memoirs of the Life of Dr. Samuel Clarke* (London, 1730), 5–6.) The first Latin translation of Rohault for undergraduate use, by John Clarke, appeared in 1697, and it subsequently appeared in several increasingly 'Newtonianized' editions. Note also that the standard mid-eighteenth-century presentation of Newtonian natural philosophy for children—the very popular and extensively reprinted work by 'Tom Telescope', *The Newtonian System of Philosophy Adapted to the Capacities of Young Gentlemen and Ladies* (London, 1761)—follows the format of Descartes' *Principia* rather than that of Newton's *Principia*, moving from matter theory, to cosmology, the theory of the earth, plants and animals, and human capacities.

whereby all substances could be broken down into smallest parts.[5] Aristotle made it clear that these smallest parts were not atoms, because when combined they could not produce a new substance, only a mixture of heterogeneous constituents.[6] But this did not prevent a number of advocates of atomism using *minima naturalia* as a basis for their natural philosophies. Daniel Sennert, for example, argued that heterogeneous mixtures consisting of such parts may be simple mixtures, like a mixture of wine and water or an alloy of gold and silver, but alternatively some may be mixtures having different properties from any of their parts, and in this latter case they may have a principle of formal, as opposed to merely accidental, unity.[7] Such mixtures take on a corpuscularian form and what results are corpuscles whose properties are fundamental, even though they themselves are made up from smaller parts.[8] They are unified as substances by their specific forms, and in this respect are very different from Democritean atoms, which Sennert rejected because of their inability to provide an efficient cause for the generation and preservation of things.[9] If Sennert found solace in Aristotle for his corpuscularianism, that of his contemporary Nicholas Hill was motivated in part by Neoplatonist sources such as Patrizi.[10] Basing himself on a Neoplatonist metaphysics of light, for example, he identified the active principle underlying nature with light,[11] maintaining that it works through the formation of atoms, which are very varied in shape and underlie all change in natural phenomena, from local motion to generation and corruption.[12]

It might be tempting to see such accounts as a stage on the way to a fully fledged mechanist corpuscularianism of the kind developed in Beeckman, Hobbes, and Descartes, but the situation was more complicated than this.[13] In the first place

---

[5] See John E. Murdoch, 'The Medieval and Renaissance Tradition of *Minima Naturalia*', in Christoph Lüthy, John E. Murdoch, and William R. Newman, eds, *Late Medieval and Early Modern Corpuscular Matter Theories* (Leiden, 2001), 91–131.

[6] Aristotle, *De gen. et corrupt.*, 327$^b$33–328$^a$18.

[7] Daniel Sennert, *Hypomnemata physica* (Frankfurt, 1636), 120. On the development of Sennert's corpuscularianism, see Emily Michael, 'Sennert's Sea Change: Atoms and Causes', in Christoph Lüthy, John E. Murdoch, and William R. Newman, eds, *Late Medieval and Early Modern Corpuscular Matter Theories* (Leiden, 2001), 331–62.

[8] This kind of approach was challenged in Sebastian Basso, *Philosophia naturalis adversus Aristotelem* (Geneva, 1621), who insists that all qualities and properties of mixtures of composites are qualities or properties of their constituents.

[9] See Michael, 'Sennert's Sea Change', 356–62.

[10] See Stephen Clucas, 'The Atomism of the Cavendish Circle: A Reappraisal', *The Seventeenth Century* 9 (1994), 247–73; and idem, 'Corpuscular Matter Theory in the Northumberland Circle', in Christoph Lüthy, John E. Murdoch, and William R. Newman, eds, *Late Medieval and Early Modern Corpuscular Matter Theories* (Leiden, 2001), 181–207.

[11] Nicholas Hill, *Philosophia Epicurea*, 86.          [12] Ibid., 36.

[13] See Keith Hutchison, 'What Happened to Occult Qualities in the Scientific Revolution?', *Isis* 73 (1982), 233–53; Ron Millen, 'The Manifestation of Occult Qualities in the Scientific Revolution', in M. J. Osler and P. J. Farber, eds, *Religion, Science, and Worldview* (Cambridge, 1985), 185–216; John Henry, 'Occult Qualities and the Experimental Philosophy: Active Principles in Pre-Newtonian Matter Theory', *History of Science* 24 (1986), 335–81; idem, 'Robert Hooke, The Incongruous Mechanist', in Michael Hunter and Simon Schaffer, eds, *Robert Hooke: New Studies* (Woodbridge, 1989), 149–80; and J. E. McGuire, 'Force, Active Principles and Newton's Invisible Realm', *Ambix* 15 (1968), 154–208.

there remained a divide well into the century between those, most notably Gassendi and Gassendians such as Charleton, who saw corpuscularianism primarily in terms of matter theory, with the shape and surface texture of atoms doing most of the explanatory work, and those who saw it primarily (like Descartes) or exclusively (like Huygens) in terms of mechanics. It is important to note in this context that the division here did not necessarily fall along qualitative/quantitative lines. What drove the matter theory approach in many cases were clearly quantitative considerations. Bacon, for example, had pressed for staunchly quantitative procedures in his investigations into specific weights and chemical reactions,[14] but what he wanted was numerical proportions. For Bacon, quantification was numerical not geometrical, whereas what mechanism (following mechanics) offered was quantification through geometrical representation, something of no relevance whatever to the investigation of chemical processes that matter theorists were undertaking. Second, those corpuscularians whose interest was in parts of natural philosophy remote from mechanics, for example those interested in iatrochemistry, could make little use of micro-corpuscularian interactions described purely in mechanical terms in picturing what was happening at a microscopic level.[15] And by mechanists' own criteria, picturability was crucial to understanding how physical processes operated. Third, mechanism remained a promissory note at a level of abstraction far removed from real physical processes, even in Descartes, who went furthest in this respect. Natural philosophers engaged in physical enquiry often simply ran out of the rather meagre resources offered by mechanism—where parsimony in explanatory principles was crucial—and were prepared to employ any means to keep the project going, often, but not always, in the hope that they could come back and rework the material in mechanist terms. Fourth, many who were committed to mechanism as the appropriate form of explanation for physical processes, perhaps even including such intractable phenomena as cohesion and magnetism, saw mechanism as being in need of supplementation when it came to the organic realm, or when one was considering goal-directed processes such as the development of the foetus and the formation of the earth.

We shall return to these questions, in some cases in detail, when we have looked at just what the varieties of mechanism offer, for just as there are different forms of non-mechanist corpuscularianism, so too mechanism is by no means a single natural-philosophical movement. Indeed, our first task must be to provide some general characterization of mechanism, by no means an easy undertaking.[16] There are, however, three features around which most of the issues hinge. First, the most

---

[14] See Gaukroger, *Francis Bacon*, ch. 6.

[15] See e.g. William R. Newman, 'The Corpuscular Theory of J. B. van Helmont and Its Medieval Sources', *Vivarium* 31 (1993), 161–91, and idem, 'Boyle's Debt to Corpuscular Alchemy', in Michael Hunter, ed., *Robert Boyle Reconsidered* (Cambridge, 1994), 107–18.

[16] One of the most concerted attempts to characterize mechanism is J. E. McGuire, 'Boyles' Conception of Nature', *Journal of the History of Ideas* 33 (1972), 523–42. Cf. C. D. Broad, *Mind and its Place in Nature* (London, 1925), 45; and Margaret J. Osler, 'How Mechanical was the Mechanical Philosophy?', in Christoph Lüthy, John E. Murdoch, and William R. Newman, eds, *Late Medieval and Early Modern Corpuscular Matter Theories* (Leiden, 2001), 423–39.

distinctive feature of mechanism—something it has in common with most varieties of corpuscularianism—is the homogeneity of the corpuscles: instead of a variety of different ultimate elements, there is only one kind of matter, and it is to this single kind of matter that all physical processes must ultimately be referred. This is a radical curtailment of explanatory resources, and we shall be exploring what lies behind it. Second, we need to investigate whether there is an explanatory price to be paid for this move to homogenous matter, in that all qualitative effects—including the organic realm—now have to be accounted for in terms of the one kind of matter. There are two complementary ways in which this question was dealt with. The explanatory resources offered by a homogeneous matter theory were expanded, most notably by postulating corpuscles differing in shape and size (traditional Epicurean atomism), or in terms of size, speed, and direction of motion (the mechanist tradition). At the same time, the *explanandum* was contracted radically, by arguing—or maintaining, for arguments are actually thin on the ground in this respect—that the qualitative variety manifest at the macroscopic level was merely apparent. Third, in the course of the seventeenth century, the foundational role of matter theory began to be challenged by mechanics, which offered motion as the basic explanatory tool. Some kinds of material explanation were incompatible with the new mechanical theories, but with the rise of corpuscularianism a form of mutual support between matter theory and mechanics became possible, in the form of mechanism. Mechanism offered a bridge between matter theory and mechanics, potentially to the benefit of both. Matter theory stood to gain from the quantitative standing of mechanics, whereas mechanics, which was often derided as being a set of mathematical disciplines that had no physical relevance, stood to gain from the physical model provided by matter theory. As it turned out, any substantial connection was very difficult to secure, and the importance of the connection was most evident at the level of mutual legitimation, which usually took the form of a promissory note rather than anything concrete, although there can be no doubt that it did act as a guide and constraint.

Mechanism existed in many varieties—one self-styled Cartesian mechanist, William Petty, even argued for male and female atoms[17]—and it is difficult to characterize in the abstract since it is driven by a number of different considerations, and as a result each major variety seems to depart from a feature of mechanism central to the others. As I shall be construing it, ideal-type mechanism has the distinctive feature that it reduces all physical processes to the activity of inert corpuscles making up macroscopic objects, where the behaviour of these corpuscles can be described exhaustively in terms of mechanics and geometry, and where they act exclusively by means of efficient causes, which require spatial and temporal contact between the cause and the effect. The simplest mechanist model is one in which we have small corpuscles of inert matter moving in an otherwise empty space and interacting with one another.[18] We can assume that the corpuscles contain no empty spaces, that they are spherical, and that they are all of the same order of magnitude. The space in which they

---

[17] See Robert Kargon, 'William Petty's Mechanical Philosophy', *Isis* 56 (1965), 63–6: 65.

[18] This model is close to what Milič Čapek calls the 'corpuscular-kinetic view of nature' in his *The Philosophical Impact of Contemporary Physics* (New York, 1961): see esp. ch. 6.

move is a continuous, complete, isotropic, three-dimensional container which acts as a reference frame for the location of bodies. As regards matter, we can think of it as being simply full space. Being full space, matter derives most of its most fundamental properties from the space it occupies: it is three-dimensional, and its basic properties do not vary depending purely on location. Also, it is homogeneous—uniformly dense—at the atomistic level, variations in density at the macroscopic level arising because of variations in the distribution of matter in space. But it also has many properties that empty space doesn't. It is discontinuous, coming in discrete bits, and it is not complete because there are gaps between these pieces of matter. Its most distinctive property, and the one that marks it out most decisively from empty space, is its impenetrability, and this can be thought of as following from the conception of matter as full space: after all, if it is already full it cannot be made fuller. As for motion, this is not reducible to matter, space, and time because there could be a universe with these but in which there was no motion; but it does depend on them since it can be defined as change in spatial location of matter in time. Time is conceived on this model as being independent of motion, so that there would still be time in a motionless universe; and as independent of matter, so that there would still be time in an empty universe.[19] Finally, the universe is causally closed: by contrast with the Aristotelian cosmos, there can be no spontaneous or arbitrary beginnings of a sequence of causes.[20]

No mechanist system adopts all the details of this ideal type, but it will help us pose some general questions about the aims of mechanism which attention to individual systems might obscure. Paramount among these are the explanatory ambitions of mechanism. Consider the basic idea of corpuscles moving in empty space, and interacting with one another. We can ask whether the corpuscles themselves, or their interactions, are likely candidates in the explanation of macroscopic phenomena. One feature of the corpuscles we have postulated is that, because they consist simply of full space, they are all identical with one another. This seems an unlikely basis for a theory that purports to explain a broad range of qualitative macroscopic phenomena. It might seem, for example, that for chemical reactions, a range of corpuscles having different chemical properties might be needed, whether the mercury-sulphur-salt theory of the Paracelsians or the expanded spirit-oil-salt-water-earth theory.[21] One alternative for corpuscularians who do not wish to postulate more than one kind of matter is to allow the homogeneous corpuscles different shapes and sizes, another is to allow them different sizes and motions. If there is to be any hope at all of explanatory

---

[19] Whether it was considered independent of space is not evident from any purely natural-philosophical discussion, although many seventeenth-century natural philosophers conceived of immortal souls as purely spiritual non-spatial entities which persisted in time. On the other hand, something that was purely spatial, but not temporal, such as a geometrical figure, would generally speaking not be treated as really existing, but rather as an abstraction, in that endurance seems to be tied up with existence in a fundamental way, although even here there are exceptions, with Malebranche, an arch-mechanist in many respects, treating geometrical figures as independently existing archetypes that persist outside time.

[20] See Graeme Hunter, 'The Fate of Thomas Hobbes', *Studia Leibnitiana* 21 (1989), 5–20.

[21] See e.g. Boyle's account in his *Sceptical Chemist*: Boyle, *Works*, i. 544.

success, however, it is crucial in both cases to attempt to mitigate the problem from the other end at the same time, for example by treating macroscopic qualitative differences as psychic additions of the perceiving mind. In other words, what one has got to do is to reduce the range of the *explanandum* radically. This is a very problematic exercise for, on the face of it, it is ad hoc and question-begging. Tailoring the *explanandum* to fit the *explanans* is, however, crucial to this kind of enterprise and, as we shall see, it is one of the more problematic aspects of the reductionist programme that mechanism engages in at the level of matter theory.

## GASSENDI AND THE LEGITIMACY OF ATOMISM

Many of the corpuscularian natural philosophies of the seventeenth century were presented as largely *sui generis*, rejecting any connection to earlier versions of corpuscularianism, either because of the unwelcome materialist connotations of these earlier forms (Boyle), or because they were conceived to be doing something different (Beeckman and Descartes). But there was one influential strand of corpuscularianism that took the form of a revival of ancient atomism. The atomist accounts of Democritus, Leucippos, Epicurus, and Lucretius were familiar to Renaissance and early-modern thinkers, although they were known, with the exception of Lucretius (whose *De rerum natura* had been in circulation as early as 1473), second-hand through the accounts in Aristotle, Diogenes Laertius, Plutarch, Sextus Empiricus, and Cicero. Epicurean atomism—the most considered form of the doctrine—was widely condemned as a form of atheism throughout late antiquity, the Middle Ages, and the Renaissance, and had been considered to be profoundly anti-Christian by almost all commentators.[22] Its offences against religion and good sense were legion: polytheism, the denial of creation and divine providence, the assertion of the infinite number of and eternity of atoms, mortalism, the denial of incorporeal reality, the assertion of the infinite extent of the universe and the plurality of worlds, the formative role it gives to chance in the formation of the world, the naturalistic construal of the first cause, the rejection of teleology, its perceived determinism, and finally its hedonistic ethics.[23] Its core natural-philosophical credentials were widely believed to have been destroyed by Aristotle's arguments against the Democritean version of partless atoms. If corpuscularianism—whatever the details—was to be substituted for Aristotelian natural philosophy, there were some philosophers at least who believed that the first task was to secure its credentials as a legitimate way of pursuing natural philosophy. The most concerted attempt along these lines was that of Gassendi.

It is important to note from the outset that, although Gassendi's natural philosophy takes the form of a systematic matter theory—with Cartesianism it was one of the two great mechanist systems of the second half of the seventeenth century—he came to natural philosophy via a very different route from Descartes, through humanist studies, and his approach could not be more different from that of Descartes. One of his prime concerns was to build up detailed historical evidence for his natural-philosophical position, something wholly alien to Descartes' approach. His aim was to establish that atomism had been the pre-eminent natural-philosophical tradition in antiquity, and to show in detail how this had been obscured by a combination of slander and mistaken criticisms, mainly at the hands of Aristotle.

This project has precedents in both religious and earlier natural-philosophical disputes over historical origins. The sixteenth and seventeenth centuries were a time of interdenominational rivalry, and a time of questioning of the legitimacy of doctrines and practices within particular denominations. By far the most important lines along which such battles were fought were historical ones. In 1588, for example, the first volume of Cardinal Caesar Baronius' massive *Annales ecclesiastici* appeared, in which the author, who had unparalleled access to the resources of the Vatican libraries, set out on his task of arranging annals of the documents and citations of the Roman Church 'from the creation of the world to the present', a work that reached thirteen folio volumes at his death in 1607. Isaac Casaubon was one of the first to respond in detail,[24] and in the 1620s Archbishop Laud, realizing that it was crucial for the Protestant Church to answer this work if it was to establish its legitimacy, was pressing both Isaac's son Meric and Gerard Vossius to continue the work, and Protestant scholars were still undertaking responses into the 1650s. This was a high-profile dispute, but vindication through origins and history was not confined to such religious debates. In 1581, Patrizi had mounted a defence of Platonism in his *Discussionum Peripateticarum* which took the form of an enquiry into the origins of philosophy and philosophical dispute, offering a detailed, highly destructive investigation of Aristotle's behaviour towards his predecessors and contemporaries, which bore close parallels to the subsequent sectarian disputes over the origins of the Church. Bacon continued this line of attack and, while he singled Aristotle out, he extended his criticism to Plato and to the whole tradition of ancient thought, with an exception being made only for Democritus. The tracing of movements back to their origins to legitimate or expose them was not, then, confined to religious controversies, but rather it was a general feature of humanistic discourse, and those who came from this background, notably Patrizi, Bacon, and Gassendi, found this a natural way of engaging natural philosophy. The idea was to show up errors and falsifications in the other side so that gradually the legitimacy of a religious or philosophical tradition was established. Gassendi's claim was that such a process reveals atomism, not Aristotelianism, to be the most viable natural-philosophical system, and as a consequence it was atomism that was the appropriate partner for Christianity.

Gassendi's interest in the Greek atomists was not initially a natural-philosophical one. In Book 1 of his *Exercitationes*, published in 1624, he had criticized Aristotle for transforming philosophy into mere disputation, but it was not until two years later that he developed an interest in Epicurus, and it was not until his meeting with Beeckman in 1629 that he extended his research to include Epicurean natural

---

[24] Casaubon's response was published in the year of his death: Isaac Casaubon, *De rebus sacris et ecclesiasticis Exercitationes xvi* (London, 1614). See the discussion in Spiller, *'Concerning Natural Philosophy'*, 2–4.

philosophy.[25] Gassendi's patron, Peiresc, had been engaged in a project of 'universal history' whereby the humanist methods of rediscovery of ancient Greece and Rome had been extended to all cultures, both ancient Near-Eastern cultures (Scaliger) and the history of France (Pasquier), and Peiresc himself had been instrumental in introducing epigraphy and numismatics into the resources for assessment of historical evidence. Peiresc—who moved with ease from questions of verification of documentary accounts of historical events into the natural-historical study of stones, minerals, plants, and animals—evidently encouraged Gassendi because he saw the recovery of Epicureanism as a contribution towards the humanist goal of reconstructing the history of the ancient world.[26]

Unlike many of his contemporaries, who confined their criticism of Aristotle to his natural philosophy, Gassendi engaged Aristotelianism as a comprehensive system and set out to replace it with something which, he tried to show, works at the same level of comprehension, namely atomism, although it is relevant here that his project of replacing Aristotelianism with Epicureanism effectively began in the mid-1620s, before he took an interest in natural philosophy.[27] Once he had developed this interest, however, atomism came to serve not just as an alternative foundation for natural philosophy but as an alternative foundation for the whole of knowledge, something that might be seen as being on a par, at the level of ambition, with the fifteenth- and sixteenth-century Neoplatonist systems. And like sixteenth-century Neoplatonists such as Patrizi, who tried to highlight original errors in Aristotle's rejection of his predecessors, so too Gassendi (who was almost certainly influenced in his early *Exercitationes* by Patrizi's *Discussionum Peripateticarum*[28]) believed that atomism could be vindicated fully only if the original Aristotelian arguments against the existence of atoms could be met in detail. This required the establishment of Epicurean doctrine on the basis of reliable texts and a contextual understanding of what was at stake in the disputes between Aristotle and various atomists. On the other hand, a contextual understanding quickly reveals what critics of Epicureanism had consistently pointed to as one of the aspects of atomist philosophy most at odds with Christian teaching: its 'atheism'. Epicurean natural philosophy ultimately has an ethical motivation: unless we study physics we will be subject to delusions about the role of the gods in the ordering of the world and about the afterlife. We need to grasp the basic structure of the world if we are to be happy. On this conception, knowledge of the natural world is not an end in itself but a means to an end: and that

[25] See Bernard Rochot, *Les Travaux de Gassendi sur Epicure et sur l'atomisme, 1619–1658* (Paris, 1944), 34–41. The meeting is described in Isaac Beeckman, *Journal tenu par Isaac Beeckman de 1604 à 1634*, ed. Cornelius de Waard (4 vols, The Hague, 1939–53), iii. 123–4.

[26] The case is made in Lynn Sumida Joy, *Gassendi the Atomist: Advocate of History in an Age of Science* (Cambridge, 1987), 43.

[27] This pre-natural-philosophy version of project has parallels with Lipsius' attempt to replace Aristotelianism with Stoicism, although Lipsius provided a defence of Stoic natural philosophy in his *Physiologiae Stoicorum Libri Tres* (Antwerp, 1604). On Gassendi's move to rehabilitate Epicureanism in the 1620s, see Margaret J. Osler, *Divine Will and the Mechanical Philosophy: Gassendi and Descartes on Contingency and Necessity in the Created World* (Cambridge, 1994), ch. 2.

[28] See Rochot's introduction to Pierre Gassendi, *Dissertations en forme de paradoxes contre les Aristoteliciens*, ed. and trans. Bernard Rochot (Paris, 1959), xi.

end is freedom from unwarranted fears, something to be achieved through a genuine understanding of how natural processes affect us.

Epicurus starts from three basic premises. He puts them this way:

*First* that nothing comes into being out of what is not. For in that case everything would come into being out of everything, with no need for seeds. [*Second*], if that which disappears were destroyed into what is not, all things would have perished, for lack of that into which they dissolved. [*Third*], the totality of things was always such as it is now, and always will be since there is nothing into which it changes, and since besides the totality there is nothing which could pass into it and produce the change.[29]

It was a commonplace of Greek thought that the world could not have been created from nothing, and so what there was in the world must have always been there. Epicurus wanted not just to claim that no matter comes into existence, however, but also that no new kinds of things come into existence. The phrase 'with no need for seeds' means that, if there were the sudden appearance of new species then there wouldn't be any permanent and individualized species of things: if anything could be generated from anything, and more specifically if something could be generated from something unlike itself, then there would be no stability of species. He concluded from this that only like can generate like. The second premiss, that nothing can go out of existence, rests on the a priori argument that if things could go out of existence, and if, by the first argument, nothing new came into existence, and finally if the world had no beginning, then everything would have gone out of existence by now. The third premiss is that the sum of things must always be the same. In one interpretation, this simply follows from the other two, for if nothing comes into existence and nothing goes out of existence, the contents of the universe remain the same. But Epicurus' third premiss is intended to go further. He wanted to infer from this that any explanation of things that holds now has been and always will be valid. And this explanation, in Epicurus' view, must be in terms of atomism, because that is where the fundamental continuity lies.

Epicurus took the view, *contra* Plato and Aristotle, that unchanging reality does not lie either beyond or behind the sensible world, but rather in it, at the microscopic level. There is a level of the sensible world itself which provides a reference point for understanding its changes. The Epicurean universe consisted of atoms and the void, nothing else. Atoms themselves are constitutive of matter: they are space full of matter, and, because they are by definition full, contain no empty space within themselves. Sensible bodies are compounds of atoms and the void. Atoms have size but they are too small to be seen. They also have shape, but at least some atomists, such as Lucretius, argued that there are only a finite number of shapes, on the grounds that if the number of possible shapes were infinite we should have to admit that there may be infinitely large bodies. Finally, they also have weight, but since the matter of which they are constituted is uniform, their weight will be directly proportional to their size, and hence will not be a fundamental property. Weight was measured from earliest antiquity using a balance, and what happens when we measure weight using a

---

[29] *Letter to Herodotus*: Long and Sedley, *The Hellenistic Philosophers*: ii. 18 [text]/i. 25 [trans.].

balance is that the heavier side descends and the lighter side rises. Consequently it is natural to assume that atoms will move downwards in a void unless they are hindered in some way, and Epicurus and atomists after him did assume this.[30]

On the Epicurean picture, all physical processes can be explained by means of the shape, size, weight, and direction of motion of atoms, and nothing else should be invoked. But in fact there is one other kind of thing introduced, the 'swerve' (*parenklisis*). The downward motion of atoms is very fast but of uniform speed, Epicurus tells us. But if atoms were completely unimpeded then they would be carried vertically downwards by their weight, all at the same uniform speed, and in these circumstances they would never meet. Consequently no worlds would ever have been formed out of the original atomic rain. But worlds do in fact exist. The explanation for this cannot lie in a variation in atomic speeds for Epicurus, because on his account heavy bodies do not fall faster than lighter ones, as Aristotle and others maintained. If the speed of atoms does not vary, Epicurus argued, the only conclusion we can come to is that the atoms cannot all have been constantly moving directly downwards. It is here that he introduced what he referred to as a minute swerve of atoms in the atomic rain, a slight deviation from the original path. This swerve is a rare, random event, brought in as an extra hypothesis to save the phenomena. Once a swerve has occurred, the swerving atom will collide with other atoms and a third type of atomic motion will be set up: the atoms will be jolted from their downward paths by collisions from all sides. It is, then, the swerve of atoms that builds into the universe an element of indeterminacy: the movements of an atom, and therefore any effects of its movement, are not entirely predictable. It gives rise to a third kind of force affecting atoms other than their downward uniform motion caused by their weight, and the swerve itself. This third kind of motion Epicurus referred to as the 'blows' or impacts that arise when atoms collide. Such impacts particularly affect light atoms, and if a light atom is trapped between two heavy ones and they collide, it can be driven in an upwards direction.

Epicureanism offered three main natural-philosophical challenges: indivisibility, materialism, and determinism. Gassendi's responses to these are crucial to his defence of atomism. The indivisibility objection was an especially difficult problem, and derived from Aristotle. In Book Δ of the *Physics*, Aristotle called into question the very idea of a body without parts. The argument is that a thing without parts can only move incidentally, and cannot move considered by itself. First he shows that there is a real distinction between the movement of parts considered by themselves, and their movements considered in relation to the motion of the whole. If we consider the case of a wheel rolling along a surface, for example, then we can see that there is a difference in the motions of the parts near the centre, the parts on the rim, and the whole, so there is not just one movement but several. Bearing this distinction in mind, consider a man sitting in a moving boat. A partless thing can move relatively, but it cannot move considered in its own right. For imagine two equal adjacent spaces, one lying between points *A* and *B*, and the other between *B* and *C*, and consider a body occupying the space *AB* which moves to occupy the space *BC*. At the time at which

---

[30] See Long and Sedley, *The Hellenistic Philosophers*: i. 46–52, and ii. 41–9, on atomic motion. See also ch. 7 of Furley, *Cosmic Problems*.

the motion occurs, there are three possibilities: the body is partly in *AB* and partly in *BC*, it is at *AB*, or it is at *BC*. The atomist cannot accept the first possibility because if the body were partly in one space and partly in another then it would clearly have parts. But if it were at *AB* it would not be moving but at rest, and if it were at *BC* it would not be moving but 'would have moved'.

There are two ways one might deal with this argument, and Epicurus seems to have urged both.[31] The first is to concede that the atom is theoretically divisible, but to hold onto the claim that it is physically indivisible. Epicurus did this, and it is the core of Gassendi's response. Before we turn to this, however, it is important to realize that Aristotle's objection requires a little more. What Aristotle's argument, if successful, shows is that an indivisible body could not move except on the supposition that time, motion, and extension are themselves composed of indivisible units; and he claimed to have demonstrated the impossibility of this. Epicurus seems to have accepted the conclusion that all these things must be composed of indivisibles if any are, and moreover he seems to have been happy to accept that they were in fact composed of indivisibles. That is to say, he seems to have accepted that not only were there atoms of matter (in the sense of smallest amounts of matter), but also atoms of time, atoms of space, and atoms of motion.[32] On this account, there are indivisible units of motion and indivisible units of space and time, such that one unit of motion involves traversing one unit of space in one unit of time; and in this case (he agreed with Aristotle) it is never true to say 'it is moving' but only 'it has moved'. Accepting Aristotle's contention that faster and slower motion entails the divisibility of time and distance, he developed the theory that there are no *real* differences in speed, and undertook to explain away the apparent differences in the speeds of visible moving bodies. The upshot is that it is only compounds—visible bodies made up from atoms—that exhibit differences in speed. The question is how these differences are to be explained, if the atoms that compose these compounds all move with the same speed. All compounds, in Epicurean theory, are composed of aggregates of atoms which jostle continually with one another in never-ceasing motion. A compound will move if all its component atoms undergo a net motion in the same direction over a period of time. When we consider those periods of time that are too small to be perceived, namely the indivisible units of time distinguishable only in thought, the atoms in a compound must be supposed to be moving in every direction, as a result of collisions with each other. The motion of a compound is the overall tendency of its component atoms taken over a continuous period of time, that is, a multiple, large enough to be perceived, of indivisible units of time.[33]

---

[31] There are other possibilities which I shall not discuss: see e.g. the discussion of 'minimal parts' in David Konstan, 'Problems in Epicurean Physics', *Isis* 70 (1979), 394–418.

[32] The issues raised here and complex and go well beyond our present concerns: for details of the relevant disputes in antiquity see Richard Sorabji, *Time, Creation and the Continuum: Theories in Antiquity and the Early Middle Ages* (London, 1983), idem, *Matter, Space and Motion: Theories in Antiquity and Their Sequel* (London, 1988), and Michael J. White, *The Continuous and the Discrete: Ancient Physical Theories from a Contemporary Perspective* (Oxford, 1992).

[33] Walter Charleton, Gassendi's English expositor, sets out these these doctrines in modern form in Book 3, ch. 9 of his *Physiologia Epicuro-Gassendo-Charltoniana.*

This kind of approach is open to Epicurus because he wants to explain differences at the macroscopic level in terms of the size, shape, and direction of motion of atoms, so it does not matter that they all travel at the same speed. But it is not open to Gassendi, because he does want to invoke differences in speed at a fundamental level. This is an indispensable part of the mechanization of atomism. It leaves Gassendi with the strategy of making a sharp distinction between physical and geometrical atomism. The *locus classicus* for this question in Gassendi is the problem of whether geometrical points have parts.[34]

This problem is traditionally one about the point at which lines intersect, for example whether an indivisible point can be the extremity of more than one line, or the intersection of lines, and it raises the fundamental issue of whether continuous magnitudes such as lines are composed of points, and if so, why and how the line would not then cease to be a continuous magnitude and become a discontinuous one. The specific version of the problem to which Gassendi addressed himself was posed by Jean-Baptiste Poysson, a French lawyer, to a number of correspondents, including Mersenne. It was whether an extended magnitude could on some occasions be treated as a genuinely mathematical point, that is, as indivisible.[35] Gassendi's first response[36] was somewhat unsatisfactory, and although he argued that sensible magnitudes of physical bodies cannot be compared with geometrical points (which Euclid explicitly defines as things that have no parts), he did occasionally run together geometrical and physical questions in the letter.[37] Nevertheless, the thrust of his argument is clear: one cannot expect the same kind of demonstration to apply to sensible physical questions and a priori mathematical ones,[38] a conclusion that accords perfectly with Aristotle's division of the sciences. The approach is borne out in Gassendi's treatment of atomic collisions, where his concern was less with kinematics as with providing an account of why bodies are deflected in oblique collisions, which he explained in terms of the fibres on one side of the body being touched first, which sets up a disequilibrium in the body, which in turn causes it to roll.[39] Mathematics deals with fictions—or, in Aristotelian terms, abstractions—whereas sensible things are real. In this first response, Gassendi did not have access to the replies of Mersenne's

---

[34] See Joy, *Gassendi the Atomist*, ch. 5, whose account guides my discussion in what follows. It is of interest that this problem, in slightly different versions, was the first recorded natural-philosophical/mathematical problem to have exercised Descartes and the first to have exercised Newton. Descartes met Beeckman in November 1618 when he asked Beeckman to translate this problem, which was posted on a placard, from Flemish for him: see Adrien Baillet, *La Vie de Monsieur Descartes* (2 vols, Paris, 1691), i. 43, and Gaukroger, *Descartes, An Intellectual Biography*, 68–9. Newton opens his early *Questiones* (1664) with the question 'Whither it be mathematicall points: or Mathematicall points & parts: or a simple entity before division indistinct: or individualls i.e. Atoms': J. E. McGuire and Martin Tamny, eds, *Certain Philosophical Questions: Newton's Trinity Notebook* (Cambridge, 1983), 336.

[35] See Mersenne, *Correspondance*, v. 285.

[36] Gassendi to Mersenne, 2 November 1635: Mersenne, *Correspondance*, v. 444–53.

[37] e.g. in his treatment of a sphere touching a plane surface: see Joy, *Gassendi the Atomist*, 87–8. More generally, on the problem of the continuum and its parts in the early-modern era, see Thomas Holden, *The Architecture of Matter: Galileo to Kant* (Oxford, 2004).

[38] Mersenne, *Correspondance*, v. 450.        [39] Gassendi, *Opera*, i. 360–1.

other correspondents, and he was moved to continue the debate when he had seen them. Four parties to the debate discussed the problem in terms of geometrical optics: Mersenne himself; Ismael Boulliau, a pro-Copernican writer on optics, astronomy, and mathematics; Jean-Baptiste Morin, physician, astronomer, astrologer, and anti-Copernican, anti-atomist natural philosopher; and Christophe Villiers, physician and chemist. Villiers dealt with the case of reflection of light by a plane mirror, but the other three concentrated on the case of a parabolic mirror reflecting light rays to a single focal point.[40] This focus is indeed a single point, and the geometry determines it as a mathematical point, yet it clearly has multiple rays converging on it. In other words, it is identifiable both geometrically and sensibly, the first treating it as a genuine point, the second as a discontinuous magnitude. These responses were designed to show that the situation described by Poysson does in fact occur, without concerning themselves about the discrepancy between continuous and discontinuous magnitudes.

Gassendi's second letter to Mersenne was written after he had seen some of the other responses,[41] including those of Mersenne and Boulliau, and he objected to what he saw as the drawing of mathematical conclusions from optics. The objection can perhaps best be put as saying that mathematical demonstrations of the properties of physical points and lines are not demonstrations of these lines per se but only under particular descriptions, to the extent that they satisfy the requirements of mathematical points and lines. The error consists in then treating the demonstration as if it were concerned with the physical points and lines per se. He applied the same considerations to astronomy, in particular to the controversy over Copernicanism, where he was unwilling to allow mathematical accounts anything more than the status of hypotheses, compatible with several different physical interpretations. 'Points, lines, and surfaces', he told Mersenne, 'are mere hypotheses . . . constructed by mathematicians.'[42] But it is not just that we should be circumspect about what mathematics can tell us about sensible things. We should also be circumspect about the relevance of the behaviour of sensible things to mathematics, for Mersenne and Boulliau treated light as if it were something incorporeal, in order to deal with it mathematically.[43]

It will be clear from Gassendi's response that his concern was not to understand how a quantitative treatment of physical phenomena might be possible, but rather to deny that mathematical arguments about the impossibility of ultimately discontinuous magnitudes have any application in the case of physical entities. 'It is not permitted,' he tells us in the *Syntagma*, 'to transfer into Physics something abstractly demonstrated in Geometry.'[44] Indeed, Gassendi is in effect prepared to cut off avenues of quantification to protect physically indivisible atoms. Yet this physical

---

[40] Mersenne had already discussed the optics of parabolic mirrors in detail in his *Quaestiones celeberrimae in Genesim* (Paris, 1623), cols. 513–15.

[41] Gassendi to Mersenne, 13 December 1635: Mersenne, *Correspondance*, v. 532–7.

[42] Ibid. 534. Gassendi does believe there are physical grounds for preferring a heliocentric theory, such as the retrogression of Mercury, Venus, Mars, Jupiter, and Saturn (*Opera*, iii. 515–16), and he appears to take the greater simplicity of heliocentric explanations as a mark in favour of their truth (ibid. 506).

[43] Mersenne, *Correspondance*, v. 534–5.     [44] Gassendi, *Opera*, i. 265.

indivisibility is not established or even defended in any of these arguments: it is simply asserted. In fact, as Descartes would show, virtually the whole range of benefits that corpuscularian matter theory brings can be accommodated without the notion of physical indivisibility if one gives up the notion of a void, for in Cartesian matter theory, corpuscles typically come in two definite sizes, with smaller pieces of no lower size limit and indeterminate shape filling the interstices between these.[45] The upshot of this is that, instead of moving in a void, the corpuscles move in a fluid. There are, of course, some initial disadvantages of this model, the most notable being how to account for the apparent production of vacua by lowering pressure. But there are also some initial advantages, such as the ability to avoid cases where physical influence seems to be transmitted other than by contact, especially in the case of the planetary motions.

The second issue, that of materialism, is one that traditionally dogged the acceptance of atomism. We need to distinguish between Democritean atomism and that of Epicurus on this question.[46] Democritus is an eliminativist: all that exists in the world is atoms and the void, and his view is that these are all we need to concern ourselves with. The macroscopic bodies that these make up are not real in their own right: only their atomic components are real. Correlatively, the distinctive qualities of atoms, such as their size, shape, and weight, are real, but the distinctive qualities of macroscopic bodies, such as colour, sweetness, bitterness, heat, and cold were objects of belief only. Epicurus, by contrast, construed, macroscopic bodies made of atoms, 'compounds', as real in their own right, despite the fact that, unlike atoms, they are not permanent. He also treated their properties as being real, because they satisfy a sensory criterion of existence.[47] The Democritean view that such qualities are unreal is contradicted by the evidence of the senses. We taste what is sweet, we feel cold, and so on. Therefore sweetness and cold are just as real as atoms. This view is quite distinctive, rejecting as it does both Democritus' reductionism but also the essentialist reductionism of the Platonist and Aristotelian doctrines that changing realities could not exist.

---

[45] See e.g. ch. 6 of *Le Monde*: Descartes, *Œuvres*, x. 31–6.

[46] See David Furley, 'Democritus and Epicurus on Sensible Qualities', in Jacques Brunschwig and Martha C. Nussbaum, eds, *Passions and Perceptions* (Cambridge, 1993), 72–94.

[47] See Long and Sedley, *The Hellenistic Philosophers*, i. 78–101/ii. 83–103. Sensation is in fact just the first criterion, although by far the most important. The second criterion is provided by general concepts or preconceptions, and it is the repeated experiences preserved by memory that give rise to these preconceptions, which make possible the use of language: when we hear the word 'man', for example, we have a preconception of the kind of object to which the name refers. The preconceptions or general concepts thus classify experiences and fix the limits of variation. Since our general notions merely register the similarities and differences found in immediate experience, they are themselves 'true' and may be used as criteria. Thus Epicurus sets up a correspondence among words, concepts, and the data of experience without invoking Platonic Ideas or Aristotelian essences and accidents. There is also a third criterion: feelings. All sensations are feelings in the sense of experiences, but when Epicurus talks of feelings as a criterion he refers to pleasure and pain. Generally, the basic sensations are our guides to the existence of the objects sensed; the general concepts or preconceptions help us to describe our sensations properly and to formulate correct propositions; the feelings of pleasure and pain are the criteria of how we should act.

The evidence of the senses plays a similarly determining role in Gassendi, because

It is not the senses themselves but the intellect that makes the error; and when it makes a mistake, it is not the fault of the senses but of the intellect, whose responsibility it is as the higher and dominant faculty before it pronounced what a thing is like, to inquire which of the different appearances produced in the senses (each one of them is the result of a necessity that produces them as they are) is in conformity with the thing.[48]

Just what Gassendi is claiming here is not clear, however. Aristotle had maintained that we have the sense organs we do because they naturally display to us the nature of the world, and a sense organ functioning normally under optimal conditions cannot mislead, and is automatically veridical.[49] Descartes, by contrast, maintained that 'the proper purpose of sensory perceptions given me by nature is simply to inform the mind of what is beneficial or harmful for the mind/body composite'.[50] On this latter view, sense organs could not in themselves be reliable as a guide to how the world is because this is not their role: it is only when combined with and guided by the intellect that they can perform this role. Gassendi seems to be claiming on the one hand that the cognitive work is done by the intellect not by the senses. On the other hand, he needs some form of sensory infallibility for his more general argument to go through, yet if it is the intellect and not the senses that is doing the cognitive work, then the senses can hardly provide any cognitive guide, infallible or otherwise. He cannot have it both ways.

Closely tied up with the question of perception is the issue of what exactly it is that we grasp in cognition. Gassendi's view was that we grasp 'appearances', rather than the inner or essential natures of things, and I shall return briefly to this doctrine in the next chapter; for the moment, I want to keep the focus on materialism, by contrasting Epicurus' account of what our cognitive relation to the world is with that of Gassendi. For Epicurus, the soul is composed of atoms, 'especially fine atoms' which are able to interact sympathetically with the rest of the living organism.[51] As well as these atoms, however, what is needed, Lucretius explained,[52] is something 'finer still', which is able to convey the sense-bearing movements, namely pleasure and pain, first to the other soul atoms and then to the body. The Epicurean tradition, especially Lucretius, divided the soul into the non-rational part, *anima*, and the rational part, *animus*. *Anima* represents a materialized version of the Greek *psuchē* (soul), used in something like its Homeric sense of 'life', whereas *animus* represents a materialized version of *dianoia* (mind). Both are made up of all kinds of soul atoms, but the *animus* is localized in the chest whereas *anima* is suffused throughout the body, and hence mixed with coarser atoms. The soul, *anima*, is a material body, but since soul atoms

---

[48] Gassendi, *Opera*, i. 85; trans. in Pierre Gassendi, *The Selected Works of Pierre Gassendi*, trans. Craig Brush (New York, 1972), 345–6.

[49] See Irving Block, 'Truth and Error in Aristotle's Theory of Perception', *Philosophical Quarterly* 11 (1961), 1–9; and Stephen Gaukroger, 'Aristotle on the Function of Sense Perception', *Studies in History and Philosophy of Science* 12 (1981), 75–89.

[50] Descartes, *Œuvres*, vii. 83 (Meditation 6).

[51] Long and Sedley, *The Hellenistic Philosophers*, i. 65–6/ii. 64–5.

[52] Ibid. i. 67–8/ii. 69–70.

are unusually fine and round, they do not cling together. They need to be held in place by the larger and more tightly assembled atoms of the body. That is why, if the body is destroyed, the soul atoms cannot survive as a sentient compound: on the destruction of the body, the soul will fly apart into its separate components. Conversely, since in the first instance it is the soul atoms that are capable of feeling, if these atoms are dispersed, then there is no feeling left in the remaining parts of the body. Hence at death, when the soul atoms are scattered, the body loses all feeling. When one is alive, however, it is not just the soul that has feeling: the body also has the power to feel. Lucretius was particularly concerned to refute the view that it is not the eyes but the mind (*animus*) that sees: in a living organism, sense organs are inseparable from soul-body complexes.

This is the key to what happens in sense perception in Epicurus. Like all atomic complexes, the soul-body complex is continually involved in internal movement. New movements, originating from outside, are set up whenever anything strikes the body in such a way as to affect the *anima* atoms present in it. All such effects are both sensations and also feelings of pleasure and pain, but since individual atoms have no power to feel or sense, feelings and sensations will occur only when a soul atom is part of a larger organism.

Gassendi followed Epicurus in making the perceptual process one in which atoms collide with or push one another:

In the case of the external senses perceiving objects, a motion occurs when a *species* or quality of the sensible thing encounters the external organ, and it occurs also as the nerves pass on the effect of this to the interior of the brain, where the nerves terminate, or rather where they have their origin. Thus nerves filled with spirits can be thought of as bundles of rays of spirits, and rays of spirits of this kind, which stretch from the brain to the external sense organs, cannot be pressed or pushed in the slightest way without this resulting in the brain, to which the external sense organ is linked, being affected.[53]

Moreover, while his account of the perceiving mind initially runs along Aristotelian/ Thomist lines, he is also clearly guided by the Epicurean *animus*/*anima* division of the soul, although *animus* is now shorn of its corporeality. The heading of Part 3, Book 9, ch. 2 of the *Syntagma* tells us, in suitably Thomist terminology: 'The rational soul is an incorporeal substance created by God and infused into the body as a form that informs the body.'[54] But the soul more generally comprises two parts, an incorporeal rational soul (corresponding to *animus*) and a corporeal soul that regulates vegetative and sentient functions (corresponding to *anima*). In an elaborate account of the functioning and connections between these two souls,[55] Gassendi construed the latter as an intermediary between the rational soul and the body. He allowed a range of

---

[53] Gassendi, *Opera*, ii. 403. Note that Gassendi makes a number of revisions to the Epicurean account of the transmission of visual images. The *simulacra* that strike the eye are now translated from the 'skins' of objects into light rays, and he is at pains to accommodate the fact, learned from Kepler, that the retinal image in inverted (ibid. ii. 377).

[54] Ibid. ii. 440; cf. 466, where it is described as a substantial form. See Brundell, *Pierre Gassendi*, 91–8.

[55] Gassendi, *Opera*, ii. 425–46.

genuinely cognitive operations to animals, who, unlike humans, possess only a corporeal soul, and he took the fact that animals are able to perform operations that display rudimentary apprehension and judgement to indicate that the rational and corporeal faculties operate in tandem.[56]

The ease with which Gassendi could spiritualize the Epicurean *animus* is doubtless due to the fact that the *animus/anima* distinction was in effect a materialization of earlier doctrines in which the soul and the body are separate. But this materialization was not driven by purely physical considerations: it was motivated by ethical concerns. One of the principal aims of Epicurus' psychological theory was to deny the survival of the personality after death. Hence beliefs in a system of rewards and punishments as recompense for life on earth are without justification. Epicurean philosophy has the ultimate aim, an ethical aim, in a broad sense of that term, of removing anxiety. For Epicurus, most fear death because they believe it to be the end of all sensation, and as Lucretius argued at length, if, when we are dead, we have no sensation, then we are unaffected, and therefore there are no grounds for anxiety.[57] The ease with which Gassendi could switch the *animus/anima* distinction back to an incorporeal/corporeal distinction should not obscure the fact that to do so is to undermine the whole rationale of Epicureanism. As Torquatus, the spokesman for Epicureanism, put it in Cicero's *De finibus*:

Thus natural philosophy supplies courage in the face of death; resolution to resist the terrors of religion; peace of mind, for it removes all ignorance of the mysteries of nature; self-control, for it explains the nature of the desires and distinguishes their different kinds.[58]

Such concerns are not a dispensable part of the Epicurean package. They go to the heart of why one pursues natural philosophy in the first place. Indeed, although details of the ends vary somewhat, no Hellenistic philosopher pursued natural knowledge for its own end, and Gassendi himself looked beyond natural philosophy to the natural theology that provided it with its rationale. Nevertheless, what remains of Epicureanism in Gassendi's revival is something that the ancient Epicureans would have taken to have missed the whole point of the exercise, and Gassendi's process of rehabilitation renders Epicureanism an empty shell as far as a broader natural-philosophical culture is concerned. Gassendi may have been true to the Hellenistic ideal, but he was not true to the Epicurean one. It is not that ethics was not of importance in Gassendi's attachment to Epicureanism. Rather, this ethics repudiated the Epicurean ethical aim of 'life without fear' and reinstituted the Christian notions of fear, anxiety, and repentance.[59]

This bears on the third question, determinism. Sensing and evaluating sensations are not the only functions of the mind on the Epicurean account; it is also capable of initiating action. The most detailed Epicurean theory of the will and action that we

---

[56] Ibid. 451.     [57] Long and Sedley, *The Hellenistic Philosophers*, i. 149–54/ii. 154–9.
[58] Cicero, *De finibus*, 1. 19. 64.
[59] On Gassendi's ethics, see Lisa Tunick Sarasohn, 'The Ethical and Political Philosophy of Pierre Gassendi', *Journal of the History of Philosophy* 29 (1982), 239–60; and idem, 'Motion and Morality: Pierre Gassendi, Thomas Hobbes, and the Mechanical World-View', *Journal of the History of Ideas*, 46 (1985), 363–80.

have is that of Lucretius,[60] which is in effect an atomist version of the Aristotelian theory of action. Lucretius used the Aristotelian example of starting to walk. The mind first needs images of movement, which are derived from sensation. These strike the mind, says Lucretius, and decision arises thereby. The form of this decision is that the movement of the mind stirs the atoms of the *anima* and ultimately those of the body. Lucretius' point was that these images are a necessary condition for walking, not that they are sufficient: whether we act on the basis of the images before us, indeed whether we even choose to focus our attention on them and hence think about them at all, depends on what kind of person we are at the moment they are presented to us. Actions depends on character. The Epicureans generally were anxious to show that human action is not dependent on what they thought of as 'external causes', namely the blows of other atoms on our atoms, or on what they called 'internal necessity', namely the first arrangement of atoms at birth. But it is difficult to see how character is not a form of the internal necessity that the Epicureans sought to avoid. Even worse, it is difficult to see how the first arrangement of atoms at birth is not something determined by external causes. It has sometimes been thought that the original atomic swerve might be helpful here, but this is by definition something random and unpredictable, and if it were sufficient by itself to explain voluntary actions, then determinism would have been overcome at the expense of making actions purposeless and wholly indeterminate. Indeed, it illustrates the dilemma of the Epicurean version of determinism. There were just no resources within Epicureanism that enabled it to raise the requisite questions of intention and responsibility for action, with the result that it had great difficulty conceiving of anything other than complete determinism and complete randomness. Free action is not only not the same as random action, nor is it something that lies on the spectrum between determined action and random action: this is just the wrong place to be looking, yet it is unclear where else one could look on the Epicurean account.

Gassendi introduced two traditional Christian doctrines, providence and free will, into his revamped version of Epicureanism. Providence enters the picture at quite a fundamental level. If we ignore free will for the moment, then physical processes come down to interactions between atoms, where the only kind of interaction is collision. As we have seen, Epicurus believed that weight is the original cause of the motion of such atoms, which means that they all originally move downwards (at the same speed). Because atoms would never come into contact with one another in this state, the 'swerve' is introduced to explain how contact is possible. But the swerve remained one of the weakest ingredients in traditional Epicureanism, and no gloss on it ever removed from it the air of something completely ad hoc. There were two considerations that had to be dealt with in any natural-philosophical revision. First, atoms clearly have come into contact with one another and this required explanation, as Epicureans realized. Second, as Aristotle had pointed out, the idea that they all moved in the same absolute direction, namely 'downwards', made little sense in an Epicurean cosmos, where the space in which they move is infinite and in which there is no notion of natural place. Gassendi did away with the notion of a natural

[60] Long and Sedley, *The Hellenistic Philosophers*, i. 105–6/ii. 110–12.

direction, and endowed atoms with different motions (and other qualities) at the point of creation, the motions chosen so that the resulting structure of, and processes in, the cosmos follow a divine plan:

It may be supposed that the individual atoms received from God as he created them their corpulence, or dimensions, however small, and their shapes in ineffable variety, and likewise they received the capacity [*vis*] requisite to moving, to imparting motion to others, to rolling about, and consequently the capacity to disentangle themselves, to leap away, to knock against other atoms, to turn them away, to move away from them, and similarly the capacity to take hold of each other, to attach themselves to each other, to join together, to bind each other fast, and the like, all this to the degree that he foresaw would be necessary for every purpose and effect that he destined them for.[61]

This replacement of chance by providence might seem to reverse the direction of causation in the universe, as the physical behaviour of bodies is now goal-directed, rather than being the blind outcome of chance events, some 'fortuitous concourse of atoms', as Cicero put it.[62] But the goal-directedness is not the same as that we find in Aristotelian natural philosophy. There is an intrinsic goal-directedness in the natural behaviour of bodies in the Aristotelian account: acorns grow into oak trees because that is in the nature of acorns, and they fall to the ground when released from constraints because that is in their nature as heavy bodies. But one could rely on intrinsic natures to too great an extent, as Renaissance naturalism demonstrated, and part of the motivation behind mechanism, as we have seen, is the removal of such natures. To this extent, Gassendi was within the mechanist tradition. Generally speaking, he treated goal-directedness as extrinsic: there is no end or goal internal to individual atoms that causes them to behave in the way they do. Indeed, at the level of the behaviour of individual atoms, an Epicurean and a Gassendean version of our universe would be indistinguishable. Gassendi's version has the distinct advantage that it accounts for the organized complexity that we find in the natural world, whereas it is a mystery how this comes about on the Epicurean picture, unless, as Lucretius urged, there is an infinity of worlds, in which case some of these will have organized complexity arising purely by chance, and we simply inhabit one of these. But the idea of an infinity of worlds was widely condemned,[63] and in any case, as far as Gassendi was concerned, there was a perfectly good explanation available, providence, which avoided the problems of Aristotelian intrinsic goals that had encouraged Renaissance naturalism, and which connected natural philosophy directly with natural theology, in that the study of natural philosophy was now *ipso facto* the study of God's providential design.

The trouble with providence is whether it leaves any room for free will, which Gassendi believed is a characteristic feature of the rational soul or intellect. Whereas the behaviour of inanimate things is determined by gravity/weight, and the behaviour of those things that possess only a vegetative/sensitive soul is determined by

---

[61] Gassendi, *Opera*, i. 280; trans. from Gassendi, *Selected Works*, trans. Brush, 400–1.

[62] Cicero, *De natura deorum*, Book 1, 24.

[63] See Steven J. Dick, *Plurality of Worlds: The Extraterrestrial Life Debate from Democritus to Kant* (Cambridge, 1982), ch. 2.

the 'generative faculty', the intellect, he tells us, 'by its own nature is flexible, so that having the truth as its object, it can judge one thing of an object at one time and another at another time, and it can consider different judgements to be true at different times.'[64] The trouble is what account we give of such flexibility. There seem to be two possibilities. First, we might make different judgements at different times because our judgements are random, unlike the deliveries of corporeal faculties, where the same information always provokes the same cognitive outcome. Clearly this is not what was meant, for if this were the case then, at least on the grounds of reliability, we would have good reason to prefer the corporeal faculties. Moreover, in a moral context, such a conception would be hopeless: rather than securing responsibility for action it would make free actions into random actions, by contrast with inflexible, but reliable, moral judgements. Second, we can say that the different judgements arise because they are judgements of different information. The reason we judge a thing one way on one occasion and in another way on another occasion is because we make these judgements relative to information, beliefs, background knowledge, and so on, and these change. If they are exactly the same, then to make a different judgement would be irrational, not a demonstration of free will. As Hobbes puts it in the *Short Tract on First Principles*, 'Hence appeares that the definition of a Free Agent, to be that, which, all things requisite to worke, being put, may worke, or not worke, implyes a contradiction.'[65] It is not of any help to reply to this kind of objection by pointing out that judgements of the same information may differ relative to contexts and interests which the agent is free to choose, for there is no dispute over whether the judgements may differ, but over what causes them to differ. Hobbes considered the contexts in which we evaluate things and the interests we bring to bear on them as being just as much caused by response to external agents as anything else.

Gassendi's Christianized Epicureanism was in the genre of Christianized Aristotelianism and Christianized Neoplatonism, and a good deal of the effort went into compromises and revisions that enabled systems that were in many respects disparate and contradictory to be reconciled. To some extent, this was a success and Gassendism vied successfully with Cartesianism as the dominant natural philosophy until the end of the seventeenth century.[66] But Gassendi does more violence to Epicureanism than the scholastics ever did to Aristotle, separating it from its central ethical rationale of a life without fear, and reinstituting the fear and anxiety that are the hallmark of early-modern Christianity.[67]

## BEECKMAN AND 'PHYSICO-MATHEMATICS'

Although it was Beeckman who turned Gassendi's interest in Epicureanism towards natural-philosophical questions, his approach was very different from the traditional

---

[64] Gassendi, *Opera*, ii. 824.

[65] Thomas Hobbes, *The Elements of Law*, ed. Ferdinand Tönnies (New York, 1969), 196.

[66] See Thomas M. Lennon, *The Battle of the Gods and Giants: The Legacies of Descartes and Gassendi, 1655–1715* (Princeton, 1993).

[67] See Delumeau, *Le Péché et la peur*.

atomism that Gassendi set out to renew, and his mechanism, unlike that of Gassendi, was motivated almost exclusively by considerations in mechanics. Gassendi prevaricated on the question of the inertness of matter, for example, telling us on the one hand that 'it is absurd to claim that matter is inert', but also that 'the view that atoms have a motive force or *impetus* is to be rejected', and finally that the question of whether matter is inert cannot be resolved by the human intellect.[68] Bloch has argued that we find a move towards an introduction of intrinsic causes, in the form of certain hylozoic and animist notions, in the wake of Gassendi's meeting with Hobbes in 1641, where Hobbes' own natural philosophy may well have alerted Gassendi to the dangers of leaving any goals out of nature.[69] On this issue, a micro-corpuscularianism such as Gassendi's, which derives primarily from atomist matter theory, stands in sharp contrast to one like Beeckman's, which derives from mechanics. Beeckman could not allow ambiguity on the question of the inertness of matter. He, Hobbes, and Descartes all used statics as their mechanical model, and the idea of active matter was completely alien to this discipline. Moreover, Gassendi's account of motion was a good deal less careful than his matter theory: he argued, for example, that celestial motions are 'uniform and perpetual, because of the circular form chosen by its author, according to which, lacking a beginning and an end, it can be uniform and perpetual'.[70] The Aristotelian idea that it was the 'beginning and end' of the motion that determined whether it required an extrinsic force for its maintenance rests on a conception of motion alien to seventeenth-century kinematics, and no one who came to mechanism via mechanics could countenance this notion.

Beeckman was the first person in Europe to pursue consistently and in detail the idea of a micro-mechanical approach to natural philosophy, combining corpuscularianism with the practical-mathematical tradition deriving from the Alexandrians. His corpuscularianism derived in the first instance primarily from engineers such as Hero of Alexandria and the Roman architect Vitruvius, rather than from philosophical sources such as Lucretius, although the ancient atomist tradition inevitably played some role in his thinking.[71] One of his first applications of corpuscularianism was in acoustics and harmonic theory, at a time when the prevailing accounts were arithmetical or geometrical. During the 1610s, he developed a corpuscular theory of sound and a pulsation theory of its transmission, accounting for consonance in terms of sound 'globules' emitted intermittently from a vibrating string, so that the periods of sound and silence coincided only when notes of the same pitch were sounded together simultaneously, the two periods becoming less regular in relation to one another as the intervals between the two notes moved across the spectrum from consonance to dissonance.[72] At the same time, he was the first to offer a geometrical proof of the inverse proportionality between string length and frequency. This combination of

[68] Gassendi, *Opera*, iii; i. 280; i. 275 respectively. See Antonio Clericuzio, 'Gassendi, Charleton and Boyle on Matter and Motion', in Christoph Lüthy, John E. Murdoch, and William R. Newman, eds., *Late Medieval and Early Modern Corpuscular Matter Theories* (Leiden, 2001), 467–82.

[69] Bloch, *La Philosophie de Gassendi*, 446–56.     [70] Gassendi, *Opera*, iii. 488.

[71] See Benedino Gemelli, *Isaac Beeckman: Atomista e lettore critico di Lucrezio* (Rome, 2002).

[72] See the discussion in H. Floris Cohen, *Quantifying Music* (Dordrecht, 1984), 116–61.

empirical and mathematical interests is characteristic of his approach. When he came to read Bacon in the early 1620s, for example, he was scathing about Bacon's claims that water could be transformed into air and that bodies always contract with a lowering of temperature (his practical experience in laying pipes and drains had taught him that ice has a greater volume than cold water),[73] but he also criticized Bacon for his inability to see a relation between mathematics and natural philosophy.[74]

Beeckman conceived of a redescription of all natural phenomena in terms of the shape, size, configuration, and motion of microscopic corpuscles, whose behaviour he modelled on the mechanical principles of macroscopic phenomena, in particular the behaviour of simple machines. In the second decade of the seventeenth century, he offered, on a first-hand basis, an approach to natural philosophy that went well beyond anything devised by any of his contemporaries in this respect. He had learned his skills primarily helping his father in the laying of water conduits for breweries, but he also had a medical degree, although he never practised. Well versed in the statical and optical works of Stevin, and Rudolph and Willebrord Snel, from 1618 onwards he made a living as an educational administrator, setting up a Collegium Mechanicum for craftsmen and scholars to study mechanics and its technological applications, and founding the first meteorological station in Europe in 1628.[75] He was the formative influence on Descartes, convincing him at the end of 1618 to take up natural philosophy and guiding his efforts in the direction of a mechanist micro-corpuscularianism. Yet Beeckman's natural-philosophical inquiries have a disorganized, almost random character, and although at the end of the 1620s he edited his notes on mechanics and cosmology with a view to organizing them into a book, he did not proceed with publication.[76]

Beeckman's natural philosophy appears in his daily journal, a commonplace book filled with questions ranging from embryology to celestial mechanics and from syllogistic to applied mathematics, all addressed in short entries rarely as much as a page in length. He prided himself on the spontaneous character of his entries, which he thought offered a more genuine insight into the questions posed than any prearranged programme of scholarship.[77] Rejecting Aristotelian and Neoplatonic notions of immaterial causes and agencies on the grounds that they were unintelligible and hence useless in natural philosophy,[78] he insisted that natural philosophy work in terms

---

[73] Beeckman, *Journal*, ii. 476.        [74] Ibid., iii. 51.

[75] The standard work on Beeckman is van Berkel, *Isaac Beeckman*. My account in this section draws extensively on Stephen Gaukroger and John Schuster, 'The Hydrostatic Paradox and the Origins of Cartesian Dynamics', *Studies in History and Philosophy of Science* 33 (2002): 535–72.

[76] Descartes, who was beginning to put together the material for *Le Monde* at this time and was evidently disconcerted to learn that Beeckman had a similar project in mind, directed a barrage of abuse against Beeckman, calling into question his abilities and his originality, and as a result Beeckman abandoned plans for the book. For the details of this episode, see Klaas van Berkel, 'Descartes' Debt to Beeckman', in Stephen Gaukroger, John Schuster, and John Sutton, eds, *Descartes' Natural Philosophy* (London, 2000), 46–59. The book did appear posthumously, however, edited by his brother Abraham, as Isaac Beeckman, *Mathematicao-physicarum meditationum, quaestionum, solutionum centuria* (Utrecht, 1644).

[77] Beeckman, *Journal*, ii. 99.        [78] Ibid., i. 25.

of concrete, imaginable things and processes, rather than abstract entities.[79] It was significant in Beeckman's view that no one who had to deal with the practical workings of machines would appeal to teleological processes, occult virtues, or immaterial causes to account for the functioning of a simple mechanical device. Explanations in the mechanical arts rested on the appeal to a clear picture of the structure and interaction of the constitutive parts of the apparatus. As simple mechanical and hydrodynamical devices showed, only motion or pressure can produce the rearrangement of parts and hence produce work, and for theoretical purposes, the causes of motions and pressures are other motions and pressures.

What Beeckman was demanding in natural philosophy was the application of the criterion of meaningful communication between mechanical artisans: the appeal to a picturable or imaginable structure of parts whose motions are controlled within a putative theory of mechanics.[80] His central contention was that to talk about effects you must be able to imagine how they are produced, and the exemplar of this resides in the mechanical arts, where one can command nature at a macroscopic level. Beeckman's starting point was atomism. His atoms possess only the geometrical-mechanical properties of size, shape, and impenetrability, being absolutely hard, incompressible, and non-elastic.[81] Motion is conceived as a simple state of bodies, rather than an end-directed process which they undergo. Moreover, the possession of motion is not mediated by any internal moving force, *impetus*, or virtue. All other qualities, including the four elemental qualities of Aristotle, arise from the diverse ways in which various atomic structures constituting bodies impinge upon our sense organs, and he devoted much of his matter theory to devising a four-element theory within the assumptions of his atomic doctrine.[82] Besides countering traditional modes of explanation still very much alive in Aristotelianism and Galenic medicine, Beeckman's element theory allowed him to de-emphasize atoms as explanatory elements in certain contexts. This was important, because he was impressed by arguments showing the impossibility of rebound after collision of perfectly inelastic atoms, and because he had difficulty reconciling atomic theory with the phenomenon of elasticity.[83] Accordingly, he built his traditional elements out of congeries of atoms

[79] See Beeckman to Mersenne, 1 October 1629, *Correspondance de Mersenne*, ii. 283. Cf. the demands that Descartes was to place on mathematics and 'mathematical' natural philosophy in the latter portions of the *Regulae*, as well as his insistence on the 'figurate' representation of problems to be solved, both in mathematics and in optics and natural philosophy generally. On the latter see Dennis Sepper, 'Figuring Things Out: Figurate Problem-Solving in the Early Descartes', in S. Gaukroger, J. Schuster, and J. Sutton, eds, *Descartes' Natural Philosophy* (London, 2000), 228–48.

[80] These questions are set out in more detail in Gaukroger and Schuster, 'The Hydrostatic Paradox'.

[81] Nevertheless, he came to have qualms about elasticity, noting in a diary entry for August 1620 that atomism harboured the antinomy that atoms had to be both perfectly hard and perfectly elastic: *Journal*, ii. 100.

[82] Ibid. ii. 86, 96; cf. iii. 138. This kind of move was certainly not unprecedented. The move from (an innocuous form of) atomism to the four elements of Aristotle was standard procedure in the eclectic Aristotelian natural philosophy textbooks. See e.g. Johannes Magirus, *Physiologia peripatetica ex Aristotele eiusque interpretibus collecta* (Frankfurt, 1596).

[83] *Journal*, ii. 100–1.

and manipulated the elements as functional units of explanation,[84] without, however, explaining what structural features the congeries had that enabled them to possess the required property of elasticity that their constituent parts lacked.

Beeckman's importance lies in the fact that he was the first to seek to explain the behaviour of atoms by modelling them on the principles of mechanics. By 1613 or 1614 he had formulated a concept of continued motion holding for both rectilinear and curved motions. He insisted that motion, once imparted to a body, is maintained at the same speed, unless destroyed by external resistance. In the absence of external constraints there is no reason why the state of motion of the body should alter, and a stone thrown in a void will continue forever, because there is nothing causing its state of motion to change.[85] Combining his principle of continued motion with his atomism, Beeckman was led to conclude that the only possible mode of external constraint or resistance that can be exerted on a body undergoing such continued motion is corpuscular impact. Conversely, only corpuscular collision and transfer of motion can account for the initiation of motion in stationary bodies which have resisted the passage of moving bodies. In short, only the transfer of motion can account for change in the position, arrangement, and disposition of atoms, and hence it alone furnishes the principle of all natural change.[86]

Central to such a mechanics was the task of providing rules of collision specifying the outcomes of exchanges of motion on the atomic level.[87] Since Beeckman's atoms are perfectly inelastic, he formulated rules applicable to inelastic collisions. He measured the quantity of motion of corpuscles by taking the product of their quantity of matter and their speed. Significantly, Beeckman linked his measure of motion to a dynamic interpretation of the behaviour of the beam balance. He evaluated the effective force of a body on a beam balance by taking the product of its weight and the speed of its real or potential displacement, measured by the arc length swept out in unit times during real or imaginable motions of the beam. He was able to build up a set of rules of impact by combining certain intuitively symmetrical cases of collisions with the dictates of his proto-inertial principle and an implicit concept of the conservation of the directional quantity of motion in a system. His treatment of symmetrical cases of collision and his notion of the conservation of motion owed their form and their putative legitimacy to the model of the balance beam, interpreted in a dynamic rather than static fashion. His rules fall into two broad categories: cases in which one body is actually at rest prior to collision, and cases which are notionally reduced to the first category. A rudimentary concept of inertia and the stipulation

---

[84] *Journal*, iii. 31. Beeckman's theory of light provides a good example. He held light to be corporeal and to consist in the finest particles of elemental heat or fire. Because light can be reflected and refracted (to Beeckman refraction was a form of internal reflection), it cannot consist in isolated atoms; therefore, light, heat, and fire had to be conceived as second-order homogenous composites made up of numerous atoms and void space.

[85] Ibid. i. 24–5.

[86] Beeckman even tried to explain the centrifugal tendency of bodies moving in circular motion in resisting media as the result of the combination of circular inertia and differential resistance of the medium on different parts of the body. *Journal*, i. 253.

[87] See Appendix I in *Correspondance de Mersenne*, ii. 632–44, which includes de Waard's notes.

that only external impacts can change the state of motion of a body provide the keys to interpreting instances of the first category. The body at rest is a cause of the change of speed of the impacting body and it brings about this effect by absorbing some of the quantity of motion of the moving body. Beeckman invoked an implicit principle of the directional conservation of quantity of motion to control the actual transfer of motion. In each case the two bodies are conceived to move off together after collision at a speed calculated by distributing the quantity of motion of the impinging body over the combined masses of the two bodies. For example, in the simplest case, in which one body strikes an identical body at rest, 'each body will be moved twice as slowly as the first body was moved' and 'since the same *impetus* must sustain twice as much matter as before, they must proceed twice as slowly'. And he adds, drawing an analogy between this situation and that of the mechanics of simple machines, 'it is observed in all machines that a double weight raised by the same force which previously raised a single weight, ascends twice as slowly'.[88] Instances of the second category of collision are assessed in relation to the fundamental case of collision of equal speeds in opposite directions.[89] Being perfectly inelastic and hence lacking the capacity to deform and rebound, the two atoms annul each other's motion, leaving nothing remaining to be redistributed which could cause subsequent motion. This symmetrical case, which is also generalized to cases of equal and opposite quantities of motion arising from unequal bodies moving with compensating reciprocally proportional speeds, derives from a dynamical interpretation of the equilibrium conditions of simple machines. Instances in which the quantities of motion of the bodies are not equal are handled by annulling as much motion in the larger and/or faster moving body as the smaller and/or slower body possesses.[90] This in effect reduces the smaller and/or slower body to rest. The outcome of the collision is then calculated by distributing the remaining unannulled motion of the larger and/or swifter body over the combined mass of the two bodies.

Beeckman's commitment to a dynamical interpretation of the principles of simple machines and his belief in a correspondence between these principles and the rules of corpuscular collision run right throughout his work.[91] He consistently demanded a dynamical approach to statics, the theory of simple machines and mechanics in general, including hydrostatics. This dynamical approach inheres in a set of rules or principles about the motion or tendencies to motion of bodies, which may also be read into the behaviour of fundamental corpuscles and atoms. The controlling idea is that macroscopic phenomena be explained through reduction to corpuscular-mechanical models. Beeckman's journal offers hundreds of examples of this sort of enterprise. In many cases merely qualitative reports of phenomena are so reduced; but in other cases it is a question of quantitative representations of phenomena already described in the practical-mathematical disciplines, for example in his reading of laws of collision out of exemplary findings in the interpretation of simple machines.

Various aspects of Beeckman's programme guided subsequent mechanists. While only Descartes would explicitly deploy the technique of seeking a causal rationale for

---

[88] *Journal*, i. 265–6.     [89] Ibid. 266.     [90] Ibid.
[91] See, e.g. ibid. and iii. 133–4.

quantitatively described macroscopic phenemona at the micro-corpuscularian level, the general reduction to corpuscular-mechanical models is a feature of all subsequent corpuscularian programmes outside iatrochemistry and alchemy. And the idea that it is the corpuscular-mechanical models that embody the quantitative features of one's natural philosophy will guide foundational natural-philosophical programmes, making sure that these are what will be called upon to provide the ultimate explanatory tools.

## CORPUSCULARIANISM AND MECHANISM: HOBBES

Gassendi and Beeckman offered very different routes to mechanism, as we have seen. Gassendi's is a legitimatory programme that focuses on matter theory, whereas Beeckman's approach seems to come directly out of mechanics, which it attempts to transform into natural philosophy by fleshing it out in micro-corpuscularian terms. The crucial stage in mechanism comes with the rise of concerted attempts to integrate mechanics and matter theory into a consistent whole, at the same time offering the mechanism so devised as a complete theory of the cosmos, and it is the approaches of Hobbes, whose closest affinities are with Gassendi, and Descartes, whose closest affinities are with Beeckman, that bring out most clearly what is at issue here.

Hobbes is Gassendi's alter ego. He takes what is essentially the same basic natural philosophy but makes no attempt at all to Christianize it: quite the contrary, he has no hestitation in drawing out its materialist and deterministic consequences. The Gassendi circle, after Gassendi's death in 1655, nevertheless regarded Hobbes as the greatest living philosopher, and it was one of Gassendi's chief apologists, Sorbière, who oversaw the publication of Hobbes' Latin works in Europe.[92] But in England, although Gassendi had a number of advocates,[93] and was for example a key figure for Newton in the early stages of his thinking,[94] there can be little doubt that atomism of the kind that Gassendi tried to foster suffered to some extent through association with Hobbes.

From a purely natural-philosophical point of view, Gassendi's version of corpuscularianism imports revisions from outside, whereas Hobbes' version proceeds in the other direction, starting from natural-philosophical considerations and extrapolating to other areas. While Gassendi's revisions are designed to secure orthodoxy, Hobbes' extrapolations are designed to apply the same 'scientific' procedures to areas such as politics and morality as he follows in natural philosophy. There is some sense in which

[92] See Noel Malcolm, *Aspects of Hobbes* (Oxford, 2002), 24–5.

[93] He also had some influential critics. Henry More, commenting on Gassendi's rehabilitation of Epicureanism, tells us that he 'was much amazed that a person of so commendable parts as P. Gassendus could ever have the patience to rake out such old coarse rags of that rotten dunghill to stuffe his large Volumes withall': *An Explanation of the Grand Mystery of Godliness* (London, 1660), p. vii.

[94] The influence is via Charleton. See McGuire and Tamny, *Certain Philosophical Questions: Newton's Trinity Notebook*, 26–126.

Hobbes' corpuscularianism is a 'purer' version of mechanism than is that of Gassendi, but the boundaries of natural philosophy are not sharp and Gassendi would doubtless consider providence a core natural-philosophical question.

Hobbes discovered Euclid in 'a gentleman's library' while on a continental tour in the service of Sir Gervase Clifton in 1630, and his interest in natural philosophy can be dated from his return to England in 1631, when he became associated with the 'Welbeck Academy', a group who met at the country seat of the William Cavendish, Earl of Newcastle.[95] There was significant interest in mathematics, astronomy, and mechanics in this group, and by the mid-1630s material was being prepared for publication: Walter Warner, for example, was editing Harriot's mathematical writings and in 1636 Robert Payne translated Galileo's *Della Scienza Mecanica* into English. In 1634 Hobbes accompanied William Cavendish, the third Earl of Devonshire, to Paris as his tutor, and moved in Mersenne's circle, and it is around 1635 that he took up the development of a mechanist natural philosophy, and began to apply it to mind and sensation.[96]

Of the mechanist natural philosophies that we are concerned with in this chapter, Hobbes' version did more than any other mechanist system to draw attention to the heterodox consequences that could be derived from mechanism.[97] This was partly because it was assumed that Hobbes' radical views in politics and theology were part of the same mechanist programme, which involved an uncompromising commitment to determinism, and partly because he offered a staunchly reductionist reading of mechanism, leading him close to a materialist theory of the mind. Hobbes' mature system,[98] as set out in *De corpore*, which he worked on throughout the 1640s and early 1650s, and published in 1655, offers one of the most ontologically parsimonious versions of mechanism. It also offers one of its more systematic versions. Hobbes begins by defining 'philosophy'—in his usage here the term primarily covers natural

---

[95]  See Malcolm, *Aspects of Hobbes*, ch. 1, for an account of Hobbes' intellectual development.

[96]  See Douglas M. Jesseph, 'Galileo, Hobbes, and the Book of Nature', *Perspectives on Science* 12 (2004), 191–211.

[97]  On the reaction to Hobbes, see Mintz, *The Hunting of Leviathan*.

[98]  The writings on natural philosophy prior to the appearance of *De corpore* show elements of naturalism, although there are some problems of attribution. The text known as 'Short Tract on First Principles', composed around 1630–1, which has traditionally been attributed to Hobbes, offers a very naturalistic natural philosophy, replete with active principles. However, the handwriting turns out to be that of Hobbes' close friend Robert Payne, and the tract should probably be ascribed to him: see Noel Malcolm's comments in the entry on Payne in Thomas Hobbes, *The Correspondence*, ed. Noel Malcolm (2 vols, Oxford, 1994), ii. 874. The question of authorship (as opposed to handwriting) is not quite so straightforward, however, as Hobbes' various optical writings of the 1640s repeat some of the definitions that appear in the 'Short Tract': see Jan Prins, 'Hobbes on Light and Vision', in Tom Sorell, ed., *The Cambridge Companion to Thomas Hobbes* (Cambridge, 1996), 129–56: 132. More generally, it is worth noting that Hobbes' detailed and disorganized comments on Thomas White's natural philosophy, composed in 1642–3, attribute to the sun a pulsating activity which has a decidedly naturalistic ring to it, especially in his comparison of this pulsating motion with systole and diastole: Thomas Hobbes, *Critique du De mundo de Thomas White*, ed. J. Jacquot and H. W. Jones (Paris, 1973), 162. But see Malcolm, *Aspects of Hobbes*, 80–145, for a detailed argument that the 'Short Tract' is by Payne.

philosophy, but it also includes what we might refer to as civil science—as

> such knowledge of effects or appearances, as we acquire by true ratiocination from the knowledge we have first of their causes or generation; And again, of such causes or generations as may be from knowing first their effects.[99]

The aim of philosophy is to discover the properties of things through their causes, and to establish their causes from their properties, and a number of disciplines which may have value in their own right nevertheless fall outside philosophy on this definition.[100] Theology, the doctrine of angels, and the 'doctrine of God's worship', are excluded because they are not known by natural reason; astrology is excluded because it not sufficiently well-grounded to avoid falsehoods; and natural and political history are excluded because they rely on experience or authority, not on reason. The grounds on which astrology is excluded reinforce the idea that natural philosophy as deduction of effects from causes can generate certainty. The exclusion of natural history is based on the same idea, that something that cannot generate certainty is simply not natural philosophy. Political history is also excluded, although Hobbes did hold the distinctive view that there is a truly philosophical or scientific form of politics which, unlike political history, can make sure we understand the causes of, and can avoid, civil war.[101] As far as natural philosophy is concerned, however, the only real candidate for it is matter theory. There is nothing in this understanding of natural philosophy that the most conservative Aristotelian would have difficulty accepting. The content of the proposed natural philosophy is an entirely different question, however.

In the ideal-type mechanism that I have outlined, the four basic constituents of the physical world are matter, motion, space, and time. The main physical problem is how to get by without adding forces of some kind to these.[102] But rather than seeing how these four could be used to account for the phenomena that might seem to require the postulation of forces, Hobbes begins by reducing the resources available, jettisoning space and time. This leaves him with matter and motion, and motion, he argues, is all we need to deal with apparently dynamic processes. It also rules out the existence of any spiritual substances: there is nothing substantial that is not material.[103]

Hobbes' first move is to deny the reality of space. One thing at stake here is the Aristotelian conception of space in terms of place. On Aristotle's notion of place, a body's place carries dynamical implications that mere spatial location never could. The notion had been intended to designate something absolute: a thing is not in a particular place with respect to some other thing, it is in a particular place per se.

[99] Thomas Hobbes, *The English Works of Thomas Hobbes*, ed. W. Molesworth (11 vols, London, 1839–1845), i. 3.

[100] Ibid. 10–11.     [101] Ibid. 7–9.

[102] This had been as true for Gassendi as it was for Hobbes and Descartes: see Richard S. Westfall, *Force in Newton's Physics: The Science of Dynamics in the Seventeenth Century* (London, 1971), 535–7.

[103] Shapin and Schaffer, *Leviathan and the Air Pump*, 96–9, argue that Hobbes gave up the idea of empty space because it might have served as a location for immaterial spirits, but this cannot be right. As Noel Malcolm points out, all Hobbes needed for his rejection of immaterial spirits was materialism: *Aspects of Hobbes*, 190–1.

The cosmos has an absolute directional structure, the crucial directions being up and down, for these form the basis for Aristotle's doctrine of natural place, which determines the motions of different kinds of substance.[104] In the absence of external constraint, for example, fire will tend to move upwards and heavy bodies will tend to move downwards. Place shapes the dynamic behaviour of the body. The rationale behind this lies in his general approach to the problem of change, which Aristotle characterizes in terms of a variation in properties or qualities of the thing undergoing the change. Local motion is a change in respect of place, and like all forms of change, it can be specified in terms of a *terminus a quo* and a *terminus ad quem*, where in this case the *termini* are contraries. The *terminus ad quem* provides the process with an end or goal which it realises: without it, there is no process, no motion, at all. Aristotle's concern is with a general theory of change, which includes everything from processes whose *termini* are contradictories, such as generation and corruption, to those whose *termini* are contraries, such as change of shape. The doctrine of place, with its absolute directions, is crucial to the Aristotelian doctrine of dynamics: why things move is central to how they move.

Hobbes' understanding of space is the antithesis of this. Space is not only not absolute, it is not even something that acts as a container for bodies, which he considers to be complete in themselves and in need of no such container.[105] Space is just a subjective frame of reference, not real in its own right. It is our awareness of body 'simply', that is, of body having no other attribute except that it is located somewhere. But although body certainly exists outside our minds, the space which body occupies is a purely mental construction.[106] Space is a 'phantasm', a mental abstraction, an imaginary extension: it is the system of co-ordinates or external locations which the mind constructs out of its experience of real extended things. *Real* space is space inherent in body. In other words, real space is corporeality itself: 'so that a body is to imaginary space what a thing is to the knowledge of that thing, for our knowledge of existing things is that imagination which is produced by the action of these things on our senses, and therefore imaginary space, which is the imagination of body, is the same as our knowledge of existing body.' Space is, in short, 'privation of body'. The meaning of privation depends in the first place on our knowledge of body, and refers only to the possibility of body coming into being. Considered by itself, privation of body is a 'figment' or 'empty imagination'. A similar account is then given of time. 'As a body leaves a phantasm of its magnitude in the mind,' Hobbes maintains, 'so also a moved body leaves a phantasm of its motion, and idea of that body passing out of one space into another by continual succession.'[107] The argument is that time is not a property of bodies, and so must be something in our mind. Periods

---

[104] The main discussion is in Book Δ of the *Physics*.

[105] Hobbes, *English Works*, i. 91–4. Cf. Gassendi's argument that space is independent of body and, it would seem, even independent of God: *Opera*, i. 183.

[106] This leads Hobbes to offer a materialist account of geometry in which points, for example, are bodies whose magnitudes are sufficiently small that they can be neglected, and lines are produced by the motions of such points. See Douglas M. Jesseph, *Squaring the Circle: The War between Hobbes and Wallis* (Chicago, 1999), ch. 3.

[107] Ibid. i. 94–5.

of time such as days, months, and years are not real but merely 'computations made in our mind' when we consider the succession of states of a body in motion: times prior to and later than the present are not real but merely extrapolations from the present.

We must distinguish here between the doctrine of space as mere privation and the question of the existence of a vacuum. For Hobbes, the former was a purely conceptual matter about the nature of space, whereas the existence of empty space was a more complex issue which depended on empirical questions and how easily these could be accommodated within his natural philosophy. In *De corpore*, for example, he makes it clear that there could, conceptually speaking, be empty spaces,[108] even though he defends the idea of a plenum there. His views on the plenum had been formed in his participation in the Mersenne circle, which had begun to concern itself with the Torricellian barometric experiments in 1644. At this time, Hobbes was an advocate of the classical atomist model of space, whereby atoms were separated by empty space. But reflecting on the apparent appearance of a vacuum at the top of the upturned tube of mercury, Hobbes began to worry that this might be in conflict with his theory of the transmission of light, whereby light is propagated through a medium, not by means of pressure, as Descartes had argued, but (in line with his parsimonious basic principles) by means of motion. He wrote to Mersenne on 17 February 1648,

So, to sum up my opinion about the vacuum, I still think what I told you before: that there are certain minimal spaces here and there, in which there is no body, and that these spaces occur because of the nature, or natural actions, of the sun, fire, and other heat-producing bodies.[109]

But then in a postcript he voiced a concern:

It is said that one can see through the empty space which is left in the tube when the mercury descends, from which it follows that the action of a light-producing body is being propagated through a vacuum (which I think is impossible). So I should like you to find out if you can what shape the images of the objects which are seen through that vacuum have, in case the rays of light are being transmitted not through the vacuum itself but, in a circular action, via the body of the tube which contains the vacuum.[110]

Roberval, also a member of the Mersenne circle, a friend of Hobbes, and someone who like Hobbes had assumed the existence of interparticulate vacuua, was also puzzled by the space at the top of the mercury, and performed a number of experiments in 1647 in which a flattened carp's bladder swelled when placed in the evacuated space.[111] Roberval reluctantly concluded that a vacuum could not have been created, and reverted to what was in effect the Aristotelian theory of condensation and rarefaction: a minute amount of air in the bladder had been rarefied so that it now took up more room than previously. Hobbes, however, could not allow rarefaction: matter could not be stretched or compressed. The region in which

---

[108] Douglas M. Jesseph, *Squaring the Circle: The War between Hobbes and Wallis* i. 93.
[109] Hobbes, *The Correspondence*, i. 165 [text]/167 [trans.].        [110] Ibid. 166, 168.
[111] See the discussion in Malcolm, *Aspects of Hobbes*, 193–6.

matter is present (the body) cannot be made larger or smaller with the same amount of matter remaining.[112] This forced him to opt for a plenum.

We shall return to this question in Chapter 10. For the present, it is enough to note that his rejection of rarefaction would follow directly from the idea of matter as full space. Such an idea in fact complements his definition of space as merely a privation of matter, and it is not surprising that matter takes on the traditional properties of space on his account. Above all, it takes on the properties of homogeneity and inertness, and this means that Hobbes has to account for apparent dynamic features of matter, which naturalists had made properties of matter, in some other way. Space cannot harbour any dynamic properties, nor can time, and if matter is now ruled out that leaves only motion, and indeed it is motion that does all the work usually reserved for dynamics. The interaction between bodies is restricted to physical contact between their surfaces, and it is by means of this contact that a body transfers some of its motion, or loses some of its motion, to another body. Hobbes employs two terms, *impetus* and *conatus*, that traditionally had dynamic, and, in the case of the latter, naturalistic connotations, but he uses them in a completely reductive way.[113] As regards *impetus*, he equates this with speed,[114] comparing uniform and non-uniform motions in terms of the constant and increasing amounts of *impetus*, where this *impetus* is not the cause of the uniformity or non-uniformity of the motion, but rather something that can be measured, just as motion can be, in terms of lines, triangles, parallelograms, and so on.

In his most general definition of *impetus*, Hobbes tells us that it is 'nothing else but the quantity or velocity' of *conatus* or 'endeavour', which he defines as: 'the motion made in less space and time than can be given; that is, less than can be determined or assigned by exposition or number; that is, motion made through the length of a point, and in an instant or point of time'.[115] *Conatus* and speed are different in that two things can travel at the same speed and yet the *conatus* of each could be different: the fall of a ball of wool and a bullet of lead may begin and end together, but the bullet has a greater effect than the wool. This looks as if Hobbes is saying that the bullet has greater force/momentum than the wool,[116] but then it is unclear why the infinitesimal nature of *conatus* has been singled out. What is at stake becomes a little clearer when we consider the origins of Hobbes' notion. Brandt has noted that there are three quite different sources in Hobbes' thinking about *conatus*.[117] The term first appears in

---

[112] See the remarks in *De corpore* and in *Six Lessons to the Professors of Mathematics*: *English Works*, i. 509 and vii. 224–5.

[113] See the discussion in Frithiof Brandt, *Thomas Hobbes' Mechanical Conception of Nature* (Copenhagen/London, 1928), ch. 8.

[114] Hobbes, *The English Works*, i. 219. His term is 'velocity', but his definition of 'velocity or swiftness' earlier in *De corpore* (ibid. 113) is a definition of a scalar quantity: 'Motion, in as much as a certain length may in a certain time be transmitted by it, is called VELOCITY or *swiftness*.' In his optics, however, it is clear (*contra* Descartes) that he does not consider speed and direction as separate or independent components of a motion.

[115] Ibid. i. 206.

[116] See the discussion Brandt, *Thomas Hobbes' Mechanical Conception of Nature*, 297–9.

[117] Ibid. 301–15.

the *Elements of Law* (1640) in the context of a psychological problem about appetite. Here Hobbes equates the appetite with an impulse to motion, and in his *Tractatus opticus* (1641), he treats sensation, which he argues proceeds via pressure, in terms of a slight displacement of the medium, something that he treats as falling under the notion of *conatus*. The slight—perhaps infinitesimally slight—displacement that initiates sensation is a *conatus*. Both the idea of the initiation of motion by appetite, and the pressure in the medium that initiates sensation, fall under *conatus*. To this he adds a third idea, through a consideration of gravity/weight. In the *Elements of Law*, he takes it as given that bodies possess a *conatus* in the form of gravity/weight. In the case of a falling body we take this *conatus* to be the motion of the body, but what about the body which, being supported, is stationary? Descartes, as we shall see below, insists on a 'tendency to motion' here rather than motion proper, but Hobbes, despite the fact that in a statical context *conatus* is identical with the virtual motion of a simple machine,[118] cannot accept the Cartesian view: he cannot allow a *conatus* without a motion, even an imperceptible—because infinitesimally small—one.

In sum, three notions converge on *conatus*—appetite as impulse to motion, pressure in a medium that initiates sensation, and gravity/weight as something acting to move even a stationary body—and they shape its character as something that is a beginning of motion and that is infinitesimally small (both spatially and temporally). In Chapter 23 of *De corpore*, Hobbes argues that the unifying notion that answers to these descriptions is to be found in statics. Describing the action of a beam balance, he proposes a number of definitions. Bodies are said to be of equal weight when the *conatus* of one of the bodies, pressing on one end of the beam, resists the *conatus* of the other body, pressing on the other end, so that neither of them is moved and they are equally poised. Weight itself is defined as an aggregate 'of all the endeavours, by which all points of that body, which presses the beam, tend downwards in lines parallel to one another'.[119] In other words, rest, as typified by bodies in equilibrium on a beam balance, is the outcome of an interplay of infinitesimal motions. Indeed, it is because of such infinitesimal motions that bodies have weight in the first place.

*Conatus* is the key to Hobbes' account of elasticity, which does a good deal more work in Hobbes than in other mechanists, and the model of the restitution of a bow or stretched string plays a significant role.[120] The problem of the restitution of a stretched string or bow when it is released from constraints is a difficult one. It apparently changes state from rest to motion before it comes to rest again, yet the cause of this change of state is difficult to discern. It involves neither contact action, as in collision, nor an attractive force acting from outside the body, as in magnetism or gravitation (phenomena which a mechanist would hope to mechanize at some stage). The only explanation is that there is not in fact a change of state: the bow has been in some sense in motion all along, in the form of a power to produce motion, with

[118] See Westfall, *Force in Newton's Physics*, 111.       [119] Hobbes, *The English Works*, i. 351.

[120] See H. R. Bernstein, '*Conatus*, Hobbes, and the Young Leibniz', *Studies in History and Philosophy of Science* 11 (1980), 25–37; Jamie Kassler, *Inner Music: Hobbes, Hooke and North on Internal Character* (London, 1995), 62–107; and idem, *Music, Science and Philosophy: Models in the Universe of Thought* (Aldershot, 2001), 101–24.

atoms at one side of the bow moving more quickly than those at the other side, so that it is in a state of disequilibrium. Describing the restoring action of the archer's monochord, he writes:

when the lath of a cross-bow bent doth, as soon as it is at liberty, restore itself, though to him that judges by sense, both it and all its parts seem to be at rest; yet he, that judging by reason doth not account the taking away of impediment for an efficient cause, now conceives that without an efficient cause any thing can pass from rest to motion, will conclude that the parts were already in motion before they began to restore themselves.[121]

In other words, the constituent corpuscles from which bodies are composed are perpetually in motion (as Epicurean atoms were), and it is this that maintains the body in a particular physical state, for all bodies have 'the beginning of their restitution within themselves, namely, a certain motion in their internal parts, which was there, when, before the taking away of the force, they were compressed, or extended'.[122] On this conception, bodies are still inert in the sense that they have no power or force of a naturalist kind by which motion is produced, for despite the naturalist connotations of the term *conatus*, Hobbes has reduced the power to produce motion to the motion itself.

## DESCARTES' *PRINCIPIA PHILOSOPHIAE*

The work of Beeckman, Gassendi, and Hobbes reveals two rather different, but equally essential, aspects of the mechanist programme. Beeckman is primarily concerned with accounting for what happens in the processes, particularly collision, that the mechanist takes as fundamental. By contrast, Gassendi and Hobbes devote a good deal of time to redescribing phenomena so that they are amenable to mechanist treatment. It is Descartes who combines these two projects in the most satisfactory form, providing both a comprehensive mechanist reduction and a fuller mechanical account of the underlying corpuscular interactions and the principles that regulate their behaviour.

Mechanist systems of natural philosophy were designed, in very general terms, to do something that Aristotelian natural philosophy had attempted to do but failed to achieve. Mechanism, conceived as a systematic natural philosophy, is a successor to Aristotelianism. It is designed to replace it, not, at the most fundamental level, to do something radically different. In its most highly developed form, Cartesian mechanism, it should be able to be placed side by side with Aristotelianism, as it were, and compared area by area. This is in fact what Descartes originally had in mind for his *Principia Philosophiae*: he intended that it be 'a complete textbook of philosophy' in which he would 'simply put down my true conclusions, with all the true premises from which I derive them, which I think I could do without too many words'. In the same volume, he added, he would also include a traditional textbook—most likely the *Summa philosophiae quadripartita* of Eustachius a Sancto Paulo—with notes at

---

[121] Hobbes, *The English Works*, i. 347–8.    [122] Ibid. 344.

the end of each proposition, in which his own views and those of scholastic comment-ators would be compared.[123]

Descartes' *Principia* played a pivotal role in sevententh-century natural philosophy. His early training in the subject had been through Beeckman, and between them Beeckman and Descartes set the agenda for a mechanist corpuscularianism, including the work of Gassendi and Hobbes, and it was Descartes, who served what was in effect an intellectual apprenticeship with Beeckman,[124] who was to produce the definitive system of mechanist natural philosophy, one with immense influence throughout the rest of the seventeenth century, and well into the eighteenth. During the 1630s and 1640s Descartes was far ahead of anyone else in devising a viable form of mechanism, and the appearance of *Principia Philosophiae* in 1644 established Cartesian mechan-ism as the pre-eminent system of natural philosophy, at least up to the appearance of Newton's alternative 'principles', *Principia Mathematica*, in 1687.

While Descartes' approach to natural philosophy is undeniably radical, there is one respect in which it looks more radical than it is. In the natural-philosophical text-books that the *Principia* is designed to replace, the functions of the rational soul, and human cognitive and affective states, come at the end, after physical and physiolo-gical questions have been discussed. This is because the discussion relies on what has gone earlier, but also because the culmination of the project lies in an understand-ing not just of the world but of our place in it, to the extent to which this can be captured by natural philosophy. Descartes apparently reverses this order, by treating human cognition in Part 1 of the *Principia*, before dealing with any other issues. But in fact what Part 1 deals with are the fundamental principles that establish natural philosophy as a legitimate exercise. These require us to separate the physical world from mind, in that the physical world cannot harbour the intentions, goals, and aims that we treat as characteristic of mind, and from God, in that God is not immanent in his creation but transcends it. We are supposed to be able to grasp that this is the right way to proceed by reflecting on our clear and distinct ideas of matter, mind, and God, and it is the doctrine of clear and distinct ideas that offers the sole guidance as to how we should proceed, on the grounds that we have to have grasped something clearly and distinctly if we are to be in a position to ask informed questions about it. The proper place for questions of the nature of mind, which cover not just cognit-ive states but affective ones, as well as questions of morality, comes at the end of the natural-philosophical enquiry, in the projected Part 6 of the *Principia*, just as it does

---

[123] Descartes, *Œuvres*, iii. 233. Cf. Descartes to [Charlet], [December 1640]; ibid. iii. 270, where he talks of 'a full comparison between the philosophy of the Schools and my own'. The scholastic natural philosophy textbooks included accounts of vital and cognitive functions, however, whereas the published version of the *Principia* confined itself to the nature of motion (Book 2), cosmology (Book 3), and the formation and nature of the earth (Book 4). Nevertheless, Descartes did originally intend that the treatise comprise six Books, not just the four that were published. The last two were to cover animal and human functions (including distinctively human cognitive and affective states as well as morality) respectively, and their proposed content can be reconstructed without difficulty from other writings of Descartes, giving us a treatise of six Books that match the late scholastic treatises, offering a systematic account of the world and our place in it. See my *Descartes' System of Natural Philosophy* for a full account of these questions.

[124] See my *Descartes, An Intellectual Biography*, ch. 3.

in the scholastic natural philosophy treatises that the *Principia* is explicitly designed to replace.

Descartes' starting point is the identification, on the basis of the criterion that we can only commit ourselves to what we perceive clearly and distinctly, of the basic kinds of substance, and his metaphysical categories of substance, attributes, and modes turn out to be very different from what their scholastic nomenclature might suggest, as he fills them out in a novel way, one guided by the requirements of the natural-philosophical edifice he is about to construct on them. He construes attributes as those properties of something without which it would cease to be what it is. The distinguishing features of substances, such as extension and thought, are attributes: if a body were to become unextended it would no longer be a body, for example, just as if a mind were to stop thinking it would cease to be a mind. Modes of substances include such things as a body's being in a particular state of motion or rest, or a mind's having particular memories or thoughts. A distinctive feature of this account is that modes are related to substance through their attributes: extension is the principal attribute of corporeal substance and the modes of corporeal substance are ways of being extended. Despite the fact that what modal state something is in is contingent, in a way that its attributes are not, modes depend on the essence of substance because they depend on the attributes of substance. Shape, for example, is a mode of corporeal bodies, and whatever shape a corporeal body has is dependent on the fact that it is extended. Moreover, its particular extension must be manifested in some particular shape. Similarly, being in some mental state is a mode of the mind, and whatever mental state a mind is in is dependent on the fact that the mind is characterized by the attribute of thinking, where this attribute must be manifested in some particular mental state.

On Descartes' account, substances can be distinguished by means of their attributes, as thinking and extended substances, and this is the way 'in which they are most clearly and distinctly understood'.[125] But they can also be distinguished by means of their modes, as when we think of a body having various shapes but retaining the same volume. In setting out this modal distinction, Descartes makes the crucial move, explaining that: 'We shall best understand the many different modes of thought, such as understanding, imagining, remembering, willing, etc., and also the diverse modes of extension or those pertaining to extension, such as all figures, and situation and movements of parts, if we regard them only as modes of the things in which they are.'[126] The importance of this is that, when we seek to understand motion—when we seek to grasp it in clear and distinct terms—we need to consider it simply as a mode of a substance, without considering the causes responsible for motion. Consequently, Descartes can and does proceed with an extensive discussion of motion before introducing causes, contrary to the Aristotelian procedure, whereby motion cannot even be identified (e.g. as being between contraries, or contradictories) without specifying its causes.

---

[125] *Principia*, Book 1, art. 63. The *Principia* comprises vol. viiiA of Descartes, *Œuvres*. For convenience, I shall not refer to them by the page number, however, but by Part and article number.
[126] Ibid. art. 65.

Crucial to this discussion is his account of place and space, which he identifies with 'body' (that is, material extension), and his rejection of the doctrine of absolute direction. The identification of place and space with matter proceeds directly via an argument from clarity and distinctness. Our clear and distinct idea of matter tells us that the nature of body 'consists in extension alone'. A crucial part of the criterion of clarity and distinctness here is whether we can imagine a substance to lack some quality. Descartes argues that we can imagine a body lacking hardness, colour, weight, and other sensory qualities, but we cannot imagine it lacking extension. He gives the example of hardness: we can imagine bodies always receding from us as we approach them, so that we are never able to touch them, but we do not think that such bodies thereby fail to be bodies, so we can imagine bodies without hardness.[127] The consequences of the claim that the nature of body consists in extension for our understanding of space are then spelled out:

> The terms 'place' and 'space', then, do not signify anything different from the body which is said to be in a place. They merely refer to its size, shape, and position relative to other bodies. To determine position, we have to look at various other bodies which we regard as immobile; and in relation to different bodies we may say that the same thing is both changing and not changing its place at the same time.[128]

What Descartes is rejecting here above all is a directional notion of space, and the fact that he speaks of 'place and space' indicates that what is at stake is not just the Aristotelian notion of place, which clearly assumes absolute directions, but also the Epicurean notion of space, which is no less directional in that atoms naturally fall downwards, which gives Epicurean space an intrinsic directionality. Descartes counters these doctrines in a distinctive way, by invoking the notion of the relativity of motion.

The concern that lies behind the doctrine of relativity of motion is the need to impose some reference point against which motions can be judged to have taken place. If space itself has no intrinsic directions, and if the reference point cannot be fixed by a global system of co-ordinates—Cartesian material extension is of 'indefinite' extent, which means there is no centre, or boundaries that we can use as reference points—then this reference point is going to be conventional and relative. The reference point against which we judge motion has to be local on Descartes' account, and indeed takes the form of identifying a body that we deem to be stationary, then determining motions in respect to that body.[129] Motion is defined as 'the transference of one part of matter or of one body from the vicinity of those bodies immediately contiguous with it and considered as being at rest, into the vicinity of others'. This definition is proposed as an alternative to that 'of common usage', whereby motion is identified with 'the force (*vis*) or action (*actio*) that brings about the transference', and he opposes this latter view because he considers

> that motion is always in the moving body, as opposed to the body that brings about the motion. The two are not normally distinguished with sufficient care; and I want to make it clear that the motion of something that moves is, like the lack of motion that is in a thing at

---

[127] *Principia*, Book 2 art. 4.     [128] Ibid. art. 13.     [129] Ibid. art. 13.

rest, a mere mode of that thing and not itself a subsistent thing, just as shape is a mere mode
of a thing that has shape. [130]

At this point we encounter a deep problem in Descartes' account.[131] Because one of
his main concerns is to deny the Aristotelian doctrine that the motion of (terrestrial)
bodies is something that naturally comes to an end, he talks of rest being the opposite of (as opposed to the outcome of) motion. This claim, along with the claim that
'nothing moves by virtue of its own nature toward its opposite or own destruction',
can then be joined as premises in his argument that bodies in motion will remain
in that state.[132] But his modal construal of motion and rest seems to operate with
two rather different conceptions of the relation between motion and rest, one operative when we are considering isolated bodies and the other when we are considering
interactions between bodies. His first 'law of nature' states that 'each thing, as far as
it is in its power, always remains in the same state'. It is clear from context that this
covers changes of speed, as well as moving bodies coming to a stop: bodies have no
more reason to alter speed than they do to stop, and this is central to his understanding of how bodies behave in the absence of external forces. However, he also tells
us that motions at the same speed are never contrary to one another: the contrary
opposition is that 'between motion and rest, or even between rapidity of motion and
slowness of motion', which looks like he is treating differences in speed on a par with
the difference between motion and rest, so that rest is just that case of motion which
takes the value of zero. On the other hand, he also insists that 'rest is the contrary of
motion'. Here motion and rest are taken generically as different and contrary modes
of a body. This conception is operative primarily when Descartes talks about interaction between bodies, as in collision. As we shall see when we come to his rules of
collision, moving bodies, whatever their speed, and bodies at rest do not behave in the
same way. The outcome of a collision between bodies moving at different speeds, and
the outcome of a collision between two bodies one of which is at rest, are quite different. Similarly, the outcomes of the collision between a moving smaller body with a
stationary larger one, and that between a stationary smaller body with a larger moving
one, are different.

What lies at the basis of this ambiguous understanding of the relation between rest
and motion is complex, but the source of the problem can be discerned in the origins of the Cartesian project in natural philosophy. In *Le Monde*, which the *Principia*
follows closely in the details of its matter theory and cosmology—but where the argument is presented in straightforward natural-philosophical terms, not reformulated
in the vocabulary of clear and distinct ideas—dynamical models are more in evidence, or at least closer to the surface, than in the *Principia*. It is of some importance
here that Descartes' earliest exercises in physical theory were in hydrostatics, and he
developed his dynamical vocabulary in statics and hydrostatics.[133] Statics and hydrostatics lend themselves well to a sharp distinction of kind between rest and motion,
which correspond to equilibrium and departure from equilibrium respectively. Hence

---

[130] Ibid. art. 25.          [131] For a full discussion see Gaukroger, *Descartes' System*, 103–14.
[132] *Principia*, Book 2 art. 37.          [133] We shall return to Descartes's hydrostatics in Ch. 10.

it is natural that when Descartes thinks of forces, notions of equilibrium come to the fore, and there is a conflict between this way of thinking of things and a kinematic way of thinking of motion and rest.

This is evident in *Le Monde* in his two treatments of the stone in a sling. In the first of these (ch. 6) the motion of an unconstrained body can only be rectilinear: since a body's tendency to move is instantaneous, this tendency to move must be rectilinear, because only rectilinear motion can be determined in an instant.[134] By contrast, in ch. 13, where Descartes is considering what causes a stone moved in a sling to pull on the string[135] (see Fig. 8.1), he argues that the tendency of the stone to move at a tangent (ACG) to the circular path it is following is to be analysed in terms of two components of this tendency. One (VXY) is a radial tendency outwards, the other is the motion along the circular path ABF which, we are told, is in no way impeded by the sling. In other words, the circular motion of the stone in the sling is not caused by any external constraint, including anything imposed by the sling: the body naturally follows this path. It is instructive here that Descartes does not seem particularly concerned to specify how a body behaves in the absence of forces, because the bodies he deals with always move within a system of constraints, just as in statics: the aim is to understand the instantaneous collisions of non-elastic bodies. One does not ask what would happen if the forces were removed, because the understanding of the action of these forces is the point of the exercise. Note also that what Descartes is concerned with (ch. 13) is not so much circular inertia as circular equilibrium, namely, the idea that a body moves in a continuous circular orbit because the forces acting upon it are exactly balanced, so that the net force is zero. The confusion arises because Descartes slides between this static notion of equilibrium (which involves the untenable but intuitively appealing assumption that some motions are dynamically unbalanced) and the dynamic notion of inertia. As a result, he evidently construes the circular motion of a body in a sling as resulting from an equilibrium between the tangential tendency of the body and its radial tendency.

These tensions persist in the *Principia*, though they are not as close to the surface, because a new element intervenes, which adds a new layer of complexity. In the *Principia* Descartes' aim is to legitimate his natural philosophy in terms of clear and distinct ideas, which means he has to translate his natural philosophy into a new language, as it were, one sanctioned by clarity and distinctness, and this requires that they be presented and defended in a vocabulary that invokes nothing more than geometry and kinematics. What we get in the *Principia* is a translation of Cartesian natural philosophy into a canonical form, although we occasionally have to look beyond the canonical formulation to understand the rationale for specific natural-philosophical claims. This is evident in his principle of the conservation of motion and his three laws of nature, which form the operational core of his system. At Part 2, art. 36, we are told that God is the primary cause of motion and that he always maintains an equal quantity of it in the universe. Descartes talks of the same amount of 'motion and rest' being conserved in the universe as a whole, distributed differently

---

[134] *Œuvres*, xi. 45–6.        [135] Ibid. 85–6.

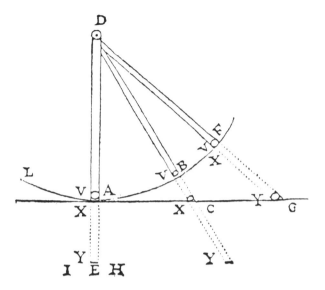

**Figure 8.1**

in different parts of the universe at different times. What is conserved is not the total amount of speed in the universe, however, for motion is a mode of a body, and so not something separate from it. The amount of motion in the universe is a function not just of speed but of the quantity or size of the matter having that speed, that is, the extent of the universe over which that speed is distributed, so that 'we must think that when one part of matter moves twice as fast as another which is twice as large, there is as much motion in the smaller as in the larger'. In other words, what Descartes considers to be conserved is the product of size and speed, understood as a scalar quantity. Now this is just one of many things that might be conserved on the basis of the argument given: all we can really conclude is that something involving some power of speed or velocity is conserved. Why this particular version should have been chosen is not indicated, but the answer is not difficult to find. The statics of simple machines provides a model in the law of the lever, where conserved force is equal to the product of weight and instantaneous displacement. Descartes sets out the principle to Mersenne, telling him that

if you have a balance in equilibrium and you place on it the smallest weight that is able to make it turn, then it will turn very slowly, whereas if you put twice this weight on it, it will turn more than twice as fast. And in contrast, if you take a fan in your hand, without your having to use any force except that needed to support it, you can raise and lower it with the same speed that it would fall by itself in the air if you let it go; but to raise and lower it twice as fast, you have to employ the same force, which will be more than double the other, since that one was nil.[136]

136 Descartes to Mersenne, 2 Feb. 1643: Ibid. iii. 614.

What Descartes has done here is simply translated from the statical case to the kinematic one, leaving weight much as it is and transforming instantaneous displacement into speed.[137]

The immutability of God that underlies the conservation of 'motion' (size times speed) is manifested in the form of laws of nature which are 'the secondary and particular causes of the various motions that we notice in individual bodies'. The first of these laws of nature specifies what form the conservation of motion takes. Just as bodies retain their shape, so they retain their state of rest if they are at rest, and their state of motion if they are in motion. More generally, in absence of external causes a body will retain its state of motion or rest. The rationale behind this is that 'rest is the opposite of motion, and nothing moves by virtue of its own nature toward its opposite or its own destruction'.[138] In the case of remaining in the same state of motion (i.e. maintaining the same speed), as opposed to just remaining in motion, his rationale depends on the idea that different states of motion depend on different amounts of motion and rest, for this is the only way change of speed can be accommodated.

The first law deals with scalar quantities and, by itself, tells us nothing about the direction of motion. But motion is always motion in a particular direction (even if relatively defined). Descartes deals with direction by means of his account of modes. Extension is the principal attribute of corporeal substance in Descartes' metaphysics, and the modes of corporeal substance are ways of being extended: the particular extension must be manifested in some shape, in some state of rest or motion, and so on for all the modes. Such modes—we can call them first-order modes—are the particular ways in which the attributes of substance exist or are manifested.[139] In the case of motion, however, there is also a second-order mode, a mode that qualifies the mode of motion, and this is 'determination'.[140] While shape and state of motion/rest are properties—modes—in terms of which the attributes of substances must be expressed, determination is a second-order mode in terms of which the first-order mode of motion must be expressed.

The first law of nature is designed to establish that first-order modes do not change without an external cause. The second law is designed to establish that the second-order modes do not change without an external cause, where the only second-order mode that Descartes mentions is determination, which is a directional quantity.[141] The law tells us that 'everything that moves is determined in the individual instants which can be specified as it moves, to continue its motion in a given direction along a straight line, and never along a curved line'.[142] This completes the account of an isolated body, and Descartes is constantly at pains to point out that in nature we will

---

[137] See Westfall, *Force in Newton's Physics*, 75.          [138] *Principia*, Book 2 art. 37.

[139] See the discussion in Peter McLaughlin, 'Force, Determination and Impact', in Stephen Gaukroger, John Schuster, and John Sutton, eds, *Descartes' Natural Philosophy* (London, 2000), 81–112.

[140] See Descartes to Clerselier, 17 February 1645: *Œuvres*, iv. 185.

[141] On determination see Alan Gabbey, 'Force and Inertia in the Seventeenth Century: Descartes and Newton', in Stephen Gaukroger, ed., *Descartes: Philosophy, Mathematics and Physics* (New York, 1980), 230–320; and Peter McLaughlin, 'Force, Determination and Impact'.

[142] *Principia*, Book 2 art. 39.

never actually find such behaviour, because the motion of bodies always ceases in the terrestrial realm owing to a number of causes, many of which we may be unaware of, and their motion is never rectilinear because in a plenum more complex looped motions are required for the translation of bodies.

The transition to the kinds of principles that have a more direct applicability to the phenomena Descartes sets out to explain—and the origin and structure of solar systems will be paramount among these—begins in the second part of the discussion of the second law. The title of Part 2, art. 39, which sets out the second law, tells us that 'all motion is, of itself, along straight lines; and consequently, bodies that are moving in a circle always tend to move away from the centre of the circle that they are describing'. Here we get to what, for Descartes, will be the cutting edge of his cosmology: a force that acts radially out from the centre, centrifugal force.[143] The two laws of nature that he has already provided employ minimal, non-dynamic, and relatively uncontentious premisses. The principal premiss is God's immutability, and he has managed to construe motion and rest in such a way that immutability rules out moving bodies coming to rest because of some internal principle. On the other hand, what these laws of nature give us is, as it stands, not a great deal of use in the cosmological arguments for which Part 2 is really just a preparation. The introduction of centrifugal force changes all this, partly because it is a dynamic notion.

The aim is to let centrifugal force ride on the relatively uncontentious arguments establishing the first two laws. But what Descartes needs for his cosmology is something that is not provided by his account of these two laws. For his cosmology he needs bodies to have a radial tendency outwards from the centre of rotation as well as a tangential tendency. He explains 'how bodies that are rotated strive to move away from the centre of their motion', and 'that all the matter of the heavens strives similarly to move away from certain centres'.[144] If a ball is placed in a hollow tube, for example, and the tube is rotated from one of its ends, the ball moves outwards from the centre.[145] Descartes realizes of course that once the ball leaves the tube—once the constraints on the motion of the ball are removed—it will not continue to move radially but will now move at a tangent to the centre of rotation. The point is that in a cosmological context, the constraints are never removed because the universe is packed with homogeneous matter, so that light, for example, will always be transmitted radially outwards from a centrally rotating sun, simply in virtue of its rotation. Cartesian optics and cosmology depend crucially upon the existence of a force acting radially outwards. In *Le Monde*, we were offered two contradictory accounts, as Descartes tried to think through rotation partly in terms of statics. Here in the *Principia*, the inconsistencies have been ironed out to some extent, for the radial tendency of the body now looks like a consequence of the fact that the cosmos

---

[143] Centrifugal force is a highly problematic notion. In the seventeenth century, certainly in such key figures as Descartes and Huygens, and perhaps even initially by Newton, it was treated as a force directed radially outwards that acts on a body revolving about a centre: as opposed to the modern understanding, whereby it is a reaction by this body to whatever it is (e.g. the sling) that is constraining it to move in a circle.

[144] *Principia*, Book 3 arts. 58 and 60 respectively.     [145] Ibid. art. 59.

is a plenum, and such a tendency would not exist if the body were projected through empty space.[146]

This does not mean, however, that the statical model is absent from Descartes' discussion, for it reappears with a vengeance in his rules of collision that accompany the third law of nature, which takes us away from the behaviour of isolated bodies described in the first two laws to the behaviour of bodies in collision.[147] The third law states that 'a body upon coming into contact with a stronger one, loses none of its motion; but that, upon coming into contact with a weaker one, it loses as much as it transfers to that weaker body'.[148] In demonstrating the third law, Descartes makes crucial use of the distinction between the first-order mode, motion, and the second-order mode, determination. The motion of a body can remain intact, he tells us, while its determination changes. This plays a crucial role in Descartes' account of collision because the colliding bodies are always perfectly inelastic. A hard tennis ball striking a court is reflected from its surface, for example (see Fig. 8.2).[149] But if the force of motion (as manifest in the speed of the body), and direction of motion were the same thing, then the ball would first have to stop before it changed direction, and if it stopped a new cause would be needed for it to move again. But there is no such new cause available: therefore, its force or speed is not affected in the impact, only the direction of its motion, which is changed. If we make Descartes' distinction between speed and determination, then we can understand how the speed might be conserved, while direction is altered.[150] Determination, unlike speed, is a composite mode and therefore not preserved in the way that speed is. The speed of the ball before being reflected is represented by the line AB, and after reflection by a line of the same length BF. The line AB also represents the determination of the ball, since determination is after all a mode of the motion,[151] and it can be resolved into two orthogonal lines: AC, which is directly opposed to the surface CBE, and AH, which is parallel to the surface so not involved in the collision. Because determination AH is not involved in the collision that results in the reflection, it is preserved, remaining a component of the determination of the reflected ball. Since the ball arrives at F from B in the

---

[146] Contrary to what I argued in *Descartes' System*, 120–1.

[147] See Stephen Gaukroger, 'The Foundational Role of Hydrostatics and Statics in Descartes' Natural Philosophy', in Stephen Gaukroger, John Schuster, and John Sutton, eds, *Descartes' Natural Philosophy* (London, 2000), 60–80; and Peter McLaughlin, 'Contraries and Counterweights: Descartes' Statical Theory of Impact', *The Monist* 84 (2001), 562–81.

[148] *Principia*, Book 2 art. 40.

[149] The example is taken from *La Dioptrique*: *Œuvres* vi. 93–6, trans. in Descartes, *The World and Other Writings* (Cambridge, 1998), 76–8. Tennis balls in the seventeenth century were hard, unlike modern (lawn) tennis balls.

[150] The idea has some intuitive plausibility. Compare Beeckman's entry in his *Journal* for 25–9 July 1619: 'If the sail of a ship is taken down and it is carried only by its prior *impetus*, it can be guided by its rudder in such a way that, moving in a semicircle towards the place from which it came, it is moved along a line by which it had come, returning by one and the same *impetus*', i. 330.

[151] Note also that, like motion, it is a magnitude: Descartes wrote to Clerselier on 17 February that, in collision, a body can pass to another more than half its speed and 'more than half its determination': *Œuvres*, iv. 186. In the end, however, it seems that determination turns out to resist any completely consistent reading. See McLaughlin, 'Force, Determination and Impact' for the best statement of the difficulties, and a realistic solution to them.

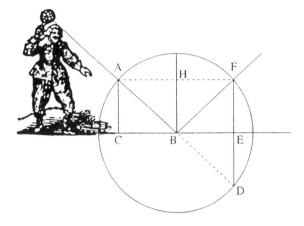

**Figure 8.2**

same time it took to travel from A to B—AB and BF represent the same speeds—the orthogonal components of BF will be HF and EF. In other words, AC has been replaced by EF, which, simply in virtue of resolving the motion into its orthogonal components, must have the opposite direction.

The rules of collision that accompany the third law of nature set out how inelastic bodies behave in collinear collisions. The collisions are each regulated by conservation of motion, and speed and/or determination can be altered as a result of collision, and there are seven basic laws describing seven initial states, the last having two variants (see Fig. 8.3).[152] The Rules describe three kinds of case: simple opposition, where bodies of equal size and speed have different determinations; double opposition between states of motion and determinations, where one body is moving and the other at rest, and where their determinations are opposed; and double opposition between intermediate states of motion and determinations, where both bodies move in the same direction but one overtakes the other. There is a statical model behind these cases.[153] In Rule 1 for example, we have a collision between two bodies of equal size and speed but different collinear determinations. The outcome is determined by the statical principle that if the arms of a balance are of equal length and the weights are equal, then the scale is in equilibrium and the conflict is a draw. What happens is the bodies' determinations are reversed so they move away from one another after impact. Rule 2 describes the case of a collision between two bodies of the same speed, but different sizes and different determinations. The outcome here is determined by

---

[152] The illustration here is from my copy of the 1659 edition of the *Principes*, published in Paris by Le Gras, which I believe is the first illustration of the different types of collision. Note that, following the marginal illustration of Book 2 art. 46 in the first edition of the *Principia*, the bodies are represented as cubes not spheres. As Peter McLaughlin rightly insists in his 'Force, Determination and Impact', the colliding bodies are in fact better represented as cubes than spheres because considerations of surface area of impact play a role once the Rules begin to be applied.

[153] See the exemplary account in McLaughlin, 'Force, Determination and Impact', 97–102.

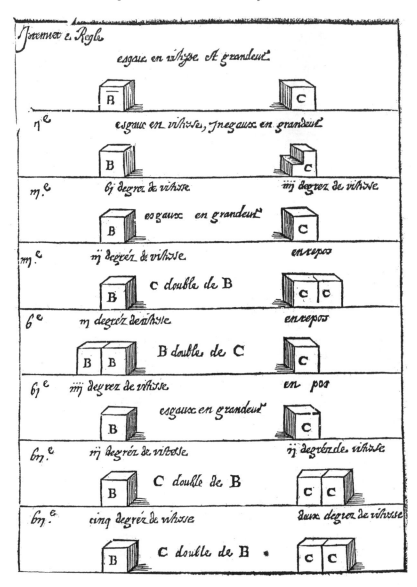

**Figure 8.3**

the statical principle that if the lengths of the arm are equal, the heavier body wins. What happens is that the determination of the lighter body is reversed, with speed unaffected. Rule 3 describes the case of a collision between two bodies of the same size, but different speeds and different determinations. The outcome here is determined by the statical principle that if the weights are equal, the longer arm determines the winner, where the analogue of the longer arm is greater speed. What happens is that the determination of the slower body is reversed, and the bodies move together with a speed that is the average of the two initial speeds.

All these Rules are problematic, if only as rules of inelastic collision, and in Rule 6, for example, it is wholly unclear how Descartes arrives at the division of speeds after impact.[154] I want to focus, however, on the especially problematic Rule 4, for here we can see the statics that ultimately underlies Descartes' account coming to the surface even more clearly, for Rule 4 is completely mysterious until we grasp its underpinnings in statics. Rule 4 tells us that when a smaller moving body encounters a larger stationary one, it rebounds with its original speed, leaving the larger body unaffected. Rule 5 tells us that when a larger moving body encounters a smaller stationary one, then both proceed in the direction of the motion after impact with a speed equal to the product of the size of the larger body times the speed of the larger body, divided by the sum of the two sizes. This is peculiar for a number of reasons. Rule 4 specifies that a smaller body can never move a larger one, no matter what its speed, and no matter how slight the difference in size. Descartes recognizes the oddity of what he is claiming, telling us that 'experience seems to contradict the rules I have just explained',[155] and noting explicitly in the introduction to Rule 4 that it may not hold when the body is surrounded by air or some other fluid. More importantly, given his definition of motion, which body is moving and which is stationary is a matter of determining the appropriate reference point, and it would be very easy to find a reference point from which the larger body would be the moving body and the smaller body the stationary one, but then we would be in the situation described by Rule 5, which provides a completely different outcome.

It is not too difficult to understand why Descartes should have insisted on Rule 4, for it underpins his optics, and it is perhaps his realization that it is needed for his optics that led him to change his mind on this question, for five years earlier he had written to Mersenne on two occasions allowing that a smaller moving body can dislodge a larger stationary one, and even indicating how the resultant speed is determined.[156] In seeking to explain why light rays, which follow rectilinear paths, behave in particular geometrically defined ways when they are reflected or refracted, he models light micro-mechanically. In reflection, for example, light corpuscles strike a larger body and are reflected from its surface. Kinematically specified laws of collision, of the kind Descartes provides, should be enough to describe the various kinds of interaction possible here, and in this way should underpin an explanation of why light behaves in particular geometrically defined ways when it encounters a reflecting surface, or when it moves from one optical medium to another. The linchpins of this treatment are his accounts of reflection and refraction, and we can confine our attention to the former. Descartes starts from the idea that when a light ray strikes a reflecting surface

---

[154] Shea makes a good stab at sorting out what Descartes' reasoning/guesswork might have been. See William R. Shea, *The Magic of Numbers and Motion* (Canton, Mass., 1991), 296–7.

[155] *Principia*, Book 3 art. 53.

[156] Descartes to Mersenne, 25 December 1639: *Œuvres*, ii. 627; and 28 October 1640: *Œuvres*, iii. 210–11.

obliquely, the angle of incidence equals the angle of reflection. To show why this happens, he resolves the ray into components, and he distinguishes the speed of the ray and its determination. In fleshing out the geometry of the situation in physical terms, Descartes simply has to imagine the light ray being composed of minute corpuscles and striking a larger body. Now if such a body were to be moved by a light corpuscle then of course the light corpuscle would have to transfer some of its motion to the larger body, in which case it would be retarded, and not only its direction but its speed would be affected. And if this happened, the angle of reflection would not then equal the angle of incidence: rather, the situation would be more like refraction, where a change in the speed of the light ray causes the bending of the ray. The kinematics have got to match what we know about the geometry of reflection, and the geometry of reflection does not deal with approximations: geometrical optics is just a particular interpretation of geometry, which is the paradigm of exactness. In providing a physical model for the geometrical behaviour of light rays, this exactness, which is of the essence of geometry, cannot be lost. If the geometrical analysis of the behaviour of light shows that the angle of incidence equals the angle of reflection, it equals it exactly, whether the light is striking a raindrop or the ocean. And if that is the case, the light corpuscle cannot move the body from whose surface it is reflected.

This explains why Rule 4 is so important for Descartes, but it does not explain what he thinks makes Rule 4 correct. If one looks to Descartes for a rationale for the law, what one finds is a physical claim—that a smaller moving body colliding with a larger stationary one cannot affect the state of the larger body—filled out in quasi-scholastic natural-philosophical terms. There are two important premises in Descartes' treatment. The first is that rest has as much reality as does motion: rest is not simply a 'privation' of motion as the scholastics had argued. The second is that rest and motion are opposed to one another: they are modal contraries. We must therefore think of the interaction of the bodies in terms of the smaller having a particular quantity of motion, and the larger having a particular quantity of rest. These are opposing states, so the bodies will be in dynamic opposition, and Rule 4 therefore describes a contest, as it were, between a larger body at rest and a smaller body in motion.[157] The bodies exercise a force to resist changes of their states, and the magnitude of this force Descartes considers to be a function of their size. A body in motion cannot, for that reason alone, have more force than one at rest; nor can greater speed confer greater force upon it. Either of these would undermine the ontological equivalence of rest and motion that Descartes wants to defend. Now, bearing this in mind, we can ask what happens when the smaller moving body collides with a larger stationary one. Clearly they cannot both remain in the same state in collision, so there will have to be a change of state. And since the smaller or 'weaker' body can hardly change the state of the larger or 'stronger' one, it is the smaller one that has its state changed (the direction of its motion is reversed), the larger body remaining unaffected in the process.

This account explains why it has to be an all-or-nothing matter. We might be tempted to ask why the smaller body should not move the larger one if the smaller

---

[157] See the discussion in Gabbey, 'Force and Inertia in the Seventeenth Century'.

body had sufficient speed, or if the difference in size were very marginal. The answer to the first question is that the ontological equivalence of motion and rest makes the speed of the smaller body irrelevant to the outcome of the collision. The answer to the second is that, because of the irrelevance of speed, the only remaining factor is size. Still, it does seem somewhat peculiar that the outcome would be the same irrespective of whether the difference in size were very significant, or whether they were almost exactly the same size. The peculiarity is removed immediately once we think of the situation in terms of statics, however. Imagine the bodies as occupying the two pans of an (idealized frictionless) beam balance. The arm will always be tipped down on the side of the heavier, no matter how slight the difference in weight. That this is indeed the reasoning behind Descartes' account is made clear in a letter to Hobbes in which Descartes responds to Hobbes' claim that the extent to which a body is moved is proportional to the force exerted on it, so that even the smallest force will move a body to some extent. Descartes replies:

His assumption that *what does not yield to the smallest force cannot be moved by any force at all* has no semblance of truth. Does anyone think that a weight of 100 pounds in a balance would yield to a weight of one pound placed in the other pan of the scale simply because it yields to a weight of 200 pounds?[158]

What Rule 4 seems to do is to reduce the question to one of statics, by removing considerations of speed. And the means by which it does this is through the principle of the ontological equivalence of motion and rest. Descartes' statement of this equivalence has often been seen as an important move in the direction of a proper understanding of the principle of inertia, as a step on the road from seeing rest simply as a privation of motion, to treating rest and uniform rectilinear motion as being dynamically on the same footing, as being states that require no force for their maintenance. This will be the route followed by Newton, and he may well have been directed along this route by reading Descartes. But it is not so clear that this captures the direction of Descartes' own thinking here. Quite the contrary, the principle of the ontological equivalence of motion and rest, which in a physical context such as the rules of collision amounts to a dynamical equivalence, is in fact a step in a completely different direction for Descartes. The ontological or dynamical equivalence of motion and rest means that what holds for rest holds for motion. Statics tells us about the behaviour of bodies at rest: perhaps it can be built upon to deal with bodies in motion, if motion can somehow be seen to be a variation on rest (a departure from an equilibrium state). If, like Descartes, one has developed one's principal dynamical concepts in the context of statics, one is going to be forced into this kind of manœuvre at times, and far from what is involved here being a translation of dynamical concepts into kinematic terms, what we seem to have is the pursuit of a dynamics for which there is no kinematic rationale. Once we consider the cosmology that this natural philosophy is designed to ground, however, it becomes clear that a kinematic rationale is of less urgency in Cartesian cosmology than it is in one in which bodies are moving through an empty space.

---

[158] Descartes to Mersenne for Hobbes, [21 January 1641]: *Œuvres*, iii. 287.

## CARTESIAN COSMOLOGY

In Cartesian cosmology, planets move because they are moved by a rotating fluid in which they are embedded. Because the universe is a plenum, for any part of it to move it is necessary that other parts of it move, and the simplest form of motion which takes the form of displacement is going to be a closed curve. There are a number of such displacements around various centres (solar systems) and they carry bodies around with them, with distance from the centre depending on how large and animated the body is. The immediate problem for Descartes lies less in his kinematics than in the fact that he has provided us with a number of basic laws regulating the behaviour of perfectly inelastic bodies either completely isolated from one another or acting upon one another in pairs in the absence of any surrounding matter. The difficulty is that bodies in Descartes' cosmos are neither perfectly inelastic nor do they exist in isolation from one another. Somehow, he needs to capture the internal material constitution of bodies and the material constitution of their immediate environment, in terms which remain mechanical. Above all, since the body moves by means of the fluid medium in which it is embedded, understanding the motion of the body is above all understanding the motion of the fluid. Cartesian kinematics cannot be used to deal with planetary motion in a direct way, for example, by treating planets as if they were perfectly inelastic bodies moving through a void. Rather, the role of the kinematics is to enable us to understand how the behaviour of the body results from the behaviour of its constituent parts, where the kinematics is primarily directed towards these constituent parts. However, this is only a first approximation, for the motion of the body depends not just on the behaviour of these constituent parts but also on the behaviour of the medium that surrounds it, so the behaviour of the medium also needs to be analysed in terms of its own constituent parts.

In the Cartesian cosmos, fluids cause, rather than offer resistance to, the motion of bodies embedded in them. Because of this, it is crucial that the motion of the constituent parts of fluids do not routinely impede the motion of solid bodies in any way, as we might initially have expected. As for a body at rest embedded in a fluid, Descartes maintains that the parts of the fluid, which are in constant motion, act upon the stationary body equally from all sides, so that the net effect is zero, and the body remains at rest. In the case of a moving body, however, the moving parts of the fluid help or reinforce the motion, allowing a large body to be moved by small force. The fluid will impede the body if it is moving faster than the particles of the fluid but, within limits, it may also acquire motion from the fluid. A solid body immersed in a fluid will be carried along by it and indeed by Descartes' definition of motion must not be considered to be moving, because there is no transference with respect to contiguous bodies. In other words, the speed of a body in a fluid will depend to a large extent upon the speed of the parts of the fluid, and this is a crucial result for Descartes' cosmology, as it is the main ingredient in the explanation of why planets remain in stable orbits. It is worth remembering, in this context, that within geocentric cosmology, the crystalline spheres had increasingly been interpreted in fluid terms, and, with the breakdown of the sharp distinction between physical and astronomical questions, by the early decades of the seventeenth century this seems to have been a widespread view.[159] For many it was a way of keeping the crystalline spheres in the wake of Tycho's demonstration that comets pass through the orbits of planets, which rules out shells of ice or crystal maintaining them in their orbits. The liquefaction of the crystalline spheres was a relatively painless way of rethinking the question of what kept planets and the fixed stars in their orbits, especially for those (like Bacon, as we have seen) who accepted some form of geocentric theory. But there was also an attraction for someone like Descartes, who wanted to account for all physical processes in terms of a physical theory that restricted physical interaction to contact action. Indeed, in Descartes' case the motivation for postulating a fluid medium is even stronger, because he has a well-developed theory of how bodies behave in fluids. By contrast, his rules of collision, which might well be used to provide a model for bodies colliding in an otherwise empty space, have no bearing on the motion of separated bodies.

If fluid cosmology has some orthodox precedents, however, Descartes's advocacy of multiple heliocentric systems does not. In the course of arguing that the intensity of the light of the sun is such that it must be a source of light, by contrast with the planets and the moon, which merely reflect light, he makes a move that neither Copernicus, nor Kepler, nor Galileo ever did:

if we consider how bright and glittering the rays of the fixed stars are, despite the fact that they are at an immense distant from us and from the sun, we will not find it hard to accept that they are like the sun. Thus if we were as close to one of them as we are to the sun, that star would in all probability appear as large and luminous as the sun.[160]

No one between Bruno and Descartes in the *Principia* had advocated, in print, a multiple heliocentric cosmos of infinite or indefinite extent, but after Descartes it becomes accepted as part of the heliocentric picture.[161] Because it has a centre around which the planets and fixed stars revolve, both Copernican and Keplerian spaces have an intrinsic directionality, a notion that Descartes definitively rejects, as we have seen. Descartes' cosmos has an indefinite number of planetary solar systems, each of them rotating around its own central sun, and each of these suns itself revolving on its own axis. His illustration of the system (see Fig. 8.4), where Y, $f$, F, S etc. are suns, leaves no doubt at all that he is advocating a multiple heliocentric system, with each sun at the centre of a vortex of rotating fluid matter that carries its planets along with it, 'and we will understand that numerous others exist, above, below, and beyond the plane of this figure, scattered throughout all the dimensions of space'.[162]

Descartes' defence of this system relies extensively on the fact that our perception of the apparent rest or motion of the planets is relative to our own rest or motion, and we may be unable to tell whether, and to what degree, the cause of their apparent motion is a motion which we undergo, but of which we may be unaware, or whether it is due

---

[159] See Donahue, 'The Solid Planetary Spheres in Post-Copernican Natural Philosophy'.
[160] *Principia*, Book 3 art. 9.
[161] See Thomas Kuhn, *The Copernican Revolution* (Cambridge, Mass., 1957), 189.
[162] *Principia*, Book 3 art. 23.

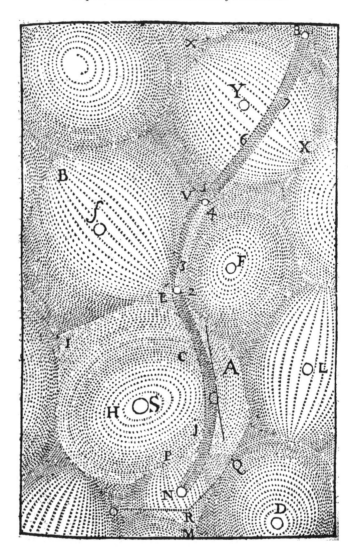

**Figure 8.4**

to a motion in what we are observing. The celestial fluid carries the earth along in its orbit, but it is at rest with respect to this fluid and, therefore, on Descartes' kinematic definition of motion and rest, which relates them only to contiguous bodies, it is also at rest per se. Note, however, that there is still a difference between the earth and the sun on this kind of definition: whereas the sun 'does not move from one place to another', in the case of the earth, we are told that 'the earth is at rest in its heaven which nevertheless carries it along'.[163] The situation is not straightforward. When Descartes explains in what sense no motion must be attributed to the earth, he distinguishes between the term as vulgarly understood and the precise use of the term, and concludes that in neither case can motion be attributed to the earth.[164] On the vulgar use of the term, people determine motion in terms of points on the earth considered to be motionless, and in this case it would be proper to talk of the other planets as moving but not the earth. On the precise definition, it would be wrong to conclude from the fact that the earth 'floats in a fluid heaven whose parts are extremely mobile and that the fixed stars always remain in the same position relative to one another' that we could treat these fixed stars as motionless and use this to establish that the earth moves, for the fixed stars are not contiguous with the earth, and therefore cannot be used to determine motion. This account has sometimes been interpreted as a relativist gloss to disguise Descartes' Copernicanism, but this is unlikely for his explicit advocacy of a multiply heliocentric system is far more radical that standard versions of Copernicanism.[165] His account does in fact make sense in terms of his understanding of motion, and this understanding has its ultimate rationale in the criterion of clarity and distinctness. Descartes' definition of motion is indeed complex but it is motivated by an attempt to provide something purely kinematic, a motivation which in turn derives primarily from his own concern with providing foundational notions that are clear and distinct. On Descartes' understanding, the earth has no power to move itself, and even if it did, it would not move in a circle, but in a straight line. The reason it moves in a circle is because it is dragged along by the surrounding fluid, something whose motion it does not affect in any way. Does this nevertheless mean it moves? That depends on what idea of motion one uses. We must remember here that the Aristotelian idea of motion as the actualization of a potentiality was not at all an intuitively clear notion, and indeed was unintelligible in some of the standard definitions, and also that, when pressed, there was no universally accepted understanding of motion. The earth certainly moves relative to the sun, particularly if one thinks of it in dynamic terms, and there is a force which Descartes associates with rotation, which acts radially out from the centre of the rotation, which is present in the earth and which would not be present if the earth were not revolving, but this is a revolution relative to the sun, not relative to the fluid carrying the body.[166] In sum, in

---

[163] Ibid. arts. 21 and 26 respectively.     [164] Ibid. art. 29.

[165] The theory that ours was not the only solar system was singled out in many of the condemnations of Cartesianism. Proposition 5 of the Condemnation of the Faculty of Theology at Louvain, 1662, condemns the claim that any world would have to have the same kind of matter as ours. Article 6 of the Congregation of the Priests of the Oratory, General Congregation of the Oratorians Residing in Paris, 1678, condemns the claim that 'there is no repugnance in God's creating several worlds at the same time'. Proposition 13 of the Prohibited Propositions of the Fifteenth General Congress of the Society of Jesus, 1706, condemns the claim that 'beyond the heavens, there really exists a space filled by bodies or by matter'. I take these from the extracts of condemnations given in the Appendix in Roger Ariew, John Cottingham, and Tom Sorell, *Descartes' Meditations: Background Source Materials* (Cambridge, 1998), 252–60. A comprehensive discussion of condemnations of Cartesianism was provided in 1705 by Jean Du Hamel in his *Quaedam recentiorum philosophorum ac praesertim Cartesii propositiones damnatae ac prohibitae* (Paris).

[166] *Principia*, Book 3 art. 29.

Descartes' view, the claim that the earth does not move has been based upon a completely misconceived understanding of motion, which in turn rests upon fundamental misconceptions about the nature of space and matter: the original context in which the claims about the earth being at rest or moving were made is a context that completely fails to satisfy the criterion of clarity and distinctness, and so Descartes simply refuses to engage with it.

The planetary model that Descartes operates with is set out in these terms:

Let us assume that the matter of the heavens, in which the planets are situated, revolves unceasingly, like a vortex having the sun as its centre, and that those of its parts that are close to the sun move more quickly than those further away, and that all planets (among which we include the earth) always remain suspended among the same parts of this celestial matter. For by that alone, and without any other devices, all their phenomena are easily understood. Thus if some straws are floating in the eddy of a river, where the water doubles back on itself and forms a vortex as it swirls, we can see that it carries them along and makes them move in circles with it. Further, we can often see that some of these straws rotate about their own centres, and that those that are closer to the centre of the vortex that contains them complete their circle more rapidly than those that are further away from it. Finally, we see that, although these whirlpools always attempt a circular motion, they practically never describe perfect circles, but sometimes become too great in width or in length. Thus we can easily imagine that all the same things happen to the planets; and this is all we need to explain all their remaining phenomena.[167]

The planets are carried in a vortex around the sun, with their periods approximately proportional to their distance from the sun, but two of the planets, the earth and Jupiter, also have moons that Descartes is aware of, and he explains the motion of these in terms of vortices as well, the period of the moons of Jupiter again being proportional to their distance from the centre. He is careful to note, however, that the centres of planets will not always necessarily be in exactly the same plane, and that the orbits they describe will not always be perfectly circular.[168] On the first question, variation of the planets in latitude, he notes slight variations from the ecliptic in the planes of other planets, but points out that all these planes pass through the centre of the sun. On the second question, the longitudinal motion of the planets, he notes that the planets appear more distant from the sun at particular times in their orbits. It is possible that Descartes knew of Kepler's work on planetary orbits, since Beeckman was studying Kepler carefully from the middle of 1628 and there is some reason to think that he showed this material to Descartes at their meetings at the end of 1628 and early 1629,[169] but if he did, there is no evidence that Descartes is referring to elliptical orbits here when he talks of orbits not being perfectly circular. It is true that he talks of the shape of the orbit of the moon as 'coming close to that of an ellipse',[170] but he never extends this to the orbits of the planets, and in any case what he is referring to is not a strict ellipse, which has two foci, but rather a shape distorted so that it resembles an ellipse, but still has a single centre. We are in the

[167] *Principia*, Book 3 art. 30.          [168] Ibid. art. 34.
[169] See Schuster, *Descartes and the Scientific Revolution, 1618–1634*, ii. 566–79.
[170] *Principia*, Book 3 art. 153.

realm of a mix of mechanics and matter theory here, where contingencies, not precise mathematics, determine the shapes of orbits, although it is worth remembering that, as we saw earlier, in Kepler's account, the 'natural' orbits—those that correspond to the geometrical archetypes—are circular, and it is the planets' librations, caused by complex magnetic and quasi-magnetic features of their physical make-up, that results in elliptical orbits. Both Kepler and Descartes treat circular orbits as natural, the difference is that Kepler is mathematically serious about the exact shape of the orbits that planets actually describe, whereas for Descartes the exact shape is a contingent physical question, determined by differing vortical pressures. For Descartes, planets always tend to move in circular orbits, 'but inasmuch as all the bodies in the universe are contiguous and act on one another, the motion of each is affected by the motions of all the others, and therefore varies in innumerable ways'.[171]

This is evident in Descartes' dismissal of the detailed observations and calculations of Tycho and others, which placed comets between the earth and the sun. Descartes' view is that they must be located outside the orbit of Saturn, and his reasons for holding this depend not upon more detailed observations or more detailed calculations, but upon the observation that they

require this extremely vast space between the sphere of Saturn and the fixed stars in order to complete all their journeys, for these are so varied, so immense, and so dissimilar to the stability of the fixed stars and to the regular revolutions of the planets around the sun, that they seem inexplicable by any laws of nature without this space.[172]

In other words, the underlying mechanical and matter-theoretic principles of Cartesian cosmology require that they be the objects most distant from the centre of our solar system and, when Descartes comes to discuss comets in detail, the assumed mass or size of these objects is also determined wholly by these principles.

Descartes fully realizes what is at issue here, and in effect he defends his general procedure in telling us that if what he deduces, from his basic principles or causes, 'is in exact agreement with all natural phenomena, then it seems that it would be an injustice to God to believe that the causes of the effects that are in nature and which we have thus discovered are false'.[173] He talks of deducing these 'in a mathematical sequence', by which he presumably means synthetically, from first principles, since there is no mathematical demonstration of any kind in the *Principia*. The crucial phrase is that about an injustice to God, which is a clear signal that what is at issue is our starting out from (divinely guaranteed) clear and distinct principles and proceeding in a way that preserves this clarity and distinctness: if we can do this then, as he makes clear in the *Meditationes* and in Part 1 of the *Principia*, we will not go astray, because God has guaranteed that what we perceive clearly and distinctly is true. Nevertheless, Descartes is careful to point to the hypothetical nature of his own enterprise: *if* we start from clear and distinct principles and proceed in the appropriate way then we cannot go wrong, but of course not everyone is going to take Descartes' word for it that his principles actually satisfy these criteria, so he is content to have them treated

---

[171] Ibid. art.157    [172] Ibid. art. 41.    [173] Ibid. art. 43.

as hypotheses, so long as it is recognized that what he will deduce from them will 'agree entirely with the phenomena'.[174]

One reason that these disclaimers come at this point is that Descartes is now about to present his matter theory, and this is something for which he cannot plausibly claim anything more than a hypothetical status. In beginning his discussion of matter theory, he notes those basic principles which he takes himself to have established: the homogeneity and divisibility of matter, and the conservation of motion (that is, the product of size and speed). What remains to be done is to determine the size of the parts into which this matter is divided, the speed at which they move, and the shape of the loops in which they move. There are an infinite number of possibilities here, so Descartes proposes we make a number of assumptions on these questions, and see whether these assumptions enable us to deduce the phenomena as they appear.

The first is that God divided matter into parts of a single size, the average of the various sizes of the parts of matter that now exist. Second, we assume that he introduced into the universe the same total amount of matter that it still contains. Finally, we assume that God

caused them all to begin to move with equal force, [1] each one separately around its own centre, by which means they formed a fluid body, such as I judge the heavens to be, and [2] also several together around certain other centres equidistant from each other, arranged in the universe as we see the centres of the fixed stars to be now, as well as around other more numerous points, equal in number to the planets. Thus, for example, he transported all the matter which is in the region AEI [Fig. 8.4] all together around the centre S, and, similarly, transported all the parts of matter that occupied the space AEV around the centre F, and so on, so that these parts formed as many vortices as there are now celestial bodies in the world.[175]

Although the parts of matter in the universe cannot begin by having a spherical shape, their rotation, and the consequent breaking off of their corners, gradually wears down their shape so that they become spherical. However, not everything can be spherical in a plenum, and the broken corners and edges of the original parts of matter must fill the regions between these spheres, and in order to do this they must be extremely tiny, as well as being very active, for, in the process of being broken off from the original pieces, they must have acquired significant speed because they are driven by the larger parts from which they initially derive through narrow gaps. Moreover, these very small parts of matter—'subtle matter' in Descartes's terminology—have a large surface area in proportion to their volume. Both the degree of activity and the large surface area : volume ratio turn out to be mechanically important properties, since both of these can affect the solidity of a body.[176] This is significant, since it means that once we leave the idealized context of the rules of collision, the quantity of motion that a body has is a function of more than the product of size and speed: the degree of agitation of subtle matter is in fact significantly greater than the product of its size

[174] *Principia*, Book 3 art. 44     [175] Ibid. art. 46.     [176] Ibid. art. 125.

and speed.[177] Descartes has no way of quantifying the extra quantity of motion generated by these new factors, yet without them, as he realizes, he cannot construct a viable cosmology.

It is not just cosmology but above all his optics that dictates what the different sizes of matter are going to be. Descartes distinguishes between three sizes of parts of matter, or 'elements' as he terms them.[178] The first is subtle matter, extremely fine and active, the second is the spherical globules from which subtle matter derives in the process of rubbing and grinding. A third kind is now introduced, composed of especially bulky parts. Descartes maintains that everything is composed of these three elements: 'the sun and the fixed stars of the first, the heavens of the second, and the earth, the planets, and the comets of the third'. Moreover, these three elements are sufficient to provide the material basis for Descartes' optics, for the first element makes up those bodies that produce light, namely suns and stars; the second element makes up the medium in which light is propagated, namely the celestial fluid; and those bodies that refract and reflect light, such as the planets, are made up from the third element.

As a significant amount of subtle matter is formed—more than is needed to fill the area between the parts of second matter—the globules (*boules*) of second matter begin to be pushed radially outwards through the action of centrifugal force, and the excess subtle matter takes its place in the more central regions, ultimately forming the sun S and the fixed stars F and *f* (Fig. 8.4 p. 306). Here we have the elements of Descartes' account of the production and transmission of light. Using the example of the stone in a sling to demonstrate the existence of a radial tendency away from the centre, he sets out to explain how the light from the disc of the sun is passed to the eye of an observer on earth. A globule at F (Fig. 8.5) is pushed by all those in the cone DFB but not by those outside the cone, so that if the space F were void, all those globules in the space DFB would advance to fill it.[179] Light is the effect of pressure in the globules, and an eye placed at F would receive impulses originating at all points between B and D, so that the whole disc of the sun is visible. Note that this pressure is transmitted instantaneously, and there is no interference between the globules, a point that can be illustrated if we imagine a vessel BFD containing balls of lead (Fig. 8.6), in which we make an opening at F, so that the balls descend by the force of their own weight. As soon as ball 1 moves, so, at exactly the same time do 2, 2 and 3, 3, 3, but none of the others. Moreover, it is the pressure, not the motion of the balls that does the work, and 'the force of light does not consist in any duration of motion, but only in the pressing or first preparation of motion, even though actual motion may not result from this pressure.'[180] Light is, in short, a pressure caused by a tendency to centrifugal motion.

The success of this account depends very much on the plausibility of the vortex theory. Since the system of crystalline spheres had been rejected on the grounds that

---

[177] See Edward Slowik, 'Perfect Solidity: Natural Laws and the Problem of Matter in Descartes' Universe', *History of Philosophy Quarterly* 13 (1996), 187–204, and more generally, idem, *Cartesian Spacetime: Descartes' Physics and the Relational Theory of Space and Motion* (Dordrecht, 2002).
[178] *Principia*, 3 art. 52.      [179] Ibid. art. 62.      [180] Ibid. art. 63.

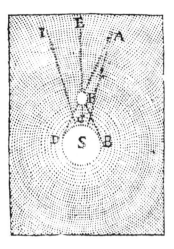

Figure 8.5

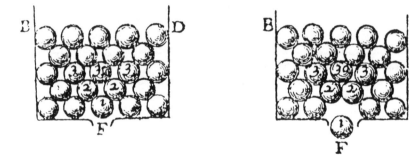

Figure 8.6

such a physical structure was not compatible with the observed motion of celestial bodies, it is clearly incumbent on Descartes to show how his vortex proposal is compatible with such observed motions, particularly with the regular, continued motions of these bodies.[181]

---

[181] Gassendi had also proposed a vortex theory, which he unaccountably traced back to Epicurus, and he evidently believed that this was the ultimate source of Descartes' account. On the Gassendean vortex theory, vortical motion was ultimately induced by an internally generated rotation, not unlike the action of Kepler's magnetic fibres, but in its effects it was physically identical to a Cartesian vortex: see Eric Aiton, *The Vortex Theory of Planetary Motions* (London, 1972), 66–7. The important point is that the two main contenders for the role of leading corpuscularian natural philosophy were committed to vortices, and Gassendeans could happily accept the Cartesian vortex theory.

The first constraint on vortices is that they cannot touch at the poles, because if they did, and they were rotating in the same direction, their motions would be combined, whereas if they were rotating in opposite directions, their motions would cancel out. Consequently, what we would expect, and what is evident from the representation in Figure 8.4 p. 306, is that the poles of some vortices touch the equators of others, and, where this is not possible, they at least have their poles as near as possible to the equators of contiguous vortices. The distribution of fixed stars in the sky suggests that the vortices are not all of equal size, but because of the way in which light is propagated, namely radially from the centre of a vortex, we can deduce that they must all be at the centre of vortices. While they are isolated in some respects from one another, however, there is a flow of subtle matter, on a cosmic scale, between vortices. What happens, in brief, is that subtle matter enters the vortex at the poles, moving to the centre and from there outwards towards the equator, where it meets the poles of other vortices and passes into these. In Figure 8.7, for example, the solar vortex AYBM rotates on its axis AB, while the neighbouring vortices K, O, L, and C rotate on their axes TT, YY, ZZ, and MM. The subtle matter from vortices K and L is able to enter at poles A and B, and that which is spun around axis AB will be expelled at Y and M, passing on to O and C, from where it will move to the centre of the vortex. The globules of second matter, however, being bulkier, are unable to conserve their motion in passing from the equator of one vortex to the pole of another, and they end up being pushed out from the centre, so that a permanent reservoir of subtle matter is formed, which constantly turns on its axis: this is the sun.[182]

One might think that the further from the centre of the vortex a body is, the greater its linear velocity; and this will indeed be an assumption in Descartes' account of the motion of comets. However, he also knew that Mercury rotates more quickly than Saturn, so speed of motion cannot be a simple function of distance from the sun. What is needed to save the appearances here is a twofold mechanism, and Descartes had already provided this in *Le Monde*.[183] What he argued was that the closer globules of second matter are to the centre of the vortex, the smaller and faster they are. But this only holds up to the orbit of the outermost planet, Saturn. Beyond Saturn, the globules move outwards with every added increment in speed.[184] The reason for this is that there is an artificial augmentation of the speed of the globules in the region between the sun and Saturn, caused by the rotation of the sun, which causes bodies contiguous to its surface to rotate more rapidly, accelerating those contiguous to these as well, but to a slightly lesser degree, and so on out to Saturn, where the effect finally peters out. The result is that, as one moves both inwards from Saturn towards the sun, and outwards from Saturn towards the periphery, the speed of the globules increases, and it follows from this that globules nearer the sun must be smaller than those further away, because if they were the same size they would have more centrifugal force, in which case they would be projected outwards beyond the latter.[185]

---

[182] Ibid. arts. 70–2.     [183] *Œuvres*, xi. 53–6.     [184] *Principia*, Book 3 art. 82.
[185] Ibid. art. 85. Aiton, *The Vortex Theory of the Planetary Motions*, 63 n. 78, notes that this implies that the stability of the vortex requires that the centrifugal force must not decrease with distance from the centre.

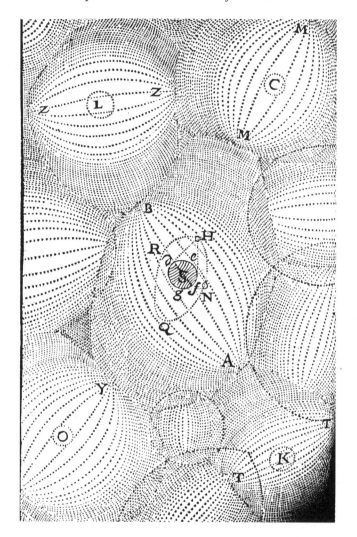

**Figure 8.7**

Subtle matter is not completely uniform in size and agitation, something that Descartes puts down to the fact that it is formed from rubbings and scrapings. Some of the larger parts of this first element are able to join together, and in the process of doing this they transfer motion to the smaller parts. The former will be found predominantly flowing in a straight line from the poles to the centre of the vortex, whereas the smaller parts, because they are smaller and more agitated, are able to circulate throughout the vortex. The larger parts of the first element have to pass around the tightly packed globules of the second element, and they become twisted into grooved threads, those coming from opposite poles being twisted in opposite directions, that is, having left- and right-handed screws. On account of their relatively small degree of agitation and their irregular surfaces, these grooved particles, on moving to the centre of the vortex, easily lock together to form large masses at the surface of the star from which they emerge. Because of their size and small degree of agitation, they appear as a spot on the surface of the sun. Descartes compares the process by which they are formed to the boiling of water which contains some substance that resists motion more than the water: it rises to the surface on boiling to form a scum, which, by a process of agglutination, comes to acquire the character of the third element. These spots can cover the whole surface of a star and cause it gradually to become invisible to observers on earth, and very occasionally the fine matter in such a covered star can break to the surface so it suddenly shines brightly, as was the case, Descartes maintains, with the 'new star' (a supernova) observed by Tycho Brahe in Cassiopeia in 1572.[186] Indeed, this account provides an explanation for why some stars can alternately appear and disappear, and why an entire vortex may occasionally be destroyed by being absorbed by other vortices.

Vortices are destroyed when the stars at their centre become occluded by spots. When the star remains free from spots, the vortex of which it is the centre cannot be destroyed, but if it becomes covered in spots, then how long it will last depends on how much it hinders the action of contiguous vortices. In Figure 8.4, for example, the location of vortex N is such that it impedes vortex S, and as its central star becomes more covered in spots, it will be swept up by vortex S.[187] A different case is that represented in Figure 8.8, where vortex C is situated between four vortices S, F, G, and H, and (above these) M and N. So long as the forces of these six surrounding vortices remain equal, vortex C cannot be completely destroyed, no matter how occluded by spots its central star is. Equilibrium between the other vortices will keep C in existence, but the universe is a place of violent activity and nothing in it will remain in equilibrium for ever.[188] As the star, through occlusion, becomes less and less active,

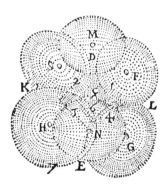

**Figure 8.8**

---

[186] *Principia*, Book 3 arts. 104–14.   [187] Ibid. art. 116.   [188] Ibid. art. 118.

the size of the vortex diminishes until finally one of the contiguous vortices engulfs it. The imagery here is that of epidemics, and it serves to force home Descartes' very radical alternative to the incorruptible heavens of the Aristotelian/Ptolemaic picture. The Cartesian universe is one in which stars die through a natural process of formation of spots, and as a result of this whole solar systems collapse. These processes are occurring all the time, and in theory are just as likely to occur in our solar system as in any other.

When vortex N (Fig. 8.4) collapses, the agglutinated material of its former central star, which is now largely constituted of the solid matter that makes up the third element, is carried into vortex S, and it is pushed towards the centre of S by the faster-moving globules at the periphery. It continues in this trajectory until it reaches a level where it has acquired a degree of agitation—which here seems to be synonymous, in kinematic language, with its degree of speed—equal to that of the surrounding globules. If this level is further out than Saturn, the body will become a comet, whose path is represented in Figure 8.4 as passing from N to C to C2.[189] If it has passed beyond Saturn inwards towards our sun, however, it will become a planet, finally reaching a layer where it has the same force to continue in its motion as the particles of the surrounding fluid in that layer. This force is a function of the density of the body, and bodies of different density will revolve at different distances from the sun, the most dense having the largest orbits: and indeed the explanation for the fact that the moon always turns the same side to the earth is given in terms of that side being less dense than the far side. The stability of each planetary orbit is secured through the fact that the planet is only in equilibrium in that orbit and cannot move either away from the centre or towards it. If the planet were to move away from the centre, it would encounter larger, slower particles that would decrease its speed and make it fall back towards the centre, whereas if it were to move towards the centre it would encounter smaller, faster particles that would augment its force and push it from the centre. Once in a stable orbit, the planet would simply be swept along by the fluid in which it was embedded. Accounting for the speed of the planets requires three mechanisms: first, speed increases as a function of distance from the centre; second, bodies between centre and the orbit of Saturn are artificially accelerated by the rotation of the sun, an acceleration that decreases as we move out from the centre until it finally dies out completely by the time we reach Saturn; and third, speed decreases between the surface of the sun and the orbit of Mercury due to a retarding solar atmosphere. As for the shape of the orbit, the solar vortex is distorted by the unequal pressures of neighbouring vortices, so that the planet does not describe an exact circle but will describe a wider loop where the pressure is less. Finally, the diurnal rotation of a planet is something that it acquires when it is first formed, and which it retains thereafter, although there is a slight diminution in speed due to the action of the surrounding medium, because, unlike its orbital motion, the diurnal motion of the earth is not due to the motion of the fluid medium and may act contrary to it.[190]

---

[189] *Principia*, Book 3 art. 126.          [190] Ibid. art. 140.

The third kind of celestial body formed from the occluded stars of collapsed vortices are the planetary satellites. Descartes talks of the two planets he knew to have moons, namely Jupiter and the earth, each being at the centre of their own vortex, which carries its satellites around with it.[191] Two possibilities are suggested as to the origins of the earth–moon relationship. Either the moon moved towards the earth before the earth began to orbit the sun (he considers that this is what happened in the case of Jupiter's moons), or, more likely, the moon, having the same density as the earth but a greater force of agitation, had to revolve at the same distance from the centre as the earth but more quickly. Both these possibilities are accounted for in the model that Descartes proposes.[192]

## THE FORMATION OF THE EARTH

The final published Part of the *Principia* considers the formation and make-up of the earth, and this was in fact the first time the earth had been an object of natural-philosophical investigation. There had of course been theories about such phenomena as earthquakes and volcanic activity, but these were considered—most notably by Aristotle—to be something that affected only the superficial layers of the earth: the earth's great mass was inert.[193] Having not only moved the earth from the centre of the cosmos, but also made it little more than a piece of refuse from another solar system, Descartes puts himself in a position where he can consider it in the same way as any other concentration of solid matter, and indeed can consider any other planet as being like the earth. The account of the formation of planets from occluded vortices is now used as a basis for a hypothetical theory of the formation of the earth, in which events are reconstructed so that the outcome of this process would result in the earth having exactly the same features as those it actually has.[194] Note that Descartes is interested only in what kind of physical processes could have resulted in the formation of the earth, not in whether it was physical processes or a supernatural act of creation that resulted in its formation: as he tells us in art. 1 of the extended French version of the *Principia*, 'it will rightly be concluded that the nature of [natural things] is the same as if they had indeed been formed in such a way, although the world was not formed in that way in the beginning, but was created directly by God'. In other words, God having decided to give the earth the characteristics it has, he could have chosen the physical process that Descartes describes and have got the same result as that he achieved by supernatural means.

The reconstruction of the earth's formation from a star and its journey into this solar system provide an indication of what its internal constitution must be like. The innermost region of the planet, marked I in Figure 8.9, is composed of subtle matter

---

[191] Ibid. art. 33.    [192] Ibid. art. 149.
[193] On theories of the earth in antiquity and in the Middle Ages, see Clarence J. Glacken, *Traces on the Rhodian Shore* (Berkeley, 1967), chs. 1–7. On Descartes's account see Jacques Roger, 'The Cartesian Model and its Role in Eighteenth-Century "Theory of the Earth"', in T. Lennon, J. Nicholas, and J. Davis, eds, *Problems of Cartesianism* (Kingston, 1982), 95–112.
[194] *Principia*, Book 4 art. 1.

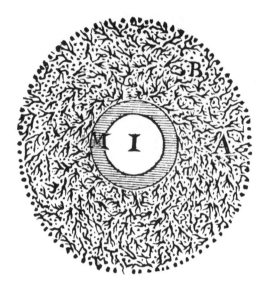

**Figure 8.9**

and is of the same consistency as the sun, except that it is not so pure. The middle region consists of dense material, of a similar consistency to sunspots, which is impervious to the globules of the second element but able to admit grooved particles and other subtle matter. Finally, the outermost region consists of particles of the third and, to a lesser extent, second element. Descartes derives the properties of the particles of third-element matter that predominates on the surface of the earth from the way in which they are formed. The particles that can be formed from the joining together of subtle matter are much larger than globules, although they are much less active, and unlike globules, which are spherical, they take their shape from the irregular scrapings from which they are formed, and so can form a large range of different shapes. Moreover, in the planet's stellar past it was formed from the subtle matter pushed to the centre of the vortex by heavier rapidly moving globules. There was great pressure towards the centre, and this remains the case as the earth moves out of its own vortex and into that of the sun, but its internal material constitution is changed by this move, for many globules at the periphery of the earth which, because of their mass/bulk, were in equilibrium with surrounding layers when they revolved close to the centre, while it was still a star, will no longer be in equilibrium once the earth has settled into a stable orbit as a planet in our solar system, and they will move towards the centre of the solar system, being replaced by heavier globules. It is this outer region that Descartes is interested in, as the two inner regions of the earth are covered by a shell of occluded material.[195]

[195] *Principia*, Book 4 art. 13.

The body that emerges from a collapsed vortex, and establishes itself in an orbiting layer of celestial fluid around the sun, is still unlike the earth as we know it in many respects, and Descartes sets out the four basic kinds of 'action' by which the different kinds of typically terrestrial phenomena are produced: these are the production of transparency by the motion of globular matter, the production of weight or gravity, the production of light, and the production of heat.[196] Consider the case of weight/gravity. Given the intense interest in gravity in the wake of the publication of Newton's *Principia*, Descartes' treatment of the phenomenon took on a great significance, and indeed became one of the key issues in disputes over the vortex theory, for, unlike the approach of Kepler and Newton whereby weight or gravity is to be explained in terms of a mutual attraction between heavy bodies and the earth, his account of weight is formulated in terms of his vortex theory. He begins with an account of the formation of spherical drops of water, whereby the celestial globules circulate in all directions around the water, exerting equal forces towards the centre at all points. In the same way, the globular matter circulating around the earth acts inwards towards the centre, giving it a spherical shape and pushing it towards those bodies we call heavy. In other words, the parts of matter do not just naturally cohere: they are pushed together by the action of the surrounding globular matter, which is squeezed to the centre as heavier matter is pushed outwards through centrifugal force, and it is this pressure that is the cause of, indeed is constitutive of, weight or gravity. In other words, weight is not an intrinsic property of bodies: nothing is intrinsically heavy. If the region around the earth were a void, then bodies would fly off its surface unless they were firmly attached, 'but since there is no such void, and since the earth is not carried along by its own motion, but is moved by the celestial matter which surrounds it and penetrates all its pores, the earth has the mode of a body that is at rest'.[197] The weight of a terrestrial body is not a function of all the matter flowing around it, however, but only of that matter which moves into the region vacated by the matter moving towards the centre, and which is therefore equal in size to it.

As the earth enters the solar system and moves into the appropriate layer of celestial matter, there will be an exchange of matter between the earth and the fluid in which it is embedded, the smaller globules on its surface changing places with the heavier globules of the surrounding fluid, a process that forces the third-element matter to join together to form large clumps which inhibit the activity of celestial globules. The process is illustrated in Figure 8.10, which represents various stages in the earth's formation, beginning on the top right and moving clockwise. At first, the highest region of the earth, A, is divided into two kinds of body, B, which is rare, fluid, and transparent, and C, which is hard, dense, and opaque. The reason for this is that the parts of C have been pressed downwards by celestial globules and have adhered to one another. But C is not completely homogeneous, and under pressure parts of C which are less inclined to bind with one another because of their shape (long as opposed

[196] Ibid. arts. 14–31.
[197] Ibid. art. 22. Unfortunately, as Régis and others were later to point out, if weight results from circulation of surrounding matter, it should be directed not towards the centre but towards the axis of rotation. See e.g. Pierre-Sylvan Régis, *Système de philosophie* (3 vols, Paris, 1690), i. 443.

to branching) are forced up and form a separate layer between A and C, namely B, which is neither completely solid like rock nor completely fluid like water. Particles of D, some of which are hard and some flexible, can separate and unite with C, on the one hand, and C itself could separate into several regions as a result of a mixture of different particles. On the other hand, this separation is responsible for the formation of a rind or shell, E, at the interface between D and B. In this way, the make-up of the planets comes to be relatively stable, but because of the action of the sun in lighting and heating the earth, a layer of agitated matter, F (see Fig. 8.11 upper half) is formed beneath E, trapped between two hard layers, and causing fissures in E to occur. As depicted in the lower illustration of Figure 8.11, fissures can occasionally erupt violently, emitting the liquid (D) and vapours (F) trapped between the two concentric crusts, causing the thick outer crust to crack and tilt, which is how continents (4 in Fig. 8.11), mountain ranges (8), and oceans (3, 6) are formed. Here, B is air, C is a thick crust from which metals originate, D is water, E is the surface of the earth, comprising stones, clay, sand, and mud, and F is air.[198]

The bulk of Part 4 of the *Principia* is devoted to what is in many ways a reformulation of the traditional theory of the elements: air (arts. 45–7), water (arts. 48–56), earth (arts. 57–79), and fire (arts. 80–132). The most significant part of this discussion is Descartes' application of his cosmology to account for the tides. Galileo, Descartes, and Newton each had a distinctive and elaborate account

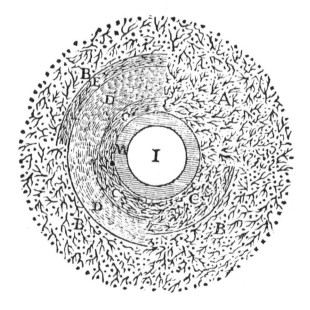

Figure 8.10

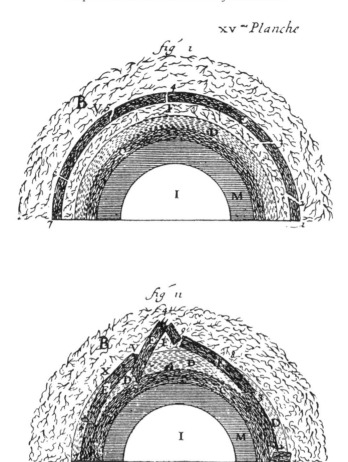

Figure 8.11

of the tides, accounts that gave each of them much trouble, and which in each case was unsuccessful, although each was a significant improvement upon the last. Mechanics and matter theory are linked in an especially complex and delicate way in the particularly intractable phenomenon of the tides, and it was an important testing ground for one's cosmology as the degree of fine tuning required highlights any inadequacies very starkly. The system that Descartes proposes in the *Principia* requires a balance of mechanics and matter theory which was to act as a model for many natural philosophers throughout the seventeenth and eighteenth centuries, offering a good fit between mechanics and matter theory.

In general terms, Descartes' cosmological system provided the first complete physical system of the universe which could be seen as an alternative to that of Aristotle, and it formed the starting point for every serious cosmological system at least until Newton's *Principia Mathematica* appeared forty-three years later. Indeed, for some of the leading natural philosophers and mathematicians of continental Europe, which was the undisputed centre of these disciplines in the eighteenth century, the Cartesian system was deemed to have significant advantages over Newtonian cosmology well into the third decade of that century, despite the bans that were put on the teaching of Cartesianism in France and elsewhere during the second half of the seventeenth century.[199] Yet the Cartesian system is not just the first great comprehensive mechanist natural-philosophical system, it is also in an important respect the last, as doubts begin to be raised as to whether a quantitative physical theory—in a mechanist or any other variety—is best pursued in traditional natural-philosophical terms. Even in Descartes' own terms, it was problematic: the mature Cartesian system is a failure by the standard of the original aspiration of Beeckman and Descartes, which was to produce a quantitative natural philosophy, a 'physico-mathematics'.[200] This is a complex debate, and not a decisive one, even with the appearance of Newton's *Principia*, which offers a very different way of pursuing physical theory, and indeed a different model of natural philosophy.

[199] Generally, see McClaughlin, 'Censorship and Defenders of the Cartesian Faith in France (1640–1720)', and Schmaltz, 'What has Cartesianism to do with Jansenism?' On the reaction to his account of the formation of the earth see Peter Harrison, 'The Influence of Cartesian Cosmology in England', in Stephen Gaukroger, John Schuster, and John Sutton, eds, *Descartes' Natural Philosophy* (London, 2000), 168–92. On the reaction to his account of transubstantiation, see Armogathe, *Theologia Cartesiana*. On the reaction to the account of *bêtes machines*, see Leonora G. Rosenfield, *From Beast-Machine to Man-Machine* (New York, 1968), and Jean-Claude Beaune, *L'Automate et ses mobiles* (Paris, 1980). By the 1750s, there was extensive hostility to Cartesian natural philosophy even in France: see Laurence W. B. Brockliss, *French Higher Education in the Seventeenth and Eighteenth Centuries* (Oxford, 1987), 353–8, 376–80, 366.

[200] Cf. Daniel Garber, 'A Different Descartes: Descartes and the Programme for a Mathematical Physics in his Correspondence', in Stephen Gaukroger, John Schuster, and John Sutton, eds, *Descartes' Natural Philosophy* (London, 2000), 113–30.

# 9

# The Scope of Mechanism

Mechanism has its natural home in physical theory, but physical theory did not by any means exhaust natural philosophy, and its claims as a model for natural-philosophical enquiry generally went well beyond physical theory. In this chapter, I want to focus on three areas of particular concern to mechanists, concerns that highlight the legitimatory aspects of the mechanist project in natural philosophy. The first is the question of how mechanists deal with the explanatory load placed on their systems by a combination of minimal explanatory resources and ambitious explanatory aims, and in particular the role that the doctrine of primary and secondary qualities plays in this respect, especially in Malebranche's reworking of Cartesianism. Second, I want to examine the attempt to extend mechanism into the realms of vital and cognitive functions, phenomena that were treated as part of natural philosophy in the early-modern period, and which generated a great deal of controversy. Finally, I shall raise some issues prompted by the relation between natural philosophy, expanded into the biological realm, and the traditional practice of clinical medicine, which harbours a very different model of understanding biological processes as they relate to illness and health.

## PRIMARY AND SECONDARY QUALITIES

The way in which natural philosophy is pursued in those parts of Descartes' *Principia* that we have been concerned with up to this point diverges from that of the scholastic tradition significantly, both in the first principles it considers necessary if natural philosophy is to be pursued on a viable basis, and in the physical and cosmological doctrines that emerge. But like the mechanist systems of Gassendi and Hobbes, it is in the same broad genre as scholastic natural philosophy in that it aims to provide a theory of the world and our place in it. In another respect, however, the mechanist systems stand in stark contrast to scholastic natural philosophy in that, compared to Aristotelian natural philosophy, they have far more restricted explanatory resources but a far more comprehensive *explanandum*: whereas Aristotelian natural philosophy restricts itself to *natural* phenomena, those which follow from the natures of things, corpuscularian natural philosophies generally purport to account for all phenomena, natural and non-natural (the motion of projectiles, the effect of mechanical devices such as levers and screws, and so on). Mechanism, in particular, purports to explain the whole of the physical realm, for, viewing things at a corpuscular level, there is a sense in which everything acts according to its nature, and all physical behaviour can always be traced back to the motions of the constituent corpuscles of things. But this places an unbearable explanatory load on mechanism, and some partitioning of the *explanandum* is required for its explanatory project to even get started. The instrument of this partitioning is the doctrine of primary and secondary qualities.

The question of the scope of natural philosophy was raised in regard to corpuscularianism in a pre-mechanist context in Bacon. As we have seen, Bacon had argued that natural philosophy should deal with artificial or violent phenomena as well as natural ones, and he had rejected Aristotelianism on these grounds. But it is not that Aristotelianism had restricted itself to natural phenomena, as if this were a choice that Aristotle had made, a choice that could be revised or overturned in the light of experience. The procedure of accounting for the behaviour of bodies in terms of underlying principles meant that one could explain only what was generated by those principles, and these were principles that determined the natural behaviour of the body, which in turn meant that this, and only this, is what could be explained. One thing one might do to go beyond the Aristotelian conception would be to turn to the discipline that dealt with 'violent' or 'non-natural' phenomena such as the motion of projectiles, namely mechanics, and seek some underlying rationale there. But there were some, such as Bacon himself, who thought that mechanics was a purely mathematical discipline of no natural-philosophical relevance, whereas for those who believed that mechanics held the key to restructuring natural philosophy, some way had to be found of connecting mechanics with natural philosophy, and this proved extremely elusive. And in any case, it clearly required a rethinking of natural philosophy, a rethinking that made it receptive to the requirements of mechanics.

One such rethinking lay in the abandonment of Aristotle's first principles and their replacement by something that generated all varieties of physical behaviour, whether natural or unnatural. Micro-corpuscularianism potentially provided the requisite new foundations here, but it lacked the focus of Aristotelianism. The Aristotelian *explanans* generated a particular kind of *explanandum*: what requires explanation is circumscribed in advance, and explanatory resources are specifically geared towards it. Micro-corpuscularianism is devoid of any such focus: the *explanandum* is undifferentiated. This is simply a consequence of attempting to account for any physical phenomenon. But what in fact happens is that micro-corpuscularianism seems to lose contact with the physical world, and its applicability is in effect limited to those idealized situations that it is able to generate from its first principles, which can be restricted to something as simple as those involving only collinear collisions between spherical corpuscles. A related problem is that these first principles offer minimal explanatory resources: shape, and speed and direction of motion, for example, by contrast with Aristotelian essential natures. Hence one of the main programmes of the micro-corpuscularian project is the tailoring of the *explanandum*: it has to be radically reduced to accommodate such minimal explanatory resources. This was facilitated via the doctrine of primary and secondary qualities.

To put the matter in its starkest terms, mechanist natural philosophies had access to potentially very powerful explanatory resources—powerful in virtue of their great economy and universality—but they had difficulty identifying anything that they could actually explain, except highly idealized phenomena. To vindicate this, these highly idealized phenomena are argued to be constitutive of the *explanandum*, either because those phenomena that cannot be accommodated to these can be excluded in various ways as being as 'secondary', as in the doctrine of primary and secondary qualities, or as not really existing at all, as in the elimination of appeal to 'vital' activities in organic phenomena. The distinction between primary and secondary qualities in effect mirrors the natural/unnatural Aristotelian partitioning of phenomena into those that one was required to explain and those that one wasn't required to explain, a distinction that often takes the form of that between occult and manifest qualities,[1] except that the partition now separates macroscopic primary qualities that are generated exclusively by micro-corpuscularian states, with which they share their properties, from those that do not share their properties with the micro-corpuscularian states that generate them, and so are treated as being not genuine phenomena at all, requiring redescription (in the case of colour for example) or elimination (as with 'life'). The distinction between primary and secondary qualities is mechanism's most powerful tool. But it is also its most question-begging one, for its rationale lies less in its ability to contract the range of the *explanandum* to manageable proportions, as in its ability to restrict any phenomena capable of explanation to those explicable by mechanism.

The primary/secondary qualities divide achieves this by a means that, on the face of it, is independent of what one's natural-philosophical commitments are, by drawing a distinction between qualities that are in the object independently of an observer, and qualities that are relative to the observer. A distinction between properties that exist in nature and those that are relative to the observer had been proposed in a natural-philosophical context as early as Democritus. Democritus was concerned to establish that all that exists in nature are atoms and the void, and among the arguments that he used to establish this was a form of relativity argument associated with Protagoras, to the effect that such phenomena as hot and cold do not exist in nature but are merely relative to us. Protagoras' relativism had in fact been predominantly moral, and although it had general epistemological consequences, its application to natural-philosophical issues was questionable. If the relativity argument was to be used to establish the general claim that macroscopic qualities were somehow not real whereas microscopic ones were, it would have to show that microscopic qualities are independent of us whereas macroscopic ones were not, something it manifestly could not do. It is therefore not surprising that Democritus' atomist successors did not restrict reality to the microscopic level: while insisting that everything is composed of atoms, Epicurus, for example, did not deny reality to combinations of atoms, or to the distinctive sensory qualities that such combinations took on, qualities that were not to be found at the atomic level.

The appearance of the relativity argument in a natural-philosophical context occurs with the debates over Copernicanism, and it is Galileo who makes two formative moves. First, as we have seen, he maintains a principle of relativity of motion, namely our inability to detect those motions in which we share. Second, in

---

[1] On the connection between the Aristotelian occult/manifest distinction and the primary/secondary quality distinction, see Hutchison, 'What Happened to Occult Qualities in the Scientific Revolution?'.

*Il Saggiatore* (1623), in setting out to show that heat is a form of motion, he advocates a distinction between those qualities that bodies actually possess and those that are psychic additions of the perceiving mind:

Now I say that whenever I conceive any material or corporeal substance, I immediately feel the need to think of it as bounded, and as having this or that shape; as being large or small in relation to other things, and in some specific place at any given time; as being in motion or at rest; as touching or not touching some other body; and as being one in number, or few, or many. From these conditions I cannot separate such a substance by any stretch of my imagination. But that it be white or red, bitter or sweet, noisy or silent, and of sweet or foul odour, my mind does not feel compelled to bring in as necessary accompaniments. Without the senses as our guides, reason or imagination unaided would probably never arrive at qualities like these. Hence I think that tastes, odours, colours, and so on are no more than mere names so far as the object in which we place them is concerned, and that they reside only in consciousness.[2]

Instead of the microscopic/macroscopic distinction so crucial to corpuscularian matter theory, here we get one formulated in terms of those properties or qualities that we can conceive a body not having, and those we cannot conceive of a body lacking. The former are qualities that result from our interactions with bodies. The latter, by contrast, would exist even if there were no such interactions, and it is these with which natural philosophy concerns itself.

There is a parallel here with the procedures of identifying how a body behaves either when it is in a state of equilibrium (the hydrostatics model) or in the absence of constraints (the kinematic model), and then showing how this behaviour is modified as it departs from an equilibrium state or comes under the action of constraints. What does the work in the present case, however, is not a physical theory but a theory of perception, and more generally a theory of perceptual cognition. The demands on this theory of perceptual cognition are significant: it must show how a physical world that contains only the properties describable in mechanical terms can produce the rich qualitative variation that we experience. At a general level, the problems inherent in the project are evident from Descartes' proposal for how this might be achieved in Rule 12 of his *Regulae*, dating from 1626–8. He appeals here to shape rather than motion, or a combination of the two, but the underlying principle, as well as the underlying problems, are the same. 'The concept of shape', he writes, 'is so simple and common that it is involved in everything perceivable by the senses'. In contrast to the Aristotelian account, whereby our visual perception of shape is dependent on our perception of colour, in that without differences in colour or shade we cannot visually distinguish boundaries, he makes our perception of colour dependent upon our perception of shape:

Whatever you may suppose colour to be, you will not deny that it is extended and so has shape. So what problematic consequences would follow if—avoiding the useless assumption and pointless invention of some new entity, and not denying what others have said on the subject of colour—we simply abstract every feature of colour except its shape, and conceive of

---

[2] Galileo, *Discoveries and Opinions of Galileo*, trans. Stillman Drake (Garden City, NY 1957), 273–9.

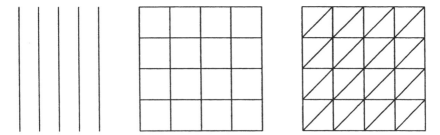

**Figure 9.1**

the difference between white, blue, red etc. as being like the difference between these or similar figures [Fig. 9.1]. The same can be said about everything that can be perceived by the senses, since we can be sure that the infinite multiplicity of figures is sufficient for the expression of all the differences in perceptible things.[3]

Descartes invites us to picture nature as if it were comprised exclusively of shapes, but is this even remotely plausible? We can, perhaps, imagine all colours being represented in terms of a variety of patterns of lines, but what is being asked of us is far more than that. The line patterns must not only represent differences in colours, but also differences between colours, temperatures, tastes, smells, and so on. There must at least be different kinds of shapes to which each sense organ responds. The idea of there being an infinite number of possible shapes does not help here, partly because this suggests that sense organs can distinguish infinitely complex shapes, which we have no reason to believe, but more importantly because what we need to know is not how many shapes there can be but how the relevant kinds of shapes are distinguished. Another factor is that some sense organs can distinguish many kinds of things at the same time: I can feel that something is round, hard, slimy, has a smooth surface, is very close to me, and so on. Again, it seems likely that different kinds of shapes would be needed here.

Within a few years of setting out this account, Descartes had developed a theory of colour where, simplifying somewhat, the colours that we experience are our responses to particular kinds of corpuscles being reflected off the surface of an object, where this surface has purely physical properties that cause the light corpuscles reflecting off it to rotate or spin. Our visual perceptual system is 'ordained by nature' to respond to these rotations by perceiving colours.[4] Descartes' account of the production of colour and its visual cognition is comprehensive, going far beyond anything else available, but the limits to its reductive strategy are obvious. For one thing, we are given no account of how the perception of colour is actually produced. As Walter Charleton put it, 'where is the Oedipus that can discover any *Analogy* betwixt the Retina Tunica, Optick Nerve, Brain, or Soul therein resident, and any one Colour?'[5] Moreover, there

---

[3] Descartes, *Œuvres*, x. 413.
[4] Ibid. vi. 130 (*La Dioptrique*, Discours 6).
[5] Charleton, *Physiologia Epicuro-Gassendo-Charltoniana*, 197.

is no suggestion that Descartes' account of colour perception is generalizable to other senses, or indeed to visual perception of other qualities such as tone and brightness (not to be confused with degree of illumination). In fact, it is not even adequate at a phenomenological level as an account of colour, for it would limit the colours we perceive to those of the spectrum, whereas most of the colours we perceive are not spectral colours at all: we perceive myriad shades of brown for example, a colour that has no place in the spectrum.

Yet if this reduction of sensory qualities to such properties as shape and motion is so inherently implausible, how do we explain its widespread support among early-modern natural philosophers? One important consideration is the collapse of the Aristotelian theory of perceptual cognition. There were two main respects in which it was found unsatisfactory: one turned on the nature of *species*, the other on developments in optics and physiology. We saw in Chapter 7 that in the early seventeenth century there was uncertainty and dispute among scholastic philosophers over just what is grasped in sense perception. The notion of 'objective being' worked well in those cases where in sense perception we grasped the essence of the thing perceived, but it was increasingly conceded that there were in fact no such cases, and some natural philosophers outside the scholastic tradition, such as Mersenne and Gassendi, had concluded that this had implications for the standing of our knowledge. Gassendi concluded that knowledge of essences of the kind that Aristotelians sought was in fact impossible given the sensory faculties we have.[6] What we grasp in sense perception are not inner essences but surface emissions.[7] Consequently, the natural-philosophical system that we can construct is one that must take appearances, not essences, as its subject matter, for we have no access to the latter. Gassendi himself sees this as a *via media* between Aristotelian dogmatism and scepticism.[8]

A second set of considerations turned on developments in optics. Aristotle had maintained that we have the sense organs we do because they naturally display to us the nature of the world, and his account of the optics and physiology of visual perception turned on what he took its function to be. Among other things, the optics and physiology had to be construed in such a way as to yield perceptual images that resembled what was perceived, because veridicality lay in resemblance. An accurate picture of the world, which is what our sense organs were designed to yield under optimal conditions, was a picture that looked exactly like that world. But Kepler had shown in detail in Chapter 5 of his *Ad vitellionem paralipomena* (1605) that the visual image was formed not on the crystalline humour but on the retina, and he showed beyond any doubt that the retinal image was inverted,[9] and this unexpected discovery suggested that the sensory and cognitive organs were not simply passive receivers of information. Aristotle had started from the assumption that perceptual cognition must yield a picture of the world which is just like the world, and any optics and physiology would have to show how this was achieved. But Kepler's work showed that

---

[6] Gassendi, *Opera*, ii. 456.     [7] Ibid. 463.     [8] See Brundell, *Pierre Gassendi*, 100.

[9] See the discussion in Lindberg, *Theories of Vision*, ch. 9. *Ad vitellionem* is available in an excellent English translation as Johannes Kepler, *Optics*, trans. William H. Donahue (Santa Fe, 2000).

the optics and physiology that Aristotle's account yielded turned out to be completely wrong.

When Descartes took up questions of visual cognition in the 1620s, he started from a new understanding of the optics and physiology of vision, and used this understanding to explore what form visual cognition might take. This reverses the direction of enquiry. Instead of working from an understanding of what we expect perception to do, we begin instead with the physical/physiological processes involved in perception and ask what the outcome of these processes is. The difficulty in following this path, especially if one construes not just the physical world, but also the physical processes involved in its perception, in mechanist terms, lies in accounting for our cognitive response. This was an issue for all mechanists, and Descartes is by far the most receptive to the complexity of the questions here. Hobbes, for example, had developed a mechanistic understanding of the optics and physiology of perception in the 1630s, but his findings were pre-empted by the publication of Descartes' *Discours* and *Dioptrique* in 1637. His reaction to these was to maintain that Descartes had not gone far enough in mechanizing perception: since vision is ultimately just motion in Hobbes' view, 'it follows that what sees is also formally and strictly speaking nothing other than what is moved',[10] namely something corporeal. But in fact Descartes' account is highly mechanized, and the dualism that Hobbes rejects plays a role only in human cognition, by which stage all perceptual processes other than intellectual judgement have been accounted for. The principal problem that Descartes deals with, a problem crucial to the success of a mechanist account of perception, but one that Hobbes does not even consider, is whether an account that simply outlined the causal processes involved in perception could capture something we recognized as a perceptual process in the first place.

The faculties involved in perceptual cognition—the 'external' sense organs, the common sense, the memory, and the imagination—had traditionally been construed in corporeal terms, with attention having been given to localization of faculties in the brain by anatomists. But the construal of some level of cognitive functioning in corporeal terms had been associated with various attempts to render matter itself sentient, by invoking the idea of a 'sensitive soul' regulating the corporeal processes from inside. To the extent that he is concerned to show that organic processes, including some cognitive operations, can be construed wholly mechanistically, Descartes has to make sure that his account is compatible with the inertness of matter. His aim is to show that the structure and behaviour of bodies are to be explained in the same way that we explain the structure and behaviour of machines, and in doing this he wants to show how a form of genuine cognition can occur in the absence of intellectual faculties. In other words, he wants to account for automata—self-moving bodies—in purely mechanistic terms. All animal perception comes in this category, as does any human perception that does not involve self-awareness.

In the case of visual cognition, we can distinguish between mere response to a visual stimulus, in which the parts of the automaton simply react in a fixed way; visual

---

[10] Hobbes, 'Tractatus opticus: prima edizione integrale', ed. F. Alessio, *Revista Critica di Storia dela Filosofia* 18 (1963), 147–88: 207.

awareness, in which the perceiver has a mental representation of the object or state of affairs that caused the visual stimulus in the first place; and perceptual judgement, the power to reflect on and make a judgement about this representation, such as a judgement as to its veridicality. Descartes restricts the last to human beings, for in his view it requires the possession of a mind/rational soul. The first is a reflex action that we find not just in animals and humans, but potentially in anything with what he considers to be a circulatory system, which includes not only the circulation of blood in animals but also the movement of sap in plants. So, for example, he includes the reflex behaviour of 'sensitive' plants, such as *Mimosa pudica*, which is extremely sensitive to touch, the leaflets of the bipinnate leaves folding together at the slightest contact with the fingers.[11] A plant apparently capable of sensation was very difficult to explain on the traditional view of sensation, because plants were thought of as being regulated by a vegetative soul, responsible for lower functions such as nutrition, while animals, as well as having a vegetative soul, also had a sensitive soul, which conferred on them the power of sensation.[12] Because Descartes rejects this theory, treating plants and animals along the same mechanistic lines as being composed solely of inert matter, there is no problem in principle with plant sensation for him. Circulation is all that is needed for such reflex action, for if a stimulus affecting one part of the body is to have a systematic effect on something other than the immediate area of contact, it is by means of circulation that the parts of the organism are connected.[13] Most animal and non-conscious human perceptual activities are different from this, going well beyond reflex response and involving representations of the world. An automaton could react directly to the corpuscular action that makes up light without actually *seeing* anything, as a genuine machine might, but this is not how Descartes describes the visual process in automata in *L'Homme*. He tells us, for example, that the 'figures traced in the spirits on the [pineal] gland, where the seat of imagination and common sense is, should be taken to be ideas, that is, to be the forms or images that the rational soul will consider directly when, being united to this machine, it will imagine or will sense any object'.[14] This indicates that there are representations on the pineal gland of the automaton. It is in fact difficult to see how they could not have perceptual representations if we are to talk about visual cognition. And it makes no sense to talk about them having representations but not being aware of the content of these representations. Arnauld, on most questions Descartes' most thoughtful follower, senses the problem, objecting that:

As far as the souls of the brute animals are concerned, M. Descartes elsewhere suggests clearly enough that they have none. All they have is a body with a certain configuration, made up of

[11] Descartes to Mersenne, 23 August 1638: *Œuvres*, ii. 329.

[12] On the traditional Galenic account the vegetative soul is located in the liver, where it operates through the veins, the natural powers of the animal soul are located in the heart, where it operates through the arteries, and its sensitive power is located in the brain, operating through the nerves. This tripartite division had implications for the development of the embryo, in that, on Galen's account, the brain, heart, and liver had to develop first.

[13] For a detailed account of these questions, see Gaukroger, *Descartes' System of Natural Philosophy*, ch. 7.

[14] Descartes, *Œuvres*, x. 176.

various organs in such a way that all the operations that we observe can be produced in it and by means of it. But I think that in order for this conviction to find faith in the minds of men, it must be proved by very valid reasons. For at first sight it is hard to believe that, without the help of any soul, the light reflected from the body of a wolf into the eyes of a sheep could move the very thin optic nerves, and that upon that motion reaching the brain, animal spirits are diffused through the nerves in such a way as is necessary to make the sheep flee.[15]

Specifically, the problem is that, while Descartes can allow that automata have representations, it is not immediately clear how he can allow that they grasp the content of these representations if they are not aware of them as representations: if, unlike human beings, they cannot make judgements about them as representations, for example about their veridicality. The behaviour of automata is such that they must be construed as responding to perceptual and other cognitive stimuli in a genuinely cognitive way, that is, in a way that goes beyond a simple stimulus–response arc. In other words, their behaviour indicates that they are sentient. But they are not conscious: they have no awareness of their own cognitive states as such and so cannot make judgements as to their content. Consequently, Descartes has to account for the behaviour of sentient but non-conscious automata. Because automata are literally 'mindless', this can be done only in terms of a mechanistic physiology. The task is the difficult one of capturing the difference between sentient and non-sentient behaviour, and setting out how this is reflected in differences at the level of a mechanistic physiology.

Descartes' solution, in brief, is twofold.[16] In the first place, he distinguishes between being affected by causes and being affected by signs. When our eyes are affected by rotating light corpuscles, we experience a sensation of colour. The rotating light corpuscles cause us to be in a certain physical state, and this enables them to signify to us something that we experience as colour, and the experience of colour would not occur unless we were able to respond to the sign in a particular way. That is to say, the light rays by themselves do not cause us to see colour, because we would not see colour unless there were something in us that enabled us to respond to this particular kind of motion as a sign of something else. Second, he construes this ability to respond to light of certain kinds in terms of a certain natural configuration of the brain. The brain is fitted out, by God, so as to respond in the appropriate way. This 'hard wiring' makes sure you get the right kind of representations: that you see light, that is, have a visual image that displays colours and shapes, when stimulated in the requisite way. It is not something in nature that causes us to have visual images, it is a combination of a stimulation produced by nature and certain features of an animal's physiology that results in a particular kind of representation, a visual perception. This is clearly different from what happens when an act of perceptual judgement is made, but is it so different from what happens when, say, a plant bends towards the light, or the foetus develops into a fully formed member of the species, which are similar kinds of process on Descartes' account? I think the difference might be characterized in this way. In the case of embryology, as we shall see later, Descartes effectively denies that

[15]  Ibid. vii. 205.
[16]  For details, see the discussion in Gaukroger, *Descartes' System*, 196–213.

a functional understanding of the development of the foetus—such as one that says that the foetus develops in the way it does so that it can become an adult of the species—tells us anything at all, and he replaces it with a mechanical-causal story. In the case of perceptual cognition in automata, by contrast, he does not deny that there is a functional story to be told, but rather indicates how the functional story can be translated into the terms of a mechanistic physiology without losing the key insight that perception of *x* by *y* involves *x meaning something to y*, so that, for example, *y* perceives *x* as a wolf. What is needed is the capacity to translate the visual stimulation, which might be characterized as agitation of the corpuscles making up the retina, into the requisite perceptual representation, that is, one that conveys the idea of a wolf. This can be achieved by the requisite corporeal organs in the brain, whose action can be described in mechanistic terms, supplemented by an account of signification which is compatible with the physical processes described in this mechanistic account and requires no other physical processes than those described.

Among the many questions raised by this account, that of the nature of representation came to dominate discussion in the form of the doctrine of ideas.[17] The problem of perceptual representation was compounded by a novel understanding of cognitive agency. Descartes' view had been that only creatures with a rational soul are capable of perceptual judgement. By the time Malebranche comes to formulate his account of perceptual cognition, this doctrine has been transformed from one that maintains that mind is necessary for human perceptual cognition, to the doctrine that the mind is responsible for perceptual cognition: that what sees and judges is not the person, but the person's mind. This shift is encouraged by the disputes over 'objective being'; by developments in optics which show that the retinal image (and, on the Cartesian account, the pineal image) does not resemble its sources in the world; by considerations of intellectual cognition where one can engage in cogitative activity without perceptual input, and which, therefore, seems to be something that the mind alone engages in; and by worries about the location of perceptual experiences such as pains, worries prompted by phenomena such as phantom limbs, where a pain is sensed as being in a limb which has in fact been amputated, allegedly showing that pains must actually be in the mind or the brain, and are merely experienced as if they were in the limb, in both the normal case and the phantom limb case.[18] The upshot is

---

[17] See Richard A. Watson, *The Downfall of Cartesianism, 1673–1712* (The Hague, 1966), and Yolton, *Perceptual Acquaintance*.

[18] See Descartes to Plempius for Fromondus, 3 October 1637: 'He expresses surprise that . . . I recognize no sensation save that which takes place in the brain. On this point I hope that all doctors and surgeons will help me to persuade him; for they know that those whose limbs have recently been amputated often think they still feel pain in the parts they no longer possess. I once knew a girl who had a serious wound in her hands and had her whole arm amputated because of creeping gangrene. Whenever the surgeon approached her they blindfolded her eyes so that she would be more tractable, and the place where her arm had been was so covered with bandages that for some weeks she did not know that she had lost it. Meanwhile she complained of feeling various pains in her fingers, wrist, and forearm; and this was obviously due to the condition of the nerves in her arm which formerly led from her brain to those parts of her body. This would certainly not have happened if the feeling or, as he says, sensation of pain occurred outside the brain.' Descartes, *Œuvres*, i. 420. One response to this use of phantom limb arguments is to model phantom limb

that Descartes, somewhat ambiguously, glosses talk of people making judgements by speaking of the mind 'inspecting images'. Arnauld, as we shall see below, resists this interpretation of the Cartesian doctrine, insisting that we do not see visual representations of the world but rather see the world by means of visual representations, and this has implications for the agent of vision also, for there is now no need to think in terms of a mind grasping mental representations: instead we can think in terms of a mind capable of the activity of visual representation as being necessary for visual perception of the world, without denying that it is the person, not her mind or her brain, that actually does the seeing. But Arnauld's was a minority view, and a relatively underdeveloped one, and the most influential treatment of the question in the Cartesian tradition was that of Malebranche.

In examining Malebranche's account, it should be noted from the outset that there is an extra factor in Cartesianism in the second half of the seventeenth century, namely the Augustinian doctrine of divine illumination.[19] The chief critic of Malebranche's theory of ideas, Arnauld, also subscribed to this doctrine, and both of them assume that clear and distinct grasp is ultimately dependent upon divine illumination. Moreover, both share the view that the function of our sense organs cannot be to display to us the nature of the corporeal world but that they serve rather to notify us of our bodily needs in a quick and economical way.[20] Malebranche maintains that, before the Fall, Adam had grasped this and he never relied on his senses to judge the nature of bodies.[21] Since the Fall, however, we have become very dependent on our bodies, with the result that we rely on our senses in respects in which this is inappropriate. Put in this way, it is clear that it is not our senses as such that deceive us, but rather the natural judgements that invariably accompany sensations, and which we make involuntarily. The degree of error involved varies. In his account of this question, Malebranche distinguishes between our judgement of primary qualities and our judgement of secondary qualities. He denies that the senses are trustworthy guides to the discovery of such primary qualities of objects as size, shape, motion, and location; but we are not completely deceived about the characteristics of bodies, for we are right in believing that bodies have some size, shape, location, speed, and direction of movement, even if we are wrong in supposing them to have the ones they appear to our senses to have. The deception worked on our senses is much more complete in the case of the secondary qualities such as colour, warmth, sound, odour, texture, and so forth. These, Malebranche tells us, 'in fact are not and never were outside us'. They are purely mental qualities, and the fact we are more mistaken about secondary qualities, which are states of the mind, than we are about primary qualities, which are states

---

pains on referred pains: see M. R. Bennett and P. M. S. Hacker, *Philosophical Foundations of Neuroscience* (Oxford, 2003), 123–4.

[19] See Henri Gouhier, *Cartésianisme et augustinisme au XVIIᵉ siècle* (Paris, 1978).

[20] See Descartes, *Principia*, Book 2, art. 3. So far as I have been able to determine, this doctrine united Cartesians of every variety, and formed a focus for some anti-Cartesian criticism, e.g. in Gerardus de Vries, 'Dissertatio de sensuum usu in philosophando', in idem, *Exercitationes rationales de deo, divinisque perfectionibus accedunt ejusdem disseretationes de Infinito* (Utrecht, 1685), 358–99.

[21] *La Recherche*, Book 1 ch. 5 p. 1 *La Recherche* appeared in a number of extensively revised and expanded editions. I shall refer to it by Book, chapter, and section number.

of bodies, suggests to Malebranche that we have a clearer idea of extension than we do of mind; exactly the opposite of Descartes' view,[22] but something assumed by many mechanists, even if they did not espouse it as bluntly as Hobbes, Gassendi, and some later Cartesians.

Our mistaking something which is merely a mode of the mind for an independently existing external quality occurs, Malebranche argues, because we confuse four things.[23] The first is the action of an object on our sense organ, such as when the minute parts of a body press against our skin; the second is the effect this has in our body, namely the transmission of this action along the nerve fibres to our brain; the third is the modification of the mind that accompanies the event that occurs in our brain, such as the feeling of warmth; the fourth is the natural judgement we involuntarily make about this sensation, for example the belief that the warmth we feel is actually in the object touched and in the hand that touches it. In general, we confuse sensations and the qualities of objects that accompany them. In acting on our sense organ, all that happens is that the minute parts of the body that are sensed, such as light corpuscles, or the rapidly vibrating parts of touched objects, come into contact with the surface of our skin. Because these parts are imperceptibly small, however, we suppose that what we sense—colour in the first case, warmth in the second—belongs to the object sensed. Consequently, 'almost everyone believes that the heat he feels, for example, is in the fire causing it, that light is in the air, and that colours are on coloured objects'.[24] But when the object responsible for the sensation is actually visible, such as when we are pricked by a needle, or when we are tickled by a feather, we do not make this mistake: we do not conclude that the pricking or the tickling are in the needle or the feather.[25] This being the case, why should we assume that where it is invisible, like the rapid motion of corpuscles, the warmth that we feel is a quality of the object? Malebranche's conclusion is that whether we take the sensory quality to be a property of the body is a function of the extent to which what is responsible for the sensation is visible to us. The corpuscles responsible for our sensation of light are among the smallest and therefore the least perceptible, and this is why, at least when we rely exclusively on sensation for our knowledge of the world, we are led to think that bodies are coloured. A parallel phenomenon occurs in respect to the intensity of a sensation and its source. In the case of strong sensations, we take the quality to be in ourselves: when we immerse our hand in water so hot that we have a burning sensation, we take the pain to be in us and not in the water. But with weak sensations, as when we immerse our hand in lukewarm water, we take the quality to be in the water and not in us.[26]

Malebranche has a distinctive account of the difference between primary and secondary qualities. He restricts the term 'idea' to our concepts of primary qualities, and he considers these to resemble the bodies that they represent. Such primary qualities

---

[22] There are complex issues here about the extent to which Descartes is committed to the transparency of the mind: see Marleen Rozemond, 'The Nature of the Mind', in Stephen Gaukroger, ed., *The Blackwell Guide to Descartes' Meditations* (Oxford, 2006), 48–66.

[23] *La Recherche*, Book 1 ch. 10 p. 6.

[24] Ibid. ch. 11 p. 1.      [25] Ibid. ch. 11 p. 2.      [26] Ibid ch. 12 p. 2.

are those that we can conceive in geometrical or mechanical terms. Our concepts of secondary qualities, by contrast, merely signal or signify to the mind some bodily state, which they do not resemble in any way, and Malebranche reserves the term 'sensations' for these. Ideas and sensations are completely different kinds of things on this view. Ideas are perceived by the intellect and Malebranche argues in detail that we perceive them in what he calls 'intelligible extension'.[27] These ideas exist not in the world or in our own mind, but rather in God, as archetypes, and we perceive them directly in God. The best way to think of this claim is in terms of a geometrical model, on which it is almost certainly based. Here the idea is that when we grasp the properties of circles, triangles, and other such figures, these figures exist neither in the corporeal world, for they are abstract, nor in the individual mind, for they have objective qualities that no exercise of will can change. Malebranche's Platonist/Neoplatonist idea is that they exist in a separate realm, and this realm (here is the Neoplatonist gloss) is a divine one. Similarly with other general ideas, on Malebranche's model: they exist in a purely intelligible realm, which he identifies with God. When it comes to perception, however, both ideas and sensations are needed. The intellect only perceives intelligible extension, whereas if we are to distinguish bodies we need to endow them with sensible qualities such as colours. But if we need to endow bodies with sensible qualities in order to be aware of them visually, aurally, and so on, then we do not perceive them directly. What we perceive are representations of bodies, or 'ideas'.

Arnauld objected to a number of doctrines in Malebranche's theory of ideas, but we can confine our attention to the view that we perceive not objects but representations of them, for this will become one of the defining features of post-Cartesian epistemology. Arnauld argues that thinking, knowing and perceiving are the same kind of activity, and the 'idea' of an object and the 'perception' of the object are one and the same thing.[28] This idea-perception stands both in a relation to the mind, and to the object perceived in so far as it is objectively in the mind. The former relation is most aptly captured by the term 'perception', while the latter is most aptly captured by the term 'idea'. So while perception is unequivocally a single act, the two complementary ingredients of this act can be designated differently. Arnauld argues that the misunderstandings arise only when, like Malebranche, one construes the having of the idea and the perception as two distinct things or processes. When one does this one is led to introduce a superfluous entity over and above the object and the perception, namely the 'idea' as a hypostatized representation, something that is also encouraged by a conflation of 'the idea of an object' and 'that object conceived'. Arnauld accepts that all thought or perception is representational, and he agrees that we see ideas immediately and objects mediately: what he denies is that this means that ideas are separate entities which stand proxy for objects. It is by means of ideas that we see external objects, but this does not mean that we see the idea but not the object. The

[27] Ibid. Book 3 p. 2. On Malebranche's account of the nature of ideas, see Steven Nadler, *Malebranche and Ideas* (Oxford, 1992).

[28] See, in particular, Arnauld, *On True and False Ideas*, 65–101. On the dispute between Malebranche and Arnauld, see Steven Nadler, *Arnauld and the Cartesian Philosophy of Ideas* (Manchester, 1989).

crucial point is that we *have* a visual representation of an object, we do not *see* a visual representation of an object: to have a visual representation of an object is just the same thing as seeing that object. Ideas are perceptual acts not perceptual objects.

Whatever their differences over the nature of the representation by which perceptual cognition takes place, Arnauld and Malebranche agree that perceptual cognition necessarily involves representations, and that our sensory representations of the natural world are systematically misleading if taken as guides to how the world really is. The question naturally arises here why we are subject to such systematic misapprehensions, and Malebranche and Arnauld are generally speaking in agreement on the answer to this question. Malebranche points out that what deceives us is not so much the senses as the natural judgements that always accompany sensation. Our sensations are always accompanied by certain involuntary judgements, and the purpose of these is the same as that of sensation: they enable the mind to move swiftly to attend to the body's needs. Our involuntary belief that painful and burning sensations belong to some part of our own body, for example, is, while strictly false, nonetheless very useful. The purpose of sensation being to make us aware of our body's needs, we often need to be alert to these immediately. If we experienced sensations as modifications of our mind, which is what they really are, then we would have to make a conscious inference from the state of our bodies, thereby failing to attend to the body's needs immediately. Our false belief that pains are in our body, for example, is crucial if we are to remove our body from something harmful to it. Colours, likewise, enable us to pick out distant bodies—such as predators—much more easily than uncoloured bodies would. Arnauld gives the best statement of the doctrine:

It must not be imagined that there is nothing in [a body] which causes it to appear to me to be of one colour rather than another. This is surely due to a different arrangement of the small parts of their surface, which is responsible for the corpuscles which are reflected from the [body] towards our eyes stimulating the fibres of the optic nerve in different ways. But because our soul would find it too difficult to discern the difference in these stimulations, which is only one of degree, God has decided in this respect to give us the means to discern them more easily by those sensations of different colours, which he has willed be caused in our soul on the occasion of these various stimulations of the optic nerve, just as tapestry workers have a pattern, which they call a 'rough pattern', where the various shades of the same colour are indicated by completely different colours, so that they are less liable to mistake them.[29]

On this account, colour is a form of perceptual enhancement that enables us to distinguish things visually in a more effective way, and put in this way, there seem to be parallels between the strategy adopted by Malebranche and Arnauld and the evolutionary epistemologies that were developed in the wake of Darwinism. But in fact the two are profoundly different at the level of what motivates them. The evolutionary approach to epistemology is designed to make something that is not scientific, or not sufficiently scientific, namely epistemology, part of a scientific enterprise. The strategy of Malebranche and Arnauld is designed to take us in the opposite direction. They hold that we are mistaken, not in seeing the world as intrinsically coloured,

---

[29] See, in particular, Arnauld, *On True and False Ideas*, 65–101; 131–2.

because that is a natural involuntary judgement, but only when we take these natural involuntary judgements to inform us of the true nature or properties of bodies. Malebranche, in particular, stresses that if, by a voluntary judgement of our own making, we endorse the natural judgements aroused in us, then it is we who are responsible for the deception.[30]

What has in effect happened is that sensations and sensory qualities have been excised from the cognitive domain. They are no longer something that natural philosophy is called upon to account for. There is no guidance as to where we must go if we want to answer questions about them—as if, once they are outside the cognitive domain, it no longer matters very much how we deal with them—but it is worth noting that in Malebranche the issue takes on a quasi-moral tone, and one is left in little doubt that, for him, judging that objects are genuinely coloured is a perverse misuse of a God-given faculty, a sign of man's fallen nature. And it is noteworthy in this respect that the great defender of 'orthodox' Cartesianism of the 1670s, Poisson, tells his readers that he came to Cartesianism when he realized the full implications of Augustine's teaching that truth was goodness and error evil, and that the task of Cartesian philosophy is to make good what we lost with the Fall.[31]

## BIOMECHANICS

If the doctrine of primary and secondary qualities removed from the purview of natural philosophy a wide range of phenomena whose explanation had traditionally been thought to be part of natural philosophy, there still remained phenomena that could not be removed in this way, but which seemed to go beyond mechanically describable processes. In particular, traditional natural philosophy had included an account of vital phenomena, and these seemed to be intimately tied up with the realization of intrinsic goals, and impervious to mechanistic reduction.

One of the principal ways in which many advocates of mechanism contrasted their project with Aristotelian natural philosophy was on the question of teleology. In the case of mechanics, optics, and cosmology, there were, outside the question of the formation of the earth, few reasons to question the elimination of teleology once Aristotelianism had been abandoned. Physiology was a different matter, however, and among the phenomena that a mechanized physiology had to deal with were a number of processes that seemed clearly goal-directed. Here at least, it was not a question of Aristotle's misguided concern to provide teleological explanations where they weren't needed, but rather that of how one could possibly avoid reference to goals in explaining these processes. The question of the apparent goal-directedness of

---

[30] Cf. Arnauld and Nicole, who insist that the reliability of our senses derives not merely from the senses themselves but also 'from the reasoning that distinguishes when we ought and when we ought not to believe them'—Antoine Arnauld and Pierre Nicole, *La Logique ou l'art de penser*, ed. P. Claire and F. Girbal (Paris, 1965), 337—then proceeding to draw consequences for the doctrine of the eucharist, which appears to contradict the senses if unchecked by reason.

[31] Nicolas Joseph Poisson, *Commentaire . . . sur la Méthode de Mr. Descartes* (Paris, 1671), 'Avis au Lecteur', unpag.

certain physiological processes constitutes the most serious challenge to a mechanist physiology, and Descartes deals with the issue head on, eliminating any element of goal-directedness in the key case of foetal development, but his target is intrinsic, not extrinsic, goals.

There are a number of similarities between Descartes' account of the formation of the earth and his description of the formation of the foetus in the *Description du corps humain*. Both had traditionally been construed as intrinsically goal-directed processes, and it is important to appreciate that Descartes' concern is not with goal-directedness as such, but with intrinsic goal-directedness. He does not deny that God guides the development of the embryo any more than he denies that God guides the formation of the earth as a habitat for human beings. But he does not assert it either because, contrary to Gassendi, he does not believe that natural philosophy gives us reliable guidance in these matters. Extrinsic goal-directedness simply does not fall within the domain of natural philosophy for Descartes. It would do so only if the goal-directedness were somehow internalized by the body so guided, but this would be to allow processes in the body that he believed were incompatible with the inertness of matter. At one level, Descartes is not denying that there is a question as to why foetal matter behaves in such a way that the foetus develops into an adult of a particular species. What he is saying is that the explanation for that is not something *internal* to the development of the foetus but *external* to it: God made it so, and God is the only final cause. What Descartes is concerned with in his natural philosophy are internal or intrinsic causes, and these are missing in the case of foetal development. What is at issue, then, is intrinsic goal-directedness. Such intrinsic or internally generated goal-directedness is a feature of Aristotelian natural philosophy, where it was thought to be characteristic of any natural process. There, organic processes, such as a seed developing into a tree, and inorganic processes, such as the fall of a body to the earth, are put down to intrinsic goal-directedness. Mechanism dismantles the conceptual apparatus whereby processes are construed as being intrinsically goal-directed, because it removes the doctrine of forms, which is crucial to the notion of something striving to realize its natural state. And for Descartes, at least, it does this not just in the cases where goal-directedness seems an artificial way to construe what happens once Aristotelianism has been abandoned, but also in cases where this remains a natural way of construing what occurs, such as in the development of the foetus.

Most biological processes can be thought of in goal-directed terms: nutrition, respiration, excretion, sleep, etc. But then many purely physical processes can be thought of in goal-directed terms, and Aristotle had thought that the explanation of the fall of heavy bodies to the ground had to display the goal-directedness of this process: bodies fall to the ground because this is their natural place, and when they are unconstrained, it is in the nature of heavy bodies to behave in this way. This raises the problem of where we draw the line. We may concede that a process can be described in terms of a goal without conceding that goal-directedness plays any genuine part in explaining the process. Unless we think that teleology plays a part in any natural organic process, for example, we will not be inclined to think that growth in the form of putting on fat in adolescents or adults requires explanation in terms of ends or goals. On the other hand, we may be inclined to think that the development of the foetus does require an explanation in terms of ends or goals: it develops in this way because it is developing into a horse, or a person, or a bird. In the middle of these two is a grey area. We can think of Descartes' strategy as pushing foetal development into the grey area, in which case the question of the right kind of explanation will no longer be judged by a priori considerations about whether goals are relevant, but by how effective whatever concrete explanation one comes up with is in accounting for the detail.

More schematically, although Descartes does not lay out his plan for dealing with this question explicitly, it seems clear that a threefold strategy must lie behind any thoroughgoing mechanist approach to embryology. First, ordinary growth is accounted for in a way that makes no references to goals. This is covered in the third section of the *Description du corps humain*, which deals with nutrition.[32] Important here is his account of how the requisite form of nourishment gets to the right part of the body. This is, of course, something one might be inclined to think of in goal-directed terms, but Descartes's approach is resolutely mechanical. Can we seriously suppose, he asks, that each bodily part can choose and guide the parts of the food to the appropriate place? To do so would be 'to attribute more intelligence to these than even our soul has'.[33] Rather, he argues, there are only two factors that can be responsible for the movement of nutrients to the appropriate place: their initial position in relation to that organ, and the size and shape of the pores in the membranes through which the nutrients pass, and in this connection he looks at the paths which the blood takes around the body and discusses the sieving effects of the pores.

Second, the process of formation and maturation of the foetus is treated simply as a species of growth: it involves a significantly greater increase in complexity and internal differentiation of parts than the process of growth from childhood to adulthood, of course, but this in itself does not make it qualitatively different. Third, Descartes must show how the development from a low degree of complexity and internal differentiation to a high degree of complexity and differentiation is something that can be handled in the same mechanistic terms. What this strategy allows one to do is to provide a general account of growth, in terms of how raw material is introduced into the organism from outside and transformed into the kinds of highly differentiated material making up bones, blood, muscle, etc. Then, having done this, one shows how the kind of account developed in this way can be extended to the case where the organs are not being built up but are actually being formed anew.

The basic explanatory tool in Descartes' account is a fermentation-like process that produces heat and a breakdown of matter when the seeds of the two sexes are combined.[34] These parts then subsequently recombine simply under the action of heat, and the expansion and increased pressure this produces. The rectilinear tendency of the parts projected under this pressure and the barriers to rectilinear motion cause various forms of branching and the collection of matter at different termini of this branching, a process which depends on degree of fluidity, degree of agitation, size of pores in the membranes formed, and various other mechanically conceived variables.[35]

---

[32] *Œuvres*, xi. 245–52.    [33] Ibid. 251.    [34] Ibid. 250–86.
[35] This account is taken over, and transmitted to an English audience, in Kenelm Digby, *Two Treatises*, 217–23.

The question here is whether, in making no reference to intrinsic ends or goals, Descartes has deprived himself of an essential ingredient in any satisfactory explanation of this development. Ideally the kind of picture he wants, as I have indicated, is that where the development of the foetus can be seen as a variant on the assimilation of nutrients, like adolescent growth, getting fat, and getting thin. No one would see putting on weight as a process directed towards a state in which one is fat: this would be to get the causality the wrong way around. Similarly, it is the (mechanistically construable) chemical and mechanical processes that occur in the foetus and the womb that cause it to develop into an adult of a particular species, not the fact that it is going to develop into a member of a particular species that causes the particular chemical and mechanical processes to occur in the way they do. Indeed, Descartes is even prepared to allow spontaneous generation along these lines, writing in his *Primae cogitationes circa generationem animalium* that 'since so few things are required to make an animal, it is hardly surprising to see so many animals, worms, and insects form spontaneously in all putrefying matter'.[36]

We must not forget that what is at issue here is the replacement of intrinsic by extrinsic goals. Descartes does not deny that the development of the embryo is a goal-directed process, and the womb of a particular animal does not just happen to have passages of the right kind, or chemical processes of the right kind. God has created the womb with these passages and chemical processes in order that material placed there can undergo a particular kind of foetal development. The upshot of Descartes' position is that the goals that direct this development are not intrinsic and hence not part of the subject matter of natural philosophy. Boyle argues in much the same way in connection with the idea of 'living' things. Rejecting the Aristotelian doctrine of intrinsic specific forms, he argues that there is no essential difference between living and non-living things, defining life as a special case of motion or activity that arises from a specific organization of corpuscles which has been preordained in God's original design of nature.[37] This general line of argument has a crucial parallel with the primary/secondary quality distinction, namely that as the *explanandum* of mechanist natural philosophy expands beyond the range of mechanics, massive surgery has to be performed on the new domains to remove those areas not amenable to mechanistic treatment. This is often undertaken with remarkable ingenuity, not just in securing gains for a mechanistic natural philosophy but also for Christian orthodoxy: goals are taken out of the realm of the material and placed firmly back in the realm of the divine. The replacement of intrinsic by extrinsic goals in the case of foetal development secures a sharp divide between the natural and the supernatural, ridding individual material things of any role in their own development and placing all such goals in the divine realm. This is the ultimate fulfilment of the theological rationale behind mechanism as conceived by Mersenne in the 1620s.

There are two fundamental issues at stake here: that of biomechanics versus a goal-directed understanding of organic processes, and that of preformation versus epigenesis, that is, whether the future organism is specified in advance, or whether it emerges

[36] Descartes, *Œuvres*, xi. 506.
[37] Boyle, 'Three Considerations about Subordinate Forms', *Works*, iii. 127–8.

through interaction with the local environment.[38] Gassendi is a mechanist on fundamental physical and cosmological questions, for example, but he draws the line at developmental physiology, where the kind of organized complexity that emerges is, he believes, simply beyond the resources of biomechanics.[39] He makes the point in his set of objections to the fourth of Descartes' *Meditationes*, in the process bringing out its importance for the project of understanding God through his creation:

Your rejection of the use of final causes in natural philosophy might have been correct in other contexts, but since we are dealing with God here, there is a danger that you might be abandoning the principal argument by which to establish, by natural light, the wisdom, providence, and power of God. . . . How or where can you obtain better evidence for the existence of such a God than from the function of the different parts of plants, animals, man and yourself (or your body), given that you bear the likeness of God. . . . You will say that it is the physical causes of shape and position that should be investigated, and that those who revert to final causes rather than active or material causes are foolish. But no mortal can understand or explain the active principle that produces the observed form and arrangement of the valves that serve as the openings to the vessels in the chambers of the heart, in what circumstances and from what sources the material with which it constructs them is obtained, what it uses and how it uses it, or what is needed to make sure that it is of the requisite firmness, consistency, fit, flexibility, size, shape, and position. Since, I say, no natural philosopher can understand and explain these and similar structures, why should he not at least marvel at this extraordinary functioning and the ineffable providence that has fashioned these valves so well for their function?[40]

To the extent that what is at issue here is the scope of biomechanics, the Cartesian response to this objection would be that it fails to distinguish clearly enough between questions of intrinsic and extrinsic causation. Descartes is not maintaining that the foetus just happens, by an accident of nature, to develop in a particular way; on the contrary, God has designed the womb and connecting passages in each species of animal in such a way that animals of different species emerge at the foetal stage. But one might accept this, and accept that biomechanics is the only way to proceed, and still remain puzzled as to how, for example, such a process could produce significant variety in individuals yet retain exceptionless fixity of species, or how the sequential production of organs could result in anything more than a composite of organs which lacked a unifying principle that would take it into the realm of the living, however this is construed.

The case of Malebranche is instructive here. Malebranche is unequivocally committed to mechanism. He accepts Descartes' mechanistic account of the formation of the world in the face of a great deal of theological criticism,[41] and he accepts his account of *bêtes machines* in the face of almost universal hostility.[42] He is a staunch advocate of biomechanics, but could not understand how epigenesis

---

[38] There are other options, such a pangenesis and simple pre-existence, which we can safely ignore here.

[39] On Gassendi's account of developmental physiology see Saul Fisher, 'Gassendi's Atomist Account of Generation and Heredity in Animals and Plants', *Perspectives on Science* 11 (2003), 484–512.

[40] Descartes, *Œuvres*, vii. 309.    [41] Malebranche, *Recherche*, Book 6 Pt 2, ch. 4.

[42] Ibid. Book 4 ch. 11, and Book 5 ch. 3.

by means of the mechanical (or mechanically construed) processes of fermentation, pressure, and expansion could produce the fully formed organism. Noting that Descartes treated developmental physiology along the lines of his account of the formation of the cosmos, he argues that in the former case we need to think of goals that are at least realized intrinsically, and hence in an important sense are built into the organism itself, thereby undermining the idea that foetal development can be treated along the lines of nutrition:

There is a great difference between the formation of living and organised bodies, and that of the vortices of which the universe is composed. An organised body contains infinitely many parts that are mutually dependent upon one another in relation to particular ends, and which must be formed if they are to work as a whole. For there is no need to follow Aristotle in thinking that the heart is the first part to live and the last to die. The heart cannot beat without the influence of the animal spirits, nor can these be passed throughout the heart in the absence of the nerves, and the nerves originate in the brain, which is where they receive the spirits. Moreover, the heart cannot beat and pump blood through the arteries unless they, and the veins that return the blood to it, have been formed. In short, it is clear that the machine cannot work until it is complete, and hence that the heart cannot live by itself. Thus, from the time of the appearance of this projecting point that is the heart in the setting egg, the chicken is alive; and for the same reason, note, a women's child is alive from the moment it is conceived, because life begins when the spirits cause the organs to function, which cannot occur unless they have been formed and connected. It would, then, be quite wrong to pretend to explain the formation of animals and plants and their parts one after the other, on the basis of simple and general laws dealing with the transmission of motion, for they are connected to one another in ways that depend on the different ends and different uses in different species.[43]

On the face of it, Malebranche faces a dilemma here. For how can he contemplate the idea of goals that are realized intrinsically and yet remain committed to biomechanics? The postulation of extrinsic causation as far as goals are concerned allows Descartes to remove such questions from the ambit of natural philosophy. A mechanist who finds this problematic can hardly return to the Aristotelian notion of intrinsic causes because the mechanist programme rests in large part on a rejection of the Aristotelian forms that provide the basis for understanding intrinsic goals. Moreover, mechanism does not in itself offer any resources to think through notions of intrinsic goals. But in fact, the solution does not lie in anything as radical as rethinking the nature of causation in mechanism. Rather, it turns on the question of epigenesis versus preformation.

This question goes to the heart of mechanism as an explanatory model. Corpuscularians generally derided Aristotelian explanations as unintelligible, and as we have seen it was Beeckman, above anyone else, who equated intelligibility and explanatory power with the appeal to a picturable or imaginable structure of parts whose motions are controlled within a putative theory of mechanics. The notion of picturability pervaded post-Aristotelian natural philosophies, and both epigenetic and preformation

---

[43] Malebranche, *Recherche*, Book 6 Pt 2, ch. 4. Malebranche, *Œuvres*, ii. 343–4. Cf. his *Méditations Chrétiennes*: *Œuvres* x. 721.

models were strongly associated with picturable processes.[44] On the epigenetic model, for example, conception could be pictured by analogy with magnetism, whereby a piece of iron coming into the sphere of attraction of the magnet has its properties transformed by the passing of something incorporeal between them. But this was an unlikely model for a mechanist, even if magnetic attraction could be mechanized, whereas the idea that the organism was preformed and that conception initiated a process of growth, was both easily visualizable and could be mechanized without difficulty along Cartesian lines.

Preformation had three distinct advantages for Malebranche. First, it was exactly the kind of doctrine that a biomechanical model of embryology needed. It required no recourse to intrinsic goals, while at the same time accounting fully for the very specific organized complexity of the developed embryo. The process of embryonic development was essentially like that from infancy to maturity: it was primarily a question of growth with qualitative changes in embryonic development being essentially no different from qualitative changes such as the onset of puberty. The driving force behind the changes was not goals but nutrition: preformation allows the whole developmental process to be accounted for mechanistically in a simple and intuitively appealing way. Second, as I have indicated, Malebranche, in common with many late seventeenth-century Cartesians, combined his Cartesianism with several distinctly Augustinian doctrines. The combination of mechanism—a doctrine that many saw as harmful to Christianity and which, to the extent that it denied intrinsic goal-directedness, was associated with Epicurean atheism—with Augustinian orthodoxy was formidable. Preformation helped cement this union, for it had explicit precedents in Augustine's theory of pre-existence, whereby 'certain seeds of all things which are generated in a corporeal and visible fashion lie hidden in the corporeal elements of this world'.[45] Third, microscopy seemed to vindicate preformation to such an extent that it very effectively dislodged epigenetic theories, sweeping everything before it in France between 1670 and 1705, for example.[46] In fact, microscopic evidence was quite inconclusive, but even those microscopists who were guarded in their reports often unwittingly leant support to preformationists in their language and in the images they used. Malpighi's work, for example, was widely used to support preformation, even though, while he believed that the rudimentary parts of an organism were present before the incubation of an egg, he did not appear to hold that these rudiments existed in the female egg before fertilization, as oval preformationists such as Malebranche held. Yet, as Wilson points out, 'it must be admitted that he supplied phrases, ideas, and the authority of his observations to such philosophical

[44] See Daniel Fouke, 'Mechanical and "Organical" Models in Seventeenth-Century Explanations of Biological Reproduction', *Science in Context* 3 (1989), 365–82; and Catherine Wilson, *The Invisible World: Early Modern Philosophy and the Invention of the Microscope* (Princeton, 1995), ch. 4. More generally, see Linda van Speybroek, Dani de Waele, and Gertrudis van de Vijver, 'Theories in Early Embryology: Close Connections between Epigenesis, Preformationism, and Self-Organization', *Annals of the New York Academy of Sciences* 981 (2002), 7–49.

[45] Augustine, *De trinitate* 3. 8.

[46] See Jacques Roger, *Les Sciences de la vie dans la pensée française du XVIIIème siècle* (2nd edn, Paris, 1971), 256–93, on theories of oval preformation.

preformationists as Malebranche and Leibniz, who were the agents responsible for disseminating and popularizing the doctrine'.[47]

For Malebranche, preformation was the key to biomechanics. It solved the one nagging problem for mechanists, which was that Descartes' account made the story that the mechanist had to tell impossibly difficult. He had both denied the existence of any goal-directed processes and insisted on starting from undifferentiated matter, something so elementary and amorphous that not only was the amount of work the mechanical processes had to do very great, but it was not even clear how mechanism alone could muster the resources to achieve this. Malebranche's advocacy of preformation shifted questions of how specific organized complexity arose more completely into the realm of extrinsic causation than did Descartes' epigenetic account, and this shifted the problems out of the realm of what was required of a mechanistic explanation. The same policy that drove Malebranche's advocacy of the distinction between primary and secondary qualities, namely the removal of unmechanizable phenomena from the *explanandum* of natural philosophy, can be seen here at work in his biomechanics.

Just how well preformation meets the requirements of mechanism is evident if we compare it not just with Descartes' attempt to reconcile mechanism and epigenesis, but also with those accounts that see a need to supplement mechanism when it comes to developmental processes, and biological processes more generally. One such approach is that of the Cambridge Platonist Ralph Cudworth. The Cambridge Platonists saw themselves as offering a bulwark against naturalism, materialism, and determinism, and they saw material things as a special kind of spiritual manifestation.[48] Nevertheless, both the leading members of the movement, Cudworth and More, believed in the independent existence of that manifestation of spirit which we call matter, and both hold that the fact that spirit is prior to matter in no way denigrates the ontological standing of matter. Indeed, Cudworth accepts the mechanist criticisms of occult qualities, praising atomism because it makes it possible to understand the corporeal world, whereas talk of forms and qualities will explain nothing. Cartesianism, however, he rejects on the grounds that it allows only the categories of the extended and the cogitative, and on the grounds that Descartes conceives of the latter in terms of consciousness. This restricts us to a choice between a universe in which everything works mechanically and independently of God, at least after he has created it, and a universe which God is called upon to maintain at every instant. Cudworth maintains that Descartes opts for the former view, driving out 'all final and mental causality' from the world and allowing only mechanical causation.

Cudworth's own position, by contrast, is that it is absurd to imagine divine interference in every earthly event, but that mechanical processes alone are insufficient.[49] He therefore attempts to defend a combination of mechanism and teleology, not by

[47] Wilson, *The Invisible World*, 122.

[48] See Ernst Cassirer, *The Platonic Renaissance in England* (Austin, 1953); John Passmore, *Ralph Cudworth: An Interpretation* (Cambridge, 1951); and A. Rupert Hall, *Henry More: Magic, Religion and Experiment* (Oxford, 1990).

[49] Cudworth, *The True Intellectual System*, i. 146.

conceiving of mechanism teleologically, but by attempting to construe these as two independent but complementary processes. To this end, he postulates the existence of 'a plastick or spermatick nature', a shaping principle in the world, above the purely mechanical processes, and distinct from God himself, for

although it be true, that the works of nature are dispensed by a divine law and command, yet this is not to be understood in a vulgar sense, as if they were all effected by the mere force of a verbal law or outward command, because inanimate things are not commendable nor governable by such a law. And therefore besides the divine will and pleasure, there must needs be some other immediate agent and executioner provided, for the producing of every effect; since not so much as a stone, or other heavy body, could at any time fall downward, merely by the force of a verbal law, without any other efficient cause; but either God himself must either immediately impel it, or else there must be some other subordinate cause in nature of that motion. Wherefore the divine law and command, by which the things of nature are administred, must be conceived to be the real appointment of some energetick, effectual, and operative cause for the production of every effect.[50]

This plastick nature is active within us as vital energy, and manifests itself in the goal-directed actions that we unwittingly perform, such as instinctual behaviour. It is the unconscious tool of a superior will, working without understanding 'the Reason of what itself doth', an impersonal, unconscious nature that directs the course of events in the universe according to the ideas of the divine architect. The elements of the material world, the atoms, may be governed by mechanical laws, but the mechanical processes are in turn governed by higher final causes.

But there are problems here both for those who are above all committed to mechanism, and for those whose concern is to combat naturalism. We can think of Cudworth as advocating a form of dualism, but with the material or corporeal part reduced down almost to nonentity. This reduction is achieved at great cost, however, for the domain of the incorporeal becomes so enlarged and all-inclusive that Cudworth's dualism loses a good deal of its theological significance. To the extent to which he is a dualist, his is a dualism of force and matter, activity and passivity, not a dualism of mind and body; and he is able to make the identification of the active with the incorporeal plausible only by regarding as incorporeal whatever is not merely the passive recipient of pushes and pulls. This means that incorporeality is no longer a guarantee of immortality. What Cudworth has done is to blur the sharp distinction between the human mind and other kinds of entity. The basis for his distinction is not the contrast between thinking and non-thinking, but between the teleological and the mechanical. What links animals and human beings on this account are instincts, and the central feature of instincts is that they are goal-directed, and hence not mechanical. Wherever ends are pursued, something incorporeal is involved, virtually by definition.

The problem here is that, on Cudworth's account of plastick nature, the agent need not be conscious of the goals. But once we grant the presence in nature of powers capable of pursuing ends without deliberating about them, we can no longer argue that,

50 Cudworth, *The True Intellectual System*, i. 147.

wherever ends are pursued, there must be a designing mind; nor, in these circumstances, can we assume that purely material and non-deliberative forces could never of themselves seek one objective rather than another. In other words, the middle ground between dualism and naturalism tends to collapse into naturalism. Given Cudworth's aims in advocating his doctrine, this is at least as bad as the corpuscularian materialism he ascribes to Hobbes. Moreover, the introduction of levels of goal-directed activity could hardly be attractive to a Cartesian, for it would ultimately just reproduce, by another name, the vegetative and sensitive souls that Cartesian physiology is devoted to expelling, as being of no explanatory value, and it is on these questions that Cartesian physiology is at its strongest.

## NATURAL PHILOSOPHY AND MEDICINE

Cartesian biomechanics suggests a view of medical disciplines as ultimately being part of natural philosophy, by contrast with a traditional understanding of medicine as a clinical discipline. Such an understanding was certainly not new with Descartes; and Bacon, for example, had thought of natural philosophy manifesting its usefulness through its ability to inform medical practice, above all in the possibility that it might suggest a way of retarding the ageing process in human beings.[51]

Throughout the the seventeenth century there were regular bitter disputes over the standing of medicine, what kind of practice it was, what kind of connection it had with other disciplines, and whether its future was one of autonomy or one of integration into, or subsumption under, a broader natural-philosophical culture. The dispute lay primarily in the demarcation between the responsibilities of apothecaries and those of physicians, and it was largely seeded along Galenist versus Paracelsian conceptions of medicine.[52] Galenists saw disease in terms of an imbalance in humours, so that every illness is essentially individual, and the remedy must be specific to the person, the place, the time of the year, the part afflicted, and so on. Paracelsians and Helmontians, by contrast, thought of diseases as separately classifiable entities, having definite universally identifiable causes and anatomical effects, and so the medicines prescribed were for the illness, not the person, and could be dispensed by apothecaries. This dispute was one in which the Royal Society became embroiled, and antagonistic relations developed between it and the Royal College of Physicians. By the end of the seventeenth century, the issues had been resolved decisively in favour of the physicians. Since the apothecaries and their natural-philosophical supporters set out to

---

[51] See Gaukroger, *Francis Bacon*, 95–100.

[52] See, e.g. P. M. Rattansi, 'The Helmontian-Galenist Controversy in Restoration England', *Ambix* 12 (1964), 1–23; Allen G. Debus, *The English Paracelsians* (New York, 1965), ch. 4; A. Rupert Hall, 'Medicine and the Royal Society', in Allen G. Debus, ed., *Medicine in Seventeenth Century England* (Berkeley, 1974), 421–52; Harold J. Cook, 'The New Philosophy and Medicine', in David C. Lindberg and Robert S. Westman, eds, *Reappraisals of the Scientific Revolution* (Cambridge, 1990), 397–436: 418–21.

replace the diagnostic practices and remedies of Galenic physicians, and since as a result their claims for their natural-philosophical systems rested on success in the shared
domain of diagnosis and remedy, they had to adopt results-orientated strategies, and
this was a battle they could not win.[53]

As we have seen, there were reservations about various parts of the mechanist
programme in biomechanics among Cartesians, explicitly about animal sensation
and development physiology. But the general aim of the mechanist programme—
whatever concerns one might have about the understanding of colours, of the sensations of heat and warmth, whatever concerns one might have over goal-directed activities—is where possible to move these squarely outside the responsibility of natural
philosophy. Nevertheless, the ingenuity with which Descartes and the mechanist tradition generally deal with these questions should not be allowed to obscure the fact
that areas of what one might properly consider cognitive enquiry are removed from
the purview of natural philosophy, and simply drop out of consideration. There is, of
course, a significant difference between dismissing colours as secondary qualities and
reducing out vital and goal-directed phenomena in biomechanics. If one gets one's
account of colours wrong then nothing much of practical consequence follows,[54] but
in the case of biomechanics there are clear connections with medicine. Indeed, it is
medicine that largely motivates this study in the first place: as Descartes wrote to the
Marquis of Newcastle in 1645, 'the conservation of health has been at all times the
principal end of my studies'.[55] Yet it is difficult to see that there could be a place for
a concept of health in Cartesian biomechanics, for the very notion of health would
seem to embody a normative conception of well-being that falls squarely outside
natural-philosophical enquiry, conceived in mechanist terms.[56]

This was certainly not a problem specific to Descartes' version of biomechanics,
and it also underlay the resistance to iatrochemical remedies. By contrast with
France, where the conservative Galenist Paris Medical Faculty forbade the sale of
all chemical remedies in the country in 1615, the first national pharmacopoeia
in England, *Pharmacopoeia Londonensis* (1618) published by the Royal College of

---

[53] Andrew Wear, *Knowledge and Practice in English Medicine, 1550–1680* (Cambridge, 2000),
chs. 8 and 9; and more generally Roger French, *Medicine Before Science*.

[54] It did have consequences in painting, however. The late seventeenth-century Academic school
of French painting defended the primacy of shape over colour on explicitly Cartesian grounds,
treating colour as a danger that could seduce one away from the truth. See Christopher Allen, 'La
tradition du classicisme' (Ph.D. thesis, University of Sydney, 1990), 25–47.

[55] Descartes to the Marquis of Newcastle, October 1645: *Œuvres*, iv. 329.

[56] In June 1646, Descartes told Chanut that 'instead of finding ways to preserve life, I have
found another, much easier and surer way, which is not to fear death' (ibid. 441–2) and during the
1640s he moved closer to the traditional humanist values: see Gaukroger, *Descartes, An Intellectual
Biography*, ch. 10. But this leaves us no wiser as to what kind of goal health is. Des Chene argues
that the fact that human beings are mind/body complexes that are able to reflect on their own
well-being means that they can transcend pure biomechanics: see Dennis Des Chene, 'Life and
Health in Cartesian Natural Philosophy', in Stephen Gaukroger, John Schuster, and John Sutton,
eds, *Descartes' Natural Philosophy* (London, 2000), 723–35. The problem is that we need notions
like health for all living things, including other animals and plants.

Physicians, had included traditional chemical remedies along with traditional Galenic ones, even though the former made little sense in terms of the Galenic notion of humoural balance. The translation of van Helmont's works into English in 1648 precipitated a crisis in English medicine that was to persist over the next two decades, providing a very different way, based in iatrochemistry, of thinking about the nature of illness, and potentially transforming the status of 'empirics', who, unlike physicians, usually specialized in one type of medical treatment and were at the bottom of the medical hierarchy, along with quacks.[57] In his first published work, *Chymical, Medicinal, and Chyrurgical Address made to S. Hartlib* (1655), Boyle advocated the free communication of drug discoveries as part of Christian charity, but the work also reveals his idea of developing medicine as a body of knowledge along natural-philosophical lines: strongly in evidence are the themes of the co-operative nature of and benefits of natural philosophy, and the idea that the discovery and communication of knowledge of nature is part of a religious quest.[58] Nevertheless, unlike Helmontians who joined the Hartlib circle after 1648 and who conceived of their project as one of radical reform, not just in natural philosophy but also particularly in education, Boyle did not see the issue in terms of a wholesale replacement of Galenic ideas by Helmontian ones. He saw the aim rather as an eclectic unification of what was good in Galenism with practical developments in iatrochemistry.[59]

The difficulty with wholesale replacement was that Galenism offered something that the iatrochemical theories lacked, namely some attempt at an understanding of what it meant to say that an organism was healthy or unhealthy. The notion of humoural imbalance was on the face of it inconsistent with the Paracelsian/Helmontian view of the completeness of iatrochemistry, but, like Cartesian biomechanics, iatrochemistry had nothing to offer in its place. This made it useless to the physician, who had to work in terms of the health and well-being of patients, and so with the Galenic notion, because there was in effect nothing else on offer. The context in which these debates were pursued, however, was not one of how physicians might incorporate iatrochemical remedies into their practice, but rather one of apothecaries versus physicians, the two vying for complete control of the same terrain. In 1651, a time when the Royal College of Physicians found itself very restricted even in its ability to prosecute unlicensed practitioners because of the political turmoil, the Helmontian Noah Biggs published a highly polemical tract in effect calling for the disbanding of traditional medicine and its replacement by one based on Helmontian principles.[60] In 1665, William Johnson, responding to an attack on the Galenism of the Royal College, wrote that iatrochemists

---

[57] See Harold J. Cook, *The Decline of the Old Medical Regime in Suart London* (Ithaca, NY, 1986), and Debus, *The English Paracelsians*. On the history of the medical hierarchy in England up to the introduction of Helmontian ideas, see Margaret Pelling, *Medical Conflicts in Early Modern London: Patronage, Physicians, and Irregular Practitioners, 1550–1640* (Oxford, 2003).

[58] See Barbara B. Kaplan, *'Divulging of Useful Truths in Physick': The Medical Agenda of Robert Boyle* (Baltimore, 1993), 25.

[59] Ibid. 30–1.

[60] Noah Biggs, *Mataeotechnia medicinae praxeos* (London, 1651).

could never have gotten such a Repute in the World, but that they Politickly made an advantage of the Factious Principles then abounding in the Common People of our late Unruly times, when the Common Interest was to be carried on by crying down Humane learning; then these Illiterate fellows spit in the face of all Liberal Arts and Sciences.[61]

The result of the struggle was disaster, with both the Royal Society and the Royal College suffering. Henry Stubbe warned Boyle personally that the Royal Society and the College of Physicians were at loggerheads with one another,[62] and in his *Plus Ultra* he maintained that the Royal Society 'avowed that *All the Ancient Methods of Science were vain and useless to a physician, and did not so much as Contribute to the Cure of a Cut-finger*'.[63] Although there were some more moderate proposals, such as the recommendation of Jonathan Goddard that physicians learn to make their own medical preparations, thus making apothecaries redundant,[64] in general the Royal College and its defenders responded in kind right to the end of the century to what they saw as the attempt by natural philosophers to take over medicine.[65]

One problem with the physicians was their commitment to the practice of bleeding patients for virtually any ailment, noted in much of the Helmontian literature, often on their title pages, as with Biggs' *Mataeotechnia medicinae praxeos* which, we are told, dissects 'the errors, ignorance, impostures and supinities of the schools, in their main pillars of purges, blood-letting, fontanels or issues, and diet, &c.' There was no evidence at all for the beneficial effects of bleeding, and here the critics of traditional medicine had a potentially powerful argument, but it is significant that it never left the level of polemics, for no one systematically examined the effects of bleeding. On the other hand, the activities of iatrochemists were too piecemeal to provide a basis for medical practice, at least before Helmontianism, and then what was offered was something that had only tangential connections with successful medical practice.[66]

Boyle's view was that both Galenic and Helmontian approaches had advantages but in different areas, and that in many cases the inconsistencies were only superficial,

---

[61] William Johnson, ΑΓΥΡΤΟ–ΜΑΣΤΙΞ. *Or some Brief Animadversions upon two late Treatises* (London, 1656).

[62] Boyle, *Works*, i. p. xcv. At the end of 1660, the Royal College had rejected a request from the Royal Society, which was desperate for accommodation, to hold its weekly meetings at the Royal College, and the situation was exacerbated when the Letters Patent and Royal Charter granted in 1662 gave the Royal Society the same rights as the Royal College to carry out dissections of the bodies of executed criminals: see Margery Purver, *The Royal Society: Concept and Creation* (London, 1967), 136, 132.

[63] Henry Stubbe, *The Plus Ultra Reduced to a Non Plus* (London, 1670), sig. a2r.

[64] Jonathan Goddard, *A Discourse Setting forth the Unhappy Condition of the Practice of Physick in London* (London, 1670).

[65] An especially amusing polemical tract is Thomas Brown's *Physick lies a Bleeding, or the Apothecary turned Doctor, A Comedy Acted every Day in most Apothecaries Shops in London* (1697).

[66] This is true at least up to the appearance of Sylvius' works in the early 1670s, who took seriously not only clinical practice but also anatomy, a topic generally dismissed by Helmontians up to this point: see Allen G. Debus, *Chemistry and Medical Debate: Van Helmont to Boerhaave* (Canton, Mass., 2001), 59–64.

a line of thought that goes back at least to Daniel Sennert's *De chymicorum* (1615).[67] While accepting the traditional Galenic clinical practice of getting the patient to describe her symptoms, and to subject excreted fluids, particularly urine, to visual examination, he advocates 'a skilful and seasonable chymical examen of the other excrements, and vitiated substances of the patient's body'. Similarly, accepting a Galenic humoural theory, he argued that chemical analysis would reveal the active constituents in the humours, for

> he, that hath been by chymistry taught the nature of the several sorts of salts and sulphurs, and both beheld and considered their various actions upon one another, and upon other bodies, seems to have considerable help to discourse groundedly of the changes and operations of the humours, and other juices contained in the body, which he hath not, that hath never had *Vulcan* for his instructor. . . . And indeed, if the juices of the body were more chymically examined, especially by a naturalist, that knows the ways of making fixed bodies volatile, and volatile fixed, and knows the powers of the open air in promoting the former of those operations; it is not impossible, that both many things relating to the nature of the humours, and to the ways of sweetening, actuating, and otherwise altering them, may be detected, and the importance of such discoveries may be discerned.[68]

Note however that, although Boyle consistently held that chemical investigation held the key to the future as far as pathology and medical remedies were concerned, his conception of natural philosophy was much less reductive than that of either foundationalist mechanists or Helmontian iatrochemists. His work on air pressure, as we shall see, was motivated in large part by the post-Harvean project of understanding the action of the heart and lungs, and he explicitly rejected reductive approaches to accounting for pneumatic phenomena. Indeed, his concern to use natural philosophy to expand understanding of medical questions was more an issue of employing experimental and quantitative procedures, rather than finding some underlying micro-structure. Note also that the Helmontian commitment to understanding medical questions in chemical terms was rarely, if ever, in practice a question of micro-structure either. In practical terms, what it amounted to was rather a commitment to the use of chemical/alchemical procedures such as fermentation. In other words, what was at issue much of the time was a commitment to practices such as blood-letting and fermentation which have no overlap in themselves but are associated with activities that stand synecdochically for different kinds of enterprise. Boylean pneumatics introduced yet another kind of activity, as did Cartesian biomechanics with its model of fluids moving under pressure. What we have, then, is not clear competition between two comprehensive approaches, but rather a complex mixture of models, none of which could realistically claim to cover the area (Helmontians and Galenists both tended to ignore anatomy for example), but each of which had claims to be taken seriously in important cognate fields.

   The Boylean eclectic response at least had the virtue of holding the field together, but in itself it could not advance it very significantly. But such advance did come,

---

[67] See Allen G. Debus, *Chemistry and Medical Debate: Van Helmont to Boerhaave*, 18.
[68] Boyle, *The Usefulness of Experimental Natural Philosophy: Works*, ii. 79–80.

almost certainly under the influence of Boyle, in the work of Thomas Sydenham.[69] Sydenham was a Galenist about the nature of disease, and a staunch defender of clinical medicine, but also its greatest reformer in the seventeenth century. More than anyone else, he put clinical medicine on a natural-philosophical footing, not by translating it into iatrochemical or biomechanical terms, however, but incorporating systematic observation and testing into clinical practice. He could not remove the obstacle provided by the notion of disease as an imbalance of humours that Galenists faced when it came to epidemics and plagues, which constrained them to see plagues as derangements of the blood, but his invention of nosology, the systematic classification and listing of diseases on the basis of repeated and informed clinical observation, was a *sine qua non* of understanding epidemics, and it is instructive to note that it occurred in a Galenist rather than an iatrochemical context. The model he used had affinities with the processes of recording and building up information in a systematic manner in natural history, requiring detailed observation of the course of an illness rather than postulating underlying causes. In the 'Epistle to the Reader' which opens the *Essay concerning Human Understanding*, Locke ranks Sydenham with Boyle, Huygens, and Newton as the leaders of natural-philosophical enquiry,[70] and Sydenham's influence on Locke's understanding of natural philosophy would be crucial.

This kind of reform of clinical medicine is, in terms of strategy, at odds with foundational programmes that would seek ultimately to include medicine within a reformulated and mechanized natural philosophy. It suggests a way of proceeding that is quite different from anything we have encountered up to this point, but the divide is not one straightforwardly between clinical medicine and natural philosophy, for from the beginning of the seventeenth century we witness developments within the core of natural philosophy that point it in the same direction. These developments fall under the rubric of 'experimental philosophy', and it is to these that we now turn.

---

[69] See Thomas Sydenham, *The Entire Works of Dr Thomas Sydenham*, ed. John Swan (London, 1742). See also Andrew Cunningham, 'Thomas Sydenham: Epidemics, Experiment, and the "Good Old Cause"', in Roger French and Andrew Wear, eds, *The Medical Revolution of the Seventeenth Century* (Cambridge, 1989), 164–90.

[70] John Locke, *The Works of John Locke, Esq* (2nd edn, 3 vols, London, 1722), p. ix.

# 10

# Experimental Natural Philosophy

If one confines one's attention to systematic natural philosophies, the choice for those engaged in physical enquiry between the middle of the seventeenth century and the appearance of Newton's *Principia* in 1687 was in effect that between the natural-philosophical systems of Gassendi and Descartes.[1] But there was another option, an anti-systematic form of natural philosophy that came to be termed 'experimental philosophy'. Although it was associated above all with Boyle and the Royal Society,[2] the public call for an experimental approach can be found as early as Noah Biggs' 1651 broadside against the universities. How do the universities contribute to the discovery of truth, he asks,

> Where have we anything to do with Mechanickal *Chymistrie* the handmaid of nature, that hath outstripped the other Sects of Philosophy, by her multiplied real experiences? Where is there an examination and consecution of Experiments?[3]

The criticism is repeated in John Webster's complaint in 1654 that the Aristotelian schools wanted 'to open the cabinet of Natures rich treasure, without labour and pains, experiments and operations, tryals and observations'.[4] Henry Power, his *Experimental Philosophy* of 1664, tells us that

> This is an Age wherein (me-thinks) Philosophy comes in with a Spring-tide; and the Peripateticks may as well hope to stop the current of the tide, or (with *Xerxes*) to fetter the Ocean, as hinder the overflowing of free Philosophy; Me-thinks, I see how all the old Rubbish must be thrown away, and the rotten Buildings be overthrown, and carried away by so powerful an Inundation. These are the days that must lay a new Foundation of a more magnificent Philosophy, never to be overthrown: that will Empirically and Sensibly canvass the *Phenomena* of Nature, deducing the Causes of things from such Originals in Nature, as we observe are producible by Art, and the infallible demonstration of mechanicks.[5]

---

[1] See e.g. Lennon, *The Battle of the Gods and Giants.*

[2] See Peter Dear, '*Totius in Verba*: Rhetoric and Authority in the Early Royal Society', *Isis* 76 (1985), 145–61; Peter Anstey, 'Experimental versus Speculative Natural Philosophy', in Peter Anstey and John Schuster, eds, *The Science of Nature in the Seventeenth Century* (Dordrecht, 2005), 215–42; and Alan Shapiro, 'Newton's "Experimental Philosophy"', *Early Science and Medicine* 9 (2004), 185–217.

[3] Biggs, *Mataeotechnica*, Dedication.

[4] John Webster, *Academiarum Examen* (London, 1654), 92. 'Is there no further end', he asks, 'nor consideration in *Physicks* but onely to search, discuss, understand, and dispute of a natural movable body . . . Surely natural *Philosophy* hath a more noble, sublime, and ultimate end, than to rest in speculation, abstractive notions, mental operations, and verball disputes'. (18)

[5] Henry Power, *Experimental Philosophy in Three Books* (London 1664), 192.

Power's conception of experimental philosophy is somewhat eclectic, but his general target is what he considers to be inappropriately systematic forms of natural philosophy, and this becomes the general polemical thrust of the idea of 'experimental' philosophy from the 1660s onwards. By the end of the 1660s this idea had become firmly entrenched in British natural philosophy, finding its way into elementary textbooks by the end of the century. John Dunton, in his 1692 philosophical primer, *The Young-Students-Library*, for example, distinguishes 'speculative' from 'experimental' natural philosophy, advising the reader to shun the former and pursue the latter, which is the only 'Certain, Sure Method to gather a true Body of Philosophy, for the Antient Way of clapping up an entire building of Sciences, upon pure Contemplation, may make indeed an *Admirable Fabrick*, but the Materials are such as can promise no lasting one'.[6] The contrast was perceived to have Baconian precedents,[7] which can be seen as the first stage of experimental philosophy. In the second stage, which dates from the 1660s, experimental philosophy is renewed with a fresh vigour and pushed in a novel direction, going beyond Baconian procedures and in fact coming closer to the approach adopted by Gilbert, of which Bacon was very critical.

The issue was a core one for apologists for the Royal Society. Sprat, for example, is keen to deny Sorbière's claim that the systems of Gassendi and Descartes provide resources for the Royal Society. 'Neither of these two men', he claims, 'bear any sway amongst them; they are never named there as Dictators over men's Reasons; nor is there any extraordinary reference to their judgements.'[8] The theme of dictatorship is referred to again in the same year, 1665, by Hooke in the Preface to his *Micrographia*:

The *Understanding* is to order all the inferiour services of the lower Faculties; but yet it is to do this only as a *lawful Master*, and not as a *Tyrant*. It must not *incroach* upon their Offices, nor take upon it self the employments which belong to either of them. It must *watch* the irregularities of the Senses, but it must not go before them, or prevent their information. It must *examine*, *range*, and *dispose* of the bank which is laid up in the Memory; but it must be sure to make *distinction* between the *sober* and *well collected heap*, and the *extravagant Idea's*, and *mistaken Images*, which there it may sometimes light upon.[9]

---

[6] John Dunton, *The Young-Students-Library* (London, 1692), pp. vi col. 2—vii col. 1.

[7] This was stressed by English writers. Maclaurin, for example, seeks legitimacy for the Newtonian project in Bacon by telling us that Bacon 'is justly held amongst the restorers of true learning, but more especially the founder of *experimental philosophy* . . . He saw there was a necessity for a thorough reformation in the way of treating natural knowledge, and that all theory was to be laid aside that was not founded on experiment'. Colin Maclaurin, *An Account of Sir Isaac Newton's Philosophical Discoveries* (London, 1748), 56.

[8] Thomas Sprat, *Observations on M. de Sorbier's Voyage into England* (London, 1665), 241–2. This is, of course, the thrust of the Royal Society's motto: 'Nullius addictus iurare in verba magistri' (to swear allegiance to the words of no master). Cf. John Dryden 'To My Honoured Friend, Dr Charleton', written in 1662, the year of his election to the Royal Society: 'The longest Tyranny that ever sway'd | Was that wherein our Ancestors betray'd | Their free-born *Reason* to the *Stagirite* | And made his *Torch* their universal Night.'

[9] Robert Hooke, *Micrographia: or some Physiological Descriptions of Minute Bodies made by Magnifying Glasses* (London, 1665), Preface, sig. b2r.

But this is certainly not the only kind of argument current in the 1660s. Henry Power had provided what might be termed an argument from economy for experiments, derived from Boyle, the previous year:

When a writer, saith [Boyle], acquaints me onely with his own thoughts or conjectures, without inriching his discourse with any real Experiment or Observation, if he be mistaken in his Ratiocination, I am in some danger of erring with him, and at least am like to lose my time, without receiving any valuable compensation for so great a loss: But if a Writer endevours, by delivering new and real Observations or Experiments, to credit his Opinions, the case is much otherwayes; for, let his Opinions be never so false (his Experiments being true) I am not obliged to believe the former, and am left at my liberty to benefit myself by the latter.[10]

Two years later, Samuel Parker, in his *Free and Impartial Censure of the Platonick Philosophie*, sets out the advantages of mechanism over Aristotelianism in a way that contrasts an experimental approach with a speculative one, where the target could be seen to be rather broader than just Aristotle, and indeed to cover any speculative system, including those of Descartes and Gassendi:

For though I preferre the Mechanicall Hypotheses before any other, yet methinks their contexture is too slight and brittle to have any stress laid upon them; and I can resemble them to nothing better than your *Glasse drops*, from which, if the least part be broken, the whole *Compages* immediately dissolves and shatters into Dust and Atoms; for their parts, which rather lie than hang together, being supported only by a thin film of brittle Conjecture (not anneal'd by experience and observation) if that fail anywhere, the whole Systeme of Hypothesis unavoidably shatters. The chief reason, therefore, why I preferre the Mechanicall and Experimental Philosophie before the *Aristotelean*, is not so much because of its much greater certainty, but because it puts inquisitive men into a method to attain it, whereas the other serves but to obstruct their industry, by amusing them with empty and insignificant Notions. And therefore we may shortly expect a greater improvement of Natural Philosophie from the *Royall Society*, (if they pursue their design) then it has had in all former ages; for they having discarded all particular *Hypotheses*, and wholly addicted themselves to exact Experiments and Observations, they may not only furnish the world with a compleat *History of Nature* (which is the most useful part of *Physiologie*) but also lay firm and solid foundations to erect Hypotheses upon (though perhaps that must be the work of future Ages:) at least we shall see whether it be possible to frame any certain Hypotheses or no, which is the thing I most doubt of, because, though the *Experiments* be exact and certain, yet their *Application* to any *Hypotheses* is doubtful and uncertain; so that though the Hypotheses may have a firm basis to bottome upon, yet it can be fastned and cemented to it no other way, but by conjecture and uncertaine (though probable) applications, and therefore I doubt not but we must at last rest satisfied with true and exact Histories of Nature for use and practice; and with the handsomest and most probable Hypotheses for Delight and Ornament.[11]

The contrast between 'experimental philosophy' on the one hand, and natural philosophy as it is conceived in the natural-philosophical systems of Descartes, Gassendi, and Hobbes on the other, is by no means straightforward, and once one

---

[10] Power, *Experimental Philosophy*, Preface (unpaginated).
[11] Samuel Parker, *A Free and Impartial Censure of the Platonick Philosophie* (Oxford, 1666), 46–8.

moves from apologists to the natural philosophers themselves, it occasionally becomes blurred. Nevertheless, it is a real and fundamental distinction. In what follows, I want to tease out some aspects of the contrast by examining three cases where, I shall argue, revealing questions of 'speculative' versus 'experimental' versions of natural philosophy are at stake. The first of these, Gilbert's attempt to focus natural-philosophical inquiry around the magnet and Bacon's criticism of this approach, predates the rise of 'experimental philosophy', but, as we shall see, what is at stake is—allowing for an increase in degree of sophistication—much the same as what is at stake in the controversy between Boyle and Hobbes on the air pump, and in Newton's investigation of the production of colour by contrast with the approach adopted by Descartes.

One general issue that I shall raise in the course of this discussion is the way in which 'speculative' natural philosophy—where one grounds the behaviour of macroscopic phenomena in basic underlying principles, at the same time making claims about comprehension and completeness—necessarily involves tailoring the *explanandum* to fit the *explanans*. 'Experimental' natural philosophy, by contrast, moves in the opposite direction, tailoring the *explanans* to fit the *explanandum*. These are profound questions that have persisted in one form or another through to the present.[12] Of particular importance is the fact that they place different legitimatory constraints on natural philosophy. Mechanism is a form of matter theory, a discipline that proceeds from fundamental assumptions about the ultimate constituents of, or principles underlying, the world and attempts to show how macroscopic behaviour—considered in a generalized way—can be derived from, or accounted for in terms of, these fundamental assumptions. In the case of mechanism, for example, the aim is to show how the nature and arrangement of the constituent parts of a body causally determine its behaviour. The central claim of matter theory is that physical explanation involves the identification of the ultimate material constituents of bodies because these are what cause bodies to behave in particular ways. At the other end of the natural-philosophical spectrum is natural history, which is driven by experiment and observation, an enterprise that is usually grounded in, and legitimated by, the belief that such enquiry provided access to an understanding of God's purposes in his creation. From the end of the sixteenth century, we find a number of significant projects oscillating uneasily between these poles, uncertain as to what the right way to approach the phenomena is, and we begin to find natural philosophy, broadly defined, moving in two apparently conflicting directions. One is the attempt to transform matter theory in a mechanist direction, to re-establish the priority of a wholly transformed and renewed matter theory as the fundamental natural-philosophical discipline: we have looked at this strategy in the last two chapters. The other, which is the subject of this chapter, can be seen as being in some respects an attempt to extend the natural-historical tradition in such a way that questions of empirical evidence and reliability gradually come to guide those of organization.

---

[12] See e.g. Nancy Cartwright, *How the Laws of Physics Lie* (Oxford, 1983); idem, *The Dappled World: A Study of the Boundaries of Science* (Cambridge, 1999); and Giere, *Science without Laws*.

It should be noted from the outset that throughout the seventeenth century, the lines of demarcation retain some degree of fluidity, in a way that is very revealing of the fundamental problems facing the natural-philosophical enterprise. It is perhaps only to be expected that Descartes and natural philosophers in the Cartesian tradition, who are concerned to base natural philosophy in a well-developed mechanistic matter theory, find themselves moving towards the natural-historical end of the spectrum once they start dealing with recalcitrant meteorological questions and terrestrial phenomena generally.[13] But the move in the other direction, from natural history to matter theory, is at first more surprising, at least before we reflect on its motivation. Boyle, for example, can be taken as representative of the natural-historical tradition, yet he engages in a concerted attempt to develop a mechanistic matter theory. What is particularly interesting here is the transfer of natural-historical concerns and procedures to matter theory. The techniques for collection and assessment of evidence in legal and biblical hermeneutics, and then in civic history and natural history, dealt with inaccessible events or facts that could not be seen, or heard, or repeated by the investigator. Matter theory likewise postulated inaccessible events—the corpuscularian theories that come to the fore in the seventeenth century postulate corpuscles that are too small to be seen and whose purported action can only be detected indirectly—and practices of assessment of evidence developed in natural history and its philological models come to bear on matter theory as early as Bacon, and later in the work of Boyle and his contemporaries.

## NATURAL HISTORY AND MATTER THEORY

One difference between matter-theoretical and natural-historical approaches to natural philosophy that is of great significance concerns the question of what the appropriate type of explanation is in natural philosophy; to put it in the starkest terms, whether it consists in accounting for the phenomenon in question by seeking its underlying physical structure, or whether it consists in accounting for it by exploring its relation to other similar phenomena which do not underlie it, but exist at the same level, so to speak. In the latter case, a form of what can be described as focusing plays a crucial role. When we looked at the emblematic tradition in natural history, we saw that the emblem was designed to embody, in a highly compressed form, a wealth of detail, bringing that detail into focus around key features of the entity in question. In the tradition of experimental philosophy, we encounter an analogous form of compressed organization of material, but in a very different natural-philosophical context, where it is an experiment, rather than an emblem, that is used to focus otherwise disparate and apparently heterogeneous material.

[13] See Gaukroger, *Descartes' System*, ch. 6. As regards later Cartesianism, one might note e.g. the fact that Cartesian chemistry textbooks of the seventeenth century routinely postulated explanations in terms of shapes of corpuscles, rather than in terms of their size, speed, and direction of motion: see Hélène Metzger, *Les Doctrines chimiques en France du début du XVII<sup>e</sup> à la fin du XVIII<sup>e</sup> siècle* (Paris, 1969).

Focusing is just one side of the question however. Once we move from natural history to the attempt to incorporate natural-historical concerns into natural-philosophical practice, the traditional notion that natural philosophy has an underlying structure in matter theory does not disappear. Rather, a complex balancing act, in which explanatory considerations play a determining role, is needed to reconcile the kind of order brought to bear on material at the phenomenal level and the order inherent in any assumed basic underlying physical processes.

The issues here are not exclusive to seventeenth-century natural philosophy, and can be found in the attempts to reform medicine by Paracelsians in the sixteenth century. At a fundamental natural-philosophical level, Paracelsus draws on two different matter theory traditions in dealing with the question of what raw materials there are in nature and how they might be transformed into therapeutic substances. These are the Aristotelian theory of the four elements and the alchemical sulphur-mercury theory of metals, to which he adds a third 'principle', salt, to account for all chemical, and more importantly iatrochemical, processes. The theory of metals is in effect more fundamental than that of the elements, which become devoid of qualities in their own right on this account, and are governed by the three principles. Sulphur gives bodies oiliness, inflammability, viscosity, and structure; mercury gives them wateriness, spirit, vapour, and vivifying powers; finally, salt gives them rigidity, solidity, dryness, and earthiness. When one looks at Paracelsian practice, however, one finds the programme developed in rather different ways. On the one hand, for many Paracelsians, the basic chemical principles had particular cosmological significance, and one of the most influential of his followers, Joseph Duchesne, offered a cosmogony in the early 1600s which is very much in the tradition of transformed natural history that we looked at in Chapter 4.[14] Just as the Garden of Eden is no longer treated as something to be read allegorically but as a real physical location that can be identified in the present world, and the Flood is treated as a real historical event for which empirical evidence must be sought, so the search for a physical reconstruction of the creation of the world is of paramount importance. In Duchesne's reconstruction, the universe begins as a mass of chaotic water, which is divided by God into the sublunar and the celestial realms, the latter containing pure 'spiritual' matter. By a process of distillation, God separates out the subtle, airy, mercurial liquor from the gross, oily, sulphurous liquor, and then, from the latter, he separates out a dry, saline residue. On the other hand, one of the other leading sixteenth-century Paracelsians, Peter Severinus, takes the project in a completely different direction, instructing his readers to buy a pair of stout shoes, explore mountains, valleys, deserts, and seashores, and 'note with care the distinctions between animals, the differences of plants, the various kinds of minerals, the properties and mode of origin of everything that exists'.[15] This echoes

---

[14] Joseph Duchesne, *Liber de priscorum philosophorum* (1603), and *Ad veritatem hermeticae medicinae* (1604). On Duchesne see Allen G. Debus, *The French Paracelsians* (Cambridge, 1991), chs. 2 and 3.

[15] Peter Severinus, *Idea Medicinae Philosophicae* (The Hague, 1660), 39: cited in Debus, *The English Paracelsians*, 20. Cf. the remark in Scarburgh's oration for Harvey: 'he had studied the sea and the land, islands, and continents, mountains and valleys, woods and plains, rivers and lakes,

Paracelsus' own claim in *Liber de nymphis* that the virtues of healing herbs are invisible yet can be detected, for

It is God's will that nothing remain unknown to man as he walks in the light of nature; for all things exist for the sake of man. And since they have been created for his sake, and since it is he who needs them, he must explore everything that lies in nature.[16]

Paracelsian iatrochemistry acts as a means of organizing the domain of natural history into those things potentially of use to medicine and those not, even though the fundamental principles that Paracelsians invoke bear little relation to this practical means of organization.

The Paracelsian tradition sought some form of underlying structure, but there are two notions of underlying structure at stake. First, there is whatever it is that explains the operation of a medicine on the body. Secondly, there is the ultimate underlying structure, the structure on which everything rests. The first notion is driven by medical considerations, whereas the second is driven by a combination of Neoplatonic metaphysics and Aristotelian/alchemical matter theory considerations. Paracelsus writes as if the two were the same thing, but clearly they are not. Moreover, since the Paracelsian system is designed above all to replace the diagnostic practices and remedies of Galenic physicians, and since as a result the claims for the systems rest on success in the shared domain of diagnosis and remedy, Paracelsians were forced to adopt results-orientated strategies. Attempting to derive remedies from first principles was impractical, and as the quote from Severinus indicates, in fact the effort was needed at the level of natural history. Indeed, the organization of the domain of natural history in iatrochemical terms is in effect an alternative to organizing it in terms of fundamental natural philosophy, whether this be conceived in Neoplatonic terms, corpuscularianism, or in some other way.

One important motivation behind this contrast is the idea that the most fundamental level does not necessarily have the explanatory resources of less reductive levels. A chemical understanding of the action of pharmaceutical substances may have far greater explanatory resources than an account in terms of the basic principles, elements, or corpuscular activity underlying the chemical processes, and it may be subject to probing, through experimental varying of conditions, in a way that the more fundamental account is not. In other words, although one might argue that it is because the fundamental principles, elements, or corpuscular activity are as they are that the chemical processes occur as they do, it may be that, as far as explanatory potential is concerned, it is the level of the phenomena themselves that offers the best explanatory resources. That is to say, a non-reductive explanation—for example something that takes the form of an examination of the causal connections between the phenomena—might be the best one. No Paracelsian could envisage such a case, for reductive explanation is one of the things that marks out his project most sharply

---

and whatever mysteries they contained' (L. M. Payne, 'Sir Charles Scarburgh's Harveian Oration, 1662', *Journal of the History of Medicine* 12 (1957), 158–64: 163).

[16] Translated in Paracelsus, *Selected Writings*, ed. and trans. Jolande Jacobi (Princeton, 1958), 109.

from Galenism, but it is a possible development of this approach, one which focuses on practical explanatory power rather than natural-philosophical foundations, and it is not necessarily in conflict with assumptions about the ultimate constituents of macroscopic bodies. For this approach to become effective, however, it is important that a sense is developed of how one might organize a domain of explanation which does not simply attempt to uncover fundamental principles, but seeks out how one might forge explanatory tools from the material to hand at the level of phenomena themselves. It is Bacon and above all Gilbert who, in navigating the muddy waters between natural history and natural philosophy, make the initial moves in this direction.

## THE FOCUSING OF NATURAL-HISTORICAL ENQUIRY: GILBERT VERSUS BACON

Gilbert and Bacon were trained, respectively, in the two Renaissance professions that concerned themselves with assessing evidence: medicine and law.[17] Gilbert was President of the Royal College of Physicians and physician to both Elizabeth and James I, and Bacon held a string of senior legal and political positions, including Attorney General and Lord Keeper of the Great Seal, and culminating in the Lord Chancellorship. Both of them stressed the practical aspects of learning, both were explicitly opposed to enthusiast forms of Puritanism, and both took up an active interest in natural philosophy only when they were in their forties, after many years of activity in their professions.

Most crucially of all, both use natural history to launch their investigations into matter theory. Both take their starting point from a natural history tradition that had been developed in novel ways by Iberian writers, preoccupied with discoveries in the New World, in the sixteenth and early seventeenth centuries. We have already noted the role of the New World flora and fauna on the demise of emblematics, but the significance extends far beyond this. Sixteenth-century Iberians were among the first to question the authority of the ancients in natural history: in theories of the winds, tides, navigation, and cosmography.[18] The pioneering work of New World natural history, José de Acosta's *Historia Natural y Moral de las Indias* (1590), offered extensive accounts of winds, tides, seasonal variations, and metallurgy, as well as the ethnology and anthropology of the indigenous population of the Americas.[19] The *Historia* was translated into English in 1604 by Edward Grimston, Bacon's colleague at Gray's

---

[17] See Ian Maclean, *Interpretation and Meaning in the Renaissance*, and idem, *Logic, Signs and Nature in the Renaissance*.

[18] The question is dealt with in detail in José Antonio Maravall, *Antiguos y Modernos: Visión de la historia e dia de progresso hasta el Renacimiento* (2nd edn, Madrid, 1986). See also Víctor Navarro Brotóns and Enrique Rodríguez Galdeano, *Matemáticas, Cosmología y Humanismo en la España del Siglo XVI. Los Comentarios al Segundo Libro de la Historia Natural de Plinio de Jerónimo Muñoz* (Valencia, 1998).

[19] See the assessment of Acosta's contribution in Jorge Canizares-Esguerra, 'Iberian Science in the Renaissance: Ignored How Much Longer?', *Perspectives in Science* 12 (2004), 86–124: 96–8.

Inn,[20] and Bacon himself is very indebted to it: his treatment of civil and natural history as falling under the faculty of memory in *Novum organum* derives from Acosta for example, and he borrows extensively from him in his 'Great Instauration', particularly in the material on winds.

Nevertheless, Bacon's legal interests are mirrored in his approach to natural history, and this pulls him in a distinctive direction. For Bacon, the reform of English law was possible only if its underlying rationality, its essential structure, could be uncovered.[21] By contrast with his English contemporaries, his attempted codification of English law was on a French model that he probably learned from the French lawyer into whose professional care he had been placed in 1578,[22] and its aim was to impose order on the law by showing that its essential structure lay in a small number of underlying principles. When Bacon moved from a concern with law to a concern with natural philosophy, beginning around 1602, he retained his commitment to the idea of seeking underlying foundational principles to provide structure for an otherwise heterogeneous mass of information, in the one case common law, in the other natural history. The latter he redefined, so as to bring it closer to matter theory, and this is evident in his *Phaenomena universi*, which provides an overall account of his matter theory as an introduction to cosmological questions.[23] The work is subtitled 'natural history for the building up of philosophy', but Bacon draws a sharp distinction between what he has in mind and what had traditionally gone under that name. He mentions classical figures such as Aristotle, Pliny, and Dioscorides, but few modern naturalists by name.[24] On the other hand, his discussions of natural history occasionally draw on a group one might naturally consider to be more marginal to the enterprise: Patrizi, Telesio, Cardano, della Porta, Bruno, and Paracelsus. Remarking on this, Paula Findlen has noted that 'for anyone versed in the natural history tradition, Bacon's own natural history seems strikingly devoid of the common markers that we associate with this genre: no lengthy descriptions of flora and fauna; no discussions of etymology, number of toes and fronds, or other classificatory devices'.[25] The reason, as she points out, is that Bacon wanted to redefine natural history, which he saw as including, and perhaps being constituted primarily of, a mixture of natural magic and alchemy. He tells us at the beginning of the *Phaenomena* that the natural history that has been compiled hitherto 'is sketchy and useless, and not even of the kind

[20] *The Naturall and Morall Historie of the East and West Indies* (London, 1604). Acosta's work was widely translated. In its first ten years alone, as well as three Spanish editions, there were translations into Latin (1596), Italian (1596), French (1598 and 1600), German (1598 and 1600), and Dutch (1598). For details, see Víctor Navarro Brotóns et al., *Bibliographia Physico-Mathematica Hispanica (1475–1900)*, i. *Libros y folletos, 1475–1600* (Valencia, 1999), 67–70 (items 3–12).

[21] See Martin, *Francis Bacon*, chs. 3 and 4.

[22] Lisa Jardine and Alan Stewart, *Hostage to Fortune: The Troubled Life of Francis Bacon 1561–1626* (London, 1998), 61.

[23] For details, see Gaukroger, *Francis Bacon*, chs. 4 and 5.

[24] He refers to Gesner, Acosta, and Georgius Agricola, *De re metallica libri XII* (Basle, 1556).

[25] Paula Findlen, 'Francis Bacon and the Reform of Natural History in the Seventeenth Century', in Donald R. Kelley, ed., *History and the Disciplines: The Reclassification of Knowledge in Early Modern Europe* (Rochester, 1997), 239–60: 240.

I am seeking'.[26] Its principal defect and, we may conclude, the feature that makes it 'not even of the kind' he is seeking, is the fact that 'it has embraced the inquiry into things natural but largely spurned that into things mechanical'. The latter, he tells us, enables us to go beyond the effects of nature and probe its secrets, although its practitioners have concentrated on things 'hidden and rare' at the expense of 'common experiments and observations'. What Bacon wants to do is to establish a connection between his newly conceived natural history—that is, a batch of disciplines including natural magic and alchemy, which have been relabelled, perhaps in order to give them some air of respectability[27]—and natural philosophy as traditionally conceived, that is, as a *scientia* which offers a fundamental understanding of nature.

What drives Baconian cosmology, and natural philosophy generally, is matter theory, and he advocates a new method of discovery designed to secure a more adequate matter-theoretical understanding of causation. As we saw in Chapter 5, what Bacon is seeking from a method of discovery is the discovery of causes that are both necessary and sufficient for their effects, and he believes that his method of eliminative induction will secure this. He locates such causes at the corpuscular level: they are the microscopic 'parts' whose distribution and behaviour is responsible for the macroscopic features of bodies. An example of how the method works is given in the case of colour in *Valerius terminus*. The account is presented there as an alternative to Aristotle's,[28] yet Bacon does not mention any of the details of Aristotle's elaborate treatment, nor any of Aristotle's criticisms of atomism, and he does not engage with Aristotle at the level of just where the nature of colour is to be found. Rather, he simply takes atomism/corpuscularianism as given, in the sense that it is in the microcorpuscular structure of the coloured body that the explanation is to be found, and the point is to guide us to the correct atomistic/corpuscularian explanation.

As its starting point, the procedure takes some combination of substances that produces whiteness, that is, we start with what are in effect sufficient conditions for the production of whiteness, and then we remove from these anything not necessary for the colour. First, we note that if air and water are mixed together in small portions, the result is white, as in snow or waves. Here we have the sufficient conditions for whiteness, but not the necessary conditions, so next we increase the scope, substituting any transparent uncoloured substance for water, whence we find that glass or crystal, on being ground, become white, and albumen, which is initially a watery transparent substance, on having air beaten into it, becomes white. Third, we further increase the

[26] *The Oxford Francis Bacon*, vi. 2/3–4/5.

[27] Compare Findlen, 'Francis Bacon and the Reform of Natural History', 241: 'Natural history had come to mean something quite different to Bacon than it had traditionally connoted; like natural philosophy it was in need of reinvention . . . [Natural history] provided a rubric under which to pursue forms of inquiry that were incapable of full redemption in their current state. It provided the *via media* between the academically exalted field of natural philosophy and both the occult sciences and the crafts tradition . . . Drawing upon these various fields of knowledge and sanitizing them through their relabelling as "natural history", Bacon strove to create an approach to nature that would make its study and its practitioners more deserving of public recognition.'

[28] Bacon, *Works*, iii. 236.

scope, and ask what happens in the case of coloured substances. Amber and sapphire become white on being ground, and wine and beer become white when brought to a froth. The substances considered up to this stage have all been 'more grossly transparent than air'. Bacon next considers flame, which is less grossly transparent than air, and argues that the mixture of fire and air makes the flame whiter. The upshot of this is that water is sufficient for whiteness, but not necessary for it. He continues in the same vein, asking next whether air is necessary for whiteness. He notes that a mixture of water and oil is white, even when the air has been evaporated from it, so air is not necessary for whiteness, but is a transparent substance necessary? Bacon does not continue with the chain of questions after this point, but sets out some conclusions, namely that bodies whose parts are unequal but in simple proportion are white, those whose parts are in equal proportions are transparent, proportionately unequal colours, and absolutely unequal black. In other words, this is the conclusion that one might expect to arrive at on the basis of the method of sifting out what is necessary for the phenomenon and what is not, although Bacon himself does not provide the route to this conclusion here.

In the circumstances, one can ask what his confidence in his conclusion derives from, if he has not been able to complete the 'induction' himself. The answer is that it derives from the consequences he can draw from his account. There are two ways in which the justification for the conclusions can be assessed: by the procedure of eliminative induction that he has just set out, and by the consequences of those conclusions generated by it.[29] This two-way process, from empirical phenomena to first principles, and then from first principles to empirical phenomena, is a classic Aristotelian procedure, but the kinds of things that Aristotelians were looking for as the ultimate principles which underlie the phenomena, principles that can then be used to generate a causal understanding of those phenomena, were very different both in aim and in substance from what Gilbert and Bacon were looking for. Much of their anti-Aristotelianism rests on a rejection of Aristotle's account of forms underlying natural processes. This is particularly marked in Bacon. Like Aristotle, Bacon thinks that natural philosophy relies at the most fundamental level on a theory of matter, but whereas the potentialities and tendencies of Aristotle's physical theory seem to inhere in matter without being physically identifiable in their own right, in Bacon's account they are present at the microscopic level in a physical way, and they are occasionally manifest at the macroscopic level in a physical way: squeezing, stretching, contraction, dilation, distension.[30] For Bacon, but not for Aristotle, the causes of

[29] Bacon, *Works*, iii. 237.

[30] See, in particular, *Phenomena universi*, which looks at the behaviour of fluids, principally water and air. Bacon's first concern is with the question of how bodies can propel themselves through these fluid media, how birds can propel themselves through air, for example, and how oars can propel boats through water. What happens in these cases is that when fluids are squeezed into confined spaces, as in the case where they are immediately behind the wings and immediately behind the oar when these push backwards, they exert a force which acts in the opposite direction to the motion of the wing or the oar, with the result that the bird or the boat is pushed forwards by the air or the water, which, as a consequence of the initial compression, expands in the direction of its motion (*The Oxford Francis Bacon*, vi. 36–40/37–41.) He looks at cases of the generation of sounds by

material processes are themselves material—they are no different in kind from their effects—and one thing that natural philosophy should provide one with is a means of working back from manifest physical effects to their underlying physical causes: the aim of natural philosophy must be to enable us to identify the physically distinct states of matter that underlie macroscopic behaviour, for they are the causes of the processes we wish to explain.

The problem is that Bacon's method of eliminative induction remains a promissory note. That the ultimate explanations for the behaviour of things lie at the level of simple microscopic analogues of macroscopic processes is not something this method can show. Moreover, not only has the method had to be guided towards such microscopic processes, it runs out of steam—both in the case of colour, which we have just looked at, and in the more elaborate treatment of heat[31]—at a very early stage and is manifestly unable to take us down to the ultimate level at which necessary conditions can be identified, let alone the necessary and sufficient conditions that Bacon seeks. Bacon's natural history simply cannot connect with natural philosophy, conceived as something that reveals essential structures. But he will not accept anything less than this, as is clear from his criticisms of Gilbert. In the context of discussing extrapolation from particular cases to a general theory, Bacon accuses Gilbert of making 'a philosophy out of the observations of a loadstone.'[32] In one sense, Bacon is quite right: Gilbert does make a philosophy out of the lodestone, but what he is doing is using a magnetic device—the terrella—to focus and render manageable the domain of explanation of a crucial part of natural history, that part which, he is able to show, has direct consequences for cosmology and the theory of the earth.

Much of Gilbert's work is in a straightforward natural-history genre of recording data and compiling an account of authoritative views on the data. The approach is evident in *Nova meteorologia*, which deals with comets, the Milky Way, clouds, winds, springs and rivers, and the seas and tides.[33] He makes a compilation of ancient, medieval, and contemporary theories on these questions, but he also takes great care to record instances of observational data, indicating whether these are his own observations or have been recorded by others. Sifting through the theories he records, he rejects some and occasionally offers his own considered view on what the true account is, but often he leaves the question open. The general procedure is that a range of views on what are usually practically motivated natural-philosophical questions are

---

air pressure, the effects of forcing water under narrow arches, the behaviour of up-turned bowls of air submerged in water, the mechanism of bellows, and various other phenomena that point to the effects of pressure on fluids, distinguishing, in particular, between two kinds of case: motion 'to avoid a vacuum' and 'motion of recovery from tension' (ibid. 46/47), and he describes a number of experiments to separate out their effects.

[31] Bacon, *Works*, i. 236–68.       [32] Ibid. iii. 293.

[33] The *Nova meteorologia*, probably written in the 1580s, along with the *Physiologiae nova contra Aristotelem*, written in the 1590s, were collected for publication soon after Gilbert's death, and were known to Bacon and Harriot in the first decades of the seventeenth century, although they were published only in 1651 under the title *De mundo*. See Suzanne Kelly, *The De mundo of William Gilbert* (2 vols, Amsterdam, 1965), one volume of which is an introduction to *De mundo*, the other volume containing a facsimile of the 1651 text.

presented, observational evidence is recorded wherever possible, an attempt is made to impose some kind of order on the views and their plausibility is assessed, and occasionally a suggestion is made as to what the right account is, whether this be new or an existing account, although the discussion generally maintains an open-ended approach.

*De magnete* follows this procedure but Gilbert is able to come to a considered judgement on a far larger range of issues. Chapter 1 of the first Book of *De magnete* is devoted to a compilation of stories, reports, and known facts about magnetism from antiquity up to his own time, going through various scholastic, naturalist, and Platonic traditions. But this is no mere listing, and occasionally he criticizes the inadequate approach of his predecessors and contemporaries. Della Porta's work, for example, is treated as an untested resource,[34] something on a par with the earlier *Nova meteorologia*, but not with *De magnete*, which is more ambitious in its aims. Part 1 does cover many of the standard topics that one might expect from such a piece of natural history—the history of the discovery of lodestone, its geographical distribution, the words for it in other languages—but it quickly comes to focus on the physical properties of lodestone, notably its polarity, its ability to align itself along a north–south axis, and its attractive and repulsive powers, before moving on to the relation between iron and lodestone. Of particular interest is Gilbert's procedure—in defending his claim that lodestone is able to attract iron ore as well as iron, and that non-magnetized iron ore will attract iron ore—of setting out an experiment in which a piece of wrought-iron wire is attached to a cork floating on water, so that its unhindered movement can be observed, and another such wire is introduced, causing the former to turn. The fact that the poles of iron ore will align themselves with the earth's verticity under suitable circumstances leads him to argue that lodestone and iron ore are in fact the same thing, iron simply being an extract of the latter. The earth is a giant magnet. In support of this, he notes that lodestone and iron ore have in common certain fundamental properties: they each have poles to which they draw objects, and an equator. Moreover lodestone is found widely distributed on the surface of the earth, which suggests that it is not just an accident of local circumstances, and iron lies deep within the earth, which would explain the wide distribution of its products at the surface. The Aristotelian theory that there is an elemental earth is dismissed on the grounds that such a thing has never been found.

Part 2 of *De magnete* deals with magnetic 'coition', a term that refers to what Gilbert considers others have incorrectly called 'attraction'. For Gilbert, coition refers to a mutual process whereas attraction means one body drawing another to it by force.[35] This is an important distinction for Gilbert because he identifies forms of attraction that resemble magnetic coition but which he believes to be very different in nature. Amber attraction, which requires the amber to be rubbed, is very different from magnetism, for example. Amber is not the only substance that has this property and he distinguishes 'electrics' (*ēlektron* is the Greek term for amber)—that is, substances that, like amber, when rubbed exhibit an attractive power—from

---

[34] Gilbert, *On the Magnet*, 6.     [35] Ibid. 68, 46.

non-electrics, which are unaffected by rubbing. He also describes a device by which one might discriminate between electrics and non-electrics: a 'versorium', a finely balanced needle that turns if a rubbed electric is brought near it but which remains stationary in the presence of a rubbed non-electric. The difference between magnetic coition and amber attraction (and electric attraction generally), set out in Chapter 2 of Part 2, is that magnetic substances share in the form of the earth, a form imposed on it by its creator, and which gave it its magnetic power. Some bodies retain this form, and these are the ones that exhibit magnetic properties. Amber does not derive from the material that carries the original magnetic form, but from the composite nature of the earth, which is made up from fluid and humid material and firm and dry material. 'Electrics' have the peculiar property that the material they compose can attract other materials when rubbed, because the fluid and humid matter from which they are made up is never wholly solidified, and as a result emits an effluvium that captures small particles and pulls them inwards. Magnetic coition, by contrast, requires no rubbing to release an effluvium because it acts not by means of an effluvium, but by means of an invisible orb of virtue. It is, unlike effluvial attraction, genuine action at a distance, although the orb is finite in extent and affects only those bodies within its periphery. Any piece of iron or other magnetic material that is introduced into this orb will affect—and be affected by—the central magnet.

At this point Gilbert makes an important move. A small central spherical magnet, a 'terrella', he tells us, will mimic the magnetic action of the earth. An example of this is the way in which magnetized pieces of iron behave when placed within the 'orb of virtue' of the terrella:

A terrella sends out in an orbe its powers in proportion to its vigour and quality. But when iron or any other magnetick of convenient magnitude comes within its orbe of virtue, it is allured; but the nearer it comes to the body, the more quickly it runs up to it. They move towards the magnet, not as to a centre, nor towards its centre. For they only do this in the case of the poles themselves, when namely that which is being allured, and the pole of the loadstone, and its centre, are in the same straight line. But in the intervening spaces they tend obliquely, just as is evident in [Fig. 10.1], in which is shown how the influence is extended to the adjoining magneticks within the orbe; in the case of the poles straight out.[36]

The use of a simple device that reproduces the action of the system under examination, a system that for one reason or another is inaccessible, is something the terrella shares with instruments such as the orrery.[37] But in the case of astronomical instruments, the action is produced in different ways in the device and in the system under examination—in the case of the orrery it is produced by clockwork, for example—whereas the terrella is distinctive in that the action is postulated to be

---

[36] Ibid. 75.

[37] Note, however, that before the sixteenth century scientific instruments were often not used as such. In both antiquity and the Middle Ages, instruments for timekeeping, navigation, and surveying were often not used for these purposes but were kept as symbols of the possession of knowledge. See Derek J. de Solla Price, 'Philosophical Mechanism and Mechanical Philosophy: Some Notes towards a Philosophy of Scientific Instruments', *Annali dell'Instituto e Museo di storia della scienza*, 5 (1980), 75–85; idem, 'Of Sealing Wax and String', *Natural History* 93 (1984), 49–56.

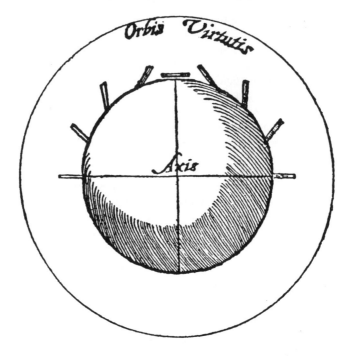

**Figure 10.1**

exactly the same. It is important to bear in mind here that Gilbert was a physician, and that anatomists had traditionally used the anatomy of an accessible animal to display the anatomy of an inaccessible one. Galen had been unable to dissect human bodies for this was forbidden in the Rome of his day, and although he urges that every opportunity should be taken to examine human cadavers (recording his observation of one such case where the flesh had been washed away by the action of a stream), this was insufficient for systematic anatomical investigation. Hence the importance of his observation that apes bore great anatomical resemblance to humans, and he had urged that, to avoid being misled, those apes closest to human beings (he considered what we now identify as barbary apes to meet this criterion) should be chosen for dissection.[38] With the revival of anatomy at Salerno from the late tenth century, the pig replaced the ape, because, as an eleventh-century Salerno anatomist puts it, 'although some animals, such as monkeys, are found to resemble ourselves in external form, there are none so like us internally as the pig, and for this reason we are going to conduct an anatomy upon this animal'.[39] Because the

[38] See Andrew Cunningham, *The Anatomical Renaissance: The Resurrection of the Anatomical Projects of the Ancients* (Aldershot, 1997), ch. 1.

[39] Twelfth-century Salerno anatomist, translated in George W. Corner, ed. and trans., *Anatomical Texts of the Earlier Middle Ages* (Washington, 1927), 51.

anatomy of the ape or the pig was postulated to resemble that of the human body so closely, the anatomy of an accessible animal could mimic that of an inaccessible one. The appearance of Vesalius' human anatomy in 1543 should not blind us to the traditions of ingenuity that earlier anatomists had developed. Unable to dissect human bodies, yet rejecting those accounts on which dissection is unnecessary—such as the Platonist view that the human body is designed to harbour the soul and so its structure mirrors the tripartite structure of the soul, a conception on which dissection is an inappropriate form of enquiry—anatomists had to think through how one had empirical access to the internal structure of the human body without dissecting it.

This is the kind of reasoning that Gilbert follows in his use of the terrella. It enables him to submit his account of the earth's magnetism to test by proxy, and in the following sections of *De magnete* it is put to great use in explaining the behaviour of magnetized bodies in the earth's orb of virtue. Books 3, 4, and 5 deal respectively with the three properties of a lodestone that is balanced and free to turn: its orientation, its deviation from the meridian, and its declination, each of these being central to questions of navigation by means of a magnetic compass. Finally, in Book 6, Gilbert explores what he considers to be the properties of a magnetic sphere for the motion of the earth. He is unable to draw consequences for the question of whether there is an annual motion, but concludes that the earth's magnetism causes it to rotate daily. More specifically, the fact that the earth is a spherical, balanced lodestone with two opposite poles causes it to turn on its axis.[40] The postulated rotation is a rotation with respect to the *primum mobile* (usually equated with the orb of the fixed stars, but Gilbert does not accept that the fixed stars all lie at the same distance from the earth) and he defends this account by recourse to an experiment in which a terrella, which is allowed to float freely on the surface of water contained in a wooden bucket, rotates if one of its poles is set facing the like pole of the earth.

By structuring his account around what can be achieved through manipulation of the terrella, Gilbert is able to bring coherence to a field of natural-historical investigation in a way that makes no appeal to fundamental natural-philosophical principles of the kind offered by the matter theory of the earlier Books of *De magnete*. Bacon objects to this approach,[41] as we have seen, and for all the radicalness of Bacon's programme, in some respects, above all in its conception of the role of basic natural-philosophical principles, he conceives of it as sharing goals with the Aristotelian one, goals that he believes the Aristotelian programme could only aspire to but which his project can realize. Gilbert, by contrast, adopts a mode of investigation that is quite different from anything Aristotle or Bacon aspired to. It is not that it is unsystematic, but rather that the systematic connections are drawn at purely phenomenal level, instead of being grounded in underlying causes. The question is what explanatory value such phenomenal connections could have.

---

[40] Gilbert, *On the Magnet*, 221.

[41] Note, however, that Bacon's knowledge of Gilbert probably did not derive from *De magnete* but from *Nova meteorologia* and *Physiologae nova*: see Marie Boas Hall, 'Bacon and Gilbert', *Journal of the History of Ideas*, 12 (1951), 466–7.

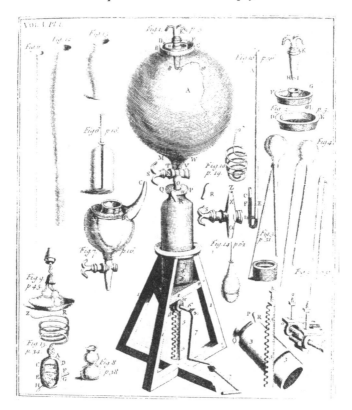

**Figure 10.2**

## THE AIR PUMP: HOBBES VERSUS BOYLE

In his *New Experiments Physico-Mechanical, Touching the Spring of Air* (1660),[42] Boyle set out reports of forty-three experiments performed with his air pump, devised with great ingenuity and skill by the instrument maker Ralph Greatorex (see Fig. 10.2) and subsequently improved by Hooke. A year later, in his *Dialogus physicus de natura aeris*,[43] Hobbes challenged Boyle's account of his experiments to produce a vacuum, initiating a dispute that was to last into the next decade, and which raised the fundamental question of what natural-philosophical understanding consisted in. In particular, it explicitly pitted 'speculative' against 'experimental' natural philosophy for the first time. How, asks Hobbes in the *Dialogus*, could Boyle have aroused 'the

---

[42] Boyle, *Works*, i. 1–117.

[43] *Thomae Hobbes malmesburiensis opera philosophica quae latine scripsit omnia*, ed. William Molesworth (5 vols, London, 1839–45), iv. 233–96; trans. as the appendix to Shapin and Schaffer, *Leviathan and the Air Pump*, 346–91.

expectations of advancing physics, when you have not established the doctrine of universal and abstract motion (which was easy and mathematical)'?[44]

The experiment identified by Boyle as 'the principal fruit' of the air pump consisted in placing a Torricellian barometer in the pump and noting the change in the level of mercury as the tube is evacuated.[45] To understand the significance of the experiment, we need to note that the appearance of an empty space at the top of a sealed tube of liquid (depending on the liquid and its height), when the full tube is inverted and placed in a dish of the same liquid, was something that attracted a variety of explanations. It was a test case for competing natural philosophies, above all for the Aristotelian theory that 'nature abhors a vacuum'. The problem had a practical side: in 1630, for example, Giovanni Baliani wrote to Galileo asking for his advice on why a long pipe he had installed to bring water over the hills to the city behaved as if there were some leak of air at the top, with the water running down both sides of the summit. Galileo replied that the reason water could not be raised above a certain height—around 34 feet—was that, like a piece of rope, water would reach a height at which it would break under its own weight. The diameter of the pipe and its total length were irrelevant: only its vertical height mattered. In the *Discorsi* of 1638, in accounting for the breaking strength of beams,[46] Galileo adapts this theory to account for cohesion: the column of 34 feet coheres due to the attraction caused by tiny vacuua between the corpuscles making up the water, an attraction that is overwhelmed by weight at 34 feet. In the course of the 1640s a number of Italian natural philosophers began looking in more detail at the phenomenon. The U-shaped tube was replaced by a glass tube with a bulb at the top, and the water level, now clearly visible, was around 34 feet. Baliani's view had been that the phenomenon was due to atmospheric pressure, and Torricelli suggested an experiment that would throw light on its cause. Thinking through the case in terms of statics, he envisaged the weight of the atmosphere balancing the weight of the column. This being the case, if in place of the water one substituted mercury, whose specific weight is fourteen times that of water, then the column of mercury should be a fourteenth the height of the column of water, as indeed it was.

One of the features of the barometer, and what made it so important, was that, like Gilbert's terrella, it could be manipulated to decide between competing accounts. Those who denied the existence of a vacuum, for example, had to provide some account of the space above the column of mercury in the sealed tube. One view, that a vapour was formed above the column, was refuted by Pascal's experiment in which a column of wine was compared with a column of water. Since wine produces vapours, on this view the wine level should be lower, whereas if the determining feature is its specific gravity, then the column of wine should be higher, because the specific weight of wine is less than that of water. Pascal was able to show that the wine column is higher. Similarly, a bubble of air could not be the explanation because the level of

---

[44] Shapin and Schaffer, *Leviathan and the Air Pump*, 379.

[45] The first published mention of Torricelli's experiments in English was in Walter Charleton's 1654 *Physiologia Epicuro-Gassendo-Charltoniana*, 348.

[46] Galileo, *Two New Sciences*, 24–6.

mercury is the same height in a closed-off tube as it is in a tube with a large bulb at the top, and it is also the same height if the length of the tube is increased. More directly, the idea that what was at stake was the weight of air and the weight of the column was tested by altering one of the variables: by taking a column of mercury to a high spot (Pascal got his brother-in-law to take it to the summit of the Puy de Dôme), and observing that there was a decrease in its height with increasing altitude.

But there were other explanations for the behaviour of the barometer, and Boyle's insertion of a barometer into his air pump suggested that it was not a question of the weight of air at all, because although the height of the column of mercury was normal in a sealed container, once the container began to be evacuated the level of the mercury fell, and this could not be due to a balance of weights because the weight of air in the container was negligible compared to that of the mercury. The variable factor, Boyle concluded, was not the weight of the air but air pressure, something reinforced in one of the other experiments (performed earlier, with a more primitive apparatus, by Roberval, as we saw in Ch. 8), in which a bladder containing a small amount of air expanded as the container in which it was placed was evacuated. Air, he concluded, is an elastic fluid that expands as external constraints are removed:

Air either consists of, or at least abounds with, parts of such a nature, that in case they be bent or compress'd by the weight of the incumbent part of the Atmosphere, or by any other Body, they do so endeavour, as much as in them lies, to free themselves from that pressure, by bearing against the contiguous Bodies that keep them bent.[47]

What is at issue in the dispute between Hobbes and Boyle is not straightforward. One thing that is clear, however, is that it is tied up with the question of just what kind of project the natural philosopher should be engaged in. We have seen that, in *De corpore*, Hobbes distinguished natural philosophy from natural history on the grounds that the latter 'is but experience, or authority, and not ratiocination'.[48] Boyle, by contrast, in his *An Examen of Mr. T. Hobbes his Dialogus Physicus de Natura Aëris*, takes Hobbes to task by asking 'what experiment or matter of fact' Hobbes has 'added to enrich the history of nature'.[49] The difference is a fundamental one. One of Hobbes' principal criticisms of Boyle's experiments, for example, is that, in invoking a restorative power in the air, Boyle is offering an account of the phenomenon which is not genuinely causal, and that such an account cannot be an explanation:

It is for a philosopher to find the true or at least very probable causes of such things. How could compressed wool or steel plates or atoms of air give your experimental philosophers the cause of restitution? Or do you offer a likely cause why in a crossbow the steel plate regains its usual straightness so swiftly?[50]

Note, however, that knowledge of causes was deemed to be conjectural by both Boyle and Hobbes, and both of them thought that, where several possible explanations were

[47] Boyle, *Works*, i. 11.

[48] Hobbes, *English Works*, i. 3. On Hobbes' classification of histories into natural, civil, and divine, and his disparagement of natural histories, see Karl Schuhmann, 'Hobbes's Concept of History', in G. A. J. Rogers and Tom Sorell, eds, *Hobbes and History* (London, 2000), 3–24.

[49] Boyle, *Works*, i. 197.

[50] Hobbes, *Opera philosophica*, iv. 247–8; trans. Shapin and Shaffer, 356–7.

available, we should seek the simplest.[51] Hobbes was insistent that causes necessitate their effects, that identical causes produce identical effects. Not only did this lie at the basis of Hobbes' understanding of mechanism, it is hard to see how it could not lie at the basis of any understanding of mechanism, Boyle's included. It is true that Hobbes pushes mechanism further than Boyle would, combining it with his reductionism to generate determinism, for example, but this is an issue about the scope of mechanism, not about its nature, and nothing in the dispute indicates that Boyle believes aspects of phenomena produced by the air pump fall outside the realm of mechanical explanation: quite the contrary, his understanding of elasticity is manifestly shaped within the context of mechanism. Within this context, the principle of 'same cause, same effect' must surely hold, otherwise one would not be able to identify the micromechanical causes of macroscopic behaviour.

The principle of 'same cause, same effect' does not, of course, rule out one effect having several different possible causes, and here again Boyle and Hobbes are in agreement, both holding that God could have produced the same effect by many different causes. Shapin and Schaffer argue that the central divide between Boyle and Hobbes here lies in their different assessments of the consequences of this for natural-philosophical enquiry. Boyle, they suggest, 'reckoned that God could produce the same effect by a number of different natural causes, and on this basis he recommended methodological caution and even nescience about the ability of natural philosophers to unveil real causes'.[52] Hobbes, by contrast, 'did not move from the admission that our knowledge of natural causes was conjectural to the tactic of bracketing off causal enquiry from the foundations of natural philosophy. For Hobbes causal statements ought to form one of the bases and starting points of any philosophical enterprise whatsoever.'[53]

In the dispute over the air pump, Boyle and Hobbes did indeed have different views on what level of explanation was appropriate, but there is nothing in Boyle's response to suggest that this was motivated by the possibility of many causes for any effect. The basic problem for Hobbes seemed to be that Boyle's proposed explanation would rule out more fundamental theories that were central to Hobbes' natural-philosophical system. Above all, Hobbes' physical optics required a medium for the transmission of light. As we have seen, it was the normal transmission of light through the space at the top of the mercury that prompted his first doubts about the existence of a vacuum in 1648.[54] For Hobbes, fundamental natural-philosophical issues had to guide one's explanations. But whereas Boyle had insisted that in addition to Hobbes' two criteria for the acceptance of a hypothesis, conceivability and necessity, one must also include 'a third, namely that it be not inconsistent with any other truth or phaenomena of nature',[55] what he offered could consistently leave open the question

---

[51] See the discussion in Malcolm, *Aspects of Hobbes*, 187–9.
[52] Shapin and Schaffer, *Leviathan and the Air Pump*, 147.     [53] Ibid. 148.
[54] Gassendi also believed that the space at the top of the tube could not be a vacuum because light, which he treated as corpuscular, was transmitted through it: *Opera*, i. 206. Unlike Hobbes, however, he did believe that it was void of air.
[55] Boyle, *Works*, i. 241.

of how light is propagated, since this is not a truth or phenomenon of nature but a hypothesis. Indeed, it is such hypotheses that the third criterion was directed towards, and he pointed out that Hobbes' notion of air as a homogeneous penetrative fluid was simply not consistent with the results of the experiment.

To help capture Hobbes' perspective on these questions, the situation might be compared with debates in astronomy. There were many ways of accounting for the motions of celestial bodies, and some of these ways carried distinct physical commitments. The Tychonic system, for example, even though it could be supported with a minimum of physical commitment, nevertheless did have physical consequences. This was, after all, why it was preferred over heliocentric systems: its physical consequences were harmless compared to those of heliocentric systems. In terms of the astronomical analogy, Boyle might be seen as proposing a system that saved the phenomena better than others, but which had an underlying physical rationale that conflicted with a body of natural philosophy that one had reason to prefer to other systems. Hobbes was not offering an astronomical system, but he was offering an account of the propagation of light, which Descartes' *Principia* had made a core cosmological issue. In these terms, Boyle's approach simply ignored fundamental natural-philosophical questions, offering what might be regarded as a one-off explanation for a phenomenon produced under conditions that could be questioned: any apparatus that produces variable pressures is particularly susceptible to leakage, for example, and Hobbes was at best sceptical that leaks had been avoided.

If we see things in this way, we can appreciate Hobbes' frustration at Boyle's approach. The frustration was shared by, and similarly exasperated, some of Boyle's continental contemporaries, notably Spinoza and Leibniz.[56] Yet the presentation of results in terms of bare facts, as it seemed to many of his critics, was not for Boyle a provisional record of research that was at a stage too early to merit systematization, or too early for appeal to fundamental causes.[57] In his earliest collection of papers, *Certain Physiological Essays*, Boyle makes it clear that he disagrees with 'some eminent Atomists' who maintain that 'no speculations in natural philosophy could be rational, wherein any other causes of things are assigned than atoms and their properties'.[58] As far as Boyle was concerned, Hobbes was treating an explanatory ideal as if it were a realistic goal. The trouble was that the explanatory ideal not only could not do any real work here, but, *contra* Hobbes, actually prevented progress. For Hobbes, progress was guided by fundamental natural-philosophical principles that showed

[56] Leibniz, e.g., wrote to Oldenburg asking him impatiently to urge Boyle to produce a systematic exposition of his views on chemistry: Leibniz to Oldenburg, 5 July 1674 and 10 May 1675, in Oldenburg, *Correspondence*, xi. 46 and 306 respectively. Spinoza also expressed reservations to Oldenburg on this score in a letter of April 1662: ibid. i. 462. Oldenburg though that Boyle and Spinoza should unite their 'mental gifts for the earnest cultivation of a genuine and solid philosophy.' (ibid. ii. 102 [text]/104 [trans]).

[57] See e.g. his comment in *Certain Physiological Essays*, that 'I am content, provided experimental learning be really promoted, to contribute even in the least plausible way to the advancement of it; and had rather not only be an under-builder, but even dig in the quarries for materials towards so useful a structure, as a solid body of natural philosophy, than not do something towards the erection of it.' *Works*, i. 307.

[58] Ibid. 308.

one what needed to be explained and what kind of explanation it required. This is an approach he shared with Beeckman, Mersenne, Gassendi, and Descartes, for, despite the differing views they held on what degree of certainty one could achieve in natural philosophy, this was the level at which it was clear that a new start in natural philosophy had been made, because this was the level at which the fundamental assumptions and principles of the new natural-philosophical system were manifest. Fundamental natural-philosophical principles did not play this role in Boyle, not because he did not subscribe to such principles—he was committed to mechanism no less than Hobbes[59]—but because he had quite a different sense of the way in which natural philosophy could best be made to work.

The form taken by natural philosophy in the air pump dispute is matter theory. Differing conceptions of what one thinks matter theory should be doing, and what its primary purposes are, may shape how one sees the natural philosophy that ultimately underlies it. Consider the case of iatrochemistry. If, like Boyle, one thinks of illness no longer in the Galenic sense as an imbalance of humours, so that every illness is essentially individual, but rather as something that has an identity in its own right, whereby the same illness can afflict several people at the same time or at different times, then the cure for the illness might be sought in some chemical treatment, a medicine, which would work, within limits, in the same way on all those afflicted.[60] Because this medicine works at a chemical level, directly on what it is that is causing an illness which is identifiable independently of the patient, matter theory had a potentially important role in expanding the range of such medicines. There are two issues here. First, there is the question of practical effectiveness: matter theory as iatrochemistry aims at supplying medicines that have genuine curative properties. The aim is wholly practical. Nothing overrides it, and no considerations are allowed to stand in the way of it. Second, there is the question of providing a rationale for the action of these medicines at the level of matter theory, and here natural-philosophical considerations re-enter the picture. Note, however, that it is not a question of understanding the chemico-physiological action of medicines: no one in the seventeenth century was remotely near such an account, and the agenda of someone like Boyle

---

[59] Note, in this connection, Boyle's refusal to become embroiled in the debates over whether there was a void in nature, and his extreme annoyance at More's attempt to use his experiments in pneumatics as irrefutable proof of the existence of the activity of an immaterial spirit on matter. Among other things, Boyle believed that More's doctrine of a Spirit of Nature was a reversion to naturalist notions that threatened to make genuinely supernatural activity redundant, a heterodoxy from which his own commitment to mechanism protected him. See Jane E. Jenkins, 'Arguing About Nothing: Henry More and Robert Boyle on the Theological Implications of the Void', in Margaret J. Osler, ed., *Rethinking the Scientific Revolution* (Cambridge, 2000), 153–79; and John Henry, 'Henry More versus Robert Boyle: The Spirit of Nature and the Nature of Providence', in Sarah Hutton, ed., *Henry More (1614–1687) Tercentenary Studies* (Dordrecht, 1990), 55–76.

[60] Galenic medicine was not without remedies of course, though they tended to be herbal rather than chemical: see Wear, *Knowledge and Practice in English Medicine*, ch. 2. The difference lay not in the provision of a remedy, even a chemical one, but in what one had to know to discover the appropriate remedy. As the English Galenist James Primerose puts it, 'Galen in his bookes of *Method*, teaches that remedies are to bee altered according to the person, place, part affected and other circumstances.' (*Popular Errours of the People in Physick*, trans. Robert Wittie (London, 1651), 20.)

was quite different from this. Boyle wasn't looking for a chemico-physiological basis for the action of medicines, but a means of identifying their essential ingredients, an identification that was relative to the means available for the isolating and extracting of 'essences'. To the extent to which natural-philosophical considerations play a role, it is that of helping us understand how it might be produced from a more convenient source or via a more convenient process, so that we might determine the required dosage in advance, so that we might discover to what extent its effects might be more general, and so on. In the *Usefulness of Natural Philosophy*, Boyle exhorts medical practitioners to look at the practices of midwives, barber surgeons, old women, American native Indians, and others: these are a potential mine of information on the powers of medicines and how to use them, not least because of the large range of different circumstances in which they have been tried.[61]

Questions at this level do not require recourse to fundamental causes, and indeed the provision of answers to them would certainly be hindered by such a search. For example, extracting the essences of substances was crucial to iatrochemistry, and it was one of the basic things to which the chemical, as opposed to medical, tradition laid claim in terms of expertise. This expertise was claimed not at the level of natural philosophy, however, but at a practical level. Early seventeenth-century chemists construed iatrochemistry in terms of fluids, not because of an underlying natural philosophy that privileged fluids (as it did in Descartes' natural philosophy for example) but because fermentation was the tried and tested way of extracting the essence of a medicine from the grossness of its matter.[62]

Boyle came to natural philosophy primarily in the first instance via iatrochemistry,[63] and indeed his commitment to corpuscularianism owed as much to the alchemical tradition stretching back to pseudo-Geber, and developed by Helmont and Boyle's early collaborator George Starkey,[64] as it did to Gassendi and Descartes. Medical questions also motivated his thinking on natural philosophy from an early stage.[65] Essays dating from 1648 and 1649, when he was in his early twenties, mention the circulation of the blood and Whistler's theory of rickets as a nutritional

---

[61] Boyle, *Works*, ii. 162 (*Usefullness*, Part 2, Essay 5, ch. 10).

[62] See French, *Medicine Before Science*, 205–7. Even the search for the Helmontian 'alkahest', an envisaged universal solvent that would dissolve all compounds into their 'simples', thereby isolating active agents in a pure form, was motivated by practical considerations. See Alan Debus, 'Fire Analysis and the Elements in the Sixteenth and the Seventeenth Centuries,' *Annals of Science* 23 (1967), 128–47; Charles Webster, 'Water as the Ultimate Principle of Nature: The Background to Boyle's Sceptical Chymist', *Ambix* 13 (1966), 96–107.

[63] See Antonio Clericuzio, 'A Redefinition of Boyle's Chemistry and Corpuscular Philosophy', *Annals of Science* 47 (1990), 562–89; idem, 'From van Helmont to Boyle: A Study of the Transmission of Helmontian Chemical and Medical Theories in Seventeenth-Century England', *British Journal for the History of Science* 26 (1993), 303–34; and idem, 'Carneades and the Chemists: A Study of *The Sceptical Chymist* and its Impact on Seventeenth-Century Chemistry', in Michael Hunter, ed., *Robert Boyle Reconsidered* (Cambridge, 1994), 79–90. See also Robert G. Frank Jr., *Harvey and the Oxford Physiologists* (Berkeley, 1980).

[64] See William R. Newman, 'The Alchemical Sources of Robert Boyle's Corpuscular Philosophy', *Annals of Science* 53 (1996), 567–85; and idem, 'Boyle's Debt to Corpuscular Alchemy'.

[65] See Kaplan, *'Divulging of Useful Truths in Physick'*, and Hunter, *Robert Boyle (1627–91)*, ch. 9.

disorder, as well as a number of dissections, and he was already thinking of biological processes in atomistic terms. This approach was distinctive of the post-Harveian generation of the 1640s and 1650s, especially those based in Oxford, whose central concern was with heat, respiration, and the nature of blood, interests that drove Boyle's own research to a large extent.[66] In the 1640s, through his association with Hartlib and others, Boyle had been subject to the influence of a combination of Helmontian chemical atomism, Gassendian atomism, and Cartesian mechanistic physiology,[67] and the author of one of the first Harveian textbooks, Nathaniel Highmore, dedicated his *The History of Generation* (1651), an attempt to interpret embryology and nutrition in atomistic terms, to Boyle.[68]

In the mid- to late-1650s, Boyle carried out extensive dissections and anatomical and physiological experiments, and in 1659 he turned to the air pump to investigate respiration more thoroughly.[69] Experiment 41 of the *New Experiments* investigated why respiration is necessary for animals, and what the role of the lungs is in respiration. A lark, a hen-sparrow, and a mouse were each placed in the chamber, which was evacuated: the animals went into convulsions, but the last two were revived by opening the container, only to be subjected again to evacuation until they died. The puzzling aspect of this for Boyle was that there remained a considerable quantity of air in the container, since the evacuation was partial. This led him to devote a long digression to respiration,[70] in length second only to his account of the 'spring' of the air. Arguing, on anatomical grounds and on the basis of vivisections of dogs, that the lungs do not move of their own accord but only follow the motion of the thorax and diaphragm, he pointed out that neither the Galenic theory that the lungs attract air, nor the Cartesian theory that air is forced into the lungs through the expansion of the thorax, was consistent with the results of the experiment. Rather, when the diaphragm and thorax dilate the lungs, the pressure becomes less on the inside than on the outside, so that contiguous air is pressed in at the open windpipe:

But of this difficulty our engine [the air pump] furnisheth us with an easy solution, since many of the former experiments have manifested, that in the case proposed, there needs not be made any . . . propulsion of the air by the swelling thorax or abdomen into the lungs; since upon the bare dilatation of the thorax, the spring of that internal air, or halituous substance that is wont to possess as much of the cavity of the chest as the lungs fill not up, being much weakened, the external and contiguous air must necessarily press in at the open wind-pipe into the lungs, as finding there less resistance than any where else about it.[71]

---

[66] See Frank, *Harvey and the Oxford Physiologists*, chs. 4–6. See also Shapiro, *John Wilkins*, ch. 5.

[67] Descartes' own mechanistic physiology remained unpublished in his lifetime (except for a few hints in *Les Passions de l'âme*), but it was available in the unauthorized work of his followers, much to Descartes' fury: Henricus Regius, *Fundamenta physices* (Amsterdam, 1646); idem, *Fundamenta medica* (Utrecht, 1647); Cornelius Hooghelande, *Cogitationes, quibus Dei existentia et animae spiritualis, et possibilis cum corpore unio, demonstrantur: necnon brevis historia oeconomiae corporis animalis proponitur, atque mechanice explicatur* (Amsterdam, 1646).

[68] On the relation between Boyle and Highmore, see Kaplan, *'Divulging of Useful Truths in Physick'*, 34–8.

[69] For details, see Frank, *Harvey and the Oxford Physiologists*, ch. 6.

[70] Boyle, *Works*, i. 99–113.     [71] Ibid. 100–1.

Traditional explanations of respiration had postulated that respiration served to cool the blood, or to help in the generation of vital spirits, or to ventilate the blood, helping it rid itself of waste products. The first and second of these Boyle countered on the basis of physiological experiments and anatomy, but in the third case he brought his air pump experiments to bear. If it were simply a case of the air sucking out waste products from the blood then, as Boyle pointed out, we would expect evacuation to be beneficial to the animals since there is increased space for the waste products, yet in fact it is clearly harmful. Alternatively, there might be a certain consistency of air that was optimal for the removal of waste products, so that if the air was too thick or too thin its ability to extract waste was affected. This is a view to which Boyle was very sympathetic,[72] and the required consistency was something to be spelled out in terms of the air's elasticity or 'spring'.

Respiration, one of the great problems bequeathed by Harvey, was, then, intimately connected with the 'spring of air'. The latter holds the key to the former: we will not understand how respiration works unless we understand the spring of the air. Now respiration is a complex empirical event: as well as the phenomena I have already mentioned, for example, Boyle devoted considerable attention to respiration in bodies immersed in fluids, notably foetal respiration and respiration in fish. Extensive anatomical and physiological work was clearly involved in the elucidation of these phenomena, as were chemical questions, but Boyle was able to focus on what might otherwise have appeared a diverse set of questions by thinking in purely mechanical terms about what was involved in the pumping action of the heart. The air pump not only allowed him to bring a completely new focus to these issues, but also to vary conditions experimentally, and the focus is in turn constrained by what can be varied in this way. This is the kind of consideration that made it look, to a critic like Hobbes (and, it should be said, to Spinoza, Leibniz, and others), as if Boyle had taken a highly contingent, highly localized topic, centred around a highly specific piece of apparatus, reporting specific results of very limited natural-philosophical significance, yet all the while giving the impression that what he was doing was as legitimate as a core form of natural philosophy.

What guided Boyle's approach to natural philosophy was not what explanatory resources a micro-mechanical corpuscularian model offered. He was committed to such a model, and it guided the kinds of explanations he was prepared to propose.[73] But it did not organize his *explanandum*. It was the air pump that shaped and brought unity and coherence to the field of enquiry. It acted as a focus for a number of contingent interests in physiology, chemistry, and mechanics, and its success lay in its ability to produce a rich range of highly controllable phenomena. At stake in the

---

[72] Nevertheless, he does not discount the possibility that there may be more to respiration than this, telling us that he is 'apt also to suspect, that the air doth something else in respiration, which hath not yet been fully explained' (ibid. 113).

[73] E.g. he explicitly rejected non-corpuscularian accounts in the case of poisons and drugs generally, whose specific and rapid action seemed to defy corpuscularian explanation: see Wilson, *The Invisible World*, 148–50.

legitimacy of this exercise was the integrity of the experiments: how carefully they had been constructed, how precise they were, whether reports of what was observed were reliable. Hobbes believed that the claims to empirical precision masked the real issue, which is that these experiments, no matter how precise, could not in themselves decide any significant natural-philosophical issues. His real concern was that they could not actually explain anything, no matter how precise they were, but he also dismissed their degree of precision. Tactically, this was a bad move. It allowed Boyle to drag Hobbes on to the experimental terrain, to make everything turn on experimental credibility, and ultimately to treat Hobbes as a failed experimenter.[74]

The legitimacy of experimental natural philosophy, as manifested in Boyle's account of his air-pump experiments, and the controversies that followed it, was not something wholly lacking in precedents. For one thing, as we saw in Chapter 6, Bacon, Galileo, and Descartes all, to varying extents, on occasion construed the question of intellectual honesty in terms of lack of commitment to a pre-given system, while at other times and in other respects they were committed to a systematic view. The difference was in some cases, especially in Galileo, the result of tactical considerations, for example the need to pre-empt the general acceptance of Tychonic astronomy as a default position in the wake of attacks on Copernicanism, by denying legitimacy to any astronomical system. In the case of Descartes, part of what was at issue was a refusal to accept any system except on the basis of a most stringent application of the criterion of clarity and distinctness, which he believed would inevitably lead to adoption of the Cartesian system. His English critics, as we have seen, construed this as a form of personal validation, and associated it with enthusiasm. By contrast, Bacon's association of an attack on the textbook tradition with his explicit and repeated valorization of communal and collective, if centrally directed, forms of natural-philosophical enquiry provided a context of legitimation not that different from Boyle's. The point I want to stress here, however, is that whatever the different reasons behind the view that there was something intellectually dishonest in falling back on a system, the idea that defending a natural-philosophical system was not the only way of pursuing natural philosophy was not new with Boyle, although (with due deference to Gilbert) carrying out a detailed natural-philosophical project along these lines may well have been.

Second, as we have already seen, Boyle had begun to consider natural philosophy as the path to natural theology from an early stage. The methods of legitimation sanctioned by the kind of Christian enquiry that Boyle was advocating include reason, experiment, and human and divine witnessing.[75] Human witnessing was a form of legitimation whose role in 'speculative' natural philosophy would be minimal, if deemed appropriate at all. But it played a significant role in Boyle's experimental natural philosophy. Moreover, it is hard to believe that the fact that the Bible, and particularly the New Testament, which provide stories of testimonies of

[74] This is brought out well in Shapin and Schaffer, *Leviathan and the Air-Pump*, chs. 4 and 5.
[75] *Reconcileableness of Reason and Religion*, Pt. 1, Essay 3: *Works*, ii. 31.

witnesses to divine deeds without the intermediary of a theology formulated in terms of pagan philosophy,[76] did not act to reinforce Boyle's confidence in witnessing. It is a core part of Protestant understanding of these texts that unmediated access to the testimony of witnesses who were present at miraculous or otherwise holy events is to be preferred to the interpolations of generations of theologians attempting to accommodate sacred teaching to pagan philosophy.

Third, many of the issues of objectivity and legitimation that underpinned the use of witnessing were being aired outside natural philosophy proper. The dispute between Hobbes and Boyle is mirrored in many ways, for example, in that between Hobbes and Hale. The very idea of working in terms of first principles is something that had been deemed impractical in other areas where Hobbes had sought to employ it. For example, in his *Dialogue between a Philosopher and a Student of the Common laws of England*,[77] Hobbes had argued that lawyers had usurped privileges of lawmaking that belonged to the sovereign, supporting this with the view that the laws were grounded in natural reason, which was consistent and certain, not in common law, which lacked these qualities, nor in any special skills of lawyers. The Chief Justice, Matthew Hale, responded by arguing that common lawyers were quite right not to speculate on the first principles of moral philosophy, seeking instead practical solutions to practical problems.[78] He writes:

Of all Kind of Subject where about y$^e$ reasoning Facultie is conversant, there is none of So greate a difficulty for the Faculty of reason to guide it Selfe and come to any Steddiness as that of Laws. . . . And therefore it is not possible for men to come to the Same Certainty, evidence and Demonstration touching them as may be expected in Mathematicall Sciences, and they that please themselves w$^{th}$ a perswasion that they can w$^{th}$ as much evidence and Congruitie make out an unerring system of Laws and Politiques equally applicable to all States and Occasions, as Euclide demonstrates his Conclusions, deceive themselves w$^{th}$ Notions wh$^{ch}$ prove ineffectual, when they come to particul$^r$ application.[79]

Boyle's own account of his approach in *The Reconcileableness of Reason and Religion*, mirrors the common law procedure exactly:

---

[76] On biblical accounts of witnessing see David Daube, *Witnesses in Bible and Talmud* (Oxford, 1986). On the standing of divine testimony see Serjeantson, 'Testimony and Proof in Early-Modern England', 206–7.

[77] Hobbes, *English Works*, vi. 1–160.

[78] J. H. Baker, ed., *The Reports of John Spelman* (2 vols, London, 1971), i. 29, cited in Rose-Mary Sargent, *The Diffident Naturalist: Robert Boyle and the Philosophy of Experiment* (Chicago, 1995), 49. I have drawn on ch. 2 of Sargent's book here.

[79] 'Reflections on the Lord Chief Justice Hale on Mr Hobbes His Dialogue of the Law', in William Holdsworth, *A History of English Law* (12 vols, London, 1936), v. 502. Hale was also a natural philosopher, and published three short polemical essays on Boyle's air-pump experiment: *An essay touching the gravitation, or non-gravitation of fluids, and the reasons thereof* (London, 1673), *Difficiles nugae, or observations concerning the Toricellian experiment, and the various solutions of the same, especially touching the weight and elasticity of the air* (London, 1674), *Observations touching the principles of natural motions and especially touching rarefaction & condensation* (London, 1677). Hale's somewhat eccentric view was that the pressure in a gas was due to an impulse to return to its natural God-given volume, from which it had deviated because of artificial compression. See the discussion in Alan Cromartie, *Sir Matthew Hale, 1609–1676: Law, Religion and Natural Philosophy* (Cambridge, 1995), ch. 13.

When we are to judge, which of two disagreeing opinions is most rational, i.e. to be judged most agreeable to right reason, we ought to give sentence, not for that, which the faculty, furnished only with such and such notions, whether vulgar, or borrowed from this or that sect of philosophers, would prefer, but that, which is preferred by the faculty, furnished, either with all the evidence requisite or advantageous to make it give the right judgment in the case lying before it, or, when that cannot be had, with the best and fullest information, that it can procure.[80]

Law is not alone in this respect, as we have already seen, for there is a group of disciplines in which questions of evidence and objectivity had received significant attention: history, medicine, and natural history occupy a prominent role here along with law. Indeed, in many respects Boyle's approach can be seen as being very much in the tradition of natural history, just as Gilbert's account of magnetism can be seen to be in that tradition. What is distinctive about both of these is that they are able to provide a powerful focus that works not at the level of some supposed underlying structure, but rather at the level of the phenomena. The focus is provided by an instrument—the terrella in Gilbert's case, the air pump in Boyle's—which draws together a number of apparently divergent phenomena in a controlled way. This is especially clear in the case of Boyle's air pump, where what emerges from his descriptions is that the principle of organization of the *explanandum* lies at the same level as the *explanandum*, and that it is the *explanans* that has to be accommodated. Boyle's natural-historical and medical interests provide fertile grounds for this move, but I want to argue that we can also glimpse it at work in a core area of 'speculative' natural philosophy, optics.

## THE PRODUCTION OF COLOUR: NEWTON VERSUS DESCARTES

Descartes and Newton each produced influential discussions of the nature of colour. Descartes' account, as set out in Discourse 8 of *Les Météors* of 1637, was that white light is homogeneous but that under certain circumstances, such as refraction through a prism at a particular angle, the constituent corpuscles making up the light ray are caused to rotate at different speeds, and this in turn causes us to see different colours. Newton's view was that light is heterogeneous and that under certain circumstances, again such as refraction through a prism at a particular angle, the light ray is decomposed into its constituent rays, which are differently coloured. If we compare these cases on the question of the relation between *explanans* and *explanandum*, we see that the way in which Descartes and Newton came to their respective conclusions is radically different. Descartes built up a geometrical optics and then shifted into a wholly different register, a micro-corpuscularian physical optics, to account for colour. Newton, by contrast, did not explain colour by reference to an underlying causal realm which produces effects at the phenomenal level, but remained in the realm of geometrical optics and explored causal relations between the phenomena themselves. As Huygens, commenting on Newton's account of the heterogeneity

---

[80] Boyle, *Works*, iv. 179–80.

of light, put it in a letter to Oldenburg, 'if it were true that from their origin some rays of light are red, others blue etc., there would remain the great difficulty of explaining by the mechanical philosophy in what this diversity of colours consists.'[81] Huygens demanded that a hypothesis be offered as to how differences in motion are connected with differences in colour, 'for until this hypothesis has been found, [Newton] has not apprised us what the nature of and difference between colours is, only the accident (which is certainly very considerable) of their different refrangibility'.[82] But Newton saw the matter in a very different way. He did not accept the idea that causes are restricted to what underlies the phenomena, and therefore necessarily at a different level from the phenomena. Rather, his treatment implied that there is a way of understanding phenomena that consists in exploring the causal connections between—as opposed to underlying—them. It is this shift that I want to highlight by comparing how Descartes and Newton investigated the nature of colour.

In his early formative work on hydrostatics, Descartes developed a distinctive approach to quantitative natural philosophy. In ideal-type mechanism, one tends to think of a microscopic substructure with simple corpuscles behaving in mechanically well-defined ways, and more importantly in ways that can be quantified easily in terms of some combination of size/mass/volume and speed/direction of motion. Processes at this level are then invoked to explain macroscopic behaviour, which is assumed to be far more complex and harder to quantify. But in fact, in terms of the practicalities of developing a micro-corpuscularian programme, the reverse was the case. This is particularly clear in Descartes, who explicitly started from a quantified macroscopic phenomenon and moved to a more speculative micro-corpuscular substructure.

Descartes employed this procedure from his earliest work in physical theory, in hydrostatics. He took as his starting point Archimedean hydrostatics, as this had been developed by Stevin. Stevin, like Archimedes, had taken a rigorously mathematical approach to hydrostatics. Archimedes' treatment of the lever, for example, works by abstracting from physical quantities, and treating bodies placed on the lever as points at the centres of gravity of the bodies, which lie along a line. Once the initial abstractions have been made and a (geometrical) procedure for determining centres of gravity established, it is all a matter of geometry. Descartes' approach, by contrast, employed a procedure that purported to uncover the physical processes responsible for the phenomena that hydrostatics, of the traditional Archimedean kind, had up until that point been described only in mathematical terms. He first turned his attention to hydrostatics at the end of 1618, when, under Beeckman's guidance, he started to investigate a number of closely related problems in hydrostatics, all of which hinged in one way or another on the 'hydrostatic paradox,' as this had been brought to light and demonstrated in Stevin's

---

[81] Huygens to Oldenburg, 17 Sept. 1672: *The Correspondence of Isaac Newton*, ed. H. W. Turnbull, J. F. Scott, A. R. Hall, and Laura Tilling (7 vols, Cambridge, 1959–77), i. 235–6.

[82] Oldenburg to Newton, quoting a letter from Huygens, 18 January 1673: *Correspondence of Isaac Newton*, i. 255–6.

work.[83] Stevin had shown that a fluid can exert a total pressure on the bottom of its container that is many times greater than its weight. In particular, he showed that a fluid filling two vessels of equal base area and height exerts the same pressure on the base, irrespective of the shape of the vessel—it might be conical, for example, or cylindrical—and hence independently of the amount of fluid contained in the vessel. His proof of this theorem worked through the idea that fluid can be replaced by a solid body of the same density without affecting the pressure it exerts, and given this, the demonstration proceeds geometrically.

Descartes' approach was quite different.[84] He substituted, for Stevin's formally rigorous and conclusive geometrical demonstration, a very different kind of account which was exploratory and, by the standards of Archimedean statics, quite inconclusive. Descartes did not and could not have denied the rigour of Stevin's account. If correctness or rigour in the accepted Euclidean or Archimedean sense was not at issue, what was? Descartes pushed the problem into what he considered to be the domain of natural philosophy.[85] The geometrical account does not provide an *explanation* of the phenomenon, because it does not identify what causes the phenomenon. Fluids are physical entities made up of microscopic corpuscles the behaviour of which determines the macroscopic behaviour of the fluid, and one needs to understand the physical behaviour of the constituent corpuscles if one is to understand the behaviour of the fluid, because this is what is causally responsible for its behaviour. In broad terms, this would have accorded with the traditional view of the scope and aims of natural philosophy: physical explanation involves the identification of what causes material bodies to behave in particular ways. Whatever disputes there might have been among Platonists, Aristotelians, Stoics, and Epicureans, there was consensus on what kind of theory provided the ultimate explanation of macroscopic physical phenomena, namely a theory of matter and causation. And it was such a conception, reflected through Aristotle's categorization of the mixed mathematical sciences as subordinate to given, previously established explanatory physical principles of matter and cause, that had effectively marginalized, or at least rendered problematic, mathematical approaches to natural phenomena within natural philosophy. Descartes' initial aim, under the rubric of 'physico-mathematics', seems to have been to shift hydrostatics from the realm of practical mathematics unambiguously into the realm of natural philosophy. This he tried to achieve by redescribing, in terms of his matter theory, what it is that causes the pressure exerted by a fluid on the floor of the vessel containing it: he redescribed what causes the pressure in terms of the cumulative behaviour of postulated microscopic corpuscles making up the fluid.

---

[83] Stevin's statical works are translated in *The Principal Works of Simon Stevin*, i. 375–501.

[84] Descartes, 'Aquae comprimentis in vase ratio reddita à D. Des Cartes', in Descartes, *Œuvres* x. 67–74. For details see Gaukroger and Schuster, 'The Hydrostatic Paradox and the Origins of Cartesian Dynamics'.

[85] He does the same thing in his examination of free fall, though not as systematically. See Gaukroger, *Descartes, An Intellectual Biography*, 80–4.

This kind of procedure acts as a model for Descartes' optics, where a geometrical optics provides the analogue of the macroscopic realm, and physical optics provides the natural-philosophical underpinnings.[86] The guiding idea is that geometrical optics describes how light behaves in particular geometrically defined ways in reflection and refraction, and physical optics explains, on the basis of a theory about the physical constitution of light, why it behaves in these ways. The case of the rainbow shows just how this works.

In Discourse 8 of the *Météors*, Descartes sets out a quantitative account of the rainbow which he holds it up as a 'sample' of his 'method'.[87] And it is indeed a model in the quantification of physical phenomena—along with Galileo's account of free fall, it was the only such model in the first half of the seventeenth century. He begins his account by noting that rainbows are formed not only in the sky, but also in fountains and showers in the presence of sunlight, and this leads him to suggest the hypothesis that the phenomenon is not a uniquely celestial one but rather one caused by light reacting on drops of water. To test this hypothesis, he constructs a large glass model of the raindrop—he uses a glass chamber-pot—and fills it with rainwater. Then standing with his back to the sun, he holds up the sphere at arm's length in the sunlight, moving it up and down so that colours are produced. If we let the light come

from the part of the sky marked AFZ [see Fig. 10.3], and my eye be at point E, then when I put this sphere at the place BCD, the part of it at D seems to me wholly red and incomparably more brilliant than the rest. And whether I move towards it or step back from it, or move it to the right or the left, or even turn it in a circle around my head, then provided the line DE always makes an angle of around 42° with the line EM, which one must imagine to extend from the centre of the eye to the centre of the sun, D always appears equally red. But as soon as I made this angle DEM the slightest bit larger, the redness disappeared. And when I made it a little bit smaller it did not disappear completely in one stroke but first divided as into two less brilliant parts in which could be seen yellow, blue, and other colours. Then, looking towards the place marked K on the sphere, I perceived that, making the angle KEM around 52°, K also seemed to be coloured red, but not so brilliant as D.[88]

In an atmosphere packed with raindrops, red spots would appear on all of them that made an angle of 42° and 52°. More generally, what is produced is a primary rainbow at 42° which has red at the top and violet at the bottom, and a fainter secondary rainbow at 52° with the spectrum inverted.

The next stage in the argument is to discover what the path of the light ray is; how, for example, is a light ray coming from A affected by passing through the raindrop? Placing a black sheet of paper between A and B, and then between D and E, he finds

---

[86] See John Schuster, '*Descartes opticien:* The Construction of the Law of Refraction and the Manufacture of its Physical Rationales', in Stephen Gaukroger, John Schuster, and John Sutton, eds., *Descartes' Natural Philosophy* (London, 2000), 258–312.

[87] Descartes to [Vatier], [23 Feb. 1638]; *Œuvres*, i. 559. This is the only example that Descartes gave of his 'method'.

[88] Ibid. vi. 326–7.

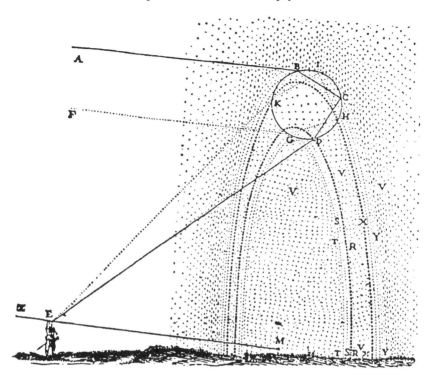

**Figure 10.3**

the red spot at D vanishes. It also vanishes when the paper is placed between B and C and then between C and D. However, he found that if he covered the whole globe but left openings at B and D, the red spot was quite visible. Ignoring the refraction by the glass from which the bowl was made, he concludes that this means that the ray from A is refracted on entering the water at B, travels to C where it is internally reflected to D, and is then refracted again on emerging at D. The secondary rainbow is formed similarly, except that, as well as the two refractions at G and K, two internal reflections are needed to account for it, at H and I.

The next question was why the primary rainbow is produced at an angle of 42° and the secondary bow at an angle of 52°. What determines the angles? The answer is the refractive index of water in relation to air. It is because of this refractive index that a light ray coming from air into water at a particular angle of incidence will be bent at a particular angle, and it is this refractive angle, together with the internal reflections, that will determine at what angle the colours will be seen. Refraction is the key thing, and Descartes now moved to focus on refraction by showing that neither curved surfaces, nor internal reflections, nor multiple refractions are needed, for the

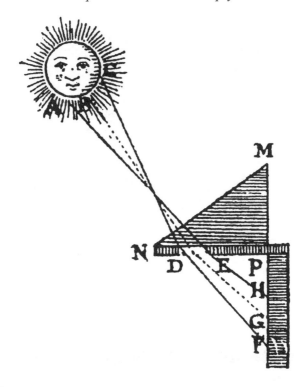

**Figure 10.4**

phenomenon can be produced with a single refraction. It can be produced with a glass prism, for example, which is of especial interest because each part of the surface of the sphere can be regarded as a minute prism. Consider the prism MNP, illustrated in Figure 10.4. When sunlight strikes the surface NM directly so that there is no appreciable refraction, and passes through a narrow aperture DE on an otherwise darkened face NP, the colours appear on the screen PHGF, red being towards F and violet towards H. For this, a single refraction is needed, for when NP is parallel to NM so that there is no appreciable refraction at all, then the colours are not produced.

Descartes now set out to explain why the colours are formed on the screen PHGF, and 'why these colours are different at H and at F, even though the refraction, shadow, and light concur there in the same way'.[89] To account for this, he shifted into a different register, from the practical mathematics that guided his geometrical optics to his micro-corpuscularian matter theory, asking us to consider the small spheres of air (second element) which transmit the pressure from the sun. These spheres

---

[89] Descartes to [Vatier], [23 Feb. 1638]; *Œuvres*, i. 331.

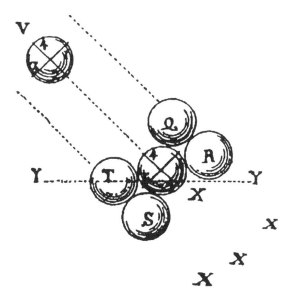

**Figure 10.5**

initially possess a motion only in the direction of their propagation, but on striking the refracting surface obliquely they acquire a rotary motion; thenceforth, they all rotate in the same direction or sense, and can either all rotate at the same speed, or neighbouring spheres can accelerate or retard their rotation, and this change in speed of rotation is invoked to explain changes in colour. Descartes' view was that what causes the differences in speed of rotation can only be the contact with the shade at D and E, since the spheres all have the same motion initially, and without the shade around the aperture DE colours are not formed. Descartes speculated that the spheres in ray EH encounter spheres moving more slowly, which retard their own motion, and the spheres in the ray DF encounter spheres moving more quickly, which accelerate their own motion. He illustrates what happens in terms of a sphere 1234 (see Fig. 10.5) that is pushed obliquely from V to X: air to water, for example. It acquires a rotary motion on reaching the surface YY because at the first instant part 3 is retarded while part 1 continues with undiminished speed. Hence the ball is compelled to rotate following the route 1234, that is, clockwise. In this case, rotation occurs simply as a result of the sphere passing from one optical medium to another.

Next, Descartes turned to the question of how different speeds of rotation are produced, resulting in different colours. We are asked to imagine sphere 1234 being surrounded by four other similar bodies, Q, R, S, T. Q and R move 'with more force' towards X than does 1234, whereas S and T have been retarded. Q and R will accelerate 1234, because their translational motion will act to push parts 4 and 1 in a clockwise direction: they will give it a greater clockwise spin. S and T, on the other hand, will have no effect on it, 'because R is disposed to move towards X faster than 1234 follows it, and T is not disposed to follow 1234 as quickly as 1234 precedes it'. This, Descartes tells us, 'explains the action of the ray DF'. It explains it because what happens is that the corpuscles that skirt the edge of D will be retarded by their contact with this edge, and they will act as S and T do. Corpuscles further away from the edge will act as do Q and R, tending to accelerate the corpuscles in the path DF. At E, the converse process occurs, and the corpuscles in the path EH are retarded.[90] This results in the production of red at F and blue or violet at H.[91] Intermediate speeds are produced in the same way, the translational motions on either side of them being different, and causing changes in their rotational velocity accordingly.

Descartes tells us that at first he doubted whether the mechanism producing colour in the prism could be the same as that producing colour in the rainbow, for the prism requires shadows whereas:

I did not notice any shadow which cut off the light [in the case of the rainbow], nor did I understand yet why they appeared only under certain angles. But when I took my pen and calculated in detail all the rays which fall on the various points of a drop of water, so as to see under what angles they would come toward our eyes after two refractions and one or two reflections, very many more of them can be seen under the angle of 41° to 42° than under any lesser one, and that none of them can be seen under a larger angle. . . . [Similarly for the secondary bow at 51° to 52°] . . . So that there is a shadow on both sides, cutting off the light which, after having passed through an infinity of raindrops illuminated by the sun, comes towards the eye under the angle of 42° or slightly less, and thus causes the primary and most important rainbow [and similarly for the secondary rainbow].[92]

The calculations depend on a knowledge of the refractive index from air to water, which he determined to be 250/187, an accurate figure. His procedure is as follows (see Fig. 10.6).[93] Rays coming from the sun, marked S, are parallel but the ray EF, for example, is refracted. The ratio FH : FC is the sine of the angle of incidence $i$ for the ray EF. When FH = 0, which is its value when it coincides with AH (which is not refracted), $i$ will be zero. Letting the radius of the drop be 10,000 units (chosen, as was the practice at the time, simply as a measure that will avoid the use of fractions),

[90] Descartes to [Vatier], [23 Feb. 1638]; *Œuvres*, i. 332–3.

[91] There is a problem here. Descartes has assumed that what holds for a ray moving from air to water also holds for a ray moving from glass to air, as in the case of the ray leaving the prism. Because of this false assumption, his account of colours gives them in the inverse order to what we would expect. Two of Descartes' correspondents pointed this out to Descartes when the *Météors* was published. See Morin to Descartes, 22 February 1638; *Œuvres* i. 546–7; and Ciermans to Descartes [March 1638]; Ibid. ii. 59–61. His reply to Morin is completely inadequate: see Ibid. 208, and Morin's reponse, ibid. 293–4. See the discussion in Alan E. Shapiro, 'Kinematic Optics: A Study of the Wave Theory of Light in the Seventeenth Century', *Archive for History of Exact Sciences* 11 (1973), 134–266: 155–9.

[92] *Œuvres*, vi. 335–6. The idea that light and shade are necessary for the spectrum had been advocated by Aristotle was in effect the default position, although it was not without its critics.

[93] Ibid. 337–41.

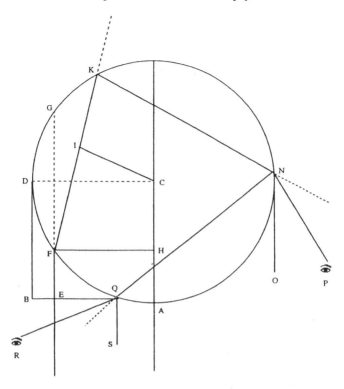

**Figure 10.6**

then when FH = 10,000, that is, when it just grazes the drop, the angle of incidence is 90°. When EF penetrates the drop and is refracted at K, it can either emerge at K or be reflected internally at K and then be refracted at N to the eye at P, or internally reflected again to Q and be refracted to the eye at R. The path FKNP, which produces the primary bow, involves one reflection and two refractions, and the path FKNQR, which produces the secondary bow, involves two refractions and two reflections. For the primary bow, we have to determine the size of the angle ONP, and for the secondary bow the angle SQR. Descartes calculates the angle ONP for the values of FH from 1,000 to 10,000 (Fig. 10.7). The calculation is based on the fact that at F the deviation $\delta$ is equal to the angle of incidence ($i$) minus the angle of refraction ($r$) measured by the angle GFK; at K the deviation is $180° - 2r$, and at N it is $i - r$. The total deviation is therefore $180° + 2i - 4r$, and since the angle ONP is $180° - \delta$, it is $4r - 2i$. Fig. 10.7 represents the case where FH = 8,000. Here, $i$ is about 40°44′.

What the calculations, as shown in Figure 10.7, demonstrate is that, whatever the angle of entry of the ray, it will exit so as to make an angle no greater than 40° 57′

| LA LIGNE<br>H F | LA LIGNE<br>C I | L'ARC<br>F G | L'ARC<br>F K | L'ANGLE<br>O N P | L'ANGLE<br>S Q R |
|---|---|---|---|---|---|
| 1000 | 748 | 168.30 | 171.25 | 5.40 | 165.45 |
| 2000 | 1496 | 156.55 | 162.48 | 11.19 | 151.29 |
| 3000 | 2244 | 145. 4 | 154. 4 | 17.56 | 136. 8 |
| 4000 | 2992 | 132.50 | 145.10 | 22.30 | 122. 4 |
| 5000 | 3740 | 120. | 136. 4 | 27.52 | 108.12 |
| 6000 | 4488 | 106.16 | 126.40 | 32.56 | 93.44 |
| 7000 | 5236 | 91. 8 | 116.51 | 37.26 | 79.25 |
| 8000 | 5984 | 73.44 | 106.30 | 40.44 | 65.46 |
| 9000 | 6732 | 51.41 | 95.22 | 40.57 | 54.25 |
| 10000 | 7480 | 0. | 83.10 | 13.40 | 69.30 |

**Figure 10.7**

with the original path of entry. In fact, as Descartes shows in carrying out more precise calculations in the range FH = 8,000 to 9,888, there is a clustering such that a large number of rays are refracted at an angle of around 41° 30'. Allowing 17' for the apparent radius of the sun, Descartes argues that the maximum angle of the interior rainbow must be at 41° 47' and the minimum angle of the outer one at 51° 37'. This account is quite compelling. It shows not only why the bows appear at the angles they do, but also why the outer boundary of the primary rainbow is more sharply defined than the inner edge of the secondary one.

There are nevertheless a number of problems with Descartes' account of the formation of colours. He was unable to explain the reverse order of colours in the secondary bow, for example, and although his account of the constitution of colour in terms of rotational velocity was a major advance on earlier theories—which tried to explain colours in terms either of a mixture of light and darkness or of a mixture of what were considered to be primary colours—he gave no means by which this rotational velocity could be measured. Indeed, rotational velocity is not dictated by any of the evidence offered by the prism: its claim is in effect that the mechanist micro-corpuscularian model that it postulates saves the appearances far better than any rival account. Descartes derived much of his factual and observational information on the rainbow from early sources, particularly from the summaries in the *Meteorologicorum libri sex* of Liebert Froidment (Fromondus), the first edition of which appeared in 1627.[94] But this material certainly did not exhaust that on colour, and in 1664 Boyle made a significant contribution to what might be termed the natural history of colour in his *Experiments and Considerations touching Colours*. Boyle takes the reader through various colour phenomena in detail, emphasizing their sheer variety and the unlikelihood of their being explained by a single natural-philosophical theory, such as Descartes' idea of varying rotational speeds of corpuscles:

And as for the Cartesians, I need not tell you, that they, supposing the sensation of light to be produced by the impulse made upon the organs of sight, by certain extremely minute and solid globules, to which the pores of the air and other diaphonous bodies are pervious, endeavour to derive the varieties of colours from the various proportion of the direct progress or motion of these globules to their circumvolution or motion about their own centre, by which varying proportion they are by this hypothesis supposed qualified to strike the optic nerve after several distinct manners, so as to produce the perception of differing colours.[95]

Boyle responded that pressure on the eye and exposure to very bright sources of illumination can generate coloured images, and that we can perceive colours in dreams, which suggests that the optic nerve can operate independently of external stimuli. He also noted that many animals and plants regularly change colour, presumably as a result of physiological processes and in some cases exposure to varying degrees of illumination. Moreover, exposure to heat causes substances to change colour, and liquids often change colour when mixed. Boyle's view was the traditional one that colours are caused by an interaction of light and matter,[96] where the surfaces of bodies were highly complex and could be affected even by changes in the degree of illumination. It is not that he prefered an Epicurean, Aristotelian, or some alchemical account of colour, for he did not. It is rather that basic micro-corpuscularian natural philosophy was, for him, not the path to follow, for to attempt to proceed in this way of necessity requires one to ignore the diversity of colour phenomena, and to focus on a small range of cases for which one's micro-corpuscularian treatment is suitable: there is nothing to support the idea that this small range of cases is even typical, however. As in the case of the air pump, Boyle looked for connections between the very diverse phenomena of colour without invoking an underlying micro-corpuscularian structure.

Two principal sources of inspiration for Newton in his early optical work were Descartes' *Dioptrique* and Boyle's *Experiments and Considerations*.[97] As we have seen, Descartes' interests lay in geometrical optics and physical optics, and Newton decided quite early on that light could not consist in pressure in the medium, as Descartes

[94] See Jean-Robert Armogathe, 'The Rainbow: A Privileged Epistemological Model', in Stephen Gaukroger, John Schuster, and John Sutton, eds, *Descartes' Natural Philosophy* (London, 2000), 249–57: 251–2.

[95] Boyle, *Works*, i. 694.

[96] This account is defended, e.g. in the best-known treatise on the rainbow: Marco Antonio De Dominis, *De radiis visus et lucis in vitris perspectivis et iride tractatus* (Venice, 1611). See Carl B. Boyer, *The Rainbow* (Princeton, 1959), ch. 7.

[97] See *Certain Philosophical Questions*, 262–72; and more generally A. Rupert Hall, *All Was Light* (Oxford, 1993), ch. 2.

had maintained.[98] But his approach to geometrical optics was tempered by Boyle's attempts to come to terms with the phenomenology of colours. And just as Boyle had used the air pump to organize and focus his *explanandum* in accounting for the elasticity of air and the action of the lungs, so Newton proceeded in a parallel way, using an instrument (a prism) in a very particular experimental arrangement to organize and focus the *explanandum*. Like Boyle, he was criticized for the narrowness of his treatment—he does not repeat the experiment many times over, he does not take into account numerous other experiments on colours, nor does he offer a natural-philosophical explanation in terms of the nature of light—and as a result his account met considerable resistance.[99]

One of Descartes' primary aims in his geometrical optics of the 1620s had been to produce lenses that brought parallel rays to a single focus. The spherical lenses used in telescopes were unable to do this, with the result that the image was significantly distorted (spherical aberration). Applying his newly discovered sine law of refraction to lenses by accommodating their curvature in terms of a series of prisms, he realized that hyperbolic and elliptical lenses would refract rays to a single point. But grinding aspherical lenses was a very difficult matter: Descartes devoted considerable time to it, constructing an intricately devised lenses grinding machine which took up a whole room, bolted to the floors and ceiling to avoid vibrations, but he had little real success. It was this problem of grinding 'Optic glasses of figures other than Spherical' to which Newton devoted attention in the years 1663–5.[100] At the beginning of 1666, Newton procured a prism, and began experimenting with it. The prism allowed one to isolate the process of image formation through refraction: to have used a lens, by contrast, would have meant one would have to deal with multiple refractions because the curvature of the lens causes incident rays to enter it at different angles.

Newton describes what he did in these terms:

I procured me a Triangular glass-Prisme, to try therewith the celebrated *Phaenomena of Colours*. And in order thereto having darkened my chamber, and made a small hole in my window-shutts, to let in a convenient quantity of the Suns light, I placed my Prisme at his entrance, that it might thereby be refracted to the opposite wall. It was at first a very pleasing divertisement, to view the vivid and intense colours produced thereby; but after a while applying my self to consider them more circumspectly, I became surprised to see them in an *oblong* form; which, according to the received laws of Refraction, I expected should have been *circular*. They were terminated at the sides with streight lines, but at the ends, the decay of light was so gradual, that it was difficult to determine justly, what was their figure; yet they seemed *semicircular*.[101]

[98] See John Hendry, 'Newton's Theory of Colour', *Centaurus* 23 (1980), 230–51.

[99] See Alan Shapiro, 'The Gradual Acceptance of Newton's Theory of Light and Colours, 1672–1727', *Perspectives on Science* 4 (1996), 59–104; and Simon Schaffer, 'Glass Works: Newton's Prisms and the Use of Experiment', in David Gooding, Trevor Pinch, and Simon Schaffer, eds, *The Uses of Experiment: Studies in the Natural Sciences* (Cambridge, 1989), 67–104.

[100] See A. Rupert Hall, 'Sir Isaac Newton's Notebook. 1661–1665', *Cambridge Historical Journal* 9 (1948), 239–50; and idem, 'Further Optical Experiments of Isaac Newton', *Annals of Science* 11 (1955), 27–43.

[101] Newton, *Correspondence*, i. 92.

There is a significant contrast here between what Newton expected to see and what he did see. On the question of what he expected to see, the light entered the room in the form of a narrow beam through a small circular hole, so it is a circular beam that is refracted through the prism. In fact, a good deal depends on the angle at which it strikes the prism, and we would expect some elongation in most cases. However, Newton's optical lectures indicate that the angle at which the beam strikes the surface of the prism is what is called the position of minimum deviation.[102] If one were to rotate the prism in relation to the light source, there would be one orientation at which rays entering the prism would be refracted to the same degree as those leaving it, so that those parallel to one another before refraction, for example, will also be parallel after refraction, and this is the angle of minimum deviation. At such an angle, one would expect the light beam to retain its circular shape, especially if one treats beams of light as if they were individual rays of the kind envisaged in geometrical optics.[103] Newton used the angle of minimum deviation, but what he found was a lozenge-shaped band which was about five times greater in length than in breadth.

He tested various possible explanations for this. One traditional explanation for the spectrum was that, because of the triangular shape of the prism, one side of the beam had to traverse a greater distance than the other, and hence the beam is disturbed or weakened more on one side than on the other, and this had led many natural philosophers to conclude that colours were a mixture of light and dark. Newton tested this by comparing the results of passing the light through the base, where the beam has to traverse the maximum distance, and near the apex, where it traverses a very short distance, only to find that the same spectrum was produced. Hence the amount of glass traversed by the beam is not an operative factor. Nor can the size of the hole through which the lights passes be a factor since, he reported, changes to the size of the hole make no difference to the spectrum produced. Moreover, placing the prism outside the window so that it was refracted before passing through the hole in the shutters and entering the darkened room made no difference either. Another possible explanation for the colours and the elongation was irregularities in the glass from which the prism was made. To test this, he took two similar prisms, one upright and one upside down, and passed the beam through these. The thought was that 'the *regular* effects of the first Prisme would be destroyed by the second Prisme, but the *irregular* ones

---

[102] Isaac Newton, *Optical Papers of Isaac Newton*; i. *The Optical Lectures, 1670–1672*, ed. Alan Shapiro (Cambridge, 1984), 53–9. See the very helpful account in Dennis L. Sepper, *Newton's Optical Writings* (New Brunswick, 1994), ch. 3, which I have made use of here.

[103] It is striking that Newton treats them in this way even after he is aware of, and has accepted, Römer's demonstration of the finite speed of transmission of light. In the *Opticks* he writes: 'Mathematicians usually consider the Rays of Light to be Lines reaching from the luminous Body to the Body illuminated, and the refraction of those Rays to be the bending or breaking of those lines in their passing from one medium into another. And thus may rays and Refractions be considered, if Light be propagated in an instant. But, by an Argument taken from the Æquations of the times of the Eclipses of *Jupiter's Satellites*, its seems that Light is propagated in time, spending in its passage from the Sun to us about seven Minutes of time: And therefore I have chosen to define Rays and Refractions in such general terms as may agree to Light in Both cases.' *Opticks: or, a Treatise of the Reflexions, Refractions, Inflexions and Colours of Light* (London, 1704), 2.

more augmented, by the multiplicity of refractions'.[104] But in fact what resulted was a colourless circular image, so irregularities could not be the cause of the colour or the elongation.

At this point, Newton began calculating and measuring. The rounded edges of the spectrum suggested that it had been elongated from a circle. Measurement of the width of the image produced by an unrefracted beam showed it to be the same as that of the spectrum: it was simply a feature of the linear propogation of light. What required explanation, therefore, is the lengthening of the spectrum in a direction perpendicular to the refracting edge of the prism. One possibility is that the rays coming from opposite ends of the sun entered the hole at different angles, and the sine law predicted that these would be refracted differently, but he calculated the difference to be very slight (about 31'), and by manipulating the prism around its axis he showed that even a deviation of 4° or 5° made no difference: the location of the colours on the wall was unchanged. This suggested either that the sine law was flawed, or that something happened to the beam once it left the prism. One possibility was that the rays making up the beam diverged on leaving the prism. Consider, for example, the Cartesian model whereby the light globules acquire a degree of rotation in passing through the prism: could not the differences in rotation cause the rays to bend? Newton remarks that he had

often seen a Tennis ball, struck with an oblique Racket, describe such a curve line. For, a circular as well as a progressive motion being communicated to it by that stroak, its parts on that side, where the motions conspire, must press and beat the contiguous Air more violently than on the other, and there excite a reluctancy and reaction of the Air proportionately greater. And for the same reason, if the Rays of light should possibly be globular bodies, and by their oblique passage out of one medium into another acquire a circulating motion, they ought to feel the greater resistance from the ambient Æther, on that side, where the motions conspire, and thence be continually bowed to one another.[105]

But he could detect no curvature: the ratio between the length and breadth of the spectrum remained constant.

'The gradual removal of these suspitions', Newton wrote in 1672, 'at length led me to the *Experimentum crucis*.'[106] The role of the 'crucial experiment' in Newton's account varied, and it played no role in his earlier report in the *Optical Lectures* nor in later reports of the experiment, but it enabled him here to bring out the kinds of consideration he thought would be decisive.[107] The new experiment was ingenious, and apparently straightforward, although, for various reasons, both good and bad, some critics were subsequently unable to reproduce the experiment.[108] Two prisms and two boards with small holes in them were set up so that the sequence was: light

---

[104] Newton, *Correspondence*, i. 93.      [105] Ibid. 94.      [106] Ibid.

[107] The extent to which this experiment has been reconstructed and idealized by Newton in the letter, which was written five years after the original experiment, is discussed in Johannes A. Lohne, 'Experimentum crucis', *Notes and Records of the Royal Society of London* 23 (1968), 169–99; and Shapiro, 'The Gradual Acceptance of Newton's Theory of Light and Colours, 1672–1727'.

[108] Mariotte, in particular, claimed that he could not establish that colour is immutable as a result of a second refraction, although many of his problems with the experiment seem to have derived from the difficulty of producing well-separated violet rays, which Newton had in fact explicitly

source (hole in shutter), first prism, first board, second board, second prism, and the wall on which final images appears (see Fig. 10.8). The boards and the second prism were in fixed position, whereas the first prism could be rotated to allow different parts of the spectrum to fall on the aperture in the second board. When violet light passed through this aperture it was refracted by the second prism to a certain point on the wall, but when red light passed through the aperture it was refracted by the second prism to a different point on the wall. One important feature of this experimental set-up is that the angle of incidence on the second prism could not vary, because both it and the boards were fixed in place: only the first prism was allowed to move. What this meant is that any difference in the position of the image on the wall could be due only to a difference in the refraction of the beam in the second prism. When he elaborated on the experiment many years later in the *Opticks* (1704), he noted that the imaged produced by the second prism are not elongated but almost circular: this circular image moved across the wall as the colour produced by the refraction shifted from red to violet.

What Newton has done in this experiment is to isolate something that can display a fundamental feature of the behaviour of light when it is refracted through a prism. Refracted light behaves differently from unrefracted light: the iris displayed on the boards was very different from the image on the wall. The conclusion he drew is that the production of colour is not something that is due to a modification of light as it is refracted through the prism; rather, there must be components of the sunlight, which behave differently, being refracted at slightly different angles along a continuous gradation from red to violet. This had immense significance for the construction of telescopes, as Newton noted,[109] for as well as the problem of correcting for the distortion produced by the wrong degree of curvature of the lens (the problem to which Descartes had directed his efforts), there was now the newly discovered problem that there would always be a small but significant difference between the refraction of the red and violet rays at the opposite ends of the spectrum, and at this point he showed how a reflecting telescope overcomes the problems of refracting telescopes in this respect.[110]

What Newton has shown in his *experimentum crucis* is described by him, in a somewhat reconstructed and idealized way, in these terms:

A naturalist would scarce expect to see ye science of those [colours] become mathematicall, & yet I dare affirm that there is as much certainty in it as in any other part of Opticks. For

---

stated was a *sine qua non* of a successful result. On the adverse French reaction to the *experimentum crucis* generally see Henry Guerlac, *Newton on the Continent* (Ithaca, 1981) ch. 4. Newton was subsequently forced to offer detailed instructions as to types of glass etc. See Schaffer, 'Glass Works: Newton's Prisms and the Uses of Experiment', 85–91.

[109] Newton, *Correspondence*, i. 95.

[110] The solution was thought by some to lie in composite lenses. Euler claimed in 1748 that an achromatic combination should be possible, and there ensued a dispute between Euler and Newtonians, who denied this. In 1757 Dolland patented a new achromatic lens, but it had no rationale in terms of physical optics, relying on chemical properties of glass rather than physical properties. See Keith Hutchison, 'Idiosyncrasy, Achromatic Lenses, and Early Romanticism', *Centaurus* 34 (1991), 125–71.

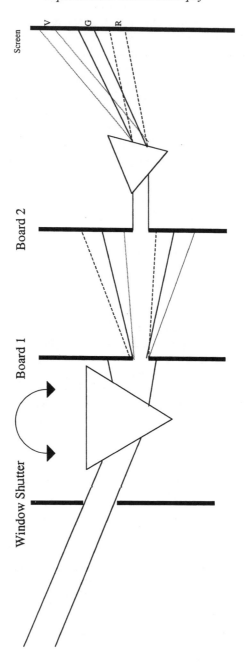

**Figure 10.8**

what I shall tell concerning them is not an Hypothesis but most rigid consequence, not conjectured by barely inferring' tis this because not otherwise or because it satisfies all phaenomena (the Philosophers universall Topick,) but evinced by ye mediation of experiments concluding directly & without any suspicion of doubt.[111]

The first point here is that the treatment of colours is mathematical. Whereas Descartes had taken his geometrical optics and then shifted into a different register to account for it in physical terms, Newton remained at the level of geometrical optics. Colours, as Newton pointed out,[112] are produced in a variety of ways which goes beyond anything that can be accounted for in a treatment that construes them in terms of mixtures of light and dark, or rotation of corpuscles. He notes for example that colours adjacent to one another in the spectrum could be mixed to produce an intermediate colour, but colours that were separated could not be mixed in this way, yet when all the colours were mixed they produced white light; and that thin strips of the wood of the shrub *Lignum nephriticum* which had been soaked in water appeared gold when refracting light but blue when reflecting it. As well as those colour-producing phenomena with which Newton was familiar, namely refractive dispersion (as in diamonds), interference (soap bubbles), and flourescence (*Lignum nephriticum*), there were other such as diffraction (feathers) and scattering (the sky), that make colour phenomena even more intractable.[113] It is worth noting here that Newton's focus in his account of his *experimentum crucis* was on the elongated shape of the spectrum rather than colour. The reason for this was that the elongation was subject to quantitative variation: Newton could keep it as part of an exercise in geometrical optics, thus ensuring that it did not leave the quantitative realm.[114] The phenomena could thus be connected mathematically, rather than in terms of a hypothetical reconstruction of an underlying microscopic physical process designed to reveal the nature of light. In other words, Newton could provide a comprehensive account of the behaviour of light without offering a theory of the nature of light, and in this sense he broke not only with Aristotelian theories but Cartesian ones as well. He was pursuing the study of light in a way that goes beyond practical mathematics and becomes part of natural philosophy, and he was able to do this because he no longer thought of natural philosophy exclusively in terms of matter theory. This shift from practical mathematics to natural philosophy, which will be our concern

---

[111] Newton, *Correspondence*, i. 96–7.     [112] Ibid. 98–9.

[113] See Alan Shapiro, *Fits, Passions, and Paroxysms* (Cambridge, 1993), 99. Note also the problem of 'boundary colours', produced when light and dark objects which abut each other are viewed through a prism, producing a spectrum which lacks a green band and is quite different from the normal one. Newton observed this spectrum: see *Certain Philosophical Questions*, 246–7.

[114] This is not the case with colour, for as Alan Shapiro notes: 'The problem of establishing the innateness and immutability of color is altogether different from that of refrangibility: first, Newton had no mathematical law to describe color changes; and second, the color of the sun's incident light appears totally different before the first refraction and ever after, once it has been resolved into colors. As Newton himself was ultimately to recognize, it is empirically impossible to prove what may be called the strong principle of color immutability for colors of the sun's light at the first refraction, since the colors are not perceptible before the first refraction and so may not be compared with the colors after that refraction to see if they have changed.' ('The Evolving Structure of Newton's Theory of White Light and Color', *Isis* 71 (1980), 211–35: 215–16.)

in the next chapter, was a crucial move not only in optics but in all the traditional Alexandrian disciplines, above all mechanics.

The second point Newton made was one about pursuing natural philosophy in a way that did not use hypotheses. The point was reinforced in the reply to Huygens published in the *Philosophical Transactions*:

> But to examine, how Colors may be explain'd hypothetically, is besides my purpose. I never intended to shew, wherein consists the Nature and Difference of colors, but only to shew, that *de facto* they are Original and Immutable qualities of the Rays which exhibit them; and to leave it to others to explicate by Mechanical *Hypotheses* the Nature and Difference of those qualities: which I take to be no difficult matter.[115]

His claim was that what he had achieved went beyond simply saving the phenomena, showing us what actually happens when light is refracted. There are two issues here. In the first place, Newton's experimental results were not quite as 'matter of fact' as he maintained: there was a protracted dispute about his account of light and colours, and particularly the *experimentum crucis*, which lasted right up to the 1720s,[116] although it should be said that there was also gradual acceptance not only of the results but of the legitimacy of this way of proceeding.[117] Second, on this way of proceeding, Newton's claim cannot be taken seriously as being about his actual work practices, where hypotheses were unavoidable,[118] but the difference is more complex than that between method of discovery and method of presentation.[119] Newton was doing something substantially different from natural philosophers such as Descartes, Gassendi, and Hobbes. He was seeking physical connections between optical phenomena, some causal (the relation between refrangibility and elongation) and some which had the status of phenomenological rules (the relation between refrangibility and colour), all the while keeping the project within natural philosophy, but without the commitment to a matter-theoretical account of underlying physical processes that was a *sine qua non* of traditional natural philosophy.[120] As was the case

---

[115] *Philosophical Transactions* 8 (1673), 6109.

[116] A further dispute over the Newtonian account was initiated at the end of the eighteenth century by Goethe, who returns to the theory that colour is a due to a mixture of light and darkness, albeit on a different basis from that on which its medieval advocates defended it: see Dennis L. Sepper, *Goethe contra Newton: Polemics and the Project for a New Science of Colour* (Cambridge, 1988).

[117] See Schaffer, 'Glass Works: Newton's Prisms and the Uses of Experiment', and Shapiro, 'The Gradual Acceptance of Newton's Theory of Light and Colours, 1672–1727'.

[118] See, specifically on optics, Alan E. Shapiro, 'Newton's Optics and Atomism', in I. Bernard Cohen and George E. Smith, eds, *The Cambridge Companion to Newton* (Cambridge, 2002), 227–55.

[119] In particular, Ben-Chaim, who rightly emphasizes Newton's move away from seeking the 'natures' of things, has, rather more contentiously, suggested that Newton sought to undermine the legitimacy of philosophical definitions of the natures of things primarily for religious reasons. See Michael Ben Chaim, 'Doctrine and Use: Newton's "Gift of Preaching"', *History of Science* 36 (1998), 169–98; see also idem, 'Locke's Ideology of "Common Sense"', *Studies in History and Philosophy of Science*, 31A (2000), 473–501.

[120] Note, however, that Newton's ability to do this varies very much from case to case and I do not want to give the impression that he can make do without matter theory *tout court*. In particular,

in Boyle, the rejection of the idea that one begins from a pre-given *explanans*, which served to organize the field of enquiry, forced Newton to devise an experimental set-up in which the *explanandum* was carved out independently. Someone preoccupied with the fundamental nature of light, such as Descartes, was unlikely to be concerned with elongation of the spectrum, which fell neither under the part of the exercise that comes under geometrical optics, nor that part which comes under the physical understanding of the nature of light. Newton was able to carve out a new explanatory space by ignoring the kind of demarcation of explanatory responsibilities that regulated Descartes' programme, by forging new connections between experimental and quantitative factors.

## ACCOMMODATING THE *EXPLANANS* TO THE *EXPLANANDUM*

The history of natural philosophy from the mid-seventeenth century onwards was driven under pressures from both 'speculative' and experimental natural philosophy, and in many ways this was one of its most distinctive features. These offer quite different conceptions of causal connections, and we can distinguish three different approaches on the basis of the cases we have looked at in this and the two previous chapters. The first is the foundationalist mechanist view, which generally speaking has a reductive notion of causation but which shares with the Aristotelian essentialist view the notion that causation is vertical, as it were: something underlying the phenomena is wholly responsible for their behaviour. At the other extreme is the view that causation connects phenomena at the same level. No advocate of experimental philosophy in the seventeenth century suggested that all causal enquiry should be restricted to the phenomenal level. Rather, what happened in the case of Boyle and Newton (and to some extent Gilbert) is that, once one moves beyond individual cases—and even within individual cases, with a complex phenomenon such as colour—causation is neither simply a question of underlying structure nor simply phenomenal, but a mixture of these. Indeed, as Newton's account of the spectrum indicates, in some respects it may not be a question of establishing causal relations but of making sense of unexpected correlations.

What emerges here is that, in the course of the 1660s, Boyle and Newton discovered that in order to account for certain phenomena in a satisfactory way they had to suspend their commitment to corpuscularianism as the sole reference point for explaining physical behaviour. Since they rejected what was in effect the only alternative comprehensive form of foundational explanation, namely an appeal to Aristotelian essences, they needed some way of organizing the phenomena under investigation other than in terms of underlying structure. Now underlying structure plays a crucial role in suggesting how the phenomena might be organized, not least in virtue of the clues it provides as to the connections between the phenomena.

his treatment of fluids in Book 2 of the *Principia* is couched entirely in terms of speculative hypotheses about the micro-structure of fluids. See George E. Smith, 'The Newtonian Style in Book II of the *Principia*', in Jed Z. Buchwald and I. Bernard Cohen, eds, *Isaac Newton's Natural Philosophy* (Cambridge, Mass., 2001), 249–313.

But, particularly in the case of the optical spectrum, these clues might turn out to be misguided, as Newton realized. One therefore has to proceed without the benefit of any supposed clues, but there is one possible source of guidance, the experimental apparatus itself. This produces a certain range of phenomena which defy explanation in fundamental terms, but which cannot be dismissed because the results themselves cannot be faulted. The only way to proceed is to take the results at face value and start from them, but from a foundationalist perspective these results show no internal coherence, because in corpuscularian terms they are anomalous. The way in which they are generated is therefore crucial, not just because this is what legitimates them but also because, if they have any coherence at all, it has something to do with the way in which they are generated. It is the way in which they are generated, for example, that holds them together as connected phenomena, and that excludes what might otherwise seem—for example, on corpuscularian grounds—to be related phenomena. The way in which the results are generated is a function of the experimental apparatus, the way in which this apparatus is manipulated, and what one is able to do with it. I suggest that what is happening here can fruitfully be described in terms of the experiment or instruments bringing a domain of investigation into focus, replacing the underlying structure that would traditionally have occupied this role. What occurs is a form of tailoring of the explanation to results produced by particular experiments or instruments, in short, a tailoring of *explanans* to *explanandum*, thereby reversing the normal direction of enquiry.

A question arises here of whether this procedure, if it is accepted at all, could only ever be provisional, whether such a piecemeal and apparently non-systematic form of understanding is genuine understanding. Three things should be noted in this connection. First, it is not a question of one side alone having to tailor things. Foundationalists always and as a matter of routine have to tailor the *explanandum* to the *explanans*, and this tailoring—by means of the doctrine of primary and secondary qualities, for example—is in fact at least as radical as anything we are concerned with here, and it is a good deal more problematic if its role is to enable foundationalism to provide the ultimate explanatory basis for all natural phenomena. Second, natural philosophers such as Boyle and Newton will typically work with both experimental and foundational agendas but in different areas. To make matters even more complicated, they may employ more than one foundational agenda: Newton will work not only with a foundationalist mechanism, but also with a foundationalist non-mechanist matter theory based on active principles when mechanism fails to yield the goods, as in the understanding of gravitation.[121] Third, even in cases where one pursues one's enquiry in purely experimental terms, there will always be a number of competing natural philosophies which act to regulate natural-philosophical discussion. It is important for Boyle, for example, in rejecting the claim that there has to be some ultimate corpuscularian account of what occurs when a tube is evacuated, that this is not taken to leave open the possibility that there may be some other ultimate explanation, an Aristotelian explanation for example. It is

---

[121] See Rob Iliffe, 'Abstract Considerations: Disciplines and the Incoherence of Newton's Natural Philosophy', *Studies in History and Philosophy of Science* 35 (2004), 427–54.

clear that, for him, if there were a fundamental explanation, it would have to be a corpuscularian one. Boyle's commitment to corpuscularianism was, as we have seen, not a commitment to the idea that all explanations must ultimately take the form of postulated interactions between corpuscles. Rather, it was a commitment to the idea that as far as fundamental processes are concerned, these take the form of interactions between corpuscles.

In short, what he was denying is that any account of physical phenomena must be couched in terms of such interactions if it is to have genuine explanatory force. In the cases that we have been concerned with, it is the experimentally established results that carry the explanatory weight and hence it is these that do the real natural-philosophical work, not the systems in which one decides to anchor them. The idea that colour is merely a secondary quality, for example, is irrelevant for Boyle and Newton in their accounts of colour. Newton didn't reserve one kind of treatment for corpuscular interaction and another for chromatic phenomena. What requires explanation isn't generated by a distinction between primary and secondary qualities, but by an identification of problematic phenomena at the phenomenal level. There was no attempt to organize the domain of investigation by replacing Aristotelian essential principles with some other kind of principle that identified the *explanandum* on what are effectively a priori grounds. The idea that a natural-philosophical system determines in advance what is to be explained and what is not was discarded. This did not mean that one should not seek a natural-philosophical system or that one should not utilize its explanatory resources. What it meant was that the abandonment of Aristotelianism brought with it the abandonment of a hard and fast way of identifying the *explanandum* of natural philosophy.

The situation was further complicated by a new ingredient that until now I have only touched upon. We have seen that Newton used a tightly controlled experiment to keep optical phenomena amenable to mathematical treatment, while at the same time making them part of natural philosophy. Advocates of experimental natural philosophy are not *ipso facto* committed to quantitative explanation any more than advocates of corpuscularianism are. But it is an assumption of, and in large part a motivation behind, at least some of the principal varieties of mechanism that the level of micro-corpuscularian explanation is going to be quantitative, since it exploits only quantifiable notions, such as speed, size, and direction of motion. Of course, this does not rule out quantifications at other levels. The interesting questions arise when, as in Descartes' account of colour, a quantified macroscopic account of colour production is redescribed in micro-corpuscularian terms, with the result that in the process we leave quantitative considerations behind and move into a speculative and qualitative realm.

In the previous two chapters we looked at some of the different attempts to transform corpuscularian matter theory along mechanist lines, and in this chapter I have explored the difference between foundationalist and experimental natural philosophies. In both cases, issues concerning the quantitative nature of the exercise impinge, but we have not yet explored these in their own right. It is to the question of a quantitative natural philosophy that we now turn.

# 11

# The Quantitative Transformation of Natural Philosophy

The goal of a quantitative natural philosophy was something that lay behind and shaped many mechanist projects in the seventeenth century. But it proved an elusive goal, even for those who, like Descartes, had originally aimed to shape their entire approach to natural philosophy around this ambition. Part of the problem was that the new natural philosophy had defined itself in terms of matter theory. It was corpuscularianism of one form or another that marked out the new philosophy from Aristotelianism, but there was nothing in corpuscularianism as such that committed one to a quantitative approach, and two of the most influential advocates of atomism, Bacon and Gassendi, had regarded mathematics and natural philosophy as wholly distinct disciplines. By contrast, there were those—such as Beeckman, Hobbes, and Descartes—who had confined the properties of corpuscles to quantitative attributes like volume/weight and speed/velocity, but they had not thereby provided a quantitative natural philosophy, because they were unable to make the transition from a micro-corpuscularian idealization to macroscopic empirical events. In particular, despite isolated successes, they failed to redirect the tradition of practical mathematics in a natural-philosophical direction. As a result, there remained deep and intractable questions about the relevance of the practical-mathematical tradition for natural-philosophical enquiry. In the first half of the seventeenth century, Descartes and Galileo were the only figures who dealt with these issues in a concerted fashion, but before we look at their proposals, we need to remind ourselves of the Aristotelian challenge.

The guiding principle behind Aristotle's approach to understanding natural processes lies in his classification of the different types of knowledge in Book E of the *Metaphysics*. We saw in Chapter 2 that Aristotle defines metaphysics, physics, and mathematics in terms of their subject matters. Metaphysics is concerned with whatever does not change and has an independent existence. 'Physics' or natural philosophy is concerned with those things that change and have an independent existence, that is, all natural phenomena. Finally, mathematics deals with those things that do not change and do not have an independent existence, namely those quantitative abstractions that we make: numbers (discontinuous magnitudes) and geometrical shapes (continuous magnitudes). The aim of scientific enquiry on this account is to determine what kind of thing the subject matter is by establishing its essential properties. The kinds of principles one employs to achieve this are determined by the subject matter of the science. To establish the essential properties of a natural object or event or process, one needs to use principles consonant with that subject matter, that is, principles that are designed to capture the essence of something which is independent and changing.

This has a very significant bearing upon the connections between the theoretical sciences, and it is particularly marked in the complex question of the relation between physics and mathematics, for it leads to the idea that physical principles must be used in physical enquiry, and mathematical principles in the very different kind of subject matter that constitutes mathematics. The two cannot be mixed, for physical and mathematical principles are essentially concerned with different kinds of subject matter. The general thrust of the Aristotelian position is that physical enquiry or demonstration cannot be pursued mathematically, any more than mathematical enquiry can be pursued physically. The point can be made in a different way by asking what one does in a physical explanation, and in particular by asking what it is that makes a physical explanation informative. Aristotle, and the whole ancient and medieval tradition after him, thought that to explain a physical phenomenon, one needed to distinguish between accidental features of a body and its essential properties, and any behaviour that could be said to be due to the body itself was due to the essential properties it had. These essential properties explained its behaviour. Such properties were material, and Aristotle argued that they could not be captured by employing mathematical or quantitative concepts.

As well as natural philosophy there also existed another discipline in antiquity, which, although it was classed under practical mathematics, dealt with physical devices: this was mechanics, the science of machines. The devices that mechanics investigated—such as the lever, the inclined plane, the wedge, the pulley, the screw, and gears—were problematic from the Aristotelian point of view in two respects. First, they were non-natural devices, that is, they added to nature rather than making manifest a natural process: as such, they came under the category of 'violent motions' rather than 'natural motions' and were not properly the subject of natural philosophy at all. Second, the mechanical disciplines were neither wholly mathematical nor wholly physical, and fell under the rubric of what Aristotle and his followers called 'mixed mathematics'.

A physical account of something—such as why celestial bodies are spherical—is an explanation that works in terms of the fundamental principles of the subject matter of physics, that is, it captures the phenomena in terms of what is changing and has an independent existence, whereas a mathematical account of something—such as the relation between the surface area and the volume of a sphere—requires a wholly different kind of explanation, one that invokes principles commensurate with the kinds of thing that mathematical entities are.[1] In *De caelo*, for example,

---

[1] See Aristotle, *Posterior Analytics*, 75ᵃ28–38: 'Since it is just those attributes within every genus which are essential and possessed by their respective subjects as such that are necessary, it is clear that both the conclusions and the premisses of demonstrations which produce scientific knowledge are essential. . . . It follows that in demonstrating we cannot pass from one genus to another.' Cf. 76ᵃ23 ff. and *De caelo,* 306ᵃ9–12.

we are offered a *physical* proof of the sphericity of the earth,[2] not a mathematical one, because we are dealing with the properties of a *physical* object. In short, distinct subject matters require distinct principles, and physics and mathematics are distinct subject matters. However, Aristotle also recognizes subordinate or mixed sciences, telling us in the *Posterior Analytics* that 'the theorem of one science cannot be demonstrated by means of another science, except where these theorems are related as subordinate to superior: for example, as optical theorems to geometry, or harmonic theorems to arithmetic'.[3] Whereas physical optics—the investigation of the nature of light and its physical properties—falls straightforwardly under physics, for example, geometrical optics 'investigates mathematical lines, but *qua* physical, not *qua* mathematical'.[4] The question of the relation between mixed mathematics, on the one hand, and the 'superior' disciplines of mathematics and physics, which did the real explanatory work on this conception, remained a vexed one throughout the Middle Ages and the Renaissance, but so long as the former remained marginal to the enterprise of natural philosophy the problems were not especially evident. By the beginning of the seventeenth century, however, the disciplines of what were conceived of as mixed mathematics were attracting a significant amount of attention, above all on the question of whether they might have any explanatory force in their own right.

The issues here in large part hinged around the problem of how to integrate mechanics into matter theory. Mechanics deals with physical processes in terms of the motions undergone by bodies and the nature of the forces responsible for these motions. Matter theory deals with how the physical behaviour of a body is determined by what it is made of, and in the seventeenth century it typically achieved this in a corpuscularian fashion, by investigating how the nature and arrangement of the constituent parts of a body determine its behaviour. Mechanical and matter-theoretic approaches to physical theory are very different, they engage fundamentally different kinds of considerations, and on the face of it offer explanations of different phenomena. We don't explain how levers, inclined planes, screws, and pulleys work in terms of matter theory. Correlatively, it is far from clear that the appropriate form of explanation of the phenomena of burning, fermentation, and differences between fluids and solids is in terms of mechanics.

Traditionally, matter theory had been constitutive of natural philosophy, and it was generally assumed from the Presocratics up to the seventeenth century that the key to understanding physical processes lay in understanding the nature of matter and its behaviour, whether this understanding took the form of a theory about how matter is regulated by external immaterial principles, by internal immaterial principles, or by the behaviour of the internal material constituents of macroscopic bodies. The traditional disciplines of practical mathematics included such areas as geometrical optics, positional astronomy, harmonics, and statics, the latter being the only area of mechanics that had been developed in any detail in antiquity. Statics, along with the other disciplines, was considered very much as a branch of mathematics, which meant—on

---

[2] *De caelo*, 297$^a$9 ff.     [3] *Post. Anal.* 75$^b$14–16.     [4] *Physics*, 194$^a$10.

the prevailing Aristotelian conception—that it dealt with abstractions and hypotheses rather than with physical reality. In other words, it was not part of natural philosophy; it was not something that one would use to explore the nature of the physical world.

## HYDROSTATICS VERSUS KINEMATICS

The discipline of mechanics has traditionally been thought of as comprising three areas: statics, dealing with bodies in a state of equilibrium; kinematics, with moving bodies; and dynamics with the forces responsible for motion. The ultimate prize of seventeenth-century physical theory was the last. Statics dealt with forces but not with motion; kinematics, on the other hand, dealt with motion but not with forces. Dynamics had to deal with both. Broadly speaking, this suggested two routes to dynamics. The first route was via statics. Since statics does not deal with moving bodies, but does deal with forces, the aim was to extrapolate from the treatment of forces used to describe stationary bodies into the realm of moving bodies, for example by asking how these forces are modified or supplemented when the stationary body begins to move in a particular way. The advantage of this approach was that statics had been pursued since antiquity in a precise, quantitative, geometrical fashion, which was exactly how seventeenth-century natural philosophers wished to pursue dynamics. The second route was via kinematics. Kinematics does not deal with forces but, at least from Galileo's *Discorsi* (1638) onwards, it does provide a precise, quantitative, geometrical account of motion, and for those who pursued this route to dynamics, the thought was that the kinematic analysis and classification of motions into various categories might yield the fundamental kinds of motion and rest, so that one could then associate different forces with these different fundamental states, and thereby explain what made them different.

Although the two routes cannot always be separated quite so easily, they lead in very different directions. Both Galileo and Descartes, for example, used models derived from hydrostatics, as well as more familiar ones from kinematics, in their work in physical theory. Galileo started with a hydrostatic model in his early work, and then abandoned it when he began to develop a kinematic model. Descartes, by contrast, had a more innovative approach to a hydrostatic model, and it guided his work in optics, cosmology, and even to some extent in physiology.

The motivation for Descartes' use of a hydrostatic model derived from his earliest work in 'physico-mathematics', as Beeckman termed it, a project in which he was guided by Beeckman. However, right from the beginning, Descartes rethought the nature of physico-mathematics and how it might be successfully pursued. Beeckman's use of hydrostatics worked with a model derived from the pseudo-Aristotelian *Mechanica problemata*.[5] Descartes took a different path, jettisoning the

---

[5] On the *Mechanica* see Henri Carteron, *La Notion de force dans la système d'Aristote* (Paris, 1923). On the influence of the *Mechanica* in the sixteenth and seventeenth centuries, see Pierre Duhem, *Les Origines de la statique* (2 vols Paris, 1905–6); Paul Lawrence Rose and Stillman Drake, 'The Pseudo-Aristotelian *Questions of Mechanics* in Renaissance Culture', *Studies in the Renaissance* 18 (1971), 65–104; and W. R. Laird, 'The Scope of Renaissance Mechanics', *Osiris* 2 (1986), 43–68.

*Mechanica* approach in favour of Archimedean statics, in the process developing, with remarkable ingenuity, a set of hydrostatically based concepts which he generalized to the whole of mechanics, ultimately building an optics and a cosmology on this basis.

The difference between the *Mechanica* model for statics and the Archimedean one is fundamental, and it bears centrally on the question of the relation between physical or natural-philosophical disciplines and mathematical ones. The Aristotelian tradition thought this question through in terms of the idea of 'subordinate sciences', although, as we shall see, some quite radical moves can be made in the genre which attempt to distance it from particular Aristotelian natural-philosophical doctrines. Galileo's early work in mechanics can be seen as falling within this tradition. The alternative is physico-mathematics, which, as Descartes came to conceive of it, cuts across the traditional conception of 'superior' and 'subordinate' sciences, and it abandons the metaphysically driven demarcation of disciplines that provides it with its rationale.[6]

The statics tradition based on the *Mechanica* offered a physical theory, whereas the Archimedean approach was purely mathematical. The contrast is most evident in their treatments of the principle of the lever. Archimedes' account abstracts from physical quantities, treating bodies placed on the lever as points, lying at the centres of gravity of the bodies, along a line. By contrast, the earlier treatment of the principle of the lever in the *Mechanica* works in terms of proportionality between weight and speed.[7] The basic principle behind this, set out in a number of passages in Aristotle,[8] is that the same force will move two bodies of different weights, but it will move the heavier body more slowly, so that the velocities of the two bodies are inversely proportional to their weights. When these weights are suspended from the ends of a lever, we have two forces acting in contrary directions, and each body moves in an arc with a force proportional to its weight times the length of the arm from which it is suspended. The one with the greater product will descend in a circular arc, but if the products are equal, they will remain in equilibrium.

Whereas Archimedes' approach made statics a mathematical discipline independent of any general theory of motion, that of the *Mechanica* made statics simply a limiting case of a general dynamical theory of motion, a theory which was resolutely physical. In other words, the *Mechanica* account came as part of a package that was driven by Aristotelian dynamics, above all by the principle of the proportionality of

---

The *Mechanica*, which is probably the work of Strato or Theophrastus, was traditionally attributed to Aristotle, an attribution which Duhem and Carteron follow. The work is Aristotelian in tenor, but has the peculiar feature that whereas Aristotelian natural philosophy confines itself to natural processes, for it is these that follow from the nature of things, the subject matter of the *Mechanica*, as is explained in the opening sentence of the work, is 'those phenomena that are produced by art despite nature, for the benefit of mankind'.

[6] Jesuit commentators adopted the term 'physico-mathematics' by the 1630s—for example Nicolo Zucchi, *Nova de machinis philosophia* (Rome, 1649)—but they used the term as synonymous with 'mixed mathematics': see Ugo Baldini, 'The Development of Jesuit "Physics" in Italy, 1550–1700: A Structural Approach', in Constance Blackwell and Sachiko Kusukawa, eds., *Philosophy in the Sixteenth and Seventeenth Centuries* (Aldershot, 1999), 248–79: 259.

[7] *Mechanica*, 850[a]39–850[b]6.         [8] The most important is *De caelo*, 301[b]4 ff.

weight and speed. This did not stop a number of sixteenth-century Italian mathematicians and natural philosophers—particularly Tartaglia, Benedetti, and Galileo—from trying to revise the package, hoping they could salvage the dynamical interpretation of the beam balance and simple machines while jettisoning the natural philosophy that lay behind it. In particular, the dynamics of Galileo's early *De motu*[9] relies on the principle underlying the *Mechanica* tradition, that of the proportionality between the force of moving a body and the speed of the body. Galileo—who by the time he wrote *De motu* (around 1590) was beginning to think in terms of the rate of fall being proportional to the specific weight of the falling body—rejected the idea that rate of fall is simply proportional to absolute weight, and interpreted the proportionality of weight and speed in such a way that bodies of the same specific weight fall at the same rate, on the grounds (which Benedetti had proposed) that a body ten times heavier than another requires ten times the force to move it, so that increased absolute weight is always balanced by increased force needed to displace that absolute weight. Duhem has claimed that this represents an extension of the Aristotelian proportionality principle,[10] but, quite the contrary, it undermines the proportionality principle. In Aristotelian natural philosophy, what moves a falling body is not something external to the body which acts against a resistance provided by the body's weight. The weight of a body is what provides its motive force, and this is why its speed is proportional to its weight. Duhem's construal only makes sense if we think of the body being pulled to the earth: in this case we can think of the external force pulling the body downwards being checked by an internal force which resists this motion. But this is wholly at odds with the fundamental tenets of Aristotelian natural philosophy. If mechanics is, in Aristotelian terms, a 'subordinate science', then what it is subordinate to is Aristotelian natural philosophy, and the direction in which Galileo (along with other sixteenth-century Italian mathematicians) was trying to move was blocked from the outset by the requirements imposed by Aristotelian natural philosophy.

Galileo was ingenious in stretching these requirements, but he could not overcome them, and it is instructive to see just how far he could get within an Aristotelian framework that had been revised so radically that it had become unstable. In his early works, he believed that hydrostatics held the key to dynamics. The hydrostatic model was developed most fully in his early account of free fall in *De motu*, where he takes issue with the Aristotelian account of projectile motion, whereby the continued motion of a projectile, once it has left the body (the cannon, or the hand, or whatever) that has projected it, is due to the surrounding medium. This account had notorious difficulties, and during the sixteenth century it was largely replaced by *impetus* theory.[11]

---

[9] Galileo, 'Dialogue on Motion', trans. in I. E. Drabkin and Stillman Drake, *Galileo on Motion and on Mechanics* (Madison, 1960), an invaluable collection of Galileo's writings; also in Drake and Drabkin, *Mechanics in Sixteenth-Century Italy*, which also contains an interesting selection of contemporary writings on mechanics, by Tartaglia, Benedetti and Guido Ubaldo del Monte.

[10] See the discussion in Duhem, *Les Origines de la statique*, i. ch. 11.

[11] For details, see Michael Wolff, *Geschichte der Impetustheorie: Untersuchungen zum Ursprung des klassischen Mechanik* (Frankfurt, 1978).

On *impetus* theory, when a projectile is launched, the launcher imparts a force to it, which is 'impressed' on the body. While remaining an external force in the sense that it originates outside the body, it is effectively internalized by that body. When the body is projected upwards, the *impetus* gradually dies down—the process can be thought of by analogy with the gradual burning up of fuel by the body (although details vary between different versions of *impetus* theory here)—and the body's motion gradually gets slower until, at the summit of its rise, it stops. The answer to the question why the body doesn't then remain suspended in the air is to be found in the balance between *impetus* and the body's natural tendency downwards. The body's natural tendency downwards has remained constant while the *impetus* that drives it upwards has been diminishing (as it has been gradually 'used up'). As the latter diminishes in relation to the former, the body will decelerate, and a point will be reached at which *impetus* and force downwards exactly balance (the apogee of the motion), after which the force downwards will predominate, and as the *impetus* gradually dies out, the body will accelerate, until finally a point will come at which there is no *impetus* left and the body will cease accelerating.

Two features of the *impetus* account were important for Galileo's purposes: it is dynamic and it has a quantitative element. *Impetus* theory invoked three forces to account for projectile motion: an external force by which the body is projected in the first place; the internalized version of this external force, *impetus*, which gradually runs out; and an internal force, *gravità*, conceived teleologically as something that enables the body to realize a natural goal, by which the body returns to its natural place. In building on *impetus* theory, Galileo retained its dynamic aspects: he was concerned to explain motion in terms of the forces responsible for it. As regards the quantitative question, *impetus* theory is quite different from Aristotle's own account. Aristotle introduced quantitative questions only in passing, in the context of a demonstration of the impossibility of motion in a void,[12] and he made speed of fall directly proportional to absolute weight and inversely proportional to the density of the medium. The latter was designed to show, *per impossibile*, that bodies would move at an infinite speed in a void, because a void has zero density. *Impetus* theory, on the other hand, offers an explanation of variations in the rate of upward and downward motion of a projectile in terms of the net balance of forces acting on or in the body.

Galileo stripped *impetus* theory down to bare essentials and rebuilt it, strengthening its quantitative aspects by applying the principles of hydrostatics, and in the process undermining its rationale in Aristotelian dynamics by relativizing the notion of weight and effectively removing any role for the doctrine of natural place. He rejected Aristotle's theory that speed of fall is directly proportional to absolute weight by citing the example of two bodies of different weights which, when dropped from a tower simultaneously, reach the ground simultaneously; and he was able to show that the claim that speed of fall is inversely proportional to the density of the medium cannot hold, because cork for example, which falls at a particular rate in air, will not fall

[12] *Physics*, 215ª24–216ª21.

at a proportionately slower rate in water, which is denser, but will rise. This points to a serious failing of the Aristotelian account of fall from the quantitative point of view: it considers the matter in terms of incommensurable quantities, making rate of fall directly proportional to the absolute weight of the body and inversely proportional to the density or specific weight of the medium. We can make these quantities commensurable either by comparing the absolute weight of the body and the absolute weight of the medium, or by comparing their respective specific weights. The first is obviously not possible, as we do not know how much medium we would have to consider. The second is viable, however, and clearly overcomes the problems with Aristotle's account. If rate of fall is directly proportional to the specific weight of the body then it is clear why two lead balls, whatever the difference in their absolute weights, will fall at the same rate. And if it is inversely proportional to the specific weight of the medium, then whether a body will rise or fall in a medium depends on whether its specific (not its absolute) weight is greater than or less than that of the medium, which explains why a material such as cork or wood—which has a higher specific weight than air but a lower specific weight than water—will fall in air but rise in water.

What Galileo was attempting to do was to model the problem of free fall on hydrostatics. The hydrostatical tradition had a well-developed account of how bodies rise in relatively dense fluids which worked in terms of comparing the specific weight of the body with the specific weight of the fluid. Galileo's idea was to argue that the fall of relatively dense bodies in air was effectively the same kind of problem—it was simply a question of treating aerostatics as a limiting case of hydrostatics—and that specific weight provided the key to the answer. In *De motu* he thought the key to the problem was to treat heavy bodies falling in air on a par with light bodies rising in water. The advantage of this was that techniques from statics could be applied directly to the present problem. Statics had been concerned with the conditions under which a body in a medium will rise or fall, where these conditions were conceived in terms of departure from an equilibrium state. Galileo attempted to generalize this analysis to cover the dynamical problem of the cause of differences in speeds of bodies moving through different media, and in doing so to render the dynamical problem amenable to the same kinds of geometrical treatment as a statical one.

His approach was to equate, as mathematically identical, the buoyant effect of the medium and the artificial lightness that an impressed force induces in a body. When a body is thrown upwards a force is impressed on it which endows it with an artificial lightness: this is an effect that alters the effective weight of the body immersed in the medium. Weight is relativized to effective weight, which is equal to the specific weight of the body minus the specific weight of the medium: when the effective weight takes a positive value the body will fall, when it takes a negative one, the body will rise.

Note two features of this account, features that will be mirrored in Descartes' hydrostatically modelled mechanics. First, there was a move to a functional understanding of weight. Galileo still recognized some distinction between downward and upward motion: the former, being a natural motion and hence having a definite goal, needs only an intrinsic cause, whereas the latter, being violent and having no aim, must always have an extrinsic cause. But his account also undermined this distinction, for it was now quite unclear in what sense the upward motion of a cork in water is any less 'natural' than its fall in air. And more importantly, we cannot ask what causes a particular downward motion in a particular case unless we know something about the medium, namely, how its specific weight compares with that of the body. It is equilibrium, rather than natural place, that is now doing the real explanatory work. This brings us to the second feature, which is that the explanation of the cause of motion is given in terms of deviation from an equilibrium state. Bodies will neither fall nor rise if they are in a state of equilibrium with the medium in which they are immersed, and when they do move, the factor that determines their motion will be, not the absolute weight of the body or that of the medium, nor the specific weight of the body or the specific weight of the medium, but the specific weight of the body minus the specific weight of the medium: just as, when two bodies are in equilibrium on the arms of a beam balance, and when we break this equilibrium by adding some further material to one of the bodies, the resulting motion of the arms of the balance is not a function of the weights of the bodies but only of the difference in their weights.

There is a sense in which the medium is constitutive of the problem here for Galileo. That is to say, he has reformulated the question of free fall so that the medium is an essential ingredient in any well-formulated question about free fall: free fall is essentially something that takes place in a medium, and the question of the nature of free fall cannot even be posed unless we ask about the contribution of the medium. To understand why, consider the beam balance case. If two bodies are not in equilibrium on a balance, then we can say that their effective weights differ, but their absolute weights are irrelevant. If the bodies are initially in equilibrium, there are several things we can do to disturb the equilibrium. We can add something to one of the pans so that it moves down and the other pan moves upward. Or we can leave the contents of the pans as they were and move the beam to the left, thereby shortening one arm and lengthening the other. The lengthening of the left arm would result in an increase in the effective weight of the contents of the left-hand pan just as much as adding more material to that pan would have. And a similar result could be achieved by leaving the contents of the pans the same, and keeping the arms the same length, but immersing the right hand pan in water. Effective weight is what matters, and this is a function of a number of factors. When we move to the case of bodies freely suspended in media, nothing changes: it is the effective weight that determines the direction and rate of motion.

It looks, then, as if one can retain formal features of the *Mechanica* account— statics as a physical discipline, which deals with the limiting case of equilibrium— while at the same time dispensing with the content of the *Mechanica*, rejecting the Aristotelian account of motive force that provided its initial rationale. But it is far from clear that this is in fact possible, even judging the matter on criteria Galileo himself would have applied. If one rejects the Aristotelian account of motive force, the explanation of equilibrium in terms of bodies' tendencies to move in arcs at speeds proportional to their weights must surely come into question, and in that case what is one left with? These principles provide the connections between statics and moving bodies. One cannot simply abandon them and assume that the connections will remain: any such connections will have lost their physical rationale. Galileo made a valiant effort in *De motu* to redirect physical theory by taking the shell of the

*Mechanica* and trying to give it a new content. But the resources he was working with were far too meagre. In particular, *impetus* was thought through exclusively in terms derived from statics. Because it was considered in terms of—and indeed measured by—the force needed by a simple machine to raise a body against its nature, it was essentially an account of vertical motion and had no application to horizontal motion. It did not refer to an extrinsic cause that altered the body's state of rest or motion, but to the capacity of a body in motion to raise itself to the height from which it fell in acquiring that motion.[13] The project was, in short, radically under-resourced conceptually, and its failure was clear to Galileo himself, since he eventually abandoned it, giving up the idea of using statics as a basis for physical theory, and replacing motions with moments in his account of the principle of the lever in his *Mecaniche* of 1602, thus severing the direct ties between statics and kinetics.[14]

Like the early Galileo, Descartes was convinced that hydrostatics could be used as model for dynamics. But his approach was completely different, avoiding the kinds of problem that forced Galileo to give up the programme at an early stage. Galileo tried to revise the *Mechanica* package with the aim of salvaging the dynamical interpretation of the beam balance and simple machines while jettisoning the natural philosophy that lay behind it, but the pivotal role this natural philosophy played meant that such a revision could never be successful. Descartes, by contrast, took up the Archimedean account, not that of the *Mechanica*. The Archimedean account came without any dynamical, or more broadly speaking physical, commitments. Descartes's aim was to produce a dynamics by putting physical flesh on the mathematical skeleton that Archimedean statics provided.

Descartes' approach in his hydrostatics, as we saw in Chapter 8, was to substitute, for Stevin's Archimedean geometrical demonstration, an exploratory account which pushed the problem into the domain of natural philosophy, asking what underlying physical arrangement caused bodies to behave in the way they did. As a result, what he was able to provide was a discussion which was undeniably inconclusive and lacking in formal rigour, but which, by contrast with Stevin's geometrical account, he believed identified what caused the phenomenon. His aim, under the rubric of 'physico-mathematics', was to shift hydrostatics from the realm of practical mathematics unambiguously into the realm of natural philosophy. This he tried to achieve by redescribing, in terms of his matter theory, what it was that caused the pressure exerted by a fluid on the floor of the vessel containing it: he redescribed what caused the pressure in terms of the cumulative behaviour of postulated microscopic corpuscles making up the fluid.

What Stevin had advocated was not just a reduction of statics to mathematics, but a severing of statics from kinetics, that is, from those parts of mechanics that study motion—kinematics and dynamics—and indeed a severing of statics from natural philosophy, howsoever conceived. The contrasting *Mechanica* tradition had relied not

---

[13] See the discussion in R. S. Westfall, *Force in Newton's Physics*, 25.

[14] See Stillman Drake, *Galileo at Work* (Chicago, 1978), ch. 2 on *De Motu* and chs. 3 and 4 on his *Mechanics*. See also Clavelin, *The Natural Philosophy of Galileo*, ch. 3. There is an English translation of the *Mecaniche* in Drabkin and Drake, *Galileo on Motion*.

just on an elementary mechanics, however, but also on Aristotelian natural philosophy, above all upon a matter theory that motivated the idea of the proportionality between weight and speed. One advantage of Stevin's isolation of statics from the rest of mechanics was that it was freed from any commitment to a particular natural philosophy. The disadvantage is that it ceased to be part of physical theory, undermining any transition from statics or hydrostatics to a dynamics, with its associated move from mathematics to natural philosophy proper. There are two questions at stake here. First, how is it possible for statics and hydrostatics to describe an empirical state of affairs, *qua* empirical state of affairs, that is, not merely *qua* abstraction? And second, how do we connect those physical features of this empirical state of affairs that are picked out by statics and hydrostatics with those physical features dealt with in other parts of physical theory; in particular, how do we connect the description of the conditions under which equilibrium occurs with an account of the forces acting on or within bodies which combine in such a way as to give rise to an equilibrium state?

Broadly speaking, there were two options open to Descartes in dealing with these questions. First, he could take the *Mechanica*-type analysis forward on the basis of the lever and simple machines, treated dynamically, to underpin a new natural philosophy that would replace Aristotle's, and then proceed to pursue physical theory generally on this basis, taking advantage of the already established connections between statics and the rest of physical theory. This was Galileo's early strategy. Or, second, he could start from Stevin's Archimedean approach in hydrostatics and try, from scratch, to provide it with physical content. He took the latter approach. What he did was to ask what natural philosophy—in effect, what theory of matter and what dynamical theory of the action of causes—enabled one to make sense of the results of Stevin's analysis. By ignoring the physical interpretation of statics central to the *Mechanica* tradition and opting for an Archimedean approach, he could not rely on any natural connection between statics and the rest of physical theory: any connections had to be forged anew. But nor was he stuck with the Aristotelian natural philosophy that came as part of the *Mechanica* package. Far from being guided by a *Mechanica*-type approach, with its grounding in Aristotelian natural philosophy, he did not even consider Aristotelian natural philosophy. Instead, he started with Stevin's mathematical account and attempted to 'physicalize' it, by fleshing it out in terms of a micro-corpuscularian theory of the material constituents of fluids. This was for him an example of 'physico-mathematics'. Far from being something in the tradition of the Aristotelian 'subordinate sciences',[15] this 'physico-mathematics' pursued a completely different route to the quantitative understanding of physical processes, attempting not to 'mix' mathematics and physics, but to translate physical problems into the quantitatively characterizable behaviour of microscopic corpuscles making up material things (bodies and fluids), and then invoking a causal register of

---

[15] *Contra* Dear, *Discipline and Experience*, who treats mathematical physics as coming out of the tradition of mixed mathematics. See also W. R. Laird, 'Galileo and the Mixed Sciences', in Daniel A. Di Liscia, Eckhard Kessler, and Charlotte Methuen, eds, *Method and Order in Renaissance Philosophy of Nature: The Aristotle Commentary Tradition* (Aldershot, 1997), 253–70.

forces, tendencies, components, and (later) 'determinations', which were completely different from Aristotelian 'principles'. What Descartes ultimately hoped to achieve by this was, at the most general level, much the same as what Galileo had hoped to achieve in his *De motu*: the extrapolation from statics—pursued in a precise, quantitative, geometrical fashion—to the whole of physical theory. But they attempted to realize this aim in quite different ways: in *De motu* Galileo attempted a radical revision of the 'subordinate sciences' tradition, whereas Descartes was in effect abandoning this tradition in favour of something wholly new. His hope was that by exploring what he took to be the latent natural-philosophical underpinnings of statics, and specifically the hydrostatic paradox, he would uncover and render explicit a wholly general natural philosophy. It was the underlying natural philosophy of Aristotle that provided the unification of mechanical disciplines offered in the *Mechanica*. If one removed that natural philosophy, then, as Galileo learned, the unification did not remain intact. Any unification had to be produced by the natural philosophy, rather than grafted on to it.

Descartes' attempt to pursue a quantitative natural philosophy by taking a macroscopic geometrical account, and then proceeding to redescribe it in terms of an underlying micro-corpuscular picture of physical behaviour, was a brilliantly original move and it did yield benefits. First in *Le Monde* and then in the *Principia*, as we have seen, Descartes aimed to provide a hydrostatically modelled mechanistic cosmology, using a micro-corpuscular theory of matter, combined with a number of laws describing the motion of the corpuscles, to set out a mechanistic cosmology which included both a celestial physics and an accounted of the nature and properties of light. He accounted for the stability of planetary orbits and the orbits of their satellites on a mechanist basis, envisaging the planets being carried in a sea of fluid matter which took the form of a vortex; moreover, he was able to account for the propagation of light from the sun in terms of the centrifugal effects of its axial rotation. Indeed, because a medium shapes the behaviour of a body directly, without having to engage any forces acting at a distance—forces which are at best poorly understood, at worst completely mysterious—a hydrostatic model had a *prima facie* case to be considered the most promising model for the ultimate prize of mechanics, dynamics.

Yet as they stood, in terms of the original aspirations of 'physico-mathematics', these projects were failures. Descartes was wholly unable to provide a quantitative natural philosophy on a systematic basis. His achievements in quantifying natural phenomena remained stubbornly in the realm of practical mathematics, and had no plausible continuity with his natural philosophy. Moreover, in his mature natural philosophy he was forced to operate with both a hydrostatic and a kinematic model simultaneously, as if they were part of the same enterprise. More specifically, he tended to use statics to provide the forces by which to fill out kinematics. This generated two sets of fundamental anomalies, an indication of just how serious and deep the problems were.

The two anomalies are of rather different kinds, although they both arise in the framework of kinematics. We have already looked at them in other contexts, so I shall be brief. The first occurs in Descartes' account of the inertial element in circular motions, where he seems straightforwardly to contradict himself: he argued that the only kind of inertial motion is rectilinear, and then went on to assume what appears to be a form of circular inertia. The second occurs in his laws of collision, where he asserted that a smaller moving body in collision with a larger stationary one would never move the larger one, something that directly contradicts our empirical intuitions about what occurs, and which has no obvious kinematic rationale.

Descartes' principle of rectilinear inertia tells us that in the absence of external forces a body will continue in a state of rest or uniform rectilinear motion, and that these are the only two inertial states of a body. He argues that since a body's tendency to move is instantaneous, this tendency to move can only be rectilinear, because only rectilinear motion can be determined in an instant. Yet as we saw in Chapter 8, Descartes was also apparently committed to the existence of circular inertia. Indeed, strictly speaking, he was committed to two kinds of circular inertia. In Chapter 13 of *Le Monde*, he treated the tugging on the string by a body whirled in a sling as being the resultant of a radial tendency outwards and the body's circular motion. The second case arose in response to the question why light rays are not retarded as they travel from the sun to the earth, to which he replied by maintaining that light corpuscles would no more lose their speed than they would their rotational velocity. 'I don't know', he writes to Ciermans, 'why you think the corpuscles of celestial matter do not maintain the rotation that gives rise to colours as well as the rectilinear motion in which light consists, for we can grasp both equally well by our reasoning.'[16] In other words, the rotation of light corpuscles needs no external force for its maintenance, any more than uniform rectilinear motion does: it is, in this sense, inertial.

The second anomaly occurs in Rule 4 of the rules for collision, which specifies that a smaller body can never move a larger one, no matter what its velocity, and no matter how slight the difference in size. As we have seen, this is a very peculiar stipulation: it does not follow from the other Rules and it is quite contrary to our empirical experience that a rapidly moving body which was very marginally smaller than a stationary body, would simply rebound on impact with the larger body, having failed to affect it at all, and leaving it in the same stationary state as it was before impact. It will be clear from the discussion in Ch. 8 that these anomalies were not simply oversights, nor simply misunderstandings, on Descartes' part. They were surface manifestations of a deep structural ambiguity in his account, which arose because Descartes modelled his kinematics on statics, and particularly on hydrostatics. It looked as if the results were being delivered by kinematics, but in fact they were being delivered to a large extent by statics, and these are two very different ways of thinking through physical problems. At the most fundamental level, they direct attention to very different kinds of issue: they pick out very different things as requiring explanation. Elements of one way of thinking through physical problems, based on statics, which is the predominant model, come into conflict with elements generated by quite a different way of thinking through the problems. This arose, for example, where the kinematics that Descartes needed to resolve a question, and the statical concepts in terms of which he tried to pursue the resolution, were in conflict, so that when he should have been

---

[16] Descartes, *Œuvres*, ii. 74.

thinking (kinematically) in terms of inertia he was in fact thinking (statically) in terms of equilibrium, and when he should have been thinking (kinematically) in terms of how unequal bodies behave when they collide, he was actually thinking (statically) in terms of how unequal bodies behave when they are placed on a balance.

## THE QUANTIFICATION OF MOTION

Galileo's interests had traditionally been in mechanics, and although these interests slipped into the background between 1608 and 1630, as he pursued his optical and physical defence of heliocentrism, there was a continuous project investigating mechanical problems generally and free fall in particular from as early as 1586 to the *Discorsi* of 1637.[17] In the long run, the *Discorsi* turns out to be even more pivotal for the development of natural philosophy in the seventeenth century than the cosmology developed by Descartes.[18] Yet in one respect, it was the result of a failure, deeply felt, on Galileo's part: the failure to develop a dynamics that might replace that of Aristotle. The inability of a radically revised version of a *Mechanica* model of statics and hydrostatics to provide the required new foundations for dynamics forced him to abandon the search for a dynamics, and instead to explore a purely descriptive—but quantitative—treatment of motion: kinematics. Yet this work turned out to be a watershed. Above all, it turned out to supply a route to dynamics that was spectacularly successful, overcoming many fundamental problems that had dogged the development of hydrostatical cosmology.

In the Third and Fourth Days of the *Discorsi,* Galileo provides the first modern full-scale kinematical treatment of motion. Three cases are singled out for attention: motion of uniform speed, naturally accelerated motion, and projectile motion. Here, kinematics is translated into practical mathematics: the treatment is thoroughly geometrical and thoroughly quantitative.[19] Space and time are the variables, and motion is treated purely in terms of change of spatial location in time, contrary to the Aristotelian view, where motion is an irreducible reality, and time merely a mental abstraction from motion. Unlike his treatment of hydrostatics, Galileo's construction of a kinematics simply dispenses with Aristotelian natural philosophy. Moreover, the placing of mechanics, in this case kinematics, at the centre of things robs matter theory of any controlling role in the formulation of basic categories which then constrain one's investigation. It is not just Aristotelian matter theory that plays no role in this investigation, but also a micro-corpuscular mechanist matter theory.

The treatment of kinematics is highly systematic, moving from the basic cases to ones of greater complexity. In the case of naturally accelerated motions, for example, Galileo begins with free fall, then proceeds to motion on a frictionless inclined plane,

---

[17] The continuity of interests is brought out well in Drake, *Galileo at Work.*

[18] This is despite the fact that the *Discorsi* was not circulated widely or rapidly, and as late as 1671 was not widely known. See Thorndike, *A History of Magic and Experimental Science*, vii. 44.

[19] Elements of the traditional treatment in terms in 'intensive magnitudes' do intrude into Galileo's account, but they are completely transformed: see Clavelin, *The Natural Philosophy of Galileo*, 278–98.

motion along a frictionless horizontal or inclined plane after free fall, and determination of the swiftest line of descent. The treatment of free fall follows on naturally from the account of uniform motion, establishing a direct relation between time and speed, so that a uniformly accelerated motion—in which we envisage a new increment of speed being added at every instant to the speed the body already has at that instant—is characterized as one in which equal increments of speed are added in equal increments of time.[20] Galileo can then proceed to establish a number of fundamental theorems. Theorem I demonstrates that in uniformly accelerated motion starting from rest, any distance traversed by the body is equal to the distance that would be traversed in the same time by a body moving at a uniform rate whose speed was halfway between that of the greatest and the least speed of the uniformly accelerating body. Theorem II, a key result, shows that in uniformly accelerated motion, distances traversed are proportional to the squares of the times.[21] Theorem III moves to the case of motion on an inclined plane, demonstrating that the times of descent of a body falling from a particular height and falling along an inclined plane from that height stand to each other as the length of the vertical and the length of the plane.[22] He then proceeds to the times of descent on planes of equal length but unequal inclination, and on planes of unequal length and inclination, before moving to a systematic study of inclined planes inscribed in circles, starting with a demonstration that bodies on any inclined planes whose vertical runs through the centre of a circle, and whose apex touches the circumference of that circle, will have equal times of descent.

The kinematics of the Third Day of the *Discorsi* deals with uniform motion and uniformly accelerated motions. The kinematics of the Fourth Day looks at what happens when we combine these two, in particular when we analyse a motion into a vertically downwards uniformly accelerated component and a horizontal uniform component. Theorem I of the Fourth Day, for example, deals with the question of horizontal projection, telling us that the curve described by a body when it descends with a motion compounded from uniform horizontal motion and a uniformly accelerated motion, is a semiparabola.[23] We shall be looking below at how Huygens extended the results of the Third Day in his treatment of the isochronous pendulum, and at the very different way in which Hooke and Newton extended the results of the Fourth Day in their investigations of centripetal force. Our principal concern will not be with kinematics as a practical-mathematical discipline, however, but with its standing as part of a natural-philosophical enterprise. It is this latter question that will be the focus of our discussion of Huygens, Hooke, and Newton. The importance of Galileo's kinematics is not just that it provided the skeleton on which a dynamics would be built, but also that his attempt to vindicate his project in kinematics against the charge that he was merely dealing with mathematical idealizations was a watershed in the development of a quantitative natural philosophy. More than any other development, it pointed the way to how one might connect practical mathematics with natural philosophy in a manner that bypasses matter-theoretical considerations.

[20] Galileo, *Two New Sciences*, trans. Stillman Drake (Madison, 1974), 154–62.
[21] Ibid. 166–7.        [22] Ibid. 175–7.        [23] Ibid. 221–2.

In order to subject the problem of projectile motion to the kind of mathematical analysis he offers, for example, Galileo had to make three assumptions. First, he had to assume that the tendency of bodies to fall to the centre of the earth can be ignored, so that they can be treated as following trajectories perpendicular to the earth's surface which, as a second assumption, he had to treat as being a true horizontal, not the surface of a sphere. Without these assumptions, as he realized, the trajectory of a projectile would cease to be parabolic, and mathematically speaking would be too complex to handle.[24] The third assumption was that the resistance of the medium could be ignored, and this is the one I want to focus on. It is far more contentious than the others, and requires a completely different kind of vindication, one that holds the key to the defence of a mathematical natural philosophy more generally. The representative of Aristotelianism in the dialogue, Simplicio, puts the point in these terms:

Besides, in my opinion it is impossible to remove the impediment of the medium so that this will not destroy the equability of the transverse motion and the rule of acceleration for falling heavy things. All these difficulties [namely, all three assumptions] make it improbable that anything demonstrated from such fickle assumptions can ever be verified in actual experiments.[25]

Galileo presented his kinematics in the form of mathematical descriptions of what happens in a void. Now the motion of bodies in a void is something we never experience and something to which we have no direct access. The motions of bodies in resisting media, by contrast, are something we regularly experience, yet these motions differ from the motions those same bodies would undergo in a void. Galileo's principle of free fall, Theorem II of the Third Day, for example, tells us that all bodies undergo a uniform acceleration in a void, but this is manifestly not the case in a resisting medium. At first sight, therefore, the principle appears to suffer from two drawbacks: it appears to tell us something about a situation that may never occur, and it appears not to tell us about situations that do normally occur. Hence there seem to be problems both about the relevance of the law and about whether it could receive any evidential support. Since we do not experience bodies falling in a void, for example, we cannot arrive at Galileo's law in any straightforward inductive way. On the other hand, since, if the law holds, its truth is contingent—bodies may just as easily have fallen at different rates in a void, or may have fallen with an unaccelerated or non-uniformly accelerated motion—it is impossible that *a priori* arguments will lead us to the law. To maintain that the law is a hypothesis open to empirical tests is of no real help either. First, the problem simply reappears at a different level. The situation described in the law does not naturally occur and cannot be experimentally induced, so in what way is it open to empirical test? And, even if the situation could somehow be experimentally induced, that would still leave the problem of how the law could be at all relevant to the case of bodies falling in resisting media. Second, the presumption behind the hypothetical construal is that the theory itself is somehow developed at a purely conceptual level and then tested empirically to determine whether it is true or not. But as we follow through Galileo's own justification of his procedure, we

---

[24] Ibid. 222–3.    [25] Ibid. 223.

see that empirical questions, and particularly experiment, are an integral part of the process, not added extras. This justification consists in an investigation of the relations that hold between a body falling in a void and that body falling in a resisting medium. Galileo took the fall of bodies in a resisting medium as his starting point and then described a series of experiments, including thought-experiments, designed to decide what factors are operative in determining the rate of fall of a body and how these factors operate.[26]

He dealt first with the traditional Aristotelian view that rate of fall is directly proportional to absolute weight. He had two arguments against this. The first was empirical: if two bodies made of the same material but of different absolute weights are dropped simultaneously from the top of a tower to the ground, they arrive at the ground simultaneously. The second was a thought experiment. If we drop, say, two lead spheres of different weights, then on the Aristotelian account the heavier will fall faster. But, suppose we tie the spheres together. The slower one would then surely slow down the faster one, and the faster one would speed up the slower, so that the resultant speed would be somewhere between the two original speeds. But the aggregate absolute weight is greater than the absolute weight of the heavier body. Hence, rate of fall cannot be directly proportional to absolute weight. Now Aristotle had also held that the rate of fall is inversely proportional to the density of the medium. Against this another thought experiment is proposed. If we let the density ratio of water to air be $n:1$, where $n$ is greater than 1 (since the specific weight of water is greater than that of air), and take a body which falls in air but floats in water (e.g. a wooden sphere), and say that this has a rate of fall of one unit in air, then it would follow that it has a rate of fall of $1/n$ units in water. But, we have already said that it floats; that is, it would not continue to move in the same direction but at a lesser rate in water, but would move in the opposite direction. So rate of fall cannot be inversely proportional to the density of the medium.

Next, Galileo made an important generalization. Instead of thinking simply in terms of rate of fall determined with respect to one body in two media or with respect to two bodies in the one medium, he considered the case of any body in any medium. First, he described an experiment that shows that the ratio between the rates of fall of bodies is not the same as the ratio of their specific weights. Gold and lead, which fall at approximately the same rate in air, behave quite differently in mercury, the former sinking, the latter rising to the surface. What this indicates is that differences in rate of fall of bodies diminishes as the density of the medium decreases. This prompted Galileo to ask what would happen in the limiting case of a void: he raised the possibility that in such a case the rate of fall of all bodies would be equal. But, until we knew the precise connection between speed, specific weight, and resistance, we would not be able to establish this. He therefore proposed an experiment in which the buoyancy effect of the medium—the ratio between the specific weight of the body and that of the medium—could be distinguished. The problem was to determine precisely what effect this ratio has on rate of fall. He compared the buoyancy effect

[26] Galileo, *Two New Sciences*, trans. Stillman Drake (Madison, 1974), 65–108.

of two media (air and water) on two bodies (ebony and lead). Given the specific weights of these substances, the buoyancy effect could easily be calculated. It turned out that it varies much more radically than the specific weight of the body: if we let the specific weights of air, water, ebony, and lead, be 1, 800, 1,000, and 10,000 respectively, then it turns out that whereas the buoyancy effect of air has a negligible effect on rates of fall of ebony and lead, the buoyancy effect of water on ebony is huge (it loses four-fifths of its effective weight) whereas its effect on lead is very small (less than one-tenth). It is the specific weight *ratios* that determine rate of fall, not the specific weights themselves. Since a void has no specific weight it cannot bear a ratio relation to the specific weight of the falling body; that is, this ratio, which is what determines differences in the rate of fall, cannot be operative in the case of a void, and so we must conclude that all bodies—whatever their specific weight—fall in a void with the same 'degree of speed' (or, as it will subsequently turn out, degree of uniformly accelerated motion). This conclusion is particularly important since on the basis of the equality of rates of fall of all bodies in a void we can proceed, at least in principle, to calculate the differences in speeds between any two bodies in any media by determining the amount by which the theoretical speed in a void will be diminished by comparing the specific weight of bodies with that of the media. To this end, Galileo carried out (largely unsuccessful) experiments to measure the specific weight of air.

There remains one problem. Bodies falling in media do not in fact accelerate uniformly. Neither specific weight nor the buoyancy effect can account for this since they are both constant (the latter being a constant for any particular body and any particular medium). This led Galileo to invoke a form of resistance to fall which is distinct from the buoyancy effect: the friction effect. The friction effect increases with the acceleration of the body since larger and larger amounts of resisting medium have to be traversed, and equilibrium is reached when the body ceases to accelerate because of friction. This state of equilibrium occurs much earlier in rarer bodies, not because the friction effect bears a direct relation to specific weight, but because the buoyancy effect is much greater in bodies of lower density and hence their motion is already greatly retarded.[27] For this reasoning to go through, however, two things have to be shown: first, that the friction effect is greater for rarer bodies; second, that it increases with speed. In order to show the first we need to isolate the friction effect experimentally from the buoyancy effect. Free fall does not allow us to do this. Galileo suggested rolling two bodies, one of cork and one of lead, down a plane which is gently inclined so as to make the motions as slow as possible and thereby to reduce the buoyancy effect. The trouble here is that the more gentle the incline the greater the surface friction, which would interfere with our isolating the friction effect (which is quite distinct from surface friction since it is an effect of the medium). He resolved these difficulties by proposing an ingenious experiment in which a cork and a lead sphere are suspended on threads of equal length and set in oscillation. The periods of oscillation remain identical for both spheres but in the case of the cork sphere the

[27] See the discussion in Paul Lawrence Rose, 'Galileo's Theory of Ballistics', *British Journal for the History of Science* 4 (1968), 156–9.

amplitude of swing is considerably reduced very quickly. This cannot be due to the greater specific weight of the lead causing it to move faster: we can begin the experiment by swinging the cork through a greater arc so that it initially moves faster but the same thing will happen eventually. Moreover, since the buoyancy effect is simply the specific weight ratio, it cannot be due to this either. It must therefore be due to the friction effect. Finally, all that remains to be shown is that the friction effect increases with speed. Again no direct experiment on freely falling bodies is possible because of the great distances that would be involved and the difficulties in measurement that would ensue. Hence the consequence that bodies projected at artificially high speeds will be retarded until they reach their natural maximum speed for that medium is of crucial importance, since an experimental situation in which this can be tested can be realized in a relatively easy and straightforward, if somewhat inexact, way. We simply fire a gun vertically downwards from a great height and measure the penetration of the bullet into the ground. We then fire the gun close to the ground and measure that penetration. The first is less than the second, which means that the bullet has been retarded.

In sum, Galileo showed, by means of a series of actual experiments and thought experiments, that rate of fall bears a complex relation to specific weight, buoyancy effect, and friction effect. By determining exactly how these factors are related to one another he was able to determine what happens when the medium is removed entirely, and this forms the content of his law of fall. It is this that secures that the law is not a mathematical abstraction or an idealization, but something that connected directly with a set of experiments and observations, as well as conceptual and mathematical arguments.

To understand the full importance of this procedure, we need to focus more closely on what exactly Galileo's law of fall tells us. It is not merely a description of what happens in one particular circumstance—fall in a void—but a description of whatever is common to all cases of free fall. What is especially significant about the case of fall in a void is that the only factors affecting the rate of fall are those that are common to all cases of fall, and fall in a void is unique in this respect since in every other case of fall there are other factors operative that are not common to every instance of fall. Thus we can state the law in two ways, as maintaining that the component of motion common to all instances of fall is a uniformly accelerated motion ($S_1$) and as maintaining that all bodies fall at the same uniformly accelerated rate in a void ($S_2$). The two statements of the law refer to the same situation, but they identify it in different ways: they provide different routes to it, as it were. This is an important part of what Galileo established. The series of experiments that we have looked at takes us from $S_1$ to $S_2$. Galileo needed to do this because $S_1$, which is the form of the law naturally suggested by purely conceptual and mathematical considerations, has a clear meaning, but it is not obvious how we could establish whether it were true or not. $S_2$ by contrast is something that we can associate with an empirically determinate mode of presentation. By itself, $S_1$ remains within the realm of mathematics, and its empirical significance is at best obscure. Empirically, we don't know where to start if we are merely told that the component of fall common to all instances of fall is a particular kind of motion. If we can show that $S_1$ refers to the same situation as $S_2$, however, then we can provide the law with determinate empirical content. It enables us to associate $S_1$ with a set of empirical procedures by which its truth can be determined, since we know that the non-universal features of fall will arise only in fall in resisting media, and the factors operative in this can be determined empirically. So what we have to do is to transform $S_1$ into $S_2$. Experiment has an absolutely crucial role to play in this enterprise, a role which, because it is not simply concerned with confirmation and falsification, has often been overlooked. And the role that it plays is that of connecting a mathematically conceived mechanics with an empirically regulated natural philosophy. It makes the vital connection that had eluded everyone else, whether in the 'mixed mathematics' or Cartesian traditions of dynamically driven statics or in the various mechanist traditions, and which will establish mechanics as a natural-philosophical discipline.

Galileo's move from the project of his early *De motu* to the *Discorsi*, which was the outcome of fifty years of reflection on mechanical problems, is indicative of a fundamental shift in thinking about mechanics. The account of motion in *De motu* is dynamic, invoking the forces responsible for motion and trying to give an account of these in terms derived from hydrostatics. After *De motu*, Galileo abandoned the hydrostatic approach to dynamics and it never again acted as a model for his dynamics. He was never able to provide a viable dynamic theory, and in his most basic mature treatment of the nature of motion, the *Discorsi*, he eschewed dynamics altogether: where forces entered the picture they entered it as the resultants of motion—such as the friction caused by a body moving through a resisting medium—rather than the causes of motion. His treatment of motion was purely kinematic.

There are a number of reasons for this shift from a hydrostatically modelled dynamics to a kinematics, and Galileo gradually realized that his hydrostatic account in *De motu* could not work. In *De motu*, as we have seen, he had argued that the solution to the problem of free fall lay in substituting specific weight for absolute weight, maintaining that the rate of fall of a body is directly proportional to its specific weight and inversely proportional to the specific weight of the medium through which it travels. But it gradually became evident that things were not so simple. If the proportionality were as *De motu* maintains, we would expect the proportions at which two bodies of different specific weights fall in one medium to be reflected in their rates of fall in a different medium. But as Galileo discovered, this does not happen.

What he came up with in the *Discorsi* was a completely different kind of explanation of free fall and projectile motion to that he had offered in *De motu*. Motion was not analysed in terms of a balance of forces but in terms of components into which the motion could be resolved, and the most fundamental component in the case of a freely falling body was its uniformly accelerated motion, because this is the only universal component in free fall. His starting point was now the fall of a body in a void, that is, in the complete absence of a medium. In other words, the medium is now no longer constitutive of the physical problem: it is not seen as something that facilitates or causes motion in some cases (such as the upward motion of a light body in a relatively dense fluid), impeding it in others (the slow fall of a heavy body in a dense medium). Rather, it is seen exclusively in terms of the resistance it offers to motion.

Galileo's later kinematics conflicted with his early hydrostatically modelled dynamics because they picked out completely different features of the physical situation as being significant. Both tried to deal with the problem of the behaviour of a body falling in a medium by construing it in terms of a more fundamental or general case where the underlying physical issues could be identified and analysed more clearly. The hydrostatic model led to the situation being generalized to the motion of bodies in fluids, whether this motion was upwards or downwards. The kinematic model led to the search for a component of motion that was common to all cases of free fall, and then an examination of how the action of this component was modified with the addition of other variables. The role of the medium was part of the condition of the problem in the first case. But in the second case, it was explicitly absent: what was identified there as holding the key to the understanding of free fall was the case where the basic physical features of the situation were to be explored by asking how a body behaves in an inert empty space.

## MECHANICS AS KINEMATICS

By the middle of the seventeenth century kinematics was beginning to look self-sufficient, no longer the poor relation of dynamics. The most significant developments in this respect were due to Christiaan Huygens.[28] His father, Constantijn Huygens, had been one of Descartes' staunchest allies and supporters during the 1640s, and Christiaan, whose prodigious mathematical and mechanical skills (he and Hooke were the two most skilled experimenters with air pumps, and quite possibly the only two people who could get them to work with any consistency) were evident from an early age, had received encouragement and advice from Descartes. His project can be seen being primarily influenced by Galilean kinematics and the 'rationalized' system of natural philosophy that Descartes set out in his *Principia*. I say 'rationalized' because, as we saw in Chapter 8, the *Principia* reformulates the natural philosophy developed fifteen years earlier in terms of 'clear and distinct ideas'.[29] This reformulation had the effect of disguising the dynamic origins of many of the ideas, and of presenting the exercise as one in kinematics. Kinematics should be quantifiable, but the only quantified part of the exercise was the laws of collision. These were so idiosyncratic, however, that they were accepted by no one, and Huygens realized at an

---

[28] Their historical significance would have been greater had Huygens published his results at the time of their discovery: as it was, almost all were first made public years after they had been developed, and indeed many of them appeared only in the *Opuscula posthuma*, ed. B. de Volder and B. Fullenius (Leiden, 1703).

[29] Although there were those (such as Gassendi) who mocked Descartes' notion of clarity and distinctness, there were influential thinkers who took it very seriously, notably Huygens, Spinoza, and Malebranche. Huygens' attitude is evident even many years after he had abandoned all the main tenets of Cartesian natural philosophy. In a letter to Bayle of 26 February 1693, after telling Bayle that he could no longer accept anything in Cartesian physics and metaphysics, he remarks that the great thing about Descartes' philosophy was that what he said could be understood, by contrast with other philosophers, 'with their qualities, substantial forms, and intentional species': Christiaan Huygens, *Œuvres complètes de Christiaan Hugens*, ed. La sociéte hollandaise des sciences (22 vols, The Hague, 1888–1950), x. 403.

early stage that any reformulation of them was going to have to be radical, and indeed was going to have to go to the core of Descartes' project. This reformulation retained certain doctrines that had always been central to the Cartesian programme, such as that of centrifugal force, as well as some that had resulted largely from its rewriting in terms of clear and distinct ideas, notably the doctrine of spatial relativity. We shall look in turn at his reformulation of the laws of collision, which resulted from an attempt to overcome the inconsistencies in Descartes' rules of collision, at his account of isochrony, which involves an ingenious development of Galileo's account of uniformly accelerated motion and is a model of how to pursue kinematics in a Galilean mould, and finally his account of centrifugal force, which combines Galilean kinematics with Cartesian cosmology. These projects demonstrate the explanatory power of kinematics, and help consolidate the idea that kinematics might actually hold the key to mechanics, banishing the forces so awkward not only for Descartes' project in the *Principia*, but for any other mechanist programme, such as those of Hobbes and Gassendi.

As we have seen, Descartes' rules of collision—motivated as they are by statical and optical as well as kinematic considerations—are not mutually consistent. Rule 4 tells us that a collinear collision between a smaller moving body and a larger stationary one leaves the larger body unaffected, the smaller one retaining its speed but rebounding, whereas Rule 5 tells us that a collinear collision between a smaller stationary body and a larger one moving towards it results in the motion of the two bodies in the direction of the original motion but with a speed less than that of the original moving body (because this speed is now distributed over two bodies). Given Descartes' account of motion in his *Principia*, speeds are always relative speeds, which means that the situation described in Rule 4 should be redescribable in terms of Rule 5, but it is not.

In *De motu corporum ex percussione*,[30] the first version of which was completed in the mid-1650s,[31] Huygens traces the problem back to a fundamental inconsistency in Descartes' principles. Descartes advocated both relativity of motion and conservation of motion, and what Huygens realized is that these are incompatible with one another. Huygens understood the relativity of motion in terms of the indistinguishability of uniform motions from one another and from rest, and this is in effect Galilean relativity rather than the Cartesian principle that whether we say something is moving or not is just relative to what contiguous bodies we designate as being stationary. Nevertheless, if Cartesian relativity holds then the milder form of relativity postulated by Huygens does. The first task is to clarify just what the adoption of relativity implies for collision.

Huygens imagined a boat moving smoothly along a canal. The experiment is very similar to that which Galileo imagined in his treatment of free fall, in which a ship passes under a bridge and bodies are dropped from the edge of the stationary bridge

---

[30] Huygens, *Œuvres*, xvi. 29–91; English trans., which I quote from here, in Richard J. Blackwell, 'Christiaan Huygens' *The Motion of Colliding Bodies*', *Isis* 68 (1977), 574–97, hereafter *The Motion of Colliding Bodies*.

[31] See Huygens, *Œuvres*, xvi, 3–14.

and the mast of the moving ship. In the case Huygens imagined, placed in the boat is a man carrying out experiments with two spherical hard bodies[32] which are suspended by strings from his hands, so that by bringing his hands together he causes the bodies to collide. A second man, who is standing on the shore, joins hands with the first as he passes, so that the two men jointly perform the same operation (Fig. 11.1). Huygens' procedure was to show how, by adjusting the frame of reference, one can account for all cases of equal bodies,[33] before moving on to unequal bodies. The most straightforward case is that of two equal bodies moving towards one another along a line joining their centres with equal speeds, for these rebound with their speeds unchanged. If the boat is moving with the same speed as one of the bodies, then what the man on the shore will see is a moving body colliding with one at rest, the latter being given a motion equal to that the former had before impact.[34] All other cases of equal bodies can then be accommodated to this symmetrical one simply by altering the speed of the boat.

**Figure 11.1**

[32] The seventeenth- and eighteenth-century terminology of collision is often misleading in that the distinction between hard and soft bodies does not exactly correspond to the distinction between elastic and inelastic bodies. Huygens did not consider his hard bodies to be elastic because elasticity is a dynamic notion and he wanted to keep the reasoning kinematic, as we shall see. But the behaviour of Huygens' hard bodies was not at all like the behaviour of Descartes' hard bodies, and the rules he provided are equivalent to the rules for elastic collisions that Wren set out in his 'Lex Naturae de Collisione Corporum', *Philosophical Transactions* 3 (11 January 1669), 867–8. Wren's laws were in response to a request from the Royal Society to investigate impact. Wallis also had a paper published, on the rules of collision for inelastic bodies, but Huygens's paper setting out the rules we are discussing was not published: see Huygens, *Œuvres*, xvi. 173–8.

[33] In Huygens' use of the term, 'equality' is a little closer to equality of mass than Descartes' usage, but it is still thought of in terms of quantity of a homogeneous matter, and so is proportional to volume.

[34] *The Motion of Colliding Bodies*, 575.

In dealing with equal bodies, Huygens postulated, as hypotheses, a principle of rectilinear inertia,[35] a principle of symmetry in the case of equal bodies with equal and opposite velocities, and a principle of relativity of motion.[36] In turning to unequal bodies, he postulated a fourth hypothesis, namely that in a collision between a larger moving body and a stationary smaller one, the former transfers some of its motion to the smaller body. Reversing the states of motion by a simple change of frame of reference, the motion transferred to the smaller body now appears as motion transferred by the smaller to the larger body in impact. In particular, *contra* Descartes, it now becomes clear that total quantity of motion cannot be conserved.[37] In his formulation of the principle of inertia, Descartes had treated speed and direction of motion as first-degree modes and second-degree modes (i.e. modes of modes) respectively, and had therefore needed separate principles covering speed and direction, whereas Huygens' principle of inertia covered uniform rectilinear motion in the one statement. Nevertheless, Huygens did not think in vectorial terms: he distinguished direction and speed, with the result that the quantity of speed, which is just the magnitude of the body times its speed, always has a positive value. Given this, and given relativity of motion, it follows that the quantity of motion is not constant in cases in which only one body reverses direction. Relativity of motion requires that the total quantity of motion is something that may increase or decrease after collision: it will vary with the frame of reference.[38]

Huygens redrafted the treatise on collision many times over a number of years, and as Westfall has noted, with each successive draft, the kinematic content grew at the expense of the dynamic,[39] reference to a *vis collisionis* being replaced by talk of transfer—or, since the transfer is relative to the frame of reference, 'apparent' transfer—of motion. Westfall takes this as an emphasis on those aspects of Descartes' treatment that had been most promising, while minimizing that element that had compromised it, but the matter is a little more complicated. Descartes himself, as we have noted, saw mechanical problems in dynamic terms, thought through largely in concepts derived from hydrostatics, which he then tried to combine with kinematics. Kinematics came to the fore in his attempt to vindicate his mechanics, in the wake of the condemnation of Galileo, in terms of clarity and distinctness, and this imposed a new set of constraints on how he set out his physical theory. What resulted was a multi-layered account in which the kinematics set the expository agenda but where dynamically motivated notions still did much of the real work. In particular, the kinematics often does not make sense in its own terms, and one has to dig down to the dynamical notions—evident in *Le Monde* but largely purged from the *Principia*—to understand what motivated his account. Yet because this is what the formulation of

---

[35] I say *a* principle of inertia because Huygens did not consider whether changes in direction were dynamically on a par with changes in speed.

[36] *The Motion of Colliding Bodies*, 574–5.

[37] Huygens argues that what is conserved is the product of the magnitude of the bodies and the square of the velocity. The question of what is preserved in collision will be the subject of a very protracted debate. See Wilson L. Scott, *The Conflict between Atomism and Conservation theory, 1644–1860* (London, 1970).

[38] *The Motion of Colliding Bodies*, 581–2.

mechanics in terms of clear and distinct ideas turns out to demand, in the *Principia* Descartes does present his basic mechanics as if it were simply a form of kinematics. Just as Malebranche will take the metaphysics of the *Meditationes* and the *Principia* at face value and work to make a consistent system out of it by subordinating everything to its most abstract and programmatic features, in the process producing something really quite novel, so too Huygens took the natural philosophy of the *Principia* and tried to make something consistent out of that by subordinating everything to its most abstract and programmatic features, and similarly, in the process he produced something novel. He tells us, Descartes

should have proposed his system of physics as an essay on what can be said with likelihood in this science, while allowing only mechanical principles.... But in seeking, as he does everywhere, to give the impression that he has found the truth, and in basing it and glorifying it in the wonderful connections set out in his writings, he has provided something which is to the detriment of the progress of philosophy. For those who accept what he says and become his disciples imagine themselves to possess an understanding of the causes of everything that can be known.[40]

One might ask why, given the role that Galilean ideas played in his kinematics, he was so concerned to defend something that looks like a Cartesian programme, especially in the light of the fact that he was in effect advocating not Cartesian relativity but Galilean relativity. The answer must lie in part in the view that, by contrast with the Cartesian programme, the kind of projects that Galileo pursued could not produce a systematic understanding of nature. As far as Huygens was concerned, the Cartesian system, no matter how flawed, provided a set of legitimate guides and constraints within which to pursue a systematic understanding of natural philosophy, something which provided genuine micro-mechanical foundations for natural philosophy: this is, after all, why the study of collision was so important, because collision, at a microscopic level, was what determined the behaviour of all macroscopic physical processes. This is evident in Huygens' response to Newton's prism experiments that we looked at in the previous chapter: only when differences in colours can be traced to differences in underlying motions can he be said to have accounted for colours.[41]

In the course of showing that two bodies whose speeds are inversely proportional to their magnitudes rebound with the same speeds they had before collision, Huygens began to work through the problem in terms of centres of gravity.[42] The principle underlying this had been demonstrated by Torricelli in his *De motu gravium* of 1644.[43] Galileo had stated, but not demonstrated, the principle that the

---

[39] Westfall, *Force in Newton's Physics*, 151.     [40] Huygens, *Œuvres*, x. 405.

[41] He adopts exactly the same attitude to Newton's account of gravity in his *Discours de la cause de la pesanteur* (1690), rejecting the idea that it consisted in attraction, and insisting that it must be explained by motion: *Œuvres*, xxi. 472.

[42] *The Motion of Colliding Bodies*, 585 ff.

[43] Evangelista Torricelli, *De motu gravium naturalitur descendentium et proiectorum libri duo* (Florence, 1644).

degrees of velocity acquired by a body in descending planes of different inclination are equal for equal vertical displacements. Torricelli demonstrated the principle in terms of the general case where bodies are joined (e.g. by a pulley or on a balance), showing, by comparing bodies tied together which lie on unequally inclined planes, that they will move only if their common centre of gravity moves.[44] Torricelli was concerned to flesh out the dynamical implications of Galilean kinematics, but Huygens moved in the opposite direction. His interest in Torricelli's principle was not in connecting up kinematics and statics but in the idea of bodies forming systems, and as a consequence acting as if they were single bodies because the centre of gravity of the system which unites them is what determines their mechanical behaviour.[45] While Torricelli had restricted his attention to vertical motion, Huygens applied it to any inertial motion. Moreover, he realized that the bodies do not have to be physically attached to one another: inertial reference frames act in the same way as a system of physical constraints. In particular, if the bodies recede from the centre of gravity with the same speeds with which they approached it before impact, the centre of gravity is not affected by the collisions and undergoes no change of motion. Simply by manipulating frames of reference, Huygens could show that the centre of gravity of an inertial system of bodies moves uniformly in a straight line before and after impact. Where Galileo and others had appealed to a force of percussion to account for the behaviour of bodies in impact, Huygens needed no such force, nor indeed a force of any kind. Huygens was concerned with bodies that are perfectly hard, and he considered these bodies to be inelastic: their speed is uninterrupted because impact is instantaneous. While Descartes had seen a need to separate speed and direction if the abrupt change of direction was not to mean that the body had to stop and then start again in a different direction, Huygens' analysis indicated that change of direction is merely relative to the frame of reference, and in the frame determined by the centre of gravity of the colliding bodies nothing happens in impact.

This ridding of mechanics of notions of force that could never attain to the clarity and distinctness that the Cartesian reformulation of natural philosophy required, is also evident in Huygens' pathbreaking work on isochrony.[46] The *Horologium oscillatorium* describes the pendulum clock invented by Huygens in late 1656. The clock overcame a number of problems that had been encountered in the proposed use of regulators for clockwork, for their use depended on the isochronism of the pendulum, but the period of the simple pendulum is also determined by amplitude, a dependence that is negligible only in the case of small amplitudes. Huygens

[44] See the discussion in Westfall, *Force in Newton's Physics*, 128–34.

[45] Before he put it to use in kinematics, Huygens explored this principle in the context of Archimedean statics, in the late 1640s: see Alan Gabbey, 'Huygens and Mechanics', in H. J. M. Bos et al., eds, *Studies on Christiaan Huygens* (Lisse, 1980), 166–99: 168.

[46] Huygens, *Œuvres*, xviii. 73–368. English trans.: *The Pendulum Clock or Geometrical Demonstrations Concerning the Motion of Pendula as Applied to Clocks*, trans. Richard J. Blackwell (Ames, Iowa: 1986). See the comprehensive discussion in Yoder, *Unrolling Time*.

therefore set out to determine what path a pendulum bob would have to trace such that its period was not a function of amplitude, and he found this path to be cycloidal. The *Horologium* is divided into four parts, each dealing with a different aspect of the problem. The first deals with the practical matters of construction and use of the pendulum clock. The second is an abstract and technical discussion of oscillation, showing the isochronism of the cycloid. The third is devoted to determining the evolutes of curves—it is the study of the locus of the centres of curvature of a curve—showing what paths a pendulum bob can be made to follow depending on the shape of the cheeks between which it is suspended, and showing in particular that the evolutes of a cycloid are cycloidal arcs. The fourth part looks at the oscillation of a compound pendulum, determining how it is related to that of a simple pendulum.

The second part is that of interest to us, and it can be divided into three main sections. The first (Propositions 1–11) deals with uniformly accelerated motion, building on the work set out in the Third Day of Galileo's *Discorsi*. These propositions describe bodies descending vertically and along inclined planes. Huygens wanted to use these in the analysis of motion along complex curved paths, and in the second section (Propositions 12–20) he provides the geometrical means for resolving such curves into the limits of a series of tangents. Finally, in the third section (Propositions 21–6), he combines the conclusions and techniques of the first two to resolve the cycloid into an infinite number of planes so that it becomes the limit of these planes. This in turn allows him to demonstrate that, for a body sliding under gravity along an inverted cycloid, the time taken to reach the bottom from any point on the curve is $\pi/2$ times the time of free fall through a distance equal to the axis, and therefore the body's oscillations about the lowest point are isochronous. The controlling idea behind this development of a theory of oscillation out of considerations of falling bodies is that of the relation between the period of cycloidal oscillation (or, in the case of small amplitudes, simple oscillation) and time of fall. Just as the period of a cycloidal pendulum varies as the square root of its length, so does the time of fall vary as a function of the square root of vertical distance fallen from rest; and just as the period of oscillation is a function of the square root of gravitational acceleration, so too is the time of fall.

The move to pursue mechanics purely in terms of kinematics is even more in evidence in the *Horologium* than it was in *De motu*. There is a conscious and explicit attempt to suppress dynamical considerations. As Westfall has shown, in the 1659 treatise upon which Part 2 of the *Horologium* is based, there is a good deal more dynamics than in the final version.[47] The final version in fact does get off to a dynamical start, beginning with three explicitly dynamical hypotheses.[48] The first states that, in the absence of gravity and the resistance of the medium, all bodies would continue in any motion they already had without change in speed and in a straight line. The second states that gravity acts in such a way as to impose a motion downwards on any uniform motion the body already has. The third states that these motions can be

---

[47] Westfall, *Force in Newton's Physics*, 159–67.     [48] *The Pendulum Clock*, 33–4.

considered separately and do not impede one another. Proposition 1, which follows these 'hypotheses', is also explicitly dynamical, to the extent of speaking of gravity 'producing' motion and of the force (*vis*) of gravity. The next two propositions, however, derive the relation of speed and time to uniformly accelerated motion in a purely kinematic fashion. Proposition 4, by contrast, offers a dynamical demonstration that speed gained in free fall is such that it will raise that body again to its initial height. But in Proposition 5 Huygens substitutes a kinematic demonstration, which is independent of Proposition 1, of the constancy of the ratio between distances traversed by a falling body in equal consecutive times. The remainder of the first section then proceeds kinematically on the minimal dynamical premisses of acceleration in free fall, and the impossibility of the centre of gravity of a system of bodies rising through the action of gravity.

The dynamics offered in Proposition 4 is quite compatible with the kinematic account that replaces it, suggesting that thinking through the question dynamically was the way in which Huygens had come to the results, but that he was prepared to present these results only in a kinematic form. There are parallels here with the practice of seventeenth-century mathematicians (Newton is an example), who may have used analytic techniques in problem-solving but insisted on presenting these results demonstratively, that is, in synthetic terms.[49] It is worth noting in this respect that in the same year that he published the *Horologium*, we find Huygens giving an explicitly dynamical demonstration that the resisting force (*incitatio*) is proportional to the arc of displacement in a cycloidal pendulum. This work, which would have provided a fitting supplement to Part 2 of the *Horologium*, is instead found in an unpublished paper on vibrations in springs.[50] Kinematics was not just Huygens' preferred mode of presentation, it was for him the only mode that revealed the basic processes clearly.

When the *Horologium* appeared in 1673, Huygens appended a number of theorems, without proofs, which he had worked out fourteen years earlier in an account of centrifugal force, *De vi centifuga*. This work was originally motivated by the problems in establishing, by experimental means, a value for the constant of gravitational acceleration for bodies falling in a void.[51] This was a very frustrating empirical exercise. Mersenne, who seems to have been the first to realize that the isochrony of the pendulum provided the most accurate basis for timing the fall of bodies, was perplexed by the fact that he found that a pendulum falls through 90° faster than a body falls the same vertical distance downwards.[52] On Mersenne's experiments, given Galileo's times-squared law, a body should fall 14 feet from rest in one second, whereas Riccioli's experiments gave a figure of 15 feet in one second.[53] After three increasingly elaborate attempts, Huygens abandoned the use of experiments to establish an

---

[49] See the comprehensive discussion in Niccolò Guicciardini, *Reading the Principia: The Debate on Newton's Mathematical Methods for Natural Philosophy from 1687–1736* (Cambridge, 1999).

[50] Huygens, *Œuvres*, xviii. 489–95. See Westfall, *Force in Newton's Physics*, 180–1.

[51] See Yoder, *Unrolling Time*, ch. 3.

[52] Marin Mersenne, *Cogitata physico-mathematica* (Paris, 1644), 38–9. Cf. idem, *Harmonie Vniverselle* (3 vols, Paris, 1636), i. *Mouvement des corps*, Book 2, 131–8.

[53] See the discussion in Alexandre Koyré, *Metaphysics and Measurement* (London, 1968), 98–110.

accurate value, and considered indirect means, notably by exploring the connection between weight and centrifugal force, telling us that 'the weight of a body is the same as the striving of matter, equal to it and moved very swiftly, to move from the centre'.[54]

This relationship between weight and centrifugal force stands at the centre of *De vi centifuga*, which deals with circular motion. Its principal aim was to provide an exact—or, in Cartesian terminology, clear and distinct—account of one of the central notions of Cartesian cosmology, centrifugal force (the term was coined by Huygens). As we have seen, centrifugal force is the notion that connects Descartes's basic mechanics and matter theory with his cosmology, and it does more work than anything else in his cosmology, being the key ingredient not only in his account of both the spacing and the stability of planetary orbits, but also in his theory of the transmission of light from the sun. In Cartesian cosmology, there is an intimate connection between centrifugal force and weight. When a body falls under its own weight, it must displace the more subtle matter in its path, forcing it upwards around the falling body. In other words, weight is something to be characterized in terms of the relation between the body and the surrounding medium, something that derives from Descartes' hydrostatic model for cosmology. But on this account, as Huygens realized, there are two outstanding problems: the rotation of the terrestrial vortex should cause falling bodies to be carried horizontally, and such bodies should fall not towards the centre of the earth but towards its axis of rotation.[55] Only an analysis of centrifugal force could resolve these questions, and to mimic the action of centrifugal force in a vortex Huygens suggested an ingenious experiment in which a wax ball is placed between two parallel threads which pass through the centre of a circular pan of water at the surface, so that the ball, which is on the surface of the water, is constrained in its motion. The pan is then rotated, but because of the constraints imposed by the threads, the ball is prevented from rotating with the water, and instead it moves to the centre where it remains. What has happened is that the rotation of the fluid had created a centripetal force, enabling Huygens to provide an experimental foundation for a vortical account of gravity.

In setting out to provide an exact account of centrifugal force, Huygens analysed it in terms of kinematics. On this analysis, centrifugal force turns out to be in many ways a mirror image of weight. As he put it in 1690, in his *Discours de la cause de la pensateur*,

The striving to move away from the centre is thus a constant effect of circular motion. And although this effect seems to be directly opposed to that of weight . . . this same striving that circulating bodies have to move away from the centre is the same thing that causes other bodies to move towards the centre . . . Thus it is in this that the weight of bodies truly consists, and it can be described in this way: it is the striving of the fluid matter—rotating in a circle around

[54] Huygens, *Œuvres*, xvii. 276.

[55] The problems had been raised at a meeting of the Académie Royale in November 1669, at which Huygens, Roberval, Mariotte, and Perrault were active participants: see Aiton, *The Vortex Theory of Planetary Motions*, 75–84.

the centre of the earth in all directions—to move away from the centre, and to push into its place the bodies that do not participate in this motion.[56]

If one suspends a stone from a cord one experiences a vertical tension downwards on the string, a tension that can be analysed in terms of statics in a straightforward way. If one now rotates the stone in a circle in the horizontal plane, one feels a similar tension, radially outwards. Huygens' intuition in trying to assimilate the second to the first is similar to that of the young Galileo, who thought that the hydrostatic account of why bodies rise in dense fluids could be generalized to enable us to understand why heavy bodies fall in air. But what Huygens draws on to explain centrifugal force is not hydrostatics but kinematics. It is kinematics that must show the identity between weight and centrifugal force. The stone's pulling on the cord when it is suspended from it, and its pulling on the cord when it is rotated in a horizontal plane, both result, on Huygens' view, from the tendency of the stone to move in the direction in which it is pulling.

Huygens began *De vi centifuga* with a summary of his general argument. If a body is constrained by a cord to move in a circular path of diameter $d$ on a horizontal gravity-free plane, then the tension on the cord due to the centrifugal tendency will equal the tension that would be exerted by the weight of the body were it suspended freely, if the body travelled the circumference of the circle in the same time that it would fall through the distance $\pi^2 d$.[57] Because the distance traversed in free fall is proportional to the square of the time, it follows, Huygens noted, that a body that moved around the circle in twice the time and maintained the same tension would require a circle with a diameter four times as large.[58] The crux of the argument is this: Let a body be constrained by a cord of radius $AB$ to follow a uniform circular motion along the arc $BD$ (Fig. 11.2), and let the tangent to the circle at $B$ be cut at $C$, the extension of a second radius that passes through $D$. The centrifugal force of the body arises from its rectilinear inertia, and $DC$ measures the distance it would have moved from the circle had it been free to follow this inertial tendency at $B$. When the angle $A$ is small, it is demonstrable that the distance between the circle and the tangent, namely $DC$, increases in proportion to the square of the length of the arc $BD$.[59] Since

---

[56] Huygens, *Œuvres*, xxi. 452, 456.    [57] Ibid. xvi. 303.    [58] Ibid. 304.

[59] Yoder notes that 'Although the derivation by which he arrived at the formula is not recorded, later propositions in both the first draft and the revision of *De Vi Centrifuga* provide the material for a reconstruction based on the proposition's accompanying diagram. He achieves the quantification by mathematically superimposing a parabola, which represents the path of a falling body that has been projected horizontally, onto a circle, around which the body is moving in a gravity-free situation. From his work in *De Circuli Magnitudine Inventa* (1654), Huygens knew that he could approximate any circle with a companion parabola whose *latus rectum* equals the diameter of a circle. The diagram . . . that accompanies the first proposition of *De Vi Centrifuga* pictures such a circle and its approximating parabola, along with the common tangent line to the one point at which they precisely agree and about which, within an infinitesimal distance on either side, the parabola can be considered to lie along the circle' (*Unrolling Time*, 19–20). I have used the simplified diagram and accompanying discussion in Richard S. Westfall, *The Construction of Modern Science* (Cambridge, 1977), 128–30. Yoder offers a detailed account.

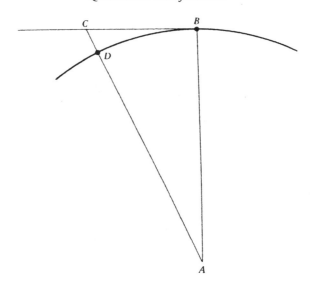

**Figure 11.2**

the angular motion is uniform, the length of the arc provides a measure of time. The conclusion is that centrifugal force is a tendency to motion by which distance would increase as the square of time. In fact, what this means is that the centrifugal tendency of a body would produce an acceleration mathematically identical to what is in effect the force of gravity. This is not the direction in which Huygens was moving, however. It would have required a turn towards dynamics, a turn that Huygens consistently resisted, and one that reflected his attachment to a foundationalist version of Cartesianism. If the paradigm of clarity and distinctness in natural philosophy, kinematics, cannot settle an issue, then appeal to such poorly understood things as forces would not.

## COSMIC DISORDER

The move from geocentrism to heliocentrism was one that had profound repercussions for conceptions of the cosmos. The shift from thinking of planetary orbits in terms of centrifugal force to one in terms of centripetal force was equally momentous, however, and had equally profound consequences. Indeed, in some ways, it was even more radical. The cosmological systems that we have examined up to now all assume that planetary orbits are a fundamental feature of the cosmos. Circular orbits may have to have their centres of rotation moved away from the earth or the sun to account for their observed motions, they may be stretched slightly out of shape, or under the influence of complex interactions between quasi-magnetic forces they may become elliptical, but orbital motion is a fundamental feature of the universe. Kepler, for example, begins his *Astronomia Nova* with these words:

The testimony of ages confirms that the motions of the planets are orbicular. It is an immediate presumption of reason, reflected in experience, that their gyrations are perfect circles.
For among figures it is circles, and among bodies the heavens, that are considered the most
perfect. However, when experience is seen to teach something different to those who pay careful attention, namely, that the planets deviate from a simple circular path, it gives rise to a
powerful sense of wonder, which at length drives men to look into causes. It is just this from
which astronomy arose among men. Astronomy's aim is considered to be to show why the
stars' motions appear to be irregular on earth, despite their being exceedingly well-ordered in
heaven . . . [60]

Before the motion of the firmament as a whole and the motions of the planets were
distinguished, Kepler tells us, the diurnal path of the heavens seemed to be close to
circles, but these were 'seen to be entwined one upon another like a yarn on a ball,
and the circles were for the most part smaller circles of the sphere, rarely the greatest
(such as here [Fig. 11.3] *ABCE, FMNG* cutting the equator *AB* in *CN*), part of them
north and part south of the greatest circle'. The astronomer's task is to unravel the
yarn. If one were to believe that 'the sun really moves through the zodiac in the space
of a year, as Ptolemy and Tycho Brahe believed, he would then have to grant that the
circuits of the three superior planets [Saturn, Jupiter, and Mars] through the ether-
ial space, composed as they are of several motions, are real spirals, not (as before) in
the manner of balled up yarn, with spirals set side by side, but more like the shape of
*panis quadragesimalis* [pretzels], as in [Fig. 11.4]'.[61] It seems clear to Kepler that one
could not prefer an account what generated such complex orbits to the Copernican
one. Note that what is at issue here is the simple motion of planets that suffer no
perturbations through interactions with the sun or with one another. We have seen
that, for Kepler, the circular motion of the sun carries the planets around in circular
orbits, but perturbations in the orbits of planets caused by the quasi-magnetic influence of the sun result in elliptical rather than circular orbits. The point here is that
the simple curve is taken to be one's starting point, and the complexities are modifications of this curve. This is equally true of the other defender of elliptical orbits,
Borelli. In his treatise on the Medicean satellites of 1666 he postulated rays emanating from a rotating sun which keep the planets in elliptical orbits, the stability of the
orbit arising from an equilibrium between the centripetal force by which the body
would move to the central sun if unimpeded, and the centrifugal force arising from
its rotation.[62] The problem was to calculate the forces by which the planets strive to

[60] Kepler, *New Astronomy*, 115.
[61] Ibid. 119. One explicitly contrary view is to be found in the matter-theoretical approach to
cosmology, e.g. in Bacon, who in his *De Augmentis Scientiarum*, in discussing the Idols of the Tribe,
tells us that the human mind presupposes and assigns to nature greater equality and uniformity
than there really is, taking as his example the contrivance of mathematicians in making all heavenly
bodies move in perfect circles, instead of, say, spirals: *Works* i. 644/iv. 432. See the discussion in
Blumenberg, *The Genesis of the Copernican World*, 40–3.
[62] Giovanni Alfonso Borelli, *Theoricae mediceorum planetarum ex causis physicis deductae*
(Florence, 1666). See the discussion in Koyré, *The Astronomical Revolution*, 467–527.

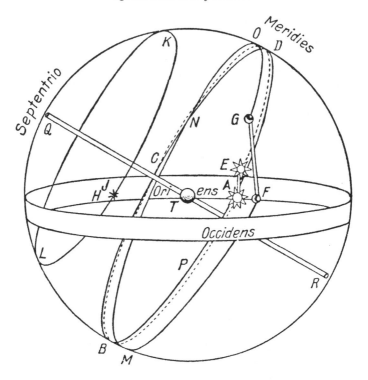

**Figure 11.3**

leave their pre-given orbits. The Cartesian system of vortices is premissed on the same assumption. Planets and their satellites have no alternative but to rotate, because rotation around central suns is a fundamental feature of the cosmos: if it were absent all motion would soon come to a stop and there would be no cosmos at all, just a block of matter. Given orbital rotation, the mechanical problem was to explain the stability of planetary and lunar orbits. There is no issue of why there are orbits in the first place: the very idea of a planet brings with it that of an orbit. Whatever disputes there might be over the shape or centres of rotation of planetary orbits, or the causes of the stability of these orbits, the orbit itself is taken as a wholly unproblematic given. The orbit is a paradigm of natural equilibrium, of a perfectly balanced motion.

Before the end of 1679, this is how almost everyone—including Newton,[63] despite his treatment of orbits in terms of centrifugal force—saw the problem. Hooke

---

[63] See D. T. Whiteside, 'Newton's Early Thoughts on Planetary Motion: A Fresh Look', *British Journal for the History of Science* 2 (1964), 117–37; idem, 'Before the *Principia*: The Maturing of Newton's Thoughts on Dynamical Astronomy, 1664–1684', *Journal for the History of Astronomy* 1 (1970), 5–19; and J. Bruce Brackenridge, *The Key to Newton's Dynamics: The Kepler Problem and the Principia* (Berkeley, 1995), 17–24.

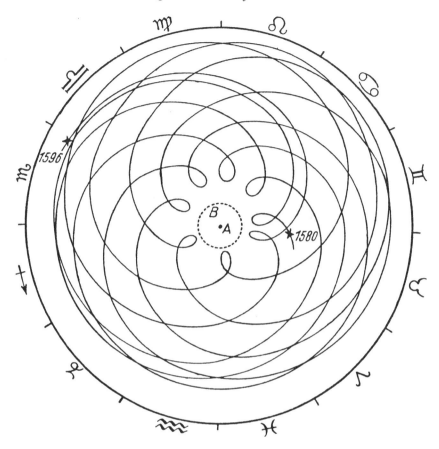

**Figure 11.4**

was the exception, and the only person to have put anything in print on the matter, although Wren, almost certainly under Hooke's influence, may also have been thinking in these terms by 1677.[64] Yet Galileo's analysis of parabolic trajectories in the Fourth Day of the *Discorsi*, in terms of a combination of a uniform rectilinear motion and an attractive accelerating force exercised by the earth, suggests that planetary orbits do not have to be taken as primitive: they are in principle analysable into components. It turned out that this analysis was very difficult to achieve in practice, and we shall touch on this question, the so-called 'Kepler problem' of determining the force required to maintain elliptical motion around a focal force centre, in the next section. A more immediately pressing question, one I now want to turn to, is why

---

[64] See Richard S. Westfall, *Never At Rest: A Biography of Isaac Newton* (Cambridge, 1980), 402–3.

no one other than Hooke actually took up this path before the end of 1679. Given the great influence of Galilean kinematics on natural philosophers such as Huygens and Newton, and given the key role of resolving motions into their components in this kinematics, something at which Huygens and Newton excelled, it is, at least on the face of it, puzzling that they did not take what seems a next logical step in the Galilean programme: why should the trajectory of an orbiting body be any different from any other curved trajectory?[65] Moreover, when the move was made, it was made by someone who was not particularly well equipped to follow it through. Hooke, though one of the most creative and ingenious thinkers of the seventeenth century, was not a creative or outstanding mathematician, and never got past the first step. Indeed, he was preoccupied by questions of force, and did not work in the kinematic tradition of thinking about mechanics in which Galileo's *Discorsi* played such a predominant role.

In November 1679, Hooke wrote to Newton asking him 'particularly if you will let me know your thoughts of that of compounding the celestiall motions of the planetts of a direct motion by the tangent & an attractive motion towards the central body.'[66] What Hooke was proposing is momentous. His point is that a body follows a rectilinear motion if unconstrained, and consequently if it follows a closed orbit, it must be deflected from its rectilinear motion by some cause, and he noted the attraction of the sun as a possible cause. This transforms the problem of orbital motion into one of understanding, not how a body strives to leave its orbit and what prevents it from doing so, but what constrains a body, which would otherwise be undergoing a rectilinear motion, to travel in an orbital motion in the first place. This is not just a technical matter. As Gal notes, Hooke's model 'portrays the planetary orbit as an *effect*—the outcome of independent, seemingly contingent physical processes'.[67] No longer are planetary orbits something fundamental and God-given, kept in place by an equally God-given balance between inward and outward tendencies. Kepler's vision of the nature of astronomy, a vision whereby the falsity of Ptolemaic and Tychonic geocentric systems was evident from the lack of regularity that planetary orbits turned out to have on their account, now appears decidedly question-begging. On the model that Hooke was proposing, there is no reason to assume that planetary motions must be regular or even orbital: if this is what they turn out to be, then this requires explanation in more fundamental terms. But despite having considered the question for over a decade,[68] Hooke had got no further with the solution by the time of his letter to Newton of 1679. Newton remarked in his reply to

[65] See Ofer Gal, *Meanest Foundations and Nobler Superstructures* (Dordrecht, 2002), 191–2.

[66] Hooke to Newton, 24 November 1670; Newton, *Correspondence*, i. 297.

[67] Gal, *Meanest Foundations*, 21.

[68] It should be said that Hooke always took upon himself huge amounts of work, more than he could manage, and that from 1666 onwards he was helping Wren redesign and rebuild London in the wake of the Great Fire, so it's not that he did not have his mind on innumerable other things at the same time. See Lisa Jardine, *The Curious Life of Robert Hooke* (London, 2003).

Hooke that he had not thought about natural-philosophical questions for some years, and had been unaware of 'your Hypotheses of compounding ye celestial motions of ye Planets, of a direct motion by the tangt to ye curve'.[69] In fact, Hooke had proposed the idea as early as 1666, in a short paper read to the Royal Society on 'the inflection of a direct motion into a curve by a supervening attractive principle',[70] and again in his Cutler lecture published in 1674, *An Attempt to Prove the Motion of the Earth*,[71] which there is reason to think Newton had in fact read.[72] But if he had, he accorded it no significance, just as he accorded no significance to Hooke's suggestion here.[73] But quite by chance he did take an interest in another matter that Hooke raised, Flamstead's reported observation of a parallax, which indirectly took him back to Hooke's question about inflection. The diurnal rotation of the earth was central to the question of the parallax, and Newton suggested an experiment to demonstrate it. Contrary to the traditional objection to the earth's diurnal rotation, which held that bodies falling from the top of a tower should reach the ground to the west of the tower, Newton reasoned that they should in fact fall to the east of the tower, because the tangential velocity of the top of the tower is greater than at its base, due to its being further away from the centre of rotation, so the falling body will in fact have a greater speed than the surface of the earth in its eastward component. The diagram (Fig. 11.5) he drew to illustrate what happens, however, shows not only the trajectory *AD* which the body would follow to the surface of the earth, but also the continuation of this trajectory to *C*, indicating what would happen if the body were free to continue to fall to the centre. In doing this, Newton inadvertently gave the problem a wholly new significance, because we are no longer dealing with free fall but in effect with orbital motion. The question is now one of the path that would be followed by a body with an initial tangential motion falling into a centre of attraction. Moreover, by representing the continued motion as a spiral, Newton made an egregious error, which Hooke was quick to point out. The resulting motion would not be one that took the body to the centre, Hooke argued: rather, it would 'circulate w^th an alternate ascent and descent',[74] following an ever-decreasing elliptical path (Fig. 11.6).

Newton realized his mistake and quickly did the calculations, attempting to show that Hooke's solution was not correct either. In fact, what he showed is that, on the assumption that gravity is constant over distance, when the body passes the diameter *AD* in Fig. 11.6, its motion will be directed not towards *N* but to somewhere between

---

[69] Newton to Hooke, 28 November 1679; Newton, *Correspondence*, ii. 300.

[70] Thomas Birch, *The History of the Royal Society of London* (4 vols, London, 1756–7), ii. 90. Birch reproduces the paper at 91–2.

[71] Gunther, *Early Science in Oxford*, 8 (*The Cutler Lectures of Robert Hooke*), 27–8. The material actually dates from four years earlier, 1670.

[72] See Westfall, *Never At Rest*, 383.

[73] See Johannes Lohne, 'Hooke versus Newton: An Analysis of the Documents in the Case of Free Fall and Planetary Motion', *Centaurus* 7 (1960), 6–52.

[74] Hooke to Newton, 9 December 1679; Newton, *Correspondence*, ii. 305.

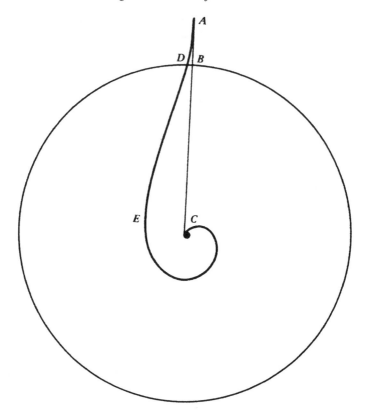

**Figure 11.5**

*N* and *D*, as in Fig. 11.7. The demonstration is revealing of the comparative ease with which Newton was able to move from the kind of analysis in terms of centrifugal force, which is how he (like Huygens) had been approaching the question, to Hooke's suggestion that the path is determined by an external force acting on the body; and indeed, mathematically, centrifugal force is easily translatable into the terms of centripetal attraction.[75] The motion of the body at *G*, he pointed out, is compounded of its tangential motion at *A* (towards *M*) and the 'innumerable converging motions successively generated by ye impresses of gravity in every moment of its passage from *A* to *G*'. These innumerable motions

    [75] See Patri J. Pugliese, 'Robert Hooke and the Dynamics of Motion in a Curved Path', in Michael Hunter and Simon Schaffer, eds., *Robert Hooke: New Studies* (Woodbridge, 1989), 181–206; François De Gandt, *Force and Geometry in Newton's Principia* (Princeton, 1995), 139–43; Gal, *Meanest Foundations*, 179–85.

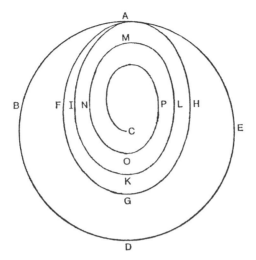

**Figure 11.6**

continually generated by gravity in its passage from *A* to *F* incline it to verge from *GN* towards *D*, and ye like motions generated in its passage from *F* to *G* incline it to verge from *GN* towards *C*. But these motions are proportional to ye time they are generated in, & the time of passing from *A* to *F* (by reason of ye longer journey & slower motion) is greater than ye time of passing from *F* to *G*. And therefore ye motions generated in *AF* shall exceed those generated in *FG* & so make ye body verge from *GN* to some coast between *N* & *D*. [76]

In his reply, Hooke pointed out that he was not assuming gravity to be constant, but to be inversely proportional to the square of distance. The problem was what the relevant curve would be under these conditions, because we have to balance changing velocities and changing distances, and Hooke simply did not know how to do this. Newton, it turns out, did, but note a difference in his approach and that of Hooke. When Newton realized that centripetal force may indeed be the key to understanding orbital motion, in a paper that may have been written within two weeks of the correspondence with Hooke,[77] he inverted Hooke's problem. Instead of asking how a body behaves under the action of an inverse square law, he assumed that the body follows an elliptical path around an attracting body at one focus, and shows that this is regulated by an inverse-square attraction. Similarly, when asked by Halley in 1684 what

[76] Newton to Hooke, 13 December 1679; Newton, *Correspondence*, ii. 308.

[77] A paper of Newton's that meets this description was first identified and published by John Herivel in 'Newtonian Studies III. The Originals of Two Propositions Discovered by Newton in December 1679?', *Archives Internationales d'Histoire des Sciences* 14 (1961), 23–34. The paper may have been written a couple of weeks after the correspondence or a couple of years after. In the latter case, it is probably not the original but a later version. On the disputes over its dating, see Westfall, *Never at Rest*, 387–8, n. 145.

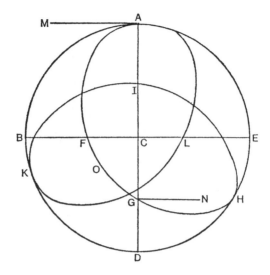

**Figure 11.7**

curve 'would be described by the Planets supposing the force of attraction towards the Sun to be reciprocal to the square of their distance from it',[78] he reversed the question, assuming an elliptical orbit and asking how it is generated.

Working back from the curve makes the mathematics much easier, but in kinematic terms it is a peculiar direction to go in. Another factor is the fact that Newton, as Kepler had done before him (compare the 'pretzels' in Fig. 11.4 with the curves in Fig. 11.7), assumes that orbits must be completely regular. The interesting thing is that, right from the start, Hooke did not take regular orbits as given, being more concerned with how orbits were generated in the first place. This is the Galilean procedure, to show how curved motions can be decomposed into rectilinear and accelerated motions, yet only Hooke saw its application to orbital motion. But Hooke also saw that this might result in orbits that are not regular, because of the various attractions that planets will be subject to. As he put it in the 1674 Cutlerian lecture:

All Coelestial Bodies Whatsoever, have an attraction or gravitating power towards their own Centers, whereby they attract not only their own parts, and keep them from flying from them, as we may observe the Earth to do, but that they also attract all the other Coelestial Bodies that are within the sphere of their activity; and consequently that not only the Sun and the Moon have an influence upon the body and the motion of the Earth, and the Earth upon them, but that [all the other planets] by their attractive powers, have a considerable influence upon its motion as in the same manner the corresponding attractive power of the Earth hath a considerable influence upon every one of their motions also.[79]

---

[78] The wording is from Halley's report of the meeting to Abraham DeMoivre. See Westfall, *Never at Rest*, 403.

[79] Gunther, *Early Science in Oxford*, viii. 27–8.

One thing that is clear is that, under these conditions, the forces determining a planet's orbit would be complex and, beyond a certain level of approximation, quite unpredictable. There would in effect be no perfectly regular orbits.[80]

This prompts the question whether there was something in Hooke's programme of research that encouraged him to think in these terms. His original motivation seems to have arisen from a straightforwardly dynamical consideration. In his first statement of the idea of bending or inflection from rectilinear motion, his Royal Society Address, he stated:

I have often wondered, why the planets should move about the sun according to COPERNICUS's supposition, being not included in any solid orbs (which the antients possibly for this reason might embrace) nor tied to it, as their center, by any visible strings; and neither depart from it beyond such a degree, nor yet move in a strait line, as all bodies, that have but one single impulse, ought to do: For a solid body, moved in a fluid, towards any part, (unless it be protruded aside by some near impulse, or be impeded in that motion by some other obviating body; or that the medium, through which it is moved, be supposed not equally penetrable every way) must perservere in its motion in a right line, and neither deflect this way or that from it. But all the celestial bodies, being regular solid bodies, and moved in a fluid, and yet moved in circular or elliptical lines, and not strait, must have some other cause, besides the first impressed impulse, that must bend their motion into that curve.[81]

This is indicative of Hooke's concerns, which stood in stark opposition to those of Huygens, for example. The opposition is nowhere clearer than on their concerns with clockwork mechanisms. Huygens couched his approach in terms of a mathematical challenge:

the simple pendulum does not naturally provide an accurate and equal measure of time since its wider motions are observed to be slower than its narrower ones. But by a geometrical method we have found a different and previously unknown way to suspend the pendulum; and we have discovered a line whose curvature is marvellously and quite rationally suited to give the required equality to the pendulum.[82]

Hooke, by contrast, was concerned not with isochrony but, as Gal puts it, with a constant and controllable force, and 'seen from this perspective, the substitution of the foliot by the pendulum, and subsequently of the pendulum by the spring are practical exercises in the manipulation of forces—*vis insita*, gravity, spring'.[83] Horology for Hooke is the art of equilibration of forces, and the challenge of accurate timekeeping lay in the ability to make different forces balance and counteract one another. In 'A manuscript concerning the invention of a longitude timekeeper', dating from around

---

[80] As E. Brian Davies points out, 'there are situations in which the dynamics of the three body problem is unpredictable because of its chaotic behaviour, and others in which the [Saari-Xia] five body problem literally has no solution beyond a certain time even though the bodies are involved in no collision': *Science in the Looking Glass* (Oxford, 2003), 168. There are noticeably chaotic orbital motions even in our solar system, particularly in the motion of the planetary satellites of Saturn and Jupiter. The most extreme is that of Hyperion, a satellite of Saturn. See Ivars Peterson, *Newton's Clock: Chaos in the Solar System* (New York, 1993), ch. 9.

[81] Birch, *The History of the Royal Society of London*, ii. 91.

[82] *The Pendulum Clock*, 11.  [83] Gal, *Meanest Foundations*, 122.

1665, Hooke, reflecting on the problem that the centre of motion of a pendulum often fails to coincide with its centre of gravity, especially in portable maritime clocks, spoke of the need to introduce 'artificial gravity': 'because natural grauity could take noe hold of it as to its motion about Its center; I contrived an artificial one which should perform the same effect.'[84] This artificial gravity was a spring, which replaced the natural gravity of the pendulum with its artificial gravity:

And as by weights there is a Naturall pendulum or perpendicular made which Galileo first applyd to the measuring of time soe by Springs is a kind of artificiall pendulum made whose vibrating motion is determined by the spring towards one determinate point, or from one determinate point, in the same manner as a perpendicular or pendulum is by grauity determind towards the center of the earth.[85]

The attempt to provide a general theory of power or force, for which gravity stands out as the central problem, can be seen to run through Hooke's work, starting with his earliest attempts at a theory of matter and power (1661), developed further in Observation VI of the *Micrographia* (1665), and coming to fruition in the 1678 Cutler lectures, *De Potentia Restitutiva, Or Of Spring*, where the spring comes to stand in for natural forces or powers generally. As Gal notes, for Hooke, 'power generates order. Not the calm stability of a revolving celestial sphere or the static perfection of the harmony of solids, but the dynamic, self-correcting, yet precarious order of his watch. And like that watch, Hooke's concept of power is constructed through springs.'[86] Hooke, motivated above all by questions of precise balance and control in instruments, had no reason to try to reformulate dynamical questions in kinematic terms, and his attempt to get to the dynamical core of physical questions enabled him to formulate these questions in a way that brought dynamical considerations to the fore. This brought with it a very different understanding of the way in which the cosmos is finely balanced, one that enabled mechanical thinking about orbital motion to reconnect directly with the Galilean project that shaped kinematic thinking.

## DYNAMICS

Newton did subsequently acknowledge that it was Hooke's letters of late 1679 that provoked him into thinking of orbital motion in terms of gravitational attraction, although he tells Halley that he had already worked out the inverse-square relation from Kepler's law that, in orbital motion, equal areas are swept out in equal times.[87]

[84] The manuscript is transcribed in Michael Wright, 'Robert Hooke's Longitude Timekeeper', in Michael Hunter and Simon Schaffer, eds., *Robert Hooke: New Studies* (Woodbridge, 1989), 63–118: 108.

[85] Ibid. 117.

[86] Gal, *Meanest Foundations*, 140. On the intimate relations between conceptualization, experimentation, and instrumentation in Hooke, see James A. Bennett, 'Robert Hooke as Mechanic and Natural Philosopher', *Notes and Records of the Royal Society* 35 (1980), 33–48.

[87] Newton to Halley 14 July 1686, *Correspondence* ii. 444–5. On Newton's earlier work on curved motions see J. Bruce Brackenridge and Michael Nauenberg, 'Curvature in Newton's Dynamics', in I. Bernard Cohen and George E. Smith, *The Cambridge Companion to Newton* (Cambridge, 2002), 85–137.

In construing orbital motion in terms of centripetal force, there were two issues in particular that Newton had to come to terms with. We have seen that Galileo and Huygens were able to apply the resources of practical mathematics to kinematics, and that Galileo, in his kinematics, had forged the connection between mathematical disciplines and natural philosophy. Newton's task was to use the resources of practical mathematics to deal with a question in dynamics, namely the 'Kepler problem' of determining the force required to maintain elliptical motion around a focal force centre. Since one of the most important respects in which natural philosophy, up to this point, had gone beyond the resources of practical mathematics was on the question of force, the quantification of force, which lay at the core of the Kepler problem, was a *sine qua non* of a successful quantitative natural philosophy. The second issue was a core conceptual question in mechanics, a problem on whose solution the success of dynamics turned, namely the nature of inertial states. If the Galilean model in kinematics was to be applied to dynamics, the question on which everything else depended was how bodies behaved in the absence of forces.

In January 1684, at a meeting of the Royal Society, Halley, Wren, and Hooke had discussed the problem of whether planetary orbits could be constructed from a linear motion and an attraction towards the sun. Hooke's proposed demonstrations did not satisfy Wren, who was unable to solve the problem himself, as was Halley. In August 1684 Halley visited Newton in Cambridge, and asked him what curve a planet would follow if the force of attraction to the sun varied with the square of the distance. Newton evidently answered immediately that it would be an ellipse, and that he had calculated it earlier. In fact, the earlier calculation, probably dating from immediately after the correspondence with Hooke, was wrong, as he realized, so he set out to prove it anew.[88]

Within a couple of months at the latest, he had a solution, if not one to exactly the question Halley had asked. It should be noted that, when Hooke sent him his suggestion of centripetal force, Newton knew that the force would not be inversely proportional to the distance. Thinking through the problem in terms of centrifugal force, Newton and Huygens had both independently demonstrated, much earlier, that the force in circular motion is proportional to $v^2/r$. In Figure 11.8, for example, where P is the planet and S the attracting body at a focus of the ellipse, Hooke's view is that the speed at P is inversely proportional to SP, the distance from the sun, whereas Newton is aware (as was Huygens) that it is in fact inversely proportional to ST, the line drawn perpendicularly from S to a point T on the tangent to the orbit at P.[89]

In his reformulated demonstration, in the wake of Halley's visit,[90] Newton began by setting out three 'hypotheses'. The first was a statement of the principle of rectilinear inertia: a body will move with a uniform rectilinear motion unless retarded by the

---

[88] See the account in Westfall, *Never at Rest*, ch. 10. The texts that we shall be concerned with can be found in Parts 2 and 4 of Isaac Newton, *Unpublished Scientific Papers of Isaac Newton*, ed. A. Rupert Hall and Marie Boas (Cambridge, 1962).

[89] See I. Bernard Cohen, *The Birth of a New Physics* (Harmondsworth, 1987), 219–21.

[90] 'On Motion in Ellipses', *Unpublished Scientific Papers of Isaac Newton*, 293–301. These propositions were subsequently reworked into *De motu*.

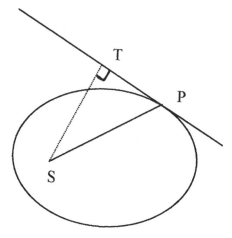

**Figure 11.8**

resistance of the medium or acted upon by an external force. The second stated the proportionality between any alteration in this path and the force altering it. Finally, the third indicated how to resolve motions into their components by means of a parallelogram of motions, so that two motions represented by lines *AB* and *AC* proportional in size to the motions (see Fig. 11.9) can be combined so as to form a parallelogram, in which case the motion will be represented by the line *AD*. The first proposition then demonstrated that a moving body in one plane that is continually attracted to a centre will sweep out equal areas in equal times (Kepler's second law). To deal with this question, he represented the continuous force of attraction in terms of discrete impulses of force acting at successive instants. In Figure 11.10, we imagine the sun to be at *A*, and a body to move initially from *B* to *C* during time *T*. If the body had received no impulse of force at *C* it would have moved, in another interval of time *T*, along the continuation of *BC* to *I*. It does receive an impulse of force at *C*, however, giving it a component of motion towards *A*. If we draw *ID* parallel to *CA*, the point *D* at which it cuts *CD* is the position of the body at the end of the second moment. Triangles *ABC* and *ACI* have equal bases—*BC* and *CI*—and an equal side—*AC*—and so are equal in area. Triangles *ACI* and *ACD* share the same base—*AC*—and stand between two parallels, so are also equal in area. Therefore the triangle *ACD* described in the second moment is equal in area to the triangle *ABC* described in the first moment. If we now let the moments of time be progressively diminished so that the force tends to a continuous action, the line *BCDEFG* becomes a curve, and a body following this curve will sweep out equal areas in equal times. One of Newton's most important achievements in this demonstration is the integration of time into the representation of the problem. The conclusion that if motion is centripetally accelerated then Kepler's area rule holds allows area swept out to be used as

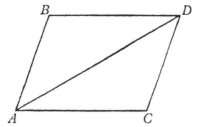

**Figure 11.9**

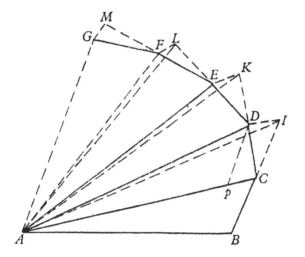

**Figure 11.10**

a way of geometrically representing time that holds of any centripetally accelerated motion.[91]

The next task is to show that a body describing an elliptical orbit around a central attracting body would be attracted in inverse proportion to the square of the distance. Newton showed first that the inverse square law holds for the apsides of a body moving in an ellipse with a centre of attraction at one of the foci (Proposition 2), and then demonstrated this for the entire perimeter of the ellipse (Proposition 3).[92] Proposition 2 attacks the problem at its most accessible points, for the curvatures are equal at

---

[91] As De Gandt notes, the law of areas, which is the first theorem of both *De Motu* and the *Principia*, 'is, as it were, the emblem of a new conception of force, disembarrassed of phantasms and indifferent to physical causes.... The regular sweeping out of areas made possible the appearance of time in the diagrams—the translation of interval of time into sizes of segments, whatever the velocity of the body on its trajectory.' (*Force and Geometry in Newton's Principia*, 272.)

[92] See the extensive treatment of the problems as they appear in *De motu*, ibid. ch. 1.

the two ends of the ellipse, which means that he could use the geometry of the circle to produce the required result, which he did, providing a demonstration that appealed to continuous forces, not discontinuous impulses of force. Proposition 3, by contrast, which deals with the more difficult general case, returns to the impulses of force, and ignores the results of Proposition 2 entirely. The crucial conclusion, however, is that all that is required for an elliptical orbit are inverse-square centripetal forces, contrary to Kepler's attempt to show that elliptical orbits are the result of a circular orbit and secondary (quasi-magnetic) forces.

Despite the success of Newton's analysis, there is a difference between the question that Halley posed and the one that Newton actually solved. Hooke, as we have seen, was concerned with the nature of centripetal force, what it is and how it acts. The question that Halley, Wren, and Hooke were interested in was, given the law of force, how one determines the trajectory. The question that Newton answers is the inverse one: given the trajectory, how does one find the law of force? In fact, Newton never explicitly solved the former question,[93] nor did he attempt to examine the nature of the force acting. But while he left the nature of gravitational force open, he could not pursue his programme in dynamics without very significant clarification of the notion of force in general.

Newton's thinking about force had a number of sources, but one important strand derived from his rejection of the Cartesian notions of space and matter, and here he was indebted to Henry More. The issues had their origins in the correspondence between Descartes and More in the late 1640s.[94] More objected to Descartes' dualism on the grounds that it is impossible to understand how a purely spiritual soul which is not spatially extended can be joined to a purely material body, which on Descartes' view is nothing but extension. He suggested that it might be better to assume that the soul, though immaterial, is also extended, and indeed that everything, even God, is extended. How otherwise could he be present in the world, he asked:

*First*, you establish a definition of matter, or of body, which is much too wide. It seems, indeed, that God is an extended thing just as much as angels are, and more generally everything that subsists by itself, so that it appears that extension is enclosed by the same limits as the absolute essence of things, which however can vary according to the variety of these very same essences. As for myself, I believe it to be clear that God is extended in this manner just because

---

[93] In Propositions 10 and 11 of Book 1 of the *Principia*, he demonstrates that if the body orbits in an ellipse, then the force acting varies with distance if it is directed towards the centre, and as the square of the distance if directed towards the focus. The Corollary of Proposition 10 states its converse, without demonstration. The closest Newton comes to a demonstration is Proposition 41 of Book 1. There is an optimistic assessment of this proposition in D. T. Whiteside, *The Mathematical Principles Underlying Newton's Principia Mathematica* (Glasgow, 1970), 16. Others are not so convinced: see Lohne, 'Hooke versus Newton', 35–6. Richard Feynman said he could not follow Newton's demonstration, and provided his own in its place: David L. Goodstein and Judith R. Goodstein, *Feynman's Lost Lecture: The Motion of Planets Around the Sun* (London, 1996), 94. De Gandt argues that the first solution to the problem is in fact that given by Johann Bernoulli in 1707: *Force and Geometry in Newton's Principia*, 8, 249–50, 257–9.

[94] On More's natural philosophy and its origins in his engagement with Cartesianism, see Alan Gabbey, 'Henry More and the Limits of Mechanism', in Sarah Hutton, ed., *Henry More (1614–1687)* (Dordrecht, 1990), 19–35.

he is omnipresent and occupies intimately the whole machine of the world as well as its singular particles. How indeed could he communicate motion to matter, which he did once, and which according to you he does even now, if he did not touch the matter of the universe in practically the closest manner, or at least had not touched it at a certain time. He would certainly not have been able to do this if he were not present everywhere and did not occupy all the spaces. God therefore . . . is an extended thing.[95]

The idea of extension cannot be used to define matter because it embraces both body and spirit, which are both extended. More's suggestion was that since matter, unlike empty space, is necessarily sensible, it should be defined by its relation to sense, i.e. by tangibility. However, Descartes insisted (on the grounds of clarity and distinctness) on avoiding all reference to sense perception, in which case, More suggested, matter should be defined by the impenetrability which it must possess and which marks it out from spirit. Spirit, though extended, is freely penetrable and cannot be touched. This means that spirit and body can coexist in the same place, and that spirits can have the same location.

In contrast to Descartes, More insisted on maintaining the classical distinction between space and things in space; these latter are things actually moving in space and not merely relatively to one another, and they occupy space in virtue of their impenetrability. More's criticism of Descartes' identification of space or extension with matter followed two main lines of attack. First, he argued that, rather than being merely the distinctive attribute of matter, extension is an attribute of being as such: something can only exist if it is spatially extended. All substance, spiritual as well as material, is extended. Second, he charged Descartes with failing to recognize the specific character both of matter and of space: matter moves in space and in virtue of its impenetrability occupies space, whereas space does not move and is unaffected by the presence or absence of matter in it.

In More's thought in the 1640s, he tended to run together space and spirit, but he subsequently came to realize that this was not quite satisfactory, and later on he distinguished sharply between the extension of spirit and the space in which that spirit, like everything else, finds itself.[96] He distinguished between space or pure immaterial extension and the 'spirit of nature' that pervades and fills it, that acts upon matter and produces various non-mechanical effects such as magnetism and gravity. Because it is inexplicable in purely mechanical terms, gravity is included among the phenomena falling under the spirit of nature.[97] Following Descartes, More did not consider it an essential property of body, but gravity cannot be explained mechanically, and therefore if there were in the world no other non-mechanical forces, unattached bodies on our moving earth would not remain on its surface, but would fly away into space. That they do not do this is a proof of the existence in nature of a 'more than mechanical', 'spiritual' agency. Indeed, without the action of a non-mechanical principle all matter in the universe would divide and disperse; there would not even be bodies,

[95] More to Descartes, 11 December 1648; Descartes, *Œuvres*, v. 238–9.

[96] On these developments see Alexandre Koyré, *From the Closed World to the Infinite Universe*, ch. 6.

[97] Henry More, *The Immortality of the Soul* (London, 1713), p. xii (Preface).

because there would be nothing to hold together the ultimate particles composing them. And of course there would be no trace of the purposeful organization that manifests itself in plants, animals, and in our solar system. All that is the work of the spirit of nature, which acts as an instrument, itself unconscious, of the divine will.

There is, then, a spirit of nature that pervades the whole of the universe and extends throughout infinite space.[98] Having established this, the question of the nature of this space itself arises. Although More prevaricated, he generally inclined towards the view that it is divine extension itself. The argument begins with the idea that 'space' is something extended. Extension, as Descartes had pointed out, cannot be an extension of nothing: distance between two bodies is real or, at the very least, a relation which has a real basis. But More did not conclude from this that empty space could not be real. Rather, he argued, it must be a real attribute of a real subject, on the grounds that there cannot be attributes without subjects. It is found not only in matter but also where no matter is present. 'Indeed', he says, 'we are unable *not* to conceive that a certain immobile extension pervading everything to infinity has always existed and will exist in all eternity, and is therefore really distinct from matter.'[99] The infinite, extended entity that pervades everything is indeed a substance, but it is not matter. It is spirit: and not *a* spirit, but *the* spirit, God. Space is not only something real, it is an attribute of God.

The influence of More on Newton was evident as early as his 'Certain Philosophical Questions' of the early 1660s.[100] Moreover *De gravitatione*, which probably dates from the mid-1680s,[101] develops some themes that derive from More. The full title of the latter is 'On the gravity/weighing-down and equilibrium of fluids', and it was designed as a treatise on fluid mechanics, but apart from a few definitions and propositions, all he completed was an introductory section. This introductory section provides his account of the nature of force and matter. Newton, inspired by More, thought that, through his separation of mind and body, Descartes had effectively denied the dependence of the material world on God, something that Newton took as tantamount to atheism. He took Descartes to task on two main issues, on his relativistic conceptions of place and motion, and on his identification of matter and extension. Descartes had thought of motion merely as change of place. Newton disagreed. 'Physical and absolute motion', he writes, 'is to be defined from other considerations

---

[98]  Ibid. 212 (Book 3, ch. 12, sect. 1).

[99]  Henry More, *Enchiridium metaphysicum* (London, 1671), 30 (ch. 6, sect. 6).

[100]  See *Certain Philosophical Questions*, 113–26.

[101]  When Hall and Hall published the text in *Unpublished Scientific Papers of Isaac Newton*, they argued that it derived from the mid-1660s, but the later dating suggested in B. J. T. Dobbs, *The Janus Face of Genius: The Role of Alchemy in Newton's Thought* (Cambridge, 1991), 130–50, is now widely accepted, e.g. by Bernard Cohen in the Introduction to his translation of Isaac Newton, *The Principia*, 47. See also, James E. McGuire, 'The Fate of the Date: The Theology of Newton's *Principia* Revisited,' in Margaret J. Osler, ed., *Rethinking the Scientific Revolution* (Cambridge, 2000), 271–96. Nevertheless, some (non-fatal) doubts have been expressed as to the basis of this new dating: see e.g. Howard Stein, 'Newton's Metaphysics', in I. Bernard Cohen and George E. Smith, eds, *The Cambridge Companion to Newton* (Cambridge, 2002), 256–307: 298–9 n. 27.

than translation, such translation being designated as merely external.' That is, change of place is something that occurs as a result of motion: motion itself needs to be characterized and explained in terms of something internal to the body, force. In Definition 5 we are told force is the causal principle of motion and rest, and that 'it is either an external one that generates or destroys or otherwise changes impressed motion in some body; or it is an internal principle by which existing motion or rest is conserved in a body, and by which any being endeavours to continue in its state and opposes resistance'. And in Definition 8 inertia is defined as 'force within a body, lest its state should be easily changed by an external exciting force'.[102]

Newton thought of motion and rest primarily in terms of the forces maintaining bodies in motion and rest, rather than the change of place that may result from the exercise of these forces. And since the force by which a body is at rest is different from the force by which it moves in a particular direction at a particular speed, motion and rest are absolute. These states in turn are different from accelerated motions, in that they require only an internal force for their maintenance, whereas accelerated motions require both an internal and an external force. Newton revised and rearranged these forces, going through a number of combinations in an effort to get them to cohere. This exercise, on which everything in Newton's dynamics was to hinge, took place in a manuscript that exists in four drafts, which we can refer to collectively as *De motu*.[103] The first draft dates from the summer of 1684, the second from late 1684, and the third from late 1684/early 1685. Newton began the second draft with four definitions:

Def. 1. I call that a *centripetal force* by which a body is attracted or impelled towards some
   point considered as the centre.
Def. 2. And that the *force of a body*, or the *force innate in a body* [*vis insita*] by which the
   body endeavours to persevere in its motion along a straight line.
Def. 3. And *resistance* that which arises from a regularly impeding motion.
Def. 4. The exponents of quantities are any other quantities proportional to the ones being
   dealt with.[104]

He then adds a five Laws ('hypotheses' in the first draft):

Law 1. A body always goes on uniformly in a straight line by its innate force if nothing
   impedes it.
Law 2. A change of the state of motion or rest is proportional to the impressed force and
   occurs along the straight line in which the latter is impressed.
Law 3. The relative motions of bodies enclosed in a given space are the same whether that
   space is at rest or whether it moves perpetually and uniformly in a straight line without
   circular motion.

---

[102] *Unpublished Scientific Papers of Isaac Newton*, 114 [text]/148 [trans.].
[103] There is a good account of these questions in Westfall, *Force in Newton's Physics*, 431–48.
[104] *Unpublished Papers of Isaac Newton*, 243 [text]/267 [trans.]. The text of *De Motu*, with extensive commentaries, can be found in De Gandt, *Force and Geometry in Newton's Principia*, ch. 1, and in Isaac Newton, *The Mathematical Papers of Isaac Newton*, ed. D. T. Whiteside (8 vols, Cambridge, 1967–81), vi

Law 4. The common centre of gravity does not alter its state of motion or rest through the mutual action of bodies. This follows from Law 3.

Law 5. The resistance of a medium is as the density of that medium and as the spherical surface of the moving body and its velocity conjointly.[105]

It is on the basis of these definitions and laws that Newton tried to account for the motions of the planets. In early drafts, he wanted to derive orbital motion from the interaction of two forces. Both are problematic, intrinsically and in relation to one another. The first is an inherent force, *vis insita*, which Newton treated as the force that maintains a body in uniform rectilinear motion. It is identical with the force by which a body resists changes to its state, and indeed appears to explain where that force comes from, for the force by which bodies are able to resist changes to their state is dependent on what state they are in: what size they are and what their velocity is. The second is a centripetal force, which continually diverts the body from that rectilinear motion. Centripetal force produces a uniform acceleration, and so is naturally thought of as the product of mass and acceleration, on the model of free fall, although as we have just seen, it is not always treated as a continuous force, but as producing discontinuous increments of motion, on the model of impact. On the way in which Hooke had thought of the matter, there was one force involved in orbital motion, that which deflects the body from its rectilinear path. Newton's conception was closer to the idea of orbits arising from an equilibrium between equal forces. The problem was that the two forces didn't seem to be commensurable, and Newton struggled, using a parallelogram of motions as a parallelogram of forces, to try and show what their resultant must be, all without success.

Newton's subsequent reworkings of *De motu* initially accentuated the inconsistencies rather than solving them, by bringing to the fore two distinct sets of dynamical concepts: one centring around the idea of absolute motion, and the other around the principle of inertia. The principle of inertia in effect undermines any attempt to determine motions in an absolute fashion, for as we have just seen, Law 3 told us that 'the relative motions of bodies enclosed in a given space are the same whether that space is at rest or whether it moves perpetually and uniformly in a straight line without circular motion'. If that is the case, then we cannot make an absolute distinction between rest and uniform rectilinear motion. Newton's first response to this was to offer a new definition of motion. Previously, he had defined it in terms of an innate force, *vis insita*, by which a body continues in a uniform rectilinear motion. But because of the problem of distinguishing rest from uniform rectilinear motion, he now included both these in his definition and made *vis insita* responsible for both of them. He defined the *vis insita* of a body as:

The innate force [*vis insita*] of matter is the power of resisting by which a body continues, as much as in it lies, in its normal state, either of resting or of moving uniformly in a straight line. And it is proportional to the body to which it belongs, nor does it differ at all from the *inertia* of mass except in our mode of conception.[106]

---

[105] *Unpublished Papers of Isaac Newton*, 243 [text]/267–8 [trans.].        [106] Ibid. 239/241.

Note that *vis insita* here is still a *power by which* a body perseveres, but also that rest is now added to the states which persevere in this way. In this version of events, Newton was saying that both uniform rectilinear motion and rest require force to persevere. *Vis insita* is conceived as an internal maintaining force: it is a separate force by which a body resists changes of state. But then Newton rethought the whole question, treating *vis insita* exclusively in terms of the force by which a body resists changes to its state, and not as the force by which a body maintains its state.

In sum, we can think of Newton's progress here in three stages. He started with a force, *vis insita*, required to maintain a body in its uniform rectilinear motion. This force also acts to resist changes to the state of the body. Second, he reflected on the fact that uniform rectilinear motion and rest should be dynamically indistinguishable, so some parity must be introduced between rest and uniform rectilinear motion. In response to this, he made *vis insita* responsible for both the maintenance of uniform rectilinear motion *and* rest. Third, he realized that there is a difference between the maintenance of motion and rest, and the resistance to change of state, and he identified the latter with a force, *vis insita*, leaving the former without a force. This meant that rest and uniform rectilinear motion no longer require a force for their maintenance: only changes of state require a force. In this way, a fundamentally new understanding of inertia was established that resolved all the problems that plagued the Galilean and Cartesian formulations.

Newtonian dynamics was in key respects a development of the Galilean model for kinematics. Indeed it is crucial for the way in which Newton conceived of dynamics that it is kinematics, not hydrostatics, that is the route to dynamics. Book 2 of the *Principia* will be largely devoted to making this point, setting out a detailed criticism of the vortex theory in which it is shown that unless there was a constant input of energy at their centres, the motion in Descartes' vortices would very quickly be evenly distributed. The hydrostatics model, as we have seen, investigated the behaviour of bodies in terms of their interaction with the surrounding medium. This was done initially in the case of a stationary medium, where a quantitative relation between the specific weights of the body and the medium was treated as the determinant of the body's motion. In its extension to cosmology, in Descartes, the medium in which the body is for all intents and purposes embedded was treated as the key to understanding the position of the body in relation to the sun, as well as the shape and speed of its orbit. On this model, every physical change has a material cause which acts through direct contact: the planets move in particular orbits, for example, because of the relative differences between the pressures and speeds of the corpuscles making up the fluids that surround the bodies, and even though the sun is distant from the planet, it can act on it via contact action because of the unbroken chain of matter connecting it to the planet. Understanding physical processes is a matter of understanding the relation between a body and the medium that surrounds it: the medium is constitutive of the problem of free fall in early Galileo and in Descartes for example, for it is the interaction between the medium and the body that defines the physical problem in the first place. This way of proceeding makes equilibrium a key physical notion, something that reinforces the idea of the naturalness of planetary orbits, which are paradigms of celestial equilibrium.

The introduction of a kinematic model into dynamics pointed physical enquiry in a wholly different direction. The starting point was now the behaviour of a body free of any constraints, where constraints are construed as anything that would cause a body to deviate from a state of rest or uniform rectilinear motion. The first step, on this model, is to analyze the behaviour of an isolated body, and then determine how this behaviour is modified as it is subjected to forces. While we do not have to consider gravitation, this approach works well. The shift from a one-body universe, to a two-body universe, to an *n*-body universe in which the only form of interaction is collision, is one in which kinematics provides the results, results that can then be explained at a more fundamental level by fleshing out these kinematic processes in dynamic terms. But once we introduce gravitation, the situation changes radically. The isolated body we begin with has to be treated as a mass point in which there are no internal differential gravitational effects, since these are dynamically complex. But this makes the shift from a one-body universe to a two-body universe very much a qualitative shift.[107] The one-body universe tells us nothing about the two-body universe in respect of the gravitational attraction that the bodies exert on one another, so that gravitation comes out as an added extra, which appears only when we have more than one body. Moreover, once we do take into account the mutual gravitational attraction of bodies, the Galilean model immediately becomes problematic for we can no longer strictly speaking begin from the behaviour of bodies at rest:

For attractions are always directed towards bodies, and—by the third law—the actions of attracting and attracted bodies are always mutual and equal; so that if there are two bodies, neither the attracting nor the attracted body can be at rest, but both . . . revolve about a common center of gravity as if by mutual attraction.[108]

More generally, the kinematic approach encourages us to see inertia as being part of the material substance of the body itself, whereas the attractive force between bodies can only be seen in terms of the effect of this material substance in the space surrounding the body or mass point. But there is something problematic about this relation between internal inertial states and external gravitational forces. Consider the simplest two-body case of gravitational attraction, free fall. Galileo had shown that all bodies fall to the earth with a uniformly accelerated motion in a void. In particular, he showed that two bodies of the same material but having different absolute weights, two lead balls for example, suspended from the same height and realised simultaneously, reach the ground simultaneously. But if one of the balls has a greater mass than the other, and if gravitational attraction is directly proportional to mass then, other things being equal, the heavier body is subject to a greater gravitational attraction, which means its rate of acceleration must be greater. The reason this doesn't happen, on Newton's account, is that the increased gravitational attraction to which more massive bodies are subject (their 'gravitational mass' in modern

---

[107] We are concerned only with the two-body case here. What Newton shows in the *Principia* is not that actual planetary orbits are elliptical, but that orbits are elliptical in a two-body approximation, and he was aware that the gravitational influence of Jupiter would lead to deviations from strict elliptical orbits in the other planets for example.

[108] Newton, *Principia*, 561 (Book 1, sect. 11).

terminology) is exactly counterbalanced by their greater inertia (their 'inertial mass' in modern terminology), manifested as resistance to acceleration. To establish this, Newton performed a number of experiments with pendulums having bobs of the same size but filled with material of different specific gravities: any difference in the ratio of inertial to gravitational mass would be manifested as a difference in the period of vibration.[109] But he could offer no theoretical account of the basis for this equivalence, because, although there is clearly a sense in which inertia and gravitation are fundamental properties in Newtonian dynamics, the Galilean model provided him with an obvious basis for understanding inertia and collision—dynamics here simply fleshes out a secure kinematic skeleton—but nothing for gravitation.[110] As a result, gravitation resists the kind of analysis and consequent clarification to which inertia has been subject.

A great deal of criticism of Newton's system turned on its failure to provide a comprehensive account of the nature of gravity, and the divide between 'speculative'—or, to use a less partisan term, 'foundationalist'—natural philosophy and experimental natural philosophy was given new life in the debates that followed the publication of the *Principia*, which, despite its derivation of a broad range of terrestrial and celestial phenomena from the basic principles of mechanics, was assimilated to a newly reformulated version of experimental natural philosophy.[111] One question at issue here is that of just what the relation between foundational natural philosophy, experimental natural philosophy, and mechanics is. More generally, this is the question of the unity of natural philosophy, and it is to this question that we now turn.

[109] See *Principia*, Book 3, Proposition 6. These experiments were originally carried out when Newton was working on *De motu*.

[110] See Brian D. Ellis, 'Newton's Concept of Motive Force', *Journal of the History of Ideas* 23 (1962), 273–8; and idem, 'The Origin and Nature of Newton's Laws of Motion', in Robert G. Colodny, ed., *Beyond the Edge of Certainty* (Englewood Cliffs, NJ, 1965), 29–68.

[111] These questions will concern us in the next volume.

# PART V

# 12

## The Unity of Knowledge

The three streams of natural philosophy that we looked at in Part IV are separated by quite definite fault lines. They are not necessarily—and certainly not in every respect—mutually exclusive ways of pursuing natural philosophy. But when Wilkins in effect combined all three in his proposal in 1660 that the Royal Society pursue 'Physico-Mathematicall-Experimentall Learning',[1] his optimism far exceeded anything actually achievable in fact, or even in principle. The truth is that the unity of natural philosophy had become deeply problematic by the 1660s, with three new models for natural-philosophical enquiry vying with two older ones.

From the thirteenth to the sixteenth centuries, there had been two models of the unity of knowledge. One was the Aristotelian notion of unity of *scientia*: the ultimate form of understanding of natural processes was one in which the essential principles underlying the behaviour of things were understood in a systematic way. The other was the Christian idea of a universe designed and created *ex nihilo* by a single God as an abode for human beings, the crucial feature of this conception being the fact that the world was the product of design, and it was only through understanding the design of the world that we had any fundamental knowledge of it. The first conception operated with a comparatively restricted notion of the purview of natural philosophy, confining it to a 'theoretical'—as opposed to a 'practical' or 'productive'—understanding of that behaviour of bodies that was generated solely by intrinsic principles. The second conception, by contrast, operated with a far more open, and less clearly defined, understanding of what fell under the rubric of natural philosophy. Natural history figured in a prominent role, for the unifying principles now lay not at the level of individual things, but at the level of divine design, which in the final analysis was the sole cause of behaviour in the natural world.

In the course of the seventeenth century, the Aristotelian notion fell into disrepute (although it did receive a highly modulated defence from Leibniz late in the century) and, perhaps because it was now freed from the constraints that Aristotelianism had imposed on natural-philosophical understanding, the 'designed cosmos' view came into its own again. The three general approaches to natural philosophy that we examined in Part IV largely determined the space within which disputes over natural-philosophical explanation took place, however, and these each provided a distinctive input into the question of the constitution of natural philosophy. What resulted was a complex interplay between these three and the two earlier conceptions, and I want

---

[1] See Shapiro, *John Wilkins*, 192.

to examine some aspects of this interplay in this chapter, with the aim of developing an overview of the role and standing of natural-philosophical enquiry by the second half of the seventeenth century, while at the same time not losing sight of the very heterogeneous make-up of natural philosophy from the third decade of the seventeenth century.

Mechanism had a particularly complex standing in relation to Aristotelian and design conceptions. It differed from them both in rejecting teleology, and because of this, at least for most of the seventeenth century, it rejected any role for notions of design in natural philosophy. It construed natural philosophy as a systematic enterprise, and nature largely as independent and autonomous as far as the physical explanations of its fundamental processes are concerned, but its rejection of individual natures led to the postulation of a fundamental level of explanation at which all physical processes ultimately find their rationale. Although this common level of explanation was that of interaction between corpuscles, the fact that both mechanism and design approaches postulated a single ultimate rationale for all physical processes (both 'natural' and 'unnatural' in Aristotelian terms) is instructive. Both conceived the totality of physical phenomena as coming within their purview, for example, a radical departure from Aristotelianism, denying the idea of accidents in nature and in many respects even denying contingency in natural processes.

Experimental philosophy by contrast offered no conception of a substantive unity of natural philosophy. It was closely connected with particular methodological rules and patterns of enquiry, but, as we have seen, many of these derived from biblical and legal hermeneutics, and certainly did not mark out natural philosophy as a distinctive enterprise, methodologically speaking. It seems to contain no intrinsic principles for the unification of natural philosophy. This may be taken as reflecting the possibility that natural philosophy is simply not a unified discipline. But such an approach would have been an unattractive way of defending the enterprise of experimental philosophy, for in the prevailing climate of competing natural-philosophical systems some anchoring in an available system would have bolstered its legitimacy, and this was painless in that, at the level of generality at which it was achieved, it required no revision to, or reinterpretation of, results. In the case of mechanism, for example, even though Boylean pneumatics and Newtonian chromatic theory were at odds with prevailing corpuscularian accounts, all this meant was that, if there were an ultimate explanation of these phenomena it would have to be a mechanist one, albeit not the mechanist one currently proposed, since this was at odds with experimentally determined phenomena. In the case of design arguments, zoology and botany could happily accommodate themselves to notions of design, since scriptural interpretation, for example, could now be guided by developments in natural history rather than vice versa. The legitimacy and standing that natural history took on as a result were immense, as the natural philosopher became a paradigm seeker after God's truths.

The geometricized natural philosophy of Huygens, Newton, and others had, on the face it, a very narrow purview, for it was basically mechanics. Like natural history it—or at least its practical-mathematical precursors—had traditionally been excluded from natural philosophy proper, but unlike natural history it could not insert itself in any straightforward way into the design programme. Because it realized one of the aims of mechanism (at least as construed by Beeckman, Mersenne, Hobbes, and Descartes), namely quantification, it was closely associated with the mechanist programme, and there was some degree of mutual reinforcement. Mechanism was essentially matter theory, however, whereas mechanics took motions and forces as its basic elements, largely avoiding talk of matter. As a result there was some competition on the question of what the basic constituents in physical processes were. To some extent, the microscope shifted the focus away from matter theory to mechanics. Mechanism, always highly speculative as far as basic micro-corpuscularian processes were concerned, had worked on the assumption that, at the micro-corpuscularian level, physical processes and their constituents were very simple: complexity came with the compound processes at the macroscopic level. It was reasonable to assume that something of the increasing simplicity in nature as one moved to the microscopic level would be made evident by microscopes. But as Hooke's *Micrographia* made graphically clear, the contrary was the case. As one moved to the microscopic level, nature became even more varied and complex than it was at the macroscopic level. What tended to happen, as a result of this, was the replacement of a matter-theoretical micro-corpuscularianism with a mechanical one. There was an outstanding problem for the strategy of moving from matter theory to mechanics, however, for the range of phenomena that could be imagined to depend on the fundamental properties of matter was a good deal broader than that one might imagine to be accounted for in terms of the laws of mechanics. An increase in the power of the *explanans* had to be weighed against what, on the face of it, was a drastic decrease in the range of the *explanandum*.

## COMMON CAUSATION

Let us begin with the motivating idea behind the mechanist notion of natural-philosophical explanation, namely that there is a fundamental level at which the kind of causal processes involved are identical for any physical phenomenon. As I have mentioned, mechanism had in common with design approaches the postulation of a single ultimate rationale for all physical processes. The corpuscularianism that replaced Aristotelian matter theory substituted, for the Aristotelian notion of cause as something that acts locally, the idea that there is a level of causation common to all physical phenomena, namely the microscopic level of atomic collisions. This acted to unify the natural-philosophical enterprise because, by contrast with the Aristotelian model, there was a fundamental level of causal interaction in which all bodies participated—'there is no motion which cannot be judged to be natural', as Gassendi put it[2]—and which shaped the behaviour of the whole physical system. Hobbes' mechanist reduction had alerted natural philosophers to the dangers of simply leaving matters at that, although what exactly should be done in this respect was a matter of dispute. On the one hand, common causation provided a single point of entry for God's activity in the world, suggesting a level at which design arguments might

---

[2] Gassendi, *Opera*, iii. 487.

obtain a straightforward purchase. But this assumed that mechanism gave a complete account of the corporeal realm, and many who were committed to mechanism, at some level, were unable to see how it could account for all physical phenomena. The problems raised by the mechanist idea of common causation provided the best entry into the issues of the completeness and unity of natural philosophy from a mechanist perspective.

One point on which early-modern natural philosophers were agreed was the complete lack of explanatory power in purported explanations offered within Aristotelian natural philosophy. In one important respect, this criticism was based on a misconception, for on the *scientia* model that Aristotelians followed, the aim of the exercise was not explanation but demonstration.[3] But mechanists now dictated the terms of the debate, and by these terms Aristotelianism had nothing to offer. 'Aristotelians', Hobbes tells us in the first chapter of *Leviathan*, 'say, For the cause of *Vision*, that the thing seen, sendeth forth on every side a *visible species* (in English) *a visible shew, apparition,* or *aspect,* or *a being seen*; the receiving whereof into the Eye, is *Seeing*.'[4] These same Aristotelians, Descartes points out, admit that what they call motion is not well understood: trying to clarify it, they define it as 'the act of being which is in potency, in so far as it is in potency', which Descartes finds completely unintelligible.[5] Gassendi agrees. 'Great God!', he writes, 'Is there a stomach in the world strong enough to digest that? What we were after was the explanation for something very familiar, but this is so complicated that nothing is clear now.'[6] And Glanvill similarly has some fun at the expense of Aristotelians:

Even the most common productions are here resolv'd into *Celestial influences, Elemental combinations, active* and *passive* principles, and such *generalities*; while the particular manner of them is as hidden as *sympathies*. And if we follow manifest qualities beyond the empty signification of their names; we shall find them as *occult*, as those which are professedly *so*. That heavy Bodies descend by *gravity*, is no better an account then we might expect from a *Rustick*: and again, that *Gravity* is a quality whereby an heavy body descends, is an impertinent *Circle*, and teacheth nothing.[7]

In general, advocates of mechanism had no difficulty showing the circularity and pathological awkwardness of such explanations (or such accounts construed as explanations). Nevertheless, abandoning the idea of invoking essential natures to explain physical behaviour brought new explanatory problems.

Aristotelian natural philosophy had been premissed on the idea that understanding the nature of something enables one to understand its properties. More precisely, its claim was that it enabled one to understand those of its properties that followed from its nature, and it enabled one to understand the behaviour that derived from

---

[3] See Alan Gabbey, 'Mechanical Philosophies and Their Explanations', in Christoph Lüthy, John E. Murdoch, and William R. Newman, eds, *Late Medieval and Early Modern Corpuscular Matter Theories* (Leiden, 2001), 441–65.

[4] Thomas Hobbes, *Leviathan or The Matter, Forme and Power of a Commonwealth Ecclesiasticall and Civil* (London, 1651), 4.

[5] Descartes, *Œuvres*, xi. 39 (*Le Monde*, ch. 7).      [6] Gassendi, *Opera*, iii. 186.

[7] Glanvill, *Scepsis Scientifica*, 126.

those properties. The behaviour of bodies that is the result of contingencies in the world, that is, that behaviour that does not derive from something essential to the body, falls outside the domain of natural philosophy. Consequently, there are many physical processes in the world that are not explicable in terms of Aristotelian natural philosophy, and it is not just that these are not explicable in fact, they are not explicable in principle. There is a natural-philosophical explanation for why water pours to the ground when released from constraints, for example, but not for why and how it is lifted by a mechanical device.[8] Aristotelian natural philosophy deals with the natural behaviour of bodies, not any other kind of behaviour they might undergo.

Bacon's primary criticism of Aristotelian natural philosophy, as we have seen, was that it was directed towards an understanding of the wrong kinds of processes. What we should be concerning ourselves with are 'artificial' processes, those by which we might constrain and control natural phenomena. To meet this demand, what is needed is not a system that excludes natural processes, since these still need to be understood if they are to be controlled, but rather a system that includes both natural and unnatural processes. There were two models for this in the natural philosophies of the Hellenistic era. Stoicism offered a holistic view of the cosmos in which everything was in effect natural, for everything was connected with everything else: the universe of beings was conceived as an immense physical organism organized around an internal principle that, by the analogy with living beings, is vital spirit or *pneuma*. This kind of model, which became popular in eclectic Neoplatonist and Aristotelian versions in the sixteenth century, was, in the move from naturalism to corpuscularianism, effectively abandoned after then, as we have seen, Spinoza being the only significant exception. Epicureanism, by contrast, offered a picture with no such intrinsic connections but in which the ultimate constituents of the universe, atoms, exhibited an absolute uniformity of behaviour (leaving to one side the problematic 'swerve', which was abandoned by early-modern advocates of atomism). On the Epicurean model, extrinsic connections fulfilled the same function that intrinsic ones did in the Stoic picture, so that in both cases there was a single fundamental level at which everything physical could be accounted for, and the cosmic system was deterministic.

This is in contrast to earlier systems, those of Plato and Aristotle. For Plato, exceptionless regularity was to be found in the Forms rather than in sensible phenomena. The classic notion of determinism—of a system in which every state of affairs is a necessary consequence of a chain of preceding causes—was almost entirely absent

---

[8] We saw in ch. 11 how Galileo and others, in the late sixteenth century, attempted to use the pseudo-Aristotelian *Mechanica* to extend a radically revised Peripatetic natural philosophy to 'unnatural' phenomena. Had this approach been successful, it would have transformed Aristotelian natural philosophy into an account of both natural and unnatural phenomena. The project was, however, not merely a failure, but, in Aristotelian terms, quite incoherent. There are other kinds of attempt which, had they been successful might have achieved the same kind of thing: note, e.g. the attempt of Niccolò Cabeo to use Aristotle's account of meteorology, which, because of the nature of the subject matter, dispenses with final and formal causes and confines itself to material and efficient causes, as a general model in natural philosophy: *Commentaria in libros Meteorologicorum* (4 vols Rome, 1646).

from Aristotle's approach also. More important for Aristotle was the contrast between the absolute necessity and invariance that applies to the motions of celestial bodies, to mathematical truths, and to certain attributes of being in the sublunary world such as human mortality and, on the other hand, the irregularity and variation of many aspects of the sublunary world, where the most that can be said of many things is that they happen for the most part but not always, and where there are many accidental connections that fall outside the scope of natural-philosophical knowledge altogether. Aristotle's picture of the consequences of an event was not one of chains of cause and effect interwoven in a nexus extending to infinity, but rather, in an analogy used by David Balme, one resembling the ripples caused by the throwing of a stone into a pond, which spread out and combine with the ripples caused by other stones, but eventually die away and come to nothing.[9] And conversely, Aristotle could assert that there are fresh beginnings (*archai*), not confined to human agency, without supposing that there is a deterministic causal nexus occasionally interrupted by undetermined events, for he simply did not see the question in these terms.[10]

The possibility of uncaused events was a basic point of contention between the Aristotelian and the Stoic views. Aristotle held that there are events that result from chance rather than necessity, where chance events are those 'unnatural' events which natural philosophy is not called upon to explain, whereas all natural processes are associated with necessity because they are the result of the activity of intrinsic causes. Aristotle's interest, however, was not so much in cause as in explanation. He gives the example of a man who goes to the market and by chance meets someone who owes him money.[11] The questions to be asked about this accidental meeting are whether it has an explanation, whether it has a cause, and whether it is necessitated by the processes that lead the man and his debtor to the market. That coincidences do not have explanations is a reasonably straightforward point. We may well be able to explain why the man arrives at the market at $t_1$, and we may be able to explain why the debtor arrives there at $t_2$, but if, *ex hypothesi*, the meeting is a coincidence, then we will not have an explanation of why $t_1 = t_2$, and indeed it is not even clear what the demand for such an explanation would amount to. Surely if we could explain it we would no longer say that it was a coincidence. The question is whether this lack of explanation means there is a lack of cause. On the face of it, it does. For if we think of an explanation simply as something that states a cause, then if we have an explanation, we clearly have a cause. But what if we cannot explain it? There might still be a cause, but one that we cannot find or recognize. Someone who doesn't accept that there are such things as accidental, coincidental, or chance events will maintain that all events are caused: the fact that we cannot explain all events simply means that we cannot find the requisite cause. So lack of explanation does not necessarily mean lack of cause. But Aristotle tended to treat causes as simply what explanations identify as the relevant factors. This makes causes

[9] David M. Balme, 'Greek Science and Mechanism I', *Classical Quarterly* 33 (1939), 129–38.

[10] See the discussions in Richard Sorabji, *Necessity, Cause and Blame: Perspectives on Aristotle's Theory* (London, 1980); and Sarah Waterlow, *Nature, Change and Agency in Aristotle's Physics* (Oxford, 1982).

[11] Aristotle, *Physics*, 196$^a$1–5.

context-relative: what will count as a cause will be determined by the kind of explanation one is seeking. On such a view, to say that a coincidence lacks an explanation is indeed to say that it lacks a cause. Finally, there is a third factor: necessitation. Necessitation is independent of both explanation and causation. As we have just seen, to provide the cause of the man's being at the market at a particular time and to provide the cause of the debtor's being at the market at the same time is not to provide the cause of their being at the market simultaneously. We want to be able to make the distinction between intentional outcomes and accidental outcomes, between the case where the man went to the market so that he might meet his debtor, and the case where it was a purely chance encounter. In the first case, the cause of the man's being at the market at a particular time plus the cause of the debtor's also being at the market at that particular time will add up to a cause of their both being at the market at the same time, for the causal chains are genuinely connected. But in the case where the meeting is accidental, there is simply no cause for their being at the market at the same time. Necessitation, however, is different. Something is a necessitating condition if its outcome is inevitable, and necessitating conditions are simply sufficient conditions. If there are sufficient conditions for a man's being at the market at a particular time and sufficient conditions for the debtor's being at the market at that time, then there are sufficient conditions for them both being at the market at the same time.

The relation between explanation, causation, and necessitation is, then, quite complex on the Aristotelian approach. On the Stoic and Epicurean accounts, by contrast, it is straightforward. In the latter, we assume that, at some level of description, everything in the universe is causally connected with everything else: as a consequence, there are no events for which there are no connecting causal chains, provided we are prepared to search back far enough through causal ancestors. Explanations are simply statements of cause, and causes always necessitate their effects. Indeed they are treated as if they were simply sufficient conditions for the effect. There are clear parallels between the Aristotle/Stoic divide and the experimentalist/foundationalist one. Both Aristotle and the experimentalists were unconcerned about some fundamental level at which all events are connected, the former because he did not even contemplate such a level, the latter because it was too remote from their natural-philosophical practice. By contrast, both the Stoics and the Atomists, and their early-modern foundationalist mechanist successors, took the view that there is a causal chain connecting any event with behaviour at the fundamental level. Hobbes, for example, was adamant that causes always necessitate their effects. And like the Stoics, Hobbes drew out what he saw as the implications for the question of voluntary acts. For Hobbes, as for the Stoics, to deny that voluntary acts have been necessary all along is to envisage a failure of causation: it is to envisage uncaused events, and this is impossible.

The distinctive features of the mechanist approach resulted—at least in its ideal-type form—from the combination of three things: a view that causation takes place at the fundamental level of corpuscularian activity; a view that at this fundamental level everything is homogeneous and causally connected in a causally closed system; and a view that this is exceptionless, that apparently teleological and apparently intentional acts in fact operate within the confines of this notion of causation.

The issues can be traced back in part to Epicureanism. Of the two Hellenistic systems of antiquity, Epicureanism is the more problematic on the question of causation. Atoms are homogeneous and behave in identical ways in identical circumstances, but how exactly are they connected? The Stoics had postulated intrinsic connections, on the model of the relation between the organs of a body, between events in the cosmos, whether microscopic or macroscopic, and these events are thereby connected in nature. But atoms are not like this: each atom is quite independent of all the others in the sense that, unless they are colliding with one another, their behaviour is unaffected by any other atom. For Aristotle and the Stoics, bodies act differently depending on their natures, whereas for the Epicureans, bodies have no individual natures. They are completely homogeneous and that is why their fundamental behaviour—namely, the behaviour that basic matter theory sets out to capture, as opposed to any ad hoc hypotheses connecting corpuscular shape with sensory qualities for example—is the same. Yet the question can be posed: what is it that makes such atoms, or corpuscles more generally, behave in the way they do? Descartes, for example, postulated a conservation principle and three laws of nature which regulate all corpuscular interactions.[12] If matter is inert, if it is devoid of the powers, potentialities, and activities of the Aristotelian and naturalist traditions, what is the source of its behaviour? Neither Descartes nor any other mechanist attempted to derive the laws of nature from the constitution of matter: that is to say, it does not follow from anything in any mechanist account of matter that bodies will continue in a motion of uniform speed, or in a straight line, in the absence of constraints. Indeed, although the ground had been prepared by Beeckman, it was Descartes, in his *Principia*, who pointed the way to thinking of the behaviour of bodies in terms of motion rather than matter, that is, in terms of mechanics rather than matter theory. This is the logical direction for mechanism in many ways. It was part of the mechanist programme as envisaged by Mersenne in the 1620s that insistence on extrinsic causation rids the natural realm of the kinds of intrinsic activities that had begun to replace the supernatural in sixteenth-century naturalism. This makes God the only causally active agent, a metaphysical view with which Descartes struggled, with no clear or satisfactory outcome.[13]

The core problem was set out by succinctly by Boyle, when he pointed out that corpuscles are bits of inert matter: to talk of them obeying or following laws is at best an inappropriate metaphor. In his *Free Enquiry Into the Vulgarly Receiv'd Notion of Nature* (1686), he notes that 'a law being but a *notional rule of acting according to the declared will of a superior*, it is plain that nothing but an intellectual being can

---

[12] Whether the conservation law, in particular, holds in the case of corpuscular interactions brought about by undetermined human acts of will (which seem to change the total amount of motion in the universe) is a contentious matter that we cannot go in to here. See Daniel Garber, 'Mind, Body, and the Laws of Nature in Descartes and Leibniz', in *Midwest Studies in Philosophy* 8 (1983), 105–33; Alan Gabbey, 'The Mechanical Philosophy and its Problems: Mechanical Explanations, Impenetrability, and Perpetual Motion', in J. C. Pitt, ed., *Change and Progress in Modern Science* (Dordrecht, 1985), 9–84; and Peter McLaughlin, 'Descartes on Mind–Body Interaction and the Conservation of Motion', *Philosophical Review* 102 (1993), 155–82.

[13] See Martial Guéroult, 'The Metaphysics and Physics of Force in Descartes', in Stephen Gaukroger, ed., *Descartes: Philosophy, Mathematics and Physics* (Brighton, 1980), 196–229.

be properly capable of receiving and acting by a law.'[14] In 1691, in the *Christian Virtuoso*, he goes further, telling us that 'inanimate bodies are utterly incapable of understanding what a law is, or what it enjoins, or when they act conformably or unconformably to it; and therefore the actions of inanimate bodies, which cannot incite or moderate their own actions, are produced by real power, not by laws'.[15] Yet Boyle himself prevaricates, and at one point in the *Free Enquiry* uses an image almost certainly derived from *impetus* theory in an attempt to clarify how God might transfer motive force into the natural realm: 'all bodies, once in the state of actual motion, whatever cause first brought them to it, are moved by an internal principle: as, for instance, an arrow, that actually flies in the air towards a mark, moves by some principle or other residing within itself'.[16]

By contrast, there were those who responded to this kind of problem by restricting any causal powers to the divine level, and those who responded by endowing matter with causal powers, and making matter theory a foundation of mechanics. Before the publication of Newton's *Principia*, there was one detailed defence of the first position, in Malebranche's *De la recherche de la vérité*, the first edition of which appeared in 1674–5, and about ten years later Newton had set out a defence of the latter in *De gravitatione*.[17] One way in which one can see the contrast between Malebranche and Newton is in terms of Cartesianism. Malebranche's project can be described as the rationalization of Cartesianism as represented in Descartes' *Principia*. Descartes' metaphysics and natural philosophy were stripped down to bare essentials, and built up again on a new basis. In the process, it took on a number of new features: above all, it effectively subordinated everything to epistemology, incorporated a phenomenalist account of the natural realm, and advocated a thoroughgoing occasionalist account of causation. Malebranche saw what he was doing as a rationalization and development of the Cartesian programme, however, and although it was a radical rereading of Descartes in some respects, it was not only a recognizable development of the Cartesian programme, but one very much in accord with the project that Huygens was pursuing, and one that was to become the canonical version of Cartesianism for many. Newton by contrast, although like other serious natural philosophers of his

---

[14] Boyle, *Works*, v. 170. This may be a response to Hale's statement that 'the Law of Nature, and the Power of Nature, is no other but the wise instituted Law of the most wise, powerful, and intelligent Being, as really and truly as an Edict of *Trajan* or *Justinian* was a *Law* of *Trajan* or Justinian': *The Primitive Origination of Mankind*, 346.

[15] Ibid. 521.

[16] Ibid. 209. See the discussion in Peter Anstey, *The Philosophy of Robert Boyle* (London, 2000), 132–4.

[17] Both Malebranche's and Newton's construal of natural philosophy were to be immensely influential. In Malebranche's case, this was through the phenomenalist metaphysics of *La Recherche*, which was to have a profound influence on Berkeley and Hume—see Charles J. McCracken, *Malebranche and British Philosophy* (Oxford, 1983)—as well as on the group of mathematicians and natural philosophers who formed around him in the 1690s—see André Robinet, 'Le groupe malebranchiste introducteur du calcul infinitésimal en France', *Revue d'histoire des sciences* 13 (1960), 287–308; idem, *Malebranche de l'Académie des sciences. L'œuvre scientifique, 1674–1715* (Paris, 1970), 47–62. Newton's influence was not via *De gravitatione*, which remained unpublished and unknown until the twentieth century, but through the Queries added to the *Opticks*, the General Scholium added to the *Principia*, and a few related writings.

generation he began as a Cartesian, came to reject Cartesianism. In *De gravitatione*, he construes Descartes' separation of mind and body—one of the most fundamental preconditions for mechanism for Descartes and for Malebranche—as a denial of the dependence of the material world on God: the ultimate cause of atheism, he writes, is 'this notion of bodies having, as it were, a complete, absolute and independent reality in themselves'.[18] Yet in one sense, he and Malebranche are at one on this question. Malebranche revised Cartesianism to bring out the complete dependence of bodies on God, just as Newton rejected Cartesianism because it makes bodies too independent of God.

Another systematic difference between the two turns on the question of the autonomy of mechanics. Mechanism had stripped matter of any intrinsic powers, with the result that the capacities of matter were confined to those that enabled it to move in particular ways and to transmit motion. Malebranche followed Huygens in treating natural philosophy in terms of kinematics, taking this as the paradigm of clarity and distinctness: this substituted a mathematical theory of motion, with bodies effectively regarded as little more than transmitters of motion, for matter theory.[19] In the *Principia*, Newton treats bodies in this way in his mechanics: at the most basic level, they are construed as idealized mass points devoid of spatial extension. The difference is that he did not think mechanics the end of the matter, if only because these mass points exercised gravitational attraction, whereas Huygens and, in a more systematic way, Malebranche attempted to construe kinematics as in effect being constitutive of natural philosophy. What drives this contrast are considerations of the explanatory force of mechanics, but it is clear from both Malebranche's and Newton's accounts that a factor of paramount importance in assessing explanatory adequacy was how divine activity is connected with natural processes. In particular, there was a pressing question of the way in which God is active at a natural level.

Malebranche's vision of a physical theory is indebted primarily to the natural philosophy set out in Descartes' *Principia*. As we have seen, Descartes offered a conception of a natural philosophy that was 'clear and distinct', and it achieved this (or purported to do so) by employing no notion that was obscure. Obscurity arose primarily, both for the late scholastic systems and for Descartes' own, when it came to the dynamical underpinnings of motion. The difference was that these were an inseparable part of the programme in the late scholastic systems, because an understanding of why something moves is a prerequisite to understanding how it moves. Descartes reversed this, arguing that we should first understand how something moves and only then should we look at causes. His account of the second stage remained comparatively underdeveloped, and in the subsequent history of Cartesian natural philosophy, broadly construed, this feature was not necessarily considered a drawback but actually started to be seen as a strength. One direction one might go in, following this Cartesian model, is to eschew any attempt to provide an independent account of the causes of motion. Rather, one might pursue the project of how things move under every

---

[18] *Unpublished Papers of Isaac Newton*, 110 [text]/144 [trans.].

[19] For Malebranche's work in kinematics, see e.g. his *Des lois de mouvement*: *Œuvres complètes*, xviiB, 29–197. See Mouy, *Le Développement de la physique cartésienne 1646–1712*, ch. 4.

conceivable type of mechanically characterizable circumstance, and see what dynamical implications fall out from this. This is the Huygens/Malebranche route, and it would be a formative influence on the project of rational mechanics in the eighteenth century. The aim was to try and get by without any explicit or independent account of force, determine what is left after an exhaustive analysis of motion, and then see what sense could be made of this residue.[20]

Malebranche took the account of Descartes' *Principia* and represented it in a systematic fashion, ridding it of inconsistencies and ambiguities. While Descartes' own project led in different directions at different times, and contained unreconciled tensions, Malebranche pursued a single trajectory systematically to its logical conclusions. Descartes, for example, had postulated three different kinds of substance—infinite substance (God), finite spiritual substance (mind), and finite extended substance (matter)—but he provided no discussion of the systematic relations between the three. Malebranche by contrast saw this as the key to his foundationalist project, and it is not difficult to appreciate how he could have taken Descartes' lack of clarity on these fundamental relations as the cause of the latter's apparent prevarication. Descartes' account of the mind–body relation, for example, varied from a naturalistic account of cognitive states in *L'Homme* and a naturalistic account of affective states in *Les Passions de l'âme*, to a sharp dualism in the *Meditationes*, yet he seemed unwilling to accept the consequences of this in the latter, insisting that the soul directly experiences bodily states. When it came to a choice between a sharp separation between body and mind in the form of occasionalism, and a blending of mind and body in the doctrine of the 'substantial unity of mind and body', he explicitly chose the latter, because the fact that occasionalism makes more metaphysical sense is outweighed by its wholly counterintuitive consequences.[21]

Malebranche, by contrast, refused to balance such considerations, believing that if something makes metaphysical sense it provides a route we must follow, and he embraced occasionalism without qualms. Consideration of the metaphysics of substance forces us, in Malebranche's view, to hold that there are in effect two substances. Mind is a kind of intermediary between God and matter, which are wholly distinct from one another: it either shares in God, in so far as it is pure intellect, or shares in matter, in so far as it is attached to a body.[22] This view of mind had a number of unwelcome consequences: in effect it committed Malebranche to Averroism, in that a disembodied mind would be identical with God,[23] and it failed to secure free will. But as a foundation for natural philosophy, the gap opened up between the divine and the natural had its advantages. On the phenomenalist path taken by Malebranche, there was a self-sufficient level of description of physical phenomena that eschewed any reference to 'occult qualities' such as forces, and this was the level at which natural

---

[20] See Stephen Gaukroger, 'The Metaphysics of Impenetrability: Euler's Conception of Force', *British Journal for the History of Science* 15 (1982), 132–54.

[21] See the discussion in Gaukroger, *Descartes, An Intellectual Biography*, 388–94.

[22] Malebranche, *La Recherche*, Preface.

[23] Malebranche tried, unsuccessfully, to avoid this consequence by appeal to his notion of a *sentiment intérieur*, a form of self-knowledge that would be required to provide the disembodied soul with an identity: see the discussion in Andrew Pyle, *Malebranche* (London, 2003), ch. 8.

philosophy, now reduced to mechanics, which was in turn reduced to kinematics, operated. Note that on Malebranche's account, the phenomenal realm is completely free of any intrinsic causal powers. This rules out the kind of enquiry to which 'experimental' natural philosophy is devoted, for there could be no causal process at this level. Causation is restricted to God's divine activity, and only God can bring about any changes in nature because there are no intrinsic powers that could initiate a causal process at this level. The claim of the experimentalists was that real demonstrable causal processes are clearly manifest at the phenomenal level, and indeed they are able to be manipulated, allowing us to test their nature and effects, whereas reference to a more fundamental level is usually merely speculative in causal terms. Malebranche's account challenged this in two ways. First, it ruled out causation at the phenomenal level: in terms of the reality of the causal processes invoked for example, there could be no difference between the cases that Boyle and Newton invoked in their pneumatics and optics, and the corpuscular collisions that foundational mechanists invoked to explain these. In neither case were the causal processes invoked genuine, because what was being identified as the causal agent in both cases was something that in fact lacked causal powers. Second, for Malebranche, causal processes were initiated exclusively in the supernatural realm. There was ultimately no natural explanation for natural processes: all one could do was confine oneself to the phenomenal level.

This way of putting things, where the contrast is between a view on which all causation is supernatural and one in which there are real causal processes at the phenomenal level, makes it look as if Malebranchian occasionalism should have provided support for a Newtonian agnostic view on the ultimate nature of gravity. But matters are more complicated. The Galilean kinematic model forced Newton to treat gravitation and inertia as fundamentally different kinds of thing: while both the source and the effects of inertia fall squarely under mechanics, in the case of gravitation the source of the force does not lie in the mechanical realm. Malebranche restricted forces and causal powers generally to the divine realm (this is in large part what gave him such problems accounting for free will), but Newton did not treat mechanics as constitutive of natural philosophy. The difference lies in the fact that kinematics includes no forces, whereas dynamics does, and to the extent to which one pursues dynamics, there is more motivation to explore the physical origins of those forces with which it deals, but which do not have a mechanical origin. Newton certainly thought that all forces derived ultimately from God, and he believed that this must be taken into account in understanding them, telling us that 'whatever cannot exist independently of God cannot be truly understood independently of the Idea of God',[24] but these forces took the form of natural causes, and if they could not be located in the realm of mechanics, then they must lie in the material constitution of things in Newton's view.

*De gravitatione* tells us nothing about the source of gravity (the 'gravity' in question is in fact weight—the 'weighing down' studied in hydrostatics—as the later parts of the treatise make clear), but it does provide a matter-theoretical basis for mechanics, and here Newton departs from mechanism quite significantly. On

---

[24] *Unpublished Papers of Isaac Newton*, 110 [text]/144 [trans.].

Newton's account of matter, it is force, rather than extension, that characterizes matter. In his hypothetical reconstruction of God's creation of matter,[25] God first makes some region of space impervious to already existing bodies: he creates an impenetrable region of space. Impenetrability, which had been merely a derived essence of matter for Descartes (anything that comprises material extension is necessarily impenetrable on Descartes' account), now becomes its only essence. Secondly, having established this region of impenetrability, he allows it to move, according to certain laws. Third, this mobile impenetrable region is opaque (we can think of this, for example, in terms of the ability to reflect or refract light corpuscles) and hence such regions are perceptible. And because it is impenetrable, it is tangible. It is a body. For the existence of such bodies, Newton tells us, 'nothing is required but extension and the action of the divine will'. These two are radically distinct however: 'extension is eternal, infinite, uncreated, uniform throughout, not in the least mobile, nor capable of inducing change of motion in bodies or change of thought in the mind; whereas body is opposite in every respect'.[26] In short, in *De gravitatione* we have a conception of matter according to which it is essentially active, or more precisely, it is a passive mass activated by an active principle. This is a notion that Newton developed in his alchemical studies,[27] which offered his only means of systematic empirical study of matter theory.

Malebranche and Newton offered conceptions of natural philosophy whose chief contrast, I suggest, turns on the question of whether God's activity in the natural realm is unmediated or mediated. In the case of Malebranche, mechanics came to be conceived as being constitutive of natural philosophy, and the paradigmatic way in which this works is via phenomenalism, for mechanics provides a precise quantitative account of the effects of forces whose sources, if they lie outside the mechanical realm, are not something that fall under natural philosophy. For Newton by contrast, the mediation was effected via matter theory, which provides the proximate source of the forces with which dynamics deals. In some respects, this reading is at odds with the picture of Newton and his followers eschewing investigation of gravitational force, and his opponents demanding that he give an account of gravitational force. But if we attend more closely to what the various parties were actually asking for, we can see that the situation is a little more complex. Newton was denying that his inability to provide an account of the nature and source of gravitation vitiates his mechanics, which is all the *Principia* offers. He was also denying that his mechanics is in any way incomplete without an account of the nature and source of gravitation, because he believed that these questions fall outside mechanics. These are the issues on which he was at odds with critics such as Huygens, who were in effect saying that, if gravitation

---

[25] Ibid. 106/139–40.    [26] Ibid. 111/145.

[27] Newton's approach to alchemy is complex in that he combined matter theory and physico-theology. As Dobbs puts it, 'what Newton hoped to gain from alchemy was a precise knowledge of the operations of the Deity in organising and vivifying the inert particles of matter in the microcosm': B. J. T. Dobbs, 'Newton as Final Cause and First Mover', in Margaret J. Osler, *Rethinking the Scientific Revolution* (Cambridge, 2000), 25–39: 38. See also idem, *The Foundations of Newton's Alchemy: or 'The Hunting of the Greene Lyon'* (Cambridge, 1975), 213–25, and idem, *The Janus Face of Genius*, 185–209.

does indeed play the role that Newton claims for it, it must be accounted for mech-anically. The suggestion in Huygens was that this account is going to lie at the micro-corpuscular level, but it is now mechanics, not matter theory, that describes events at this level, for matter has been wholly mechanized. Huygens' demand was, then, that the source of gravity be something that can be accounted for within mechanics, and that not only can no mechanics make any claims to completeness or comprehensive-ness until this has been achieved, but that to deny that this can be done within one's mechanics is tantamount to an admission that that mechanics is seriously deficient.

The difference between Newton and Huygens over what falls within mechanics went the heart of the adequacy of mechanism, for on the Newtonian conception mechanism is but one of a number of disciplines that make up the resources we need to pursue natural philosophy, and there is no reason to suppose that these disciplines are intrinsically connected: indeed, it is their apparent lack of any connection that makes the situation so problematic. It is interesting in this context that one of the prime purposes of alchemy in Newton's programme was the exploration of otherwise inaccessible underlying microscopic principles: one must gauge what is going on at the hidden, microscopic level by means of their manifest chemical reactions at the macroscopic level. Alchemy acts as a kind of inferential microscope. And what it reveals is in some ways rather similar to what was revealed by optical microscopes. Mechanism had assumed that mechanics and matter theory could be combined at the microscopic level, but in fact those who took succour from microscopy were not those who saw micro-corpuscularian interactions as involving nothing but bulk, speed, and direction, but rather those who advocated a more traditional qualitative form of matter theory, or whose concern was with experimental philosophy and natural history. The problem was that what was seen through the microscope was a world that was in many respects more complex and varied than the macroscopic world.

Advocates of more traditional forms of corpuscularianism, which worked with shapes and textures, even though they had undoubtedly expected something simpler at the microscopic level, were not so worried by this. The project of Gassendi and his followers was very much locked into ancient debates over atomism versus the continuum. As a result, someone like Charleton, who introduced Gassendi's natural philosophy into England in the mid-century, could construe what he saw, or what he heard reported, as a vindication of corpuscularian over Aristotelian accounts of the nature of matter. Charleton's view is that apparent sympathies, action at a distance, and the subjective features of the world such as love at first sight, are all to be accounted for in terms of the various qualitatively distinct forms of physical connections between atoms, so that

in every Curious and Insensible Attraction of one bodie by another, nature makes use of cer-tain slender Hooks, Lines, Chains, or the like intercedent Instruments, continued from the Attrahent to the Attracted, and likewise . . . in every Secret Repulsion or Sejunction, she useth certain small Goads, Poles, Levers or the like protruding Instruments, continued from the Repellent to the Repulsed bodie.[28]

---

[28] Charleton, *Physiologia Epicuro-Gassendo-Charltoniana*, 344

The contrast he draws is with Aristotelians, who

Not being able ever to explicate an insensible Propriety, from those narrow and barren Principles: they thought it a sufficient Salvo for their Ignorance, simply to affirme all such Properties to be *Occult*; and . . . they blushed not to charge Nature Herself with too much Closeness and Obscurity, in that point, as if she intended that all Qualities, that are *Insensible*, should also be *Inexplicable*.[29]

Charleton believed the microscope vindicated atomism, not in that it shows us atoms, but rather in that the continuities at the macroscopic level are shown up at the microscopic level to consist of mountains and valleys, so that the 'superfice of no body can be so exactly smooth and polite, as to be devoid of all unevenness or asperity, every common microscope discovering numerous inequalities in the surface of even the best cut Diamond, and the finest Chrystal'.[30] As Catherine Wilson points out, for Charleton continuity was just a question of perceptual blurring: the microscope reveals the uniformity of a metal surface to be in fact irregular, and water must be like fine sand, though even the microscope does not reveal this.[31] In short, if the issue is atomism versus the continuum, then the microscopic observations point decisively in favour of atomism, and the fact that limited magnification does not allow them to reveal the atoms themselves is not a pressing issue.

But for those advocating forms of mechanism more closely allied with developments in mechanics, that is, those which construe the fundamental properties in terms of motion, it was far from clear what to conclude. Certainly there was no observation of, and no prospect of observation of, colliding corpuscles. Indeed, it is difficult to know exactly what one could expect to see at a corpuscular level. Glanvill thought that we should be able see what Adam—whose 'sight could inform him whether the Loadstone doth attract by Atomical *Effluviums*'—saw without the aid of microscopes,[32] but there was some confusion about what was visible and what was not. Boyle speculated that, had we sufficiently powerful microscopes, we might see how 'those little protuberances and cavities do interrupt and dilate the light' and produce the colours 'we attribute to the visible object',[33] and Henry Power talks of using the microscope to see 'the Solary Atoms of Light (or *globuli aetheri* of the renowned *Des-Cartes*)'.[34] But it is hard to see what Power has in mind here: surely not the globules striking corpuscles and acquiring a rotation, for we see by means of the globules, we do not see the globules.[35] There was deep confusion on the fundamental question of just what one would expect to discern by microscopic observation

---

[29] Ibid. 342. Compare the remarks of Friedrich Schrader, that the microscope shows the actual preformed plant lying hidden in the seed, not some speculated 'potential' plant: *De microscopiorum usu in naturali scientia et anatome* (Göttingen, 1681), 16

[30] Charleton, *Physiologia Epicuro-Gassendo-Charltoniana*, 97.

[31] Wilson, *The Invisible World*, 57–8. I have followed Wilson's exemplary account in a number of respects here.

[32] See ibid. 63–4.     [33] Boyle, *Works*, v. 680.

[34] Power, *Experimental Philosophy*, Preface.

[35] The general point was grasped by Mersenne: 'Even if we could enter into the interior of things, we would not understand them any better, for we cannot perceive anything except exterior accidents.' *La Verite des sciences*, 9.

as far as fundamental physical processes were concerned. Nor was it by any means just optics that posed the problems. The closer to mechanics that mechanism gets, the less appropriate the microscopic/macroscopic distinction becomes. In short, as far as mechanism was concerned, far from lending support, the microscope served rather to highlight its speculative character. The microscopic world as uncovered by the microscope, as Hooke's *Micrographia* demonstrates, revealed novelties in natural history—botany, zoology, mineralogy—areas that had never been pursued in terms of a postulated underlying microscopic structure, but almost nothing of relevance to those areas of natural philosophy that had been premissed on the idea of an underlying microscopic structure.

This had consequences for the idea that the unity of natural philosophy consisted in some ultimate level of causation that lay at the corpuscular level. If the postulation of such a level was doomed to remain in the realm of the speculative, untouched by the one discipline that opened up the microscopic world directly, then the principle of unity itself looked decidedly speculative and self-serving. Of course, there were other ways of delving into the microscopic realm, most notably alchemy/chemistry, where the hope was that underlying processes could be manipulated to yield visible, and perhaps even quantifiable, effects at the macroscopic level. This was certainly to be Newton's approach, and as the century progressed matter theorists understandably began to lose interest in microscopy.[36] At the same time, mechanics was construing physical properties no longer in terms of corpuscles but in terms of what came to be known as mass points—centres of mass whose actual extension was not relevant at the abstract level at which mechanics worked—and no one thought of these as being microscopic in the sense that they would be revealed by a suitably powerful microscope. With the development of mechanics in Huygens and Newton, physical properties no longer automatically translated into material properties, and mechanics and matter theory started to come apart in a way that made it increasingly difficult to identify a unique and sufficiently comprehensive level of common causation.

In general terms, the idea that natural philosophy could be unified by referring all processes back to a level of common causation had a number of problems. This level of common causation should, ideally, have identified a small number of simple primary qualities that were fully quantified, and the interactions between corpuscles having only these qualities should then have given rise to the complex macroscopic world of secondary qualities. But with the rise of microscopy the reverse appeared to be the case: it was the macroscopic world that yielded to quantification, the microscopic processes remaining in the realm of speculation. Moreover, it is unclear how the microscopic/macroscopic distinction functions when taken out of its original home of matter theory: whether processes are microscopic or macroscopic is irrelevant in mechanics. We saw in Chapter 9 that the primary/secondary distinction came to replace the microscopic/macroscopic distinction as a way of proceeding that was more in tune with the requirements of mechanics. This provided a means of doing something that had always been at the core of corpuscularianism from Democritean

[36] Wilson notes that by 1692, 'Hooke was already complaining of a reaction against the microscope, of boredom and disenchantment' (*The Invisible World*, 67).

atomism onwards, namely identifying what might be termed a fundamental level of reality. Despite Democritus, it could not plausibly be argued that the microscopic world was more real than the macroscopic one. But it could be argued that the world of primary qualities was more real than that of secondary qualities: that primary qualities were really in the world whereas secondary qualities were merely psychic additions of the perceiving mind. Natural philosophy thus became focused on the former, and since the realm of primary qualities was what natural philosophy dealt with, it was to this extent unified in a substantial sense. But the shift from microscopic/macroscopic to primary qualities/secondary qualities was also a shift from something that had an intuitive and unambiguous grounding in matter theory, to something that was contentious and speculative, lacking empirical support and support from microscopy, and perhaps even hindering empirical enquiry by pointing it in a wholly inappropriate direction, as the case of Newtonian chromatics indicates.

## POLITICO-THEOLOGY AND NATURAL PHILOSOPHY

Common causation, were it successful, would unify natural philosophy, conceived in micro-corpuscularian terms.[37] But common causation is restricted to natural philosophy, and tells us nothing about areas of cognitive endeavour outside natural philosophy. This raises the question whether there are any general lessons to be learned from the successes (real or imagined) of natural philosophy, and whether there might be specific implications for the other areas of cognitive endeavour. However, it is impossible to raise this issue fruitfully without asking more fundamental questions about the aims of cognitive enquiry, and in what respect natural philosophy realizes these aims. In particular, it can be asked whether a discipline that proceeds in a fashion wholly different from that of natural philosophy could be a genuine form of cognitive enquiry, whether there could be quite different models for cognitive enquiry, with theology and natural philosophy, for example, each taking different routes. This option became less attractive after the Pomponazzi affair, although ill-conceived and ill-fated attempts by thinkers such as Bruno to establish a general set of what were, broadly speaking, philosophical criteria that might regulate any form of cognitive enquiry set back any hopes of establishing philosophy as the ultimate arbiter. The problem lay in part in the fact that the natural philosophy which was at the cutting edge of new developments seemed to have no single or uncontentious strategy, compared with theology for example, when it came to the question of the point of cognitive enquiry in the first place.

In classical antiquity, philosophers considered the ultimate goals of knowledge to be wisdom and happiness. Christianity transplanted these goals into a purely spiritual realm, so that they could be realized fully only in a union with God, which was not realizable until after death. Despite an attempt to revive the classical conception by some Renaissance thinkers, knowledge had been transformed in the process, and

---

[37] In principle, this would not prevent either experimental or physico-mathematical forms of natural philosophy doing much of the explanatory work, so long as they could be anchored, as it were, in micro-corpuscularianism. In fact, as we have seen, matters are a little more complex.

the notion that, in pursuing natural philosophy for example, one was pursuing wisdom and happiness, now took on a somewhat problematic aspect. It was far from clear that natural philosophy could produce wisdom and happiness any more than could mathematics or medicine. It was not that wisdom and happiness were abandoned as worthwhile goals, but rather that it was no longer clear how they were to be realized through natural philosophy. It is in this context that the aims and goals of natural philosophy were rethought, with truth and use, which are not intrinsically connected, coming to replace wisdom and happiness, which are intrinsically connected, in that wisdom was conceived to produce to the highest form of happiness. The urgency with which Bacon tried to connect truth and use into an integrated whole was driven ultimately by an attempt to fashion a notion of cognitive enquiry and its cultural standing that would replace the integrated notions of wisdom and happiness that the central role of natural philosophy was making obsolete. What emerged were problems and concerns that are distinctive of Western modernity.

Were natural philosophy just one cognitive discipline among many, this would not have been a significant problem. However, as we have seen, as early as the thirteenth century, natural philosophy had become the key to cognitive enquiry generally. In writers such as Pomponazzi, Telesio, Bruno, and Hobbes it had come close to exhausting the range of cognitive disciplines. But if natural philosophy, so conceived, could not achieve these goals, the question had to be posed whether cognitive enquiry generally was the right place to be looking for wisdom and happiness. The Baconian reform of natural philosophy had made usefulness a central aim but, quite apart from the fact that such usefulness was not much in evidence in the seventeenth century, much more needed to be said if natural philosophy was to play the cognitive and cultural roles than Bacon and his successors had in mind for it.

One way in which this difficulty was met was to remodel natural philosophy along the lines of a natural history which had in effect become a natural theology. Here natural philosophy takes over the Christianized aims of wisdom and happiness by transforming itself into something which for all intents and purposes was a form of Christianity. We have already looked at such an approach in its Boylean form,[38] and it results in a reshaping of both natural philosophy and Christianity, something that I shall be exploring in later volumes. There is also another way of meeting the challenge, however, one in which the autonomy and self-contained nature of natural philosophy is emphasized, and where an attempt is made to legitimate natural-philosophical enquiry by showing how it generates the wisdom and happiness

---

[38] Note, however, that Boyle never believed that natural theology could replace revelation. In the appendix to the *Christian Virtuoso*, he tells us that 'if we believe God to be the author of things, it is rational to conceive that he may have made them commensurate, rather to his own designs in them, then to notions we men may best be able to frame of them' (*Works*, i. 466). In his early 'Essay of the Holy Scriptures', in the course of rejecting an anti-Trinitarian view of the Socinians, Boyle claimed that the Socinians were 'incomparable Masters of Reason', but at the same time staunchly denied that scripture could be judged against the criteria of reason. Later, in *A Discourse Concerning Things above Reason* (1681), he made it clear that many doctrinal matters are intrinsically beyond reason. See Jan W. Wojcik, 'Pursuing Knowledge: Robert Boyle and Isaac Newton', in Margaret Osler, ed, *Rethinking the Scientific Revolution* (Cambridge, 2000), 183–200: 188–9.

that had seemed to many to have become the preserve of religious experience and understanding. Spinoza, combining a defence of the value of the traditional interrelated goals of wisdom and happiness with a wholly uncompromising defence of the kind of methodological approach on which mechanism rests as the only possible approach in cognitive enquiry, set out a novel conception of the nature of wisdom and happiness based directly and exclusively on considerations drawn from natural-philosophical practice. What Spinoza tried to show is that a mechanist natural philosophy, suitably interpreted, can supply us with an understanding of the world and our place in it which is a comprehensive alternative to that offered by Judaeo-Christian teaching and aspirations.

There were two ingredients in Spinoza's project. One was a reassessment of the nature of religious understanding generally and revelation in particular, the other an attempt to provide a new account of self-understanding and freedom that is guided by the same general principles that guide the development of a mechanist natural philosophy. The first of these projects traded on developments in biblical hermeneutics that can be traced as far back as Valla, although Spinoza put a particularly radical gloss on these. The second is largely without precedent, although in some ways Spinoza's conception of natural philosophy, despite its thoroughgoing mechanism, had affinities with Renaissance naturalists, especially Telesio.

Descartes argued that we can assess the veracity of our beliefs to the extent to which we can present them to ourselves clearly and distinctly, for clarity and distinctness offer divinely guaranteed criteria by which to judge the reliability of ideas and beliefs. We can imagine two directions in which the Cartesian project might proceed. One is to argue that we should distinguish those ideas capable of clear and distinct presentation, and concentrate on these, leaving those not amenable to the criterion of clarity and distinctness to one side. The other is to insist that, to the extent to which we are concerned with questions of knowledge and truth, all cognitive claims, without exception, must be subjected to the criterion of clarity and distinctness. Cartesianism was most highly developed in the Netherlands from the mid-1630s onwards,[39] and it is there that we can find the clearest expressions of these conflicting trajectories.

Descartes himself certainly considered that many theological questions cannot be subjected to the criterion of clarity and distinctness because of the radical transcendence of God. God is not present in the world and his purposes are inscrutable to us. As a consequence, in contrast to Boylean physico-theology for example, for Descartes natural knowledge will never lead us to knowledge of the divine. The natural and supernatural realms are firmly partitioned from one another. This line of thought receives a distinctive development in the Dutch Cartesian Johannes de Raey, who argued that clarity and distinctness are not general properties of ideas, that is, something to which all ideas are susceptible, but are rather a feature of a select group of ideas, namely the metaphysically grounded concepts of Cartesian natural philosophy.[40] Consequently,

---

[39] See Theo Verbeek, *Descartes and the Dutch: Early Reactions to Cartesian Philosophy, 1637–50* (Carbondale, 1992).

[40] The argument was first set out in his *De libertate et servitute* (1666), published in an expanded version in his *Cogitata de interpretatione* (Amsterdam, 1692), 425–37.

the point of starting philosophical enquiry from doubt is not to make obscure and confused ideas into clear and distinct ones, but to separate out the two kinds of ideas and the disciplines appropriate to them. Clear and distinct ideas are appropriate in philosophy (paradigmatically natural philosophy) alone and cannot be applied to other disciplines, such as theology. Raey did not deny that scriptural interpretation, for example, delivers truth, only that our grasp of that truth can be in terms of clear and distinct ideas. In this way, his distinction, now reformulated in Cartesian terms, mirrors the traditional divide between natural-philosophical demonstration and theological interpretation: they are two fundamentally different kinds of activity, taking different roads to different truths.

The opposite route was developed in ground made fertile by the Dutch liberal theologian Johannes Cocceius, and radicalized by Cartesianism, and in the 1650s there ensued a struggle between the Cartesio-Cocceans and the conservative Aristotelians led by Gisbert Voetius.[41] The Cartesio-Coccean position was set out by Christopher Wittich in 1653,[42] his central claim being that Scripture is written in the language of the vulgar for their consumption, not in the language of truth. The latter he construed in terms of Descartes' criterion of clarity and distinctness. The consequence of this approach for scriptural interpretation was drawn out explicitly by another Dutch Cartesian, Lodewijk Meyer. Meyer noted that it follows that since scripture is not written in clear and distinct terms, but since God's revelation could not contradict or in any way conflict with the natural light of reason, Cartesian clear and distinct ideas should provide the standard by which to judge scriptural interpretation. The Cartesian criterion of clarity and distinctness must be used to judge any cognitive claims, including scriptural interpretation.[43] There is a sense in which Spinoza, whose approach has its origins in Cartesianism,[44] has a foot in both camps. On the one hand, he argued that there were a number of competing systems of morality, only one of which—that set out in the *Ethica*—employed the criterion of clarity and distinctness, and this marked it out from all others, which were not the kinds of system that could employ this criterion, because, he maintains, their goal is not truth. But he also held that, to the extent that one makes rational cognitive claims, to the extent that one is concerned with the ultimate basis of morality as opposed to simply seeking to secure moral behaviour, there there was only one form of genuine understanding possible, and this was that which followed the criterion of clarity and distinctness. In other words, the same cognitive criteria that hold in natural philosophy must hold

[41] See Theo Verbeek, 'Tradition and Novelty: Descartes and Some Cartesians', in Tom Sorell, ed., *The Rise of Modern Philosophy* (Oxford, 1993), 167–96; idem, 'From "Learned Ignorance" to Scepticism: Descartes and Calvinist Orthodoxy', in Richard H. Popkin and Arjo Vanderjagt, eds, *Scepticism and Irreligion in the Seventeenth and Eighteenth Centuries* (Leiden, 1993), 31–45; Ernestine van der Wall, 'Orthodoxy and Scepticism in the Early Dutch Enlightenment', in Popkin and Vanderjagt, *Scepticism and Irreligion*, 121–41; and Israel, *Radical Enlightenment*, 23–8. More generally, see Jonathan I. Israel, *The Dutch Republic: Its Rise, Greatness, and Fall 1477–1806* (Oxford, 1995), chs. 27, 28, and 30.

[42] Christopher Wittich, *Dissertationes Duae* (Amsterdam, 1653).

[43] Lodewijk Meyer, *Philosophia S. Scripturae Interpres* (Amsterdam, 1666).

[44] On Spinoza's intellectual development see Steven Nadler, *Spinoza: A Life* (Cambrige, 1999).

in the case of any cognitive claims, including those of scriptural interpreters. Spinoza sought not only to undermine the divide between natural-philosophical demonstration and theological interpretation, but to establish the former as the only procedure that could yield knowledge.

Spinoza translated the traditional aims of wisdom and happiness into what he called piety and peace. Although one of his favourite strategies was to give the impression that he was showing the compatibility of his system with traditional values, only for it to turn out that the terms standardly used to refer to those values have shifted meaning in an ingenious way in the course of the argument, piety and peace are more closely related to the original pair than the terminology might suggest, and they are intrinsically interdependent. This interdependence arises from his construal of religion generally in terms of a politico-theology that raises the question of what authority derives from, and in particular what religious and political authority derive from, and what the scope of that authority is. Philosophy, by contrast, is not construed in terms of authority at all, because the application of criteria of certainty in philosophy means that we do not need to defer to authority. Authority is appropriate only where we cannot decide the issue for ourselves. We obey a sovereign's decisions, for example, not because we have accepted the reasoning behind them: if we only obeyed in the cases where we understood and agreed with the reasoning behind decisions, we would hardly be granting any authority at all to the sovereign.[45] Similarly in the case of a prophet, one of the authors of scripture. The prophet interprets God's decrees as they are revealed to him, and we accept what he says because we accept his authority.

But how do we know that the prophet is a genuine prophet? Spinoza discussed three traditional signs of prophecy.[46] The first is the vividness of the prophetic experience, but as he pointed out, dreams and hallucinations can be vivid. The second is the performance of miracles, but again these might not be genuine (Spinoza's view was that there are in fact no genuine miracles[47]), and in order to establish their credentials we must establish that they are performed by a genuine prophet, so there is a circularity. The pressing problem in establishing genuine prophecy here is that the experience of the prophet is strictly private. His experience is an 'inward testimony' and cannot be shared with others: unlike the philosopher offering an argument, he cannot bring others into a state of mind the same as his own. We cannot experience what the prophet experiences and assess it for ourselves. There is no question of being taught to be a prophet, or learning to be a prophet, and this is what distinguishes the activity of 'interpretation' in which the prophet engages from the reasoning of the philosopher.

This brings us to the third sign, that 'the minds of prophets are directed exclusively towards what is right and good'. We judge the credentials of a prophet from the

---

[45] Benedict Spinoza, *Tractatus theologico-politicus*, trans. Samuel Shirley (Leiden, 1991), 300 (*Adnotationes in Tractatum theologico-politicorum*, ch. ii).

[46] *Tractatus*, trans. Shirley, 233–4. See the exemplary discussion in Theo Verbeek, *Spinoza's Theologico-Political Treatise* (Aldershot, 2003), chs. 3 and 4.

[47] *Tractatus*, trans. Shirley, 124.

morality of his teachings and his behaviour, but this morality is in turn measured by the standards of reason, which thereby act as the ultimate grounds for judgement.[48] Three points are worth noting about this conclusion. First, just as a political system is to be judged with respect to peace, that is, with respect to its ability to secure peace, so revelation is to be judged with respect to its ability to secure piety in those who accept it. Just as sovereigns exercise authority but do not reveal truth, so too in Spinoza's politico-theology, prophets also exercise authority but do not reveal truth. Prophecy is to be assessed in terms of its practical upshot, just as government is. Truth is the exclusive preserve of philosophy.

Second, assent to revelation requires an act of will, whereas the will is irrelevant to knowledge, on Spinoza's view. This contrasts both with the traditional view of how we come to know the existence of God, and with the Cartesian view. In the first case, as we have seen, knowledge is construed as something motivated, in that we start from something that we judge to be true, and set out to elucidate and demonstrate it: the scepticism and anguish said to result from such a procedure when we set out from the judgement that God does not exist are taken as a *reductio* of the original judgement. In the Cartesian case, made clear in Descartes himself and even more explicitly in Malebranche, volition is a component in knowledge, for to believe something is to freely assent to its truth.[49] But for Spinoza a cognitive judgement cannot involve an act of volition. It is not as if we decide something is true and then assent to its truth: once we have applied cognitive criteria to a belief and demonstrated its truth, that is the end of the matter. Talk of assent is only relevant where we accept something on authority. Crucial to this distinction is Spinoza's account in the opening chapters of *Tractatus theologico-politicus* on the difference between prophecy and philosophy in terms of the imagination and the intellect. Prophecy, he maintained, is the work of the imagination alone, without any input from the intellect. This explains why prophets are able to achieve things that are beyond the intellect, why they use literary forms such as parables and allegories that have no relation to logical demonstration, why prophecy is sporadic, how those with no learning at all can be prophets, why prophecy lacks intrinsic certainty, and why it reflects the personality, belief, and temperament of the prophet.[50] In the light of this, it would be misguided to expect that prophecy could enlighten us as to truth generally, and natural-philosophical truths in particular. It is entirely appropriate that it be judged by its ability to induce piety in those who accept it, but entirely inappropriate that it be judged by its ability to reveal or establish truths about the world.

Third, as we have seen, the traditional view of atheism was that, since there were no intellectual grounds for atheism, it was motivated by immorality: immoral people, fearful of the consequences of their behaviour, denied the existence of God in the hope that they could escape punishment. Conversely, immoral behaviour, or impiety,

---

[48] *Tractatus*, trans. Shirley, 234.

[49] See Michael Della Rocca, 'Judgement and Will', in Stephen Gaukroger, ed., *The Blackwell Guide to Descartes' Meditations* (Oxford, 2006), 142–59; and more generally Susan James, *Passion and Action: The Emotions in Seventeenth-Century Philosophy* (Oxford, 1997).

[50] See the discussion in Verbeek, *Spinoza's Theologico-Political Treatise*, ch. 3.

was also the standard way of identifying atheists. Spinoza wished to establish that the worth of a system is to be judged by the piety to which it leads those adhering to that system. And he argued that his own system, despite advancing many of the theses characteristic of atheism—denial of a transcendent God, determinism, denial of providence, etc.—in fact induced piety, and should therefore be treated in this respect as being on a par with those religious beliefs that induced piety. It is easy to see an analogy with the case of Copernicanism here: Spinoza sets out to show that his system 'saves the appearances'—in this case induces the piety that is a universal goal—just as well as do systems of religious belief. The issue then arises whether one of these equivalent systems is the 'real' system, and there is no doubt that he wanted to establish that there is one system that has the relevant credentials in this respect, namely the one he proposed himself, and which he set out in detail in his *Ethica*.[51]

Before we look at this system, however, it will help to have an idea of what the kind of knowledge that Spinoza sought looks like. In his early *Tractatus de Intellectus Emendatione*, he distinguished between various classes of knowledge, or purported knowledge, rejecting hearsay knowledge (knowledge that simply comes from upbringing and tradition), knowledge based on accidental comparison of similar occurrences (such as knowledge that people are mortal), and knowledge that I have of a cause through an effect, as when I deduce the union of mind and body from the fact of sensation, for example. Spinoza rejected these three kinds of knowledge, because they do not serve to increase the power of the understanding. Two other kinds, however, he did accept: knowledge in which an effect is deduced from a cause, and the kind of unmediated grasp of truth that Spinoza, following Descartes, refers to in terms of *intuitus*. The latter has Cartesian precedents, and is the kind of knowledge we have of the *cogito*. The former is a bit more idiosyncratic. In Axiom 4 of the *Ethica*, we are told that 'the knowledge of an effect depends on, and involves, the knowledge of the cause'. For Spinoza, to say that $A$ causes $B$ is to say that $B$ is dependent upon $A$ for its existence and nature. This dependence between things is 'expressed in' or 'conceived through' a dependence between ideas, where the idea of $B$ is dependent upon the idea of $A$ if its truth must be established by reference to the idea of $A$. The conclusions of a mathematical proof for example are dependent upon the premises, and the model for the relation of 'rational dependence' between ideas here is clearly mathematics. More problematically, it is also a model for 'causality', which is the relation that exists between $A$ and $B$ when the existence and nature of $B$ must be explained in terms of $A$. Through proof we *explain* a conclusion, and if the premises are self-evident, we explain it completely. In other words, causal relations and deductive relations are exactly the same thing: reality and conception coincide, so that relations between ideas correspond exactly to relations in reality.

---

[51] On the *Ethica* see Martial Guéroult, *Spinoza* (2 vols, Paris, 1968); Edwin M. Curley, *Spinoza's Metaphysics: An Essay in Interpretation* (Cambridge, Mass., 1969); and, particularly on the scholastic background to Spinoza's metaphysics, Harry Austryn Wolfson, *The Philosophy of Spinoza* (2 vols, New York, 1969). I have used the translations in Spinoza, *Collected Works, i,* trans. E. Curley (Princeton, 1985).

The argument is designed to establish *intuitus* and deduction as the two sources of knowledge. *Intuitus* provides us with certainties immanent in the mind, and deduction shows us how these can be used to produce new knowledge. In this respect Spinoza believed he was following Descartes, but he immediately went on to reject a crucial part of Descartes' procedure, the method of doubt. True ideas, Spinoza believed, contain their own certainty. Certainty is just 'the objective essence of a thing', that is, the thing as it is represented in the understanding. It follows that the mind in possession of true ideas cannot fail to know that they are true: no truly sincere doubt can reach them, and they require no guarantee. Once we have identified fictitious, false, or doubtful ideas, we are in no danger of confusing them with true ideas, and Spinoza believed that they can be identified quite straightforwardly. A fictitious idea is identified primarily by its lack of determinateness. We can arbitrarily imagine its objects as existing or not existing; we can arbitrarily attribute such and such a predicate to a being whose nature is known to us imperfectly—for example, we can imagine that the mind is square. The fictitious idea is the idea that permits an alternative. But if we possess the true idea of something, its indeterminateness disappears. To anyone who knew the entire course of nature the existence of a being would be either a necessity or an impossibility, and anyone who knew the nature of the mind could not suppose it to be square. A false idea, by contrast, attributes to a subject a predicate that is not deduced from its nature, because the mind conceives its nature only in a confused, indistinct manner. Doubt springs from error. Descartes' hyperbolic doubt, for example, was possible only because of a false belief in the possible existence of a deceitful God. A true idea, on the contrary, is a completely determinate idea that contains the cause of everything that can be stated or denied concerning its object. We have a true idea of a well-regulated mechanism of a clock, for example, when the relation between its parts is conceived distinctly, even though the mechanism may not be realized: there may actually exist no such clock. What constitutes a true idea is not its correspondence with an external reality but what Spinoza calls its 'intrinsic character'.

Spinoza was clearly thinking here of the power of the understanding to form, purely from within its own resources, true ideas in mathematics. It begins with simple ideas which must be true since, being simple, they have to be wholly determinate. It then forms complex ideas by linking these simple ideas. The idea of a sphere, for example, has its origin in the rotation of a semicircle around its diameter. Each such idea is a wholly determinate essence, and the mind never has to pass through universal, abstract axioms in order to grasp them. The problem is that while this account may be seem plausible for mathematics, it seems unlikely that knowledge of nature could be arrived at in this way. Spinoza believed it can be, however. The key to it is methodical analysis of the conditions of the problem. Knowledge of nature can be achieved purely through the understanding if the understanding is able to represent a true essence that is the universal cause of all the effects of nature, just as the essence of a circle is the cause of all its properties. From the idea of the true essence, the understanding deduces, objectively, the idea of all other things, so that our minds reproduce nature as perfectly as possible. Now the nature which the understanding deduces from the objective essence of the principle underlying nature cannot, Spinoza tells us, 'be a succession of singular things subject to change, but must be a succession of fixed, eternal things'. To understand what these fixed, eternal things are, we need to remember that Descartes postulates in nature fixed essences and eternal truths, such as extension, the conservation of motion, and the laws of collision. Spinoza's 'fixed, eternal things' are also the whole set of laws which constitute the permanent structure of nature; they are laws 'according to which all singular things happen and are regulated'. But this means that they are also particular essences, well-defined and determinate verities (just as the essence of a right angle or of a circle is a determinate essence in mathematics), although they are present throughout nature and play the role of universals. Generally speaking, just as we deduce one mathematical truth from another without ever reaching the end of the chain or using it to form a whole, Spinoza saw each of the 'fixed, eternal things' as nothing more than a link in a chain or a moment in a progression, and not as part of a whole. And just as in mathematics, so too in the most general case, for Spinoza, one's deduction must always be orientated toward the solution of the problem that was its point of departure. In the most general case, the problem is nothing less than that of human nature and its union with God. This is the problem that his *Ethica* is directed to.

The *Ethica* begins with a consideration of what exists, and Spinoza very quickly comes to the remarkable conclusion that, contrary to the Cartesian view that there are three substances—God, mind, and matter—there is in fact only one substance, God. The demonstration takes the form of a version of the ontological argument. Spinoza, like Anselm and Descartes before him, does not use the ontological argument to establish the existence of God, in the sense of setting out an argument designed to convince someone who doubts or does not believe that God exists. The argument is directed not so much at God's existence as to what God's existence consists in, because what they were concerned with is the nature of God, and as a means of approaching this question they establish that God's existence is such that he must have certain distinctive features. Because of the extremely heterodox conclusion that Spinoza draws, this feature is particularly clear from his version of the argument. The ontological argument is usually taken to show that there is at least one thing that exists, namely God. Spinoza argues that it also shows that there is at most one thing that exists, and hence, as he puts it in Proposition 14 of Book 1 of the *Ethica*, that 'there can be, or be conceived, no other substance than God'. The reasoning runs thus: Spinoza defines God as a 'substance consisting of infinite attributes, each of which expresses eternal and infinite essence.'[52] God cannot be caused by anything else and hence must be *causa sui;* but if something is *causa sui* its essence must involve its existence. Therefore God necessarily exists. This part of the argument can be expressed in more traditional terminology, along these lines: God has every perfection, and not only can something that has every perfection not rely on something outside itself for its existence, but its existence is just one of its perfections. Next Spinoza moves to the wholly original part of the argument. 'There can be, or be conceived, no other substance than God',[53] he tells us, because God expresses all the attributes of substance, and were something

---

[52] Spinoza, *Ethics*, Book 1, def. 6.   [53] Ibid. def. 14.

else to express one of these attributes (which it would have to were it to be a substance) then there would exist two substances with the same attribute, which is impossible, because attributes express essence, which is distinctive and unique. The only conclusion to be drawn is that God is identical with the totality of what exists.

Now although nothing can exist apart from God, however, distinct things can exist *in* God. Existence *in* God is a term of the art in Spinoza, and there are two things we must grasp to understand just what is being claimed. First, we must remember that Spinoza associated causation and deduction, so that *A*'s being the cause of *B*, and *B*'s being contained in *A*, are just another way of saying that *A* is the explanation for *B*. But his account also relied on his idiosyncratic construal of the relation between substance, mode, and attribute. The *Ethica* begins with a definition of something's being *causa sui*, its own cause: 'By that which is self caused I mean that whose essence involves existence; or that whose nature can be conceived only as existing.'[54] This definition—which turns out to be the definition of everything that exists—is followed by a tripartite distinction between 'substance', 'attribute', and 'mode'. Substance is 'that which is in itself and conceived through itself'. That is to say, to conceive of it we do not need to conceive of anything else. Now Spinoza argued that whatever is conceptually independent in this way is also ontologically independent. Hence existence belongs to the very nature of substance, and every substance contains within itself the complete explanation of its own nature and existence. Spinoza saw this argument as merely drawing out inescapable logical consequences from an idea that had previously been understood only in a confused way. Many scholastic and Cartesian philosophers had assumed substances to be the ultimate constituents of reality, and, as such, self-dependent. What they had failed to see, on Spinoza's account, was the natural consequence of this assumption; namely, that *any* substance must be *causa sui*, and therefore necessarily existent. The definition of substance is not contentious in itself, only the consequence that Spinoza drew from it. The definition of a mode, by contrast, is quite idiosyncratic, although it makes sense given his account of substance. It is defined as something that cannot exist independently: a mode must be a mode *of* something. The usual way of thinking of modes is as properties or relations, but Spinoza used the term to include individual things. You and I are both modes of the divine substance, since we can both be conceived as not existing, and therefore owe the explanation of our existence to something outside ourselves. We are not self-dependent and if we exist, it is through the power of something outside of us. Finally, an attribute is defined as 'that which the intellect perceives as constituting the essence of substance'. Here Spinoza seems to be following Descartes, who argued that the essence of a substance is known clearly and distinctly through its principal attribute—for example, the essence of body is known through extension. Spinoza's claim that a substance can have more than one attribute also seems to have a precedent in Descartes, albeit not one that he follows up. Although Descartes defined the essence of matter in terms of extension, he was aware that whatever is material is also necessarily impenetrable, and he construed impenetrability as its derived

⁵⁴ Spinoza, *Ethics*, Book 1, def. 1.

essence.[55] So matter could be said to have extension and impenetrability as its essence; and in Spinoza's terminology, this would mean that its attributes would be extension and impenetrability, which would be to say that there are two different ways of perceiving what the essence of matter is.

Specifically, Spinoza identified two attributes of God: thought and extension. The first is the systematic totality of ideas; the second the systematic totality of physical objects. But this was not a statement of dualism, at least of any traditional kind. Spinoza dealt with the mind–body problem simply by arguing that ideas and physical objects are modifications of a single substance, conceived in two separate and incommensurable ways, now as mind, now as matter or extension. Neither can be reduced to the other, but we are not talking about different things when we use mental and material categories.

It follows that God is not distinct from the world but identical with it, a conclusion of many Renaissance naturalists, although Spinoza's route to, and interpretation of, this conclusion was quite different. For Spinoza, God is conceived by the human mind in two separate ways: whether contemplating the divine mind, and our own mind as part of it, or investigating the structure of the physical world, we are advancing our knowledge of God. Spinoza expressed his monism in a celebrated phrase: the world is *Deus sive Natura*—God or Nature. God is not the transcendent cause of the world, acting outside or beyond it, as Mersenne and Descartes had been anxious to establish, but its immanent cause, acting from within. Moreover, since causality is a form of necessity, and since the divine nature is eternally and necessarily as it is, everything that happens in the world happens by necessity. Just as there is no freedom of a traditional kind in the physical world, a view that was held by all mechanists, so Spinoza takes his construal of the mental and the physical as being ontologically the same thing to mean that neither is there any freedom of a traditional kind in the mental world. An effect follows from its cause with the rigid necessity of a mathematical proof. Every human action, as a mode of God, arises out of the same unbreakable chain of necessity, and therefore such ideas as 'chance' and 'freedom' cannot be given the significance that they have traditionally been taken to have. Things could have been otherwise only if God could have been otherwise: but God could not have been otherwise, since to be God he has to have every perfection, and nothing that did not have every perfection could have been God.

Finally, God is the only 'free' cause, since he alone is self-creating. In so far as we think of God in this way we understand nature as an active and creative principle, intelligible in and through itself. We understand it as *natura naturans* ('naturing nature') and under this aspect we associate it with God, mind, a creator, and atemporality. When we explain things in this way, we do not relate those things to what precedes them in time, but rather show their timeless relation to the eternal essence of God. But we can also study nature as the product of creation, as the working out of a creative endeavour or impulse. In this way, we understand it as *natura naturata* ('natured nature'), and under this aspect we associate it with nature, matter, something created, and temporality. *Natura naturans* and *natura naturata* are two sides

---

[55] See e.g. Descartes to More, 15 April 1649: *Œuvres*, v. 341–2.

of the same coin. Spinoza's metaphysics dictated that nothing exists save one substance: the self-contained, self-sustaining, and self-explanatory system that constitutes
the world. This system may be understood in two different ways, but it is one and the
same system, and indeed one and the same thing, that is being understood.

In Book 2 of the *Ethica*, Spinoza moved to the study of human nature in so far as
it can be deduced from the nature and attributes of this single substance. Only two
of God's infinite attributes are known, namely extension and thought, and each of
these is simple, infinite, and eternal. Human nature, on the other hand, which comprises body and soul, is characterized by duration, change, multiplicity, birth, and
death. The initial problem is, therefore, how human nature can spring from divine
nature, when the two are so different. The best way to see Spinoza's answer to this
is to consider the way he drew on Cartesian natural philosophy. Like Huygens and
Malebranche, it was the rationalized system of Descartes' *Principia*, in which physical theory is reformulated in terms of clarity and distinctness, that Spinoza saw as
the core of the natural-philosophical project, and indeed Spinoza, whose first publication was a rewriting of Cartesian philosophy in axiomatic terms, generated his philosophical results almost exclusively through systematization, drawing unforeseen and
unexpected consequences from a rich and powerful system, and driving it in novel
directions. In the present case, the starting point was Descartes' claim that bodies
are distinguished from one another only in so far as they are moving with respect
to one another. The quantity of motion in the universe is constant, albeit distributed differently from instant to instant, and the laws governing the distribution of
motion—laws of inertia and laws of collision—are eternally true. Spinoza construed
the constant quantity of motion in the universe as a mode of the attribute of extension: it is an eternal mode, like the attribute itself, and it is an infinite mode since it
signifies an element of immutability in that aspect of the universe taken as a whole. In
other words, while there is change at the individual level, at the total level there is no
change, since the quantity of motion is unchanging. So the one substance that exists,
considered in terms of its attribute of extension, has an eternal and infinite mode,
namely: a fixed quantity of motion. This same substance, under its other attribute,
mind, also has an infinite mode: namely, 'infinite intellect', or the intellect of God,
which contains everything else.

The real novelties in the Spinozean system come, however, when we turn from
infinite to finite modes. A finite mode of extension, body, is nothing but a material
extension with parts formed by some portions moving with respect to others in such a
way that the whole persists for a certain time. In this we can find nothing that links the
body to the eternal essence of the attribute of extension. Rather, the existence of the
body *qua* body is due to its interactions with other finite modes. That is, other bodies
have transferred motion to it, but these in turn have received their motion from other
bodies, and so on. And what is true of the modes of extension is also true of the modes
of thought, or ideas, for the order of objects in our thought reproduces the order of
realities in extension, in accordance with the correspondence of attributes. From this
it follows that a finite mode has a manner of existing quite different from that of an
infinite mode or an attribute. In the infinite mode and the attribute, essence is merged
with existence. But the finite mode, considered from the standpoint of its essence, is

merely possible, since it begins to exist only when another finite mode produces it, and ceases to exist as soon as another finite mode excludes it. On Spinoza's account, existence in the sense of duration—simple persistence through time—is existence to the extent that it is distinct from essence, and finite beings are peculiar in that they have the cause of their existence outside themselves: it is not part of their essence that they exist. Indeed he treats the finite world, with its external causality and its mere duration, as deficient in that it cannot be deduced immediately from the nature of any of the attributes of the one substance. But this one substance is nevertheless responsible for it, since it is responsible for everything. Spinoza puts this by saying that God is not the immanent cause but the remote cause of the finite world. But this is problematic. Remote causes are still immanent in that they are not transcendent. And since he thinks of causation in terms of deductive entailment, remote inferences are in logical terms just as direct as immediate ones. So it's not clear that Spinoza can capture the way in which God is remote. On the other hand, if God is not remote, this makes us simply part of God, and in consequence divine, which is incompatible with our role as merely part of a totality: the doctrine of one substance begins to resemble the Averroistic doctrine of one mind.

Despite this, Spinoza's conception of human nature offered a powerful model of self-realization, albeit one that had to wait until the end of the eighteenth century before it began to have a significant philosophical currency. For Spinoza, the human being consists of a body and a mind, which he describes respectively as an actual mode of extension and an actual mode of thought constituted by the idea of this body. To understand the obscure characterization of the latter, we must remember that the attribute of thought and the attribute of extension—both attributes of the one substance—each provide us with a complete and adequate knowledge of essence. Thought and extension each represent reality as it essentially is, and each attribute gives a *complete* account of that reality. Hence every mode—including every object in the system of time and change—can be described in both mental and in physical terms, and if we are not acquainted with the ideas that express the reality of a physical object, this is merely the result of our confused perception. In our own case, however, we know both the mental and the physical expression of a single finite mode. The mind, Spinoza tells us, is a particular *idea*, namely 'the idea of the body'.[56] This idea is 'not simple, but composed of many ideas',[57] and to each of its components there corresponds a bodily process that is its 'object' or *ideatum*. The obscurity here is largely terminological. Normally, when we say that an idea is an idea *of* some object, we do not mean to suggest that the idea and the object are intimately connected, like our mind and our body for example. After all, we can have ideas of fictional objects, of objects that we are unacquainted with, and so on. Normally, the word 'of' means 'about', and the 'object' of an idea is what is represented or thought about in the idea. For Spinoza, however, the only genuine cognitive relation that could exist between an idea and a material thing is the relation that exists between an idea, which is a mode of the single substance conceived under the attribute of thought, and the very same mode conceived under the attribute of extension. For Spinoza, 'the idea of

---

[56] Spinoza, *Ethics*, Book 2, prop. 13.     [57] Ibid. prop. 15.

the body and the body itself—that is, mind and body—are one and the same individual thing, conceived now under the attribute of thought now under the attribute of extension'.[58] Mind and body are one and the same thing: nevertheless, to describe a thing as mind and to describe it as body is to situate it within two separate and incommensurable systems. The details of the systems cannot be mutually substituted, so there cannot be a causal relation between the two.

Spinoza conceived of the human being as a part of, or a finite mode in, nature. Now all finite modes persist and retain their identity only so long as a certain distribution of motion and rest is preserved among the system of simple bodies composing them. Human beings constantly suffer changes of state or modifications of their nature in interactions with their environment; but because they are relatively complex organisms they can be changed in a great variety of ways without their 'actual essence' as particular things being destroyed. The identity of any particular thing in nature depends on its power of self-maintenance, and the 'actual essence' of any particular thing is simply this tendency to self-maintenance which, in spite of external causes, makes it the particular thing that it is. This is the point of Spinoza's statement in the *Ethica* that 'the *conatus* by which each thing endeavours to persist in its own being is nothing more than the actual essence of the thing itself'.[59] The greater the power of self-maintenance of the particular thing in the face of external causes, the greater the reality (that is, the greater the identity) it has, and the more clearly it can be distinguished as having a definite nature and individuality. Within Spinoza's definitions, it is necessarily true that every finite thing, including the human being, endeavours to preserve itself and to increase its power of self-maintenance. The *conatus* is a necessary feature of everything in nature, because this tendency to self-maintenance is involved in the definition of what it is to be a distinct and identifiable thing. Thus, human beings maintain their identity or individuality through self-maintenance, something which is not the outcome of choice or decision but occurs naturally and necessarily in all things in nature. Particular things that are less complex in their structure than persons are susceptible to fewer modifications and have less individuality as distinct things: their cohesion is liable to disruption by a comparatively narrower range of external causes.

Anything can be conceived as a part of nature, either under the attribute of thought or under the attribute of extension. Only human beings, however, have that degree of complexity such that, conceived under the attribute of thought, they can be said to be self-conscious, or be said to have minds consisting of ideas that reflect the effects of external causes in modifying that balance of motion and rest which constitutes the human body. A modification arising out of body's interaction with other things may result in either an increase or a decrease in *conatus*. Every increase in *conatus* is by definition a pleasure, every decrease a pain. Spinoza defined the word 'pleasure' as 'the passion by which the mind passes to a higher state of perfection' and he defined 'pain' as 'the passion by which it passes to a lower state of perfection'.[60] In this way, the degree of power or perfection of any finite thing depends on the degree to which it

---

[58] Spinoza, *Ethics*, Book 2, scholium to prop. 21.　　　[59] Ibid. prop. 7.
[60] Ibid. Book 3, prop. 11.

is causally active, and not passive, in relation to things other than itself. The one abso-lutely powerful and perfect being, God or nature, is in all respects active and in no respects passive. A finite mode, such as a human being, has a greater power and per-fection in so far as its successive states or modifications are less the effects of external causes and are more the effects of preceding changes within itself. This means that a human being, conceived as a finite mode of thought, has greater power or perfection to the extent that the succession of ideas that constitute its mind are linked together as causes to effects. In other words, someone is active and not passive to the extent that their succession of ideas is a logical one. Most human minds consist of a sequence of ideas such that the causes of these ideas are external to the sequence; the sequence is therefore not in itself intelligible, as a self-contained sequence is. The power and per-fection of an individual mind is increased in proportion as it becomes less passive and more active and self-contained in the production of ideas.[61]

On Spinoza's account, the individual, at any moment of its existence, is, regarded as a body, in a condition to be stimulated or depressed in vitality by contact with certain things; this condition or 'determination' is completely explicable by purely physical laws, and in terms of physical equilibrium, and of the recent disturbances in this equilibrium, a conception highly reminiscent of Galenic medicine. The same situation can also be characterized in different terms: lack of freedom consists in being moved by causes of which we are unaware because our ideas are confused, in which case the transition to freedom is made solely by our ideas becoming adequate. The transition from inadequate ideas to adequate ones is, in effect, the transition from passivity to activity of the mind. When our ideas are adequate, we are no longer moved by something external to us; what initiates our movement is within us, and by definition we are free. It is crucial for Spinoza that rational understanding is not merely a means to something else. It is at the same time both means and end. The goals which the understanding reveals are the goals of freedom and rationality, and these are one and the same. This freedom, which consists in knowing the causes that move one, and thus making the causes internal and not external to the agent, entails the belief that 'free will' is among the illusions, the confused ideas, that the person who is genuinely free has discarded.

In this way, then, in a project that clearly has Epicurean and Stoic precedents, Spinoza recaptured the notions of wisdom and happiness, removing them from the religious world which they had inhabited since the Patristic era, and restoring them to the secular realm, a secular realm in which natural philosophy provided a comprehensive and complete form of understanding of the world and our place in it. Needless to say, this provoked a response of unprecedented hostility, which outdid that accorded even to Epicurus and Hobbes. But the wholesale rejection of Spinoza's ideas, outside an underground movement,[62] was not just due to a

---

[61] Spinoza was less explicit about what constitutes such an increase in the power or perfection of a human being conceived as a particular extended thing or body, and he didn't clearly explain what the equivalent in physical terms is of the transition from an illogical association of ideas to logically coherent thoughts.

[62] See Israel, *Radical Enlightenment, passim.*

failure by his contemporaries to come to terms with Spinozism: Malebranche and Leibniz certainly tried to come to terms with it, for example, and it shaped their own thinking on questions of causation, freedom, and the mind. Nor was it due to Spinoza being someone 'ahead of his time'. The idea of imposing rigorous criteria of assessment of biblical interpretation had precedents stretching back as far as Valla and had been assimilated by Protestant theologians, many of whom had not shirked from drawing attention to contradictions and discrepancies. Moreover, Spinoza's natural philosophy was in many respects simply a dogmatic restatement of Descartes' *Principia*, of which he managed to systematize only the early parts. The reasons why the Spinozean programme was not taken up by his contemporaries and immediate successors is, I suggest, rather to be found in intrinsic difficulties in his system, and above all its failure to meet the demands of the natural philosophy he advocated.

The paradigm of knowledge for Spinoza was a mechanist natural philosophy formulated along the lines of a doctrine of clarity and distinctness. Spinoza's version of this latter doctrine did not match that of Descartes in every detail, and above all it was not tied in to a programme of systematic doubt. One feature of the Cartesian doctrine, that assessment of veracity is a matter of inspection of ideas, was retained however. The difference was that, for Descartes, while there were some questions—such as the existence of God, the nature of matter, and the nature of the mind—where inspection of ideas was sufficient to reveal everything, there was a large range of empirical questions where clarity and distinctness were necessary, but not sufficient, conditions for understanding. In the latter case it was a question of presenting ideas to oneself in such a way that one could formulate clear and distinct questions. Questions such as the number of satellites of Jupiter are not the kind of thing that could be discovered through an examination of one's clear and distinct ideas alone, because they are empirical questions. For Spinoza, by contrast, while such questions are as a matter of fact empirical for us, this is simply due to the inadequacy of our understanding of the universe, and if we had a full grasp we would understand that there are no contingencies but only necessities. If Jupiter has four moons this is because it could not but have four moons: it is in the nature of things that it have four moons and it could not have been otherwise.

This puts a load on the notion of a clear and distinct idea that it cannot possibly bear. Indeed, it is not even clear that it can bear the load it carries in its paradigm case, physical theory. As we have seen in the case of Spinoza's contemporary and neighbour, Huygens,[63] the rigorous application of the doctrine to physical theory did not act to expand the range of natural-philosophical knowledge, but to contract it into kinematics. The model that underlay Huygens' understanding of clarity and distinctness was that of axiomatic geometrical demonstration, and it was the application of this notion to the study of motion that prevented him from introducing forces into mechanics. Spinoza employed the same model but in a way that he considered captured what it is about mathematical demonstration that confers its certainty and conviction, namely clarity and distinctness. But such clarity and distinctness, to the extent that it goes beyond merely the demands of

---

[63] On the relation between Spinoza and Huygens, see Nadler, *Spinoza*, 221–2.

rigorous argument, which are generally accepted, far from embodying the essence of geometrical demonstration, in fact becomes little more than a metaphorical extension of the idea of geometrical demonstration. Yet just how counterproductive the notion could be was evident even in its least contentious and (outside geometry itself) most literal form, in mechanics. The reaction of Huygens and Spinoza to Boyle's experimental approach to pneumatics was one of incomprehension: they simply could not understand how an approach that was not systematic, that did not start from foundational clear and distinct ideas, and deduce the phenomena from principles formulated in terms of these ideas, could yield genuine explanations. They were unable to take Boyle's work at face value and assess its merits before proceeding to ask how it fitted in with their canons of explanation. But at least in Huygens' case, Boyle's approach to explanation is being compared with a canon that has genuine explanatory power: the issue is whether axiomatic demonstration from foundational principles is the only possible legitimate form of explanation. The case of Spinoza is far more egregious in this respect, for the canon of explanation that does the real work in Spinoza's system is not something uncontentiously legitimate: it is a highly contentious metaphorical extension of the clarity and distinction in evidence in a geometrical demonstration.

Spinoza's proposal of a general methodological criterion has close affinities with Descartes' early attempt to extrapolate a general theory of method from his discovery of a 'universal mathematics',[64] and some of the basic problems can be traced back to Descartes. Around 1620, Descartes began musing on how a calibrated multi-limbed compass, an instrument called the proportional compass, which had been used, among other things, for the calculation of compound interest, could enable one to resolve not just arithmetical problems such as this, but also geometrical problems, such as the trisection of angles. Up to this point, geometry and arithmetic had been treated as distinct unrelated disciplines: on the Aristotelian definition, for example, they deal with continuous and discontinuous magnitudes respectively. But reflection on just what manipulation of the proportional compass does, namely the generation of continued proportions, led Descartes to the realization that underlying both arithmetic and geometry is a more fundamental mathematical discipline, a general theory of proportions, which he termed 'universal mathematics' (*mathesis universalis*). This discipline, he argued, underlies all mathematical disciplines, not just the theoretical disciplines of geometry and arithmetic but also the practical ones such as astronomy and harmonics. This discovery was followed up in two different—and, as it turned out, conflicting—directions, a mathematical one and a non-mathematical one. The first was the development of a structural theory of equations, algebra, which enabled Descartes to solve mathematical problems that had defied the efforts of geometers. This provided striking evidence that Descartes had in fact discovered a more fundamental underlying discipline, one with great problem-solving power. The second development was an attempt to discover an even more fundamental level, in which Descartes moved to the idea that just as universal mathematics underlies all the mathematical disciplines, so it itself is perhaps simply

---

[64] See Gaukroger, *Descartes, An Intellectual Biography*, ch. 4.

a reflection of something even more fundamental, namely universal method, which covers all knowledge and is not restricted to mathematics. The guiding idea behind this was that, if there is a form of presentation of mathematical ideas such that one can grasp their truth or falsity clearly and without doubt, one can ask more generally what it is that confers this character on these mathematical ideas. The problem for Descartes was that his understanding of what it was to present mathematical ideas in clear and distinct terms, namely in terms of primitive operations on line lengths, broke down once he started to deal with certain complex mathematical operations.[65] The application of the method in the case of mathematics can be illustrated by the operation of addition. It is not as clear as it possibly could be from the formula $2 + 2 = 4$ that 2 and 2, when added together, do actually equal 4: we need to understand the symbols, operators, and the nature of the operations. But when we represent numbers as line lengths or dots, we grasp the truth of the proposition immediately. It is immediately clear from putting one pair of dots, :, next to another pair of dots, :, that what we obtain is : :. There is no room for mistake or confusion. But a discrepancy arose in the *Regulae* between the concern to represent the operations of arithmetic algebraically, in structural terms, and the concern to provide a vindication of arithmetical processes in terms of operations so clear and distinct that one could not fail to assent to them. When, in the uncompleted Rules 19–21 of the *Regulae*, he turned to 'problems that must be set up in terms of several equations in several unknowns', that is, higher-order root extractions, the vindication in terms of clear and distinct ideas broke down completely, as we end up with line-length vindications involving geometrical constructions of such extreme complexity that their degree of clarity and distinctness is manifestly less than the operations they are supposed to vindicate. And in the case of imaginary roots, any connection between Descartes' algebraic procedures and the vindication in terms of line lengths broke down completely, for there is no line-length construction available at all. This did not lead Descartes to give up the doctrine of clear and distinct ideas however; rather, in its subsequent development, its model shifted from mathematics to the *cogito ergo sum*, which acts as a paradigm case of cognitive grasp. Here we have something that achieves at least one aspect of what universal method was supposed to achieve, the provision of a means of making the conceptual content of a proposition so transparent that in grasping it we immediately grasp its truth or falsity. But the breakdown of the doctrine in mathematics—which had been not only the paradigm case for its application but, in the form of the more modest doctrine of universal mathematics, had been the only area in which it was able to demonstrate that it was genuinely able to produce results—was a serious blow to its general legitimacy. And the further one moved from the mathematical case, the more problematic and contentious the criterion became.

This was especially problematic for the Spinozean project for, as we have seen, Spinoza modelled clarity and distinctness on mathematical demonstration to an extent unthinkable even in Descartes, collapsing causal relations into deductive ones so that empirical enquiry became a form of quasi-mathematical deduction. Yet Spinoza's

[65] See Gaukroger, *Descartes, An Intellectual Biography*, ch. 5.

confidence was misplaced, for he had never put his original conception of clear and distinct ideas to the test in mathematically demanding cases, as Descartes did, or physically demanding cases such as the formation of the earth, where anyone working in the area would immediately see talk of mathematical necessity as completely inappropriate, and indeed as something that would effectively prevent any study of the earth getting off the ground. It is salutary to note in this regard that on the one occasion on which Spinoza turned his attention to systematic natural philosophy, namely his axiomatization of Descartes' *Principia*, he confined his attention to the wholly programmatic early sections of the *Principia*, stopping well before reaching any physical theory of macroscopic observable processes. Contemporary natural philosophers who found Spinoza's project unacceptable were well aware of the wholly idealized nature of his notion of certainty. Only Huygens insisted on working with a notion of clarity and distinctness that imposed similar standards of demonstration, but what he was after—over and above genuine mathematical rigour in mechanics, which is uncontentious—was a reduction of mechanics to kinematics, because he considered that it is forces that undermine the clarity and distinctness of mechanics. For Huygens, then, advocacy of a criterion of clarity and distinctness restricted genuine knowledge to a very limited domain. For Spinoza, however, it was not the domain that was limited—quite the contrary, this was now expanded to cover the whole of cognitive enquiry—but the kind of grasp that one could have of it. By contrast with Huygens' approach, this had the result of diluting any strengths that the criterion might have.

This is not to say that the very distinctive accounts of issues such as the nature of the mind, freedom of the will, and the nature of person that Spinoza provided, and which generated much of the hostility to his philosophy, can be passed over on the grounds that the programme of reconsidering all ideas in terms of clarity and distinctness, which generated these doctrines, is fatally flawed. Quite the contrary, these make up a powerful and lasting contribution to the philosophical tradition. Spinoza's doctrine of what subsequently came to be known as 'neutral monism', the doctrine that the mental and the physical are different forms of description of the world and not two different kinds of substance, remains a major contender for a theory of mind, by contrast with Malebranche's occasionalism and Leibniz's pre-established harmony for example. His denial of freedom of the will, if taken not as a question about whether we are free or not, but as a question about what exactly the notion of free will is supposed to secure, remains a major philosophical challenge. For if the problem to which it is directed is that of how we secure responsibility for behaviour (particularly morally culpable behaviour), there is a real question as to whether, having gone through a process of practical reasoning in which we have weighed the options and decided that a particular course of action is the right or appropriate one, we do in fact make someone responsible for how they behave by adding an extra stage in the process in which the person then chooses whether or not to act upon that decision, not on further reflective grounds (since these would be part of the process of reflective reasoning) but apparently on no rational grounds at all, just on the basis that they were able to act or not act on the decision to which their reasoning had led them. Such a process, far from securing responsibility for action, would randomize moral behaviour. Finally, there is Spinoza's doctrine of the person, which cultivates a notion whereby one makes oneself into a moral agent—and more generally into a human being—by taking responsibility for one's life, something that Spinoza construed in purely cognitive terms, although we do not have to follow him in this respect. Here we have a compelling alternative to traditional understandings of morality and humanity, an alternative that was to be developed from the end of the eighteenth century. Whatever the merits of these doctrines, however, they cannot be made to depend on Spinoza's general programme of re-examination of our ideas in terms of clarity and distinctness. Rather, they need to be assessed on their own merits, but Spinoza offered them as inseparable parts of a package, which very effectively prevented this. The situation changed only when they were replanted in the fertile climate of German Romanticism at the end of the eighteenth century, and it is instructive that this was a climate in which the idea of a purely cognitive route to self-realization had no viability.[66]

That it was the German Romantics who resurrected the Spinozean project is enlightening, for their proto-vitalistic understanding of the cosmos was very far from the mechanism that provided the basis for physical enquiry in Spinoza. But it was Spinoza's notion of *conatus* that attracted them, and it was this very notion, suggestive of Renaissance naturalism and explicitly tied to the pantheism of which naturalists were traditionally accused, that seemed to undermine the mechanist credentials of Spinoza's project. It is noteworthy, for example, that the way in which he described *conatus* precludes its being mechanized along Hobbesian lines. Nor would it help to partition the physical and the mental descriptions of the universe, *natura naturata* and *natura naturans*, and confine *conatus* exclusively to the latter. The sticking point here is the idea that *natura naturata* and *natura naturans* are the same thing, and in admitting *conatus* as an indispensable ingredient in the latter one is in effect saying it is really there in nature, however one ultimately chooses to describe nature.[67] The removal of active powers from nature, which is the hallmark of mechanism, is compromised by the idea that there is a mode of description of nature in which such active powers are indispensable. After all, Cudworth was arguing that there is a level of description of natural processes—the purely physical level—at which mechanism is perfectly adequate, but that once one starts dealing with organic processes it needs to be described in terms of active powers. This is, of course, not what Spinoza was arguing, but the way in which *conatus* only becomes evident as we move into the organic realm, and particularly into the human realm, does encourage the notion that modes of description and levels of description at least converge, and might well end up being the same thing for explanatory purposes, in that one mode of description might be more appropriate for the inorganic and another for the organic. And in that case, the price one pays, by mechanist standards, may seem greater in the case of Spinoza than in Cudworth, for the Spinozean system does have (in one mode of description) active powers at the level of brute matter.

---

[66] See e.g. Heinrich Heine, *Zur Geschichte der Religion und Philosophie in Deutschland* (Halle, 1887), and the discussion in Charles Taylor, *Hegel* (Cambridge, 1975), ch. 1. I shall be returning to these questions in a subsequent volume.

[67] The transfer of *conatus* from the mental to the physical in fact mirrors Spinoza's transfer of determinism from the physical to the mental.

What made the Spinozean system particularly unattractive from the point of view of natural philosophy, however, is that by 1677, when the *Ethica* appeared, there was a widespread awareness that there was something fundamentally wrong with Descartes' laws of collision, yet Spinoza reproduced a version of Rule 4, whereby a smaller moving body cannot affect a larger heavier one, while at the same time asserting that all motion was relative.[68] One of the most manifest problems in Cartesian mechanics is simply skirted over, with no awareness of the depth or fundamental nature of the problem. He tells us that he 'ought to have explained and demonstrated these things more fully. But I have already said that I intended something else, and brought these things forward only because I can easily deduce from them the things I have decided to demonstrate.'[69] This is where Spinoza's project began to look decidedly odd. The oddness derived not so much from the fact that he treated these basic principles as if they were conceptual truths, for Huygens to some extent did that also (as would the eighteenth-century tradition of rational mechanics), but rather from the view that the conceptual truths in question are so secure that it is as if there could be no question of their not being mutually consistent. We grasp their truth so clearly and distinctly that we know we could not be mistaken. But it turns out that we are mistaken, and this must put in doubt the idea that simple reflection (as opposed, for example, to the detailed exploration of consequences) is adequate to establish truth. It might be thought that a geometrical model had misled Spinoza here, but *reductio ad contradictionem* was a standard demonstrative device in geometry, and postulated axioms were not immune from assessment in terms of their consequences. Moreover, the problem was not just that the mechanical principles from which Spinoza wanted to extrapolate are flawed, but that these principles acted as a model for the deductive structure of the Spinozean system. Deduction was treated as an essentially one-way process, with no procedure for identifying mistaken principles in terms of their consequences.

Another principle inconsistent with the principle of relativity was the conservation of the total quantity of motion: it was rejected by Huygens in the 1650s and abandoned by Wren and Wallis in their 1669 papers on collision in the *Philosophical Transactions*, where Huygens' own account was discussed. Yet the role of this principle in Spinoza's system was as fundamental as the principle of relativity. It played a crucial role in his metaphysics, as we have seen, for the constant quantity of motion in the universe, which is an eternal and infinite mode of the attribute of extension, signifies an element of immutability in that aspect of the universe taken as a whole: while there is change at the individual level, at the total level there is no change, since the quantity of motion is unchanging. But if conservation of quantity of motion, as Spinoza conceived it, is not viable, and indeed if it is inconsistent with his other key natural-philosophical principles, then it could not play the metaphysical role that he imposed on it. The translation of natural-philosophical principles into conceptual truths/metaphysical principles is a high-risk strategy (one that Kant would also pursue in the case of the nature of space), and Spinoza's is an extreme case of premature

---

[68] *Ethics*, Book 2, prop. 13.     [69] Ibid.

translation. The worst thing that could happen to a natural-philosophical model for knowledge which claims to paradigmatically manifest clarity and distinctness is for the natural philosophy on which it is based to turn out to be not merely inadequate but self-contradictory. After all, the content of the particular natural-philosophical principles set out was not incidental to Spinoza's account: it stood at the very core of his project. In this respect, no one with an active commitment to natural philosophy could have considered the Spinozean proposal seriously as an adequate account of the role of natural philosophy in knowledge more broadly. It was simply ignored by natural philosophers, and it lacked any natural-philosophical legitimacy.

## PHYSICO-THEOLOGY AND NATURAL PHILOSOPHY

'The method of interpreting Scripture is no different from the method of interpreting Nature and is in fact in complete accord with it,' Spinoza tells us in the *Tractatus theologico-politicus*.[70] In effect, this could be a statement of the central claim of the main alternative to Spinozism, which traced the unity of knowledge back to the unified design that underlies the created world and our place in it. Spinoza had raised the key question of the authority of scriptural interpretation, but although he broached this question in a distinctive manner, he was certainly not the first to raise it. The problem of authority of scriptural interpretation was one that had begun to occupy many writers from the sixteenth century onwards, and by the mid-seventeenth century there was something of a crisis of authority in this respect.[71] Spinoza used this crisis to undermine the claims of the Bible to provide anything more than a model of moral behaviour and guidance, one that did not have any intrinsically privileged standing, and which, he argued, in fact turns out to be inferior to the conception of the world and our place in it offered by the kind of philosophical system that he set out to provide. But there was another way of dealing with the crisis of authority, which was to bolster it with support from natural philosophy. This was the model wherein natural philosophy guided scriptural interpretation, not in a potentially antagonistic way as in Spinoza, but in a way that ensured coherence and empirical adequacy for scriptural statements about the natural realm.

In understanding how such a model functioned, it is helpful to contrast it with the idea of common causation. Aristotle had allowed new beginnings to arise in nature, new things to come into existence, but the Stoic/Epicurean notion of activity in the cosmos as being generated by chains of causes introduced a principle of causal closure, which mechanists embraced with enthusiasm. On the Epicurean model, however, the world had come about by chance, for the atoms making it up would never have come into contact were it not for an initial 'swerve' which initiated a series of collisions, and the swerve was a random event in an otherwise deterministic universe. The question provoked by such a conception was whether a world that came about by chance in

---

[70] *Tractatus*, trans. Shirley, 141.
[71] Generally on this question see Henning Graf Reventlow, *The Authority of the Bible and the Rise of the Modern World* (Philadelphia, 1985).

this way could have any regular structure, and in particular whether it could have the kind of regular structure we know our world to have. To seventeenth-century natural philosophers, nature appeared to have not only regular structure but a unified structure of the kind that one associates with artefacts—something that was reinforced by the revelation of the beauty and complex symmetry of microscopic structure—and indeed many traditional arguments for the existence of a creating deity had rested on this feature of the world. There seemed to be an economy of means underlying the world that was far more potent than that which the common causation view had tried to capture, because common causation itself could not account for the artefactual nature of the world, the way in which its parts cohered in a manner that could not have come about by chance. Moreover, the assumption that the world was an artefact had consequences for natural-philosophical enquiry that marked it out from the common causation view. For if it were indeed an artefact, this would indicate that there are many as yet undiscovered depths and connections in the world which it is the duty of the natural philosopher to seek out, for these lead us to a fuller understanding of the design lying behind the world, and in consequence a fuller understanding of its designer.

In the most general terms, the task of the new physico-theology, one which took developments in natural philosophy seriously, and which treated natural philosophy itself as an ally potentially on a par with revelation, was to reconcile apparently divergent accounts to present a unified picture. Unlike the Thomist notion of a metaphysical bridge between theology and natural philosophy, however, what we now witness is a far more direct connection between natural philosophy and revelation, one that 'triangulates' enquiry, as it were, so that two different and apparently quite independent streams converge on the truth. There may initially be an assumption in favour of revelation in this enterprise, but there was nothing to prevent natural-philosophical considerations prevailing where necessary.

There were a number of ways of carrying out this exercise, and some were more successful than others. One strategy was the attempts of Cudworth and More to rediscover an original philosophy—deriving from Adam and Moses, and formulated in its extant (but deficient) form by Plato—which underlay Christianity, and to reconcile this with recent developments in Cartesian natural philosophy. More, for example, tells us that he and Descartes were both united in a holy purpose, and

we are both setting out from the same *Lists*, though taking severall ways, the one travelling on the lower *Road* of *Democritism*, amidst the thick dust of *Atoms* and flying particles of *Matter*, the other tracing over the high and airey Hills of Platonism, in that more thin and subtle Region of *Immateriality*, meet together notwithstanding at last (and certainly not without a Providence) at the same *Goale*, namely at the entrance of the holy Bible, dedicating our joint Labours to the use and glory of the Christian Church.[72]

Cudworth offered a more integrated account, construing atomism as coming in the forms of Democriteanism, where the atoms are physical, and Pythagoreanism, where the atoms are spiritual. In the long first chapter of his *True Intellectual System*, he

---

[72] Henry More, *A Collection of Several Philosophical Writings* (London, 1662), p. xii.

sets out to show that Democritean atomism is in fact a degenerate version of what was originally a dualistic doctrine in which the explanatory work was done by the spiritual categories. While Cudworth's monumental project may have attracted some admirers, however, it does not seem to have attracted followers, and this way of proceeding came to little.

A different kind of project, still very ambitious and often sharing assumptions about an original Adamic and Mosaic philosophy that underpinned Christianity, but in a more traditional physico-theological genre, was that of attempting to reconcile new natural-philosophical theories of the formation of the cosmos, and particularly the formation of the earth, with the account in Genesis. Instead of engaging fundamental speculative natural-philosophical questions, as Cudworth did, a connection was established between the empirical claims offered in natural-philosophical accounts about the stages in the formation of the earth and the natural processes that occur at these stages, and what are interpreted as empirical claims about the stages in the formation of the earth, and the cosmos in general, in Genesis. On the face of it, this was a high risk strategy. The attempts of Paracelsians such as Duchesne to fill out the events described in Genesis in terms of physical and chemical processes had been at best heterodox, for example, and it was unclear that the thoroughgoing naturalization that they had offered added to our understanding of these events: it had just been a Paracelsian story about origins, saving the 'appearances' (as described in Genesis), and little more than a speculative gloss lacking any independent vindication. By contrast, there was the comprehensive mechanist account of the formation of the earth, based purely on natural-philosophical considerations, presented in Book 4 of Descartes' *Principia*. Here was an account integrated into a broader natural-philosophical picture whose plausibility and explanatory power were widely recognized. But, as we saw in Ch. 8, not only did Descartes describe the process as if there were no divine goals shaping the earth as a habitat for human beings, but the stages identified seemed to be at odds with those described in Genesis.[73] In particular, on the Cartesian account, the earth was formed well after stars such as the sun, and its habitat was shaped by processes that were common to any planet, not just those other planets in our solar system but also those that Descartes considered, by analogy, must exist in other solar systems.

Yet as Burnet put it in his *Sacred Theory of the Earth*, 'We are not to suppose that any truth concerning the natural world can be an enemy to religion: for Truth cannot be an Enemy to Truth, God is not divided against himself.'[74] The strategy that Burnet

---

[73] See Descartes to Chanut, 6 June 1647: 'It is true that the six days of creation are described in Genesis in such a way as to make man appear its principal object; but it could be argued that the story in Genesis is written for man, and so it is chiefly the things that concern him that the Holy Spirit wished particularly to relate, and that he did not speak of anything except in its relation to man. Preachers, whose concern is to spur us on to the love of God, commonly lay before us the various benefits we derive from other creatures and say that God made them for us. They do not bring to our attention the other ends for which he might be said to have made them, because this would be irrelevant to our purpose.' Descartes, *Œuvres*, v. 55.

[74] Thomas Burnet, *The Theory of the Earth: Containing an Original of an Account of the Earth, and of all the Changes Which it Hath Undergone, or is to Undergo Till the Consumation of All Things. The First Two Books, Concerning the Deluge, and Concerning Paradise* (London, 1684), a2.

in effect adopted is one of triangulation on the shared truth of revelation and natural philosophy, 'shared' in the strong sense that revelation and natural philosophy deal with exactly the same truth, not different kinds of truth in any sense (an assumption shared with Spinoza but not, for example, with Descartes and Malebranche). The area in which he pursued this enterprise is particularly well suited to such an approach. Just as Genesis had traditionally been subject to significant puzzles over interpretation (many of which derived from the fact that the text presents two different accounts of creation, at 1: 1–2: 3 and 2: 4–2: 25), from the Church Fathers onwards but particularly as the new biblical criticism developed from the beginning of the sixteenth century, so too natural-philosophical theories of the formation of the earth were far less secure than the mechanically inspired foundations of natural philosophy to which writers such as Descartes had devoted far more attention. From the point of view of physico-theology, both had potentially much to gain from the insights of the other.

Because the question of the formation of the earth raised issues about the design of the earth as a habitat for human beings, among the pressing questions were not just geology and fossils, but also chronology and human history. The issues were summed up by Stillingfleet in 1662 in his *Origines sacrae*:

As the tempers and Genius's of Ages and Times alter, so do the arms and weapons which Atheists imploy against Religion; the most popular pretences of the Atheists of our Age, have been the irreconcileableness of the Account of Times in Scripture with that of the Learned and ancient Heathen Nations; the inconsistency of the belief of the Scriptures with the principles of reason; and the account which may be given of the Origine of things from the principles of Philosophy without the Scriptures.[75]

In the first Book of *Origines*, Stillingfleet tells us, he has

manifested that there is no ground of credibility in the account of ancient times given by any Heathen Nations different from the Scriptures which I have with so much care and diligence enquired into, that from thence we may hope to hear no more of men before *Adam* to salve the Authority of the Scriptures by, which yet was intended only as a design to undermine them; but I have not thought the frivolous pretences of the Author of that Hypothesis worth particular mentioning, supposing it sufficient to give a clear account of things without particular citation of Authors, where it was not of great concernment for the understanding of the thing it self.[76]

The 'frivolous author' in question is Isaac de La Peyrère, whose *Men before Adam*, published in 1655,[77] initiated a long-running dispute on biblical chronology. The plausibility of La Peyrère's case depended to a large extent on two factors: the presence of humans in the New World and Oceania, which were separated from Europe

---

[75] Edward Stillingfleet, *Origines Sacrae, or a Rational Account of the Grounds of Christian Faith, as to the Truth and Divine Authority of the Scriptures, And the matter therein contained* (London, 1662), 'The Preface to the Reader' (unpaginated).

[76] Ibid.

[77] Isaac Lapeyrère, *Prae-Adamitae, sive exercitatio super versibus duodecimo, decimotertio, & decimoquarto, capitis quinti Epistolae D. Pauli ad Romanos* bound with *Systema theologicum ex Praeadamitarum hypothesi* ([Amsterdam], 1655). An English version appeared in the same year: *A Theological Systeme Upon the Presvpposition that Men were before Adam* (London, 1655).

both geographically and culturally, with no record of ancestors of modern Europeans having travelled to these places; and chronologies such as those of ancient civilizations and of Chinese emperors which went back significantly further than Adamic times. To reconcile these facts with biblical chronology, La Peyrère argued that the Pentateuch, the first five books of the Bible, did not present a universal record of human history, but only a history of the Hebrews. Adam was the first Jew that God created, but he was not the first human, as was evident, La Peyrère maintained, from the existence of human beings in remote parts of the world which, given the time-scale presented in the Bible, could have had no contact with any of our ancestors. He concluded that there must have been separate creations, and that Adam was not the first man but simply the first Jew. Gentiles had been created much earlier. On this reading, biblical claims to universal history were wholly contrary to the evidence, and particular episodes such as the Flood were not universal cataclysms but simply local events confined to Jewish history.

The question of the veracity of Jewish history was one whose importance had emerged as early as the late second century in the thinking of Theophilus, Bishop of Antioch, who found that the acceptance of Christianity was significantly hampered by its lack of antiquity. Its novelty and radical difference from everything that preceded it had been one of its greatest features in its Pauline version, but a century and a half later it had become a hindrance, as it seemed unlikely to its critics that something barely a century old could make claims to be the true religion. Theophilus turned to the Old Testament, which he believed prophesied the coming of Christ, and which simply in virtue of this had a continuity with Christianity, so that Christianity in effect had a history as old as that of the Old Testament. Adding up the lifetimes of the patriarchs, he calculated that the world had been created 5,698 years earlier: far more ancient that the histories claimed by critics of Christianity. But claims of greatest antiquity came to be disputed, and in a context of discrepancies between different chronologies, which made matters far more complex. Discrepancies between the ancient chronology of Manetho, the Egyptian historian of the fourth century BCE, and the chronology of the Pentateuch or the Septuagint, had been known since at least the Patristic era, as Augustine had discussed the Egyptian chronologies,[78] arguing that Egyptian gods were in fact historical heroes who had learned from inspired Jewish teachers. Egyptian chronology was realigned with Jewish chronology as it was incorporated into a Christian framework of world history.[79] By the sixteenth century, chronology was modelled either exclusively on biblical chronology or on a combination of biblical chronology and the comprehensive ancient chronology of Annius of Viterbo.[80] The latter was in fact a forgery. The seventeen-volume work presented what purported to

[78] Augustine, *De civitate dei*, 12. 10.

[79] There is a comprehensive account of these questions in Anthony Grafton, *Joseph Scaliger. A Study in the History of Classical Scholarship* (2 vols, Oxford, 1983–93).

[80] Annius of Viterbo, *Antiquitatu[m] Variaru[m], volumina XVII* (17 vols, Paris, 1512). The work was first published Venice, from 1499 onwards. It was reprinted throughout the sixteenth century, the last edition being that printed in Wittenberg in 1612.

be the lost works of ancient historians such as Manetho, Berosus the Chaldean, and Metasthenes the Persian. Annius provided commentaries and organized the material into a comprehensive and unified chronology which not only discredited the standard ancient histories of Greece and Rome but filled in—that is, invented—full dynasties for all known nations, also providing etymologies that linked Gentile and biblical figures: Janus, for example, we are told derives from the Hebrew word for wine, *yanin*, and was really Noah.[81] The 'edition' of Berosus is particularly important because here Annius offered not only a universal genealogy of peoples that conforms to the Bible, but also a genealogy of 'wisdom' through Noah's sons.[82]

It is only with Scaliger's *De emendatione temporum* (1583) and *Thesaurus temporum* (1606), that we encounter a complete abandonment of Annius' dynasties, as Scaliger deploys every available form of enquiry, from the principles of philology that made him one of the pre-eminent textual critics of his time, to detailed astronomical calculations to clarify reported dating. Among his innovations, Scaliger circumvented the problem of different calendar systems that had dogged comparative studies of chronology to this time by proposing a master calendar, the Julian period, against which all other chronologies could be placed, and which began at a hypothetical time (1 January 4713 BCE) which he was sure was before creation and so did not exist, and ran almost 1700 years into the future.[83] While he did not believe that there were events that predated the biblical identification of the time of creation, however, he realized that the very careful procedures that he had used had established beyond reasonable doubt the reliability of Manetho's chronology, which identified Egyptian dynasties as early as 1336 years before the Mosaic dating of creation.[84]

---

[81] Anthony Grafton, 'Joseph Scaliger and Historical Chronology: The Rise and Fall of a Discipline', *History and Theory* 14 (1975), 156–85: 164.

[82] See Schmidt-Biggeman, *Philosophia Perennis*, 421–8.

[83] It is striking that Augustine, despite his key role in establishing a single time embracing all human history, persisted in using relative chronologies which had no relation to an overriding linear time: see Donald J. Wilcox, *The Measure of Times Past: Pre-Newtonian Chronologies and the Rhetoric of Relative Time* (Chicago, 1987), 119–29; and more generally G. W. Trompf, *The Idea of Historical Recurrence in Western Thought: From Antiquity to the Reformation* (Berkeley, 1979). Scaliger started from the procedure of the early sixth-century Roman scholar, Dionysius Exiguus, for drawing up a table of dates for Easter based on the birth of Christ. He realized that if he knew the phase of the moon and the day of the week, i.e. if he could fix the date in the 19-year lunar cycle and the 28-year solar cycles, then he could locate the date within a longer cycle which was the product of these, namely a 532-year cycle. Scaliger wanted a cycle that enabled him to establish a universal chronological system, however, so he needed something longer. For the extra multiplier needed, he fixed on the indiction, a 15-year cycle instituted by Diocletian, which was a civil cycle intended for taxation census purposes, and which was subsequently used as the basis for dating legal and documents in the Middle Ages. Multiplying the Dionysian cycle by that of indiction gives a 7,980-year cycle, which he called the Julian period because it counted the years of the Julian calendar. There is a good summary in Wilcox, *The Measure of Times Past*, 197–203.

[84] Grafton, 'Joseph Scaliger and Historical Chronology', 170–3. The dating of creation was considered an approximation until James Ussher, after fifty years of work on the topic, provided an exact calculation in his 2,000-page *Annales veteris et Novi Testamenti* (London, 1650): 6 p.m. on Saturday, 22 October 4004 (Julian calendar) BCE. See James Barr, 'Why the World was Created in 4004 BC: Archbishop Ussher and Biblical Chronology', *Bulletin of the John Rylands University Library of Manchester* 67 (1985), 576–608. Ussher's dating was generally accepted up to the nineteenth century.

Scaliger's *Thesaurus* precipitated considerable debate in the course of the seventeenth century, and various attempts were made to save the biblical account.[85] A number of writers treated the ante diluvian dynasties as fictitious, but this was problematic because at the same time they uniformly accepted the account of the later dynasties. In his *De theologia gentili* (1641), Gerardus Vossius argued in detail, on the basis of diverse considerations—from the different names of what were supposed to be the same cities in different dynasties, to the fact that great empires had traditionally not been *sui generis* but had grown together from smaller sovereign states—that at least many of the dynasties of Mantheo were collateral rather than successive. Anthony Grafton has argued that one important consequence of Vossius' appeal to such general social questions as the nature of empires was to take the disputes to some extent out of the realm of philology into a more popular pamphlet genre, and into the realm of political and theological polemics.[86] Yet La Peyrère, who had no knowledge of Greek or Hebrew, was unfamiliar with the scholarship and debates on ancient chronologies, and was seemingly unaware of Scaliger's *Thesaurus*. It would have provided his account with significant extra weight, as his critics, who were very familiar with the debates on ancient chronologies, realized.

Perhaps La Peyrère's lack of knowledge of the literature accounts for Stillingfleet's dismissal of his views, but Stillingfleet's own account of the superiority of Jewish over classical histories in Book 1, for example, hardly engages the philological literature and is couched primarily in terms of an original source versus corruption, an original tradition by contrast with derivative and necessarily corrupted ones. In effect, Stillingfleet's strategy seemed to be to maintain that only when this issue had been decided could any other form of enquiry, including philological and chronological enquiry, begin, and of course then the only role left for them was that of identifying corruptions of an original Adamic knowledge and suggesting how these might have arisen. In this way, philological considerations could never dislodge the priority of the biblical account.

Having established, to his own satisfaction, the legitimacy of the chronology of the Bible, Stillingfleet turned, in Book 3 chapter 2 of *Origines*, to natural philosophical-questions, in particular to 'the several Hypotheses of the Philosophers who contradict Moses'. These he narrowed down to four main types: the hypothesis that the world has existed from eternity, which he associates with the Neopythagorean Ocellus Lucanus, Aristotle, and certain Platonists; the hypothesis that matter pre-existed God's formation of the world, a doctrine he attributes primarily to the Stoics but also finds in Pythagoras and Plato; the Epicurean hypothesis that accounts for the origins of the cosmos in terms of a chance concourse of atoms; and the Cartesian hypothesis that the universe formed when God imbued matter with motion. Stillingfleet's view was that, if any of these 'hypotheses' were true, then Christianity could not be: the religion of Moses would be overthrown, purported miracles would be frauds, God would not be free in his actions, the world would come about by chance, and so on.[87]

---

[85] Grafton, 'Joseph Scaliger and Historical Chronology', 173–81.          [86] Ibid. 176.
[87] Stillingfleet, *Origines Sacrae*, 421–3. See the discussion in Paolo Rossi, *The Dark Abyss of Time: The History of the Earth and the History of Nations from Hooke to Vico* (Chicago, 1984), ch. 5.

A crucial ingredient in his approach was the unity of the biblical view by contrast with the devotion to argument for its own sake that he ascribed to the Greeks:

the *difference* of the *former Philosophers* of the *Ionic sect*, after the time of *Thales*, as to the *material principle* of the *world*, one *substituting air*, another *fire* instead of *water*, rendred the *tradition* it self *suspected* among other *Philosophers*, especially when the *humour* of *innovating* in *Philosophy* was got among them, and they thought they did nothing unless they *contradicted* their *Masters*; thence came that *multiplicity* of *Sects* presently among them, and that *Philosophy* which went much on the *original tradition* of the *world*, was turned into *disputes* and *altercations*, which helped as much as to the finding out of *Truth*, as the *fighting* of two *Cocks* on a *dunghil* doth the *finding* out the *Jewel* that lyes there. For which, *scraping* and *searching* into the *natures* of *things* had been far more *proper*, then *contentions & wranglings* with each other; but by means of this *litigious humour Philosophy* from being a *design* grew to be a *meer Art*, and he was accounted the best *Philosopher*, not that searched further into the *bowels* of *nature*, but that *dressed* and *tricked* up the *notions* he had in the best *posture* of *defence* against all who came to oppose him.[88]

Here, standard arguments against the predilection of classical philosophers, particularly Aristotle, for disputation, are deployed in effect against any non-Mosaic account of the origins of the world: the claim is that the disagreement for its own sake typical of Greek philosophy can hardly offer a sound basis for an alternative to the biblical account. Stillingfleet does have independent arguments against the classical accounts—the Aristotelian argument from first mover presupposes the eternity of motion whereas in fact God can confer motion on something that is initially stationary, the idea that matter must pre-exist creation is simply in contradiction with God's powers, the variety in the world cannot be accounted for on an atomistic basis, its order and beauty cannot derive from chance, and so on—but in the main these simply pit varying views against the biblical account, and in many cases it is sufficient to refute them simply to show their incompatibility with the biblical account.

We can compare this approach with that of Matthew Hale, whose *The Primitive Origination of Mankind*, written primarily in the 1660s,[89] appeared posthumously in 1677. Although his aims were similar to those of Stillingfleet—he set out, he tells us, to show that the world had a beginning in time and that those philosophers who have offered accounts contrary to the Mosaic story are in error—his approach was very different. Hale was Chief Justice of the King's Bench, and he had a very explicit understanding of what judicial impartiality consisted in. In 1668 he set out in his diary nine attributes that he believed appropriate to the *persona* of a judge, of which two are particularly striking because of their overlap with the proposals for the reform of the natural philosopher that we looked at in Chapter 6. The fifth very much mirrors the requirements that natural philosophers such as Bacon and Descartes had seen as crucial to the development of a philosophical *persona*, stating that since coming to a judicial decision 'is a business of that importance and yet difficulty a man may be careful to keep a temperate body, with great abstinence and moderation in eating and drinking, and a temperate mind totally abandoning all manner of passion, affection,

---

[88] Stillingfleet, *Origines Sacrae*, 429.
[89] On dating see Cromartie, *Sir Matthew Hale*, 198.

and perturbation that so he may come to the business with clearness of understanding and judgment'. But it is the seventh that is particularly important in the present context, and here similarly we have a maxim that can be transferred directly from a legal to a natural-philosophical context: 'That he avoid all precipitancy and haste in examining, censuring, judging, pause and consider, turn every stone, weigh every question, every answer, every circumstance, follow the wise direction of Moses in a case of importance to inquire, ask, diligently inquire, behold if it be true and the thing be certain; all the senses, all the methods of disquisition are little enough in cases of great moment or difficulty, especially where a man can err but once.'[90]

Hale made it clear in the subtitle of the work that the investigation is one 'according to the light of nature'. In particular, he was genuinely concerned with providing a natural-philosophical answer to the question of how the New World came to be populated:

The late Discovery of the vast Continent of *America* and Islands adjacent, which appears to be as populous with Men, and as well stored with Cattel almost as any part of *Europe*, *Asia*, or *Africa*, hath occasioned some difficulty and dispute touching the Traduction of all mankind from the two common Parents supposed of all Mankind, namely *Adam* and *Eve*; but principally concerning the storing of the World with men and Cattel from those that the Sacred History tells us were preserved in the Ark.[91]

The evidence is then set out, and the conclusion that some have drawn summed up in these terms:

That since by all Circumstances it is apparent that *America* hath been very long inhabited, and possibly as long as any other Continent in the World, and since it is of all hands agreed that the supposed common Parents of the rest of Mankind, *Adam, Noah* and his three sons, had their habitations in some parts of *Asia*, and since we have no probable Evidence that any of their Descendents traduced the first Colonies of the *American* Plantations into *America*, being so divided from the rest of the World, the access thither so difficult, and Navigation the only means of such a Migration being of a far later perfection than what could answer such a Population of so great a Continent: That consequently the *Americans* derive not their Original either from *Adam*, or at least not from *Noah*; but either had an Eternal Succession, or if they had a Beginning, they were *Aborigines*, and multiplied from other common Stocks than what the *Mosaical* History imports.[92]

Hale's response went beyond Stillingfleet's in an important respect.[93] Rather than just pitting scripture and natural history against one another, he was able to identify a number of auxiliary hypotheses that scriptural readings and natural history may share, but which actually lie at the root of the conflict between them. It is obvious that something has to give where there is a conflict between the scriptural accounts and natural-historical reports, but he realized that what has to give is not necessarily confined to either of these. He certainly devoted a lot of attention to showing that navigation by

---

[90] Quoted in Maija Jansson, 'Matthew Hale on Judges and Judging', *The Journal of Legal History* 9 (1988), 201–13: 207.

[91] Hale, *The Primitive Origination of Mankind*, 182.          [92] Ibid. 183.

[93] See the discussion in Rossi, *The Dark Abyss*, ch. 6.

ancestors of Noah to the Americas was in fact possible (he noted for example what a marvel of ship-building the ark must have been[94]), and that the migrations could have taken place by different peoples at different times. But he also questioned an assumption underlying both scriptural interpretation and natural history, an assumption which, if abandoned, shows that the discrepancy between the two approaches is actually far less than it has commonly been taken to be. This is the assumption of the fixity of species, something associated very much with Aristotle in natural history. Hale asked whether the American flora and fauna described by writers such as Acosta were actually completely unrelated to European species, for example, or whether they may have been in some way a development of them. Arguing that there may have been significant geological changes in the 4,000 years separating us from the Flood, so that areas previously above sea level are now below it, and vice versa,[95] he also began to question whether these radical geological transformations might be matched in transformations of species. There are, he argued, several ways in which the divergence between American and European/Asian species could be accounted for. He pointed to a number of mechanisms whereby variations could be produced: the mixing of characteristics ('anomalous production') in offspring, especially in fowl, noting that new varieties regularly occur in this way, as they do from 'the promiscuous couplings of Males and Females of several *Species*, whereby there arise a sort of Brutes that were not in the first Creation'[96]; the routine variation in features such as colour and shape in plants between parent and offspring; the changes that culturing and environment can produce, such as the size of certain fish in relation to the size of the pond that they live in; and he noted the widespread theory, citing Harvey as an authority, holding that individual features of offspring, such as facial characteristics, depend on the image or idea that the mother had in her mind at the point of conception.[97]

An important part of Hale's argument rests on his account of fossils. There are, he tells us, two accounts of the origins 'of these Petrified Shells'. The first is, although they can be found at great distances from the sea and at great heights, they were in fact deposited there by the sea, either by the Flood or because the face of the earth was very different in the past from what it is now. The second is that, because they occur at such a distance from the sea, because they may have shapes of things not found in the seas nearest to them or indeed in any seas, and because they are made of stone which is not found in the sea but rather only in the places where the fossils themselves are found, these fossils can only be 'the Effects of the Plastick power of the Earth'.[98] Hale himself found the rarity of fossils evidence against the second hypothesis, maintaining that (as with plants) they would be produced annually if the plastick power theory were true. Nevertheless, he did allow that some arise *de novo*, postulating 'Seminal Ferments' produced by the earth.

The difficulty of providing a satisfactory account of fossils either in scriptural terms or in terms of natural history is clear from Hale's own unhappy solution, yet fossils seemed to manifest created beauty and harmony in a particularly striking way. If the united forces of natural history and scripture were to open up creation to closer

[94] Hale, *Primitive Origination*, 194.     [95] Ibid. 193.     [96] Ibid. 199.
[97] Ibid. 200.     [98] Ibid. 192.

investigation, then accounting for fossils was going to play a key role. By the end of the 1660s there had appeared two important works in the natural history/physico-theology genre which dealt directly with the question of fossils. The first was Hooke's *Lectures and Discourses on Earthquakes* (1668).[99] Like Hale, Hooke rejected both the view that the fossils have been transported from the sea (he denied the Flood lasted long enough or could have had sufficient power to achieve this), and the plastick nature thesis. He examined the idea that they have an organic origin, that the process that produces them mimics, in minerals, processes that produce plants and animals,[100] the difference being that whereas in the case of the vegetable and mineral kingdoms the external shape is evidence of an internal functional form, in the case of fossils we have only the outward surfaces. But if this is the case, Hooke argued, we need to know, first, how the bodies have been transported from the place in which they were formed into that in which they are found; and second, why they are made of a substance different from that from which they were originally formed. Hooke believed he had an account that provides a satisfactory answer to these questions, and this takes the form of eleven 'propositions'. The first is that fossils comprise either vegetable or animal bodies

converted into Stone, by having their Pores fill'd up with some petrifying liquid Substance . . . or else they are the lasting Impressions made on them at first, whilst a yielding Substance by the immediate Application of such Animal or Vegetable Body was so shaped, and that there was nothing else concurring to their Production, save only the yeilding of the matter to receive the Impression, such as heated Wax affords to the Seal; or else a subsiding or hardening of the Matter, after by some kind of Fluidity it had perfectly fill'd or inclosed the figuring Vegetable or Animal Substance, after the manner as a Statue is made of Plaster of Paris . . .[101]

This process Hooke considered to require some extraordinary cause, and he identified a number of possibilities, such as exhalations from earthquakes, crystallization from a saline solution, the drying of glutinous matter forming sand into a hard stone, or the freezing or compression of these bodies over a long period. Whatever the process, Hooke was sure that a great part of the surface of the earth had undergone transformation since creation, in particular that parts now land were once sea and vice versa. Above all, land that was once flat may have been transformed by earthquakes, turning it into the highest mountains, as in the case of the Alps: indeed, Hooke argued that most of the irregularities on the earth's surface are due to earthquakes. His later theory of the effects of the earth's rotation is important here, for the rotation not only causes

[99] The full title is: 'Lectures and Discourses of Earthquakes, and Subterraneous Eruptions. Explicating the Causes of the Rugged and Uneven face of the Earth; and What Reasons may be given for the frequent finding of Shells and other Sea and Land Petrified Substances, scattered over the whole Terrestrial Superficies'. The lectures appear as Part 5 of Robert Hooke, *The Posthumous Works . . . containing his Cutlerian Lectures and other Discourses* (London, 1705). On Hooke's geology see David Oldroyd, 'Robert Hooke's Methodology of Science as Exemplified in his Discourse of Earthquakes', *British Journal for the History of Science* 6 (1972), 109–30; Rhoda Rappaport, 'Hooke on Earthquakes: Lectures, Strategy and Audience,' *British Journal for the History of Science* 19 (1986), 129–46; Yushi Ito, 'Hooke's Cyclic Theory of the Earth in the Context of Seventeenth Century England', *British Journal for the History of Science* 21 (1988), 295–314.

[100] Hooke, *The Posthumous Works*, 289.       [101] Ibid. 290.

the surface to have an ellipsoidal envelope of water, but also, because of the centrifugal forces produced, it has different effects at the poles and the equator. He also speculated that the earth's poles are shifting so that equatorial regions move towards the poles, with the effect that the crust is subject to gradually changing forces, giving rise to earthquakes and to variations in the extent to which particular regions are covered by the seas.[102] Indeed, Hooke offered a geological account of how God might have brought about the Flood, which he could have caused by the activity of earthquakes temporarily flattening the surface of the earth, which would have resulted in its surface being covered with water.[103] Most radically of all, Hooke argued that 'there have been many other Species of Creatures in former Ages, of which we can find none at present; and that 'tis not unlikely also but that there may be divers new kinds now, which have not been from the beginning.'[104] This comes close to an abandonment of the idea of eternal species: Hooke's idea was that what varieties of species there are now is essentially a function of what kind of environment those species find themselves in, and earlier varieties might not only have been quite different but might even not be recognized by us as being of the same species.[105]

In the year after Hooke gave his first lectures on earthquakes, Nicolaus Steno published his *Prodromus*, in which he set out how the earth's history might be recoverable from rocks, and fossils in particular: given that a substance has a certain shape and has been produced by natural processes, he asked, how, simply by examining this substance, are we to discover where and how it has been produced?[106] Steno was particularly concerned to show how natural-historical and scriptural accounts parallel and reinforce one another, and in particular to remove any discrepancies between his six-stage geological chronology of the earth and the biblical one. He went to some pains, for example, to show that the Flood can be accounted for if we assume that the earth's central fire is surrounded by huge reservoirs of water, normally kept from the surface by collapsed strata of rocks but which can be forced to the surface by pressure from the subterranean fire, a pressure which causes the subterranean caverns to expand and raises the sea floor. The result is that the earth, being in its early stages of formation and having a flatter surface than it does now, and having its non-active subterranean cavities filled with soil, is wholly flooded.[107] This is not just an exercise in reconciliation, however, but one in which natural history guides our interpretation of scripture, filling out our understanding of exactly what happened in the events reported in the Bible.[108]

[102] Ibid. 350–6 (lectures from 1686/7). See David Oldroyd, 'Geological Controversy in the Seventeenth Century: '"Hooke vs Wallis" and its Aftermath', in Michael Hunter and Simon Schaffer, eds, *Robert Hooke: New Studies* (Woodbridge, 1989), 207–33.

[103] Hooke, *The Posthumous Works*, 328.        [104] Ibid. 291.        [105] Ibid. 327.

[106] Nicolaus Steno, *De solido intra solidum naturaliter contento dissertationis prodromus* (Florence, 1669). An English translation by Henry Oldenburg appeared two years later: *The Prodromus to a dissertation concerning solids naturally contained within solids laying a foundation for the rendering a rational accompt both of the frame and the several changes of the masse of the earth . . . Englished by H. O.* (London, 1671). A convenient modern edition is *Opera philosophica*, ed. V. Maar (2 vols, Copenhagen, 1910).

[107] Steno, *Opera*, ii. 223.        [108] See the account in Rossi, *The Dark Abyss*, ch. 4.

The work that cemented this approach and exposed it to a wide audience, in the process effectively transforming the public perception of physico-theology, is that of Burnet, beginning with the publication of the Latin original of his *Sacred Theory of the Earth* in 1680.[109] Burnet's view was that Genesis was written to accommodate the capacities of the ignorant, and that a literal reading of Genesis simply encourages atheism, a view that had also been held by Henry More.[110] Genesis had to be interpreted with the help of natural history/natural philosophy and Burnet considered that the resources for such an interpretation were presented by Descartes' formative theory of the earth in Book 4 of the *Principia*:

An eminent Philosopher of this Age, *Monsieur des Cartes*, hath made use of the like *Hypothesis* to explain the irregular form of the present Earth; though he never dream'd of the Deluge, nor thought that first Orb built over the Abysse, to have been any more than a transient crust, and not a real habitable World that lasted for more than sixteen hundred years, as we suppose it to have been. And though he hath, in my opinion, in the formation of that first Orb, and upon the dissolution of it, committed some great oversights, whereof we have given an account in the Latin treatise; however he saw a necessity of such a thing, and of the disruption of it, to bring the Earth into that form and posture wherein we now find it.[111]

Descartes' account was widely regarded as the first of the new theories of the earth, and he was 'the first world maker this Century has produced', as John Keill, the defender of a Newtonian theory of the earth, put it in 1698.[112] Henry More had seen in Descartes' theory of the earth a number of hints that he had in fact uncovered the true philosophy underlying Genesis. He noted that, like Genesis but unlike Aristotle, there were three kinds of matter postulated in Descartes; that the solar origins of the earth is a Mosaic doctrine but one not demonstrated until Descartes; and it is also a Mosaic doctrine that the suns and planets are generated by the heavens and the aetherial matter in them.[113] In this respect, Burnet was following a programme that had been initiated by More in the 1660s. And at a very general level, the programme had parallels with what natural philosophers were doing in other contexts. Just as Newton had fleshed out a Galilean kinematic project in dynamic terms with such success, so filling out Descartes' rational reconstruction of the earth's formation as a real historical process was another instance of the consolidation of physical theory by fleshing out. After all, what standing could the Cartesian account have if it was just left as it was, as a hypothetical rational reconstruction, and what better way was there to test its reality than by filling it out in terms of the real historical processes described in revelation?

[109] *Telluris theoria sacra: orbis nostri originem et mutationes generales, quas aut jam subiit aut olim subiturus est, complectens...* (London, 1680). The later books appeared as: *Telluris theoria sacra. Libri duo posteriores de conflagratione mundi et de futuro atatu rerum* (London, 1689). New English versions appeared in 1690 (Books 3 and 4) and in 1691 (Books 1 and 2), and there is a convenient modern edition of these: Thomas Burnet, *The Sacred Theory of the Earth* (London, 1965).

[110] See Harrison, 'Cartesian Cosmology in England', 180–1.

[111] Burnet, *The Sacred Theory of the Earth*, 93.

[112] John Keill, *An Examination of Dr Burnet's Theory of the Earth* (London, 1698), 14. See Harrison, 'Cartesian Cosmology in England', 168.

[113] More, *A Collection*, 79–80.

Of course, not everyone was so happy to accord Cartesian natural philosophy such a central place (even More began to have his doubts as time progressed), but the point is that the whole relationship between natural philosophy and revelation has been radically altered. Whether one adapted a natural philosophy or devised a new one, the aim was now to produce a symbiotic union. This development found its clearest expression in theories of the earth, but the idea that natural philosophy is a means of seeking evidence of God's activity in nature would become widespread in the 1680s and 1690s, particularly in England, and Newton for example would consider the stability of planetary orbits to be evidence of God's constant intervention.

Such a radical transformation of the relation between natural philosophy and religious thought generally could not leave the *relata* unaffected. Natural philosophy, as we have seen, began to take on an explicitly religious aspect as early as Boyle, but this was not the only form the transformation of natural philosophy took on by any means. Nor indeed was the transformation wholly confined to physico-theology. We saw earlier that Spinoza's metaphysics, modelled as it was on natural philosophy, presented itself as a competitor to religion in what Spinoza considered to be its sole legitimate function, the inculcation of piety. Spinoza's project was certainly not one in physico-theology, but it attempted to bring natural philosophy and revelation together onto common ground, just as physico-theology did. This move to a common ground was, of course, a way of establishing competition between scriptural authority and the clarity and distinctness of natural philosophy for Spinoza, whereas it was a prerequisite to a highly integrated form of co-operation for the physico-theologists. But both in effect treated natural philosophy and the interpretation of revelation as being ultimately part of the same enterprise, for better or worse. The consequences for religion were explicitly radical in the Spinozean programme, which called for a fundamental reassessment of religious authority. But the alliance that physico-theology attempted to establish also had profound consequences for religious authority, as natural theology came to be considered increasingly to fall within the domain of natural philosophy rather than that of theology. In some respects, such as the religious role that the Boylean natural philosopher took on, these were quite explicit, while in other respects they were implicit, until the appearance of deism in the 1680s began to make evident the radical possibilities of natural theology. At that point, a 'scientific culture' developed in the West that was very different from anything that had gone before, as the Enlightenment heralded a wholly new conception of the world and our place in it.

# Conclusion

Natural philosophy in the seventeenth century was a highly heterogeneous enterprise, incorporating disciplines—above all natural history and practical mathematics—that had no place in traditional conceptions, and which in many respects fitted poorly with the newly reformulated corpuscularian matter theory that stood as a direct competitor to traditional natural philosophy. On the other hand, revelation, which had been separate from, and occasionally in competition with, natural philosophy gradually came to be incorporated directly into a broadened form of the natural-philosophical enterprise, reshaping it in a fundamental way. What we find, with growing momentum as the seventeenth century progresses, are repeated, and increasingly successful, attempts to ally natural philosophy with revelation in an attempt to share an entirely new cultural role for natural philosophy.

The problems created by the introduction of Aristotelianism in the thirteenth century had been held at bay, if not resolved, in the traditional Thomist view that natural philosophy, conceived as dealing with justification and demonstration, and revelation, conceived as expressing unique overriding truths, could be bridged by metaphysics. I have argued that the failure of such bridging becomes evident at the beginning of the sixteenth century in the Pomponazzi affair, as it emerged that reconciliation between Aristotelian natural philosophy and Christian theology was going to be at best problematic and contentious. To renounce reconciliation and let natural philosophy—whether of an Aristotelian, Platonist, or less traditional kind—take an autonomous path was fraught with danger, however, as the phenomenon of Renaissance naturalism demonstrated. The problem was compounded when the integrity of Aristotelian natural philosophy was threatened by developments in disciplines that fell outside natural philosophy on the Aristotelian conception (and, it should be said, on all traditional conceptions, including those of Platonists and Epicureans). Claims were made in these disciplines that had a direct bearing on, and were occasionally in direct competition with, natural-philosophical views.

I have singled out two areas for detailed consideration in this respect, natural history and practical mathematics, as well as drawing attention to areas such as medicine which had always had a problematic standing in relation to natural philosophy. In particular, the practical-mathematical discipline of astronomy became a trigger for a number of problems in the wake of Tycho's astronomical observations of the 1570s. It provoked the questions of what the relation was between a discipline that, in 'saving the appearances', was, first, unable to save them adequately within the confines of Aristotelian natural philosophy, and second, was able to save them only in a way that appeared to question the credibility of scriptural accounts of the nature of the earth and celestial bodies. The first played a crucial role in the attempts to secure natural-philosophical standing for the practical-mathematical disciplines, which was to result not only in the rehabilitation of mechanics, but also in the emergence of a natural-philosophical programme, mechanism, that was to rival Aristotelian natural philosophy, and to carry much of the legitimatory weight of the new developments in natural philosophy in the seventeenth century. The second engaged fundamental questions that went beyond those raised by the Pomponazzi affair, questions that revived a problem that the Thomist notion of metaphysics had to a large extent obscured, namely that, no matter how successful one's metaphysics was in the bridging exercise, Aristotelian natural philosophy had never presented a wholly satisfactory conception of the natural realm as far as Christian theology was concerned, because it failed to capture the single origin of the natural world and the fundamental assumption that the world was the product of design. Once these latter issues came to the fore, Aristotelianism, now in a weakened state, began to look like the wrong kind of partner for Christianity, whereas the new disciplines, as well as displacing Aristotelianism in matter theory and physical theory more generally, were in a sufficiently early stage of development that they could be connected with a religious view of the natural world and our place in it, providing that this religious view was not completely closed to developments in natural philosophy. Since there was some common understanding of—indeed common sources of—canons of explanation and the nature of evidence between natural history and biblical criticism, the relation between accounts of natural events in revelation and the natural-historical understanding of such events was a particularly promising area as far as convergence of interests was concerned.

What emerged from this was a conception of revelation and natural philosophy as being mutually reinforcing, a reinforcement consolidated through a process of 'triangulation', towards the shared truth of revelation and natural philosophy. In this way, the nature of the natural-philosophical exercise was transformed and provided with a unique vindication and legitimacy. The combination of revelation and natural philosophy—the two 'books' superposed into a single volume, as it were—produced a unique kind of enterprise, quite different from that of any other scientific culture, and one that was largely responsible for the subsequent uniqueness of the development of natural philosophy in the West. This uniqueness derives in large part from the legitimatory aspirations that it takes on in the course of the seventeenth century, and I have attempted to reconstruct how these legitimatory aspirations were formed. The kind of momentum that lay behind the legitimatory consolidation of the natural-philosophical enterprise from the seventeenth century onwards, a momentum that marked it out from every other scientific culture, was generated not by the intrinsic merits of its programme in celestial mechanics or matter theory but by a natural-theological imperative.

Comparison with other scientific cultures—earlier cultures and those outside the West—suggests that the development of a successful celestial mechanics, in Newton's *Principia*, might well have gradually brought to a close the natural-philosophical programme of the late sixteenth, seventeenth, and early eighteenth centuries. One crucial difference seems to be the diverse directions in which the programme was proceeding, so that as mechanics took on an increasingly phenomenological character in the eighteenth century and began to shed its role as the paradigm of natural-philosophical enquiry, the development of an intensive programme in natural history pushed this to the fore of questioning about the nature and relevance of natural-philosophical enquiry generally. The beginning of this programme effectively comes with Burnet's *Sacred Theory of the Earth*, above all because of the extensive public reaction this work provoked. These are matters to be considered in the next volume. But note the kind of consideration that is appropriate. We are dealing with a cultural set of circumstances, largely played out along national lines. What happened was something that was driven in large part by culturally specific concerns about the standing of revelation, and the outcome was a fusion of revelation and natural philosophy, transforming the latter into part of a distinctive kind of legitimatory enterprise. Areas such as mechanics became part of natural philosophy proper in the seventeenth century, as we have seen, thereby leaving what had been generally considered the realm of mathematical idealizations, but because natural philosophy itself had been transformed, it was no longer a question simply of solving technical problems which could be shown to be fundamental to understanding real physical processes. Rather, mechanics, along with astronomy, became tied in with a novel legitimatory project which had taken on aspects of scriptural interpretation, and as a result its ultimate aims ended up as a part of the natural-philosophical programme into which it had been drawn, goals that were construed along the lines of a discovery of a unique truth. It was only with this development that many of the distinctive features of modern conceptions of the role and standing of science in our culture came into existence.

The novel legitimatory project that emerged in the England of the 1680s, and which encompassed and redirected natural philosophy, while it attempted to unify the enterprise in various ways, was nevertheless unable to impose a top-down unity. The three projects that I have concentrated on in Part IV—mechanism, experimental natural philosophy, and mechanics—followed different and largely autonomous paths, and did not end up as integral parts of the same enterprise. Rather, connections tended to be established on a local-needs basis, and it was primarily support that guided such needs: although clarification and elucidations were occasionally sought, for example, these tended to be pursued internally in the vast majority of cases. The idea that disciplinary connections might be forged through what were in effect one-off, pressing local needs was anathema to those natural philosophers who saw themselves at the forefront of a new project in natural philosophy, one that would provide a wholesale replacement for traditional Aristotelian natural philosophy. There was an overwhelming belief that, if a piecemeal connection, no matter how well it worked, was at odds with, or failed to connect adequately with a unified picture of nature (typically one spelled out in terms of its microscopic constituents, taken to be characterizable in terms of basic physics), then it was at best fundamentally incomplete and at worst mistaken. This attitude was evident in the reactions to Boylean pneumatics and Newtonian chromatics, but it has persisted, with regular waxing and waning in its fortunes, up to the present time. The question we need to consider, and one to which we shall be returning in subsequent volumes, is to what extent this idea that there is or could be a unified picture of nature obscures what actually happens in scientific practice on issues of reconciliation of conflicting approaches. It will be clear from the discussion in this volume that other discourses, not least in medicine and the biological arena generally, added an extra dimension of complexity, as did developments in theology and especially biblical hermeneutics, which formed part of the loose natural-philosophical package that emerged in the 1680s. But the sources of the metaphysical idea that the ultimate aim of science must be a unified picture of nature were very varied, and the problems were compounded by the fact that it was usually such a fundamental assumption as to remain effectively a priori, neither examined critically nor probed in terms of evidence.

Because, from the beginning, I have stressed the importance of taking full cognizance of the fact that the transformation of the nature and goals of natural philosophy was not something achieved just in conceptual or institutional terms, but also by means of a transformation of the *persona* of the natural philosopher, I believe we shall be better prepared to probe this question. For the presentation of a unified picture of nature might not just be part of a particular conception of scientific enquiry, but also part of the *raison d'être* of the natural philosopher/scientist, something that secures a particular kind of standing or authority outside a narrowly conceived technical expertise. More generally, this is a dimension that has been missing from discussions of early-modern natural philosophy to date, yet, as I have urged, it provides an indispensable key to how natural philosophy came to be inserted into early-modern culture more generally. The range of factors that acted to restructure the nature of what might be termed natural-philosophical authority was complex, involving very different kinds of determinants: the exigencies of the Italian patronage system, the classificatory problems posed by New World flora and fauna, local forms of anti-Aristotelianism, the attempt to forestall acceptance of a Tychonic system in astronomy, the stress on practical understanding in Tudor and Stuart England, attempts to provide foundations for knowledge that trump traditional notions of natural-philosophical authority, to change natural philosophy from a speculative to a practical discipline, to incorporate practical mathematics into natural philosophy, to establish the autonomy of medicine with respect to natural philosophy, and so on. The transformation of the *persona* of the natural philosopher was crucial to changing conceptions of the nature and goals of natural philosophy, and reliability of character was crucial in a way that it had not been previously, as a concern with objectivity and impartiality became the hallmarks of the natural philosopher. As natural philosophy repositioned itself in the intellectual domain, the natural philosopher took on a new kind of authority, becoming uniquely qualified to undertake, or at least provide cognitive standards for, any kind of enquiry. It is here, more than anywhere else, that the cultural origins of the modern standing of science lie.

# Bibliography of Works Cited

Abra de Raconis, Charles François d'. *Totius philosophiae, hoc est logicae, moralis, physicae, et metaphysicae* (2 vols, Paris, 1633).

Acosta, José de. *Historia natvral y moral de las Indias, en qve se tratan las cosas notables del cielo, y elementos, metales, plantas, y animales dellas: y los ritos, y ceremonias, leyes, y gouierno, y guerras de los Indios* (Seville, 1590).

———— *The Naturall and Morall Historie of the East and West Indies*, trans. Edward Grimston (London, 1604).

Adams, Marilyn McCord. *William Ockham* (2 vols, Notre Dame, Ind., 1987).

Adas, Michael. *Machines as the Measure of Man: Science, Technology, and Ideologies of Western Dominance* (Ithaca, NY, 1989).

Agricola, Georgius. *De re metallica libri XII* (Basle, 1556).

Aiton, Eric J. *The Vortex Theory of the Planetary Motions* (London, 1972).

———— 'Johannes Kepler and the *Mysterium Cosmographicum*', *Sudhoffs Archiv* 62 (1977), 174–94.

Albertus, Magnus. *Opera omnia*, ed. Augustus Borgnet (38 vols, Paris, 1890–9).

Albrecht, Michael. *Eklektik. Eine Begriffsgeschichte mit Hinweisen auf die Philosophie- und Wissenschaftsgeschichte* (Stuttgart/Bad Canstatt, 1994).

Alciati, Andrea. *Emblemata cum commentarijs amplistimis* (Padua, 1621; facsimile copy New York, 1976).

Allen, Christopher. 'La tradition du classicisme' (Ph.D. thesis, University of Sydney, 1990).

Amico, Giovanni Battista. *De Motibus corporum coelestium iuxta principia peripatetica sine eccentris et epicyclis* (Venice, 1536).

Anderson, Francis. *The Philosophy of Francis Bacon* (New York, 1971).

Annas, Julia. *The Morality of Happiness* (Oxford, 1993).

Annius of Viterbo. *Antiquitatu[m] Variaru[m]* (17 vols, Paris, 1512).

Anon. *The Character of a Town-Gallant; exposing the extravagant fopperies of som vain self-conceited pretenders to gentility and good breeding* (London, 1675).

Anselm of Canterbury. *Basic Writings*, trans. S. N. Deane (2nd edn, La Salle, Ill., 1962).

———— *Opera omnia*, ed. Franciscus Salesius Schmitt (2 vols, Stuttgart, 1968).

Anstey, Peter. *The Philosophy of Robert Boyle* (London, 2000).

———— 'Experimental versus Speculative Natural Philosophy', in Peter Anstey and John Schuster, eds, *The Science of Nature in the Seventeenth Century* (Dordrecht, 2005), 215–42.

Applebaum, Wilbur. 'Keplerian Astronomy after Kepler: Researches and Problems', *History of Science* 34 (1996), 451–504.

Aquinas, Thomas. *Opera omnia*, ed. S. E. Fretté and P. Maré (34 vols, Paris, 1874–89).

———— *Scriptorum super libros sententiarum*, ed. R. P. Mandonnet and Maria Fabianus Moos (3 vols, Paris, 1929–33).

———— *Summa Theologica*, trans. Fathers of the English Dominican Province (2 vols, Chicago, 1952).

———— *On the Unity of the Intellect Against the Averroists*, trans. Beatriz H. Zedler (Milwaukee, 1968).

——*Summa contra Gentiles*, trans. A. C. Pegis, J. F. Anderson, V. J. Bourke, and C. J. O'Neil (4 vols, Notre Dame, 1975).

Ariès, Phillipe. *Religion populaire et réforme liturgique* (Paris, 1975).

Ariew, Roger. *Descartes and the Last Scholastics* (Ithaca, NY, 1999).

——Cottingham, John, and Sorell, Tom, eds. *Descartes' Meditations: Background Source Materials* (Cambridge, 1998).

Aristotle. *Aristotle's Physics I, II*, ed. and trans. William Charlton (Oxford, 1970).

Armogathe, Jean-Robert. *Theologia cartesiana: l'explication physique de l'Eucharistie chez Descartes et Dom Desgabets* (The Hague, 1977).

——'The Rainbow: A Privileged Epistemological Model', in Stephen Gaukroger, John Schuster, and John Sutton, eds, *Descartes' Natural Philosophy* (London, 2000), 249–57.

Armstrong, Arthur H. *The Architecture of the Intelligible Universe in the Philosophy of Plotinus* (Cambridge, 1940).

Arnauld, Antoine. *On True and False Ideas*, trans. and introd. Stephen Gaukroger (Manchester, 1990).

——and Nicole, Pierre. *La Logique ou l'Art de Penser*, ed. P. Claire and F. Girbal (Paris, 1965).

Arnold, Matthew. *God and the Bible* (New York, 1893).

Arriaga, Roderigo de. *Cursus philosophicus* (Antwerp, 1632).

Ashworth Jr., William B. 'Natural History and the Emblematic World View', in David C. Lindberg and Robert S. Westman, eds, *Reappraisals of the Scientific Revolution* (Cambridge, 1990), 303–32.

——'Emblematic Natural History of the Renaissance', in N. Jardine, J. A. Secord, and E. C. Spary, eds, *Cultures of Natural History* (Cambridge, 1996), 17–37.

Auerbach, Eric. *Mimesis* (Princeton, 1968).

Augustine of Hippo. *The City of God*, trans. Marcus Dods (2 vols, Edinburgh, 1872).

Averroes. *Tahāfut al-Tahāfut: The Incoherence of the Incoherence*, trans. with introd. and notes by Simon van den Bergh (London, 1954).

——'Averroes on the Principles of Nature: The Middle Commentary on Aristotle's *Physics, I, II*', trans. Steven Harvey (Ph.D. thesis, Harvard University, 1977).

Aversa, Raphael. *Logica Institutionibus Praeviis Quaestionibus Contexta* (Rome, 1623).

Avicenna. *Le Livre de science*, trans. Mohammad Achena and Henri Massé (2 vols, Paris, 1955).

Bachelard, Gaston. *Le Nouvel Esprit scientifique* (Paris, 1934).

——*La Formation de l'esprit scientifique* (Paris, 1938).

Bacon, Francis. *The Works of Francis Bacon*, ed. James Spedding, Robert Leslie Ellis, and Douglas Denon Heath (14 vols, London, 1857–74).

——*The Oxford Francis Bacon*, ed. Lisa Jardine and Graham Rees (15 vols, Oxford, 1996– ).

Bacon, Roger. *The 'Opus Maius' of Roger Bacon*, ed. J. H. Bridges (3 vols, Oxford, 1897–1900).

Badaloni, Nicola. 'I fratelli Della Porta e la cultura magica a Napoli nel'500', *Studi Storici* 1 (1959–60), 677–715.

Baillet, Adrien. *La Vie de Monsieur Descartes* (2 vols, Paris, 1691).

Baker, John Hamilton, ed. *The Reports of John Spelman* (2 vols, London, 1971).

Baldini, Ugo. 'The Development of Jesuit "Physics" in Italy, 1550–1700: A Structural Approach', in Constance Blackwell and Sachiko Kusukawa, eds, *Philosophy in the Sixteenth and Seventeenth Centuries* (Aldershot, 1999), 248–79.

Balme, David M. 'Greek Science and Mechanism I', *Classical Quarterly* 33 (1939), 129–38.

Barbour, Julian B. *Absolute or Relative Motion: A Study from a Machian Point of View of the Discovery and the Structure of Dynamical Theories* (Cambridge, 1989).

Barenblatt, Daniel. *A Plague upon Humanity: The Hidden History of Japan's Biological Warfare Program* (New York, 2005).

Barker, Peter. 'Stoic Contributions to Early Modern Science', in Margaret J. Osler, ed., *Atoms, Pneuma, and Tranquillity: Epicurean and Stoic Themes in European Thought* (Cambridge, 1991), 135–54.

—— 'The Optical Theory of Comets from Apian to Kepler', *Physis* 30 (1993), 1–25.

—— 'The Role of Religion in the Lutheran Response to Copernicus', in Margaret J. Osler, ed., *Rethinking the Scientific Revolution* (Cambridge, 2000), 59–88.

—— and Goldstein, Bernard R. 'Realism and Instrumentalism in Sixteenth-Century Astronomy: A Reappraisal', *Perspectives on Science* 6 (1998), 232–58.

Barlow, William. *The Navigator's Supply* (London, 1597).

Barnes, Jonathan. 'Aristotle's Theory of Demonstration', in Jonathan Barnes, Malcolm Schofield, and Richard Sorabji, eds, *Articles on Aristotle*, i. *Science* (London, 1975), 65–87.

Barr, James. 'Why the World was Created in 4004BC: Archbishop Ussher and Biblical Chronology', *Bulletin of the John Rylands University Library of Manchester* 67 (1985), 576–608.

Barrow, John D., and Tipler, Frank J. *The Anthropic Cosmological Principle* (Oxford, 1986).

Basso, Sebastian. *Philosophia naturalis adversus Aristotelem, in quibus abstrusa veterum Physiologia restauratur, & Aristotelis errores solidis rationibus refelluntur* (Geneva, 1621).

Baudouin, François. *De institvtione historiae vniuersae et eivs cum iurisprvdentia coniunctione,* ΠΡΟΛΕΓΟΜΕΝΩΝ libri II (Paris, 1561).

Beaune, Jean-Claude. *L'Automate et ses mobiles* (Paris, 1980).

Bebbington, David W. 'Science and Evangelical Theology in Britain from Wesley to Orr', in David N. Livingstone, D. G. Hart, and Mark A. Noll, eds, *Evangelicals and Science in Historical Perspective* (Oxford, 1999), 120–41.

Beckwirth, Sarah. *Christ's Body: Identity, Culture and Society in Late Medieval Writings* (London, 1993).

Beeckman, Isaac. *Mathematicao-physicarum meditationum, quaestionum, solutionum centuria* (Utrecht, 1644).

—— *Journal tenu par Isaac Beeckman de 1604 à 1634*, ed. Cornelius de Waard (4 vols, The Hague, 1939–53).

Ben-Chaim, Michael. 'Doctrine and Use: Newton's "Gift of Preaching"', *History of Science* 36 (1998), 169–98.

—— 'Locke's Ideology of "Common Sense"', *Studies in History and Philosophy of Science*, 31A (2000), 473–501.

Ben-David, Joseph. *The Scientist's Role in Society* (Chicago, 1984).

Benn, Alfred W. *The History of English Rationalism in the Nineteenth Century* (2 vols, London, 1906).

Bennett, J. A. 'Robert Hooke as Mechanic and Natural Philosopher', *Notes and Records of the Royal Society* 35 (1980), 33–48.

—— *The Mathematical Science of Christopher Wren* (Cambridge, 1982).

—— 'The Challenge of Practical Mathematics', in Stephen Pumfrey, Paolo L. Rossi, and Maurice Slawinski, eds, *Science, Culture and Popular Belief in Renaissance Europe* (Manchester, 1991), 176–90.

Bennett, M. R., and Hacker, P. M. S. *Philosophical Foundations of Neuroscience* (Oxford, 2003).

Berkel, Klaas van. *Isaac Beeckman (1588–1637) en de mechanisierung van het wereldbeeld* (Amsterdam, 1983).

_____ 'A Note on Rudolphus Snellius and the Early History of Mathematics in Leiden', in C. Hay, ed., *Mathematics from Manuscript to Print, 1300–1600* (Oxford, 1988), 156–61.

_____ 'Descartes' Debt to Beeckman: Inspiration, Cooperation, Conflict', in Stephen Gaukroger, John Schuster, and John Sutton, eds, *Descartes' Natural Philosophy* (London, 2000), 46–59.

Berman, Harold J. *Law and Revolution: The Formation of the Western Legal Tradition* (Cambridge, Mass., 1983).

_____ *Law and Revolution*, ii. *The Impact of the Protestant Reformations on the Western Legal Tradition* (Cambridge, Mass., 2003).

Bernal, J. D. *The Social Function of Science* (London, 1939).

Bernstein, H. R. '*Conatus*, Hobbes, and the Young Leibniz', *Studies in History and Philosophy of Science* 11 (1980), 25–37.

Biagioli, Mario. 'The Social Status of Italian Mathematicians', *History of Science* 27 (1989), 41–95.

_____ *Galileo Courtier, The Practice of Science in the Culture of Absolutism* (Chicago, 1993).

_____ 'Replication or Monopoly? The Economies of Invention and Discovery in Galileo's Observations of 1610', in Jürgen Renn, ed., *Galileo in Context* (Cambridge, 2001), 277–320.

Bianchi, Luca. 'Censure, liberté et progrès intellectuel à l'Université de Paris au XIII$^e$ siècle', *Archives d'histoire doctrinale et littéraire du Moyen Âge* 63 (1996), 45–93.

Biggs, Noah. *Mataeotechnia medicinae praxeos. The vanity of the craft of physick. Or, A new dispensatory* (London, 1651).

Binet, Etienne. *Essay des merveilles de nature et des plus nobles artifices* (Rouen, 1621).

Birch, Thomas. *The History of the Royal Society of London, For Improving of Natural Knowledge, From Its First Rise* (4 vols, London, 1756–7).

Bjurstrom, Per. 'Baroque Theater and the Jesuits', in Rudolph Wittkower and Orma B. Jaffe, eds, *Baroque Art: The Jesuit Contribution* (New York, 1972), 99–110.

Black, Edwin. *War Against the Weak: Eugenics and America's Campaign to Create a Master Race* (New York, 2001).

Blackwell, Constance. 'The Case of Honoré Fabri and the Historiography of Sixteenth and Seventeenth Century Jesuit Aristotelianism in Protestant History of Philosophy: Sturm, Morhof and Brucker', *Nouvelles de la Republique des Lettres* (1995), 49–77.

_____ 'Thales Philosophus: The Beginning of Philosophy as a Discipline', in Donald R. Kelley, ed., *History and the Disciplines: The Reclassification of Knowledge in Early Modern Europe* (Rochester, 1997), 61–82.

Blackwell, Richard J. 'Christiaan Huygens' *The Motion of Colliding Bodies*', *Isis* 68 (1977), 574–97.

_____ *Galileo, Bellarmine, and the Bible* (Notre Dame, 1991).

Blair, Ann. *The Theater of Nature* (Princeton, 1997).

Bloch, Olivier. *La Philosophie de Gassendi* (The Hague, 1971).

Block, Irving. 'Truth and Error in Aristotle's Theory of Perception', *Philosophical Quarterly* 11 (1961), 1–9.

Blumenberg, Hans. *The Legitimacy of the Modern Age* (Cambridge, Mass., 1983).

_____ *The Genesis of the Copernican World* (Cambridge, Mass., 1987).

Blundeville, Thomas. *Exercises containing sixe Treatises* (London, 1594).

_____ *Theoriques of the seven Planets* (London, 1602).

Bobonich, Christopher. *Plato's Utopia Recast: His Later Ethics and Politics* (Oxford, 2002).

Bodin, Jean. *Methodus ad facilem historiarum cognitionem* (Paris, 1566).

Bodin, Jean. *Universae naturae theatrum* (Lyon, 1596).

Boethius of Dacia. *On the Supreme Good*, ed. and trans. J. F. Wippel (Toronto, 1987).

Booth, Emily. *'A Subtle and Mysterious Machine': The Medical World of Walter Charleton (1619–1670)* (Dordrecht, 2005).

Borelli, Giovanni Alfonso. *Theoricae mediceorum planetarum ex causis physicis deductae* (Florence, 1666).

Bowersock, Glen W. *Hellenism in Late Antiquity* (Ann Arbor, 1990).

Bowler, Peter J. *Reconciling Science and Religion: The Debate in Early Twentieth-Century Britain* (Chicago, 2001).

Boyer, Carl B. *The Rainbow* (Princeton, 1959).

Boyle, Robert. *The Works of the Honourable Robert Boyle*, ed. Thomas Birch (6 vols, London, 1772).

Brackenridge, J. Bruce. *The Key to Newton's Dynamics: The Kepler Problem and the Principia* (Berkeley, 1995).

—— and Nauenberg, Michael. 'Curvature in Newton's Dynamics', in I. Bernard Cohen and George E. Smith, eds, *The Cambridge Companion to Newton* (Cambridge, 2002), 85–137.

Brague, Rémi. *Eccentric Culture: A Theory of Western Civilization* (South Bend, Ind., 2002).

Brandt, Frithiof. *Thomas Hobbes' Mechanical Conception of Nature* (Copenhagen/London, 1928).

Broad, C. D. *Mind and its Place in Nature* (London, 1925).

Brockliss, Laurence W. B. *French Higher Education in the Seventeenth and Eighteenth Centuries* (Oxford, 1987).

—— 'Copernicus in the University: The French Experience', in John Henry and Sarah Hutton, eds, *New Perspectives on Renaissance Thought* (London, 1990), 190–213.

—— 'The Scientific Revolution in France', in Roy Porter and Mikulas Teich, eds, *The Scientific Revolution in National Context* (Cambridge, 1992), 55–89.

—— 'Rapports de structure et de contenu entre les *Principia* et les cours de philosophie des collèges', in Jean-Robert Armogathe and Giulia Belgioioso, eds, *Descartes: Principia Philosophiae, 1644–1994* (Naples, 1996), 491–516.

Brooke, John Hedley. *Science and Religion: Some Historical Perspectives* (Cambridge, 1991).

—— and Cantor, Geoffrey. *Reconstructing Nature: The Engagement of Science and Religion* (Oxford, 1998).

Brown, H. V. B. 'Avicenna and the Christian Philosophers in Baghdad', in S. M. Stern, Albert Hourani, and Vivian Brown, eds, *Islamic Philosophy and the Classical Tradition* (Columbia, SC, 1972), 35–48.

Brown, Peter. *Augustine of Hippo, A Biography* (London, 1967).

—— *Power and Persuasion in Late Antiquity: Towards a Christian Empire* (Madison, 1988).

—— *The Body and Society: Men, Women, and Sexual Renunciation in Early Christianity* (London, 1989).

Brown, Theodore M. 'The Rise of Baconianism in Seventeenth-Century England: A Perspective on Science and Society during the Scientific Revolution', in *Science and History: Studies in Honor of Edward Rosen*, Studia Copernica 16 (Wrocław, 1978), 501–22.

Brown, Thomas. *Physick lies a Bleeding, or the Apothecary turned Doctor, A Comedy Acted every Day in most Apothecaries Shops in London* (London, 1697).

Brundell, Barry. *Pierre Gassendi: From Aristotelianism to a New Natural Philosophy* (Dordrecht, 1987).

Bruno, Giordano. *La cena de le ceneri Descritta in cinque dialogi* (London, 1584).

—— *De la causa, principio et vno* (London, 1584).

_____ *De l'infinito vniuerso et mondi* (London, 1585).

_____ *De gl'heroici furori* (London, 1585).

_____ *De triplici minimo et mensvra ad trivm specvlatiuarum scientiarum* (Frankfurt, 1591).

_____ *The Ash Wednesday Supper*, trans. S. Jaki (The Hague, 1975).

_____ *Cause, Principle and Unity*, ed. Richard J. Blackwell and Robert de Lucca (Cambridge, 1998).

Buckley, Michael J. *At the Origins of Modern Atheism* (New Haven, 1987).

Budd, Susan. *Varieties of Unbelief: Atheists and Unbelievers in English Society 1850–1960* (London, 1977).

Budé, Guillaume. *Annotationes . . . in quatuor et viginti Pandectarum libros* (Paris, 1535).

Bullinger, Heinrich. *Der Widertoeufferen ursprung, fürgang, Secten, waesen, fürnemme vnd gemeine jrer leer Artickel* (Zurich, 1560).

Burke, Peter. *The Renaissance Sense of the Past* (London, 1969).

_____ *The Italian Renaissance: Culture and Society in Italy* (Princeton, 1986).

Burkert, Walter. 'Platon oder Pythagoras? Zum Ursprung des Wortes "Philosophie" ', *Hermes* 88 (1960), 159–77.

Burnet, Thomas. *Telluris theoria sacra: orbis nostri originem et mutationes generales, quas aut jam subiit aut olim subiturus est, complectens . . .* (London, 1680).

_____ *The Theory of the Earth: Containing an Original of an Account of the Earth, and of all the Changes Which it Hath Undergone, or is to Undergo Till the Consumation of All Things. The First Two Books, Concerning the Deluge, and Concerning Paradise* (London, 1684).

_____ *Telluris theoria sacra. Libri duo posteriores de conflagratione mundi et de futuro atatu rerum* (London, 1689).

_____ *The Sacred Theory of the Earth* (London, 1965).

Burns, Norman T. *Christian Mortalism from Tyndale to Milton* (Cambridge, Mass., 1972).

Burtt, Edwin Arthur. *The Metaphysical Origins of Modern Physical Science: A Historical and Critical Essay* (London, 1924).

Bush, Vannevar. *Science, the Endless Frontier: A Report to the President by Vannevar Bush, Director of the Office of Scientific Research and Development* (Washington, 1945).

Butler, Edward C. *Western Mysticism: The Teaching of Augustine, Gregory and Bernard on Contemplation and the Contemplative Life* (New York, 1966).

Butterfield, Herbert. *The Origins of Modern Science* (London, 1949).

Bylebyl, Jerome J. 'Medicine, Philosophy and Humanism in Renaissance Italy', in John W. Shirley and F. David Hoeniger, eds, *Science and the Arts in the Renaissance* (Washington, 1986), 27–49.

Bynum, Catherine Walker. *Jesus as Mother: Studies in Spirituality of the High Middle Ages* (Berkeley, 1982).

Cabeo, Niccolò. *Philosophia Magnetica, in qua magnetis natura penitus explicatur* (Cologne, 1629).

_____ *Commentaria in libros Meteorologicorum* (4 vols, Rome, 1646).

Cabero, Chrystostomus. *Brevis summularum recapitulatio* (Valladolid, 1623).

Cabral, Regis. 'Herbert Butterfield (1900–79) as a Christian Historian of Science', *Studies in History and Philosophy of Science* 27 (1996), 547–64.

Cahan, David. 'Helmholtz and the Civilizing Power of Science', in David Cahan, ed., *Hermann von Helmholtz and the Foundations of Nineteenth-Century Science* (Berkeley, 1993), 559–601.

Calvin, John. *Commentaries on the First Book of Moses Called Genesis*, trans. John King (2 vols, Edinburgh, 1847–50).

Canizares-Esguerra, Jorge. 'Iberian Science in the Renaissance: Ignored How Much Longer?', *Perspectives in Science* 12 (2004), 86–124.

Cano, Melchior. *Locorum Theologicorum Libri Duodecim* (Cologne, 1574).

Čapek, Milič. *The Philosophical Impact of Contemporary Physics* (New York, 1961).

Capizzi, Antonio. *The Cosmic Republic: Notes for a Non-Peripapetic History of the Birth of Philosophy in Greece* (Amsterdam, 1990).

Cardano, Girolamo. *De subtilitate libri XXI* (Nuremberg, 1550).

—— *De rerum varietate libri XVII* (Basle, 1557).

Cardwell, Donald S. L. *The Organisation of Science in England* (London, 1972).

Carlyle, Robert W., and Carlyle, Alexander J. *A History of Medieval Political Theory in the West* (6 vols, Edinburgh, 1970).

Carmody, F. J. 'The Planetary Theory of Ibn-Rushd', *Osiris* 10 (1952), 556–86.

Carnap, Rudolph. 'Intellectual Autobiography', in Paul Arthur Schilpp, ed., *The Philosophy of Rudolph Carnap* (La Salle, Ill., 1963), 3–84.

Carteron, Henri. *La Notion de force dans la système d'Aristote* (Paris, 1923).

Cartwright, Nancy. *How the Laws of Physics Lie* (Oxford, 1983).

—— *The Dappled World: A Study of the Boundaries of Science* (Cambridge, 1999).

Carus, Paul. *The Religion of Science* (Chicago, 1893).

Casaubon, Isaac. *De rebus sacris et ecclesiasticis Exercitationes xvi* (London, 1614).

Casaubon, Meric. *A Treatise concerning Enthusiasme* (London, 1655).

—— *Of Credulity and Incredulity in Things Natural, Civill and Divine* (London, 1668).

—— *A Letter to Pierre Moulin . . . Concerning natural experimental Philosophie, and some books lately set about it* (Cambridge, 1669).

Cassirer, Ernst. *The Platonic Renaissance in England* (Austin, 1953).

—— *The Individual and the Cosmos in Renaissance Philosophy* (Philadelphia, 1963).

—— Kristeller, Paul Oskar, and Randall Jr., John Herman, eds and trans. *The Renaissance Philosophy of Man* (Chicago, 1948).

Cat, Jordi, Cartwright, Nancy, and Chang, Hasok. 'Otto Neurath: Politics and the Unity of Science', in Peter Galison and David J. Stump, eds, *The Disunity of Science* (Stanford, 1996), 347–69.

Caussin, Nicolas. *Electorum symbolorum et parabolarum historicarum syntagmata* (Paris, 1618).

—— *La Cour sainte ou l'institution chrétienne des Grands* (Paris, 1624).

—— *Eloquentiae sacrae et humanae parallela* (Paris, 1624).

Cavendish, Margaret, Duchess of Newcastle. *Observations upon Experimental Philosophy to which is added The Description of a New Blazing World* (London, 1666).

Celaya, Juan de. *Expositio magistri ioannis de gelaya valentini in quattuor libros de celo & mundi Aristotelis cum questionibus eiusdem* (Paris, 1518).

Chadwick, Owen. 'Evolution and the Churches', in Colin A. Russell, ed., *Science and Religious Belief: A Selection of Recent Historical Studies* (London, 1973), 282–93.

Chant, Colin. 'Science in Orthodox Europe', in David Goodman and Colin A. Russell, eds, *The Rise of Scientific Europe, 1500–1800* (London, 1991), 333–60.

Chantraine, Pierre. *Dictionnaire étymologique de la langue grecque, histoire des mots* (4 vols, Paris, 1968–80).

Charleton, Walter. *The Darknes of Atheism Dispelled by the Light of Nature. A Physico-Theological Treatise* (London, 1652).

—— *Physiologia Epicuro-Gassendo-Charltoniana: or A Fabrick of Science Natural, upon the Hypothesis of Atoms* (London, 1654).

Cicero, Marcus Tullius. *The Works of Cicero*, Loeb edition: various eds and trans. (28 vols, Cambridge, Mass., 1914– ).

Clagett, Marshall. *The Science of Mechanics in the Middle Ages* (Madison, 1959).

Clavelin, Maurice. *The Natural Philosophy of Galileo* (Cambridge, Mass., 1974).

Clement of Alexandria. *Stromata Buch I–IV*, ed. Otto von Stählin (Berlin, 1960).

Clericuzio, Antonio, 'A Redefinition of Boyle's Chemistry and Corpuscular Philosophy', *Annals of Science* 47 (1990), 562–89.

_____ 'From Van Helmont to Boyle: A Study of the Transmission of Helmontian Chemical and Medical Theories in Seventeenth-Century England', *British Journal for the History of Science* 26 (1993), 303–34.

_____ 'Carneades and the Chemists: A Study of *The Sceptical Chymist* and its Impact on Seventeenth-Century Chemistry', in Michael Hunter, ed., *Robert Boyle Reconsidered* (Cambridge, 1994), 79–90.

_____ 'Gassendi, Charleton and Boyle on Matter and Motion', in Christoph Lüthy, John E. Murdoch, and William R. Newman, eds, *Late Medieval and Early Modern Corpuscular Matter Theories* (Leiden, 2001), 467–82.

Clucas, Stephen. 'The Atomism of the Cavendish Circle: A Reappraisal', *The Seventeenth Century* 9 (1994), 247–73.

_____ 'Corpuscular Matter Theory in the Northumberland Circle', in Christoph Lüthy, John E. Murdoch, and William R. Newman, eds, *Late Medieval and Early Modern Corpuscular Matter Theories* (Leiden, 2001), 181–207.

_____ '*Simulacra et Signacula*: Memory, Magic and Metaphysics in Brunian Mnemonics', in Hilary Gatti, ed., *Giordano Bruno: Philosophy of the Renaissance* (Aldershot, 2002), 273–97.

Cochrane, Charles Norris. *Christianity and Classical Culture* (rev. edn, Oxford, 1944).

Cohen, H. Floris. *Quantifying Music* (Dordrecht, 1984).

_____ *The Scientific Revolution: A Historiographical Inquiry* (Chicago, 1994).

Cohen, I. Bernard. *The Birth of a New Physics* (Harmondsworth, 1987).

Coimbra Commentators. *In octo libros physicorum Aristotelis* (Coimbra, 1592).

_____ *In quattuor libros De coelo* (Lisbon, 1593).

_____ *In libros Aristotelis qui Parva naturalia appellantur* (Lyon, 1594).

_____ *In libros Meteorum* (Lyon, 1594).

_____ *In tres libros De anima* (Coimbra, 1598).

Colish, Marcia L. *The Mirror of Language: A Study in the Medieval Theory of Knowledge* (New Haven, 1968).

_____ *The Stoic Tradition from Antiquity to the Early Middle Ages* (2 vols, Leiden, 1985).

_____ *Medieval Foundations of the Western Intellectual Tradition, 400–1400* (New Haven, 1997).

Colquhoun, Patrick. *A Treatise on Indigence; exhibiting a general view of the national resources for productive labour; with propositions for ameliorating the condition of the poor, and improving the moral habits and increasing the comforts of the labouring people* (London, 1806).

Compayré, Gabriel. *Histoire critique des doctrines de l'éducation en France* (2 vols, Paris, 1879).

Contamine, Philippe. *Guerre, État et Société à la fin du moyen âge* (Paris, 1972).

Cook, Harold J. *The Decline of the Old Medical Regime in Stuart London* (Ithaca, NY, 1986).

_____ 'The New Philosophy and Medicine', in David C. Lindberg and Robert S. Westman, eds, *Reappraisals of the Scientific Revolution* (Cambridge, 1990), 397–436.

Copenhaver, Brian, ed. and trans. *The Greek Corpus Hermeticum and the Latin Asclepius in a new English Translation, with Notes and Introduction* (Cambridge, 1992).

_____ and Schmitt, Charles B., *Renaissance Philosophy* (Oxford, 1992).

Copernicus, Nicolaus. *De revolutionibus orbium coelestium* (Nuremberg, 1543).

—— *On the Revolution of the Heavenly Spheres*, trans. C. G. Wallis, in *Britannica Great Books* 16 (Chicago, 1952), 501–838.

Corner, George W., ed. and trans. *Anatomical Texts of the Earlier Middle Ages* (Washington, 1927).

Cornford, Francis Macdonald. *Plato's Cosmology* (London, 1937).

Cornwall, John. *Hitler's Scientists: Science, War, and the Devil's Pact* (New York, 2003).

Coton, Pierre. *Sermons sur les principales et plus difficiles matieres de la fay* (Paris, 1617).

Courcelle, Pierre-Paul. *La Consolation de Philosophie dans la tradition littéraire. Antécédents et postérité de Boèce* (Paris, 1967).

Cox, Jeffrey. *The English Churches in a Secular Society: Lambeth, 1870–1930* (Oxford, 1982).

Craven, William G. *Giovanni Della Mirandola, Symbol of His Age* (Geneva, 1981).

Creath, Richard. 'The Unity of Science: Carnap, Neurath, and Beyond', in Peter Galison and David J. Stump, eds, *The Disunity of Science* (Stanford, 1996), 158–69.

Croll, Oswald. *Basilica chymica* (London, 1635).

Cromartie, Alan. *Sir Matthew Hale, 1609–1676: Law, Religion and Natural Philosophy* (Cambridge, 1995).

Crombie, Alistair C. *Robert Grosseteste and the Origins of Experimental Science, 1100–1700* (Oxford, 1971).

Cronin, Timothy J. *Objective Being in Descartes and in Suárez* (Rome, 1966).

Cudworth, Ralph. *The True Intellectual System of the Universe* (2nd edn, 2 vols, London, 1743).

Cunningham, Andrew. 'Thomas Sydenham: Epidemics, Experiment, and the "Good Old Cause"', in Roger French and Andrew Wear, eds, *The Medical Revolution of the Seventeenth Century* (Cambridge, 1989), 164–90.

—— *The Anatomical Renaissance: The Resurrection of the Anatomical Projects of the Ancients* (Aldershot, 1997).

Curley, Edwin M. *Spinoza's Metaphysics: An Essay in Interpretation* (Cambridge, Mass., 1969).

Dainville, François de. *La Naissance de l'humanisme moderne* (Paris, 1940).

Dalbiez, Roland. 'Les sources scolastiques de la théorie cartésienne de l'être objectif', *Revue d'Histoire de la Philosophie* 3 (1929), 464–72.

Daston, Lorraine. *Classical Probability in the Enlightenment* (Princeton, 1988).

Daube, David. *Witnesses in Bible and Talmud* (Oxford, 1986).

David of Dinant. *Davidis de Dinanto Quaternulorum Fragmenta*, ed. M. Kurdzialek (Warsaw, 1963).

Davidson, Donald. *Inquiries into Truth and Interpretation* (Oxford, 1984).

Davies, E. Brian. *Science in the Looking Glass: What Do Scientists Really Know?* (Oxford, 2003).

Davies, Paul. *God and the New Physics* (Harmondsworth, 1983).

Dawkins, Richard. *The Selfish Gene* (London, 1978).

De Gandt, François. *Force and Geometry in Newton's Principia* (Princeton, 1995).

Dear, Peter. '*Totius in Verba*: Rhetoric and Authority in the Early Royal Society', *Isis* 76 (1985), 145–61.

—— *Mersenne and the Learning of the Schools* (Ithaca, NY, 1988).

—— 'From Truth to Disinterestedness in the Seventeenth Century', *Social Studies of Science* 22 (1992), 619–31.

—— *Discipline and Experience: The Mathematical Way in the Scientific Revolution* (Chicago, 1995).

Debus, Allen G. *The English Paracelsians* (New York, 1965).

–––– 'Fire Analysis and the Elements in the Sixteenth and the Seventeenth Centuries', *Annals of Science* 23 (1967), 128–47.

–––– *The French Paracelsians* (Cambridge, 1991).

–––– *Chemistry and Medical Debate: Van Helmont to Boerhaave* (Canton, Mass., 2001).

Della Rocca, Michael. 'Judgement and Will', in Stephen Gaukroger, ed., *The Blackwell Guide to Descartes' Meditations* (Oxford, 2006), 142–59.

Delumeau, Jean. *Le Catholicisme entre Luther et Voltaire* (Paris, 1971).

–––– *La Peur en occident (XIV^e–XVIII^e siècles): Une cité assiégée* (Paris, 1978).

–––– *Le Péché et la peur: La culpabilisation en occident, XIII^e–XVIII^e siècles* (Paris, 1983).

–––– *Rassurer et protéger: Le sentiment de sécurité dans l'occident d'autrefois* (Paris, 1989).

–––– *L'Aveu et le pardon* (Paris, 1992).

Den Hartog, Jacob Pieter. *Mechanics* (New York, 1961).

Denifle, Heinrich, and Châtelain, Émile, eds, *Chartularium Universitatis Parisiensis* (4 vols, Paris, 1889–97).

Des Chene, Dennis. *Physiologia: Natural Philosophy in Late Aristotelian and Cartesian Thought* (Ithaca, NY, 1996).

–––– *Life's Form: Late Aristotelian Conceptions of the Soul* (Ithaca, NY, 2000).

–––– 'Life and Health in Cartesian Natural Philosophy', in Stephen Gaukroger, John Schuster, and John Sutton, eds, *Descartes' Natural Philosophy* (London, 2000), 723–35.

–––– *Spirits and Clocks* (Ithaca, NY, 2001).

Descartes, René. *Œuvres de Descartes*, ed. Charles Adam and Paul Tannery (2nd edn, 11 vols, Paris, 1974–86).

–––– *Principles of Philosophy*, eds and trans. Valentine R. Miller and Reese P. Miller (Dordrecht, 1991).

–––– *The World and Other Writings*, ed. and trans. Stephen Gaukroger (Cambridge, 1998).

Detienne, Marcel. *Maîtres de vérité dans la grèce archaïque* (Paris, 1990).

–––– and Vernant, Jean-Pierre. *Les Ruses d'intelligence: la metis des grecs* (Paris, 1974).

Dettloff, Werner. *Die Entwicklung der Akzeptations- und Verdienstlehre von Duns Skotus bis Luther* (Münster, 1963).

Detwald, Jonathan. *Aristocratic Experience and the Origins of Modern Culture: France, 1570–1715* (Berkeley, 1993).

Devillairs, Laurence. *Descartes et la conaissance de dieu* (Paris, 2004).

Dewey, John. 'Unity of Science as a Social Problem', in Otto Neurath, Rudolph Carnap, and Charles Morris, eds, *Foundations of the Unity of Science* (2 vols, Chicago, 1970), i. 32–3.

Di Napoli, Giovanni. *L'immortalità dell'anima nel Rinascimento* (Turin, 1963).

Dick, Steven J. *Plurality of Worlds: The Extraterrestrial Life Debate from Democritus to Kant* (Cambridge, 1982).

Diderot, Denis. *Encyclopèdie ou Dictionnaire Raisonné des Sciences, des Arts et des Métiers* (17 vols, Paris, 1751–65).

Digby, Kenelm. *Two Treatises: In the One of Which, The Nature of Bodies; In the Other, The Nature of Mans Soule, is Looked into: In Way of Discovery of the Immortality of Reasonable Soules* (Paris 1644).

Dijksterhuis, Eduard Jan. *The Mechanization of the World Picture* (Oxford, 1961).

Diogenes Laertius. *Lives of Eminent Philosophers*, with an English trans. by R. D. Hicks (Loeb edn: 2 vols, Cambridge, Mass., 1972).

(Pseudo-)Dionysius the Areopagite. *Opera Omnia: Coelistis Hierarchia. Ecclesiastica Hierarchia. Diuina nomina. Mystica theologia. Duodecim epistolae* (Venice, 1556).

Dixsaut, Monique. *Le Naturel Philosophe: Essai sur les Dialogues de Platon* (Paris, 1985).

Dobbs, Betty Jo Teeter. *The Foundations of Newton's Alchemy: or 'The Hunting of the Greene Lyon'* (Cambridge, 1975).

—— *The Janus Face of Genius: The Role of Alchemy in Newton's Thought* (Cambridge, 1991).

—— 'Newton as Final Cause and First Mover', in Margaret J. Osler, *Rethinking the Scientific Revolution* (Cambridge, 2000), 25–39.

Dod, Bernard. 'Aristoteles Latinus', in N. Kretzman, Anthony Kenny, and Jan Pinborg, eds, *The Cambridge History of Later Medieval Philosophy* (Cambridge, 1982), 45–79.

Domanski, Juliusz. *La Philosophie, théorie ou manière de vivre?: les controverses de l'Antiquité à la Renaissance* (Fribourg/Paris, 1996).

Domingues, Beatriz Helena. *Tradição na Modernidade e Modernidade na Tradição: A Modernidade Ibérica e a Revolução Copernicana* (Rio de Janeiro, 1996).

—— 'Spain and the Dawn of Modern Science', *Metascience* 7 (1998), 298–312.

Dominis, Marco Antonio de. *De radiis visus et lucis in vitris perspectivis et iride tractatus* (Venice, 1611).

Donahue, William H. 'The Solid Planetary Spheres in Post-Copernican Natural Philosophy', in Robert S. Westman, ed., *The Copernican Achievement* (Berkeley, 1975), 244–75.

—— *The Dissolution of the Celestial Spheres* (New York, 1981).

Drake, Stillman. *Galileo Studies* (Ann Arbor, 1970).

—— *Galileo at Work: A Scientific Biography* (Chicago, 1978).

—— and Drabkin, I. E. ed. and trans. *Mechanics in Sixteenth-Century Italy* (Madison, 1969).

Draper, John William. *History of the Conflict between Religion and Science* (London, 1875).

Duchesne, Joseph. *Liber de priscorum philosophorum* (1603).

—— *Ad veritatem hermeticae medicinae* (1604).

Du Hamel, Jean. *Quaedam recentiorum philosophorum ac praesertim Cartesii propositiones damnatae ac prohibitae* (Paris, 1705).

Duff, Antony. 'Moral Philosophy as Applied Science?', *Philosophy* 63 (1988), 105–10.

Duhem, Pierre. *Les Origines de la statique* (2 vols, Paris, 1905–6).

—— *To Save the Phenomena* (Chicago, 1969).

Dunton, John. *The Young-Students-Library, Containing Extracts and Abridgments of the Most Valuable Books* (London, 1692).

Dupleix, Scipion. *Corps de philosophie, contenant la logique, l'ethique, la physique, et la metaphysique* (Geneva, 1623).

Durantel, J. *Saint Thomas et le Pseudo-Denis* (Paris, 1919).

Ebeling, Gerhard. *Evangelische Evangelienauslegung* (Munich, 1942).

Edgerton, Samuel Y. *The Heritage of Giotto's Geometry: Art and Science on the Eve of the Scientific Revolution* (Ithaca, NY, 1991).

Edwards, John. *Brief Remarks upon Mr. Whiston's New Theory of the Earth* (London, 1697).

Eisenman, Robert. *James the Brother of Jesus* (New York, 1998).

Ellis, Brian D. 'Newton's Concept of Motive Force', *Journal of the History of Ideas* 23 (1962), 273–8.

—— 'The Origin and Nature of Newton's Laws of Motion,' in Robert G. Colodny, ed., *Beyond the Edge of Certainty* (Englewood Cliffs, NJ, 1965), 29–68.

Ellis, Ieuan. *Seven Against Christ: A Study of Essays and Reviews* (Leiden, 1980).

Emilsson, Eyjólfur Kjalar. *Plotinus on Sense-Perception: A Philosophical Study* (Cambridge, 1988).

Erasmus, Hendrik J. *The Origins of Rome in Historiography from Petrarch to Perizonius* (Assen, 1962).

Erickson, Carolly. *The Medieval Vision: Essays in History and Perception* (New York, 1976).

Eustachius a Sancto Paulo. *Summa philosophiae quadripartita, de rebus Dialecticis, Ethicis, Physicis, & Metaphysicis* (Cologne, 1629).

Evans, Gillian R. *Philosophy and Theology in the Middle Ages* (London, 1993).

Evelyn, John. *Sylva; or, A Discourse of Forest-Trees, and the Propagation of Timber in His Majesties Dominions* (London, 1679).

Fabri, Honoré. *Controversiae logicae: In quibus selectae Disputationes discussae, non parum lucis Analyticae asserunt* (Lyon, 1646).

Fara, Patricia. *Sympathetic Attractions: Magnetic Practices, Beliefs, and Symbolism in Eighteenth-Century England* (Princeton, 1996).

——— *Newton: The Making of Genius* (London, 2002).

Faret, Nicolas. *L'Honneste Homme. Ov l'Art de plaire a la court* (Paris, 1630).

——— *The Honest Man: or, the Art to Please in Court* (London, 1632).

Fattori, Marta. '"Vafer Baconus": la storia della censura del *De augmentis scientiarum*', *Nouvelles de la République des lettres* (2000), 97–130.

——— 'Altri documenti inediti dell'Archivio del Sant'Uffizio sulla censura del *De augmentis scientiarum* di Francis Bacon', *Nouvelles de la République des lettres* (2001), 121–30.

——— 'La diffusione di Francis Bacon nel libertinismo francese', *Rivista di storia della filosofia* 57 (2002), 225–42.

——— 'Sir Francis Bacon and the Holy Office', *British Journal for the History of Philosophy* 13 (2005), 21–49.

Febvre, Lucien. *The Problem of Unbelief in the Sixteenth Century: The Religion of Rabelais* (Cambridge, Mass., 1982).

Feingold, Mordechai. *The Mathematicians' Apprenticeship: Science, Universities and Society in England, 1560–1640* (Cambridge, 1984).

Ferreiro, Larrie D. 'Ships and Science: *The Birth of Naval Architecture in the Scientific Revolution, 1600–1800* (Cambridge, Mass., 2006).

Feyerabend, Paul. *Against Method* (London, 1975).

Ficino, Marsilio. *Opera omnia* (2 vols, Basle, 1576).

——— *Platonic Theology,* ed. James Hankins and William Bowen, trans. Michael J. B. Allen and John Warden (6 vols, Cambridge, Mass., 2001–   ).

Field, Judith V. *Kepler's Geometrical Cosmology* (London, 1988).

Findlen, Paula. 'Francis Bacon and the Reform of Natural History in the Seventeenth Century', in Donald R. Kelley, ed., *History and the Disciplines: The Reclassification of Knowledge in Early Modern Europe* (Rochester, 1997), 239–60.

Finocchiaro, Maurice A. 'Philosophy versus Religion and Science versus Religion: The Trials of Bruno and Galileo', in Hilary Gatti, ed., *Giordano Bruno: Philosopher of the Renaissance* (Aldershot, 2002), 51–96.

Firpi, Luigi. *Il processo di Giordano Bruno* (Rome, 1993).

Fisch, H. 'The Scientist as Priest: A Note on Robert Boyle's Natural Theology', *Isis* 44 (1953), 252–65.

Fisher, Saul. 'Gassendi's Atomist Account of Generation and Heredity in Animals and Plants', *Perspectives on Science* 11 (2003), 484–512.

Fleck, Ludwig. *Entstehung und Entwicklung einer wissenschaftlichen Tatsache* (Basle, 1935).

Fögen, Marie Theres. *Die Enteignung der Wahrsager* (Frankfurt, 1993).

Fontenelle, Bernard le Bovier de. *Œuvres de Monsieur de Fontenelle . . . nouvelle édition* (10 vols, Paris, 1762).

Fothergill-Payne, Louise. 'Seneca's Role in Popularizing Epicurus in the Sixteenth Century', in Margaret J. Osler, ed., *Atoms, Pneuma, and Tranquillity: Epicurean and Stoic Themes in European Thought* (Cambridge, 1991), 115–34.

Foucault, Michel. *Les Mots et les choses* (Paris, 1966).

Fouke, Daniel. 'Mechanical and "Organical" Models in Seventeenth-Century Explanations of Biological Reproduction', *Science in Context* 3 (1989), 365–82.

Fowler, Colin F. *Descartes on the Human Soul: Philosophy and the Demands of Christian Doctrine* (Dordrecht, 1999).

Fracastoro, Girolamo. *Homocentrica: Sive de Stellis* (Venice, 1538).

Frank Jr., Robert G. *Harvey and the Oxford Physiologists* (Berkeley, 1980).

Franklin, Julian. *Jean Bodin and the Sixteenth Century Revolution in the Methodology of Law and History* (New York, 1963).

Freddoso, Alfred J. 'God's Concurrence with Secondary Causes: Why Conservation is Not Enough', *Philosophical Perspectives* 5 (1991), 553–85.

____ 'God's General Concurrence with Secondary Causes: Pitfalls and Prospects', *American Catholic Philosophical Quarterly* 67 (1994), 131–56.

____ 'Ockham on Faith and Reason', in Paul Spade, ed., *Cambridge Companion to Ockham* (Cambridge, 1999), 326–49.

Frede, Michael. *Essays in Ancient Philosophy* (Oxford, 1987).

Freeman, Charles. *The Closing of the Western Mind: The Rise of Faith and the Fall of Reason* (London, 2003).

French, Roger. *Ancient Natural History* (London, 1994).

____ *Medicine Before Science: The Rational and Learned Doctor from the Middle Ages to the Enlightenment* (Cambridge, 2003).

____ and Cunningham, Andrew. *Before Science: The Invention of the Friars' Natural Philosophy* (London, 1996).

Freudenthal, Gad. *Aristotle's Theory of Material Substance: Heat and Pneuma, Form and Soul* (Oxford, 1995).

Froidment [Fromondus], Liebert. *Meteorologicorum libri sex* (Antwerp, 1627).

Fumaroli, Marc. *L'Âge de l'eloquence: Rhétorique et 'res literaria' de la Renaissance au seuil de l'époque classique* (Geneva, 1980).

Funkenstein, Amos. *Theology and Scientific Imagination from the Middle Ages to the Seventeenth Century* (Princeton, 1986).

Furley, David. *Cosmic Problems: Essays on Greek and Roman Philosophy of Nature* (Cambridge, 1989).

____ 'Democritus and Epicurus on Sensible Qualities', in Jacques Brunschwig and Martha C. Nussbaum, eds, *Passions and Perceptions* (Cambridge, 1993), 72–94.

Fyfe, Aileen. 'The Reception of William Paley's *Natural Theology* in the University of Cambridge', *British Journal for the History of Science* 30 (1997), 35–59.

____ *Science and Salvation: Evangelical Popular Science Publishing in Victorian Britain* (Chicago, 2004).

Gabbey, Alan. 'Force and Inertia in the Seventeenth Century: Descartes and Newton', in Stephen Gaukroger, ed., *Descartes: Philosophy, Mathematics and Physics* (New York, 1980), 230–320.

____ 'Huygens and Mechanics', in H. J. M. Bos et al., eds, *Studies on Christiaan Huygens* (Lisse, 1980), 166–99.

____ 'The Mechanical Philosophy and its Problems: Mechanical Explanations, Impenetrability, and Perpetual Motion', in J. C. Pitt, ed., *Change and Progress in Modern Science* (Dordrecht, 1985), 9–84.

____ 'Henry More and the Limits of Mechanism', in Sarah Hutton, ed., *Henry More (1614–1687) Tercentenary Studies* (Dordrecht, 1990), 19–35.

_____ 'The *Principia Philosophiae* as a Treatise in Natural Philosophy', in Jean-Robert Armogathe and Giulia Belgioiso, eds, *Descartes: Principia Philosophiae, 1644–1994* (Naples, 1996), 517–29.

_____ 'Mechanical Philosophies and Their Explanations', in Christoph Lüthy, John E. Murdoch, and William R. Newman, eds, *Late Medieval and Early Modern Corpuscular Matter Theories* (Leiden, 2001), 441–65.

Gal, Ofer. *Meanest Foundations and Nobler Superstructures: Hooke, Newton and the 'Compounding of the Celestiall Motions of the Planetts'* (Dordrecht, 2002).

Galileo Galilei. *Le Operazioni del compasso geometrico et militare* (Padua, 1606).

_____ *Sidereus nuncius* (Venice, 1610).

_____ *Il Saggiatore* (Rome, 1623).

_____ *Dialogo sopre i due massimi sistemi del mondo* (Florence, 1632).

_____ *Discorsi et demonstrazione matematiche intorno à due nove scienze* (Leiden, 1637).

_____ *Dialogue Concerning the Two Chief World Systems—Ptolemaic and Copernican*, trans. Stillman Drake (Berkeley, 1953).

_____ *Discoveries and Opinions of Galileo*, trans. Stillman Drake (Garden City, NY, 1957).

_____ *The Controversy on the Comets of 1618*, ed. and trans. Stillman Drake (Philadelphia, 1960).

_____ *Galileo on Motion and on Mechanics*, eds and trans. I. E. Drabkin and Stillman. Drake (Madison, 1960).

_____ *Two New Sciences: Including Centers of Gravity and Force of Percussion*, trans. Stillman. Drake (Madison, 1974).

_____ *Operations of the Geometric and Military Compass 1606*, ed. and trans. Stillman Drake (Washington DC, 1978).

_____ *Sidereus Nuncius or The Sidereal Messenger*, trans. and introd. Albert van Helden (Chicago, 1989).

Galison, Peter. 'Aufbau/Bauhaus: Logical Positivism and Architectual Modernism', *Critical Inquiry* 16 (1990), 709–52.

_____ 'Introduction: The Context of Disunity', in Peter Galison and David J. Stump, eds, *The Disunity of Science* (Stanford, 1996), 1–33.

_____ *Image and Logic: A Material Culture of Microphysics* (Chicago, 1997).

Galluzzi, Paolo. 'L'Accademia de Cimento: Gusti' del principe, filosofia e ideologia dell' esperimento', *Quaderni Storici* 48 (1981), 788–844.

_____ 'Gassendi and *l'Affaire Galilée* of the Laws of Motion', *Science in Context* 13 (2000), 509–45.

Galton, Francis. *English Men of Science: Their Nature and Nurture* (New York, 1875).

Garasse, François. *La Doctrine curieuse des beaux esprits de ce temps, ou prétendus tels* (2 vols, Paris, 1623).

Garber, Daniel. 'Mind, Body, and the Laws of Nature in Descartes and Leibniz', in *Midwest Studies in Philosophy* 8 (1983), 105–33.

_____ 'A Different Descartes: Descartes and the Programme for a Mathematical Physics in his Correspondence', in Stephen Gaukroger, John Schuster, and John Sutton, eds, *Descartes' Natural Philosophy* (London, 2000), 113–30.

Garin, Pierre. *La Théorie de l'idée suivant l'école thomiste* (2 vols, Paris, 1932).

Gascoigne, John. 'A Reappraisal of the Role of the Universities in the Scientific Revolution', in David C. Lindberg and Robert S. Westman, eds, *Reappraisals of the Scientific Revolution* (Cambridge, 1990), 207–60.

Gassendi, Pierre. *Opera Omnia* (6 vols, Lyon, 1658).

Gassendi, Pierre. *Dissertations en forme de paradoxes contre les Aristoteliciens*, ed. and trans. Bernard Rochot (Paris, 1959).

——— *The Selected Works of Pierre Gassendi*, trans. Craig Brush (New York, 1972).

Gaukroger, Stephen. 'Bachelard and the Problem of Epistemological Analysis', *Studies in History and Philosophy of Science* 7 (1976), 189–244.

——— 'Aristotle on Intelligible Matter', *Phronesis* 25 (1980), 187–97.

——— 'Aristotle on the Function of Sense Perception', *Studies in History and Philosophy of Science* 12 (1981), 75–89.

——— 'The One and the Many: Aristotle on the Individuation of Numbers', *Classical Quarterly* 32 (1982), 312–22.

——— 'The Metaphysics of Impenetrability: Euler's Conception of Force', *British Journal for the History of Science* 15 (1982), 132–54.

——— *Cartesian Logic: An Essay on Descartes's Conception of Inference* (Oxford, 1989).

——— *Descartes, An Intellectual Biography* (Oxford, 1995).

——— 'The Role of the Ontological Argument', *Indian Philosophical Quarterly* 23 (1996), 169–80.

——— 'Justification, Truth, and the Development of Science', *Studies in History and Philosophy of Science* 29 (1998), 97–112.

——— 'The Role of Matter Theory in Baconian and Cartesian Cosmologies', *Perspectives on Science* 8 (2000), 201–22.

——— 'The Foundational Role of Hydrostatics and Statics in Descartes' Natural Philosophy', in Stephen Gaukroger, John Schuster, and John Sutton, eds, *Descartes' Natural Philosophy* (London, 2000), 60–80.

——— *Francis Bacon and the Transformation of Early Modern Philosophy* (Cambridge, 2001).

——— 'Objectivity, History of', in N. J. Smelser and Paul B. Baltes, eds, *International Encyclopedia of the Social and Behavioural Sciences* (Oxford, 2001), xvi. 10785–9.

——— *Descartes' System of Natural Philosophy* (Cambridge, 2002).

——— and Schuster, John. 'The Hydrostatic Paradox and the Origins of Cartesian Dynamics', *Studies in History and Philosophy of Science* 33 (2002), 535–72.

Gemelli, Benedino. *Isaac Beeckman: Atomista e lettore critico di Lucrezio* (Rome, 2002).

George of Trebizond. *Comparatio philosophorum Platonis et Aristotelis* (Venice, 1523).

Gernet, Louis. *Anthropologie de la Grèce antique* (Paris, 1968).

Gesner, Conrad. *Historia animalium* (5 vols, Zurich, 1551–87).

Gibbon, Edward. *Essai sur l'étude de la littérature* (London, 1761).

Gibson, R. W. *Francis Bacon: A Bibliography of his Works and of Baconiana, to the Year 1750* (Oxford, 1950).

Giere, Ronald N. *Science without Laws* (Chicago, 1999).

Gieysztor, Aleksander. 'Management and Resources', Hilde de Ridder-Symoens, ed., *A History of the University in Europe*, i. *Universities in the Middle Ages* (Cambridge, 1992), 108–43.

Gilbert, Neal W. *Renaissance Concepts of Method* (New York, 1960).

——— 'The Early Italian Humanists and Disputation', in A. Molho and J. Tedeschi, eds, *Renaissance Studies in Honor of Hans Baron* (Florence, 1971), 203–36.

Gilbert, William. *De magnete, magnetisque corporibus, et de magno magnete tellure: Physiologia nova plurimis et argumentis et experimentis demonstrata* (London, 1600).

——— *On the Magnet*, trans. Silvanus P. Thompson (New York, 1958).

Gilmore, Allan A. 'Augustine and the Critical Method', *Harvard Theological Review* 39 (1946), 141–63.

Gilson, Étienne. *La Philosophie de St. Bonaventure* (Paris, 1945).

_____ *History of Christian Philosophy in the Middle Ages* (London, 1955).

_____ 'Autour de Pomponazzi: problématique de l'immortalité de l'âme en Italie au début du XVI$^e$ siècle', *Archives d'histoire doctrinale et littéraire du moyen âge* 18 (1961), 163–279.

_____ *The Christian Philosophy of Saint Augustine* (London, 1961).

_____ *The Christian Philosophy of Saint Thomas Aquinas* (London, 1961).

Gingerich, Owen. 'Islamic Astronomy', in idem, *The Great Copernicus Chase and Other Adventures in Astronomical History* (Cambridge, 1992), 43–56.

Giorgio, Francesco. *De harmonia mundi totius cantica tria* (Venice, 1525).

Glacken, Clarence J. *Traces on the Rhodian Shore* (Berkeley, 1967).

Glanvill, Joseph. *Scepsis Scientifica: or, Confest Ignorance, the way to Science; in an Essay of The Vanity of Dogmatizing, and Confident Opinion* (London, 1665).

_____ *Scire/i Tuum Nihil Est; or, the Author's Defence of the Vanity of Dogmatising* (London, 1665).

_____ *Plus Ultra* (London, 1668).

_____ *A Praefatory Answer to Mr. Henry Stubbe* (London, 1671).

_____ *Philosophia Pia, or, A discourse of the religious temper and tendencies of the experimental philosophy which is profest by the Royal Society to which is annext a recommendation and defence of reason in the affairs of religion* (London, 1671).

_____ *The Zealous and Impartial Protestant* (London, 1681).

Gmelig-Nijboer, Caroline Aleid. *Conrad Gesner's Historia Animalium: An Inventory of Renaissance Zoology* (Meppel, 1977).

Goddard, Jonathan. *A Discourse Setting forth the Unhappy Condition of the Practice of Physick in London* (London, 1670).

Godman, Peter. *The Silent Masters: Latin Literature and Censors in the High Middle Ages* (Princeton, 2000).

Gomez, Joaquim F. 'Pedro da Fonseca: Sixteenth Century Portuguese Philosopher', *International Philosophical Quarterly* 6 (1966), 632–44.

Goodman, David. 'Iberian Science: Navigation, Empire and Counter-Reformation', in David Goodman and Colin A. Russell, eds, *The Rise of Scientific Europe, 1500–1800* (London, 1991), 117–44.

Goodman, Lenn. *Avicenna* (London, 1992).

Goodstein, David L. and Goodstein, Judith R. *Feynman's Lost Lecture: The Motion of Planets Around the Sun* (London, 1996).

Gouhier, Henri. *Cartésianisme et augustinisme au XVII$^e$ siècle* (Paris, 1978).

Grafton, Anthony. 'Joseph Scaliger and Historical Chronology: the Rise and Fall of a Discipline', *History and Theory* 14 (1975), 156–85.

_____ *Joseph Scaliger. A Study in the History of Classical Scholarship* (2 vols, Oxford, 1983–93).

_____ *New World, Ancient Texts: The Power of Tradition and the Shock of Discovery* (Cambridge, Mass., 1992).

Grandami, Jacques. *Nova demonstratio immobilitatis terrae petita ex virtute magnetica* (La Flèche, 1645).

Grant, Edward. 'Aristotelianism and the Longevity of the Medieval World View', *History of Science* 16 (1978), 93–106.

_____ *Planets, Stars, and Orbs: The Medieval Cosmos, 1200–1687* (Cambridge, 1996).

Gray, John. *Heresies* (London, 2004).

Greenblatt, Stephen. *Marvelous Possessions: The Wonder of the New World* (Chicago, 1991).

Gregory, Richard. *Discovery: Or the Spirit and Service of Science* (London, 1916).

Gribbin, John. *Science: A History 1543–2001* (London, 2002).

Gualazzini, Ugo. *Ricerche sulle scuole pre-universitarie del medioevo: contributo di indagini sul sorgere delle università* (Milan, 1943).

Guerlac, Henry. *Newton on the Continent* (Ithaca, NY, 1981).

Guéroult, Martial. *Spinoza* (2 vols, Paris, 1968).

_____ 'The Metaphysics and Physics of Force in Descartes', in Stephen Gaukroger, ed., *Descartes: Philosophy, Mathematics and Physics* (Brighton, 1980), 196–229.

Guicciardini, Niccolò. *Reading the Principia: The Debate on Newton's Mathematical Methods for Natural Philosophy from 1687–1736* (Cambridge, 1999).

Guillaumont, Antoine. *Aux origines du monachisme chrétien: Pour une phénoménologie du monachisme* (Bégrolles-en-Mauge, 1979).

Guilmartin, John F. *Gunpowder and Galleys: Changing Technology and Mediterranean Warfare at Sea in the Sixteenth Century* (Cambridge, 1974).

Gunther, Robert T. *Early Science in Oxford* (15 vols, Oxford, 1923–67).

Guthrie, William K. C. *Socrates* (Cambridge, 1971).

_____ *The Sophists* (Cambridge, 1971).

Hacking, Ian. 'The Disunities of the Sciences', in Peter Galison and David J. Stump, eds, *The Disunity of Science* (Stanford, 1996), 37–74.

Hadot, Ilsetraut. *Seneca und die griechisch-römische Tradition der Seeleneitlung* (Berlin, 1969).

Hadot, Pierre. *Philosophy as a Way of Life: Spiritual Exercises from Socrates to Foucault* (Oxford, 1995).

_____ *Plotinus or the Simplicity of Vision* (Chicago, 1998).

_____ *What Is Ancient Philosophy?* (Cambridge, Mass., 2002).

Hale, Matthew. *An essay touching the gravitation, or non-gravitation of fluids, and the reasons thereof* (London, 1673).

_____ *Difficles nugae, or observations concerning the Toricellian experiment, and the various solutions of the same, especially touching the weight and elasticity of the air* (London, 1674).

_____ *Observations touching the principles of natural motions and especially touching rarefaction & condensation* (London, 1677).

_____ *The Primitive Origination of Mankind, Considered and Examined According to the Light of Nature* (London, 1677).

Hall, A. Rupert. 'Sir Isaac Newton's Notebook. 1661–1665', *Cambridge Historical Journal* 9 (1948), 239–50.

_____ *Ballistics in the Seventeenth Century: A Study of the Relations between Science and War with Reference Particularly to England* (Cambridge, 1952).

_____ 'Further Optical Experiments of Isaac Newton', *Annals of Science* 11 (1955), 27–43.

_____ 'Medicine and the Royal Society', in Allen G. Debus, ed., *Medicine in Seventeenth Century England* (Berkeley, 1974), 421–52.

_____ 'What Did the Industrial Revolution in Britain Owe to Science?', in Neil McKenrick, ed., *Historical Perspectives: Studies in English Thought and Society in Honour of J. H. Plumb* (London, 1974), 129–51.

_____ 'Gunnery, Science, and the Royal Society', in John G. Burke, ed., *The Uses of Science in the Age of Newton* (Berkeley, 1983), 111–42.

_____ *Henry More: Magic, Religion and Experiment* (Oxford, 1990).

_____ *All Was Light: An Introduction to Newton's Opticks* (Oxford, 1993).

Hall, Marie Boas. 'Bacon and Gilbert', *Journal of the History of Ideas* 12 (1951), 466–7.

_____ 'Oldenburg, The *Philosophical Transactions*, and Technology', in John G. Burke, ed., *The Uses of Science in the Age of Newton* (Berkeley, 1983), 21–47.

Hankins, James. *Plato in the Italian Renaissance* (Leiden, 1994).

Hanson, Richard. *The Search for the Christian Doctrine of God* (Edinburgh, 1988).

Hargreave, D. 'Reconstructing the Planetary Motions of the Eudoxian System', *Scripta Mathematica* 28 (1970), 335–45.

Harnack, Adolf von. *Marcion: das Evangelium vom fremden Gott* (Leipzig, 1921).

Harrison, Peter. *The Bible, Protestantism, and the Rise of Natural Science* (Cambridge, 1998).

—— 'The Influence of Cartesian Cosmology in England', in Stephen Gaukroger, John Schuster, and John Sutton, eds, *Descartes' Natural Philosophy* (London, 2000), 168–92.

—— 'The Natural Philosopher and the Virtues', in Conal Condren, Stephen Gaukroger, and Ian Hunter, eds, *The Philosopher in Early Modern Europe: The Nature of a Contested Identity* (Cambridge, 2006), 202–28.

Hawking, Stephen. *A Brief History of Time* (London, 1988).

Headley, John M. *Tommaso Campanella and the Transformation of the World* (Princeton, 1997).

Hedwig, Klaus. *Sphaera Lucis: Studien zur Intelligibilität des Seienden im Kontext der mittelalterlichen Lichtspekulation* (Münster, 1980).

Heer, Friedrich. *The Holy Roman Empire* (London, 1968).

Heine, Heinrich. *Zur Geschichte der Religion und Philosophie in Deutschland* (Halle, 1887).

Heinzmann, Richard. *Die Unsterblick der Seele und die Auferstehung des Leibes: eine problemgeschichtliche Untersuchung der frühscholastischen Sentenzen- und Summenliteratur von Anselm von Laon bis Wilhelm von Auxerre* (Münster, 1965).

Helden, Albert van. 'Galileo and the Telescope', in Paolo Galluzi, ed., *Novità celesti e crisi del sapere* (Florence, 1984), 150–7.

Helmholtz, Hermann von. *Science and Culture: Popular and Philosophical Essays*, ed. D. Cahan (Chicago, 1995).

Hendry, John. 'Newton's Theory of Colour', *Centaurus* 23 (1980), 230–51.

Henriques, Ursula. *Religious Toleration in England, 1787–1833* (London, 1961).

Henry, John. 'Occult Qualities and the Experimental Philosophy: Active Principles in Pre-Newtonian Matter Theory', *History of Science* 24 (1986), 335–81.

—— 'Robert Hooke, The Incongruous Mechanist', in Michael Hunter and Simon Schaffer, eds, *Robert Hooke: New Studies* (Woodbridge, 1989), 149–80.

—— 'Henry More versus Robert Boyle: The Spirit of Nature and the Nature of Providence', in Sarah Hutton, ed., *Henry More (1614–1687) Tercentenary Studies* (Dordrecht, 1990), 55–76.

Herivel, John W. 'Newtonian Studies III. The Originals of Two Propositions Discovered by Newton in December 1679?', *Archives Internationales d'Histoire des Sciences* 14 (1961), 23–34.

Heyd, Michael. *'Be Sober and Reasonable': The Critique of Enthusiasm in the Seventeenth and Early Eighteenth Centuries* (Leiden, 1995).

Highmore, Nathaniel. *The History of Generation* (London, 1651).

Hill, Christopher. *Milton and the English Revolution* (London, 1977).

Hill, D. K. 'The Projection Argument in Galileo and Copernicus: Rhetorical Strategy in the Defence of the New System', *Annals of Science* 41 (1984), 109–33.

Hill, Nicholas. *Philosophia Epicurea, Democritiana, Theophrastica, proposita simpliciter, non edocta* (Paris, 1601).

Hinchcliff, Peter. *Benjamin Jowett and the Christian Religion* (Oxford, 1987).

Hisette, Roland. *Enquête sur les 219 articles condamnés à Paris le 12 Mars 1277* (Louvain/Paris, 1977).

—— 'Etienne Tempier et ses condamnations', *Recherches de théologie ancienne et médiévale* 47 (1980), 231–70.

Hobbes, Thomas. *Leviathan or The Matter, Forme and Power of a Commonwealth Ecclesiasticall and Civil* (London, 1651).

———— *The English Works of Thomas Hobbes*, ed. William Molesworth (11 vols, London, 1839–45).

———— *Thomae Hobbes malmesburiensis opera philosophica quae latine scripsit omnia*, ed. William Molesworth (5 vols, London, 1839–45).

———— 'Tractatus opticus: prima edizione integrale', ed. F. Alessio, *Revista Critica di Storia dela Filosofia* 18 (1963), 147–88.

———— *The Elements of Law*, ed. Ferdinand Tönnies (New York, 1969).

———— *Critique du De mundo de Thomas White*, ed. J. Jacquot and H. W. Jones (Paris, 1973).

———— *The Correspondence*, ed. Noel Malcolm (2 vols, Oxford, 1994).

Hoffmann, Manfred. *Erkenntnis und Verwirklichung der wahren Theologie nach Erasmus von Rotterdam* (Tübingen, 1972).

Hofmann, Karl. *Der Dictatus Papae Gregors VII* (Paderborn, 1933).

Hofstadter, Richard, and Metzger, Walter. *The Development of Academic Freedom in the United States* (New York, 1955).

Holden, Thomas. *The Architecture of Matter: Galileo to Kant* (Oxford, 2004).

Holdsworth, William. *A History of English Law* (12 vols, London, 1936).

Hollinger, David A. 'The Defense of Democracy and Robert K. Merton's Formulation of the Scientific Ethos', *Knowledge and Society* 4 (1983), 1–15.

———— 'Science as a Weapon in *Kulturkämpfe* in the United States During and After World War II', *Isis* 86 (1995), 440–54.

Holton, Gerald. *Einstein, History and Other Passions* (Cambridge, Mass., 1996).

Holtzmann, Robert. *Geschichte der sächsischen Kaiserzeit (900–1024)* (Munich, 1941).

Hooghelande, Cornelius. *Cogitationes, quibus Dei existentia et animae spiritualis, et possibilis cum corpore unio, demonstrantur: necnon brevis historia oeconomiae corporis animalis proponitur, atque mechanice explicatur* (Amsterdam, 1646).

Hooke, Robert. *Micrographia: or some Physiological Descriptions of Minute Bodies made by Magnifying Glasses* (London, 1665).

———— *An Attempt to Prove the Motion of the Earth* (London, 1674).

———— *Lectures De Potentia Restitutiva, or of Spring* (London, 1678).

———— *The Posthumous Works . . . containing his Cutlerian Lectures and other Discourses* (London, 1705).

———— *Diary, 1672–80*, ed. H. W. Robinson and W. Adams (London, 1935).

Horkheimer, Max. 'Reason Against Itself: Some Remarks on Enlightenment', in James Schmidt, ed., *What is Enlightenment? Eighteenth-Century Answers and Twentieth-Century Questions* (Berkeley, 1996), 359–67.

Howard, Edward. *Remarks on the New Philosophy of Descartes* (London, 1700).

Hsia, R. Po-Chia. *Social Discipline in the Reformation* (London, 1989).

Huff, Toby E. *The Rise of Early Modern Science: Islam, China, and the West* (Cambridge, 1993).

Hume, David. *Dialogues Concerning Natural Religion*, ed. and introd. Norman Kemp Smith (Indianapolis, 1947).

Hunter, Graeme. 'The Fate of Thomas Hobbes', *Studia Leibnitiana* 21 (1989), 5–20.

Hunter, Ian. *Rival Enlightenments: Civil and Metaphysical Philosophy in Early Modern Germany* (Cambridge, 2001).

Hunter, Michael. *The Royal Society and its Fellows 1660–1700* (2nd edn, Oxford, 1994).

———— *Science and the Shape of Orthodoxy: Intellectual Change in Late Seventeenth-Century Britain* (Woodbridge, 1995).

_____ *Robert Boyle (1627–91): Scrupulosity and Science* (Woodbridge, 2002).

Huppert, George. *The Idea of Perfect History: Historical Erudition and Historical Philosophy in Renaissance France* (Urbana, 1970).

Hutchison, Keith. 'What Happened to Occult Qualities in the Scientific Revolution?', *Isis* 73 (1982), 233–53.

_____ 'Supernaturalism and the Mechanical Philosophy', *History of Science* 21 (1983), 297–333.

_____ 'Idiosyncrasy, Achromatic Lenses, and Early Romanticism', *Centaurus* 34 (1991), 125–71.

Huxley, Julian. 'Science and Religion', in F. S. Marvin, ed., *Science and Civilization* (Oxford, 1923), 279–329.

_____ *Religion without Revelation* (London, 1927).

Huxley, Thomas Henry. *Collected Essays* (9 vols, New York, 1893–4).

Huygens, Christiaan. *Opuscula posthuma*, ed. B. de Volder and B. Fullenius (Leiden, 1703).

_____ *Œuvres complètes de Christiaan Hugens*, ed. La Sociéte hollandaise des sciences (22 vols, The Hague, 1888–1950).

_____ *The Pendulum Clock or Geometrical Demonstrations Concerning the Motion of Pendula as Applied to Clocks*, trans. Richard J. Blackwell (Ames, Iowa, 1986).

Hylson-Smith, Kenneth. *Evangelicals in the Church of England 1734–1984* (Edinburgh, 1989).

Iliffe, Rob. ' "Is He Like Other Men?": The Meaning of the *Principia Mathematica* and the Author as Idol', in Gerald Maclean, ed., *Culture and Society in the Stuart Restoration* (Cambridge, 1995), 159–76.

_____ 'Abstract Considerations: Disciplines and the Incoherence of Newton's Natural Philosophy', *Studies in History and Philosophy of Science* 35 (2004), 427–54.

Iserloh, Erwin. *Gnade und Eucharistie in der philosophischen Theologie des Wilhelm von Ockham: Ihre Bedeutung für die Ursachen der Reformation* (Wiesbaden, 1956).

Israel, Jonathan I. *The Dutch Republic: Its Rise, Greatness, and Fall 1477–1806* (Oxford, 1995).

_____ *Radical Enlightenment: Philosophy and the Making of Modernity 1650–1750* (Oxford, 2001).

Ito, Yushi. 'Hooke's Cyclic Theory of the Earth in the Context of Seventeenth Century England', *British Journal for the History of Science* 21 (1988), 295–314.

Ivry, Alfred L. 'Al-Kindi as Philosopher: The Aristotelian and Neoplatonic Dimensions', in S. M. Stern, Albert Hourani, and Vivian Brown, eds, *Islamic Philosophy and the Classical Tradition* (Columbia, SC., 1972), 117–40.

Jacquart, Danielle. 'Aristotelian Thought in Salerno', in Peter Dronke, ed., *A History of Twelfth-Century Western Philosophy* (Cambridge, 1988), 407–28.

Jaeger, Werner. *The Theology of the Early Greek Philosophers* (Oxford, 1947).

James, Susan. *Passion and Action: The Emotions in Seventeenth-Century Philosophy* (Oxford, 1997).

Jansson, Maija. 'Matthew Hale on Judges and Judging', *The Journal of Legal History* 9 (1988), 201–13.

Jardine, Lisa. *Francis Bacon: Discovery and the Art of Discourse* (Cambridge, 1974).

_____ *On A Grander Scale: The Outstanding Career of Christopher Wren* (London, 2002).

_____ *The Curious Life of Robert Hooke: The Man Who Measured London* (London, 2003).

_____ and Kelley, Donald R. 'Lorenzo Valla and the Intellectual Origins of Humanist Dialectic', *Journal of the History of Philosophy* 15 (1977), 143–64.

Jardine, Lisa, and Stewart, Alan. *Hostage to Fortune: The Troubled Life of Francis Bacon 1561–1626* (London, 1998).

Jardine, Nicholas. 'Galileo's Road to Truth and the Demonstrative Regress', *Studies in History of Science* 7 (1976), 277–318.

—— 'The Significance of the Celestial Orbs', *Journal of the History of Astronomy* 13 (1982), 168–94.

—— *The Birth of History and Philosophy of Science: Kepler's* A Defence of Tycho against Ursus *with Essays on its Provenance and Significance* (Cambridge, 1988).

—— 'Epistemology of the Sciences', in Charles Schmitt, Quentin Skinner, and Eckhard Kessler, eds, *The Cambridge History of Renaissance Philosophy* (Cambridge, 1988), 685–711.

Jarrell, Richard A. 'The Contemporaries of Tycho Brahe', in René Taton and Curtis Wilson, eds, *Planetary Astronomy from the Renaissance to the Rise of Astrophysics, Part A: Tycho Brahe to Newton* (Cambridge, 1989), 22–32.

Jenkins, Jane E. 'Arguing About Nothing: Henry More and Robert Boyle on the Theological Implications of the Void', in Margaret J. Osler, ed., *Rethinking the Scientific Revolution* (Cambridge, 2000), 153–79.

Jensen, J. Vernon. 'The X Club: Fraternity of Victorian Scientists', *British Journal for the History of Science* 5 (1970/1), 63–72.

Jesseph, Douglas M. *Squaring the Circle: The War between Hobbes and Wallis* (Chicago, 1999).

—— 'Galileo, Hobbes, and the Book of Nature', *Perspectives on Science* 12 (2004), 191–211.

Johns, Adrian. *The Nature of the Book* (Chicago, 1998).

Johnson, Francis J. *Astronomical Thought in Renaissance England* (Baltimore, 1937).

Johnson, William. ΑΓΥΡΤΟ—ΜΑΣΤΙΞ. Or some Brief Animadversions upon two late Treatises (London, 1656).

Johnston, Mark D. *The Evangelical Rhetoric of Ramón Llull* (New York, 1996).

Jolivet, Jacques. 'The Arabic Inheritance', in Peter Dronke, ed., *A History of Twelfth-Century Western Philosophy* (Cambridge, 1988), 113–48.

Jolley, Nicholas. 'The Reception of Descartes' Philosophy', in John Cottingham, ed., *The Cambridge Companion to Descartes* (Cambridge, 1992), 393–423.

Jonas, Hans. *The Gnostic Religion* (2nd edn, Boston, 1963).

Jones, Howard. *The Epicurean Tradition* (London, 1989).

Joy, Lynn Sumida. *Gassendi the Atomist: Advocate of History in an Age of Science* (Cambridge, 1987).

Kahn, Charles H. *The Verb 'Be' in Ancient Greek* (Dordrecht, 1973).

Kantorowicz, Ernst. *The King's Two Bodies: A Study in Medieval Political Theology* (Princeton, 1957).

Kaplan, Barbara B. *'Divulging of Useful Truths in Physick': The Medical Agenda of Robert Boyle* (Baltimore, 1993).

Kapp, Ernest. 'Syllogistic', in J. Barnes, M. Schofield, and R. Sorabji, eds, *Articles on Aristotle*, i. *Science* (London, 1975), 35–49.

Kargon, Robert Hugh. 'William Petty's Mechanical Philosophy', *Isis* 56 (1965), 63–6.

Kassler, Jamie. *Inner Music: Hobbes, Hooke and North on Internal Character* (London, 1995).

—— *Music, Science and Philosophy: Models in the Universe of Thought* (Aldershot, 2001).

Keckermann, Batholomew. *Gymnasium logicum, id est, De usu & exercitatione logicae artis absolutiori & pleniori, libri tres* (London, 1606).

Keill, John. *An Examination of Dr Burnet's Theory of the Earth* (London, 1698).

Kelley, Donald R. *The Foundations of Modern Historical Scholarship: Language, Law, and History in the French Renaissance* (New York, 1970).

Kelly, Suzanne. *The De mundo of William Gilbert* (2 vols, Amsterdam, 1965).

Kennedy, George. *A New History of Classical Rhetoric* (Princeton, 1994).

Keohane, Nannerl. *Philosophy and the State in France: The Renaissance to the Enlightenment* (Princeton, 1980).

Kepler, Johannes. *Ad vitellionem paralipomena, quibus Astronomiae pars optica traditvr* (Frankfurt, 1605).

—— *Dissertatio cum Nuncio Sidereo* (Prague, 1610).

—— *Johannis Kepler Astronomi Opera Omnia*, ed. C. Frisch (8 vols, Frankfurt, 1858–71).

—— *Johannes Kepler Gesammelte Werke*, ed. W. von Dyck, M. Caspar, F. Hammer, M. List, and V. Bialas (Munich, 1937–  ).

—— *Epitome of Copernican Astronomy*, Books 4 and 5, trans. C. G. Wallis, in *Britannica Great Books* 16 (Chicago, 1952), 843–1004.

—— *New Astronomy*, trans. William H. Donahue (Cambridge, 1992).

—— *The Harmony of the World*, trans., ed., notes by E. J. Aiton, A. M. Duncan, and J. V. Field (Philadelphia, 1997).

—— *Optics*, trans. William H. Donahue (Santa Fe, 2000).

Kessler, Eckhard. 'The Transformation of Aristotelianism During the Renaissance', in John Henry and Sarah Hutton, eds, *New Perspectives in Renaissance Thought* (London, 1990), 137–47.

Kieckhefer, Richard. *Repression of Heresy in Medieval Germany* (Philadelphia, 1979).

Kiernan, Victor. 'Evangelicalism and the French Revolution', *Past and Present* 1 (1952), 44–56.

Kimmich, Dorothee. *Epikureische Aufklärungen: Philosophische und poetische Konzepte der Selbstorge* (Darmstadt, 1993).

King, William. *The Original Works of William King, LL.D.* (3 vols, London, 1776).

Kircher, Athanasius. *Magnes sive de arte magnetica* (Rome, 1641).

Kitcher, Philip. 'The Ends of the Sciences', in Brian Leiter, ed., *The Future for Philosophy* (Oxford, 2004), 208–29.

Klein, Jacob. *Greek Mathematical Thought and the Origin of Algebra* (Cambridge, Mass., 1968).

Klibansky, Raymond. *The Continuity of the Platonic Tradition During the Middle Ages* (London, 1950).

Knowles, David. *The Evolution of Medieval Thought* (London, 1962).

Knox, Dilwyn. 'Ideas on Gestures and Universal Languages, *c.*1550–1650', in J. Henry and S. Hutton, eds, *New Perspectives on Renaissance Thought* (London, 1990), 101–36.

Knox, Robert. *An Historical Relation of the Island Ceylon, in the East-Indies* (London, 1681).

Kołakowski, Leslek. *Positivist Philosophy from Hume to the Vienna Circle* (Harmondsworth, 1972).

Konstan, David. 'Problems in Epicurean Physics', *Isis* 70 (1979), 394–418.

Kors, Alan Charles. *Atheism in France, 1650–1729*, i. *The Orthodox Sources of Disbelief* (Princeton, 1990).

Koyré, Alexandre. *From the Closed World to the Infinite Universe* (Baltimore, 1957).

—— *Metaphysics and Measurement* (London, 1968)

—— *The Astronomical Revolution* (Paris/London/Ithaca, 1973).

—— *Galileo Studies* (Hassocks, 1978).

Kristeller, Paul Oskar. *The Philosophy of Marsilio Ficino* (New York, 1943).

—— *Eight Philosophers of the Renaissance* (Stanford, 1964).

—— *Renaissance Thought and its Sources* (New York, 1979).

Kuhn, Thomas. *The Copernican Revolution* (Cambridge, Mass., 1957).

Kuhn, Thomas. *The Structure of Scientific Revolutions* (2nd edn, Chicago, 1962).

_____ *The Essential Tension* (Chicago, 1977).

Kusukawa, Sachiko. *The Transformation of Natural Philosophy: The Case of Philip Melanchthon* (Cambridge, 1995).

La Cerda, Melchior de. *Usus et exercitatio demonstrationis* (Cologne, 1617).

La Peyrère, Isaac de. *Prae-Adamitae, sive exercitatio super versibus duodecimo, decimotertio, & decimoquarto, capitis quinti Epistolae D. Pauli ad Romanos* bound with *Systema theologicum ex Praeadamitarum hypothesi* ([Amsterdam], 1655).

_____ *A Theological Systeme Upon the Presvpposition that Men were before Adam* (London, 1655).

Laird, W. Roy. 'The Scope of Renaissance Mechanics', *Osiris* 2 (1986), 43–68.

_____ 'Galileo and the Mixed Sciences', in Daniel A. Di Liscia, Eckhard Kessler, and Charlotte Methuen, eds, *Method and Order in Renaissance Philosophy of Nature: The Aristotle Commentary Tradition* (Aldershot, 1997), 253–70.

Lakatos, Imre. 'Falsification and the Methodology of Scientific Research Programmes', in Imre Lakatos and Alan Musgrave, eds, *Criticism and the Growth of Knowledge* (Cambridge, 1970), 91–196.

Lamberton, Robert. *Homer the Theologian* (Berkeley, 1986).

Landes, David S. *The Wealth and Poverty of Nations: Why Some are So Rich and Some are So Poor* (New York, 1999).

_____ *The Unbound Prometheus: Technological Change and Industrial Development in Western Europe from 1750 to the Present* (2nd edn, Cambridge, 2003).

Lang, Helen S. *The Order of Nature in Aristotle's Physics* (Cambridge, 1998).

Langdon-Davies, John. 'Science and God', *The Spectator*, 31 January 1931, 137–8.

Lattis, James M. *Between Copernicus and Galileo: Christoph Clavius and the Collapse of Ptolemaic Cosmology* (Chicago, 1994).

Launoy, Jean. *De varia Aristotelis in Academia Parisiensi Fortuna* (Paris, 1653).

Le Fanu, James. *The Rise and Fall of Modern Medicine* (London, 1999).

Le Goff, Jacques. *Les Intellectuels au moyen âge* (Paris, 1957).

_____ 'The Universities and the Public Authorities in the Middle Ages and the Renaissance', in idem, *Time, Work, and Culture in the Middle Ages* (Chicago, 1980), 135–49.

Le Moyne, Pierre. *Les peintures Morales* (Paris, 1640).

Lear, Jonathan. *Aristotle and Logical Theory* (Cambridge, 1980).

Leclercq, Jean. *L'Amour des lettres et le désir de Dieu: Initiation aux auteurs monastiques du moyen âge* (Paris, 1957).

L'Ecluse, Charles. *Exoticorum libri decem* (Leiden, 1605).

Leff, Gordon. *Medieval Thought* (Harmondsworth, 1958).

_____ *William of Ockham: The Metamorphosis of Scholastic Discourse* (Manchester, 1975).

_____ 'The *Trivium* and the Three Philosophies', in Hilde de Ridder-Symoens, ed., *A History of the University in Europe*, i. *Universities in the Middle Ages* (Cambridge, 1992), 307–36.

Lennon, Thomas M. *The Battle of the Gods and Giants: The Legacies of Descartes and Gassendi, 1655–1715* (Princeton, 1993).

Lenoble, Robert. *Mersenne ou la naissance de la mécanique* (2nd edn, Paris, 1971).

Lettinck, Paul. *Aristotle's Physics and its Reception in the Arabic World* (Leiden, 1994).

Levi, Anthony. *Renaissance and Reformation: The Intellectual Genesis* (New Haven, 2002).

Lewis, Bernard. *The Muslim Discovery of Europe* (London, 2000).

Liebeschütz, Hans. 'The Debate on Philosophical Learning During the Transition Period (900–1018)', in A. H. Armstrong, ed., *The Cambridge History of Later Greek and Early Medieval Philosophy* (Cambridge, 1970), 587–610.

Lightman, Bernard. ' "The Voices of Nature": Popularising Victorian Science', in Bernard Lightman, ed., *Victorian Science in Context* (Chicago, 1997), 187–211.

―――― 'The Story of Nature: Victorian Popularizers and Scientific Narrative', *Victorian Review* 25 (1999), 1–29.

―――― 'Huxley and Scientific Agnosticism: The Strange History of a Failed Rhetorical Strategy', *British Journal for the History of Science* 35 (2002), 271–89.

Lindberg, David C. *Theories of Vision from al-Kindi to Kepler* (Chicago, 1976).

Lindquist, Svante. 'A Wagnerian Theme in the History of Science: Scientific Glassblowing and the Role of Instrumentation', in Tore Frängsmayr, ed., *Solomon's House Revisited* (Canton, Mass., 1990), 160–83.

Linneaus, Carolus. *L'Équilibre de la nature*, trans B. Jasmin, introd. C. Limoges (Paris, 1972).

Lipsius, Justus. *De Constantia* (Leiden, 1584).

―――― *Manducationis ad Stoicam philosophiam libri tres* (Antwerp, 1604).

―――― *Physiologiae Stoicorum Libri Tres* (Antwerp, 1604).

Litt, Thomas. *Les Corps celestes dans l'univers de Saint Thomas d'Aquin* (Louvain, 1963).

Lloyd, Geoffrey E. R. *Magic, Reason and Experience: Studies in the Origins and Development of Greek Science* (Cambridge, 1979)

―――― *The Revolutions of Wisdom: Studies in the Claims and Practice of Ancient Greek Science* (Berkeley, 1987).

―――― 'The Definition, Status, and Methods of the Medical *Technē* in the Fifth and Fourth Centuries', in A. C. Bowen, ed., *Science and Philosophy in Classical Greece* (London, 1991), 249–60.

―――― *Adversaries and Authorities: Investigations into Ancient Greek and Chinese Science* (Cambridge, 1996).

―――― *The Ambitions of Curiosity: Understanding the World in Ancient Greece and China* (Cambridge, 2002).

Locke, John. *The Works of John Locke, Esq*, 2nd edn (3 vols, London, 1722).

Lohne, Johannes A. 'Hooke versus Newton: An Analysis of the Documents in the Case of Free Fall and Planetary Motion', *Centaurus* 7 (1960), 6–52.

―――― 'Experimentum crucis', *Notes and Records of the Royal Society of London* 23 (1968), 169–99.

Lohr, Charles H. 'Jesuit Aristotelianism and Sixteenth-Century Metaphysics', in G. Fletcher and M. B. Scheute, eds, *Paradosis* (New York, 1976), 203–20.

―――― 'The Medieval Interpretation of Aristotle', in Norman Kretzmann, Anthony Kenny, and Jan Pinborg, eds, *The Cambridge History of Later Medieval Philosophy* (Cambridge, 1982), 80–98.

―――― 'Metaphysics', in Charles B. Schmitt, Quentin Skinner, and Eckhard Kessler, eds, *The Cambridge History of Renaissance Philosophy* (Cambridge, 1988), 537–638.

―――― 'The Sixteenth Century Transformation of the Aristotelian Division of the Speculative Sciences', in D. Kelley and R. Popkin, eds, *The Shapes of Knowledge from the Renaissance to the Enlightenment* (Dordrecht, 1991), 49–58.

―――― 'Metaphysics and Natural Philosophy as Sciences: The Catholic and Protestant Views in the Sixteenth and Seventeenth Centuries', in Constance Blackwell and Sachiko Kusukawa, eds, *Philosophy in the Sixteenth and Seventeenth Centuries* (Aldershot, 1999), 280–95.

Lojacono, Ettore. 'Socrate e l'honnête homme nells cultura dell'autunno del Rinascimento francese e in René Descartes', in Ettore Lojacono, ed., *Socrate in Occidente* (Florence, 2004), 103–46.

Long, Anthony A., and Sedley, David N., eds, *The Hellenistic Philosophers* (2 vols, Cambridge, 1987).

López Piñero, José María. *Ciencia y Técnica en la Sociedad Española de los Siglos XVI y XVII* (Barcelona, 1979).

Lounsbury, Floyd G. 'Maya Numeration, Computation, and Calendrical Astronomy', in Charles Coulton Gillespie, ed., *Dictionary of Scientific Biography* (New York, 1981), xv. 759–818.

Maccagnolo, Enzo. 'David of Dinant and the Beginnings of Aristotelianism in Paris', in Peter Dronke, ed., *A History of Twelfth-Century Western Philosophy* (Cambridge, 1988), 429–42.

Macculloch, Diarmaid. *Reformation: Europe's House Divided, 1490–1700* (London, 2003).

MacDowell, Douglas M. *The Law in Classical Athens* (London, 1978).

Maclaurin, Colin. *An Account of Sir Isaac Newton's Philosophical Discoveries* (London, 1748).

Maclean, Ian. *Interpretation and Meaning in the Renaissance: The Case of Law* (Cambridge, 1992).

Macleod, Roy. 'A Victorian Scientific Network: The X-Club', *Notes and Records of the Royal Society* 24 (1969), 305–22.

McClaughlin, Trevor. 'Censorship and Defenders of the Cartesian Faith in France (1640–1720)', *Journal of the History of Ideas* 40 (1979), 563–81.

McCracken, Charles J. *Malebranche and British Philosophy* (Oxford, 1983).

McEvoy, James. *The Philosophy of Robert Grosseteste* (Oxford, 1986).

McGuire, J. E. 'Force, Active Principles and Newton's Invisible Realm', *Ambix* 15 (1968), 154–208.

⸻ 'Boyles' Conception of Nature', *Journal of the History of Ideas* 33 (1972), 523–42.

⸻ 'The Fate of the Date: The Theology of Newton's *Principia* Revisited', in Margaret J. Osler, ed., *Rethinking the Scientific Revolution* (Cambridge, 2000), 271–96.

McKendrick, Neil. 'The Role of Science in the Industrial Revolution: A Study of Josiah Wedgwood as a Scientist and Industrial Chemist', in M. Teich and R. Porter, eds, *Changing Perspectives in the History of Science* (London, 1973), 274–319.

McLaughlin, Peter. 'Descartes on Mind–Body Interaction and the Conservation of Motion', *Philosophical Review* 102 (1993), 155–82.

⸻ 'Force, Determination and Impact', in Stephen Gaukroger, John Schuster, and John Sutton, eds, *Descartes' Natural Philosophy* (London, 2000), 81–112.

⸻ 'Contraries and Counterweights: Descartes' Statical Theory of Impact', *The Monist* 84 (2001), 562–81.

⸻ *Logic, Signs and Nature in the Renaissance: The Case of Learned Medicine* (Cambridge 2001).

Macy, Gary. 'The Doctrine of Transubstantiation in the Middle Ages', *Journal of Ecclesiastical History* 45 (1994), 11–44.

Magirus, Johannes. *Physiologia peripatetica ex Aristotele eiusque interpretibus collecta* (Frankfurt, 1596).

Malcolm, Noel. *Aspects of Hobbes* (Oxford, 2002).

Malebranche, Nicholas. *Œuvres complètes*, ed. André Robinet (20 vols, Paris 1958–78).

Malingrey, Anne Marie. *Philosophia: Étude d'un groupe des mots dans la littérature grecque, des Présocratiques au IVᵉ siècle après J.-C.* (Paris, 1961).

Mandonnet, Pierre. *Siger de Brabant et l'averroïsme latin au XIIIᵐᵉ siècle, 2ᵐᵉ partie: Textes inédits* (2nd edn, Louvain, 1908).

Manning, John. *The Emblem* (London, 2002).

Mansfeld, Jaap. 'Bad World and Demiurge: A "Gnostic" Motif from Parmenides and Empedocles to Lucretius and Philo', in R. van den Broeck, ed., *Studies in Gnosticism and Hellenistic Religions* (Leiden, 1981), 261–314.

Manuel, Frank, and Manuel, Fritzie. *Utopian Thought in the Western World* (Cambridge, Mass., 1979).

Maravall, José Antonio. *Antiguos y Modernos: Visión de la historia y dia de progresso hasta el Renacimiento* (2nd edn, Madrid, 1986).

Marcel, Raymond. ' "Saint" Socrate, patron de l'humanisme', *Revue internationale de philosophie* 5 (1951), 135–43.

Margolis, Howard. 'Tycho's System and Galileo's *Dialogue*', *Studies in History and Philosophy of Science* 22 (1991), 259–75.

Marincola, John. *Authority and Tradition in Ancient Historiography* (Cambridge, 1997).

Marion, Jean-Luc. *Sur la théologie blanche de Descartes* (Paris, 1981).

Markgraf, George. *Historia naturalis Brasiliencis* (Leiden, 1648).

Marrone, Steven P. *William of Auvergne and Robert Grosseteste: New Ideas of Truth in the Early Thirteenth Century* (Princeton, 1983).

Marsden, George M. *Fundamentalism and American Culture: The Shaping of Twentieth Century Evangelicalism, 1870–1925* (Oxford, 1980).

Marsh, Peter T. *The Victorian Church in Decline* (London, 1969).

Marsilius of Padua. *Defensor Pacis*, trans. and introd. Alan Gewirth (Toronto, 1980).

Martens, Rhonda. *Kepler's Philosophy and the New Astronomy* (Princeton, 2000).

Martin, Julian. *Francis Bacon, the State, and the Reform of Natural Philosophy* (Cambridge, 1992).

Mason, Mary E. *Active Life and Contemplative Life: A Study of the Concepts from Plato to the Present* (Milwaukee, 1961).

Mathias, Peter. *The First Industrial Nation: An Economic History of Britain, 1700–1914* (London, 1983).

Maxwell, James Clerk. 'Are There Real Analogies in Nature?', in Lewis Campbell and William Garnett, *The Life of James Clerk Maxwell, with a Selection from his Correspondence and Occasional Writings and a Sketch of his Contributions to Science* (London, 1882), 235–44.

Mayaud, Pierre-Noël. *Le Conflit entre l'Astronomie Nouvelle et l'Écriture Sainte aux XVIᵉ et XVIIᵉ siècles* (5 vols, Paris, 2005).

Melanchthon, Philip. *Commentarius de anima* (Wittenberg, 1540).

Mendoça, Francisco de. *Viridarium sacrae et profanae eruditionis* (Lyon, 1635).

Mercati, Angelo. *Il Sommario de processo di G. Bruno* (Vatican City, 1942).

Mercer, Christia. 'The Vitality and Importance of Early Modern Aristotelianism', in Tom Sorell, ed., *The Rise of Modern Philosophy* (Oxford, 1993), 33–67.

Mersenne, Marin. *Quaestiones celeberrimae in Genesim* (Paris, 1623).

——— *L'Impiete des Deistes, Athees et Libertins de ce temps, combatuë, & renuersee de point en point par raisons tirees de la Philosophie, & de la Theologie* (Paris, 1624).

——— *La Verite des Sciences, contre les Septiqves ou Pyrrhoniens* (Paris, 1625).

——— *Harmonie Universelle* (3 vols, Paris, 1636).

——— *Cogitata physico-mathematica* (Paris, 1644).

——— *Correspondance du P. Marin Mersenne, religieux minime*, ed. Cornelius de Waard, R. Pintard, B. Rochot, and A. Baelieu (17 vols, Paris, 1932–88).

Merton, Robert K. *Science, Technology and Society in Seventeenth-Century England* (New York, 1970).

——— *The Sociology of Science*, ed. N. Storer (Chicago, 1973).

Metzger, Hélène. *Les Doctrines chimiques en France du début du XVIIᵉ à la fin du XVIIIᵉ siècle* (Paris, 1969).

Meyendorff, Jean. *Le Christ dans la théologie byzantine* (Paris, 1969).

Meyer, Lodewijk. *Philosophia S. Scripturae Interpres: Exercitatio paradoxica in qua veram Philosophiam infallibilem S. Literas interpretandi Normam esse apodictice demonstratur & discrepantes ab hac sententiae expenduntur ac refelluntur* (Amsterdam, 1666).

Michael, Emily. 'Sennert's Sea Change: Atoms and Causes', in Christoph Lüthy, John E. Murdoch, and William R. Newman, eds, *Late Medieval and Early Modern Corpuscular Matter Theories* (Leiden, 2001), 331–62.

_____ and Michael, Fred S. 'Two Early Modern Concepts of Mind: Reflecting Substance vs. Thinking Substance', *Journal of the History of Philosophy* 27 (1989), 29–48.

Middleton, W. E. Knowles. *The Experimenters: A Study of the Accademia del Cimento* (Baltimore, 1971).

Mikkeli, Heikki. *An Aristotelian Response to Humanism: Jacopo Zabarella on the Nature of Arts and Sciences* (Helsinki, 1992).

Mill, John Stuart. *On Liberty* (London, 1859).

Millen, Ron. 'The Manifestation of Occult Qualities in the Scientific Revolution', in M. J. Osler and P. J. Farber, eds, *Religion, Science, and Worldview* (Cambridge, 1985), 185–216.

Mintz, Samuel I. *The Hunting of Leviathan* (Cambridge, 1962).

Mokyr, Joel. *The Lever of Riches: Technological Creativity and Economic Progress* (New York, 1990).

Momigliano, Arnaldo D. *Studies in Historiography* (New York, 1966)

_____ *Alien Wisdom: The Limits of Hellenization* (Cambridge, 1971).

_____ *The Classical Foundations of Modern Historiography* (Berkeley, 1990).

Montaigne, Michel de. *Essais*, ed. Maurice Rat (2 vols, Paris, 1965).

Monte, Guido Ubaldo del. *Mechanicorum Liber* (Pesaro, 1577).

Mooney, Chris. *The Republican War on Science* (New York, 2005).

Moore, Robert I. *The Formation of a Persecuting Society: Power and Deviance in Western Europe 950–1250* (Oxford, 1981).

Morall, John B. *Political Thought in Medieval Times* (Toronto, 1980).

More, Henry. *Observations on Anthroposophia Theomagica and Anima Magica Abscondita of Eugenius Philalethes* ([London], 1650).

_____ *Enthusiasmus Triumphatus, Or, A Discourse of the Nature, Causes, Kinds, and Cure, of Enthusiasme* (London, 1656).

_____ *An Explanation of the Grand Mystery of Godliness* (London, 1660).

_____ *A Collection of Several Philosophical Writings* (London, 1662).

_____ *Enchiridium metaphysicum sive de rebus incorporeis succincta et luculenta dissertatio* (London, 1671).

_____ *The Immortality of the Soul, So far forth as it is demonstrable from the Knowledge of Nature, and the Light of Reason* (London, 1713).

Morris, Charles. *Pragmatism and the Crisis of Democracy* (Chicago, 1934).

Moss, Jean Dietz. *Novelties in the Heavens: Rhetoric and Science in the Copernican Controversy* (Chicago, 1993).

Mouy, Paul. *Le Développement de la physique cartésienne 1646–1712* (Paris, 1934).

Moxon, Joseph. *A Tutor to Astronomy and Geography* (London, 1686).

Müller-Hill, Benno. *Murderous Science: Elimination by Scientific Selection of Jews, Gypsies, and Others, Germany 1933–1945* (Oxford, 1988).

Muños Iglesias, Salvador. 'El decreto tridentino sobre la Vulgata y su interpretación por los teólogos des siglo XVI', *Estudios biblicos* 5 (1946), 145–69.

Murdoch, John E. 'The Medieval and Renaissance Tradition of *Minima Naturalia*', in Christoph Lüthy, John E. Murdoch, and William R. Newman, eds, *Late Medieval and Early Modern Corpuscular Matter Theories* (Leiden, 2001), 91–131.

Muslow, Martin. *Frühneuzeitliche Selbsterhaltung: Telesio und die Naturphilosophie der Renaissance* (Tübingen, 1998).

Nabod, Valentin. *Astronomicarum institutionum libri III* (Venice, 1580).

Nadal, Jeronimo. *Adnotationes et Meditationes in Evangelia* (Anvers, 1594).

Nadler, Steven. *Arnauld and the Cartesian Philosophy of Ideas* (Manchester, 1989).

——— *Malebranche and Ideas* (Oxford, 1992).

——— *Spinoza: A Life* (Cambridge, 1999).

Nakayama, Shigeru. 'Japanese Scientific Thought', in Charles Coulton Gillespie, ed., *Dictionary of Scientific Biography* (New York, 1981), xv. 728–58.

Nardi, Bruno. *Saggi sull'aristotelismo padovano dal secolo XIV al XVI* (Florence, 1958).

Nardi, Paolo. 'Relations with Authority', in Hilde de Ridder-Symoens, ed., *A History of the University in Europe*, i. *Universities in the Middle Ages* (Cambridge, 1992), 77–107.

Navarro Brotóns, Víctor. 'Contribución a la Historia del Copernicanismo en España', *Cuadernos Hispanoamericanos* 283 (1974), 3–24.

——— 'The Reception of Copernicus in Sixteenth-Century Spain: The Case of Diego de Zúñiga', *Isis* 86 (1995), 52–78.

——— and Rodríguez Galdeano, Enrique. *Matemáticas, Cosmología y Humanismo en la España del Siglo XVI. Los Comentarios al Segundo Libro de la Historia Natural de Plinio de Jerónimo Muñoz* (Valencia, 1998).

——— and Salavert Fabiani, Vincente L., Rosselló Botey, Victoria and Darás Romá, Víctor. *Bibliographia Physico-Mathematica Hispanica (1475–1900)*, i. *Libros y folletos, 1475–1600* (Valencia, 1999).

Needham, Joseph. *Science and Civilisation in China* (7 vols, in 50 sects., Cambridge, 1954– ).

Nelson, Benjamin. *On the Roads to Modernity: Conscience, Science, and Civilizations* (Towota, NJ, 1981).

Netton, Ian Richard. *Muslim Neoplatonists: An Introduction to the Thought of the Brethren of Purity* (London, 1982).

Neurath, Otto. 'Unified Science as Encyclopedic Integration', in Otto Neurath, Rudolph Carnap, and Charles Morris, eds, *Foundations of the Unity of Science* (2 vols, Chicago, 1970), i. 1–27.

Newman, William R. 'The Corpuscular Theory of J. B. van Helmont and Its Medieval Sources', *Vivarium* 31 (1993), 161–91.

——— 'Boyle's Debt to Corpuscular Alchemy', in Michael Hunter, ed., *Robert Boyle Reconsidered* (Cambridge, 1994), 107–18.

——— 'The Alchemical Sources of Robert Boyle's Corpuscular Philosophy', *Annals of Science* 53 (1996), 567–85.

Newton, Isaac. *Opticks: or, a Treatise of the Reflexions, Refractions, Inflexions and Colours of Light* (London, 1704).

——— *The Correspondence of Isaac Newton*, ed. H. W. Turnbull, J. F. Scott, A. R. Hall, and Laura Tilling (7 vols, Cambridge, 1959–77).

——— *Unpublished Scientific Papers of Isaac Newton*, ed. A. Rupert Hall and Marie Boas (Cambridge, 1962).

——— *The Mathematical Papers of Isaac Newton*, ed. D. T. Whiteside (8 vols, Cambridge, 1967–81).

——— *Certain Philosophical Questions: Newton's Trinity Notebook*, introductory essay, ed. and trans. James E. McGuire and Martin Tamny (Cambridge, 1983).

——— *Optical Papers of Isaac Newton*, i. *The Optical Lectures, 1670–1672*, ed. Alan Shapiro (Cambridge, 1984).

——— *The Principia: Mathematical Principles of Natural Philosophy*, ed. and trans. I. Bernard Cohen and Anne Whitman (Berkeley, 1999).

Nicholas of Autrecourt. *The Universal Treatise of Nicholas of Autrecourt*, trans. Leonard Kennedy, Richard Arnold, and Arthur Millward (Milwaukee, 1971).

Nichomachus of Gerasa. 'Introduction to Arithmetic', trans. Martin L. D'Ooge, in *Britannica Great Books* 11 (Chicago, 1952), 811–48.

Nietzsche, Friedrich. *Basic Writings of Nietzsche*, trans. and ed. Walter Kaufman (New York, 1968).

Nifo, Agostino. *In Aristotelis libros de coelo et mundo* (Naples, 1517).

_____ *De immortalitate animae libellum Petrum Pomponatium Mantuanum* (Venice, 1518).

Noakes, Richard. '*Punch* and Comic Journalism in Mid-Victorian Britain', in Geoffrey Cantor et al., *Science in the Nineteenth-Century Periodical: Reading the Magazine of Nature* (Cambridge, 2004), 91–122.

Norman, Robert. *The nevve, attractive shewing the nature, propertie, and manifold vertues of the loadstone, with the declination of the needle, touched therewith, vnder the plaine of the horizon* (London, 1614).

Nussbaum, Martha. *The Therapy of Desire: Theory and Practice in Hellenistic Ethics* (Princeton, 1994).

Oakley, Francis. *The Western Church in the Middle Ages* (Ithaca, NY, 1979).

_____ *Omnipotence, Covenant and Order* (Ithaca, NY, 1984).

Oestreich, Gerhard. *Neostoicism and the Early Modern State* (Cambridge, 1982).

Ockham, William. *Quodlibetal Questions*, trans. A. J. Freddoso and F. E. Kelley (2 vols, New Haven, 1991).

Oldenburg, Henry. *The Correspondence of Henry Oldenburg*, ed. A. Rupert Hall and Marie Boas Hall (13 vols, Madison, 1965–75).

Oldroyd, David. 'Robert Hooke's Methodology of Science as Exemplified in his Discourse of Earthquakes', *British Journal for the History of Science* 6 (1972), 109–30.

_____ 'Geological Controversy in the Seventeenth Century: "Hooke vs Wallis" and its Aftermath', in Michael Hunter and Simon Schaffer, eds, *Robert Hooke: New Studies* (Woodbridge, 1989), 207–33.

Olson, Richard G. 'Tory-High Church Opposition to Science and Scientism in the Eighteenth Century: The Works of John Arbuthnot, Jonathan Swift, and Samuel Johnson', in John G. Burke, *The Uses of Science in the Age of Newton* (Berkeley, 1983), 171–204.

Ong, Walter J. *Ramus, Method and the Decay of Dialogue* (Cambridge, Mass., 1983).

Oresme, Nicole. *Le Livre du ciel et du monde*, ed. Albert D. Menut and Alexander J. Denomy, trans. and introd. Albert D. Menut (Madison, 1968).

Origen. *The Song of Songs, Commentary and Homilies*, trans. R. P. Lawson (London, 1957).

Osler, Margaret J. 'Fortune, Fate, and Divination: Gassendi's Voluntarist Theology and the Baptism of Epicureanism', in Margaret J. Osler, ed., *Atoms, Pneuma, and Tranquillity: Epicurean and Stoic Themes in European Thought* (Cambridge, 1991).

_____ *Divine Will and the Mechanical Philosophy: Gassendi and Descartes on Contingency and Necessity in the Created World* (Cambridge, 1994).

_____ 'How Mechanical Was The Mechanical Philosophy?', in Christoph Lüthy, John E. Murdoch, and William R. Newman, eds, *Late Medieval and Early Modern Corpuscular Matter Theories* (Leiden, 2001), 423–39.

Ostwald, Friedrich Wilhelm. *Monism as the Goal of Civilization* (Hamburg, 1913).

Otegem, Matthijs van. *A Bibliography of the Works of Descartes (1637–1704)* (2 vols, Utrecht, 2002).

Overton, Richard. *Mans Mortallitie* (Amsterdam [false imprint, actually London], 1643).

Ozment, Stephen. *The Age of Reform, 1250–1550* (New Haven, 1980).

Pagden, Anthony. *European Encounters with the New World: From Renaissance to Romanticism* (New Haven, 1993).

Paley, William. *Natural Theology: or, Evidences of the Existence and Attributes of the Deity, collected from the Appearances of Nature* (London, 1802).

Pannenberg, Wolfhart. *Die Prädestinationslehre des Duns Skotus* (Göttingen, 1954).

Paracelsus. *Selected Writings*, ed. and trans. Jolande Jacobi (Princeton, 1958).

Parker, Geoffrey. *The Army of Flanders and the Spanish Road, 1567–1659: The Logistics of Spanish Victory and Defeat in the Low Countries' Wars* (Oxford, 1972).

Parker, Richard A. 'Egyptian Astronomy, Astrology, and Calendrical Reckoning', in Charles Coulton Gillespie, ed., *Dictionary of Scientific Biography* (New York, 1981), xv, 706–27.

Parker, Samuel. *A Free and Impartial Censure of the Platonick Philosophie* (Oxford, 1666).

Passmore, John. *Ralph Cudworth: An Interpretation* (Cambridge, 1951).

Patrizi, Francesco. *Discussionum Peripateticarum tomi IV, quibus Aristotelica philosophiae universa historia atque dogmata cum veterum placitis collata, elegantur et erudite declarantur* (Basle, 1581).

—— *Nova de universis philosophia* (Ferrara, 1591).

Payne, L. M. 'Sir Charles Scarburgh's Harveian Oration, 1662', *Journal of the History of Medicine* 12 (1957), 158–64.

Pedersen, Olaf. 'Galileo and the Council of Trent: The Galileo Affair Revisited', *Journal for the History of Astronomy* 14 (1983), 1–29.

Peghaire, Julien. *Intellectus et ratio selon S. Thomas d'Aquin* (Paris and Ottawa, 1936).

Pelikan, Jaroslav. *Christianity and Classical Culture* (New Haven, 1993).

Pelletier, Gérard. *Palatium reginae eloquentiae* (Paris, 1641).

Pelling, Margaret. *Medical Conflicts in Early Modern London: Patronage, Physicians, and Irregular Practitioners, 1550–1640* (Oxford, 2003).

Péna, Jean. *Euclidis optica et catoptrica* (Paris, 1557).

Pereira, Benedictus. *De communibus omnium rerum naturalium principiis et affectionibus, Libri Quindecim* (Rome, 1576).

—— *Prior tomus Commentariorum et Disputationem in Genesim* (Lyon, 1590).

Pérez-Ramos, Antonio. *Francis Bacon's Idea of Science and the Maker's Knowledge Tradition* (Oxford, 1988).

Peters, Francis E. *The Harvest of Hellenism* (New York, 1970).

Peterson, Ivars. *Newton's Clock: Chaos in the Solar System* (New York, 1993).

Petrarch, Francesco. *Opera* (Basle, 1554).

—— *Invectivarum contra medicum libri IV*, ed. P. G. Ricci (Florence, 1950).

Peucer, Caspar. *Elementa doctrinae de circulis coelestibus et primo motu* (Wittenberg, 1551).

Peurbach, Georg. *Theoricae novae planetarum* (Wittenberg, 1542).

Picard, Gabriel. 'Essai sur la connaissance sensible d'après les scolastiques', *Archives de philosophie* 4/1 (1926), 1–93.

Pigeaud, Jackie. *La Maladie de l'âme: Étude sur la relation de l'âme et du corps dans la tradition médico-philosophique antique* (Paris, 1981).

Pingree, David. 'History of Mathematical Astronomy in India', in Charles Coulton Gillespie, ed., *Dictionary of Scientific Biography* (New York, 1981), xv. 533–633.

Pintard, René. *Le Libertinage érudit dans la première moitié du XVII^e siècle* (2 vols, Paris, 1943).

Plutarch. *Moralia*, various eds. and trans., Loeb Classical Library (15 vols, Cambridge, Mass, 1927–69).

Poisson, Nicolas Joseph. *Commentaire . . . sur la Méthode de Mr. Descartes* (Paris, 1671).

Pollot, Laurent. *Dialogues contre la pluralité des religions et l'athéism* (La Rochelle, 1595).

Pomponazzi, Pietro. *De immortalitate animae* (Padua, 1516).

—— *Tractatus acutissimi utillimi et mere peripatetici* (Venice, 1525).

—— *De naturalium effectuum causis sive de incantationibus* (Basle, 1556).

Pomponazzi, Pietro. *De fato* (Basle, 1567).

Pontano, Giovanni. *De rebus coelestibus libri XIIII* (Basle, 1556).

Popkin, Richard H. 'Cartesianism and Biblical Criticism', in Thomas M. Lennon, John M. Nicholas, and John W. Davis, eds, *Problems of Cartesianism* (Kingston and Monteal, 1982), 61–82.

Popper, Karl R. *The Open Society and its Enemies* (2 vols, London, 1945).

\_\_\_\_ *The Poverty of Historicism* (London, 1957).

\_\_\_\_ *The Logic of Scientific Discovery* (revd edn, London, 1968).

\_\_\_\_ *Objective Knowledge* (London, 1972).

Porta, Giambattista Della. *Magiae Natvralis Libri Viginti in Qvibvs Scientiarum Naturalium diuitiae demonstratur* (Frankfurt, 1597).

Power, Henry. *Experimental Philosophy in Three Books* (London 1664).

Preus, James S. *From Shadow to Promise: Old Testament Interpretation from Augustine to the Young Luther* (Cambridge, Mass., 1969).

Price, Derek J. de Solla. 'Philosophical Mechanism and Mechanical Philosophy: Some Notes towards a Philosophy of Scientific Instruments', *Annali dell'Instituto e Museo di storia della scienza* 5 (1980), 75–85.

\_\_\_\_ 'Of Sealing Wax and String', *Natural History* 93 (1984), 49–56.

Priestley, Joseph. *An Essay on the First Principles of Government; and on the nature of political, civil, and religious liberty* (London, 1768).

Primerose, James. *Popular Errours of the People in Physick*, trans. Robert Wittie (London, 1651).

Principe, Lawrence M. *The Aspiring Adept: Robert Boyle and his Alchemical Quest* (Princeton, 2000).

Prins, Jan. 'Hobbes on Light and Vision', in Tom Sorell, ed., *The Cambridge Companion to Thomas Hobbes* (Cambridge, 1996), 129–56.

Ptolemy, Claudius. *The Almagest*, trans. R. Cateby Taliaferro, in *Britannica Great Books* 16 (Chicago, 1952), 1–465.

\_\_\_\_ 'The Arabic Version of Ptolemy's *Planetary Hypotheses*', ed. and trans. Bernard R. Goldstein, *Transactions of the American Philosophical Society* 57/4 (1967), 3–55.

Pugliese, Patri J. 'Robert Hooke and the Dynamics of Motion in a Curved Path', in Michael Hunter and Simon Schaffer, eds, *Robert Hooke: New Studies* (Woodbridge, 1989), 181–206.

Pumfrey, Stephen. 'William Gilbert's Magnetic Philosophy, 1580–1684: The Creation and Dissolution of a Discipline' (Ph.D. thesis, The Warburg Institute, London, 1987).

\_\_\_\_ 'Magnetical Philosophy and Astronomy, 1600–1650', in René Taton and Curtis Wilson, eds, *Planetary Astronomy from the Renaissance to the Rise of Astrophysics, Part A: Tycho Brahe to Newton* (Cambridge, 1989), 45–53.

\_\_\_\_ 'Neo-Aristotelianism and the Magnetic Philosophy', in John Henry and Sarah Hutton, eds, *New Perspectives on Renaissance Thought* (London, 1990), 177–89.

Purshall, Conyers. *An Essay at the Mechanism of the Macrocosm: or the Dependence of Effects upon their Causes* (London, 1707).

Purver, Margery. *The Royal Society: Concept and Creation* (London, 1967).

Putnam, George H. *The Censorship of the Church of Rome and its Influence on the Production and Distribution of Literature* (2 vols, New York, 1906–7).

Pyenson, Lewis. *Cultural Imperialism and Exact Sciences: German Expansion Overseas, 1900–1930* (New York, 1985).

_____ *Empire of Reason: Exact Sciences in Indonesia, 1840–1940* (Leiden, 1989).

_____ *Civilizing Missions: Exact Sciences and French Overseas Expansion, 1830–1940* (Baltimore, 1993).

Pyle, Andrew. *Malebranche* (London, 2003).

Rabbow, Paul. *Seelenführung: Methodik der Exerzitien in der Antike* (Munich, 1954).

Raey, Johannes de. *Cogitata de interpretatione* (Amsterdam, 1692).

Randall, John H. *The School of Padua and the Emergence of Modern Science* (Padua, 1961).

Randles, W. G. L. *The Unmaking of the Medieval Christian Cosmos, 1500–1760: From Solid Heavens to Boundless Æther* (Aldershot, 1999).

Ranea, Alberto Guillermo. 'A "Science for *honnêtes hommes*": *La Recherche de la Vérité* and the Deconstruction of Experimental Knowledge', in Stephen Gaukroger, John Schuster, and John Sutton, eds, *Descartes' Natural Philosophy* (London, 2000), 313–29.

Rankin, Herbert D. *Sophists, Socratics and Cynics* (London, 1983).

Rapoport, Anatol. 'Scientific Approach to Ethics', *Science* 150 (1957), 796–9.

Rappaport, Rhoda. 'Hooke on Earthquakes: Lectures, Strategy and Audience,' *British Journal for the History of Science* 19 (1986), 129–46.

Rashed, Roshi, ed. *Encyclopedia of the History of Arabic Science* (3 vols, London, 1996).

Rattansi, Piro M. 'The Helmontian-Galenist Controversy in Restoration England', *Ambix* 12 (1964), 1–23.

Reeds, Karen. *Botany in Medieval and Renaissance Universities* (New York, 1991).

Régis, Pierre-Sylvan. *Système de philosophie* (3 vols, Paris, 1690).

Regius, Henricus. *Fundamenta physices* (Amsterdam, 1646).

_____ *Fundamenta medica* (Utrecht, 1647).

Reichenbach, Hans. *The Rise of Scientific Philosophy* (Berkeley, 1951).

Reisch, George A. *How the Cold War Transformed Philosophy of Science: To the Icy Slopes of Logic* (Cambridge, 2005).

Reusch, Heinrich. *Die 'Indices Librorum Prohibitorum' des sechzehnten Jahrhunderts* (Nieuwkoop, 1961).

Reventlow, Henning Graf. *The Authority of the Bible and the Rise of the Modern World* (Philadelphia, 1985).

Rheticus, Georg Joachim. *Narratio prima* (Danzig, 1540).

Riccioli, Giovanni Battista. *Amalgestvm novum* (3 vols, Bologna, 1651).

Ridley, Mark. *A Short Treatise of Magneticall Bodies and Motions* (London, 1613).

Rist, John M. *Plotinus: The Road to Reality* (Cambridge, 1967).

_____ *Stoic Philosophy* (Cambridge, 1969).

Riverius, Lazarus. *Opera medica universa: quibus continentur I. Institutionum medicarum, libri quinque. II. Praxeos medicae, libri septemdecim. III. Observationum medicarum, centuriae quatuor* (3 vols, in 1, Lyons, 1663).

Robinet, André. 'Le groupe malebranchiste introducteur du calcul infinitésimal en France', *Revue d'histoire des sciences* 13 (1960), 287–308.

_____ *Malebranche de l'Académie des sciences. L'œuvre scientifique, 1674–1715* (Paris, 1970).

Rochemonteix, Camille de. *Un Collège des jesuits au XVII^e et au XVIII^e siècles* (4 vols, Le Mans, 1889).

Rochot, Bernard. *Les Travaux de Gassendi sur Epicure et sur l'atomisme, 1619–1658* (Paris, 1944).

Roger, Jacques. *Les Sciences de la vie dans la pensée française du XVIIIème siècle: la génération des animaux de Descartes à l'Encyclopédie* (2nd edn, Paris, 1971).

Roger, Jacques. 'The Cartesian Model and its Role in Eighteenth-Century "Theory of the Earth" ', in T. Lennon, J. Nicholas, and J. Davis, eds, *Problems of Cartesianism* (Kingston, 1982), 95–112.

Rogerson, John. *Old Testament Criticism in the Nineteenth Century* (London, 1984).

Rohault, Jacques. *Traité de physique* (Paris, 1671).

Roques, René. *L'Univers dionysien: structure hiérarchique du monde selon le Pseudo-Denys* (Paris, 1983).

Rose, Paul Lawrence. 'Galileo's Theory of Ballistics', *British Journal for the History of Science* 4 (1968), 156–9.

———— and Drake, Stillman. 'The Pseudo-Aristotelian *Questions of Mechanics* in Renaissance Culture', *Studies in the Renaissance* 18 (1971), 65–104.

Rosen, Edward, ed. and trans. *Three Copernican Treatises* (New York, 1971).

Rosenfield, Leonora G. *From Beast-Machine to Man-Machine* (New York, 1968).

Ross, Alexander. *The new planet no planet, or, The earth no wandring star, except in the wandring heads of Galileans* (London, 1646).

Rossi, Paolo. *The Dark Abyss of Time: The History of the Earth and the History of Nations from Hooke to Vico* (Chicago, 1984).

Rovighi, Sophia Vanni. *L'immortalita dell'anima nei maestri francescani del secolo XIII* (Milan, 1936).

Rowland, Ingrid. 'Giordano Bruno and Neapolitan Neoplatonism', in Hilary Gatti, ed., *Giordano Bruno: Philosopher of the Renaissance* (Aldershot, 2002), 97–119.

Royal College of Physicians. *Pharmacopoea Londinensis in qua medicamenta antiqua et nova vsitatissima, sedulò collecta, accuratissimè examinata, quotidiana experientia confirmata describuntur* (London, 1618).

Rozemond, Marleen. 'The Nature of the Mind', in Stephen Gaukroger, ed., *The Blackwell Guide to Descartes' Meditations* (Oxford, 2006), 48–66.

Rubin, Miri. *Corpus Christi: The Eucharist in Late Medieval Culture* (Cambridge, 1991).

Rüegg, Walter. 'Themes', in Hilde de Ridder-Symoens, ed., *A History of the University in Europe* i.*Universities in the Middle Ages* (Cambridge, 1992), 3–34.

Runciman, Steven. *The Medieval Manichee: A Study of the Christian Dualist Heresy* (Cambridge, 1982).

Ruse, Michael. *The Evolution–Creation Struggle* (Cambridge, Mass., 2005).

———— and Wilson, Edward O. 'Moral Philosophy as Applied Science', *Philosophy* 61 (1986), 173–92.

Russell, Jeffrey Burton. *Dissent and Reform in the Early Middle Ages* (Berkeley, 1965).

Saʿid al-Andalusi. *Book of the Category of Nations*, trans. and ed. Semaʿayn I. Salem and Alok Kumar (Austin, 1991).

Santas, Gerasimos Xenophon. *Socrates: Philosophy in Plato's Early Dialogues* (London, 1979).

Sarasohn, Lisa Tunick. 'The Ethical and Political Philosophy of Pierre Gassendi', *Journal of the History of Philosophy* 29 (1982), 239–60.

———— 'Motion and Morality: Pierre Gassendi, Thomas Hobbes, and the Mechanical World-View', *Journal of the History of Ideas*, 46 (1985), 363–80.

———— 'Epicureanism and the Creation of a Privatist Ethic in Early Seventeenth-Century France', in Margaret J. Osler, ed., *Atoms, Pneuma, and Tranquillity: Epicurean and Stoic Themes in European Thought* (Cambridge, 1991), 175–96.

Sargent, Rose-Mary. *The Diffident Naturalist: Robert Boyle and the Philosophy of Experiment* (Chicago, 1995).

Scaglione, Aldo. *The Liberal Arts and the Jesuit College System* (Amsterdam, 1986).

Scaliger, Joseph. *Iul. Caesaris F. opus nuvum de emendatione temporum in octo libros tributum* (Geneva, 1583).

_____ *Thesavrvs temporvm. Evsebii Pamphili Caesareae Palaestinae Episcopi Chronicorum canonum omnimodae historiae libri duo* (Leyden, 1606).

Schaffer, Simon. 'Glass Works: Newton's Prisms and the Use of Experiment', in David Gooding, Trevor Pinch, and Simon Schaffer, eds, *The Uses of Experiment: Studies in the Natural Sciences* (Cambridge, 1989), 67–104.

Schipperges, Heinrich. *Weltbild und Wissenschaft: Eröffnungsreden zu den Naturforschersammlungen 1822 bis 1972* (Hildesheim, 1976).

Schlick, Moritz. *Problems of Ethics* (New York, 1939).

Schmaltz, Tad M. 'What has Cartesianism to do with Jansenism?', *Journal of the History of Ideas* 60 (1999), 37–56.

Schmidt-Biggemann, Wilhelm. 'Apokalyptische Universalwissenschaft: Johann Heinrich Alsteds *Diatribe de mille annis apocalypticis*', *Pietismus und Neuzeit*, 14 (1988), 50–71.

_____ *Philosophia Perennis: Historical Outlines of Western Spirituality in Ancient, Medieval and Early Modern Thought* (Dordrecht, 2005).

Schmitt, Charles. 'Perennial Philosophy: From Agostino Steuco to Leibniz', *Journal of the History of Ideas* 27 (1966), 505–32.

_____ *Aristotle in the Renaissance* (Cambridge, Mass., 1983).

_____ 'Philoponus' Commentary on Aristotle's *Physics* in the Sixteenth Century', in Richard Sorabji, ed., *Philoponus and the Rejection of Aristotelian Science* (London, 1987), 210–30.

_____ 'The Rise of the Philosophical Textbook', in Charles B. Schmitt, Quentin Skinner, and Eckhard Kessler, eds, *The Cambridge History of Renaissance Philosophy* (Cambridge, 1988), 792–804.

Schofield, Christine. 'The Tychonic and Semi-Tychonic World Systems', in René Taton and Curtis Wilson, eds, *Planetary Astronomy from the Renaissance to the Rise of Astrophysics, Part A: Tycho Brahe to Newton* (Cambridge, 1989), 33–44.

[Schoock, Martinus.] *Admiranda methodus novae philosophiae Renati Descartes* (Utrecht, 1643).

Schrader, Friedrich. *De microscopiorum usu in naturali scientia et anatome* (Göttingen, 1681).

Schröder, Winfried. *Ursprünge des Atheismus: Untersuchungen zur Metaphysik- und Religionskritik des 17. und 18. Jahrhunderts* (Stuttgart/Bad Canstatt, 1998).

Schuhmann, Karl. 'Hobbes's Concept of History', in G. A. J. Rogers and Tom Sorell, eds, *Hobbes and History* (London, 2000), 3–24.

Schuster, John. *Descartes and the Scientific Revolution, 1618–1634* (2 vols, Ann Arbor, repr. of 1977 Princeton University Ph.D. thesis).

_____ '*Descartes opticien:* The Construction of the Law of Refraction and the Manufacture of its Physical Rationales', in Stephen Gaukroger, John Schuster, and John Sutton, eds, *Descartes' Natural Philosophy* (London, 2000), 258–312.

Schwarz, Werner. *Principles and Problems of Biblical Translation: Some Reformation Controversies and Their Background* (Cambridge, 1955).

Scott, Wilson L. *The Conflict between Atomism and Conservation Theory, 1644–1860* (London, 1970).

Sedley, David. 'Philoponus' Conception of Space', in Richard Sorabji, ed., *Philoponus and the Rejection of Aristotelian Science* (London, 1987), 140–53.

Sennert, Daniel. *De chymicorum cum Aristotelicis et galenicis consensu ac dissensu liber I* (Wittenberg, 1619).

Sennert, Daniel. *Hypomnemata physica* (Frankfurt, 1636).

Sepper, Dennis L. *Goethe contra Newton: Polemics and the Project for a New Science of Colour* (Cambridge, 1988).

—— *Newton's Optical Writings: A Guided Study* (New Brunswick, 1994).

—— 'Figuring Things Out: Figurate Problem-Solving in the Early Descartes', in Stephen Gaukroger, John Schuster, and John Sutton, eds, *Descartes' Natural Philosophy* (London, 2000), 228–48.

Sergeant, John. *Non Ultra, or, a Letter to a Learned Cartesian* (London, 1698).

Serjeantson, Richard W. 'Testimony and Proof in Early-Modern England', *Studies in History and Philosophy of Science* 30 (1999), 195–236.

Settle, Thomas B. 'Ostilio Ricci, A Bridge Between Alberti and Galileo', *Actes du XII^e Congrès International d'Histoire des Sciences* (Paris, 1971), 121–6.

—— 'Egnazio Danti and Mathematical Education in Late Sixteenth-Century Florence', in John Henry and Sarah Hutton, eds, *New Perspectives on Renaissance Thought* (London, 1990), 24–37.

Severinus, Peter. *Idea Medicinae Philosophicae* (The Hague, 1660).

Shadwell, Thomas. *Complete Works*, ed. Montague Summers (5 vols, London, 1927).

Shanahan, Timothy. 'Teleological Reasoning in Boyle's *Final Causes*', in Michael Hunter, ed., *Robert Boyle Reconsidered* (Cambridge, 1994), 177–92.

Shapin, Steven. *A Social History of Truth: Civility and Science in Seventeenth Century England* (Chicago, 1994).

—— *The Scientific Revolution* (Chicago, 1996).

—— and Schaffer, Simon. *Leviathan and the Air Pump: Hobbes, Boyle, and the Experimental Life* (Princeton, 1985).

Shapiro, Alan E. 'Kinematic Optics: A Study of the Wave Theory of Light in the Seventeenth Century', *Archive for History of Exact Sciences* 11 (1973), 134–266.

—— 'The Evolving Structure of Newton's Theory of White Light and Color', *Isis* 71 (1980), 211–35.

—— *Fits, Passions, and Paroxysms: Physics, Method, and Chemistry and Newton's Theories of Colored Bodies and Fits of Easy Reflection* (Cambridge, 1993).

—— 'The Gradual Acceptance of Newton's Theory of Light and Colors, 1672–1727', *Perspectives on Science* 4 (1996), 59–104.

—— 'Newton's Optics and Atomism', in I. Bernard Cohen and George E. Smith, eds, *The Cambridge Companion to Newton* (Cambridge, 2002), 227–55.

—— 'Newton's "Experimental Philosophy"', *Early Science and Medicine* 9 (2004), 185–217.

Shapiro, Barbara J. *John Wilkins, 1614–1672: An Intellectual Biography* (Berkeley, 1969).

—— *Probability and Certainty in Seventeenth-Century England: A Study of the Relationships Between Natural Science, Religion, History, Law, and Literature* (Princeton, 1983).

—— *A Culture of Fact: England, 1550–1720* (Ithaca NY, 2000).

Shea, Victor and Whitla, William, eds, *Essays and Reviews: The 1860 Text and Its Reading* (Charlottesville, Va., 2000).

Shea, William R. 'Galileo and the Church', in David C. Lindberg and Ronald L. Numbers, eds, *God and Nature: Historical Essays on the Encounter between Christianity and Science* (Berkeley, 1986), 114–35.

—— *The Magic of Numbers and Motion: The Scientific Career of René Descartes* (Canton, Mass., 1991).

Shorey, Paul. *Platonism Ancient and Modern* (Berkeley, 1938).

Sidney, Philip. *An Apology for Poetry*, ed. Geoffrey Shepherd (London, 1965).

Simplicius. *On Aristotle On the Soul 1.1–2.4*, trans. J. O. Urmson, notes by Peter Lautner (London, 1995).

Singer, Charles. *A Short History of Scientific Ideas to 1900* (Oxford, 1959).

Singer, Dorothea Waley. *Giordano Bruno, His Life and Thought: With Annotated Translation of his Work, On Infinite Universe and Worlds* (New York, 1968).

Sivin, Nathan. 'On the Word "Taoist" as a Source of Perplexity. With Special Reference to the Relations of Science and Religion in Traditional China', *History of Religions* 17 (1978), 303–30.

—— 'Why the Scientific Revolution Did Not Take Place in China—Or Didn't It?', in E. Mendelsohn, ed., *Transformation and Tradition in the Sciences* (Cambridge, 1984), 531–54.

—— 'Ruminations on the Dao and its Disputers', *Philosophy East and West* 42 (1992), 21–9.

Slowik, Edward. 'Perfect Solidity: Natural Laws and the Problem of Matter in Descartes' Universe', *History of Philosophy Quarterly* 13 (1996), 187–204.

—— *Cartesian Spacetime: Descartes' Physics and the Relational Theory of Space and Motion* (Dordrecht, 2002).

Smith, George E. 'The Newtonian Style in Book II of the *Principia*', in Jed Z. Buchwald and I. Bernard Cohen, eds, *Isaac Newton's Natural Philosophy* (Cambridge, Mass., 2001), 249–313.

Snell, Bruno. *Die Ausdrücke für den Begriff des Wissens in der vorplatonischen Philosophie* (Berlin, 1924).

Society of Jesus. *Regulae Societatis Iesu* (Rome, 1580).

Sonnert, Gerhard. *Einstein and Culture* (Amherst, 2005).

Sorabji, Richard. *Necessity, Cause and Blame: Perspectives on Aristotle's Theory* (London, 1980).

—— *Time, Creation and the Continuum: Theories in Antiquity and the Early Middle Ages* (London, 1983).

—— 'John Philoponus', in Richard Sorabji, ed., *Philoponus and the Rejection of Aristotelian Science* (London, 1987), 1–40.

—— *Matter, Space and Motion: Theories in Antiquity and Their Sequel* (London, 1988).

Sorell, Tom. *Scientism: Philosophy and the Infatuation with Science* (London, 1991).

South, Robert. *Sermons preached upon Several Occasions* (7 vols, Oxford, 1823).

Sparn, Walter. *Wiederkehr der Metaphysik: Die ontologische Frage in der lutherischen Theologie des frühen 17. Jahrhunderts* (Stuttgart, 1976).

Spencer, Herbert. *The Principles of Ethics* (2 vols, New York, 1892).

Speybroek, Linda Van, Waele, Dani de, and Vijver, Gertrudis Van de. 'Theories in Early Embryology: Close Connections between Epigenesis, Preformationism, and Self-Organization', *Annals of the New York Academy of Sciences* 981 (2002), 7–49.

Spiller, Michael R. G. *'Concerning Natural Philosophy': Meric Casaubon and the Royal Society* (The Hague, 1980).

Spinoza, Benedict. *Collected Works*, i, trans. E. Curley (Princeton, 1985).

—— *Tractatus theologico-politicus*, trans. Samuel Shirley (Leiden, 1991).

Spitz, Lewis W. *The Religious Renaissance of the German Humanists* (Cambridge, Mass., 1963).

Sprat, Thomas. *The History of the Royal-Society of London for the Improving of Natural Knowledge* (London, 1657).

—— *Observations on M. de Sorbier's Voyage into England* (London, 1665).

Steenberghen, Fernand Van. *Aristotle and the West* (Louvain, 1955).

Stegemann, Ekkehard W., and Stegemann, Wolfgang. *The Jesus Movement: A Social History of its First Century* (Edinburgh, 1999).

Stein, Howard. 'Newton's Metaphysics', in I. Bernard Cohen and George E. Smiths, eds, *The Cambridge Companion to Newton* (Cambridge, 2002), 256–307.

Stein, Peter. *Regulae Iuris: From Juristic Rules to Legal Maxims* (Edinburgh, 1966).

Stephenson, Bruce. *Kepler's Physical Astronomy* (Princeton, 1994).

—— *The Music of the Heavens: Kepler's Harmonic Astronomy* (Princeton, 1994).

Steno, Nicolaus. *De solido intra solidum naturaliter contento dissertationis prodromus* (Florence, 1669).

—— *The Prodromus to a dissertation concerning solids naturally contained within solids laying a foundation for the rendering a rational accompt both of the frame and the several changes of the masse of the earth . . . Englished by H. O.* (London, 1671).

—— *Opera philosophica*, ed. V. Maar (2 vols, Copenhagen, 1910).

Stevin, Simon. *The Principal Works of Simon Stevin*, ed. Ernst Cronie et al. (5 vols, Amsterdam, 1955–66).

Stewart, Larry. *The Rise of Public Science: Rhetoric, Technology, and Natural Philosophy in Newtonian Britain, 1660–1750* (Cambridge, 1992).

Stiglmyr, Joseph. *Das Aufkommen der pseudo-dionysischen Schriften und ihr Eindringen in die christliche Literatur* (Bonn, 1895).

Stillingfleet, Edward. *Origines Sacrae, or a Rational Account of the Grounds of Christian Faith, as to the Truth and Divine Authority of the Scriptures, And the matter therein contained* (London, 1662).

Stintzing, Roderich. *Geschichte der deutschen Rechtswissenschaft*, i. (Munich/Leipzig, 1880).

Stubbe, Henry. *A Censure upon Certain Passages contained in the History of the Royal Society* (Oxford, 1670).

—— *The Plus Ultra Reduced to a Non Plus* (London, 1670).

Suàrez, Francisco. *Metaphysicarum disputationem, in quibus, & universa theologia ordinatè traditor, & quaestiones ad amnes duodecim Aristotelis libros pertinentes, accuratè dispuntatur* (Salamanca, 1597).

Swerdlow, Noel M. 'The Derivation and First Draft of Copernicus' Planetary Theory: A Translation of the *Commentariolus* with Commentary', *Proceedings of the American Philosophical Society* 117 (1973), 423–512.

—— 'Pseudodoxia Copernicana: Or, Enquiries into Very Many Received Tenets and Commonly Presumed Truths, Mostly Concerning Spheres', *Archives internationales d'histoire des sciences* 26 (1976), 108–58.

Sydenham, Thomas. *The Entire Works of Dr Thomas Sydenham*, ed. John Swan (London, 1742).

Tanner, Norman P., ed. *Decrees of the Ecumenical Councils* (2 vols, London, 1990).

Taub, Liba Chai. *Ptolemy's Universe: The Natural Philosophical and Ethical Foundations of Ptolemy's Astronomy* (Chicago, 1993).

Taylor, Alfred E. *A Commentary on Plato's Timaeus* (Oxford, 1928).

Taylor, Charles. *Hegel* (Cambridge, 1975).

Telescope, Tom [John Newbery]. *The Newtonian System of Philosophy Adapted to the Capacities of Young Gentlemen and Ladies* (London, 1761).

Telesio, Bernardinus. *De Rerum Natura Iuxta Propria Principia Libri IX* (Naples, 1586: facsimile repr., Hildesheim, 1971).

Tertullian. *Quinti Septimi Tertulliani Opera*, ed. J. G. P. Borleffs et al. (2 vols, The Hague, 1953–4).

Thorndike, Lynn. *A History of Magic and Experimental Science* (8 vols, New York, 1923–58).

Tierney, Brian. *The Crisis of Church and State, 1050–1300, with Selected Documents* (Engle-wood Cliffs, NJ, 1964).

Topham, Jonathan R. 'The *Wesleyan-Methodist* Magazine and Religious Monthlies in Early Nineteenth-Century Britain', in Geoffrey Cantor et al., *Science in the Nineteenth-Century Periodical: Reading the Magazine of Nature* (Cambridge, 2004), 67–90.

Topsell, Edward. *The historie of fovre-footed beastes. . . . collected out of all the volumes of Con-radvs Gesner, and all other writers to this present day* (London, 1607; facsimile copy New York, 1973).

Torporley, Nathaneal. *Diclides Coelemetricae seu valuae Astronomicae Vniuersales* (London, 1602).

Torricelli, Evangelista. *De motu gravium naturalitur descendentium et proiectorum libri duo* (Florence, 1644).

Toulmin, Stephen. *Cosmopolis: The Hidden Agenda of Modernity* (New York, 1990).

Tribby, Jay. 'Dante's Restaurant: The Cultural Work of Experiment in Early Modern Tuscany', in A. Bermingham and J. Brewer, eds, *The Consumption of Culture, 1600–1800* (London, 1991), 319–37.

Tribe, Keith. *Genealogies of Capitalism* (London, 1981).

Trompf, Gary W. *The Idea of Historical Recurrence in Western Thought: From Antiquity to the Reformation* (Berkeley, 1979).

Turmel, Joseph. *Histoire des Dogmas* (6 vols, Paris, 1931–6).

Turner, Frank M. *Between Science and Religion: The Reaction to Scientific Naturalism in Late Victorian England* (New Haven, 1974).

——— 'The Victorian Crisis of Faith and the Faith That Was Lost', in Richard J. Helmstadter and Bernard Lightman, eds, *Victorian Faith in Crisis: Essays on Continuity and Change in Nineteenth-Century Religious Belief* (London, 1990), 9–38.

Ullmann, Walter. *The Medieval Idea of Law, as Represented by Lucas de Penna: A Study in Fourteenth-Century Legal Scholarship* (London, 1946).

——— *A Short History of the Papacy in the Middle Ages* (London, 1972).

Urbach, Peter. *Francis Bacon's Philosophy of Science* (La Salle, Ill., 1987).

Urvoy, Dominique. *Ibn Rushd* (London, 1991).

Ussher, James. *Annales veteris et Novi Testamenti* (London, 1650).

Valla, Laurentius. *In Latinam Novi Testamenti Interpretationem ex Collatione Graecorum Exem-plarium Adnotationes* (Paris, 1505).

Veit-Brause, Irmline. 'The Making of Modern Scientific Personae: The Scientist as a Moral Person? Emil du Bois-Reymond and His Friends', *History of the Human Sciences* 15 (2002), 19–50.

Verbeek, Theo. *Descartes and the Dutch: Early Reactions to Cartesian Philosophy, 1637–50* (Carbondale, Ill., 1992).

——— 'Tradition and Novelty: Descartes and Some Cartesians', in Tom Sorell, ed., *The Rise of Modern Philosophy* (Oxford, 1993), 167–96.

——— 'From "Learned Ignorance" to Scepticism: Descartes and Calvinist Orthodoxy', in Richard H. Popkin and Arjo Vanderjagt, eds, *Scepticism and Irreligion in the Seventeenth and Eighteenth Centuries* (Leiden, 1993), 31–45.

——— *Spinoza's Theologico-Political Treatise* (Aldershot, 2003).

Verger, Jacques. 'Patterns', in Hilde de Ridder-Symoens, ed., *A History of the University in Europe*, i. *Universities in the Middle Ages* (Cambridge, 1992), 35–74.

——— 'Teachers', in Hilde de Ridder-Symoens, ed., *A History of the University in Europe*, i. *Universities in the Middle Ages* (Cambridge, 1992), 144–68.

Vermij, R. H. 'Het copernicanisme in de Republiek', *Tijdschrift voor Geschiedenis* 106 (1993), 349–67.

Vickers, Brian. 'Analogy versus Identity: The Rejection of Occult Symbolism, 1580–1680', in Brian Vickers, ed., *Occult and Scientific Mentalities in the Renaissance* (Cambridge, 1984), 95–164.

―― 'Bacon's So-Called "Utilitarianism": Sources and Influence', in Marta Fattori, ed., *Francis Bacon, Terminologia e fortuna nel XVII secolo* (Rome, 1984), 281–313.

Vidal-Naquet, Pierre. 'La raison greque et la cité', *Raison Présente* 2 (1967), 51–61.

Vigenère, Blaide de [translation of Philostratus]. *Images ou Tableaux de Platte Peinture des deux Philostrates sophistes grecs* (Paris, 1614).

Viret, Pierre. *Instruction chrestienne en la doctrine de la loy et de l'euangile* (2 vols, Geneva, 1564).

Vlastos, Gregory. 'The Disorderly Motion in the *Timaeus*', in R. E. Allen, ed., *Studies in Plato's Metaphysics* (London, 1965), 379–99.

―― 'Creation in the *Timaeus*: Is it a Fiction?', in R. E. Allen, ed., *Studies in Plato's Metaphysics* (London, 1965), 401–19.

―― 'The Socratic Elenchus', *Oxford Studies in Ancient Philosophy* 1 (1983), 27–58.

Voelke, André-Jean. *La Philosophie comme thérapie de l'âme* (Paris, 1993).

Vossius, Gerardus Ioannis. *De theologia gentili, et physiologia Christiana; sive De origine ac progressu idolatriae* (Amsterdam, 1641).

Vries, Gerardus de. *Exercitationes rationales de deo, divinisque perfectionibus accedunt ejusdem disseretationes de Infinito; Nullibitate Spirituum; Homine Automatico; Contradictoriis Deo possibilus; Sensuum in Philosophando Usu; Cogitatione ipsa Mente; Operationibus Brutorum. In quibus passim quae de hisce philosophatur Cartesius cum rectae Rationis dictamine conferuntur* (Utrecht, 1685).

Waerden, Bartel L. van der. 'Mathematics and Astronomy in Mesopotamia', in Charles Coulton Gillespie, ed., *Dictionary of Scientific Biography* (New York, 1981), xv. 667–80.

Walker, D. P. *Spiritual and Demonic Magic from Ficino to Campanella* (London, 1969).

―― 'Medical Spirits in Philosophy and Theology from Ficino to Newton', in D. P. Walker, *Music, Spirit and Language in the Renaissance*, ed. Penelope Gouk (London, 1985), ch. 11.

Wall, Ernestine van der. 'Orthodoxy and Scepticism in the Early Dutch Enlightenment', in Richard H. Popkin and Arjo Vanderjagt, eds, *Scepticism and Irreligion in the Seventeenth and Eighteenth Centuries* (Leiden, 1993), 121–41.

Waquet, Françoise. *Le Latin ou l'empire d'un signe* (Paris, 1999).

Waterlow, Sarah. *Nature, Change and Agency in Aristotle's Physics* (Oxford, 1982).

Watson, Richard A. *The Downfall of Cartesianism, 1673–1712* (The Hague, 1966).

Watts, Michael R. *The Dissenters*, ii. *The Expansion of Evangelical Nonconformity* (Oxford, 1995).

Wear, Andrew. *Knowledge and Practice in English Medicine, 1550–1680* (Cambridge, 2000).

Webb, Beatrice. *My Apprenticeship* (London, 1926).

Webster, Charles. 'Water as the Ultimate Principle of Nature: The Background to Boyle's Sceptical Chymist', *Ambix* 13 (1966), 96–107.

―― *The Great Instauration: Science, Medicine and Reform (1626–1660)* (London, 1975).

Webster, John. *Academiarum Examen* (London, 1654).

Weisheipl, James A. 'Albertus Magnus and Universal Hylomorphism: Avicebron', in Francis J. Kovas and Robert W. Shahan, eds, *Albert the Great: Commemorative Essays* (Norman, 1980), 239–60.

Wesley, John. *A Survey of the Wisdom of God in the Creation: or a Compendium of Natural Philosophy* (2 vols, London, 1827).

Westfall, Richard S. *Force in Newton's Physics: The Science of Dynamics in the Seventeenth Century* (London, 1971).

_____ *The Construction of Modern Science* (Cambridge, 1977).

_____ *Never At Rest: A Biography of Isaac Newton* (Cambridge, 1980).

Westman, Robert S. 'The Comet and the Cosmos: Kepler, Mästlin and the Copernican Hypothesis', *Studia Copernicana* 5 (1972), 7–30.

_____ 'The Melanchthon Circle, Rheticus, and the Wittenberg Interpretation of the Copernican Theory', *Isis* 66 (1975), 165–93.

_____ 'The Astronomer's Role in the Sixteenth Century: A Preliminary Study', *History of Science* 18 (1980), 105–47.

_____ 'The Copernicans and the Churches', in David C. Lindberg and Ronald L. Numbers, eds, *God and Nature: Historical Essays on the Encounter between Christianity and Science* (Berkeley, 1986), 76–113.

Whiston, William. *Historical Memoirs of the Life of Dr. Samuel Clarke* (London, 1730).

White, Andrew Dickson. *A History of the Warfare of Science and Theology in Christendom* (2 vols, New York, 1896).

White, Michael J. *The Continuous and the Discrete: Ancient Physical Theories from a Contemporary Perspective* (Oxford, 1992).

White, Thomas. *Controversy Logick; or, The Methode to come to truth in debates of Religion* (Paris, 1659).

Whiteside, Derek Thomas. 'Newton's Early Thoughts on Planetary Motion: A Fresh Look', *British Journal for the History of Science* 2 (1964), 117–37.

_____ *The Mathematical Principles Underlying Newton's Principia Mathematica* (Glasgow, 1970).

_____ 'Before the *Principia*: The Maturing of Newton's Thoughts on Dynamical Astronomy, 1664–1684', *Journal for the History of Astronomy* 1 (1970), 5–19.

Wieland, Georg. 'The Reception and Interpretation of Aristotle's *Ethics*', in Norman Kretzmann, Anthony Kenny, and Jan Pinborg, eds, *The Cambridge History of Later Medieval Philosophy* (Cambridge, 1982), 673–86.

Wieland, Wolfgang. *Die aristotelische Physik* (Göttingen, 1970).

Wilcox, Donald J. *The Measure of Times Past: Pre-Newtonian Chronologies and the Rhetoric of Relative Time* (Chicago, 1987).

Wiles, Maurice. *Archetypal Heresy: Arianism through the Centuries* (Oxford, 1996).

Wilkins, John. *The Discovery of a New World* (London, 1638).

_____ *A Discourse Concerning a New Planet* (London, 1640).

Wilkins, John. *Mathematicall Magick. Or, the vvonders that may be performed by Mechanicall Geometry* (London, 1648).

Williams, Daniel H. *Ambrose of Milan and the End of Nicene-Arian Conflicts* (Oxford, 1995).

Wilson, Catherine. *The Invisible World: Early Modern Philosophy and the Invention of the Microscope* (Princeton, 1995).

Winkler, Mary, and Helden, Albert van. 'Representing the Heavens: Galileo and Visual Astronomy', *Isis* 83 (1992), 195–217.

Wippel, John F. 'The Condemnations of 1270 and 1277', *Journal of Medieval and Renaissance Studies* 7 (1977), 169–201.

Wittich, Christopher. *Dissertationes Duae* (Amsterdam, 1653).

Wojcik, Jan W. 'Pursuing Knowledge: Robert Boyle and Isaac Newton', in Margaret Osler, ed., *Rethinking the Scientific Revolution* (Cambridge, 2000), 183–200.

Wolff, Michael. *Geschichte der Impetustheorie: Untersuchungen zum Ursprung des klassischen Mechanik* (Frankfurt, 1978).

Wolff, Michael. 'Philoponus and the Rise of Pre-Classical Dynamics', in Richard Sorabji, ed., *Philoponus and the Rejection of Aristotelian Science* (London, 1987), 84–120.

Wolfson, Harry Austryn. *The Philosophy of Spinoza* (2 vols, New York, 1969).

Wood, P. B. 'Methodology and Apologetics: Thomas Sprat's *History of the Royal Society*', *British Journal for the History of Science* 13 (1980), 1–26.

Wren, Christopher. 'Lex Naturae de Collisione Corporum', *Philosophical Transactions* 3 (11 January 1669), 867–8.

Wren, Stephen. *Parentalia: or, memoirs of the Family of the Wrens; viz. Of Mathew Bishop of Ely, Christopher Dean of Windsor, &c. but chiefly of Sir Christopher Wren, late Surveyor-General of the Royal Buildings, President of the Royal Society, &c. &c.* (London, 1750).

Wright, Michael. 'Robert Hooke's Longitude Timekeeper', in Michael Hunter and Simon Schaffer, eds, *Robert Hooke: New Studies* (Woodbridge, 1989), 63–118.

Yates, Frances A. *Giordano Bruno and the Hermetic Tradition* (Chicago, 1964).

—— *The Art of Memory* (London, 1978).

Yoder, Joella G. *Unrolling Time: Christiaan Huygens and the Mathematization of Nature* (Cambridge, 1988).

Yolton, John W. *Thinking Matter: Materialism in Eighteenth-Century Britain* (Oxford, 1983).

—— *Perceptual Acquaintance from Descartes to Reid* (Oxford, 1984).

Zucchi, Nicolo. *Nova de machinis philosophia* (Rome, 1649).

Zúñiga, Diego de. *Commentaria in Job* (Toledo, 1584).

—— *Philosophiae prima pars, qua perfecte et eleganter quatuor scientia Metaphysica, Dialectica, Rhetorica, et Physica declarantur* (Toledo, 1597).

# Index